Rationality, Morality, and Self-Interest

Studies in Epistemology and Cognitive Theory

General Editor: Paul K. Moser, Loyola University of Chicago

A Useful Inheritance: Evolutionary Aspects of the Theory of Knowledge
by Nicholas Rescher, University of Pittsburgh

Practical Reasoning: Goal-Directed, Knowledge-Based, Action-Guiding Argumentation
by Douglas N. Walton, University of Winnipeg

Epistemology's Paradox: Is a Theory of Knowledge Possible?
by Stephen Cade Hetherington, University of New South Wales

The Intellectual Virtues and the Life of the Mind
by Jonathan L. Kvanvig, Texas A & M University

Blind Realism: An Essay on Human Knowledge and Natural Science
by Robert Almeder, Georgia State University

Epistemic Virtue and Doxastic Responsibility
by James A. Montmarquet, Tennessee State University

Rationality, Morality, and Self-Interest: Essays Honoring Mark Carl Overvold
edited by John Heil, Davidson College

Rationality, Morality, and Self-Interest

Essays Honoring Mark Carl Overvold

EDITED BY

John Heil

ROWMAN & LITTLEFIELD PUBLISHERS, INC.

ROWMAN & LITTLEFIELD PUBLISHERS, INC.

Published in the United States of America
by Rowman & Littlefield Publishers, Inc.
4720 Boston Way, Lanham, Maryland 20706

British Cataloging in Publication Information Available

Library of Congress Cataloging-in-Publication Data

Rationality, morality, and self-interest : essays honoring Mark Carl
Overvold / edited by John Heil.
p.   cm. — (Studies in epistemology and cognitive theory)
Includes bibliographical references and index.
1. Reason.   2. Ethics.   3. Self-interest.   I. Overvold, Mark Carl,
1948–1988.   II. Heil, John.   III. Series.
B73.R38   1993   170—dc20   92–36825 CIP

ISBN 0–8476–7762–1 (cloth : alk. paper)
ISBN 0–8476–7767–2 (pbk. : alk. paper)

Printed in the United States of America

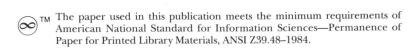

The paper used in this publication meets the minimum requirements of
American National Standard for Information Sciences—Permanence of
Paper for Printed Library Materials, ANSI Z39.48–1984.

For Leif and Jon-Mark

Mark Carl Overvold 1948–1988

Contents

Preface

Mark Carl Overvold was born February 15, 1948 in Veblan, South Dakota. He died on November 2, 1988 of cancer diagnosed less than three months earlier. At the time of his death he was associate professor of philosophy and chair of the Department of Philosophy at Virginia Commonwealth University. The papers in this volume are dedicated to his memory.

Overvold was graduated summa cum laude from St. Olaf College in 1970, and elected to Phi Beta Kappa. He received his Ph.D. from the University of Michigan in 1976, and taught at Brown University, the College of William and Mary, and the University of Texas before joining the faculty at Virginia Commonwealth University in the fall of 1977. He will be remembered as a gifted philosopher and teacher, and as an exemplary colleague. He was philosophically astute, but never arrogant; scrupulously honest, but never pompous; a person of strong conviction, but never dogmatic. He was, in all ways, an impressive man.

Many of the papers collected here were presented at a conference on the theme "Rationality, Morality, and Self-Interest," held in Overvold's honor at St. Olaf College, Northfield, Minnesota, October 18–20, 1990. Some were published in a special supplement to the *Journal of Philosophical Research* (vol. 16, 1991), some were published elsewhere, and some appear here for the first time. The latter include a paper on Butler that Overvold was completing at the time of his death. The remaining papers address topics on which Overvold worked during his tragically brief academic career. They testify to the depth of his views and to his influence on a wide range of philosophers.

This volume would not have been possible without considerable help from a number of people and organizations including Robert Audi, Thomas Carson, Harrison Hagan Heil, Brad Hooker, Adam Knapp, Paul Moser, Michael Novatny, Angelina Overvold, and Frederick Stoutland, St. Olaf College, the Philosophy Documentation Center, and Virginia Commonwealth University.

Davidson, North Carolina
October 1992

Part 1

Rationality

1

Epistemic Perspectivism*

Frederick Schmitt

Epistemic perspectivism is the view that for one important evaluative property, the property of being epistemically justified—justified in the sense required for knowledge—thinking makes it so: a subject's belief is justified in virtue of being sanctioned by the subject's outlook or perspective on justification. In this respect justified belief differs fundamentally from natural properties like being an electron or being red, for which thinking does not make it so. On perspectivism, justified belief is by its nature *perspectival belief*—belief sanctioned by the subject's epistemic perspective, by his or her judgments of justification or of justificatorily relevant properties (or by his or her epistemically guiding cognition). To say that the subject's belief is sanctioned by the perspective is not to say that it satisfies or conforms to some principle that is the content of a judgment of justification, but that it is *judged* to satisfy such a principle. Here are two examples of the view:

(a) *Reliabilist iterativism:* S is justified in believing p just in case S is justified in believing that the belief p is reliable.[1]

This is a version of perspectivism if S's perspective is taken to consist of propositions of the form "The belief p is reliable" that S is justified in believing, and the belief p is taken to be sanctioned by S's perspective when there is a proposition in the perspective corresponding to p. Laurence BonJour is committed to this view by various arguments he gives in *The Structure of Empirical Knowledge* (1985). For convenience, I use the term "reliable" where BonJour uses "likely to be true," which, it is clear, is

* This paper appears here for the first time. I would like to thank Alvin Goldman and participants at the Cincinnati Philosophy Colloquium, March 1992, for helpful comments.

1. A belief is reliable just in case it belongs to a specified class of beliefs most of which are true. Usually, the specified class is held to be the class of beliefs formed by a specified process that forms the belief in question.

supposed to be a statistical property of the form: having a feature F such that beliefs with F are generally true. I will refer to reliabilist iterativism as simply "iterativism."

  (b) *Counterfactual reflective perspectivism:* S is justified in believing p just in case S
       would on reflection believe that the proposition p is reliable.

This too is a version of perspectivism if the perspective is taken to consist of beliefs about reliability one would hold on reflection. Richard Foley (1987) proposes this view. For simplicity, I use the term "reliable" in application to a proposition where Foley says that it is the conclusion of an argument likely to be truth-preserving, with premises of which there is no reason to be suspicious. I will refer to counterfactual reflective perspectivism in what follows as simply "reflective perspectivism." There may be other versions of perspectivism. It is plausible enough to class John Pollock's (1986) view that a justified belief is one that conforms to a norm that guides the subject in cognition as a version of perspectivism. This view emphasizes the dependence of justification on background cognition as (a) and (b) do. However, guidance by a norm does not entail ascribing justification or other epistemically relevant property to the justified belief as (a) and (b) do. It is problematic whether reflective equilibrium theories of justified belief count as versions of perspectivism; they do not have either of the perspectivist features just mentioned. But I will have to set aside these theories to deal with (a) and (b).

It should be evident from these examples that perspectivism enjoys broad acceptance in current epistemology, receiving endorsement from such otherwise rival philosophers as BonJour, Foley, Pollock, and Keith Lehrer (1990). Perspectivism has indeed made such inroads in current epistemology that even staunch reliabilists like Alvin Goldman (1986) and Ernest Sosa (1991) make large concessions to it. Despite its popularity, the motivation for perspectivism has remained obscure. The burden of this paper is to assess possible motivations. My aim in doing so will be to determine whether there is any role for perspectival belief in epistemic evaluation.

What is at issue in judging perspectivism? I shall consider in detail one important issue—whether perspectival belief plays a significant role in epistemic evaluation. But there is a broader and more elusive issue I can only gesture at here. It is clear that perspectivism is supposed to contrast with reliabilism and more generally externalism. Certainly it is intended to be a form of internalism. It is actually a difficult issue whether all versions of perspectivism meet my lower bound on an internalist theory—i.e., entail what I call *mental internalism,* or the supervenience of justification on the subject's mentality. But perspectivism is at any rate distinguished from other theories of justification that do meet this lower bound—versions of coherentism, foundationalism, and accessibility internalism. At stake in the dispute between perspectivists and everyone else is whether we are to conceive of justification as conforming to a law given by ourselves or by nature. The issue between perspectivists and accessibility internalists and everybody else is whether justification is a matter of self-maintenance or maintenance by nature—whether it escapes or falls prey to a certain kind of luck. And the issue between perspectivists (and others) and externalists is whether justification escapes or involves being embedded in one's environment in an intimate way—whether justification is an ecological matter. Despite the importance of these issues, I must pass over them to discuss more fine-grained matters.

1. THE INTUITIVE CASE FOR ITERATIVISM

The intuitive case for iterativism begins with the observation that perspective affects justification in significant ways.

(i) It is uncontroversial that justification is *undermined* by justified *negative* evaluation in the sense that a subject cannot be justified in a belief if he or she justifiedly judges it unreliable. That is, S is justified in believing p only if S is not justified in believing that the belief p is unreliable. Iterativism has a ready explanation for this condition: it follows more or less immediately from the iterativist claim that S is justified in believing p only if S is justified in believing that the belief p is reliable. But of course this requirement of justified *positive* evaluation of the belief p goes much beyond the requirement of the *absence* of a justified negative evaluation that is needed to explain the example. The strength of the case for iterativism here must rest on the lack of alternative nonperspectivist explanations of undermining by justified negative evaluation. Reliabilist explanations of undermining, for example, attempt to explain it by appeal to the requirement that justified beliefs be reliable.[2]

The perspectivist can best head off such explanations by showing that the requirement of reliability is too strong. BonJour has attempted exactly this by appealing to the demon example: subjects can be justified even though their beliefs are unreliable because they are deceived by a demon. But even if we accept BonJour's example and abandon reliability, we still have the option of explaining both the example and undermining by appeal to a nonperspectivist version of coherentism. A suitable version of

---

2. See Schmitt 1992 for extensive discussion of reliabilist accounts of undermining, as well as responses to the demon example.

coherentism might entail that coherence is present in the demon example, while negative evaluation of the belief p is incoherent with the belief p. Admittedly, such a version of coherentism would require a broad conception of coherence subsuming but not entailing perspectival belief. No one has offered such a version. Most versions of coherentism simply define coherence by a list that includes sanctioning by perspective as one (optional) kind of coherence and condemnation by perspective as a kind of incoherence. And that ultimately yields no *explanation* of the phenomena to which BonJour appeals. Nevertheless, BonJour's appeal makes an unwarranted bet that no such version of coherentism can be made out—that any well-motivated version of coherentism must collapse into iterativism. Until BonJour has ruled out the sort of coherentism I have in mind, appeal to undermining and the demon example cannot favor iterativism.

(ii) The other part of the intuitive case for iterativism is the claim that intuitively perspectival belief (as understood by iterativism) *suffices* for justified belief: if S is justified in believing that the belief p is reliable, then plausibly S is justified in believing p. Suppose I must choose between exercising two processes. I believe process A to be reliable, and B to be unreliable. Surely I am justified in the belief that results from A, even if it turns out later that my belief that A is reliable was mistaken. However, it seems rather likely that reliabilism can explain this intuition. For instance, it is plausible that the inference from "A is reliable and yields the belief p" to "p" is itself a (conditionally) reliable inference: in general, when the premise is true, the conclusion tends to be true. If so, reliabilism will entail that the belief p is justified (in a propositional sense) when this inference is available (and epistemically relevant) and the premise that the belief p is reliable is justified. This is so despite the fact that A turns out to be unreliable. In short, according to reliabilism, perspectival belief entails that the belief p is reliable, and thus it suffices for justified belief. Of course, intuitively, if I exercise B, which I take to be unreliable, my belief is not justified, even though B is reliable. But our intuition here may be explained by appeal to the idea that justification is undermined by my justified belief that B is not reliable. And thus reliabilism will explain our intuition here if it explains undermining.

Now, BonJour has attempted to argue that reliabilism does not itself give a sufficient condition of justification, and if this were so, reliabilism could not explain why perspectival belief suffices for justified belief. In particular, he asks us to imagine that clairvoyant belief is (unknown to the subject) reliable, and he claims that such beliefs would not be justified. But whether clairvoyant belief counts as justified on reliabilism depends on whether the clairvoyant process counts as epistemically relevant. If pragmatic considerations like whether evaluators tend to recognize the processes or judge their reliability accurately enter into relevance, then clairvoyant belief will not be justified. The power of BonJour's example to show that reliability is not sufficient for justified belief, and to preempt a reliabilist account of the sufficiency of perspectival belief for justified belief, thus depends on ruling out pragmatic constraints on relevance. And that will be an uphill battle. As things now stand, we have no serious argument that perspectivism alone explains the sufficiency of perspectival belief for justified belief.

In short, it is relatively uncontroversial that perspectival belief is sufficient for justified belief, and that justified belief requires the absence of negative evaluation. But we have no reason to think that an iterativist account is the only one that can explain these facts. And of course we have no intuitive reason to take perspectival belief to be *necessary* for justification. So we have no intuitive case for iterativism here. There is even less of an intuitive case for reflective perspectivism.

I would now like to argue that there is a powerful intuitive case against requiring perspectival belief. To ensure that we cite an example in which justified positive evaluation is absent, it is best to choose an example of perception by a cognitively immature subject, one who lacks the cognitive resources to make or be justified in making positive evaluations. I believe it is obvious enough that we unhesitatingly ascribe justified perceptual beliefs to such subjects. But for those who need proof, let me try to produce a convincing case. What we currently know about cognitive development suggests that there is a period of cognitive development, which can vary in children from three to six, during which we ascribe perceptual beliefs, despite the fact that the subject lacks the concept of reliable belief and is thus unable to be justified in a positive evaluation. To cite just one pertinent experimental result, Willats relates the case of a girl who drew a basketball as a circle, suggesting that her line represents the occluding contour of the ball and the interior of the circle represents the surface of the ball. In short, she drew the basketball to a first approximation as it appears. However, when asked to draw the mold mark on the basketball,

> the child first drew a line *outside* the first circle, saying as she did so "I can't draw it here because it's not inside the ball." Finally she drew a line on top of the first circle, saying "And I can't draw it here because it won't show up. So I can't do it." It is hard to resist the conclusion that for this child the shape enclosed by the circle stood for the whole volume of the ball, while the circle stood for the surface of the ball, dividing the inside of the ball from the space outside. (p. 90)

The girl is unable to represent the mold mark by drawing it the way it appears. Her explanation about her inability to do this suggests that her drawing does not represent the surface of the ball or its appearance at all, but is a two-dimensional topological diagram representing the space inside and the space outside the surface of the ball. Of course when adults represent the surface of a ball, they draw it as a circle, and it might be thought that the girl was doing the same thing and intended her drawing to resemble the appearance of the ball. But the fact that she could not draw the mold mark across the circle suggests that the girl does not treat the area of the circle as appearing the way the surface of the ball appears. One explanation of why the girl does not do so would be that her artistic resources are restricted to topological representations. But this itself needs explanation. And it is not implausible that the explanation is that she lacks a concept much like our concept of visual appearance. It could be that she is prevented from representing the appearance of the ball because having the concept of appearance is necessary for successful drawing. Perhaps the recognition of appearance is needed to represent things as they appear.[3]

Yet at the same time there is little doubt that we would ascribe justification to the child's perceptual beliefs: she is justified in believing that this is a basketball, that the basketball is round, etc. It seems consistent with our knowledge of children's cognitive development that there is a stage at which we ascribe justification to the child's perceptual beliefs even though she lacks the concept of appearance. At any rate, I do not think that the discovery that children lack the concept of appearance would cause us to withdraw our attribution of justification to their perceptual beliefs. On any plausible view of reliability, however, perceptual beliefs are reliable when they are of certain types, instances of which are frequently true, and these types are defined (at least in part) by perceptual appearances. Thus a subject can have beliefs about the reliability of perceptual beliefs only if she possesses a concept of appearance. In short, it is at least consistent with our knowledge of development that there is a stage at which we ascribe justification to the child's perceptual beliefs even though she lacks the concept of reliability and is thus unable to have, and therefore to be justified in having, beliefs about reliability. Intuitively, a belief can be justified even though the subject is not justified in believing it reliable.

At this point some philosophers—Sosa (1991), for example—have wanted to distinguish between reflective and animal knowledge, ascribe the latter to small children, and deny that such knowledge requires justified belief. But I doubt whether there is any intuitive distinction of this sort: intuitively the child knows and is justified in her perceptual beliefs in the

---

3. For an interesting discussion of the significance of this case for the theory of perceptual attitudes, see Morton 1987.

same sense that I know and am justified in mine. Nor is it clear why the dichotomy is between *reflective* and animal knowledge. These are not contradictories (are they even contraries?), and it would need to be argued that all nonanimal knowledge is reflective. Of course reflection and justification for believing that one's belief is justified may well be desirable and required for mature thinkers to be justified. But whether there is such a requirement is not the issue. The issue is the source of the requirement. Does this requirement stem from the nature of justified belief itself, so that it pertains to all justified beliefs, or only from the special endowments of mature subjects under a conception of justified belief that applies more broadly? Perspectivism requires the former, but our intuitions say otherwise. I shall cover obliquely below the related question whether there is a theoretical point to making such a distinction.

2. THE RESPONSIBILITY ARGUMENT FOR ITERATIVISM

I have argued that we are far from having a full intuitive case for iterativism. Nor do I see any real prospect of one. The perspectivist must therefore supply an alternative route to the view by locating a significant epistemic role for perspectival belief. If the perspectivist can locate such a role and argue that justified belief plays just this role, that will be quite enough to establish perspectivism as the correct account of justified belief. What are the prospects for such a case? I would like to devote the rest of this paper to considering the matter in detail.

What is wanted here is an innocuous formal conception of justified belief, one that wears its evaluative significance on its sleeve, but that must nevertheless be characterized by perspectival belief. Perspectivists have in fact attempted to locate such a formal conception and to deduce perspectivism from it.

I would like to begin with the idea, deriving from the work of BonJour, that iterativism can be deduced from a conception of justified belief as *epistemically responsible belief*, or belief that results from epistemically responsible cognition. BonJour's argument is this:

> The distinguishing characteristic of epistemic justification is…its essential or internal relation to the cognitive goal of truth. It follows that one's cognitive endeavors are epistemically justified only if and to the extent that they are aimed at this goal, which means very roughly that one accepts all and only those beliefs which one has good reason to think are true. To accept a belief in the absence of such a reason, however appealing or even mandatory such an acceptance might be from some other standpoint, is to neglect the pursuit of truth; such an acceptance is, one might say, *epistemically irresponsible*. My contention here is that the idea of avoiding such

irresponsibility, of being epistemically responsible in one's believings, is the core of the notion of epistemic justification. (1985, p. 8)

It is hard to be sure of the exact order of BonJour's argument, but the following is suggested:

1. *The conception of justified belief as epistemically responsible belief.* S is justified in believing p just in case S is epistemically responsible in believing p.

2. *The conception of epistemically responsible belief as well-motivated belief.* S is epistemically responsible in believing p just in case in believing p, S aims (in the right way) at believing what is true.

3. In believing p, S aims (in the right way) at believing what is true just in case S is justified in believing that the belief p is likely to be true.

4. So S is justified in believing p just in case S is justified in believing that the belief p is likely to be true.

Conclusion 4 is of course just iterativism.

There is a serious preliminary problem with this argument. It is not plausible to suppose, as premise 3 has it, that perspectival belief entails aiming at believing what is true. Merely being justified in believing that the belief p is reliable does not entail that one is motivated in a certain way in believing p. Nor can we get around the problem by replacing the biconditionals in 3 and 4 with forward conditionals and leaving the backward conditional of 4 to the intuitive case (discussed in the last section) that perspectival belief entails justified belief. For on perspectivism, perspectival belief entails justified belief and so will once again entail aiming at true belief. I see no way to amend the argument to restore plausibility. But I am willing for the sake of discussion to pass over this problem and proceed to more central defects in the argument.

Premise 1, the conception of justified belief as epistemically responsible belief, has been endorsed by a number of philosophers, including Roderick Chisholm (1977), Hilary Kornblith (1983), and Lorraine Code (1983), but the idea remains deeply underdeveloped. There is little doubt that the status of epistemically responsible belief plays an important role in the constellation of epistemic conditions. But no one, to my knowledge, has ever carefully argued that justified belief is to be identified with epistemically responsible belief, perhaps in part because no one possesses a detailed enough account of epistemically responsible belief to fund such an argument. I will return to the plausibility of premise 1 below, but I wish to begin with the other premises.

Premises 2 and 3 together entail that epistemically responsible belief is perspectival belief. Unfortunately, this consequence seems to be false. We may adapt William Alston's examples (1989) to make the objection.

Suppose that I accept the doctrine of the Trinity, but I see that it appears logically contradictory. I reject various ways of rendering it logically consistent—e.g., by the device of relative identity. I see I have no plausible premises from which I can infer it by deduction or any other reliable inference. After long deliberation, I reject the view that anyone employs a reliable process of revelation to arrive at the doctrine. I regard this view as incompatible with what we know of human cognitive faculties. I recognize that my acceptance of the doctrine is the result of indoctrination. In short, my acceptance is not sanctioned by my perspective. On the contrary, it seems that I am justified in believing that my acceptance is unreliable. For I am justified in believing that I possess no argument for it that would afford me a reliable inference and no reliable noninferential way of arriving at the belief. One might object that I cannot maintain my acceptance of the doctrine and at the same time be justified in believing that my acceptance is unreliable. For the belief in unreliability here would be incoherent with my acceptance of the doctrine: that acceptance would support the availability of revelation or other reliable ways of arriving at the doctrine. But such incoherence is the human condition. It cannot prevent me from maintaining my acceptance and being justified in believing that my acceptance is unreliable. The most it could entail is that I cannot be justified in believing this and at the same time be justified in accepting the doctrine. That is fine. For purposes of the example, we may take the former alternative.

Let us also suppose, however, that try as I might I cannot shake my acceptance of the doctrine. I make my best effort to resist it, but I fail. Then surely I am epistemically responsible in my acceptance, despite the fact that it is not sanctioned by my perspective. We ought to reject the conclusion that epistemically responsible belief is perspectival belief. (Those who wish to segregate religious beliefs as the proper domain of faith and deny on this ground that they are susceptible to any kind of epistemic evaluation at all may choose another example—political beliefs will do just as well.)

It might be replied that my acceptance of the doctrine is not really epistemically responsible here. To be sure, my cognitive *actions* are epistemically responsible—I try to rid myself of this belief. But my *belief* is not *itself* epistemically responsible. For it does not *result* from my best efforts but rather resists them. So the objection does not succeed in showing that I can be epistemically responsible in my belief without its being perspectival.

I confess my grasp of the notion of epistemically responsible belief is not firm enough to yield intuitions about whether my actions can be epistemically responsible without my belief being so because my belief fails to result from my actions. But I am willing to concede this for the sake of argument. This concession does not, however, save the responsibility argument, for two reasons.

First, if we accept the assumption that epistemically responsible belief entails *resulting* from one's best efforts, then we lose the other direction of the equivalence between epistemically responsible and perspectival belief. We lose the claim that perspectival belief *entails* epistemically responsible belief. For, among other things, there could be perspectival beliefs that do not result from epistemically responsible actions. For example, my perspective might sanction beliefs that result from *automatic* perceptual processes or *innate* beliefs even though these do *not* result from any actions at all. Perhaps it will be replied that a belief counts as epistemically responsible when it *would* result from doing one's best. But counterfactualizing the notion of "resulting from" in the account of epistemically responsible belief, if it works here, will prevent the new account from handling the example of irresistible religious belief, since the latter belief *would* still result from my doing my best even though it does not in fact result, and so it will count as epistemically responsible once again on the counterfactualized account.

Second, let it also be noted that even if my acceptance of the doctrine of the Trinity is not epistemically responsible, it can hardly be said to be *irresponsible* either. Then we can make a different objection to 2 and 3. For presumably if, as the perspectivist equivalence for epistemically responsible belief holds, a belief is responsible when it is sanctioned by my perspective, it will be *irresponsible* when *condemned* by my perspective. But my religious belief is in fact condemned (since I regard it as unreliable). Thus the example undercuts the conclusion that epistemically responsible belief is perspectival belief even if this belief is not responsible.

These observations show that epistemically responsible belief and perspectival belief diverge. The former depends on such factors as whether a belief is irresistible, while the latter does not: an irresistible belief must be either epistemically responsible or neither epistemically responsible nor irresponsible. Either way the equivalence between epistemically responsible belief and perspectival belief breaks down. The reason is that epistemically responsible belief depends on whether the subject is doing the best he or she can in believing *p*, and one can do one's best and still believe an irresistible belief that is condemned. Perspectival belief, on the other hand, does not depend on any such thing because one can have justified beliefs about the reliability and unreliability of beliefs independently of whether they are resistible.

One might take all this to show that it was a tactical error for the perspectivist to tie justified belief to epistemically responsible belief. Epistemically responsible belief does not match up with perpectival belief in the desired way. One might maintain, however, that perspectival belief does match up with belief that aims at true belief, and that this is enough for an argument for perspectivism. But this attempt at an end run around the objection meets similar obstacles. Automatic perceptual beliefs can be perspectival without our aiming at the truth in believing them and without resulting from aiming at the truth. And again counterfactualizing aiming does not get the perspectivist out of the fire. It does not help to say that a belief is perspectival just in case it would result from our aiming if we did aim. For irresistible beliefs can fail to be perspectival even though we would believe them if we were to aim at the truth.[4]

It might be replied that my focus on irresistible belief deprives my objection of breadth, but in fact the objection generalizes to many resistible beliefs as well. Resistible beliefs will be epistemically responsible whenever one does one's best in believing them—i.e., whenever it is epistemically cost-effective not to resist them. Thus, resistible beliefs can be epistemically responsible though unjustified and nonperspectival when it is too much (epistemic) trouble to get rid of them. Indeed, the problem with a perspectivist account is a deep one, a point that has been made in effect by William Alston (1989), but cannot be repeated often enough. The account leaves out one of the chief factors in epistemically responsible belief—the cost-effectiveness of forming (or retracting) the belief. Sanctioning by one's perspective is no doubt a factor here, but it can be overridden by factors that affect cost, like control.

It might be suggested that we view perspectival belief as an *idealization* of epistemically responsible belief in which we abstract from factors such as control. If we did, then my objection to the responsibility argument would no longer apply. But what would be the advantage of measuring beliefs against such an ideal standard? By design, idealized belief does not *amount* to epistemically responsible belief. And we have at least one other ideal standard against which we can measure beliefs—namely, reliability.

Perhaps it will be suggested that perspectival belief is what we aim at directly when our ultimate aim is epistemically responsible belief. Of course we aim at true and reliable belief in aiming at epistemically responsible

---

4. It is worth noting that the example of irresistible belief also casts doubt on premise 1, the claim that justified belief is epistemically responsible belief. My irresistible religious belief is unjustified though epistemically responsible.

belief. But it might be suggested that we aim at these things indirectly and at perspectival belief directly.

I agree that justified belief is what we aim at directly when we aim at epistemically responsible belief. But I see no plausibility in the claim that we must aim directly at *perspectival* belief. It is true that one could get epistemically responsible belief by aiming at some goals in addition to true, reliable, and epistemically responsible belief. But the conditions of epistemically responsible belief do not themselves constrain us to aim at any particular such goal. All that is required is aiming at these goals guided by considerations like cost of control. Suppose the subject aims at true, reliable, and epistemically responsible belief, relying of course on beliefs about reliability to do so. Suppose the subject takes factors of cost into account in arriving at the belief p. I do not see why such a subject could not be epistemically responsible in believing p, despite that fact that she does not aim at perspectival belief. Now it might be that the subject should consider the plausibility of her metabeliefs about reliability while en route to the belief p. I do not see this as mandatory for epistemically responsible belief— what if there are no doubts about these metabeliefs, or what if there are doubts but considerations of cost militate against considering them? The negative answer I would expect here suggests that what is required of the metabeliefs about reliability on which the subject relies is that they be themselves epistemically responsible, rather than justified (contrary to what is required by perspectival belief). (That is, a qualified iterativism may be true for epistemically responsible belief, though false for justified belief.) The subject might rely on unjustified metabeliefs about reliability whose reliability it is too costly to check. But even if the subject considers their plausibility, it does not follow that she is *aiming* at perspectival belief. So we do not have a case that epistemically responsible belief entails aiming at perspectival belief.

It should be noted that nothing in this section shows that justified belief and perspectival belief diverge. In all of our examples, the beliefs are either both justified and perspectival, or neither justified nor perspectival. The point of this section has rather been that the tie between justified and perspectival belief is less problematic than that between either of these and epistemically responsible or well-motivated belief. There is no gain in appealing to the more problematic tie to establish the less problematic.

3. THE ADVISORY ARGUMENT FOR REFLECTIVE PERSPECTIVISM

I would like to turn now to another prominent argument for perspectivism which I shall call the *advisory argument*. This argument hinges on the alleged advisory nature of justified belief and the role of perspectival belief in epistemic advice-taking. The argument is that justified belief is advisable belief; the only proper advice is perspectivist advice; so justified belief is perspectival belief. This argument is suggested by remarks of Richard Foley:

> You need a way to proceed in making sense of the world from your own perspective, a way in which it is appropriate for you to proceed, given your own lights. You cannot simply read off from the world what is true, and neither can you read off what methods or procedures are likely to guarantee true beliefs. So, it is unhelpful for you to be told to believe some claim only if it is true, and it is equally unhelpful for you to be told to use only reliable methods. (Foley 1989, p. 171)

Foley's remarks suggest that what it is helpful for you to be told is to believe what you would on reflection deem reliable. Since justified belief is advisable belief, it is belief you would on reflection deem reliable—and this is perspectival belief, as defined by Foley's reflective perspectivism. Apparently the argument favors reflective perspectivism over iterativism. For it is not helpful to be told to believe what you are *justified* in believing reliable, since you do not yet know which beliefs are justified—it is the point of the advice to tell you. The advisory argument rules out iterativism, and indeed any similarly circular account of justification.

The advisory argument comes in several versions. All share the same first premise and differ in the properties they ascribe to proper advice. It will help in getting started to have a particular version before us:

1. *The advisory conception of justified belief.* Justified belief is advisable belief—belief that *conforms to* proper epistemic advice. Let us say that epistemic advice is *proper* when it is advice that would properly be offered to someone who wishes to believe what is reliable. And let us say that a belief *conforms to* epistemic advice when it satisfies the condition specified by the advice. For example, if the advice is reliabilist advice—i.e., advice to believe what is reliable—then a belief conforms to the advice just in case it is reliable. If the advice is reflective perspectivist advice, then a belief conforms to it just in case the subject would on reflection deem it reliable.

2. Proper epistemic advice is by its very nature advice that we are always able to take—where "always" means "on any occasion on which we seek to believe what conforms to the advice."

3. The only epistemic advice that we are always able to take is the advice to believe what is sanctioned by our perspective.

4. Hence, justified belief is belief sanctioned by our perspective—i.e., perspectival belief.

This version of the advisory argument focuses (in steps 2 and 3) on the sort of advice we are always *able* to take.

The argument does not explicitly assume any tie between justified belief and responsible belief, as the responsibility argument does. It might be that the questions about advisable belief we will discuss apply also to belief that aims at truth, since in aiming at truth it might be inevitable to take advice (in some sense of "taking advice"). At the same time, as we shall see, advisable belief need not be belief that aims at truth. Points about advisable belief will therefore have more general application, and the advisory conception is not committed to a conception of justified belief as well-motivated belief. For this reason, the advisory conception may be able to avoid entailing the relevance of factors, like cost of control, that do not apply to justified belief. The advisory argument may in this regard be more plausible than the responsibility argument.

In other respects, however, the advisory argument may be less plausible. A first reaction to the question whether perspectivist advice is proper might be incredulity at the question: proper advice for whom and in which circumstances? Surely it depends on whom we are talking about. Perhaps perspectivist advice is proper for people who are good at reflection, but not for others. I sympathize with this reaction, but of course if it is right there is something wrong with the advisory conception of justified belief and perhaps with perspectivism as well. If the advisory conception is good, there must be some account of propriety that varies from subject to subject only to the extent that justification does—presumably, at some level, not at all. If we say that perspectivist advice is proper for people who are good at reflection, "good at" presumably means "able to get true belief from," and it begins to look as if perspectival belief is valuable because it gets us reliable belief—a view inconsistent with perspectivism. I am willing to forgo this reaction here. I shall assume for argument's sake that there is only one kind of proper advice, and that justified belief is advisable belief. There will be enough problems with the other premises of the argument.

The version of the argument we have before us is in fact not very promising. It seems impossible to interpret "able to take advice" in such a way that premises 2 and 3 both come out true. For "able to take advice" can mean either "able to *conform* to advice" or "able to *attempt* to conform to advice." If it means the former, then premise 3 is implausible. For we have the same trouble here as with the responsibility argument: we are not able to conform to perspectivist advice in the case of irresistible beliefs.

Moreover, premise 2 is implausible. Both perspectivist and reliabilist advice are inconsistent with 2. And the premise is indeed implausible on this interpretation. Certainly it is not *generally* true of proper advice that we are always able to conform to it. We are not always, on every occasion on which we seek to do what conforms to the advice, able to conform to the advice given in cookbooks, auto maintenance manuals, pop psychology primers, or "How to Prepare for the SAT." To be sure, proper advice is tuned to some degree to the abilities of those to whom it is directed. But the degree of attunement is a product of two conflicting desiderata: the desideratum of satisfying a goal (such as producing delicious food) and the desideratum of giving advice people are able to conform to. Since not everyone is able to cook delicious food, pitching to common abilities would entail failing entirely to honor the desideratum of producing delicious food. Thus advice must be given that is to some degree *ability-insensitive*—such that some who seek the advice will occasionally be unable to conform to it. Nor can we always translate ability-insensitive advice into ability-sensitive advice by giving advice conditional on having certain abilities. For many human activities worth doing require an indefinitely large number and range of abilities—so large and diverse that one cannot expect to be able to write just those abilities into the advice.

One might try to argue for the requirement that advice be ability-sensitive—i.e., for premise 2—by appeal to the principle that "ought" implies "can." Epistemic advice specifies at some level what it is *epistemically permissible* to believe. Thus, according to this argument, it is epistemically advisable to believe p in case it is epistemically permissible to believe p. So you ought epistemically always to withhold the belief p in case it is not advisable to believe p. But since "ought" implies "can," if you ought to withhold the belief p, then you can withhold the belief p. So you can always withhold an inadvisable belief. This is supposed to establish premise 2: you are always able to conform to advice.

The trouble with appealing to the principle that "ought" implies "can" to establish premise 2 is that the same examples that lead us to question the premise also lead us to question whether "ought" implies "can." One ought to remove a soufflé from the oven immediately before serving, one ought to expand one's vocabulary before taking the SAT, and so on, regardless of whether one can. Hence "ought" does not always imply "can." So why should we assume that the *epistemic* "ought" implies "can"? Without the principle that the epistemic "ought" implies "can," we lack a persuasive argument for premise 2.

I have offered these doubts about premises 2 and 3 on the interpretation of "taking advice" as "*conforming* to the advice." What happens on the alternative interpretation of "taking advice" as merely "*attempting* to conform to the advice"? (Henceforth I shall interpret taking advice in this way unless otherwise indicated.) I am willing to concede premise 2 on this interpretation. It is plausible enough that there is no point in giving advice to people who are unable even to attempt to conform to it, and consequently it is improper to give such advice in circumstances in which people seek belief or in which it is appropriate for them to seek belief.

However, premise 3 remains implausible. For we can surely always *attempt* to conform to reliabilist advice if we can always attempt to conform to perspectivist advice. This is enough to knock down the version of the advisory argument we have been considering.

It is clear, then, that the proponent of the argument must do one of two things: either retreat to a version of the argument on which proper advice requires that we are able to conform to the advice *in some desirable class of circumstances* in which we are able to conform to perspectivist but not reliabilist advice; or complain that reliabilist advice is improper because of some *defect* other than that we are not always able to conform to the advice. Both of these ways of criticizing reliabilist advice are suggested by the remarks of Foley we quoted earlier (p. 15).

It might be objected—and Foley seems to be making this objection—that reliabilist advice is improper because it is *vacuous* in the way that alethic advice (the advice to believe what is true) is vacuous, or in the way that the stockbroker's advice to buy low and sell high is vacuous: this advice merely tells us to do what we initially sought to do—hold a true belief as to whether *p*. But the charge of vacuity clearly does not apply to reliabilist advice, since the advice does not merely tell us to do what we initially sought to do. It specifies an action *by which* we can do what we initially sought to do: we can believe what is true by believing what is reliable. Reliabilist advice is not useless because it is vacuous.

A different charge that might be made against reliabilist advice is that it is *incomplete*, rather than vacuous. For the task of believing what is reliable is a nonbasic task, and for a nonbasic task, advice must specify the basic action that we must perform by which we perform the task. Perhaps this is what Foley has in mind when he says that we cannot simply "read off from the world" what is reliable. For the task of believing what is reliable, like that of believing what is true, is nonbasic, and we need further instructions for carrying out this task.

This is true, but there is no reason why reliabilist advice, cannot be supplemented with further instructions. A natural supplement would be this: check the frequency of true beliefs in the output of a relevant process (or set of processes) available on the occasion and believe what would result from the exercise of the process if it is reliable. In taking reliabilist advice, the subject must of course rely on beliefs about frequencies of truths, about the relevance and availability of processes, and about what beliefs these processes would yield when exercised. But reliabilist advice implicitly specifies the various basic actions needed to judge what is reliable and thereby believe what is true.

I suspect that Foley has in mind a rather different and deeper complaint about the incompleteness of reliabilist advice—that it is incomplete in an important way: it fails to be what I shall call *closed*. To be closed, advice must provide the subject with some recommendation, not only about whether to believe *p*, but also about whether to hold the *advisory beliefs*, the beliefs on which the subject must rely in taking the advice. Closed advice, in other words, builds a recommendation about advisory beliefs into its advice. Of course the reliabilist does offer advice about which advisory beliefs to hold—namely, reliabilist advice. But this advice is not built into the advice about believing *p*, nor could it be. For any attempt to build it in would touch off a regress of recommendations about advisory beliefs. The subject would have to take the same recommendation about the beliefs on which he or she relies in taking the recommendation about the advisory beliefs, and so on. Now, any sort of advice would give rise to an internal regress of recommendations if we were to incorporate into it the *same* advice as a recommendation for advisory beliefs. The complaint against reliabilist advice is therefore not that it gives rise to a regress when this is done, but that it incorporates no alternative recommendation for the advisory beliefs. It sets no standards for the advisory beliefs employed in taking reliabilist advice. In this, it might be alleged, it differs from reflective perspectivist advice, which in effect incorporates a recommendation by asking one to believe what one would on reflection deem reliable. It might be claimed that the advisory beliefs on which we rely in taking this advice are beliefs about reliability that would be the products of such reflection.

However, the apparent superiority here of perspectivist advice is an illusion. Reflective perspectivist advice is not closed any more than reliabilist advice. Far from being closed, it does not incorporate any recommendation at all. In taking the advice, we do not rely on a belief about reliability that would be the product of reflection. Rather, we rely on a belief about whether we would on reflection deem the belief *p* reliable. The advice does not give us any recommendation as to which beliefs of the latter sort we are to rely on. We *could* arrive at a belief as to whether the belief *p* is reliable by reflecting or simulating reflection, but the advice does not tell us to do so.[5]

---

5. Of course reflective advice could say: reflect as to whether the belief *p* is reliable. Then it would avoid reliance on any advisory beliefs and thus vacuously be closed. But this reflective advice does not entail perspectivism under the advisory conception of justified belief. Rather it entails that a belief is justified just in case it results from reflection. That is not a perspectivist theory. The perspectivist cannot gain closure by retreating to the advice to reflect.

Lack of closure is no defect, however, since no advice could be closed (other than, trivially, advice that relies on no beliefs at all). In other words, the regress argument generalizes from showing that we cannot give a recommendation that is the *same* as the advice, as in the case of reliabilist advice, to showing that we cannot give a recommendation for *all* the beliefs on which we rely in taking advice. This is enough to lay the present objection to reliabilist advice to rest.

Let us try one final objection to reliabilist advice, related to the issue of closure: that iterated reliabilist advice-taking is ruled out as *circular*. This does finally promise to distinguish reliabilist from perspectivist advice. For in taking reliabilist advice, one relies on advisory beliefs about the reliability of the belief *p*. This requires one to judge whether beliefs belonging to a reference class of beliefs suitably related to the belief *p* are generally true. In particular, one must judge whether a certain process *R* is reliable, and hence whether the outputs of *R* are generally true. But to judge the latter, we must rely on output beliefs *q* for sufficiently many *q*. Unfortunately, taking reliabilist advice regarding these output beliefs is ruled out, since to take such advice, we must again judge whether *R* generally yields true beliefs, since the belief *q* is an output of *R*. And this is circular. Perspectivist advice, it might be claimed, does not succumb to the same charge, since it does not require relying on the same advisory beliefs at more than one order.

It is not easy to judge whether this objection has any force against reliabilist advice. Certainly it cannot be required of advice that we can take advice about advisory beliefs for any number of orders without circularity. For human beings do not have an infinite fund of beliefs on which to rely in taking advice at successive orders. Advice-taking must either terminate or must go circular at some point. There is no way out of circularity in advice-taking, as there is in a regress of justified belief, where the beliefs in the regress may result from something other than advice-taking. The difference between reliabilist and perspectivist advice is only that reliabilist advice goes circular while perspectivist advice terminates. So if there is to be any objection here, it must be that the circularity in taking reliabilist advice occurs at too early an order.

Why would it be too early? Perhaps the most persuasive line here is that advice-taking is designed to answer doubts, and reliabilist advice cannot do so because the output beliefs on which it relies must be doubted if the belief *p* is doubted. Perspectivist advice might be said to differ in this regard.

This objection has some force. I concede that when the point of taking advice is to answer a doubt, and that doubt extends to all outputs of *R*, then relying on those outputs is ruled out. It does not follow, however, that taking reliabilist advice is ruled out. This *would* follow if one *had* to rely on the other outputs of R in taking reliabilist advice. The objection does indeed show that taking reliabilist advice cannot answer doubts when all outputs of R are doubted and one is restricted to outputs of R in answering the doubts.

Despite this, there are three points to make in defense of reliabilist advice. First, these are not the only circumstances in which there are doubts. It is not always true that when a belief p is doubted, so are all the other outputs of R. There are *local* doubts that pertain to some outputs of a process and not others. We might doubt the truth of a proposition—e.g., the belief that this is an elm—and not at the same time doubt the truth of another—the belief that *that* is an elm—even though belief in these propositions would count as outputs of the same process R. Taking reliabilist advice may afford an answer to this doubt, despite the fact that one relies on outputs of R in taking the advice.

Second, when *all* the outputs of R are doubted, these doubts can sometimes be answered by relying on beliefs that are not outputs of R. Reliabilist advice-taking may rely on general and theoretical beliefs (e.g., evolutionary beliefs) about correlations between the reliability of processes and other conditions. Beliefs in such correlations must ultimately rely on output beliefs of some processes, but these need not be output beliefs of the process R. It is true that the plausibility of certain theoretical arguments for the reliability of some processes—e.g., evolutionary arguments for the reliability of inductive inference—has been called into serious question recently by Stephen Stich (1990, chapter 3), but I do not think it can seriously be denied that there are some plausible theoretical arguments for the reliability of some processes on practical grounds. Reliabilist advice-taking may therefore answer doubts in a variety of circumstances in which the outputs of R are all doubted.

Moreover, it seems that perspectivist advice-taking must simulate reliance on general beliefs in reflection if it is to answer local doubts. If a local doubt is to be answered by considering what we would on reflection believe reliable, then presumably our determination of what we would believe cannot rely solely on locally doubted beliefs. It must rely on *general* beliefs. So perspectivist advice-taking is in much the same boat regarding local skepticism as reliabilist advice-taking.

Third, perspectivist advice-taking labors under an analogous limitation. To take advice regarding the belief p, one must rely on the counterfactual psychological belief q: one would on reflection believe that the belief p is reliable. To take advice regarding the belief q, one must rely on the counterfactual psychological belief r: one would on reflection believe that the belief that one would on reflection believe that the belief p is reliable is reliable. It is hard to imagine that one would have a serious doubt about q

that did not extend to r as well, since r has a similar subject matter and is more complex than q.

These are all the criticisms of the advisory argument for reflective perspectivism that I have for the moment. There does not seem to be any way to argue from an advisory conception of justified belief to the conclusion that justified belief is perspectival belief. We have seen no ground for denying that we can take reliabilist advice.

At this point, perspectivists may try to retreat to the weaker claim that taking perspectivist advice is in a certain sense indispensable in taking advice, in a way that taking reliabilist advice is not. For in *attempting* to conform to reliabilist advice in the right way, we necessarily *conform* to *perspectivist* advice—we necessarily have a perspectival belief.[6] But if "in the right way" means "with justification," this argument runs into the same problem as the responsibility argument—irresistible religious or political beliefs we are justified in believing to be unreliable. We may attempt to conform to reliabilist advice and fail to believe what we are justified in believing reliable—fail to have a perspectival belief—because our belief resists our efforts.

4. IS PERSPECTIVIST ADVICE PROPER?

So far we have considered versions of the advisory argument that try to deduce perspectivism from the *formal* nature of advice. Perhaps we should consider a last and somewhat different version of the argument, one that tries to deduce perspectivism from the substantive nature of advice.

What ought a substantive account of proper advice look like? If the advisory conception of justified belief is to be noncircular, we shall have to avoid defining proper advice in terms of justified belief, since the direction of definition is the reverse under the advisory conception. This does not leave us with very many natural candidates for an account of proper advice. Here is the one that comes immediately to mind: proper advice is advice the taking of which tends to lead to reliable beliefs.

On this account, it is difficult to decide between reliabilist and perspectivist advice. Their effects would be similar. In favor of reliabilist advice is the fact that more subjects are able to attempt to conform to it than to perspectivist advice. For example, more subjects have the concept of reliability than have the concept of reflecting on reliability. It might seem that perspectivist advice easily makes up for this by having a higher tendency to lead to reliable belief on each occasion of advice-taking, since

---

6. This argument differs from the earlier advisory argument in supporting reliabilist iterativism rather than counterfactual reflective perspectivism.

reflecting on reliability is more apt to lead to a correct judgment of reliability than mere belief about reliability. But that depends on how good the subject is at reflection. People often become confused and indecisive as a result of reflection, or simply fail to make progress. It is a commonplace of cognitive psychology that subjects who commit fallacies or reason invalidly, when they are invited to reflect on the validity of their inference in debriefing, tend to develop rationalizations of their methods and tend to entrench their way of reasoning. The perspectivist might deny that this is genuine reflection. Perhaps not, but then the point would be that people often tend to reflect in the wrong way, and so are poor at *attempting* to take perspectivist advice. Either way, perspectivist advice has trouble. Of course, debriefing sessions are one thing and reflection in ordinary life is another. But it would not be surprising if people were even worse at reflecting under the pressures of ordinary life than in debriefing. Finally, reflection on reliability takes considerable effort that might otherwise be diverted to exercising reliable processes. This will reduce the number of reliable beliefs and count against perspectivist advice.

5. THE ARETAIC ARGUMENT FOR ITERATIVISM

There is one last hope for an argument for perspectivism—by appeal to an *aretaic* conception of justified belief, or more exactly, to a specific aretaic conception. There are many things that matter epistemically besides justified belief—abilities and dispositions to exercise reliable processes, the cognitive mechanisms that underlie such processes, powerful cognitive faculties, and justification-supporting cognitive practices, to name just a few. To have a justified belief does not, on any plausible view of justification, entail having the ability or disposition to acquire justified beliefs; in this sense one can be justified by accident. Yet such abilities and dispositions are of the first importance for successful cognition. Justification-supporting practices rely on an infrastructure of such cognitive abilities and dispositions. These abilities and dispositions are among the epistemic virtues. Clearly, however, epistemic virtues matter in large measure because of their relation to justified belief. This suggests that we might rely on our understanding of epistemic virtues to define justified belief.

An aretaic theory of justified belief is one that understands justified belief in relation to intellectual or epistemic virtues like intelligence, wisdom, perspicacity, care, imaginativeness, etc. One might begin with the observation that epistemic virtues matter because they facilitate or give rise to justified belief, and one might turn this around and say that justified beliefs are beliefs of a sort that *result* from certain epistemic virtues. Alternatively, one might say that a justified belief is one that *manifests* certain epistemic virtues, as behavior that helps others manifests the virtue of benevolence, or determination to complete a task in the face of danger manifests courage. I will focus on the latter manifestation account.

Clearly, different epistemic virtues perform different functions. The beliefs that manifest intelligence or imaginativeness need not be justified. And while wisdom and care are often manifested by justified beliefs, they need not be. We must locate a particular virtue, or a small set of virtues, that are typically manifested by justified beliefs. One proposal is that justified belief is belief of a sort that manifests *epistemic integrity* (alternatively: *epistemic autonomy*). On this account of justified belief, if it turns out that perspectival belief is belief that manifests epistemic integrity, then perspectivism follows.

What is epistemic integrity? *Moral* integrity, in one sense at least, is the practice of sticking to one's moral tenets—acting in accordance with what one believes morally right, even, or especially, in the face of opposition to doing so or of the temptation to do otherwise. A person with moral integrity does not stray from her moral judgments or principles even under threat or bribe; she does not knuckle under and act in a hypocritical or unprincipled way. Such judgments may be judgments of particular cases or of general principle. It seems that moral integrity entails a practice of acting in accordance with the moral judgments one is *justified* in making, and not merely the ones one *actually* makes. Sticking to unjustified judgments does not manifest integrity but pigheadedness. *Epistemic* integrity resembles moral integrity in being a practice of believing what is sanctioned by one's justified epistemic judgments or principles—believing what one is justified in deeming reliable—in the face of the temptation to cut corners (e.g., by wishful thinking or hasty generalization) and in the face of interference that threatens to disrupt the cognitive processes one deems reliable (e.g., interference from self-deception, cognitive biases such as recency, latency, and halo effects, confirmation bias, overconfidence, and the like). Epistemic integrity also entails a disposition to reconsider, defend, or amend one's epistemic judgments under counterevidence.

Now to state the aretaic argument for iterativism:

1. Justified belief is belief of a sort that manifests epistemic integrity.

2. The sort of belief that manifests epistemic intergrity is iterativist belief.

3. Therefore, justified belief is iterativist belief.

Is this a persuasive argument for perspectivism? Here are some problems with the argument.

First, it has force only if some aretaic conception of justified belief is plausible. Yet aretaic conceptions have little plausibility. To be sure, the idea behind an aretaic conception—that there is a significant relation between certain epistemic virtues and justified belief—is correct. But we may explain this relation without endorsing the aretaic conception itself. We need not explain the relation by saying that justified belief is belief of a sort that manifests an epistemic virtue. On the contrary, something entirely different is suggested by the observation that got us started on the aretaic conception, the observation that the practice of justification depends on certain character traits. This observation suggests that certain epistemic virtues tend to facilitate and give rise to justified beliefs. Of course not all epistemic virtues do this. Similarly, it may be that not all justified beliefs manifest certain epistemic virtues, or indeed any epistemic virtues at all.

To see this, reflect that there is nothing natural about defining a *deontic* status like justified belief—epistemically permissible belief—as belief of a sort that manifests exemplary traits or virtues. On any charitable epistemology, even those who lack virtues have scads of justified beliefs, and there is no obvious reason why what is permissible for those who are not virtuous should turn out to be what manifests the traits of those who are virtuous. To be sure, a primary point of ascribing virtues is to get people to do good deeds by emulating the deeds of the virtuous. But this no more entails that the only permissible beliefs are those of a sort that manifest virtues—that justified beliefs are always beliefs of a sort that manifest virtues—than the fact that a chief point of ascribing benevolence is to get people to do morally good deeds by emulation entails that the only permissible actions are morally good deeds. A primary point of evaluating permissible beliefs is surely to create a broad space in which people have approved beliefs even when they lack virtues. This space may be necessary to encourage people to make progress toward those virtues. People are bound to stumble in trying to emulate virtuous beliefs; these are very hard won (unlike reliable beliefs, which do not need the corresponding protection of a status of perspectival belief). More importantly, a space of permissible beliefs may be necessary if people are to maintain and use desirable beliefs though they lack virtues and indeed fail to emulate them. After all, most people fall short of most virtues, and at a certain point stop trying to emulate them. That is why less than exemplary (not very perspicacious, wise, or careful) beliefs can be justified. These are justified beliefs that do not manifest any epistemic virtues.

Of course the heroic proponent of the aretaic conception could respond by insisting that justified but less than exemplary beliefs, though they do not themselves manifest epistemic virtues, are nevertheless beliefs *of a sort* that manifest epistemic virtues. But once this "sort" has been stretched to include beliefs that do not manifest epistemic virtues, the need for an account of what a sort is becomes pressing. It will not do to say that a sort includes just those beliefs sufficiently similar overall to manifestations of epistemic virtues. It is doubtful that a justified but not very perspicacious or careful perceptual belief must be overall more similar to a perceptual belief that manifests perspicacity and care than an unjustified, perspicacious but careless belief. The latter two are, after all, similar in perspicacity. If the relevant sort of belief is to be defined by similarity to beliefs that manifest epistemic virtues, the similarity must be in some particular respect. For example, the justified belief that does not manifest virtue might be similar to the manifesting belief in respect to reliability, coherence, or whatever. The trouble is that once the relevant respect is identified, we can simply define justified belief directly in terms of that respect—in terms of reliability or coherence—and forget about manifesting virtue. Identifying the respect is equivalent to identifying the property that all justified beliefs have in common. In this case, the explanatory work in the apparently aretaic definition of justification is being done by the identified property, and the account of justified belief is, in its explanations of our intuitions about justified beliefs, nonaretaic. For these reasons, an aretaic conception of justified belief seems unpromising.

Even granting the plausibility of an aretaic conception, we may ask: why *this* aretaic conception? Why should *epistemic integrity* be chosen as the virtue justified beliefs must manifest, rather than some combination of perspicacity, care, etc.—virtues that are not always manifested by (or only by) perspectival belief? Certainly if, as I have suggested, certain epistemic virtues facilitate or give rise to justified belief, we would be hard pressed to pick out one among these deserving of the central position in an account of justification accorded to epistemic integrity by the present account. To assume that justified belief is belief that manifests epistemic integrity is to give conformity to one's perspective an importance in cognition that would need as much argument as identifying justified belief directly with perspectival belief.

A final objection to the aretaic argument is that its assumption that perspectival belief is belief of a sort that manifests epistemic integrity is doubtful at best. On one view of manifestation, the beliefs that manifest a virtue are those that result (in an appropriate way) from the virtue. On another view, they are those that somehow represent all of the qualities involved in the virtue—in the case of epistemic integrity, such qualities as a disposition to seek and maintain justified beliefs about reliability. On neither view of manifestation do perspectival beliefs always manifest epistemic integrity.[7]

I have canvassed arguments for perspectivism by appeal to formal conceptions of justified belief—responsibility, advisory, and aretaic conceptions—conceptions that seemed, at least initially, relatively innocuous, yet perhaps rich enough to yield perspectivism. Perspectival belief, whether defined by iterativism or reflective perspectivism, does not fit any of these conceptions. Our lead question was whether there is any role for a status of perspectival belief in epistemic evaluation. The answer suggested by our survey is "None." Of course I have expressed doubts about whether any of these conceptions describes justified belief. Nevertheless, I am inclined to regard epistemically responsible belief as a significant epistemic status distinct from justified belief. But my conclusion is not merely that perspectival belief is not justified belief, but that it is not epistemically responsible, advisable, or virtuous belief either. There is no role for a status of perspectival belief. No doubt BonJour is right that it is (usually) good to be justified in believing that one's belief is reliable. And Foley is right that it is (often) good to believe what results or would result from reflection on reliability. But perhaps this is because for many subjects, one's belief tends to be reliable or coherent just when one is justified in believing that one's belief is reliable, or when one reflects on reliability. The attraction of perspectival belief may trace to its association with another kind of belief—perhaps reliable belief, perhaps coherent belief—that is more intimately related to justified belief.

---

7. Similar objections may be made to versions of the aretaic argument that substitute epistemic conscientiousness or autonomy for epistemic integrity.

2

Structural Justification*

Robert Audi

Justification comes in many forms and is predicable of many kinds of things. Its primary bearers are actions and beliefs; but it may belong, globally, to entire outlooks on the world and, specifically, to individual propositions. It may also apply to persons, policies, and other complex entities which, unlike actions, are not events and, unlike propositions, do not have truth value. Even to catalogue and interconnect the bearers of justification would be a large task. My project here will not accomplish that, though it should lay some of the groundwork for doing it. My focus is on the forms of justification rather than its bearers, and I shall locate and clarify a kind which, though applicable to a great diversity of elements, is often left faceless in the crowd of justificatory notions that more often occupy philosophers. In doing this it is easiest to work with the cognitive domain; for even if we do not assume—as I certainly do not—that all justification is ultimately explicable in terms of justified belief, the domain of belief is at once central in epistemology and a good model for other territories in which justification resides. I begin with a sketch of justifcatory attributions and from there proceed to explicate the notion central in this paper.

I. FOUR KINDS OF JUSTIFICATION

(1) When I justifiedly believe something, I have *doxastic justification*—or simply *belief justification*: to have this is simply to have justified belief.[1]

* This paper is dedicated to the memory of Mark Overvold, with whom I spent many stimulating and profitable hours discussing philosophical problems related to it. It originally appeared in the *Journal of Philosophical Research* 16 (1991: 473–92). For comments on earlier drafts I thank Frederick Adams, Paul Moser, and Kevin Possin. Discussion at the Mark Overvold Conference was also helpful.
    1. The term "doxastic" in this use was suggested by Roderick Firth (1978); "belief justification" is simply the standard English equivalent which I proposed in Audi 1988. The former is more common in the literature and I will use it more often.

(2) When I do not believe something, but have a ground for believing it such that, if (other things equal) I believed it *on* that ground, I would justifiedly believe it, I have *situational justification*. This is, roughly, the presence in one's epistemic situation of a justifying ground for p.[2] Thus, while I did not—until I thought of the matter—believe that the chair beneath me minutely sags from my weight, I was previously justified *in* believing this, by virtue of my justified beliefs about the material sustaining me in relation to my weight.[3] Since one also has justifying grounds when one justifiedly believes p, situational justification occurs with, as well as without, doxastic justification. (3) We may speak of justification for propositions: we can ask if there is any justification for the view, cited without attribution in a gossip column, that Jack is guilty, or for the conclusion that Jill has left town. Call this *propositional justification*; it may exist whether or not anyone believes the proposition so justified and whether or not anyone is situationally justified in believing it. It may be, e.g., that while no one now has evidence for concluding Jill has left town (and so no one has situational justification for it), a brief investigation would unearth some and thereby confirm that indeed there was justification. Propositional justification is, then, *relative* to potential believers—being something like (genuine) evidence that is available to one or more persons indicated in the relevant context—but it is not *predicated* of any actual person. Of these three sorts of justification, propositional justification has been given least attention, common though the notion is in standard parlance.

There is a fourth notion, related to propositional justification, to which philosophers have paid still less attention. Let me bring it out by example. Imagine that Gail is a student of mine about to embark on a job search. I believe her to be good in her main fields, a capable teacher, and something of a generalist as well; but I also know that the competition is stiff. Given all that I now know and justifiedly believe, I am not justified in believing (or in disbelieving) that she will get a job on the first round. I do not, then, have

---

2. This term comes from Audi 1988. Firth used "propositional justification" here, but it seems to me that the relevant notion is *person-relative* propositional justification—a proposition's being justified *for* a person. That term is cumbersome; more important, "situational" has the virtue of calling attention to the subject's epistemic situation, which contains the ground(s) of justification. There is also a phenomenon, described in the text, which I think is more properly called propositional justification.

3. That I did not believe this until the matter came up may be controversial; in Audi 1982 I defend the implied distinction between dispositional (nonoccurrent) beliefs and— what is illustrated here—mere dispositions to believe, where the disposition to have a relevant belief is actualized by elicitors such as thinking about the grounds one has or may have.

situational justification for believing this: in what I take to be roughly equivalent terminology, the proposition that she will get a job on the first round is not justified for me. But suppose I have heard of an opening in a department which I have good reason to believe would regard Gail very highly, though I have not thought about her in connection with it and have not drawn this conclusion. As I think about the school, I conclude that they need, and will likely realize that they need, a generalist; that they are men of good will who prefer not to remain an all-male department; and they would take my recommendation very seriously. It also occurs to me that one of them has a degree from Tri-State College (which happens to be Gail's undergraduate school). Suppose further that there is an opening in a similar department, where the facts are different but reflection would also lead me, with equal warrant, to the same conclusion, though again I have not drawn it. Now imagine that the time for recommendations arrives and I am depressed as I say to Gail that I *hope* she will find something. I speak cautiously to her because I do not think I am justified in saying more, and I am suspending judgment. Suddenly, I search my memory, remember both the openings I heard about months before, and form the intention to recommend her for both. Now I may be justified in believing, and may justifiedly believe, that she will get a job on the first round. What this case shows is that while the proposition that she will get a job on the first round was initially not, on the basis of the total evidence contained in my beliefs (including my propositional knowledge), *justified* for me, it was *justifiable* for me. I want to call the kind of justification I had prior to recalling the openings and thinking about them *structural justification*.

The plausibility of calling such justification structural derives from its grounds' being available to me, by reflection, *in* my cognitive structure (internally accessible to reflection, as some epistemologists would put it) though reflection may not be needed to bring it to mind—yet not organized or pulled together in such a way as to justify me, without further ado, in believing that Gail will get a job on the first round. I have the makings of a justification, but they are *unintegrated* and so do not amount to a justification as they stand in my cognitive system: roughly, in my body of beliefs, dispositions to believe, inferential tendencies, memory, and consciousness. Once I have recalled the openings and the facts about them, the proposition that Gail will get the job is justified for me: I now have, in my body of beliefs, grounds which adequately (if minimally) support that proposition. My epistemic situation now contains *cognitively registered* grounds for the belief. Prior to my recalling the openings and forming the intention to recommend Gail for them, the proposition is only *justifiable* for me: I in some sense *have* a justification, but it is buried in my cognitive inventory, not registered in premises I believe, or displayed in my perceptual consciousness, or in any other way ready to ground my believing the proposition.

We can sharpen the contrast between structural justification and its more familiar cousin, situational justification, if we connect both with the notion of believing a proposition on the basis of a ground. There are two cases of believing to be considered here: the inferential one just illustrated, in which one believes a proposition on the basis of one or more others, and the noninferential one, in which the ground on the basis of which one believes is experiential, as in the case of believing the paper one is seeing to be white on the basis of visual impressions of white. Situational justification for believing p occurs where one's epistemic situation contains a ground, whether inferential or not, such that, should one (other things equal) believe p on the basis of that ground, one would justifiedly believe it.

Structural justification is, as it were, presituational: in order to get from structural to situational justification one must either form the appropriate belief(s) or have the relevant experience, say by recalling certain events or by introspecting. Thus, it is because I recall the openings that I have situational justification for forming the beliefs which express my (inferential) grounds for believing that Gail will get a job on the first round. When I do form these beliefs, I am situationally justified in believing that, in turn. Because I formed them as a result of accessing materials already in my cognitive system, as opposed to my making new observations or getting testimony on the subject, my original justification is properly called structural.

As this example indicates, I take the relevant structure to be not only cognitive but such that those of its aspects pertinent to the justification in question are available to the subject by reflection, including introspective reflection. If in some cases reflection, as opposed to, say, merely asking oneself a relevant question, is not needed, in others only extensive reflection will bring the justifying elements to mind. The sense in which structural justification for believing p is *had*, then, is not occurrent, but dispositional: under certain—highly variable—kinds of conditions, S can bring the justifying elements into consciousness and can form, or hold, the belief that p on the basis of them. There are, however, two ways in which reflection can bring the justifying elements into consciousness. With situational justification, the justifier is accessible through what we might call *revelatory reflection*: a belief or recollection or percept, say, is already present as a justifier of the propositional object of the belief that p—making p justified *for S*—and S need only reflect to become aware of this set of elements and, upon believing p on the basis of them, to acquire a justified belief that p. With structural justification, on the other hand, the justifiers are accessible only through *generative reflection* (or thought): the kind that, through such things as producing a belief not yet possessed, yields situational justification.[4] Generative reflection produces justification by producing new grounds, whether inferential, as in the case of newly formed beliefs expressing premises for p, or direct, as in the case of memory impressions of the state of affairs p expresses. These grounds provide situational justification, which in turn may lead to actually justified belief of p.

One might think that except in the case of doxastic justification we should not speak of justification at all, but only justifiability. It is true that a situationally justified belief that p is, if not already justified, justifiable—most notably by S's coming to hold it on the basis of the elements that justify p for S. Similarly, if S has structural justification for p, S can, by both reflection *and* coming to believe p on the basis of the justifying elements, achieve justified belief that p. In each case *believing* p is justifiable for S (whether the belief is already held or not); but in the former p itself is *justified* for S, whereas in the latter p is only *justifiable* for S. But neither situational nor structural justification is simply a "counterfactual property": granting that S's having them *implies* counterfactuals, it is not equivalent to them. Both are actual properties that S has in virtue of perceptual states, memory impressions, beliefs, and certain other psychological attributes. Indeed, even propositional justification exists not just because the proposition is justifiable in the abstract, but because someone has actual properties that make the relevant evidence accessible.

The varieties of nondoxastic justification, then, though they correspond to different sorts of justifiability, are not reducible to it. And if they are all ultimately understandable by appeal to doxastic justification, they are not species of it; they each correspond to different locutions; and distinguishing them conceptually can clarify the overall theory of justification and the diverse ways in which we may be said to have evidence. If a kind of reduction is possible by virtue of all four kinds being analyzable in terms of one, say doxastic justification, it may still be best for epistemological theory to work with each independently. It is at best cumbersome, e.g., to say, not that S has structural justification for believing p, but instead that while S does not presently have grounds for p such that S is justified in believing it, still, by reflection S can acquire grounds for p such that, if he comes to believe it on those grounds, this belief will be justified.

It should be apparent from the centrality of accessibility through reflection that the notion of structural justification as I am developing it is internalist in the following sense. The justification in question is internally

---

4. These terms are drawn from Audi 1989a, where they are associated with the distinction between justified and merely justifiable belief.

accessible to S: roughly, available to consciousness through reflection, including introspective reflection, as opposed to perceptual observation or testimony from someone else. It is not merely part of the subject's psychological or physical make-up, nor need it be a guarantor (or probabilizer) of truth independently of accessible elements. This is not to say that a counterpart notion of structural justification cannot be developed from an externalist perspective, but that is not my approach here.[5]

II. SOME VARIETIES AND DEGREES OF STRUCTURAL JUSTIFICATION

The placement example can be used to bring out the broadest division among kinds of structural justification: that between inferential and non-inferential sorts, between the kind grounded in premises for p and the kind grounded directly in, say, sensory experience. The structural justification I have for believing that Gail will get a job on the first round is inferential. For my justification comes through at least one proposition such that it is only on the basis of *it* as a (justified) premise—whether I actually draw a conclusion from it or not—that the proposition is justifiable for me. Thus, the belief of this proposition, a belief in which my structural justification would culminate if fully realized in my cognitive system, would be inferential, in the broad sense that the belief would be based on one or more other beliefs of mine and would derive its justification therefrom.[6] By contrast, my structural justification for believing that there is a relevant job opening might be noninferential; I might, e.g., have a disposition to recall a mention of the opening by a friend, and when my memory is jogged by my search for relevant information and I do recall the opening, the basis of my belief that it exists is not another proposition I believe, but rather my memorial impression of the conversation. The proposition that the opening exists is justified for me *by* memory, not by inference from anything I *believe about* my memory.[7]

---

5. If structural justification is conceived as a kind of justifiability, an externalist construal is readily imagined: p is structurally justified for S provided (roughly) S's reflecting in a suitable way would produce in S an externally satisfactory justification for p. It might, e.g., result in calculating probabilities that in fact do render p probable and produce belief of it. The accessibility of the justifiers is still internal; but on this view they must in the context also be reliable belief-producers.

6. There need not be an actual *process* of inference for this to occur; the belief might arise, and remain, as structurally rather than episodically inferential. Nothing major in this paper hinges on this difference, but for those interested it is developed and defended in Audi 1986 and, for the case of action, it is more fully elaborated in Audi 1989b, especially chapters 4–5.

7. I am sidestepping here the issue whether all noninferential justification, even in the structural case, is ultimately grounded at least partly in noninferential justification; but I

It will be obvious that structural justification, like any other kind, admits of degree. Some grounds are better than others; some inferences from grounds to a conclusion are better justified than others; and some propositions for which one has justification are also such that one has some degree of justification for their negations. For these and related reasons, structural justification may be weak as well as strong. A number of the elements of strength can be discerned as we consider some main kinds of structural justification. I shall begin with inferential cases and conclude with the remaining ones.

The first pair of cases to be noted have in common S's believing a set of adequate premises. Here "premises" does not imply that an inference is drawn but only that an inference would be appropriate; and adequacy is simply sufficiency for justification: that is, the premise set—call it q— justifies the conclusion—call it p—for S. In the first case, S believes the premises but would need to reflect a moment to see *how* q supports p. By contrast with the case of situational justification, then, S is not epistemically ready to believe p on the basis of q until S registers the connection between them, say by making the connection through reflection. This is why p is only *justifiable* for S and not, until S, say, completes sufficient reflection, *justified* for S. Call this a case of *unrealized connection*, since what S needs to pass from structural to situational justification is simply an appropriate grasp of their evidential connection. None of this implies that a connection can be made *only* through reflection. It may be obvious to me, once I think of them together, that q implies p; or I may have a standing belief to the effect that propositions of the first kind support propositions of the second, as where the first, like a falling barometer, expresses a mark of the truth of the second.

In the second case, S has registered the connection but is not appropriately disposed to believe p on the basis of q, say because S mistakenly, but with ample warrant, thinks that q is inadequate evidence for p. Call this an instance of a *mistakenly defeated connection*. Here (or in some variants of this case, at least) this epistemic belief is consistent with S's in some way having a justification for p, yet the belief prevents S's being justified in believing p, since holding that belief would be against S's own best (and reasonable) evidential judgment. We would then have another case of structural justification without situational justification.

Once we understand these cases, it becomes clear how to single out certain others. Suppose, for instance, we substitute, for believing q, a

---

hope it is clear that the reasons for (and against) saying this can be applied to structural justification as in other cases of justification.

disposition to believe it. This would put me a step further from actually focusing on my justification for p and forming a justified belief of it—where such belief-formation is the cognitive culmination of structural justification. For even upon registering the connection between q and p, I would not have q as a premise until I came to believe it. What we have here is a *doxastically unrealized premise*, since I have not formed (even "unconsciously") a belief expressing that premise. In the same way, we can get a variant of the second case, in which one mistakenly believes that q inadequately supports p. In this variant, in order to form a justified belief that p, one would need *both* to form the premise belief and to overcome the erroneous, and perhaps also unreasonable, epistemic belief. This case would combine unwarranted defeat with lack of doxastic realization.

Among the various possibilities that remain, at least one other deserves mention. It occurs where I am disposed to believe, but do not believe, q because I might mistakenly, yet with ample warrant, think I lack adequate ground for q, say because I have an argument that I quite reasonably (but wrongly) take to disprove it. Here we have a *mistakenly defeated premise*. While there would *be* an adequate ground for q, say a deeply buried but accessible memory of a proof of q, and, in virtue of that memory and my registering the proof's connection with p, I would have a justification for p, still I would not be justified in believing p (or so it would seem for at least some cases in which one quite reasonably thinks one lacks adequate justification for q or for p), and I could not (other things equal) form a justified belief of p without overcoming the mistaken tendency to resist believing q.[8]

This is not to imply that a disposition to believe, as opposed to actually believing, a proposition that is adequate evidence for p cannot itself justify one's belief of p. I leave this difficult question open; but a disposition at least cannot do so if its would-be justifying effect is defeated, as it seems to be, by the reasonable epistemic belief blocking acceptance of q. If the disposition did justify q, moreover, note that this would not in my terminology yield a case of inferential justification of the belief that p, one would be disposed to

---

8. It is arguable that if one has ample warrant to believe one lacks adequate grounds for q, then even if this is false one lacks structural *as well as* situational justification for q. If this line is correct, we might then say that S's structural justification is only prima facie, the same status S's situational justification has. It is possible, however, that the structural justification is unaffected by the mistaken epistemic belief, e.g. because if S grasped the elements that structurally justify p then the error underlying the mistaken belief would immediately come to light, whereas the justification for q, which that belief specifically concerns, is defeated by this epistemic belief. There presumably are, then, cases of the kind described in the text.

infer p from q but, not having formed a belief that q, one would not believe p on the basis of believing q.

The main cases so far described are variants of two kinds: first, those in which S believes q but lacks something that connects it with p and is required for being justified in believing p; and secondly, those in which S does not believe p but is disposed to believe q and would thereby—or at least upon suitably registering the connection between q and p—acquire situational justification for believing p. There are also cases exhibiting greater distance between the basis of S's structural justification and an actual justified belief that p. Imagine that I neither believe nor am disposed to believe that q, but am able, by reflection, to arrive at grounds for q and thereby at a disposition to believe it. Perhaps not every such case is one of having justification for p; if, e.g., I also had a much stronger tendency to arrive instead at grounds for not-q, we might think the evidence for q can merely be had by me. But we can imagine mathematical cases in which, although there is no conflicting evidence, justification is—so to speak—on my cognitive map, yet finding the right path requires my thinking about the various familiar routes and tracing them until an unfamiliar, implicit route comes into view. As this suggests, one possibility is that q is conjunctive and, even when one arrives at the conjuncts separately, one does not have them as premises for p until they somehow are combined in one's mind. The same distinction—between a disposition to believe q and a readiness to arrive at a belief by reflection—applies to S's relation to the connection between q and p. And there are many subcases which we need not even mention once the general grounds of classification are clear.

Before we move to the topic of noninferential structural justification, we should extend what has been said to the case of second-order beliefs. Epistemic beliefs whose subject is *propositions* have already been mentioned. Epistemic beliefs can also be about other *beliefs* and can defeat justification in that instance too. Thus, I might in a special case have structural justification both for p and for the proposition that I am not justified in believing p. These instances of structural justification are in tension with one another and in different situations one or the other might dominate. Thus, whether or not I actually come to believe that I am not warranted in believing p, the structural justification I have for the proposition that I am not warranted could prevent such justification as I have for p from being adequate for, say, my knowing that p should I believe p on the relevant basis. On the other hand, if my justification for the second-order epistemic belief derives from an insufficiently considered skepticism and my justification for p is excellent, this justification for p may prevail despite my tendency to deny that I have it.

With this much before us, we can be brief about the noninferential cases. Here a ground for *p*, say a visual experience, gives me a justification for *p* without doing so through my believing that that ground obtains. My memorial tendencies might justify me (structurally) in believing that John visited me once even if they supply me with no premises for this. For I might be able, by thinking about John in relation to my past visitors, to call up images, or remember events, such that they would noninferentially ground my believing John visited. Again, I am not justified *in* believing this initially; but I have a justification in the sense that, by reflection, I can put myself into a position in which I am justified in believing it and can thereby come to form an actually justified belief of it. To be sure, once my reflection elicits the justificatory grounds, I can (in principle) always *formulate* them in a way that provides an inferential justification. But to conclude from this that my justification must be inferential in the first place would be a grave error. That what justifies us in believing *p* can be given inferentially in an argument for *p* does not imply that the original function of this justifier is inferential. Indeed, if there were no noninferential justification prior to premises and formulable in them only by its retrospective (or second-order) grasp, it is at best unclear how there could be any justification at all.[9]

Similar examples can be drawn from the domains of perception, consciousness, and a priori reflection. In all of these one can have capacities whose exercise takes one to a ground for a proposition, where the distance one must reflectively traverse is such that, while one has a justification for *p*, one is not yet justified in believing it. One may need to scrutinize one's visual field and think about its contents; one may need to examine one's thoughts and feelings; one may need to draw inferences from propositions one believes. The task may be easy or difficult, long or short. But in each case there is at least one path one can take from some ground one has to a justified belief that *p*. The next section will examine these paths and their role in the cognitive structure.

III. COGNITIVE STRUCTURE AND JUSTIFICATORY PATHS

It is time to clarify the metaphor of a justificatory path. The basic idea is that of a relation, direct or indirect, between a ground—which is the origin of the path—and what that ground justifies—which is the destination of the path. This is not to paint a simple linear picture of justification; for all I am saying here, justificatory paths are only one route to justification and

---

9. This is of course part of the classical regress problem. For an opposing point of view see BonJour 1985, and for a brief reply see Audi 1988, chap. 6. Further responses to BonJour and other coherentists are given in Moser 1989.

achieve it by producing coherence. Certainly a normal cognitive system exhibits an interlocking pattern of paths, and a ground can be undermined by leading to an unacceptable destination, just as, by contrast, traceability to a solid ground can underlie justification. What implies an obviously unjustified proposition, for instance, must itself be at least diminished in its justification, quite as what is implied by an obviously justified proposition must inherit at least some degree of justification.[10] A theory of justification in which paths are central need not, then, treat beliefs as isolated strands of cognition. That there are grounds provides a basis of justification, but does not imply that this basis cannot itself be altered by either lateral or vertical pressures: for instance, by apparent inconsistencies among grounds and by disconfirmation derived from what is inferentially built upon them.

Structural justification occurs when there is an appropriate justificatory path from the justified proposition to the ground(s) of its justification. If we can understand such paths, we can understand much of what is important about structural justification. My account takes these paths to be internal and requires that they be longer than those appropriate to situational justification: to repeat, there the proposition is *justified for S* and *S* will (other things remaining equal) justifiedly believe it by simply coming to believe it on the basis of the justifying ground; in the structural case, the proposition is only *justifiable for S*, and (other things remaining equal) in order for *S* to form a justified belief of it some cognitive change must occur which creates situational justification. To speak somewhat speculatively, structural justification at least normally implies a *capacity* to believe *p*, but does not imply an inclination to believe it upon considering whether it is so; situational justification at least normally implies both a capacity to believe *p* and some inclination to believe it upon considering whether it is so.[11] This difference is connected with the point that in the latter case reflection has further to go to reach ground level.

It should be noted that while the notion of structural justification contrasts with that of situational justification, one can have both for the same proposition so long as they reside in different grounds. One could have situational justification for believing *p*, by virtue of believing premises

---

10. There is no simple transmission principle that covers all the cases here. For discussion of closure see Klein 1981; Dretske 1970, which Klein discusses critically; and Audi 1991 which suggests an account of justificatory transmission that does justice to the views of both. I offer no account of obviousness, but I take it to be relative to something like a reasonable person, to lie between self-evidence and dubiousness, and to be much closer to the former than the latter.

11. The qualification "normally" is needed because, for one thing, *S* may be unable to believe *p* because that would be highly damaging to *S*'s ego.

q, and structural justification for believing *p*, by virtue of a disposition to believe *r*, which also warrants *p*. Indeed, both of these possibilities are compatible with one's having doxastic justification as well, say because one believes *p* on the basis of *s*, which is an adequate ground for it and renders it propositionally justified. The kind of justification one has for a proposition, then, is relative both to the kind of ground that provides it and to one's cognitive relation to that ground.

It is implicit in what has been said so far that one important property of justificatory paths is *length*. Some of the factors that go into it have been illustrated. One is the number of inferential links which, in *S*'s mind, connect *q* with *p*, i.e., the number of inferences *S* would draw starting with *q* and ending with *p*, if, other things remaining equal, *S* wanted to justify *p*, began with *q* as a premise, and proceeded rationally. There would be only one link if *S* would infer *p* directly from *q*, two if the inference would go through *r* as an intermediate premise, three if it would go from *r* to *q* and then to *p*, etc. A parallel factor—where the justification is noninferential—is the number of cognitive changes needed to put *S* into a position of justified belief that *p*, for instance the number of dispositions one must realize in order to have the requisite memory impressions to ground believing that one has visited Mark's home.

We might also speak of the *depth* of a path. This is mainly a matter of how far reflection must go into memory or the recesses of consciousness or the subject matter in question, in order to yield a ground from which *S* can trace a path to *p*, e.g., by a reasoning process. Depth tends to be proportional to length, but it need not be: I may need to bring a repressed event to consciousness in order to believe *p* justifiedly, yet the resulting path might go directly from the recollection I finally ferret out to the proposition I come to believe on the basis of it. I dig deep among associations until I get the crucial thing in consciousness, but I do not reach it by an inferential path. We might also single out a kind of depth that corresponds to how far down in *S*'s evidential cognitive hierarchy the path goes, say to beliefs of what seems to *S* self-evident as opposed to merely true. This is (person-relative) *epistemic depth*—depth in the cognitive foundations—as opposed to *psychological depth*—depth measured by the difficulty of reflectively reaching the justifying ground for *p*, whether because of repression, length, or some other factor. The former is commonly a matter of the depth *of* the ground, the latter commonly a matter of the depth *to* it.

Still another variable is *embeddedness*. By this I mean the degree to which the path represents a stable cognitive feature of the agent. Some beliefs are psychologically basic in us and, in addition to being noninferential, seem to us incapable of falsity, while others are held tentatively; some images we easily mistrust, while others are too vivid to attribute to anything but reality; and so on for other sources of belief. Even a deep path need not be highly embedded; a short path certainly may be. But there are probably no simple correlations here.

Length, (psychological) depth, and embeddedness are psychological as opposed to epistemic variables. They can be used in developing a theory of justification, but are not themselves grounds for attributing it or normative in the sense appropriate to epistemic concepts of appraisal. But there are also epistemic dimensions of justificatory paths. I shall mention four.

An important element in assessing the degree of structural justification is the *adequacy* of the crucial justificatory path(s). This notion can be given an externalist construal in terms of the objective likelihood of the truth of p relative to that of S's premises for it, q—roughly, the reliability of the connection between them; but I have in mind an internalist notion. On this showing, adequacy would be a function of the justificatory power of the original ground and the strength of the ensuing links. On an externalist construal, reliability would be a matter of the truth-conduciveness of these items; and where structural justification is of the kind likely to produce *knowledge*, reliability would seem to be a crucial factor.

To illustrate adequacy construed on internalist lines, imagine an inferential chain: if q is abundantly justifiable and is traceable to p by a deductively valid inferential chain, then (other things equal) p is abundantly justified for S. Inductive links would transmit less justification. A weaker ground would generate less to begin with. Similarly, where the path is non-inferential, we can still discern these two variables: roughly, the quality of the source and the preservation of the justification it supplies.

That two or more paths can lead to the same proposition has already been suggested. This is *convergence* of paths. It can lead to overdetermination: two or more independent sources of justification, each sufficient to justify p for S. This is common, and it yields not only justification stronger than S would have by any one of the paths, but also a degree of systematization of the cognitive structure, as where S can regard p as explaining, or helping to explain, propositions from several domains with features suggesting p as their most likely explainer. The overdetermination just illustrated is justificationally *homogeneous*, in the sense that each path originates in a structural justifier; overdetermination may also be *heterogeneous*, as where one path originates in a structural justifier and another in a situational justifier. If S believes p, the heterogeneity can be threefold: the third path may originate in a doxastic justifier—one in which the belief is actually grounded. The first kind of path is potential, since S does not believe p on the basis of the relevant ground; the second kind may be potential or actual, since *S* may or may not believe *p* on the basis of the ground, and so there may or may not be an appropriate (partly causal) connection; and the third kind must be actual, since in the case of doxastic justification *S* must believe *p* on the basis of the justifying ground.

If there can be convergence, we should also expect possible *divergence*: one ground leading, by way of different links, to different propositions. A single recollection of Gail's paper may readily justify the quite different beliefs that she was articulate and that she was tall. Here there may be sufficient justification for many propositions, and certainly they can be systematized to some degree by their traceability to a common ground. That ground may, but need not, constitute or suggest an explanation of them all.

The final case to be mentioned here is *obstruction*. There is obstruction in the psychological sense of a factor that prevents formation of the belief that *p*, but there is also obstruction in the justificatory sense of a defeater, as where *p* obviously conflicts (logically or probabilistically) with another proposition, *S* is justified in believing or justifiedly believes. If the conflict is logical and obvious to *S*, then *S* is unlikely to come to believe *p*, at least where *S* already believes the competitor; but note that there can be such a conflict where *S* has better justification for *p* than for its competitor. Here we might have psychological, but not justificatory, defeat. Where *S*'s justification for the competitor is better, we would have justificatory even if not psychological defeat.

There are other dimensions of justificatory paths, but the beginnings of a theory of justificatory paths have been set out. The points made in this section should help in understanding structural justification and thereby the broad notion of having justification. I do not take this to be exactly equivalent to having evidence, but it is quite similar and structurally parallel. We also have, then, some of the basic materials for understanding the ways in which one may have evidence (see Feldman 1988 and Moser 1989). The remainder of this paper will simply bring out some general properties of structural justification and show its generalizability beyond the domain of belief.

IV. PROPERTIES OF STRUCTURAL JUSTIFICATION

Although the notion of structural justification is in some ways weaker than the other main normative notions applicable to belief, it has some of the same properties. Let me sketch two kinds, the first epistemic and the second causal and descriptive.

First, structural justification apparently has the capacity to justify other dispositions. While structural justification with respect to *p* does not justify—though it has the potential to justify—believing *p*, it can justify a disposition to believe p. Thus, I may be justified in my disposition to believe p, even though I am not justified, without further changes, *in* believing p.[12] Where I am justified in believing p, the justifying elements are such that (other things equal) if I come to believe p because of those elements, then my belief of it will be justified. Things are epistemically in order in me; what is lacking is only the normal causal connection that holds between a ground and a belief justified by it. In the case of a justified disposition to believe p, two things are needed for justified belief that p: one is the integration of the relevant ground(s), e.g., a grasp of their connection with p, which is often possible only through a grasp of their connection with one another; the second is the causal connection just mentioned. It may seem strange that one could be justified in the disposition to believe, yet not the belief, that p. But we must bear in mind that situational justification for p represents a stronger epistemic position: S is not justified in believing p unless there is some justifying ground for p, whether experiential—say, perceptual or memorial—or cognitive, such that S either has that ground or believes the relevant proposition, whereas S can have structural justification for p provided S is suitably disposed to *acquire* a ground.[13]

Second, the notion of structural justification has causal import, at least in the sense that by virtue of the properties such justification supervenes on, appeals to it can be explanatory in a broadly causal sense (this is admittedly an indirect kind of causal import, since the actual causes seem to be the supervenience base properties). Suppose I refuse to grant John's claim that we know each other only through the telephone and correspondence. By way of explanation one might note that I have structural justification for

---

12. In taking dispositions to admit of justification, I mean to be taking them to be psychologically real, though nonoccurrent and supervenient, properties of persons. Thus, to have a justified disposition is not equivalent to the truth of subjunctives like, "If S should come to believe p on the basis of the relevant grounds, S would justifiedly believe it." This sort of thing can hold of someone who does not, in the relevant sense, *have* the grounds; and it is having those grounds (reachable) in the cognitive system that grounds the justified disposition.

13. One might argue that S can have a justified disposition to believe p, without situational justification for it, because S can come to believe p other than *through* the actualization of the justified disposition, say on impulse. Suppose I do not recall John's visit (though I could if I properly searched my memory) but simply form the belief that he visited, because it facilitates thinking about him. Now I merely have, but have not "used," my structural justification (embedded in my memory) for p, and I am not justified in believing it. The belief lacks a ground, though I have a ground *for* a ground of it. The main trouble with this reasoning is that, even when I have a good justification for believing p, I can *still* come to believe it for some other, inadequate reason. The important possibility pointed out in the reasoning, then, does not discriminate between structural and situational justification.

believing that he visited me, and that we have some tendency not to believe what we have such justification for believing false. It need not be that I subliminally believe he visited (though that is possible here); rather, there are factors, such as buried memories I have not brought together, which, in ways I may not fully understand, make me resist holding the view against which I have an as yet unarticulated justification. Granted that these are the causal factors, noting my justification can serve to appeal to the operation of such factors even when we know only what sort of thing they are and not their exact identity.

A third property of structural justification is its descriptive power. Consider a rational outlook on the world, in the sense of a world view. This is a global notion which is best understood not as a group of beliefs but as a coherent set of beliefs *and* dispositions to believe, where the latter are elements of the kind rooted in or closely connected with structural justification. A rational outlook on the world is not just a matter of a set of warranted beliefs about it; it is in part a readiness to arrive at views about it, by reflection, when appropriate questions arise. This reserve from which justified views will emerge by (generative) reflection is in part what structural justification yields. Quite parallel points apply to the notion of a rational person; but here we have other propositional attitudes to consider as well as beliefs. Structural justification of the cognitive sort under discussion remains, however, an important part of the picture, and as we shall shortly see it has noncognitive analogues.

Regarding epistemic properties of structural justification, there are just two cases to be mentioned here. First, structural justification observes only limited closure. If I have it for p, and p entails (even self-evidently entails) r, it does not follow that I have it for r. Too many factors can intervene; so, while the justificatory path may perhaps carry some justification, my relation to r may be such that I am not sufficiently justified with respect to it to acquire (without new grounds not available through reflection alone) a justified belief of it.[14] Second, structural justification typically implies a potential for knowledge, but does not imply actual knowledge, even when p is true and there are no untoward conditions of the kind specified in the literature in showing that justified true belief is not sufficient for knowledge. The obvious point here is that knowing entails believing, and structural justification, since it does not imply believing, cannot imply knowing. But an equally important point is that there are cases in which one has a

---

14. Again, the issue is transmission of justification, and for reasons given in Audi 1991 I maintain that while some degree of justification does transmit it may not be sufficient for overall justification at the end of the chain.

perfectly good justification yet does not know, even when the proposition in question is true. Think of a justified belief that one's train will be about on time; one rarely knows such a thing, but may justifiedly believe it. On the other hand, when one's structural justification for a true proposition, p, is sufficiently strong, we may loosely speak of p as among the things S "knows." We might call this *virtual knowledge*. If you know a lot about a subject, you are commonly credited with knowing many propositions for which you would need to reflect at least briefly to discover a justificatory path. Structural justification that is accessible enough and concerns propositions one can explain and defend can generate a strong potential for knowledge even if, in strict usage, there is no knowledge without belief.

V. NONEPISTEMIC STRUCTURAL JUSTIFICATION

The main work of this paper has been to clarify a notion of justification which is easily lost in the welter of epistemic terms. But the significance of the notion is by no means limited to epistemology. Indeed, while cognitive justification has been the domain of application of my account of the notion of structural justification, that notion is really far more general. Any propositional attitude admits of structural justification, and so does action. Let us briefly consider these cases in turn.

It should be easy to see how the account of structural justifcation applies to conative attitudes. While admittedly we do not often speak of justified wants, we do speak of rational desires and of what people should or should not want given what might be called their "basic nature" as understood in terms of their ideals, beliefs, and deepest desires. I can be justified *in* wanting my daughter to assert her independence, and I can simply have a structural justification for wanting this. In the former case the want is justified for me (whether I have it or not); in the second it is only justifiable for me. In the former case I presumably have basic, rational wants, say for her to have a good life, such that I believe her asserting independence will contribute to their realization. In the latter case, I presumably have dispositions to form such wants. Where we have justificatory cognitive paths in the case of justification for believing, we have justificatory motivational paths in the case of justification for wanting. And by and large the same distinctions apply in both domains. There is, e.g., embeddedness, psychological depth, and, opposite epistemic depth, a kind of normative depth, depending on how far the path goes into the foundations of S's system of rational desires. If the path ends in a merely instrumental desire, then (other things equal) it goes less deep normatively than one ending in an intrinsic one. This is plausible at least on the assumption that the rationality of an instrumental desire depends on that of an intrinsic one.

Actions, being events and not dispositions, are ontologically different from the propositional attitudes. But the notion of structural justification still applies. It may well be that (prospective) justification for actions is equivalent to justification for intending to perform them. If not, there is a relation near enough to equivalence to enable us to understand structural justification for actions by drawing a parallel between structural justification as applied to beliefs and structural justification as applied to intentions. Similarly, we get a counterpart fourfold distinction: there is (1) justifiedly doing, (2) being justified in doing, (3) an action (type) being justified for an agent, and (4) an agent's simply having a justification for doing something. If (as I hold) the justification (and indeed the rationality) of actions is determined largely by the justification (and rationality) of the wants and beliefs underlying them, then the full assessment of action will require not only elucidation of these four notions, but connecting them with their counterparts for the wants and beliefs underlying actions. The task is large, but at least it can be better understood in relation to the framework developed in this paper.

Let me illustrate the applicability of structural justification to one case: that of rationality in relation to self-interest. It has often seemed to philosophers that rational action is, ultimately, action justified (or at least justifiable) by considerations of self-interest.[15] One way to take this is to interpret self-interest in terms of self-regarding desires, such as those for one's own pleasure, and then to argue that for every rational action, the agent has at least situational justification for it in terms of one or more beliefs to the effect that it will contribute appropriately to satisfying some such desire. But we can accommodate a wider range of prima facie rational actions (at least action types) if we substitute structural justification for situational justification here. For there may surely be things one is disposed to want whose achievement would be intuitively in one's interest, that one does not actually want and would come to want only upon some reflection on facts, experiences, concepts, etc., internally accessible to one (recall that if they are not internally accessible, then the potential justification, however significant it may be, is not structural in my sense). I omit considerations about the rationality of the relevant instrumental beliefs and the relative strengths (or rationality) of the self-interested wants in relation to one another and other wants. I also abstract from the issue of whether there are certain sorts of things which every self-interested person, or even every

---

15. For some discussion of this see Frankena 1983, which suggests that the Greeks tended to hold a version of egoism as a basis of ethics. For clarification of the difficult notion of self-interest, see Overvold 1980 and 1984.

rational one, *should* want intrinsically. The notion of structural justification is neutral with respect to these issues and at the same time provides a broader conception of rationality to work with, whether in relation to self-interest or the foundations of ethics or the theory of rationality in general.

VI. CONCLUSION

I conclude by simply listing the advantages of countenancing structural justification as a distinct kind (or form), as opposed to lumping it with what is ordinarily called being justified in believing or, sometimes, having reason to believe (or to want, or to do). First, we get a more perspicuous account of the nature and scope of justification, something particularly important given the widespread skeptical tendency to regard justification for belief as exhausted by what one can readily marshal as premises. Second, we clarify the issue of epistemic responsibility, though without a commitment to doxastic voluntarism, since we can now ask whether such responsibility should be ascribed—either in crediting or criticizing people—not only on the basis of their having grounds they can readily cite, but in terms of their possessing resources at a greater distance from consciousness. Should we, in effect, make more room for the inventory of justification by including what is not ready to hand? Responsibility may be possible not just on the basis of what one can readily say for oneself when relevantly challenged; it can be achieved even where one would need considerable reflection to meet the challenge, though perhaps only where one has at least situational justification for believing that such reflection would meet a relevant challenge. Third, countenancing structural justification also enables us to distinguish justified belief from various cases of justifiable belief, and similarly for the other propositional attitudes and for action. In making this distinction, we can clarify how the distance from the merely justifiable to the actually justified can be traveled along one or another kind of justificatory path. And fourth, by allowing so much justification to be built into the cognitive structure of the agent, we make it much easier to account for the justificatory role of experience and reason. From a single experience or a single piece of reasoning, many justificatory paths can radiate; similarly, a large range of propositions can be such that the agent could trace a path from them to a suitable ground in experience and reason. This makes it possible for the vast edifice of a person's justified beliefs, and the even more extensive network of propositions that are justified for an agent though not believed, to be seen as adequately grounded in the range of experiences, memories, and thoughts realistically attributable to normal people. Our justification goes much further than our readily accessible grounds for our actual justified beliefs; and our reserve supply of justifying elements, even if it is not sufficient to satisfy skeptics, can bring far more than our beliefs, our current experiences, and our immediate memories into the framework of experiential and rational grounds that provide foundations of justification and knowledge.

3

Epistemic Engineering Audi-Style[*]

Frederick Adams

In what follows, I shall limit my remarks solely to justification in the epistemic domain.[1] The question I shall address is whether justification admits of several different kinds or varieties, or whether justification is one kind of thing with several factors or ingredients that make it up. I tend to view epistemic justification as one kind of thing. There may be many different factors that determine whether a given belief of mine is justified. Did I have adequate evidence to justify my belief? Did I hold my belief because of the evidence? Did I realize the connection between the evidence and the belief it justifies? There are many such factors that are relevant to the determination of the justificatory status of my beliefs, but I tend to see these factors as determining the single epistemic status of my belief. That is, these factors determine whether the belief that I hold is or is not actually justified. The more of the conditions necessary for having a justified belief that I satisfy, the closer I come to having a justified belief. Any degree to which I fall short is a degree in which my belief fails to be justified. For example, if I fail to hold a specific belief, even though I possess the relevant grounds to justify that very belief were I to form it, then there is no justified

---

* I met Mark Overvold at Robert Audi's NEH Seminar on Reasons, Justification, and Knowledge in the summer of 1983. Mark quickly rallied to my defense as I maintained the somewhat unpopular thesis that if epistemic justification amounted to more than information-caused belief, it was unnecessary for knowledge. This view is now more popular and is espoused in some version by William Alston, Robert Audi, Fred Dretske, and a host of others. At the time, however, Mark was one of the few that did not look upon my view with horror or amazement. I am eternally grateful to him for coming to my aid when the dissenting members of the seminar descended upon me. An abbreviated version of this paper was published as "Audi on Structural Justification" in the *Journal of Philosophical Research* 16 (1991: 493–98).

1. Many more things than beliefs may be justified. Actions, policies, theories, lifestyles, may all be kinds of things that may be said to be justified or unjustified. However, I shall consider only the justification of beliefs and only in the context of epistemic justification for the purposes of this paper.

belief. Indeed, there is no actually justified anything, although there are grounds that would justify a certain belief, were I to acquire it. Suppose I know that the murderer walks with a limp and I know that you walk with a limp. If you are the murderer, my knowledge that the murderer walks with a limp can be a justifying ground, but first I have to believe you to be a suspect. Prior to that, I have no justified beliefs that you are the murderer. I do, of course, have the justified belief that the murder walks with a limp. But that is an actual belief and is actually justified by its grounding knowledge. I tend to think that actual justification is the only justification there is.

Robert Audi, in "Structural Justification" (this volume) advances a contrasting view according to which epistemic justification covers a variety of things and comes in a variety of forms, some of which fall short of actually justified belief. On Audi's view, there are many things that can be justified, propositions as well as beliefs and other cognitive structures, and justification can exist (and actually justify cognitive tendencies) prior to the formation of relevant beliefs that may eventually be justified. While I share many of Audi's views about knowledge and justification, I do not share his penchant for multiple varieties of actual and potential justification. There are a wealth of issues raised by Audi's views on structural justification. I cannot address all that are of interest, but I will tug at two threads: Audi's desire to maintain neutrality with respect to internalist and externalist theories of justification (I am not sure that he can maintain this neutrality), and his belief that we need to countenance many different kinds of justification (I am not yet convinced that we do).

I shall begin with some issues that continue to nag. Audi wants to distinguish at least four different kinds of justification: propositional, belief (or doxastic), situational, and structural. *Propositional justification* is justification for propositions, and it may exist whether or not anyone believes the proposition that is justified. *Belief (or doxastic) justification* is simply justified belief. This kind of justification cannot exist independently of someone's belief. *Situational justification*, Audi tells us, is a kind of justification I have when I have a ground for a belief, but do not yet have the belief. However, were I to form the belief on that ground, then I would have a justified belief. Thus, prior to the formation of the belief I have situational justification, because of the ground or basis for the belief that I do possess. Finally, there is structural justification. *Structural justification* is a kind of justification that I possess, but have not yet realized or accessed, and, hence, no actual belief of mine is justified by it yet. I have failed to draw the relevant inference or to access the relevant memory that will generate a justified belief, but all of the structure necessary to justify the belief is in place.

Audi illustrates structural justification with an example. Suppose that Gail, Audi's student, is looking for a job. While Audi knows well Gail's considerable talents in philosophy, he is not yet justified in believing that she will land a job in this year's search. Competition is keen and the market is tight. However, suppose that Audi has heard of a job opening that would ideally match Gail's talents to the job description (although Audi has not thought of Gail when thinking of that job opening, so he has not noticed the ideal match). Suppose further that when Audi thinks about the job opening it becomes clear that the department in question needs someone with Gail's talents, prefers not to remain an all-male department, and would take Audi's recommendation of Gail very seriously. Further, suppose that one of the members of the department has a degree from Gail's undergraduate school. Suppose also that there are additional schools with openings, where the facts are different, but where Audi would, upon reflection, see an ideal match between the job and Gail's talents. From the example it is clear that Audi thinks there is a kind of justification that he has for thinking that Gail will (or may) get a job in this year's job search, although he has not considered the factors and drawn the appropriate connections. Audi says, "I want to call the kind of justification I had prior to recalling the openings and thinking about them *structural justification*" (p. 31).

How is one to evaluate the claim that there are so many different varieties of epistemic justification? For openers, although I have my doubts about the existence of Audi's different varieties of justification, let us suppose that they do exist. If these are *different kinds* of justification, what sense of "justify" do they share? Is the concept of epistemic justification *that disjunctive*? Consider propositional and doxastic justification. Propositional justification takes, as an object, a proposition—the proposition itself is justified. Doxastic justification takes as an object a belief—the belief is justified.

First, I find it hard to accept that a proposition itself (independently of a belief/believer of the proposition) can be justified. Propositions (if they exist) do not *do* anything in virtue of which they can be justified.

Second, if a proposition (unlike an agent) *can* be justified, it cannot be justified in the *same sense* of "justify" that a person's believing a proposition can be justified. On the one hand, if there is no common element in the type of justification that propositions and beliefs have, then the concept of justification is itself disjunctive—there are *not just* different kinds of things that can be justified. On the other hand, if there is a type of justification that beliefs and propositions share, then are there really two *different kinds* of justification? Or is there but one kind of justification that attaches to two different kinds of object? I am inclined to think that, at most, it would be the latter. Audi seems to think that it is the former.

Third, suppose that propositional justification is something like finger-prints on a murder weapon—the existence of the prints on the gun, under the circumstances, constitutes natural evidence (indication) of Smith's murderous deed. (Assume, if you will, that none but the murderer's prints would be on the gun, in the circumstances.) If this is the justification that accrues to propositions, why is it not the *very same* justification that accrues to beliefs? For example, for an externalist about justification, prints on the weapon, caused to be there in the right circumstances, reliably indicate Smith's guilt. Also, detective Columbo believes that Smith is guilty. His belief's being reliably caused by the prints on the weapon can, under the proper conditions, reliably indicate the truth of Columbo's belief (Columbo's belief reliably covaries with the truth). Therefore, prints on the weapon can reliably indicate the truth of a proposition *or* the truth of a properly formed belief. There can be but *one* sense of justification for beliefs *and* for propositions.

For an internalist, propositional justification may be a *problem*. How could a proposition be justified (internally) without being believed or accessed? Propositional justification seems essentially externalistic. Still, if an internalist *can* accommodate propositional justification, matters become even simpler. The proposition that Smith is guilty can be justified by the prints on the weapon, were someone to believe the proposition on that basis. Perhaps no one need actually believe the proposition in order to give an internalist rendering of propositional justification. If it can be done counterfactually, then belief justification and propositional justification are the very same. Columbo's *belief* of the *proposition* that Smith is guilty is justified, if believed on the basis of the prints (and Columbo is aware of the prints and of the relation between the prints and guilt and so on). I shall return to these matters below.

Now I turn more directly to Audi's notion of structural justification and its close relative, situational justification. My next nagging worry is that the relationship between them is *too close*. Both situational and structural justification, as Audi conceives of them, are kinds of justification that render a belief *justifiable*, but not yet *justified*. Further, for both types of justification, one major hindrance to a belief's actually being *justified* is that one either lacks entirely the belief that would be justified (or, perhaps, one believes it on some other basis—although, Audi does not explicitly set it up this way). So there is, if you will, a *cognitive gap* to be filled. In the case of situational justification, the gap is small—*S need only form the belief that p* (on the proper basis) for the belief to be *justified*. Audi's example is this:

"while I did not—until I thought of the matter—believe that the wooden chair beneath me minutely sags from my weight, I was previously justified *in* believing this, by virtue of my justified beliefs about the kind of wood sustaining me in relation to my weight" (p. 30). Under these conditions, Audi tells us, all one need do is *form* the belief that the chair sags and the belief will be justified. Still, an internalist should worry that this disposition to form a belief is, or can be, *justified* (not just *justifiable*) prior to internal access of the disposition or its ground. Indeed, nothing in the definition of situational justification rules out a case where—for whatever reason—a subject is epistemically incapable of forming the belief that would be justified, if formed. Then the justification would *not even be accessible*. This should be intolerable for an internalist about justification. The fact that the states that justify are "in the head" is not enough to make the justification internal. To be internal, there must, in principle, be access to the states that justify.

In the case of structural justification, S not only needs to form the belief that p (the one that would be justified), but S needs to *take cognitive steps* to fill the gaps between the basis (or ground) that S has and the acquisition of the belief that p it would justify (or, in some cases, S needs to eliminate mistaken defeaters). Recall Audi's example of his belief about Gail. He has memories of suitable job openings for Gail and has buried memories of connections between these jobs and Gail's undergraduate college, and so on. However, he has not yet cognitively connected these things in a way that would justify his believing that Gail will get a job this round. Further, in speaking of "justificatory paths," Audi maintained that we can "understand much of what is important about structural justification" if we can understand such paths (p. 39). If we take this quote literally, the picture that emerges is that in the path from structural justification to justified belief there are cognitive *links* or *gaps* that must be *closed*—much as switches closing in an electric circuit. Yet, pretty clearly, there is also what we may call *cognitive work* to be done along the path from situational justification to justified belief. Audi says that situational justification "normally implies both a capacity to believe p and some inclination to believe it upon considering whether it is so" (p. 39). *Considering* is cognitive work. Some cognitive switch is not yet closed—the belief to be justified has not yet formed. If anything, we are talking about differences of *degree*, not of kind, between situational and structural justification. The latter may take *more* cognitive work to become actualized than the former, but there is *work* to be done, nonetheless. (As Aristotle taught us, there can be different degrees of potentiality. We seem to have, here, different degrees of potential for justified belief.)

Even an internalist about justification must be willing to admit that what is available to our internal gaze is the deliverance of much cognitive activity—we are aware only of the tip of the cognitive iceberg. The amount of cognitive work required for traversing the path from situational justification to justified belief may be great—even though to our internal gaze it may seem that the only thing that has happened is that a belief has been formed. Thus, as with propositional and doxastic justification, it appears that, with respect to situational and structural justification, we have differences in *degree* of justification, not in *kind.* (Notice, by the way, that both of the latter kinds of justification take as objects not propositions or beliefs, but *dispositions* to believe. One can *have* these dispositions prior to being *aware* of them. So one can have situational or structural justification prior to gaining internal access to the justification. Thus, it is not clear to me that Audi can maintain his internalism with respect to them—even if he can maintain it with respect to the *beliefs* that ultimately may be *justified* at the ends of their respective paths.)

I share with Audi many views about what it takes for a belief (that one currently possesses) to be justified. The belief must be causally related to its ground of justification—one must believe because of that ground. A belief can be justified by being related to its ground by inference or directly (without a mediating inference). A belief can be *justifiable* without being *justified.* A justified belief can have its justification defeated (mistakenly, or nonmistakenly). There are a host of such features of justification that are important and are revealed in Audi's elaborate account of structural justification. I shall not try to list them all.

Where we part company, at least in this case, is that Audi is a distinguisher and I am a unifier. In my mind, all of the questions about justification that are important for epistemology have one focus: Is *S*'s currently held belief that *p* justified? Certainly we ask about "would-be" justification. Would *S* be justified if *S* believed that *p* because of these factors or those? But the payoff to the question turns on whether *S*'s actual beliefs are (or are not) justified. This can mean the difference between knowing and not knowing that *p* or between being reasonable and not being reasonable in believing that *p*. These are the important epistemic stakes.

I happen to think that what Audi has given us is a fragment of the set of would-be justification. That is how I see situational and structural justification. They are elements of the class of would-be justification. They tell us conditions under which one would be justified if one actually held beliefs with the appropriate causal histories and backgrounds. But, of course, that is all they are. *S*'s belief that *p* could never be *justified* by would-be justification—only *justifiable.*

Let me suggest that if I am right in thinking that structural justification is a species of would-be justification, then we know that truth, belief, and knowledge—some of the other important epistemic players—admit of similar treatment. There are conditions (that we could spell out) under which a proposition would be true, under which S would believe that p, and under which S would know that p. Does this mean that we need an account of "structural truth," "structural belief," and "structural knowledge," to go along with plain old truth, belief, and knowledge? Indeed, Audi is already well on his way to an account of "structural belief" with his account of dispositions to believe vs. dispositional belief, and he comes very close to something like structural knowing—he calls it "virtual knowledge"—when he maintains that structural justification implies a strong potential for knowledge "even if, in strict usage, there is no knowledge without belief" (p. 45).

With structural and situational justification, Audi has described only a part of what I am calling would-be justification. This is because he is trying to present an internalist account, but he does indicate that there could be an externalist account. It is easy to see how one might go about giving such an account. One just edges out a bit further on the justificatory path, so to speak. One goes further out than what is already stored in memory to what would be stored in memory, if one had certain kinds of experiences. For example, suppose Audi did *not* already have the buried memories that, if brought to consciousness and coupled with the proper cognitive activity, would justify his believing Gail will get a job this year. He has no structural justification. If he *did* hear of such job openings and if he *did* have such memories and *did* engage in the proper reflection, he *would* be justified in thinking that Gail will get a job first round—because the jobs are there and the connections between Gail and the jobs exist. There is *would-be* justification just waiting for him. Indeed, this is probably just Audi's "propositional" justification. Though, as I indicated earlier, it looks pretty externalistic to me.

Why do we need to think of these possibilities as different kinds of justification? Why isn't there just *one kind* of justification, *actual justification of actual beliefs*? The rest are cases of would-be justification. A belief would actually be justified under appropriate conditions—and Audi nicely sets out the details of much of the epistemic engineering required for justified belief under some of those conditions. If it is still would-be justification, however, there is *no justification* (of any kind). Not yet. One could still make the fine points about justification that Audi details concerning revelatory reflection (reflecting upon the grounds that justify a belief), generative reflection (cognitive reflection that produces necessary justifying beliefs), inferential and non-inferential justification, degrees of justification, mistakenly defeated justification, and so on.

What are the advantages of Audi's way of viewing his epistemic results over mine? Perhaps it is supposed to be that on his way we can plot out all of the relationships between the evidence for a proposition's truth, the information that one may have stored in memory, the inclinations to believe on the basis of these grounds, and so on. To my mind, this is just pointing out which epistemic circuits are available and which switches must close for the *epistemic light of justified belief to go on.* Surely we can chart the course— give the wiring diagram—without calling anything in the blueprint "justification" until the epistemic light *goes on.* As I see it, Audi is giving us an epistemic wiring diagram for justified belief. He is doing the epistemic engineering for justified belief.

Audi concludes by suggesting that in acknowledging multiple kinds of justification: (1) we obtain a more perspicuous account of the nature and scope of justification; (2) we clarify epistemic responsibility; (3) we easily distinguish the justified from the justifiable. I claim that all of this can be done with one kind of justification, viz., the kind a belief has when it is actually justified. On my view, the reason Audi gives us (1) is that we now have the epistemic wiring diagram. We can trace the source of epistemic justification. On my view, we get (2) if we can trace out a clear path from the grounds for a belief to its formation and its effects. And on my view, we can secure (3) by distinguishing the justified (circuits closed, light on) beliefs from the nonjustified (no light on or no appropriate paths from relevant grounds to target beliefs).

I close with a point that did not fit neatly anywhere above. In touting the epistemic properties of structural justification, Audi heralds its causal powers. He gives an example in which he refuses to grant that he knows John only through telephone conversations and correspondence (p. 43). Audi appeals to the existence of buried memories of meetings with John that he has not brought together or accessed in order to justify his tendency to believe he has met with John face to face. Let us suppose that there was at least one prior meeting with John buried in Audi's memory. This, he claims, constitutes structural justification for his inclination to believe that he has met John before, even though he cannot recall the meeting now.[2] Audi says that such structural justification has "causal import" (p. 43). I take it that the

---

2. I do not see why the "seeming to recall having met" sort of experience that must accompany such phenomena is not sufficient to justify (actually justify an existing belief) Audi's belief that he met John before. However, this is not the point I am currently stalking.

idea is that the buried memory of the meeting with John both *causes and justifies* Audi's tendency to believe that he has met John before. He appeals to supervenience of structural justification to explain the causal power of structural justification. However, this raises problems similar to those in the war over broad vs. narrow mental content. Not only must a mental state have broad content, but its having that content must be a causal factor, if broad content is to be a causal factor. (I will resist a replay of the now all too familiar Twin-Earth examples and lessons drawn; see Horgan and Timmons in this volume.) Similarly, not only must a mental state have justification, but its having it must be a causal factor to do the work Audi suggests. We can imagine two buried memories, one real the other only a quasi-memory, similar in content but not tied to a genuine experience of the subject. The literature on personal identity is littered with examples of recording memories of one person and planting them in another person's brain. When transferred, they are only "quasi-memories" because they are not memories of experiences actually had by the person in whom they are implanted. If the memories and quasi-memories are brain-identical in their intrinsic physical properties, they will have identical causal powers. Thus, if one of them (the real memory) has supervening epistemic properties, it will be causally equipotent to the fake memory. How can the mere fact that the real memory has justificatory properties supervening on it give it causal power? For the fake (or quasi-) memory has the very same causal power. In the case of broad content, recall, in order to show that broad content is causally empowering, it is not enough to show that a belief with a broad content causes something. Epistemology faces the same challenge. For causal powers to be sensitive to justification, one must show that it is in virtue of the state's *having justification* that it can acquire causal power. Since Audi has not yet established that this is so, he may have, at this point, overstated structural justification's credits. Even if this trick can be turned, however, I think Audi is again threatened with giving up his neutrality on internalism vs. externalism. For surely, if structural justification has the capacity to justify other dispositions to believe, this need not be an internal matter (internal in the epistemic sense), it may be external (as external as wide or broad mental content).

4

Motivational Ties[*]

Alfred R. Mele

Must a rational ass equidistant from two equally attractive bales of hay starve for lack of a reason to prefer one bale to the other?[1] Must a human being who wants *A* neither more nor less than he wants an alternative, *B*, fail to pursue either option? Surely, one suspects, some practical resolution is possible. Surely, ties of either sort need not result in death or paralysis. But why?

My concern here is with human beings and wanting or motivation, not with asses and reasons. My guiding question, crudely framed, is this: How is intentional behavior possible in instances of motivational ties?

1. QUESTIONS AND GROUND RULES

The tighter the connection between motivation and intentional action, the more intriguing our question becomes. Donald Davidson has advanced the following principle linking wanting to intentional action:

> If an agent wants to do *x* more than he wants to do *y* and he believes himself free to do either *x* or *y*, then he will intentionally do *x* if he does either *x* or *y* intentionally. (Davidson 1970/1980, p. 23)

If an agent realizes that *x* and *y* are mutually exclusive alternatives and he wants to do neither more than the other, he might do something else

* This paper is derived from Mele 1992, chapter 3.5–7. An earlier version was presented at the 1990 meetings of the American Philosophical Association, Eastern Division; Robert Frazier provided useful commentary. The paper presented at the Overvold Conference, "Wanting and Wanting Most," was the bulk of Mele 1992, chapter 3; Peter Vallentyne served, instructively, as commentator. Robert Audi and John Heil offered constructive criticism of a draft of this paper. I am grateful to all of them for their help.

1. This question is traditionally associated with Buridan. However, Ullmann-Margalit and Morgenbesser (1977, p. 759n.) report that the example of the ass does not appear in his known writings. For interesting recent discussions of "Buridan cases," see Bratman 1985 and 1987.

entirely, of course—something that he wants to do more. But if there is nothing else that he wants more to do, what happens? One might suggest that the agent will at least want to do *either* x or y more than he wants to do neither: Perhaps even though he wants x and y equally, he has another want, a want to do either, that is stronger than any competitor. But, of course, he cannot just do *either*; if he is to do either, he must do one or the other. But which, given that he wants them equally? If he simply *picks* one or adopts some randomizing selection procedure such as tossing a coin and then acts accordingly, must the motivational tie have been dissolved? Or might he intentionally do x (or y) while still wanting equally strongly to perform the alternative? Might something other than his wanting to do one more than he wants to do the other account for what he does?

Davidson's answer to this last question appears to be "No." He maintains that "only if an agent values one line of action more highly than any alternative does he act intentionally in the present, or harbour intentions for the future" (Davidson 1985, p. 200). And, for Davidson, the valuing at issue is to be understood motivationally: "I think of evaluative judgments as conative propositional attitudes" (p. 206). He claims as well that when, there being no intrinsic grounds for preference, we resort to extrinsic grounds, such as the result of a coin toss, our "need to choose has caused [us] to prefer the alternative indicated by the toss" (p. 200). Taking "prefer" to imply "want more," the claim suggests that, for Davidson, the practical outcome of a motivational tie of the sort at issue depends upon the tie's being broken—upon the agent's coming to want to perform one of the actions more than he wants to perform the other. Is this right?

Now for some ground rules. First, I shall suppose, both for the sake of argument and for stylistic reasons, that to *want* to A is to have some motivation to A, the content of which features a representation of the agent's (prospective) A-ing,[2] and that wanting to A more than one wants to B is strictly a matter of relative motivational force.[3] Second, I shall assume

---

2. This characterization is redundant if all motivation to A features a representation of the agent's (current or prospective) A-ing. However, we sometimes identify a state as motivation to A even when we take it to involve no such representation. For example, if a young child habitually strikes other children who anger him, we may say that his anger at little Billy is, for him, motivation to strike Billy, even though we regard the anger, not as incorporating a desire to hit—nor a representation of hitting Billy—but as *issuing* in a desire with that representational content.

3. "S wants to A more than she wants to B," as I understand the sentence, is true by default when S wants to A and has no desire to B. Perhaps it is true that utterances of the form in question *conversationally imply* that S has some desire to B. But there is nothing stronger than conversational implicature here; in particular, no logical entailment. Consider a coach's assertion to his team: "They want to win more than you do; in fact,

that distinctions blurred by the former supposition can be recaptured by distinguishing among types of wants, in the broad sense of the term just stipulated. Thus, for example, we can distinguish between appetitive and nonappetitive wants, affective and nonaffective wants, and so on.

2. THE POSSIBILITY OF MOTIVATIONAL TIES

In this age of mass production, we seem often to be faced with alternatives equivalent in all relevant respects. I see several shirts of the same size, style, and color in the bargain basement, or several toothbrushes similarly related, and I buy *one*. But why *that* one? Did I want most to buy *it*? How can that be the case, if I recognized that none of the shirts, or toothbrushes, was any better or worse than the others?

One might suggest that in all such cases agents judge it best to purchase an item selected and are accordingly most motivated to buy it. However implausible this suggestion may seem, it is worth pursuing—at least briefly.

In a well-known paper, Nisbett and Wilson (1977, pp. 243–44) report the results of a study in which fifty-two subjects were invited to evaluate "four identical pairs of nylon stockings" (for additional details and discussion, see Wilson and Nisbett 1978). Stockings at the far right of the display were judged superior to "the left-most by a factor of almost four to one." Here, the position of an item in an array apparently has a marked influence on evaluation, and we properly expect motivational strength to follow suit.

Other things being equal, the individuals who judged the right-most stockings to be of the highest quality would buy them, if they were to buy any of the four pairs. But even someone who judged the stockings to be of equal value might, with good reason, purchase the right-most pair. Nisbett and Wilson speculate that the evaluative favoring of the right-most stockings may be accounted for by the subjects' carrying "into the judgment task the consumer's habit of 'shopping around,' holding off on choice of early-seen garments on the left in favor of later-seen garments on the right" (Nisbett and Wilson 1977, p. 244). Even a shopper who judges an array of inspected items to be qualitatively identical, however, may reasonably want to purchase the last one inspected more than the others, simply because it is at his fingertips. And his buying the one he does might accord with some evaluative principle of his concerning efficiency.[4] This, of course, is why Buridan's ass is placed between two *equidistant* bales of hay.

---

you don't want to win at all." What follows the "in fact" is not a retraction of the initial assertion. Indeed, it serves to reinforce the claim.

4. This point is not offered as an objection to Nisbett and Wilson's conjecture. The conjecture concerns the *rating* of purchasable items; my point is about the *purchasing* of items and attitudes toward the purchasing acts. This distinction will be addressed shortly.

Let us consider, then, a case in which an agent is equidistant from a pair of items even while he is inspecting them. Suppose that he wants a copy of a certain book and that he spies a pair, each wrapped in cellophane, on a shelf. He picks both up, one in each hand; and he looks at each in turn, starting at the left. If he finds no qualitative differences, what happens next? Well, perhaps he takes the book looked at last to the cashier, owing to something like the above-mentioned consumer's habit. And if we can reasonably appeal to habit in this way, we lack here a clear instance of a motivational tie. For, owing to his consumer's habit, the agent may be more motivated to select the book that he did than he would otherwise have been, and more motivated to select this one than the alternative.

Does the very *inspection* of the items confront our agent with a motivational tie? Not necessarily. Perhaps he carried into the inspection task his "reader's habit" of starting at the left. Owing to that habit, he might have been more motivated to start at the left than at the right.

One might think that if we grant habits of the sort in question a role in determining motivational strength, we can achieve a motivational tie by counterbalancing the agent's habit with his giving a slightly higher evaluative rating to the book first viewed. But this presupposes a conception of the operation of the habit that may well be too crude. Perhaps the habit enhances motivation to select the item last inspected only when the agent gives no other item in the array a higher evaluative rating.

It is evident by now that clear instances of motivational ties are not as easy to come by as one might have thought. One source of the problem merits special emphasis. An evaluative tie is not sufficient for a motivational tie. For example, even if our book-buyer does not take either copy of the book to be superior to the other, he may be more motivated to buy the one viewed last, owing to the motivational influence of habit. Of course, evaluative ranking of purchasable items is one thing and evaluative ranking of *acts* of purchasing another. For reasons of efficiency, I may judge it better to buy the stockings that I am now holding than to buy the qualitatively identical ones that I saw earlier twenty feet to the left, even though I take the stockings to be equally good. But I see no compelling reason to maintain that our book-buyer explicitly judged it best to purchase the book that he did. Wanting more does not entail judging better, as familiar examples of akratic behavior (or "weakness of will") indicate (for a defense of this thesis, see Mele 1987, chapters 3 and 6).

3. PRACTICAL RESOLUTION OF A MOTIVATIONAL TIE

Ironically, relatively clear instances of motivational ties might be easier to find when alternative objects are *not* identical (in the mass-production sense). Alan, who wants to see a movie tonight, has narrowed the options to two films scheduled to be shown simultaneously at the same theater complex. He finds the prospect of seeing each equally attractive and, we may suppose, he is no more motivated to see one than the other.

Imagine that Alan decides to drive to the theater this evening and to resolve the issue there by tossing a coin if a look at the movie posters and the like leaves him undecided. Later, while standing in line at the theater, Alan resorts to a coin toss. Setting aside questions about the etiology of Alan's assignments of heads and tails, let us suppose that movie A wins the toss and that Alan purchases a ticket for A.

I have already mentioned Davidson's claim that when, in a situation like Alan's, we resort to a strategy like his, our "need to choose has caused [us] to prefer the alternative indicated by the toss." Taking "prefer" to imply "want more," this suggests that Alan's coin toss, in conjunction with other features of the case, has one or both of the following results: (1) Alan's motivation to see A tonight (or to purchase a ticket for A) increases; (2) Alan's motivation to see B tonight (or to purchase a ticket for B) decreases. Both are genuine possibilities, and a motivational shift may well be a normal feature of cases of the sort at issue. But I shall suggest that there is another possibility as well, a theoretically interesting one that is excluded by Davidson's contention.

Before the further possibility is identified, we would do well to inquire about the grounds for Davidson's claim. The functional connection between wanting and action has at least two dimensions. First, the representational content of an agent's want to A identifies a practical goal (or subgoal), the agent's A-ing, so that "action-wants" provide practical direction, as it were. Second, wants have an inclinational or conative dimension. They incline agents to act on them. If we suppose (i) that we intentionally A only if we are moved to A, (ii) that wants move us to act in virtue of their motivational strength alone (*what* they move us to do, however, depends on their content), and (iii) that only wants are capable of moving us to act, in the pertinent sense of the term—or, more cautiously, that any motivational state is so only in virtue of its incorporating a want or wants, and that a motivational state's capacity to move us to act is encompassed in the capacity of the incorporated want or wants to do so—we are well on our way to Davidson's view about the motivational outcome of random selection. For, given these suppositions, if the motivational strength of the pertinent wants were equal in a case like Alan's, there would be nothing to account for his being moved to act by one of the competing wants rather than the other.

Although (i) is certainly in need of elaboration, I shall simply grant it for the sake of argument. Now, (ii) is, I think, true of wanting, standardly conceived. And a popular philosophical convention treats "want" as a blanket term for all motivation. But it may be that when the standard conception and the convention are combined as in (iii) something goes awry.

Consider this conjecture. Faced with the motivational tie at issue, Alan selects a coin-tossing procedure for settling what he will do. Having settled upon this procedure (and assignments of heads and tails),[5] and having tossed the coin, he forms a purchasing intention in accordance with the result of the toss; and, as it happens in this particular case, he acts on that intention *even though the motivational tie persists.* If the capacity of intentions to move agents to act is not wholly encompassed in the (relative) motivational strength of incorporated wants, the conjecture might be true.

Here is a hypothesis. When a desire to A that one has at t issues (in the "normal way") in an intentional A-ing at t, it does so by issuing in and sustaining an intention to A (or an intention to try to A) of which the following is true: Acquisition of the intention initiates the A-ing, and the intention, once it is in place, sustains and guides the A-ing.[6] Further, an agent who intends to A (beginning) at once—who *proximally* intends to A—will A intentionally beginning straightaway, unless something prevents his doing so or thwarts his efforts. (This latter suggestion is hardly a bold one.) Sources of prevention and of thwarted efforts include the agent's lacking the ability to A, the unfriendliness of his environment, his bungling an attempt, and his being more motivated to do at the time something, B, that is incompatible with his A-ing. However, being *equally* motivated to perform some competing action is not a preventive or thwarting condition.

This conjunctive hypothesis does not require that proximal intentions generally, nor even *effective* proximal intentions particularly, incorporate preponderant motivational strength. It leaves open, for example, the possibility that intentions move us by virtue of their having some executive quality that is not reducible to desire strength. (On the executive nature of intentions, see Mele 1990 and 1992, chapters 9 and 10.)

---

5. In some cases, assignments of heads and tails will themselves raise problems about motivational ties. But let us simply suppose that Alan is in the habit of assigning heads to the alternative he represents first and that his representing A *first* is not motivationally explained.

6. Compare Myles Brand's (1984, p. 127) contention that "desiring is an intention-former" and Hector Castañeda's (1975, p. 284) claim that "wantings are characteristically inclinations to intend...." See also Mele 1990.

The latitude provided is attractive. An agent who makes the transition from merely wanting to A—even preponderantly—to intending to A is commonly regarded as having made progress toward action. And this progress cannot be articulated wholly in terms of motivational strength. Someone who, wanting to A more than he wants to do anything incompatible with his A-ing, forms an intention to A, need not now want more strongly to A (either absolutely or relative to alternatives) than he did a few moments earlier. (Indeed, owing in part to the enhanced salience of the prospect of A-ing attendant, in a particular case, upon forming the intention, one's absolute motivation to A might even diminish a bit. Consider a long-term bachelor who, having finally decided to marry Susan, is now feeling considerably more anxious about the quality of married life than he was just prior to reaching the decision, with the result that his motivation to marry Susan is slightly attenuated.) Still, it certainly looks as though, in forming an intention, the agent has made practical progress. And even if his (absolute or relative) motivation to A *were* to increase, why should *this* be counted as progress, given that he was already preponderantly motivated to A anyway?

Against the background of a view of action that accords beliefs, desires, intentions, and the like, a causal role in the production of intentional behavior, we should expect the progress characteristic of the transition from wanting to intending to have some *causal* significance. Now, the formation or acquisition of an intention need not augment the agent's *cognitive/representational* condition in a way required for the production of intentional behavior. After all, the pertinent know-how, beliefs, plans, and the like are sometimes present already, awaiting the agent's decision. I have suggested that motivational strength need not be altered either. Still, it seems, even in the absence of a change of either sort, there is practical progress in the move from wanting to intending—progress whose causal significance, if any, must be located elsewhere, perhaps in some further, executive dimension of intention.

Consideration of a case not involving a motivational tie will prove useful. Sally is preponderantly motivated to avenge an insult, and she knows that this is so. However, she has moral qualms about behaving vengefully in this instance, and she is consequently attempting to decide what to do. Eventually, she decides to indulge her desire for vengeance, even though she thinks that doing so is morally improper; and she acts accordingly. Here, Sally's practical progress consists in her now being *settled*, as we might say, upon taking a course of action—one that she was already preponderantly motivated to take.[7]

If Sally's progress lies in her coming to be settled upon a course of action, the same may be said of Alan. The result of the coin toss settles for him the matter that had been unsettled. And, one naturally supposes, his being settled upon purchasing the designated ticket will issue in his purchasing it, provided that nothing prevents this.

One might be tempted to infer from Alan's purchasing the ticket for A that he wanted to purchase that ticket more than he wanted to purchase a ticket for B. But the question before us now is whether this inference is required, whether we can make sense of Alan's behavior *only* on the supposition that he wanted most to purchase an A ticket. I have suggested an alternative; and if the alternative is a genuine one, it has significant implications for the theory of motivation. Most important, not all states that move us to action need be understood as moving us to A in virtue of their incorporating *preponderant* motivation to A.

I have been suggesting that, faced with a motivational tie between options A and B, an agent might intentionally A without having come to want to A more than to B. My focus has been on the connection between the motivational condition of an agent and the behavior that it promotes. Call that a *forward* connection. It might be claimed that some *backward* or historical connection, in a case like Alan's, requires that the agent want to A more than to B. More concretely, one might contend, for example, that an agent's recognizing the result of a randomizing procedure as A-favoring, in a case of the kind in question, provides him with a new reason to A, and that—other things being equal—this will strengthen his desire to A relative to his competing desire to B.

Unpacking "other things being equal" here is not easy. (It rarely is.) And without some qualification, the claim would obviously be false. For example, seeing that the coin has come up heads, S might unexpectedly experience disappointment and now want the losing alternative more. Further, setting aside cases of this kind, why can't the acquisition of the new reason issue in an intention to A while not issuing in a preponderance of motivation to A? After all, the point of the toss is to settle matters; and if matters would be settled by the formation or acquisition of an intention even in the absence of a change in relative desire-strength, why suppose that the intention-promoting new reason must (also) be a desire-enhancing

---

7. I shall not attempt to provide an account of "being settled" in this paper. For a partial characterization, see Mele 1990. A much fuller account is offered in Mele 1992, chapter 9.

reason? Why can't acquisition of the new reason go directly to the heart of the matter, as it were, without (also) bringing it about that the agent wants more to A than to B?

Even if a reading of the ceteris paribus clause could be found, however, on which the claim about enhanced desire-strength is true, that would not imply that whenever agents faced with a motivational tie employ a randomizing procedure and then intend and act accordingly, they want to perform the action performed more than the relevant alternative. That inference is blocked by the ceteris paribus clause. What is needed is an additional premise, or argument, to the effect that when other things are not equal in instances of motivational ties in which agents resort to a randomizing procedure, agents intentionally A only if their desire to A is strengthened relative to the competing desire—which leads us quickly back to *forward* connections. If (1) the hypothesis expressed earlier about the connection between intention and intentional action is correct and (2) intending to A (as I have suggested here and argued elsewhere) does not require wanting to A more than one wants to perform any relevant alternative, cases are easily imagined in which one's motivation to A is not increased relative to the pertinent alternative by an A-favoring flip of the coin and one nevertheless intentionally A-s (see Mele 1987, chapters 3 and 7; 1990; and 1992, chapter 9). (Recipe for constructing cases: Identify something about S or his circumstances that precludes a shift to wanting to A more than to B upon viewing what he knows is an A-favoring toss, but without preventing him from intending to A, which intention he acquires.) The issue at hand turns upon forward connections and the nature of intentions, not upon the effects of randomizing procedures on desire strength in normal cases.

Again, I am willing to grant that *normally*, in cases of the sort in question, agents want most to do what they do. Even when an arbitrary picking is substituted for a coin toss, an agent might, after picking, want to perform the action picked more than the alternative. If the picking is identified with the formation of an intention, he might want more to act as he intends than to act otherwise. Then again, motivated by a desire to do either A or B in an instance of a motivational tie, perhaps an agent may simply arbitrarily select one alternative without possessing or acquiring at the time a selection-referring or intention-referring desire (e.g., a desire to execute his intention to A or a desire to conform his behavior to his selection of an alternative). Perhaps in some instances of motivational ties, picking or intending an alternative, A, settles matters without the assistance of a desire whose content refers to the agent's picking or intending A and without his wanting to A more than he wants to B. In any event, I have not been able to locate a convincing argument that the practical resolution of a motivational tie between an A-ing and a B-ing requires that the agent come to want one more than the other. And I have sketched grounds for thinking that no such argument is forthcoming. On the conception of intention to which I have alluded (a conception defended at length in Mele 1992), there is no *need* for a preponderant want of the identified kinds in the production of intentional action. In the absence of such a need, an agent may intentionally A while wanting just as much to do something, B, that he deems an open alternative to an A-ing.

4. WANTS, INTENTIONS, AND MOTIVATIONAL STRENGTH

In a very broad sense of "want," intentions are at least partially constituted by wants. Earlier, I characterized wanting to A, in a broad, technical sense of the term, as having motivation to A, the content of which features a representation of the agent's (current or prospective) A-ing. If intending to A encompasses the possession of motivation to A, as is standardly thought, then intending to A encompasses wanting to A, on the characterization at issue. (Obviously, an intention to A has the requisite representational property.) Now, even if wants not incorporated in intentions move us to act in virtue of their motivational strength alone, the supposition that intentions incorporate wants does not entail that *intentions* move us only by virtue of the motivational strength of the incorporated wants. Again, intention may have a motivational feature not wholly encompassed in the strength of incorporated wants.

One might attempt to find resources for rebutting this last suggestion in a certain conception of motivational strength. It has often been observed that the motivational strength of a want cannot be determined by the felt intensity of the want, if our intentional behavior is to accord uniformly with our strongest wants: Sometimes, our most affectively intense wants are not the wants on which we act. Nor is want-strength universally fixed by agents' assessments or evaluations of the objects of the wants, as garden-variety instances of akratic action show (Mele 1987, chapters 3 and 6). Some might be tempted by a certain quasi-functional account of motivational strength according to which the motivational strength of a state is simply a measure of its capacity to produce appropriate intentional behavior. On such an account, if the capacity of an agent's intention to A to result in an attempt to A is greater than the capacity of his competing desire to B to result in an attempt to B, the intention has more motivational strength than the desire.

Notice what the thesis—that wants move us to act in virtue of their motivational strength alone (thesis (ii) above)—amounts to, on this account of motivational strength: Wants move us to act in virtue of their capacity to move us to act. This is far from satisfying. Matters would be improved significantly if features of wants on which that capacity rests were identified. Of course, on the account of motivational strength at issue, the *motivational strength* of wants cannot, without vicious circularity, be offered as such a feature.

Suppose that, other things being equal, intentions to A have a greater "capacity" to produce appropriate intentional behavior than do *mere* wants to A—that is, wants that are neither identical with nor incorporated into intentions. This supposed fact need not be accounted for by maintaining that intentions possess to a greater degree some determinate feature that they share with mere wants. The difference in question might be explicable, for example, on the alternative hypothesis that intentions and mere wants have different functional roles in the production of intentional action. Perhaps, as I suggested earlier, the specifically actional function of mere wants is to prompt and sustain suitable intentions, while that of intentions is to initiate, sustain, and guide intentional action. The motivational element in each state might play a different functional role. In that case, it would be misleading to suggest that there is some single motivational property, namely, action-causing strength, that an agent's intentions and mere wants have in varying degrees. And if motivational commensurability of the sort at issue is rejected, the door is wide open to the possibility that occasionally, wanting equally strongly to A and to B and recognizing that we cannot do both, we intentionally A.

In the absence of a compelling reason to maintain, roughly, that we intentionally do only what we want most to do, we should leave it open that motivational ties may, in some instances, be practically resolved while the tie remains. Of course, we will want to have at our disposal some account of how this can happen. And I have sketched a pertinent hypothesis about the standard functional connection between intentions and intentional actions. Generating a detailed account of the place of intentions in the etiology of intentional actions is a project for another day.[8]

---

8. For various elements in such an account, see Mele 1989; for a fuller account, see Mele 1992, part 2.

5

Deriving Morality from Rationality*

Holly M. Smith

I. INTRODUCTION

From its earliest beginnings, Western philosophy has attempted to forge a strong link between rationality and morality. Contemporary social contractarian theories derive a good deal of their attractiveness from their claim to have achieved this goal. Such theories argue that the principles of justice, or the principles of morality, issue from a contract that rational individuals would agree to initially, and would comply with once implemented. These theories present moral norms as issuing from rational choice, and so claim to establish the desired connection between morality and rationality.

David Gauthier is the most recent advocate of this approach in his attempt to provide a contractarian justification for moral behavior. In defending his enterprise, Gauthier explicitly invokes the desirability of establishing what he calls "the deep connection" between reason and morality.[1] He asserts that "The main task of our moral theory [is] the generation of moral constraints as rational" (p. 7) and develops this thought in the following passage:

> The language of morals is…surely that of reason. What theory of morals, we might…ask, can ever serve any useful purpose, unless it can show that all the duties it recommends are also truly endorsed by each individual's reason?…But are moral duties rationally grounded? This we shall seek to prove, showing that reason has a practical role related to but transcending individual interest, so that principles of

* A version of this paper orignally appeared in P. Vallentyne, ed., *Contractarianism and Rational Choice: Essays on David Gauthier's* Morals by Agreement, © Cambridge University Press 1991, and is used by permission. I am grateful to Michael Bratman, David Copp, Peter Danielson, Alan Nelson, David Schmidtz, and George Smith for comments on earlier versions.

1. Gauthier 1986, p. 4; page numbers introduced parenthetically refer to this work unless otherwise indicated.

action that prescribe duties overriding advantage may be rationally justified. We shall defend the traditional conception of morality as a rational constraint on the pursuit of individual interest....Our enquiry will lead us to the rational basis for a morality. (pp. 1–2)

Thus it is essential to the success of Gauthier's project in his own eyes that he can indeed establish the link between rationality and morality. And in taking this stance he joins a venerable Western tradition advocating the importance of this link.

I shall argue, however, that Gauthier fails to show that morality is based on rationality. To see how his argument falls short, let me very briefly describe his main line of thought. Gauthier begins with Hobbes's and Rawls's idea that society is a "cooperative endeavor for mutual advantage." Human beings, living in isolation from each other, can only expect to do poorly in their struggle to survive and flourish. Social cooperation would enable each person to fare better than he or she could do in isolation. Unfortunately, the more common types of potentially profitable cooperation are ones in which individuals' direct pursuit of self-interest paradoxically produces an outcome in which each person is worse off than he would have been if everyone had acted less selfishly. Consider a case in which you and I are two fishermen inhabiting adjoining properties along a dangerous coastline. Hidden sandbars often cause our boats to run aground and our catch to be lost. Each of us can expect two such accidents in the coming year, one on our own sandbar, and one on our neighbor's sandbar. If either of us erected a lighthouse, it would prevent any accidents on the adjacent sandbar. The cost to each of us of a single accident is $500, while the cost per year of erecting and maintaining a lighthouse is $600. In these circumstances, if each of us considers only our own welfare, neither will build a lighthouse, since the annual cost exceeds the benefit by $100. But each of us fares worse under this arrangement (where we each suffer an annual loss of $1000 from accidents) than under an arrangement in which both of us build a lighthouse, for each lighthouse benefits *both* its builder and his neighbor (if both build, each suffers a yearly cost of only $600).

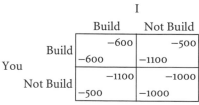

Figure 1.

The dilemma posed by this situation is represented in figure 1. In classic prisoner's dilemmas such as this one, an optimal outcome cannot be reached by each agent pursuing his or her own interest. It could be reached, however, if behavior were constrained by principles prohibiting purely selfish behavior: for example, a principle requiring each fisherman to build a lighthouse. According to Gauthier, such principles, if they impartially constrain the pursuit of direct self-interest, qualify as *moral* principles. But Gauthier also argues that it is *rational* for each individual to adopt and comply with such principles—rational in the standard sense of maximizing one's own self-interest. The core of Gauthier's project is to argue for this thesis, which if true would establish morality as part of the theory of rational choice.

When mutually beneficial outcomes are available through cooperation, but purely selfish behavior would disadvantage everyone, individuals have reason to work together to secure mutual benefits. However, many different cooperative arrangements are often available in a given case. For example, one cooperative arrangement just described in the fisherman case has each of us building our own lighthouse; but a second arrangement, also to the advantage of each, would have each of us building our own lighthouse, but you paying me $50 to defray my expenses; a third would involve my instead paying you $50 to defray your expenses; and so forth. Individuals who might benefit greatly under one arrangement would do far less well under an alternative arrangement that favored others. In these circumstances, members of the group must bargain with each other to determine which particular arrangement they will adopt. Gauthier argues that rational, fully informed people will bargain according to what he labels the "Principle of Maximin Relative Benefit." Bargains reached in accord with this principle mandate cooperative arrangements in which the benefits created by cooperation are distributed so that the return to each individual is proportionate to the contribution (under some interpretation) that he or she brings to the cooperative enterprise. Individuals will bargain with each other to establish the basic terms of their future social interaction—the principles of morality and justice that will govern them—and will agree to norms that require distributing the benefits of interaction proportionally to the contributions of each interactor. Thus Gauthier argues that they would agree to norms requiring promise-keeping, truth-telling, and fair dealing, because adherence to such norms permits people to cooperate in ways that may be expected to render the benefits of concrete interactions proportionate to the contribution provided by each party.

People in the state of nature, bargaining with each other to establish mutually beneficial constraints on purely selfish behavior, must look to the future in arriving at their agreement, in the sense that they recognize it is pointless to agree on constraints with which no one will later comply. Thus Gauthier must show that people would indeed comply with the constraints—i.e., the moral principles—agreed to in the original bargain, for otherwise no bargain will be struck.

Hobbes was driven to solve this compliance problem by invoking an all-powerful sovereign to enforce terms of the bargain by threats of harm to disobedient citizens. Many contract theorists have agreed with Hobbes that compliance cannot be secured without coercive measures of some kind. Perhaps Gauthier's most distinctive contribution to contractarian theory is his argument that coercion is unnecessary to secure compliance. He argues that it is rational for a would-be bargainer to "dispose himself" to comply with the terms of the initial bargain so long as he expects similar compliance from others. Agents so disposed may occasionally be exploited by others who take advantage of their willingness to comply with agreements made. But, Gauthier argues, given plausible assumptions about human abilities to ascertain each others' dispositions—assumptions that human beings are "translucent," although not completely "transparent," to each other—a person who disposes herself to comply with fair bargains will enjoy opportunities for beneficial cooperation that will be denied to persons lacking this disposition. Because of these opportunities, she maximizes her self-interest by disposing herself to comply. And, Gauthier argues, having disposed herself to comply, it is rational for her actually to comply when the occasion arises, even when she would maximize her utility by violating the agreement. Thus compliance with socially adopted norms can be secured by largely voluntary means, and each would-be cooperator knows there is a point to agreeing to the bargain, since each will have reason to comply with the bargain once made.

II. THE RATIONALITY OF COMPLIANCE

I shall begin by examining Gauthier's core argument for the rationality of compliance. To understand Gauthier's official statement of it, we must first introduce his definitions of several key terms. First, Gauthier defines a "constrained maximizer" as

> (i) someone who is conditionally disposed to base her actions on a joint strategy or practice should the utility she expects were everyone so to base his action be no less than what she would expect were everyone to employ individual strategies, and approach what she would expect from the cooperative outcome determined by minimax relative concession; (ii) someone who actually acts on this conditional

disposition should her expected utility be greater than what she would expect were everyone to employ individual strategies. (p. 167)[2]

In terms of our fisherman example, what this means is that you are a constrained maximizer if (i) you form the intention to build your lighthouse if I build mine, and the intention not to build your lighthouse if I do not build mine (since the utility you would receive if both you and I build our lighthouses exceeds what you would receive if neither of us built one); and moreover (ii) you actually *do* build your lighthouse if, and only if, you expect me to build mine (since your expected utility of building a lighthouse only exceeds what you would get if we both fail to build lighthouses in a case where you expect me to build mine as well). A *straightforward maximizer*, by contrast, is someone "who seeks to maximize his utility given the strategies of those with whom he interacts"—i.e. a normal maximizer of expected utility (p. 167). In Gauthier's initial statement of his argument, he assumes that the agents involved are *transparent* to each other—i.e., each is "directly aware…whether he is interacting with straightforward or constrained maximizers" (pp. 173–74). For the sake of greater plausibility, this assumption is then weakened to the assumption that the agents are merely *translucent*—i.e., ones whose dispositions "to cooperate or not may be ascertained by others, not with certainty, but as more than mere guesswork" (p. 174). Because it is simpler to state the argument using the stronger assumption of transparency, I shall initially stick with it. Gauthier's own statement of his argument goes as follows:

---

2. Gauthier uses the term "disposition" to describe constrained maximization. It is troubling that he never explains what this crucial term means. Since it is difficult to get a grip on the logic of the argument without an explication of "disposition," I have made the most natural assumption, namely that a disposition is an intention to perform a certain kind of act. This explication preserves an important feature that Gauthier wants, namely that the later choice to perform the act is genuinely a free act. My informal formulation of constrained maximization (immediately following in the text) differs slightly from Gauthier's formal definition. Strictly speaking, Gauthier's (somewhat unclear) definition only stipulates what a constrained maximizer does if (in our case) she expects her partner to build his lighthouse; it does not stipulate what she does if she expects her partner *not* to build his lighthouse. However, it is clear from Gauthier's discussion that constrained maximization requires the person to form, and carry out, the intention not to build her lighthouse if she expects her partner not to build. It is this aspect of the disposition that protects the constrained maximizer from exploitation by straightforward maximizers. My informal characterization of constained maximization assumes the case of transparency, in which the agent knows that her partner will form, and carry out, the intention to build (or the intention not to build, as the case may be). In the case of translucency, in which the agent may assign probabilities less than one to each possible action of her partner, constrained maximization could be stated as "forming and carrying out the intention to build if the expected utility to her of doing so exceeds her expected utility if both partners fail to build; and forming and carrying out the intention not to build otherwise."

Suppose I adopt straightforward maximization. Then I must expect the others to employ maximizing individual strategies in interacting with me; so do I, and expect a utility, u. Suppose I adopt constrained maximization. Then if the others are conditionally disposed to constrained maximization, I may expect them to base their actions on a cooperative joint strategy in interacting with me; so do I, and expect a utility u'. If they are not so disposed, I employ a maximizing strategy and expect u as before. If the probability that others are disposed to constrained maximization is p, then my overall expected utility is $[pu' + (1 - p)u]$. Since u' is greater than u, $[pu' + (1 - p)u]$ is greater than u for any value of p other than 0 (and for $p = 0$, the two are equal). Therefore, to maximize my overall expectation of utility, I should adopt constrained maximization. (p. 172)[3]

Having argued that it will maximize an agent's expected utility to adopt constrained maximization, Gauthier then claims that *since* it is rational to choose to be a constrained maximizer, it is *also* rational to carry out that choice—i.e., to cooperate when the time comes (p. 186). Let us lay this argument out, somewhat less technically, in terms of our example of the fishermen. We may envision the situation as a symmetrical one, in which each of us is faced with the same choice. The argument may be stated as follows:

1. I can now choose between constrained maximization (*CM*) or straightforward maximization (*SM*), and my choice will bring about my actually carrying out the chosen option. The options are: (a) *CM*, forming the intention to build if you build, or not build if you do not; and then actually building if I expect you to build, or not building if I expect you not to build; (b) *SM*, forming the intention not to build whatever you do; and then actually not building whatever I expect you to do.

2. Each of us is transparent, so each will be aware of the other's choice, and will know that the other will actually carry out that choice.

3. If I choose *CM*, then (a) if you choose *CM*, you will build and I will build; (b) if instead you choose *SM*, you will not build, and I will not build either.

---

3. This argument contains what appears to be a (recurrent) misstatement, namely that others are "conditionally disposed" to constrained maximization. There is never any question of people being *conditionally disposed* to constrained maximization; constrained maximization is already itself a disposition to form certain conditional intentions, and to carry one of them out when the specified conditions occur. "A constrained maximizer is conditionally disposed to cooperate in ways that, followed by all, would yield nearly optimal and fair outcomes, and does cooperate in such ways when she may actually expect to benefit" (p. 177). Notice also, as David Schmidtz has pointed out to me, that although Gauthier here describes his argument as showing that *CM* maximizes expected utility, it is more properly described as showing that *CM* is the dominant strategy (in cases of transparency).

4. If I choose *SM*, then (a) if you choose *CM*, you will not build, and I will not build; (b) if instead you choose *SM*, you will not build, and I will not build either.

5. Hence if you choose *SM*, it makes no difference to my utility whether I choose *CM* or *SM*; whereas if you choose *CM*, I maximize my utility by choosing *CM* and inducing you to build.

6. So it is rational for me to choose *CM*.

7. If I am rational to choose *CM*, then it is rational for me to carry it out when the time comes (e.g. to build my lighthouse if you build yours).

Notice a highly significant feature of this argument: if successful, it entails that I should adopt *CM* and follow it when interacting with you, *even if you and I will only interact on this single occasion, and even if our interaction will have no effect on my future opportunities to cooperate with other individuals.* Gauthier rejects solutions to prisoner's dilemmas that rely on iterated occasions for cooperation, and takes himself to have shown that it is rational to cooperate even in the single-interaction case (169–70).

III. COMMENT ON PREMISES 1 AND 2

I have deliberately phrased premises 1 and 2 so as to reveal certain aspects of Gauthier's argument that his own language tends to obscure.

Let me comment briefly upon these aspects. First, I have worded premise 1 to bring out Gauthier's assumption that the choice of constrained maximization at t_1 will actually lead me to form the appropriate unconditional intention at t_2 and then perform the chosen act at t_3. For example, if I form the intention at t_2 of building my lighthouse, then I *will* build it at t_3. There is no possibility that I will fail to carry out what *CM* requires of me. We might call this assumption the *Causal Efficacy Thesis*: the thesis that forming an intention to do *A* will cause the performance of *A*. Gauthier's calculation of my expected utility in choosing *CM* implicitly incorporates this assumption (for, if I could backslide on an intention to build my lighthouse, the expected utility of intending to build would not simply equal the expected utility of both of us building lighthouses). Indeed, given the truth of the transparency assumption, and the fact that, if you have chosen *CM*, you will only build your lighthouse if you know I will build mine, Gauthier needs the truth of the Causal Efficacy Thesis to establish that my choosing *CM* will induce you to build and so maximize my utility. He also needs it to rule out the possibility of my adopting a strategy like the following one:

KM   Forming the intention to build if you build, or not to build if you do not build; and then not building *whatever* you do.[4]

Under conditions of translucency, adopting *KM* rather than *CM* might well maximize an agent's utility because it would enable him to mislead other agents about his future actions. However, *KM* is ruled out by the assumption of causal efficacy. But we should at least note the extreme strength of this assumption. I find it quite implausible to assume that any intention of mine *inevitably* causes my subsequent carrying out of that intention: some do, but some do not. Upgrading the *kind* of mental state I form (to a commitment or resolution) does not change this fact. Of course we often change our minds when we acquire new information, or when we adopt new values. Gauthier (1984, p. 159) wants to set such cases aside. But even in cases where none of these factors matters it is implausible to suppose our commitments always compel our future acts—especially in the kind of case in question, where considerations of utility press the agent to change her mind when the time comes. Indeed, if the Causal Efficacy Thesis were true, it is hard to see how prisoner's dilemmas could have been the deep historical problem for social cooperation that they have been. However, in order to turn to other aspects of the argument, I will nonetheless provisionally grant Gauthier the truth of the thesis.

Would it raise difficulties for Gauthier's argument if my forming an intention to do *A* only caused me to do *A sometimes*, say, 60% of the time? Suppose you and I are both *CM*'s, and I form the intention to build—but in this particular case, I will not carry through. Since I am transparent, you will detect my future failure to build, and so will form the intention not to build, and will not build. But since you are also transparent to me, I will detect your intention not to build, and so, by *CM*, should form the intention not to build myself. But by hypothesis, I have formed the intention to *build*. It appears as though failure of the Causal Efficacy Thesis would be inconsistent with Gauthier's other assumptions.

---

4. Some people object to *KM* on the grounds that one could never intentionally adopt it, since that would involve simultaneously committing oneself to (a) intending at t_1 to do *A*, and (b) intending at t_2 *not* to do *A*. It is claimed that one cannot, at least rationally, commit oneself to this sort of inconsistent intention formation. Even if this is true, at most it would show that *KM* could not be recommended to agents by a *decision-guide*, i.e. a prescription to be used in their actual decision-making. It would not show that *KM* fails to be the best disposition actually to have (even if one could not rationally bring it about that one has this disposition). If the Causal Efficacy Thesis were not true, then *KM* might well be the best disposition for an agent to have in a prisoner's dilemma under conditions of translucency.

There is a related problem here, which is that Gauthier makes no provision for the possibility that either prospective partner might fail to carry out the intention to cooperate, not because of any change of mind, but rather because circumstances conspire to make cooperation impossible (e.g., I intend to build my lighthouse, but then am unable to purchase the requisite building materials).[5] Part of this problem could be evaded by stating the constrained maximization intention as a *doubly* conditional intention, namely an intention to cooperate, if others do, and if the world permits. Such a restatement would mean that potential partners to whom one was transparent would have to know not just one's intentions and future trustworthiness, but also whether the world would permit cooperation. But epistemic relations between potential partners would remain complex, and perhaps involve the kind of inconsistencies just described, in any case where the world will not permit cooperation.

It is worth pointing out that Gauthier's adoption of the Causal Efficacy Thesis appears to raise a special problem for him. In his discussion of deterrence cases, he explicitly rules out cases in which the agent is *im*perfectly rational, unable fully to control her behavior in terms of her considered preferences. As an instance of such a case, he describes an agent whose cool preference not to retaliate will be overcome by her feelings of anger, rage or panic at the moment action is called for. Gauthier stipulates that he only wants cases in which the person can control her behavior at the time when the choice to retaliate or not must be made. Second, Gauthier rules out cases in which the person, in expressing her intention, delegates her power to choose, by arranging that some other person or some preprogrammed device, capable of ignoring her preferences, will ensure that if the threatener strikes, retaliation will ensue (Gauthier 1984b, pp. 100–105.] Thus we are explicitly confined to cases in which, at the time of action, the agent is rational and in control of what she chooses and does. Clearly Gauthier wants the same conditions to hold in compliance cases as in deterrence ones.

These restrictions may appear to rule out the Causal Efficacy Thesis, because it may appear that if a person is *caused* to do A, then she is not exercising rational choice to do A at the time of the action. However, my view, and I suspect Gauthier's as well, is that the Causal Efficacy Thesis is *not* ruled out by the requirement that the person choose rationally at the time she decides whether or not to carry out her intention. (Notice a potentially confusing switch in terminology here: "choose rationally" does not mean, as it usually does in Gauthier's and my texts, "perform the best act"; rather it

---

5. David Schmidtz pointed this out to me.

means something like "make a reasoned choice given one's evidence.")
Since I believe causation is compatible with rational choice, all this
requirement entails is that the causal chain initiated by her forming the
intention to do *A* must operate by causing her *to choose rationally to perform
A.* It must cause her, for example, to deliberate rationally in selecting her
alternative. Thus forming the intention to build a lighthouse must cause her
to believe that building a lighthouse is best. Since Gauthier is not interested
in misinformed or irrational agents, this belief must be true. But we know
that it would not be best for her to build a lighthouse unless she has
previously formed the intention of doing so (since building a lighthouse, by
itself, merely *decreases* her utility). Thus forming the intention to build must
not only cause her to believe retaliation would be best, it must *in addition
make* it the case that building *is* best. So far, however, we have not
established that forming this intention would make it best to build. Now, to
support the final conclusion of his argument, Gauthier invokes a principle
which asserts that if it is rational (best) to form an intention, then it is
rational (best) to carry it out; see § v below. Thus if we could establish that
it is rational for the agent to form the intention to build, then we could
derive the needed conclusion here, namely that forming the intention to
build does indeed make it best to build. However, we cannot at this point in
the argument help ourselves to the assumption that it is rational to form the
intention to build, since this is precisely what we are trying to prove. We
cannot argue that the intention is rational because it would cause the
intended act to be performed, and then turn around and argue that the act
itself is best because the earlier intention to perform it was rational. Given
Gauthier's desired constraints, the intention is only rational if it would
cause the intended act to be performed *rationally,* i.e., if it would make the
intended act best. And we cannot prove this until we have proved the
intention is rational. There seems to be an unavoidable circularity in the
argument here.

The second point to notice is that I have stated the transparency
assumption (in premise 2) to bring out the fact that it incorporates not
merely the assumption that each person will be aware of the other's choice,
but also the assumption that each person will know *that the other will
actually carry out that choice.* Gauthier himself tends to discuss the
transparency assumption in terms that suggest it merely implies that each
person is aware of the other person's current mental state, e.g, the other
person's current choice or intention. For example, he states that "a person's
expectations about how others will interact with him depend strictly on his
own choice of disposition only if that *choice* is known by the others" (p. 173,
my emphasis). However, it is clear that Gauthier both needs and relies on

the much stronger assumption that others not only know the person's current choice, but also predict infallibly whether or not the person will carry out that choice. For example, Gauthier defines "transparency" as a state in which "each is directly aware...whether he is interacting with straightforward or constrained maximizers (pp. 173–74). Since, as we have just seen, a constrained maximizer is one who *will* carry out her intentions, it follows that awareness that you are a constrained maximizer involves the true belief, not only that you are forming certain conditional intentions, but also that you will carry one of them out when the condition is satisfied. If I did not have this infallible ability to predict your future acts, Gauthier could not argue (as he does) that I maximize my expected utility by choosing *CM*, since I would sometimes be cheated by defecting partners. Correspondingly, Gauthier's translucency assumption is an assumption that agents' abilities to detect each others' intentions *and* to predict future fulfillment of those intentions surpass mere guesswork. My point here is not to reject these assumptions, but rather to indicate clearly how strong they are, and at least to raise doubts about their credibility.

IV. DOES *CM* MAXIMIZE EXPECTED UTILITY?

Now let us turn to premise 3, which spells out what the consequences will be if I choose *CM* as opposed to *SM*. Here the argument runs into trouble. The first major problem is that Gauthier mistakenly assumes both that (a) my only options are *CM* and *SM*, and (b) my partner's only options are *CM* and *SM*. He then argues that *CM* is my best response to the possibility of these choices on the part of my partner. Both these assumptions seem false—there is no reason to suppose that our options are limited in this fashion. Since discussion of what additional options might be rational for me to choose is complicated, I will restrict myself here to pointing out that my partner has a variety of alternatives, and that *CM* is not my best response to many of these. I may, for example, face a partner who has chosen what we may call "unconditional cooperation":[6]

UC Building one's lighthouse whatever one's partner does.

Or I may face someone who has chosen "radical cooperation":

RC Building one's lighthouse if and only if one's partner has chosen unconditional cooperation.

---

6. I am grateful to David Schmidtz for pointing out to me the relevance of this alternative option.

How would someone who has chosen *CM* fare against a partner who has chosen *UC*? It is obvious that the best choice is *SM* rather than *CM*, since the straightforward maximizer will always obtain –500 while the constrained maximizer will only obtain –600. Similarly, against a partner who has chosen *RC*, one will maximize utility by choosing *UC* rather than *CM*, for in this way one will achieve a constant return of –600 rather than –1000. Of course a partner who chooses *UC* or *RC* may not be rational, since this choice will not fare well against all possible configurations of partners and their choices (although it is certainly arguable that someone choosing *UC* is *moral*). But *CM* is hardly an attractive option if it only succeeds against perfectly rational partners. Since many people are in fact irrational, an acceptable option must work against all comers, be they rational or not.[7] Hence Gauthier's argument that *CM* maximizes utility is significantly incomplete, since it does not take account of cases in which the chooser's partner will select some other option (perhaps an irrational one) besides either *CM* or *SM*. To establish whether *CM* is superior, we would have to know how many potential partners have chosen *SM*, *CM*, *UC*, *RC*, and all the other options that could be defined; how transparent or translucent these individuals are; what the stakes are in possible interactions with them; and so forth. Gauthier has not performed this task for us, and we can have no advance reason to suppose that *CM* will emerge ever or often as the best policy.

But even if we restrict ourselves to partners who choose either *CM* or *SM*, Gauthier's argument is less compelling than he realizes. Let us look at his first claim:

> If I choose *CM*, then (a) if you choose *CM*, you will build and I will build.

Why, precisely, is it supposed to be the case that if I choose *CM*, then if you choose *CM* as well, you will build and I will build? Each of us is transparent, so each of us knows the other's choice, plus the fact that the other will carry out that choice. But how does each of us make the relevant choice?

---

7. The importance of establishing the rationality of a strategy against irrational opponents has been recognized since von Neumann and Morgenstern (1953, p. 3 2) concluded that "...the rules of rational behavior must provide definitely for the possibility of irrational conduct on the part of others." (von Neumann and Morgenstern 1953, p. 32; as quoted in Skyrms 1992, chapter 6). Even Gauthier, who argues that *CM* rather than *SM* is rational, evidently concedes that *CM* must succeed against irrational dispositions, of which (in his view) *SM* is one. David Copp (1991, p. 3) describes the contractarian strategy as arguing that there is a set of moral requirements such that a population of fully rational people would agree to comply with them. But if this argument assumes that each person may presuppose the rationality of everyone else in agreeing to comply with these requirements, it idealizes our actual situation beyond any usefulness.

There are actually *two* crucial choices that each of us must make here: the choice between *CM* and *SM*, and the choice (if *CM* is selected) of which unconditional intention to form, the intention to build or the intention not to build. Let us simplify matters by assuming that you have already chosen *CM*, and of course I know this. What should I predict you will do if I choose *CM*? Gauthier seems to assume that I may simply predict that you will form the intention to build your lighthouse, and then build it. But matters are much more complex than this. Given your choice of *CM*, what I *can* predict is that you will form the intention to build and carry it out if and only if you predict that I will form the unconditional intention to build and then carry out this intention. But how can I assume you can make this prediction about me? Your position vis-à-vis me is perfectly parallel to my position vis-à-vis you. Even if you know that I choose *CM*, all you can infer from this is that I will form the intention to build and carry it out *if and only if* I predict you will build. You cannot infer that I will intend and build, simpliciter. But if you cannot infer this, then you will not build. And I will not form the intention to build and then carry it out unless I believe you will build. Neither of us, knowing the other has chosen *CM*, has sufficient information to predict on that basis what the other will do, so neither of us can decide which intention to form or which act to carry out.

What we have just seen is that if "transparency" is interpreted as Gauthier officially interprets it, namely as awareness on the part of another agent whether he is interacting with a constrained or straightforward maximizer, then transparency is not sufficient to allow two transparent constrained maximizers to predict what the other will do, or to choose any intention or action themselves, since that choice depends on their making this prediction. We might try to avoid this by allowing Gauthier a *maximum* notion of transparency, namely the assumption that each agent just directly knows (or truly believes) what (unconditional) intention the other agent forms, and knows that the other will carry out that intention. But even this will not solve the problem. To see this all we need to do is notice that it is perfectly consistent with our both being constrained maximizers that we both form the intention *not* to build, and then carry out that intention. (For being a *CM may* involve forming the intention not to build if you predict the other agent will not build, and then not building yourself; if both of us do this, then we both still qualify as choosing and carrying out *CM*.) Thus it is *not* possible, contrary to Gauthier's argument, to show that if we both choose *CM*, and we are both transparent to each other in this maximum sense, then we will both form the intention to build and then carry out those intentions. We might instead both form and act on the intention *not* to build. But if it is false that two constrained maximizers will necessarily cooperate, it is false that my choosing *CM* when you have chosen *CM* necessarily produces greater utility for me than my choosing *SM*: they might produce the very same utility—the utility I receive if neither of us builds a lighthouse.

It might be hoped that a reformulation of constrained maximization could be found according to which it would necessarily be the case that if two transparent partners both choose *CM*, then they will both build. Unfortunately, such reformulations do not seem to be available. Consider the following simple candidate:

> *CM′* Forming the intention to build, and carrying out that intention.

Two agents, both of whom adopt *CM′*, will necessarily both build their lighthouses. But adopting *CM′* leaves each of them vulnerable to straightforward maximizers, since it directs the agent to build regardless of what her partner does. To avoid this we need to incorporate the kind of clause adopted by Gauthier, which dictates adopting the same intention as one's partner; and to secure joint building, rather than joint nonbuilding, we need an additional clause that provides pressure, so to speak, in the direction of building. The following option might be thought to solve the problem:

> *CM″* (i) Forming the intention to build if one's partner will build, or forming the intention not to build if one's partner will not build; and (ii) carrying out whichever intention one forms; and (iii) forming the intention to build and actually building if one's partner forms the intention to comply with (i) and (ii).

It may appear that *CM″* secures the result Gauthier wants, since if both you and I adopt *CM″*, then each of us forms the intention to comply with clauses (i) and (ii), and hence each of us must comply with clause (iii)—so we both build our lighthouses. However, *CM″* must be rejected, for it does not prescribe a consistent set of intentions. For suppose you have adopted clauses (i) and (ii), but not clause (iii), and you also form the intention not to build (as we have seen, nothing in clauses (i) and (ii) rules this out). Then, by *CM″*, I must *both* form the intention to build (since that is required by clause (iii)), and *also* form the intention not to build (since that is required by clause (i)). But these intentions, and their attendant actions, are inconsistent. In general, every reformulation of *CM* I have inspected is vulnerable to some problem or another: either it does not guarantee joint compliance, or it leaves the agent vulnerable to exploitation by a partner who does not adopt *CM*, or it delivers inconsistent prescriptions. Unless a successful version of *CM* is forthcoming, we must conclude joint adoption of constrained maximization cannot secure joint compliance as Gauthier's argument assumes.[8]

On Gauthier's original presentation of his argument, I never do worse if I choose *CM* than if I choose *SM*, and in one case out of four possible types of case, I will do better. On my construal of the argument (assuming my partner chooses either *SM* or *CM*), I never do worse if I choose *CM*, and in

---

8. Peter Danielson (1991) recognizes this difficulty, and formulates a version of *CM* that he claims avoids the problem. He introduces the notion of a "metastrategy," that is, "a function that takes each of the other player's choices (or metastrategies) into a choice." He then introduces the metastrategy *CC* (intended to be roughly similar to Gauthier's *CM*) which is defined as "*CC* = *UC* → *C*; *MAX* → *D*; *CC* → *C*" (where *UC* and *MAX* are other metastrategies). But *this* definition is clearly illegitimate, since it refers to the very concept being defined (*CC* itself). Danielson states that *CC* can be defined "extensionally" in terms of the game matrix, but this cannot be correct, since he explicitly recognizes (his figures 1 and 2, pp. 293, 295) that a first order game (in which the agents' options are ordinary actions) may have the same matrix as a second-order game (in which the agents' options are metastrategies). Thus game matrices alone cannot define metastrategies, since such matrices do not distinguish them from ordinary actions or choices. Indeed, since a "metastrategy" is *defined* as a strategy from another player's choice or metastrategy to a choice, it is difficult to see how a metastrategy could be individuated (much less implemented, as Danielson himself realizes), without some reference to the other player's choice or metastrategy. In other work Danielson attempts to solve this problem by use of a quotational device which I have not had the opportunity to examine.

Richmond Campbell (1988) suggests the following formulation of *CM* to get around this problem: "In a choice situation involving strategic interaction a person has the *CM* disposition iff: (1) she has property *R* and (2) she will cooperate with other agents interacting with her iff she believes that each of them has property R." Property *R* is any property that *SM*'s will not have, such as the property of being ready to reciprocate cooperation when making the second move in *sequential* prisoner's dilemmas (p. 351). It is true that *SM*'s will not have the property Campbell describes, so that someone who adopts *CM* will not be exploited by *SM*'s. However, there will be other defecting agents who *would* reciprocate cooperation in sequential prisoner's dilemmas, but who would *not* cooperate in simultaneous prisoner's dilemmas; an agent adopting Campbell's version of *CM* would be vulnerable to exploitation by these agents. *SM* agents do not exhaust the list of possible noncooperative agents that *CM* agents must be protected against. We cannot, of course, without problematic circularity, simply define a *CM* agent as one who cooperates with all and only other *CM* agents (or ones she believes to be *CM* agents). There is a deep problem here about whether the kind of relation Gauthier needs between *CM* partners is incoherent: it may be that his conditions will only be met if the decision of each partner *causes* the decision of the other partner—a type of causal interaction that cannot be countenanced.

Donald Regan (1980, chapters 8–10) discusses analogous problems of coordination that might face act utilitarians. He introduces a new version of utilitarianism that, he argues, enables agents who follow it to protect themselves from "exploitation" by others, and yet enables them as a group to secure the greatest utility available to them as a group. The daunting complexity of this new theory leaves me uncertain as to its success; but readers interested in pursuing this problem for Gauthier would be well repaid to study Regan's contribution.

one case (where you also choose *CM*) out of four I *may* do better. This is getting to be pretty slim pickings as support for the rationality of choosing *CM*. It becomes even slimmer when we move from the strong transparency assumption to the more realistic translucency assumption Gauthier himself uses. Under the transparency assumption, *CM* is a safe choice, since I can never be exploited by straightforward maximizers: I can always recognize them in advance and protect myself. But under the translucency assumption, *CM* is no longer safe: it exposes me to exploitation by undetected straightforward maximizers. Both I and potential partners can resort to the *pretense* of being a constrained maximizer, and then prey on those who are deceived. The issue then is whether the gain possibly available through adopting *CM* is outweighed by the risk of exploitation that it creates.

Gauthier argues that under the translucency assumption, it is rational to choose *CM* only if the ratio between the probability that an interaction involving *CM*s will result in cooperation and the probability that an interaction involving *CM*s and *SM*s will involve exploitation and defection, is greater than the ratio between the gain from defection and the gain through cooperation (p. 176). In arguing that this will often happen, Gauthier assumes that two constrained maximizers who successfully identify each other will always cooperate. What we have seen is that they will *not* always cooperate. Hence the probability that an interaction involving *CM*s will result in cooperation is lower than Gauthier assumes (although we cannot say how much lower). Therefore it takes a correspondingly *lower* ratio between the gain from defection and the gain through cooperation for it to be rational to choose *CM*. The less people stand to gain from defection, the more likely it is that *CM* is rational; but the more people stand to gain from defection, the less likely it is that *CM* is rational. The rationality of choosing *CM* is not undermined for *every* case by the phenomenon I have described. What I have shown, however, is that the number of cases in which it is rational to choose *CM* is smaller than Gauthier supposes, and it may be significantly smaller. And, as we saw at the beginning of this section, it may not be rational at all if one's potential partners adopt options such as *UC* or *RC* rather than *CM* or *SM*. All this may dramatically reduce the number of occasions on which it is rational to dispose oneself to act morally, and so may considerably shrink the scope of the justification for moral action that Gauthier is trying to provide.

V. THE RATIONALITY OF CARRYING OUT RATIONAL INTENTIONS

In the preceding section I argued that Gauthier succeeds in showing the rationality of choosing constrained maximization in fewer cases than he realizes. Let us now turn to the question of whether it is really rational for me to carry out constrained maximization even in the cases where it is rational to choose it in advance. Item 7 of Gauthier's argument asserts that it is: that, for example, if I rationally choose *CM* and form the intention to build my lighthouse, then it is rational for me actually to build the lighthouse when the time comes.[9]

Why does Gauthier think it is rational for me to carry out my chosen policy? He admits that doing so is not rational in the usual sense of maximizing utility. It appears that what he relies on here is a general principle, which we may label the Rationality of Perseverance Principle:

> RPP   If it is rational for an agent to form the intention to do *A*, then it is rational for the agent actually to do *A* when the time comes (assuming the agent acquires no new information, and has not altered her values).

Gauthier asserts, for example: "If it is rational for me to adopt an intention to do *x* in circumstances *c*, and if *c* comes about...then it is rational for me to carry out *x*;" and also, "if [a person's] dispositions to choose are rational, then surely her choices are also rational" (1984, p. 159; 1986, p. 186).

Unfortunately, and surprisingly, Gauthier offers no positive argument in favor of the Rationality of Perseverance Principle. The only argument he appears to provide is the concession that if the agent will suffer from some future weakness or imperfection (such as weakness of will), then it will *not* be rational for her to persevere in carrying out an intention (pp. 184–86).[10] But of course this does not provide positive evidence that rationality requires perfect agents to persevere.

---

9. Part of this claim is the claim that if I rationally choose *CM*, and seeing that you will not build your lighthouse, form the intention not to build my lighthouse, then it is rational for me to carry out this intention as well. But no one disputes that carrying out this particular intention is rational.

10. In discussing what it would be rational to do for agents who are subject to weaknesses or imperfections, Gauthier states that such rationality constitutes "a second-best rationality," and denies that any lesson can be drawn from this about the dispositions and choices that are rational for the perfect actor (pp. 185–86). This seems to be a mistake. It is rational, simpliciter, to do the best one can in the face, so to speak, of the materials that have been given to one. An imperfect agent, one afflicted with future weakness of will, does the best she can in the face of *this* material. The material is imperfect, but her rationality in dealing with this material is not imperfect or "second-best." Similarly an agent facing a threatener, or a straightforward maximizer, does the best she can in the face of this material. The agents she faces are also imperfect (on Gauthier's view), but this does not show that her rationality in dealing with these agents is imperfect. I can see no principled difference between doing the best one can vis-à-vis one's own future imperfections and doing the best one can vis-à-vis other agents' imperfections.

Indeed, it is difficult to know how one could argue for the rationality of perseverance. On the face of it, intentions and the intended acts are two distinct events, sometimes having different features and different consequences. Hence the appropriateness of an intention appears to imply nothing conclusive about the appropriateness of the intended act. I may, for example, have promised to form a certain intention, but not promised to carry it out; in such a case I am obliged to form the intention, but not obliged to carry it out, especially if my doing so would be undesirable.[11]

The natural move here for a defender of perseverance would be to appeal to intuitions about rationality in various cases. Unfortunately, such appeals do not appear to support the principle. In standard cases, where the consequences of the intention are the same as those of the intended act, where the agent is rational to form an intention at t_1 to perform A rather than B at t_2, and where she receives no new information and does not change her values by t_2, we all agree that she then would be rational at t_2 to carry out her intention by performing A. But we cannot use this fact to support the claim that the existence of her prior intention to do A *makes it* rational to do A, since it would be rational for her to do A whether or not she had ever formed that prior intention. She has all the same reasons to do A at t_2 that she had at t_1; if it was reasonable to choose A over B at the earlier time, of course it is reasonable to choose it now. Someone attempting to support the Rationality of Perseverance Principle by appeal to this kind of case would have to resort to a different scenario, one involving two possible worlds, identical to each other except that in the first world the agent forms a rational prior intention to do A while in the second world the agent forms no prior intention. It would then have to be claimed that at the time of action the first agent has *more* reason to do A than the second agent. I myself have no inclination to think this: the two agents appear to me to have precisely equal reason to do A.

Gauthier needs the strong interpretation of the *RPP*, according to which the rationality of the earlier intention *makes* the later action rational. Otherwise, in the kinds of cases with which we are specifically concerned, that is, cases where the agent's reasons for forming the intention to do A are independent of his reasons for actually doing A, the action would have to be judged irrational according to the normal utility-maximizing criterion of rationality. This presumption of irrationality could only be overturned by

---

11. Since this paper was written, I have discovered that similar arguments to those in this paragraph (and a case similar to my subsequent telepathic terrorist case) have already been presented by Gregory Kavka (1984, pp. 155–59). A second independent and insightful discussion of what I call *RPP* (keyed to another article of Kavka's) is contained in Bratman 1987, pp. 101–6.

the strong interpretation of the *RPP*. But it is precisely in such cases that we feel the greatest conviction that the agent's reasons for forming the intention to do *A* seem not to carry over *at all* as reasons to do *A* itself. Consider the case of a government official negotiating with a terrorist. The terrorist, an infallible mind reader, threatens to blow up a planeload of innocent people unless the official forms the mental intention of releasing the terrorist's imprisoned comrades. When, and only when, the official forms this intention (a psychological event the terrorist will detect telepathically), the bomb will be disarmed. Clearly under these circumstances it would be rational for the official to form the intention of releasing the terrorist's comrades. Once he has formed the required intention and the terrorist has permanently disarmed his bomb, it seems equally clear that it would be rational for the official to change his mind and *not* release the comrades. Indeed we would view a terrorist who merely demanded the formation of intentions as extremely stupid. Here, then, is a clear-cut case where it is rational to form an intention, and yet irrational to carry it out, contrary to the implications of the Rationality of Perseverance Principle.[12] Gauthier might argue that his acceptance of the Causal Efficacy Thesis shows that it is causally impossible for the official both to form the intention to release the comrades and then to change his mind. But this does not show that refusing to release the comrades is *rational*, i.e., the best act. Gauthier assumes throughout that the agent has genuine alternatives available to him at t_2, i.e., that he *could* release the comrades. And if he could release them, it is open to us to assess this act as the best one.

It may fix this conclusion even more firmly in our minds to notice that Gauthier needs an extremely strong perseverance principle: not just the assertion that prior intentions create *some* reason to carry them out, but rather the assertion that prior intentions create *conclusive* reason to carry them out. For if the reason to comply created by one's earlier intention is not conclusive, there will always be danger that the disutility of compliance will outweigh the reason in favor of compliance created by the earlier intention, and defection will turn out to be rational after all. The complete counterintuitiveness of such a strong perseverance principle can be seen if we merely raise the stakes at issue in a given case. Consider a case in which a telepathic burglar threatens to steal all my household valuables. I know that if I form the intention of blowing up the house with the burglar and myself inside, it is nearly certain that he will be deterred. I form this intention, but

---

12. Gauthier regards deterrence cases and compliance cases as completely parallel, so he would not dismiss such a case as irrelevant to his argument about compliance with morality (pp. 184–87).

unfortunately he is not deterred. According to the Strong Perseverance Principle, it is now rational for me to blow up the house and kill myself, merely because I previously formed the intention of doing so under these circumstances. But no one, I think, would want to agree to this. Gauthier's guiding hope in his project is to provide a foundation for moral norms on norms of rationality, because the latter's binding status is much more easily accepted. But if it turns out that the norms of rationality include such principles as perseverance, it appears they may demand greater self-sacrifice from us than even morality typically does, and will be even more difficult to accept. If morality requires rationality of perseverance as its foundation, we are probably worse off than we are with a morality that has no separate foundation.

It is also worth noting that nothing in Gauthier's argument for the rationality of choosing constrained maximization really turns on the fact that the means by which I effect my subsequent compliance is a choice to form a certain *intention*. We could restate the entire argument, just as effectively, to show that it would maximize my utility to perform *any* present act that would bring about my subsequent choosing to build a lighthouse. For example, suppose that tonight I open a magazine to an article I want to read tomorrow. Tomorrow I read the article, its mentioning lighthouses triggers the idea that I might build one, and that is precisely what I do. Suppose also that I am transparent to you, in the sense that you detect my opening the magazine tonight and accurately predict that it will stimulate me tomorrow to build a lighthouse. You are a (suitably defined) constrained maximizer. If Gauthier's argument were correct, my opening the magazine in these circumstances would induce you to build your lighthouse as well, and we would have evaded the prisoner's dilemma. Hence, since it would (on Gauthier's argument) maximize utility for me to open the magazine, rationality requires that I do so. But, when the time came for me to build the lighthouse, Gauthier would be unable to argue that building the lighthouse is also rational for me, since he can invoke no prior intention on my part to establish its rationality. Since there is no difference between the utility I can secure by forming an intention and the utility I can secure by opening the magazine, there is no way for Gauthier to argue that I must form the intention rather than open the magazine. Agents who bring about their own compliance with moral rules by such means as opening magazines cannot be said to be rational when they do comply.[13]

---

13. It is clear that in opening the magazine I have no intention to build a lighthouse. We might investigate whether I could *deliberately* secure my building the lighthouse by performing some act today that would bring about my building the lighthouse tomorrow,

We should note the flip side of Gauthier's reliance on intentions to make subsequent compliance rational. Imagine a case in which one's partner has performed the cooperative act, even though one did not oneself adopt constrained maximization, or form the intention to cooperate. In such a case Gauthier must say that it is not rational, and hence not moral, for one to cooperate, since no prior intention to cooperate makes it rational now. (And, since belatedly forming such an intention would have no effect on one's partner's action, there is no reason to do so, even if such an intention, if rational, would make one's cooperating rational.) This seems a clear case in which the recommendations generated by Gauthier's system diverge sharply from those of ordinary morality, which would recommend cooperation even if one had not originally intended to cooperate.

I conclude that the Rationality of Perseverance Principle is false.[14] If this is correct, then Gauthier has not shown that it is rational to carry out constrained maximization, even in those cases where it is rational to adopt it. It follows from this that he has not shown that it is rational to abide with

---

without at the time of the act intending to build a lighthouse (it might be claimed, for example, that doing A with the intention of bringing about my doing B shows that I *do* have the intention of doing B at the time I do A). I am not at all sure this latter claim is correct, but I shall not try to discuss it here. The important point for us here is that my act of opening the magazine is rational, i.e. utility-maximizing, whether or not *I* believe it will have the desired effect. And if I open the magazine in ignorance of its effect, I can hardly be said to have the intention of bringing about that effect.

Gauthier might try to assert (and there is some textual evidence that he believes) an analog of the Perseverance Principle: that if it is best (rational) for me to do act A (partly because it will bring about later act B), then when the time comes it must be best (rational) for me to do B as well. Clearly this is incorrect. Suppose a business student has only two choices: to accept a job with Firm A, or to accept a job with Firm B. If she accepts the job with Firm A, she will subsequently cheat a client out of $100, be caught, and sentenced to spend a month in jail. If she accepts the job with Firm B, she will subsequently cheat a client out of $100,000, be caught, and sentenced to spend ten years in jail. Given the prospects, it would be best for her to accept the job with Firm A—and best partly because this job will result in her stealing (merely) $100. But it hardly follows that it would then be best (or rational) for her to cheat the client out of $100. She may be destined to do this by her earlier choice, but we can still criticize her action. (See above, footnote 9, for discussion of whether such cases are sufficiently parallel to the ones in which Gauthier is interested.) In cases such as this, one might question whether act B (stealing $100) is part of what makes act A (accepting the job with Firm A) best—it would be more intuitive to say that act A is best *despite* its leading to act B. But the analogue to the Perseverance Principle just articulated is only significant if it applies to subsequent acts (such as stealing the $100) that are not rational or best taken in themselves.

14. Copp (1991, § 3) also argues that actual compliance is irrational even if the *CM* disposition is rational (except in the sense that the *CM*'s preferences have changed, in virtue of her adoption of *CM*, so that compliance necessarily becomes the utility-maximizing act).

moral rules once accepted, even if it is rational to accept them. Moreover, even if the Rationality of Perseverance Principle were true, it would not apply to cases in which an agent induces himself to comply with moral precepts by some means (such as opening a magazine) that do not involve forming an intention to perform the act of compliance. Any agent who maximizes his utility by such means cannot be said to be rational when he then complies. Whether his act of compliance is brought about by a utility-maximizing intention or a utility-maximizing act of another sort, the compliance itself is not rational.

VI. THE DERIVATION OF MORALITY FROM RATIONALITY

I have argued that Gauthier has not shown that it maximizes expected utility in a significant number of cases for a person to adopt constrained maximization. I have further argued that he has not shown, because it is false, that it is rational for a person to act according to constrained maximization even in the cases where it was rational to adopt it. Now I want to take up a harder and more important question. Suppose my previous arguments were wrong, and Gauthier had indeed shown that it is rational both to adopt constrained maximization in many cases and then to carry it out. Would the success of this argument show, as Gauthier believes it does, that morality is founded on rationality, and hence that rationality provides a "justificatory framework for moral behavior and principles" (p. 2)? If the success of Gauthier's argument *would* provide a rational justification for morality, then we would be well repaid to tinker with the details of his argument in an attempt to salvage it from my previous criticisms. But if success would not provide such a justification, then such tinkering has little or no point.

I shall assume that the point of providing morality with a justificatory framework is to defend it against the moral skeptic, who believes all moral statements are false, or meaningless, or at any rate without epistemological justification. We may characterize what Gauthier has done as arguing that individual rationality, or self-interest, requires a person to dispose herself to perform certain cooperative acts, and then actually to perform those acts when the time comes. Suppose we assume that the acts in question are precisely the same ones that morality requires. Still, the success of this argument would not show that *morality* has been provided with a justification. It would show that we have self-interested reasons to do what morality, *if it were true* (or correct), would demand—but it would not show that morality *is* true (or correct). Such an argument would merely show an interesting coincidence between the purported claims of morality and the real claims of self-interest.[15] In order for Gauthier to answer the moral skeptic, he must do something more. But precisely what?

One promising strategy for answering the moral skeptic would be to find premises that the skeptic must accept, and then to show that certain moral statements follow from those premises. I believe that Gauthier can be interpreted as trying to follow precisely this strategy. He puts forward certain premises that he believes everyone must accept, and then argues that moral statements can be derived from them. In his case the premises are not factual statements, or definitions of moral terms, but rather normative principles of individual rationality. If these principles cannot be rejected, or at any rate are more readily acceptable than morality itself, then if moral principles can be shown to follow from them, morality will have been provided with a suitable foundation. We need not follow the cognitivist in granting that the principles of individual rationality are *true*, but whatever variety of acceptability they do have will be fully inherited by the moral principles that can be shown to follow from them.[16] The moral skeptic will be hard put to reject such principles.

How, precisely, is the argument supposed to go? Gauthier posits the following two axioms of individual rationality (where *RPP* is our old friend the rationality of perseverance, and *RMX* is a *qualified* version of the rationality of maximizing expected utility). He characterizes these as comprising a "weak and widely accepted conception of practical rationality" (p. 17).

RPP If it is rational for an agent to form the intention of doing *A*, then it is rational for the agent actually to do *A* when the time comes (assuming the agent acquires no new information, and has not altered her values).

RMX It is rational for an agent to act so as to maximize her expected utility, unless doing so requires her to violate *RPP*. (pp. 43–44; 182–87)

He then argues that these axioms entail the following principles:

---

15. I take this to be one of the points of Copp 1991. Copp and I initiated our lines of inquiry into the force of Gauthier's argument independently; reading earlier versions of his stimulating discussion forced me to clarify for myself what I thought Gauthier was really trying to do in connecting rationality and morality.

16. Some authors have tried to follow this strategy by deriving moral statements from definitions of moral terms. For example, if we agree that "is morally obligatory" just means "would maximize the general happiness," then we can hardly reject the truth of the statement "It is morally obligatory to maximize the general happiness." The weakness of this version of the strategy is that a skeptic can respond, "Why should anyone care about acts that maximize the general happiness?" Gauthier's version avoids this problem, because it *starts* with normative principles that have motivational force.

I. Under circumstances C, it is rational for an agent to adopt constrained maximization and form the intention to cooperate.

II. If the agent rationally forms the intention to cooperate, then it is rational for her to carry out this intention (assuming she has acquired no new information and has not altered her values).

The phrase "circumstances C" refers to any combination of empirical factors, involving the intentions of other agents, their degree of translucency, the possible gains and losses associated with cooperation and defection, etc., that makes it true in a given case that the agent would maximize her expected utility by adopting constrained maximization. Principle I follows straightforwardly from axiom *RMX*, if we allow this form of rationality to be applied to the formation of intentions (i.e., adoption of constrained maximization) as well as to external conduct. Principle II is a straightforward special case of axiom *RPP*.

Gauthier claims that the traditional conception of morality identifies any impartial constraint on self-interested behavior as moral (pp. 2–4). On this account principle I is not a moral principle, since it in no way constrains self-interested behavior. To the contrary, it recommends adoption of constrained maximization precisely because it will maximize the agent's self-interest. Hence, if this argument provides a justification for morality, the whole weight falls on principle II. Principle II clearly does constrain self-interested behavior, since it requires the agent to cooperate even when doing so would fail to maximize her utility. Let us grant, for the sake of argument, that principle II is also impartial in some suitable sense.

Does the fact that principle II constitutes an impartial constraint on self-interested behavior show that it is a moral principle? Clearly not. Impartial constraint is *not* sufficient to show a principle is moral. Consider a rule of etiquette requiring thank-you notes to be hand-written rather than typed. Such a rule is certainly an impartial constraint, but it does not thereby qualify as a moral principle.[17] What more is required for morality? This is a difficult question, to which I will not try to supply a general answer.

---

17. Another example is the Principle of Malevolence, which prescribes any action maximizing the general unhappiness. This principle is both impartial and a constraint on self-interest (since it is often highly damaging to an agent's own interests to follow it), yet it hardly seems to be a moral principle. Other examples are supplied by club rules, legal codes, Mafia codes of honor, professional codes, administrative regulations, etc. Of course some of the prescriptions stemming from these sources will require acts that are morally right, but it does not follow that all such prescriptions coincide with morality, or that any of them *in itself* constitutes a moral prescription. The difficulty with the Principle of Malevolence is not the one I cite in the text—inappropriate deontic force—but rather inappropriate content.

But it appears to me that we can characterize what is lacking in rules of etiquette as something like *appropriate deontic force*. It is by no means easy to say what the deontic force appropriate to morality amounts to. But, borrowing from the traditional literature on the nature of morality, we might suggest the following three features:

1. Moral prescriptions are *overriding.* That is, they outweigh prescriptions from any other source when there is a conflict. In particular, they outweigh the recommendations of self-interest; or perhaps, more accurately, strong moral considerations outweigh weak considerations from any other normative sphere.

2. Moral prescriptions are *categorical.* That is, they hold independently of the agent's actual desires and aversions.

3. Moral prescriptions for action make it appropriate for agents to hold associated distinctive moral attitudes, such as guilt for personal derelictions, blame towards others who violate the prescriptions, a feeling that one is justified when one follows the prescription, etc.

The question before us is whether principle ii has the kind of deontic force required of genuine moral principles.[18] Is its recommendation overriding and categorical, and does it support attitudes of guilt and blame, etc.? I am not going to try to answer this question definitively. One can certainly argue that principle ii generates prescriptions that are both overriding and categorical. They are overriding because they always outweigh the recommendation of self-interest to maximize one's own utility, and they are categorical for the same reason: they tell the agent what to do regardless of her desires at the moment of action. (On the other hand, there is a sense in which they are neither overriding nor categorical, since these prescriptions only arise because of the agent's prior attempts to satisfy her desires and maximize her self-interest by adopting constrained maximization. This is not the kind of independence from desires that Kant, for example, had in mind.) It is far less clear that one can argue that prescriptions generated by principle ii appropriately support attitudes of blame, guilt, and so forth. I myself see no reason why an agent should feel *guilty* (or should *blame* others) for violating principle ii, which is essentially a demand that one's action and intentions show a certain form of consistency. Inconsistency is not usually the object of blame and guilt.

---

18. Gauthier's commitment to deriving principles with moral force is shown in the following passage (p. 9): "A person is conceived as an independent center of activity, endeavoring to direct his capacities and resources to the fulfillment of his interests. He considers what he can do, but initially draws no distinction between what he may and may not do. How then does he come to acknowledge this distinction? How does a person come to recognize a moral dimension to choice...?"

But this is not the point I want to make here. What I want instead to point out is that whatever deontic force principle II does possess, it inherits this force directly and solely from the Axiom of Rational Perseverance, since it is simply a special case of that axiom. If that axiom has appropriate deontic force, then principle II will as well; whereas if that axiom fails to have the appropriate force, then principle II will also fail. What this means is that principle II only qualifies as a moral principle if axiom *RPP* qualifies as a moral principle. But if axiom *RPP* qualifies as a moral principle, then Gauthier has not succeeded in deriving morality from some nonmoral source.[19] Instead he has derived morality from morality itself. This is no help against the moral skeptic. The only possible way in which such an argument could be construed as an effective response to the moral skeptic would be if the *RPP*, although moral, were somehow less questionable or more readily acceptable than other moral principles. Quite the opposite seems to be the case, as my arguments in the last section aimed at showing.

What we have discovered is that even if Gauthier had succeeded in establishing the truth of principles I and II, he would not have answered the skeptic by showing how morality can be derived from individual rationality. Either the principles he derives do not qualify as moral principles, because they lack the required deontic force, or if on the other hand, they possess that force, it is only because a covert moral principle was smuggled into the axioms of individual rationality. No amount of tinkering with the details of Gauthier's argument will circumvent this problem.

The problem is a general one, extending beyond Gauthier's project to other possible attempts to derive morality from individual rationality. It appears to be precisely the powerful deontic force of morality that makes it suspect. It looks as though *any* attempt to derive morality in the manner I have outlined here faces the same dilemma as Gauthier's attempt: either the derived principles will be deontically too weak to qualify as genuinely moral, or else the premises will be so strong that they already qualify as moral, and subject to the full blast of the skeptic's suspicion. If morality is to be defended against skepticism by an appeal to rationality, we need some better strategy than the one I have outlined here.

I conclude that the long-sought proof for the rationality of morality still eludes us, despite the hard and illuminating work Gauthier has devoted to the cause of finding it. It may elude us forever.

---

19. See pp. 5 and 17, for Gauthier's assertions that he aims to derive morality from a non-moral source.

Part II

Morality

6

On the Paradox of Deontology*

William H. Shaw

Deontological moral theories seem paradoxical because they are prepared to forbid certain actions even when those actions would prevent the occurrence of more actions of the very same sort. In the first section of this essay, I explicate this paradox, and in the following section I go on to describe and criticize some ways in which deontologists have responded to it. Thereafter, however, I offer solace to the deontologist. The third and fourth sections discuss the conditions that must be met before this paradox poses a genuine problem and the likelihood of those conditions being satisfied. Then, with a nod to rule utilitarianism, I show that the deontologist has an important, albeit pragmatic line of rebuttal, which in conjunction with other considerations raised in the essay can assist nonconsequentialists to disarm the paradox of deontology.

I

"Deontological" or "nonconsequentialist" are labels for a very wide category of moral theories, so wide that many will think that the differences within the deontological camp are more striking than the differences between it and the theories that are seen as outside it. The paradox I discuss does not presuppose a rigorous definition of these familiar terms.[1] Perhaps the only feature that matters here is that in deontological or nonconsequentialist theories the rightness (or wrongness) of an action is a function of more than the goodness or badness of its consequences. Deontologists do not eschew consequences altogether; they contend merely that there is more to morality

* I thank Jonathan Bennett for his critical comments on this essay, an earlier version of which appeared in the *Journal of Philosophical Research* 16 (1991: 393–406).

1. Along with almost all contemporary moral theorists, I assume that there is a meaningful and relevant contrast between deontological and consequentialist moral theories, however exactly that contrast is best drawn. Hare, however, has rejected the distinction altogether; see Hare 1963, p. 124.

than pursuing good outcomes. The good, in their view, does not fully determine the right.

It follows from this that a morally required or morally permitted action may sometimes be a less than optimific action. This characteristic of deontological theories is not itself paradoxical, and nonconsequentialist writers frequently insist on it: some actions, they say, are wrong to perform even though performing them would produce more good in the world than not performing them. The good envisioned is typically happiness, and in this way deontological moral theorists distance themselves from classical utilitarianism. When, however, the good is defined so as to include the absence of actions of a sort forbidden by the deontological theory, then a paradox begins to emerge.

In his famous critique of utilitarianism, Bernard Williams (1973, p. 89) observes in passing that a nonconsequentialist might hold that it was wrong of someone to break his promise even if breaking it was the only way to prevent several other people from breaking theirs. But Robert Nozick may have been the first to underscore the truly puzzling character of this moral stance. "If nonviolation of C is so important," he writes, "shouldn't that be the goal? How can a concern for the nonviolation of C lead to the refusal to violate C even when this would prevent more extensive violations of C?" (Nozick 1974, p. 30) Here Nozick puts his finger firmly on the paradox of deontology: deontological rules may forbid a particular action in certain circumstances even though performing that action in those circumstances would result in fewer actions of the forbidden type.

Whether one wants to describe this as a paradox, as I shall continue to do, depends on what one means by "paradox." But this definitional issue is unimportant, in part, because it is not obvious how a moral theorist should respond to the realization that his theory has this (or any other) paradoxical feature. Does the paradox mark some deep theoretical difficulty or does it simply show (like the "twin paradox" of relativity theory) that our pretheoretical expectations have to be adjusted in the light of our theory? The *Oxford American Dictionary*, for instance, defines paradox as "a statement etc. that seems to contradict itself or to conflict with common sense but which contains a truth," and one might simply claim that moral theorists are not so rich in truths that they can afford to discard them merely because they conflict with common sense or *appear* contradictory. In this vein, Nozick himself seems ultimately to shrug off the paradox that concerns us as an interesting, if curious feature of his moral theory.

In the case of the paradox of deontology, however, one is naturally led to ask, in Samuel Scheffler's words:

How can it be rational to forbid the performance of a morally objectionable action that would have the effect of minimizing the total number of comparably objectionable actions that were performed and would have no other morally relevant consequences? How can the minimization of morally objectionable conduct be morally unacceptable?[2]

These are important questions, and they call for a response. The deontologist must have a very compelling theory that explains and justifies the moral restrictions that lead to the paradox before he can shrug off that paradox and with it Scheffler's questions. Nozick, it bears noting, notoriously lacks such a theory.

So much then may be obvious. Any deontological moral theory should have some grounds for its particular moral restrictions, some reason for accepting them despite their leading to the paradox we are discussing. If the deontologist has a powerful enough and conclusive enough theory, then the paradox will not and should not bother him; in fact, this feature or implication of his theory will cease to seem paradoxical to him. I do not know of such a theory, but perhaps it exists or could be developed. It is safe to say, though, that many deontologists lack a theory that is conclusive enough for them to be able, credibly, to ignore the paradox and Scheffler's questions. (Many of them lack a conclusive enough theory because they lack a genuine theory altogether, appealing instead to the intuitive plausibility of the restrictions that give rise to the paradox.) Long habituated to their views, even deontologists without a sufficient theory may cease to feel anything really paradoxical about the paradox of deontology. But that is a kind of dogmatic slumber: these deontologists are in no position to ignore Scheffler's questions.

Of these questions, I shall be concerned primarily with the first. The second question can only be answered—if it can be answered at all—by elaborating the deep structure of the particular deontological theory that one favors. I do not wish to elaborate and defend any specific deontological theory here, however, because I am interested in the paradox as it applies to the whole class of deontological theories. Moreover, even if one's favored deontological theory satisfactorily explains how it can be morally unacceptable to act so as to minimize morally objectionable conduct (Scheffler's second question), one is still faced with the problem of whether it really can be rational for a theory to forbid such conduct or rational of us to accept such a theory and adhere to its normative injunctions (Scheffler's first question). This latter problem I call the *Scheffler problem*. I think that

---

2. Scheffler 1985/1988, p. 244. Scheffler explores the structure of this paradox, but he does not claim to have resolved it.

one can go some distance towards answering it and thus disarming the paradox of deontology without presupposing the truth of any particular deontological theory. But before arguing this, I wish to raise the ante by criticizing some ways in which deontologists have responded to the paradox of deontology.

II

Although Nozick draws our attention to the paradoxical implications of the deontological moral restrictions that he endorses, he ultimately, as I observed, shrugs them off, content simply to take for granted a system of natural rights that entails those restrictions. Nozick does, to be sure, contend that these restrictions—he calls them "side constraints"—reflect the Kantian principle that individuals are ends and not merely means. But this contention only pushes the paradox up one level since it fails to explain why moral agents must accept a side constraint against using people as means even when doing so would minimize the amount of non-Kantian conduct overall.

Insofar as Nozick defends his side constraints at all, he does so simply by asserting that individuals are not to be sacrificed for the greater good. There are only individuals with their separate lives, he writes; there is "no *social entity* with a good that undergoes some sacrifice for its own good" (Nozick 1974, pp. 32–33). But this waves the paradox away with an irrelevance. Utilitarians need not, and typically do not, accept the idea of a social entity with a good above and beyond the various goods of individual persons; if anything, utilitarians historically have followed Bentham in subscribing to methodological individualism. If utilitarianism permits individuals to be sacrificed to the greater good, as its critics say it does, then that greater good is simply the good of yet more individuals. Rejecting the idea of a social entity with a good above and beyond that of individual persons does not show the wrongness of a moral agent's violating C in order to prevent more extensive violations of C.

Historically, deontologists have stressed that moral agents must strive to keep their own hands clean and to refuse to allow dreadful circumstances to coerce them into doing dreadful deeds. Unlike the hypothetical utilitarian, they will not shoot an innocent Indian to prevent several innocent Indians from being shot (Williams 1973, pp. 98–99). At the end of the day, deontologists of a less absolutist sort might pull the trigger, depending on how the story is told and how many lives are at stake,[3] but they will typically deny

---

3. One variable that is widely thought to make a moral difference is whether the Indian, the shooting of whom is being proposed, is among those who will otherwise die.

either that doing so is morally mandatory or that it becomes morally man-datory as soon as the number of those who would otherwise be shot is larger than the number of those whom one is invited to shoot (as the utilitarian is alleged to believe). Even moderate deontologists endorse restrictions that it will be wrong for me to violate, at least in some cases, even though my doing so would serve to minimize violations of the very same restriction.

Yet if my violating a rule prevents other instances of rule violation, it is hard to see how the fact that it is I who does the violating could, given the cost of my refraining, be made to carry so much moral weight.[4] After all, if action *x* is wrong, then it must be wrong in virtue of certain general features of actions of that type. And the fact that it is I who performs the action in this case cannot be such a general feature. The deontologist may reply that this ignores the special responsibility that I, as a moral agent, have for my own actions. But this rejoinder will not suffice. To be sure, I control my actions in a way that others cannot, and in this sense I can be said to have a special responsibility for them. This trivial truth, however, does not establish what the deontologist wants it to establish; in particular, it fails to show the rationality of my respecting a rule when violating it would lead to less wrongdoing of the very same sort.

Some deontologists will argue, to the contrary, that this way of looking at the matter alienates me from morality; it abridges my autonomy and restricts the fulfillment of my projects. I should not be forced to do wrong, to dirty my own hands. But this standard reply will not do. First, deontological moral restrictions are themselves restrictions that constrain my conduct regardless of my projects; they are not optional; I do not choose them. Second, these restrictions prevent me from acting so as to reduce the total number of violations of those restrictions. Suppose that I care about reducing the amount of *x*-ing in the world. Then, whatever else may be said about it, to forbid me to perform an *x*-type action in order to reduce the overall amount of *x*-ing, cannot be justified on the grounds that it promotes my moral autonomy. The Scheffler problem is not resolved by stoutly insisting that people are not morally required continually to set aside their own otherwise legitimate concerns, projects, relationships, hopes, and ambitions in order to promote the good of others. That insistence is sound, but it is irrelevant here.

As Scheffler argues, deontologists will naturally be inclined to support the moral restrictions they endorse by appealing to the disvalue of violating

---

4. Thomas Nagel offers some reflections intended in part to enhance the plausibility of the deontologist's placing moral weight on the fact that it is *my* violation. I discuss Nagel below. See also Darwall 1986.

those restrictions or by appealing to some property of the victims of those violations, but these defenses fail to come to terms with the paradox (Scheffler 1982, pp. 87–90, 100). Deontological theories, that is, standardly see morality as evaluating actions from a point of view broader than that of the interests of the individual actor. These theories must, it seems, regard violations as inherently morally objectionable or undesirable, in the sense that it is morally preferable that none should occur than that any should occur. Otherwise, the claim that individuals must obey those restrictions when doing so is contrary to their interests would not be plausible. Yet, if this is so, for a theory to maintain that "there are times when we must act in such a way that a larger rather than a smaller number of violations actually takes place" does indeed seem puzzling (Scheffler 1985/1988, p. 254).

Thomas Nagel would grant that deontological theories can and do regard the violation of their restrictions as inherently and impartially objectionable. But he rejects the dominance of this impartial perspective and its concomitant neutral conception of moral value (Nagel 1986, pp. 175–85). Deontological restrictions are, he stresses, agent-relative; they provide reasons for respecting others that do not give way to a larger "agent-neutral respect free of perspective." From my perspective, in other words, the wrongness of my x-ing is not altered by the fact that, were I to x, I would reduce the overall amount of x-ing. Although I disvalue x-ing, deontological restraints provide me with an agent-relative reason for refraining from x-ing that does not yield to an impartial, agent-neutral imperative to reduce x-ing. With characteristic vividness, Nagel describes what is it like for an agent to experience a deontological constraint and why we find doing evil that good may come of it so repugnant. But this is largely moral phenomenology, as Nagel recognizes, and he offers no decisive answer to the question of why, in light of the Scheffler problem, we should remain committed to the moral importance of the internal, personal perspective and the deontological restrictions that respect it.

Nagel insists on the importance of the personal perspective, but he does not deny that deontological restrictions may conflict with the good as understood from an impartial and detached point of view. Some deontologists, however, deny the very notion of better and worse states of affairs, impersonally judged. They attack consequentialism's belief that the good determines the right by rejecting the presupposition that there is (always? sometimes?) an impersonal way of ranking the goodness of states of affairs. Thus, Bernard Williams contends that a nonconsequentialist can believe that an agent did the right thing in doing A in situation S without attaching a sense to the statement that the state of affairs which consists in the agent's doing A is better than any other state of affairs accessible to him

(Williams 1973, pp. 87–88). And Philippa Foot argues, more or less, that judgments about the goodness of states of affairs are basically speaker-relative.[5]

If utilitarianism cannot always judge states of affairs to be, impartially, better or worse, then it has a problem. The deontologist, however, does not escape the paradox by showing that states of affairs cannot always be so judged. He must further show that in circumstances where the paradox looms, one cannot impartially judge that it is worse or more objectionable that, say, five killings occur than that one occur. The deontologist can allege this, of course, but it is not clear how he could hope to show it. If his theory is at all plausible, the deontologist himself will recognize a duty of benevolence, and he will believe that when one is acting benevolently it is better, ceteris paribus, that one act such that one killing occurs and five are prevented rather than that five occur and one is prevented, if that is one's only choice.[6] This is not to beg the question against the deontologist but rather to point out that in other contexts he is perfectly prepared to judge that a situation is better if there are fewer rather than more moral violations and to grant, even insist, that this provides a reason for acting.

The deontologist may assert, however, that context is everything. Once we know that an act would be wrong, we cannot then intelligibly ask whether it would be a better for it to be done. I think to the contrary that this is perfectly intelligible and that we do it all the time—even when we refrain from so acting. This sort of deontologist writes as if it would be unintelligible for there to be conflicts between the right and the good, which displays a naïveté about the moral life of the sort that deontologists customarily impute to utilitarians. On the other hand, if the deontologist is asserting not that it would be unintelligible to ask whether the wrong act would have better results, but rather asserting that such considerations should not sway us, then he is not answering the paradox. He is simply insisting on the moral restrictions that give rise to it.

The standard responses to the Scheffler problem, to the apparent irrationality of forbidding one to do x when doing x would reduce x-ing, are, I have been arguing, inadequate. But my comments do not show the untenability of a deontological moral approach. Deontologists may well find an answer to the paradox of deontology and Scheffler's awkward questions by elaborating further one of the arguments I have canvassed or by

---

5. Foot 1985. There is more to Foot's position than I say, but the complications need not concern us here.

6. Against Elizabeth Anscombe and John Taurek and in defense of common sense, I have argued (Shaw 1980) that the numbers matter when one must decide which of two parties to assist when one cannot assist both.

developing some line of reasoning I have overlooked. Still, deontologists have their work cut out for them, and in the meantime, I offer them a strategy that, while not eliminating all their theoretical difficulties, goes some way toward disarming the Scheffler problem.

III

The paradox of deontology is supposed to arise, not simply for this or that normative theory, but rather for a whole class of theories; this explains the general and rather abstract character of the paradox. This very abstractness, however, leads one to wonder whether there really are cases—and what they would look like—in which violating some well-justified deontological moral restriction would decrease the net number of violations of that very restriction.

This question is hard to answer without adopting the perspective of some particular deontological theory and then getting down to specific moral restrictions and detailed situations. It certainly seems logically possible that circumstances could exist such that breaking one's promise will prevent others from breaking theirs or such that murdering someone will result in fewer murders than not murdering him. Bear in mind, however, that a plausible deontological system will allow various moral factors to influence its judgment about what does and does not—in a particular circumstance and all things considered—constitute wrongful promise breaking or immoral killing. The system may permit many, if not all, of its rules to be overridden by other moral considerations endorsed by the system itself. And if the deontological theory does treat some restrictions on our conduct as exceptionless, these are unlikely to be simple injunctions like "Thou shall not kill" as opposed to more complicated rules with various conditionals already built into them.[7]

It is one thing to say that a theory requires an agent to obey restriction C even though violating it would reduce C-violations overall and another thing to find such circumstances in the real world: truly dilemmatic circumstances, that is, in which no other course of action is open to the agent that would, in a deontologically permitted way, prevent the further violations or otherwise obviate the apparent "either–or" choice. That my violating C would reduce the number of C-violations poses a problem or paradox for the deontologist only if there is no other way, compatible with my respecting C, in which those violations by others can be prevented. Scheffler, Williams, Nozick, and other writers do not mention this point— perhaps, to be fair, because they take it for granted—but it bears

---

7. For an interesting example, see Alan Donagan (1978, p. 188) on torturing terrorists.

emphasizing. Suppose, for example, that I have a list of professional assassins and that my killing them would prevent a greater number of future murders. My deontological theory instructs me not to kill them. Nothing even resembling a paradox begins to emerge here unless we stipulate that there is no alternative, morally licit way in which those future murders could be prevented.

Suppose, however, that a deontological agent does indeed face a genuine "either–or" choice of whether to violate C in order to prevent a greater number of C-violations. From some deontological perspectives, it will be morally relevant how the agent got himself into this predicament. A rationalistic deontological system that does not admit the possibility of a conflict of duties can concede that someone who violates its rules may put himself in a situation where it will no longer be possible for him to obey all its precepts (Donagan 1984, pp. 305–6). Wrongdoing can get us into jams, on this view, from which we cannot extricate ourselves without violating some moral rule. Likewise, a deontologist might claim that the Scheffler problem is no embarrassment to his theory if the agent stumbled into the paradoxical situation because of conduct condemned by the theory in the first place.

The deontological theorist insists that the agent still ought not to x, even though his x-ing would prevent others from x-ing. However, since the untoward consequences of the agent's refusing to x result from an earlier moral malfeasance, the theorist contends that we are witnessing one of the paradoxes of failing to do one's duty, not a paradox of duty itself. Not everyone will be persuaded by this reasoning. After all, the hapless agent, who has done wrong but now wants to do right, still faces the Scheffler problem: if he cares about not x-ing, shouldn't he do x to prevent more x-ing? That the predicament is his fault and not that of his theory, whose consistency in commanding us not to x has been upheld, does not solve his practical dilemma.

At this point the deontologist might consider a second move. Plausible moral codes often lay down one set of rules under conditions of general compliance and another set under conditions of noncompliance. Ideally, we are required to leave our weapons at home, but not when others nevertheless persist in going about armed. In this vein, the deontologist might offer the agent who has violated some prior duty a secondary or derivative set of principles that agents should follow in these circumstances. That is, he might tell us that having made a moral mess of things, the right course of action is now, not to follow the original rules regardless of the cost, but rather to minimize the amount of moral damage.

The preceding three paragraphs illustrate the kind of casuistic reasoning to which certain deontological theories might have recourse. It is no part of my brief to show that this reasoning is sound, and in any case, the deontologist will find it difficult, I think, to maintain that only agents who have gone morally astray in the first place will confront the paradox of deontology. The more modest point of this section is, rather, that one cannot assume that the possibility of paradox poses a genuine and insurmountable difficulty for a given deontological theory without carefully examining the latter's full theoretical and casuistic resources.

IV

Let me review the argument so far. The circumstances that occasion the paradox of deontology and give rise to the Scheffler problem represent a coherent possibility, at least when those circumstances are described in general terms. But mere logical possibility is a ghostly thing. For the possibility of paradox to be genuinely troubling, at least two conditions must be met. First, we need a richly described and realistic case, where the many moral and factual variables of the world we know give way to a simple, ineluctable, and paradoxical alternative and where—arguably, anyway—this is not due to a prior failure of duty by the agent. Second, we must carefully examine the case from the perspective of a deontological theory that is both plausible and reasonably sophisticated, and it must be shown that its philosophical resources are indeed unable, in the circumstances described, to avoid the paradox of forbidding x at the cost of increased x-ing.

Will these conditions be satisfied in the real world? The three relevant answers are, of course: (a) never, (b) sometimes, and (c) frequently. The reflections of the preceding section challenge the complacent assumption that the deontological paradox is a likely occurrence—at least when we are considering credible moral theories. I therefore put answer (c) aside. Those same reflections do not suffice to establish answer (a), but I entertain it as a hypothesis in this section in order to explore its implications. Thereafter, I assume the truth of answer (b).

Suppose, then, that as a matter of empirical fact the paradox of deontology never arises, at least not for plausible and reasonably sophisticated deontological theories. There are possible worlds where nonviolation of C would lead to more extensive violations of C, but this world is not one of them. In this case the deontologist can argue, I think, that the paradox of deontology can safely be ignored. If a theorist can promulgate restriction C confident that it need never be violated in order to prevent other violations of C, then what is the problem?

The problem, a critic might claim, is that the consistent deontologist must, as a matter of abstract principle, continue to maintain that one's doing x would be wrong even if the situation were such that doing x would lead to less x-ing overall. That is true. But remember that we are assuming that the deontologist has a sophisticated and reasonably attractive moral system in terms of which he can, after having examined the specific circumstances and weighed all the relevant moral factors, account for the wrongness of my x-ing. Is it plausible for us then to say that—the overall attractiveness of the deontologist's system notwithstanding—it is irrational for him to prohibit me from x-ing because circumstances might be, *but in fact never are*, such that my x-ing would reduce the total amount of x-ing? I think not.

Some consequentialists may resist this contention and insist that even if the paradox never arises in our world, the fact that it is a logical or theoretical possibility reveals something deeply problematic about deontological moral theory. How can such a theory be plausible, they will ask. But this is not the issue here, where it is being assumed that we have in view a sophisticated deontological theory that is able to make a deep and philosophically attractive case for its particular agent-relative restrictions. It is with regard to that hypothetical theory that I assert that there would be nothing irrational about accepting its normative instructions in a world where (a) is true.

To be sure, deontologists themselves have often assumed, at least implicitly, that the acceptability of a moral theory depends on its implications for all possible worlds.[8] But I think they are mistaken to have held this view. That a moral theory has counterintuitive or paradoxical implications in other possible worlds is not automatically grounds for embarrassment in this one. No normative system's moral rules are proved irrational by imagining that an evil demon responds to every refusal to violate them with three of his own enormously more grave violations. But that is not quite the point, our critic might respond: it still needs to be shown that it is rational to prohibit me from x-ing in the demon world. But, again, I think that the deontologist can plausibly insist that, given his theory's grounds (whatever they are) for believing it wrong of me to x, prohibiting me from x-ing is not made irrational by counterfactual suppositions about remote possible worlds.

---

8. There are some important exceptions. Elizabeth Anscombe has always resisted appeals to far-out examples. And Russell Hardin (1988, p. 25) points out that Alan Donagan has abandoned his earlier view that moral theory must be "true of all possible worlds."

Perhaps, however, it depends on how remote those worlds are. In other words, the reasons why (a) is true—assuming here, still, that it is true—may make a difference. If its truth is a pure happenstance, on the order, say, of the fact that there have never been and will never be ten one-eyed redheads in my garage at one time, then the world in which (a) is true is much closer to the world in which (b) is true than if scientific law or basic facts about human nature guarantee (a)'s truth. For my own part, I think that even if (a) is only a subordinate or fortuitous truth of our world, its truth would still permit the deontologist to ignore the Scheffler problem. There is nothing irrational in adhering to a moral restriction, which is otherwise justified, even though it has a paradoxical implication in a very close possible world, if it does not, as a matter of empirical fact, have that implication in our world. But since I do not wish to assume the truth of (a), which is speculative at best, I shall not pursue this point further.

V

Let us now suppose, what I take to be the more realistic assumption, that the paradox of deontology is more than a logical possibility. It can and occasionally does arise for specific theories in real circumstances. Still, two things seem clear. First, real cases are far rarer than the possible cases philosophers can dream up in their armchairs. Second, real cases in which the relevant agent or agents would actually know that violating C would reduce the total of C-violations are rarer still. The first point has already been discussed, but the implications of the second require examination.

As critics of act utilitarianism have long urged, there are serious limitations on our ability to predict accurately the consequences of our actions. This problem is even more serious in the present case where the agent must know (or have a well-justified belief) (1) that his violating C will so affect other agents that there will be fewer violations of C than if he had refrained from violating C and (2) that there is no way, compatible with C, in which he can bring about the same (or greater) reduction in C-violations. These knowledge conditions are not easily met. Even when an agent does indeed face the deontological paradox, he is unlikely to know (1) and (2). On the other hand, an agent who believes (1) and (2) and, thus, that he faces the paradox of deontology will often not know, or be well justified in believing, (1) and (2). He may, in fact, simply be mistaken. Human beings are inclined to rationalize, and where wrongdoing tempts us, we may well embrace (1) and (2) on insufficient evidence.

Given the fact that agents are unlikely to know (1) and (2) and the fact that agents will at least sometimes falsely believe (1) and (2), then a deontological theory's insistence that one not violate C, regardless of the possibility that this might reduce the number of C-violations, gains pragmatic support. The deontologist can insist, in other words, that allowing agents to violate C, when they sincerely believe that doing so will reduce the number of C-violations, would itself result in more C-violations than would denying them the freedom to set C aside.[9] Here the deontologist takes a page from the rule utilitarian who argues that it will not be optimal to encourage or permit agents to seek directly to maximize the good. Thus, the deontologist addresses the Scheffler problem by arguing along the above lines that there is nothing irrational about insisting that agents not violate C, notwithstanding the possibility that such a violation might, in some circumstances, reduce the number of C-violations.

The Scheffler problem emerged out of the paradox of deontology this way: if a theory forbids agents from violating C, this must be because it cares about C not being violated; but if this is so, then is there not something irrational about forbidding a C-violation when it would reduce C-violations overall? A reply to this is that permitting C to be violated is not a promising strategy for reducing C-violations over the long haul. Permitting people to murder when they have good reasons for believing that this will reduce the amount of murder is not an intelligent way to prevent murder; it is better to insist that no one is permitted to murder. This point can be brought out another way. The deontologist wants moral agents to have that character and set of dispositions that firmly commit them to following his theory's rules and principles, even in Scheffler-like circumstances. Not only is this the right character for agents to have, but—the deontologist is now adding—their having it will lead to fewer moral violations than any other character available to them.

If I am right, then given the conditions necessary for the paradox to arise in the first place, given the lack of knowledge of most agents, and given the pragmatic consideration mentioned in the preceding paragraphs, it follows that it is not irrational for an otherwise philosophically convincing deontological theory to prohibit agents from x-ing even when those agents believe that they are in Scheffler-like circumstances. The proposition that a refusal to countenance violation of C best promotes adherence to C is not the deep ground upon which the deontologist justifies imposing that normative restriction on agents. The deontologist, however, can appeal to that proposition to disarm the paradox of deontology and meet the Scheffler

---

9. When this would not otherwise be permitted by the deontologist's moral system. As previously discussed, C may be overridden by other considerations internal to the moral system of which it is part, or it may presuppose various conditions for its application or have exceptions built into it.

problem. But how do things look from the point of view of the agent? His theory teaches him the wrongness of *x*-ing and instructs him, foremost, to take care not to *x*. Sometime, however, it might truly be the case—let us grant—that, were the deontological agent to *x*, then there would be less *x*-ing overall and that the agent knows this and even knows that he knows this.

Bear in mind, though, that this deontological agent does not, in general, have as strong a moral obligation to prevent an *x*-ing as he does not to *x*. This is for reasons internal to his moral system, which—whatever its specific character—is not a maximizing or value-promoting system like consequentialism. The critic who encourages the agent to *x* in order to prevent *x*-ing is inviting him to look at the matter from a directly consequentialist perspective, inviting him, in effect, to abandon the moral theory that holds his allegiance. But this invitation will not be compelling—and the deontologist will be guilty of no irrationality in declining it—if in addition to whatever positive grounds the theory offers for its moral restraints, it can claim good pragmatic or consequentialist grounds for not permitting an agent to *x* in order to reduce *x*-ing (where his system would not otherwise permit this).

The deontological agent who believes himself to be in Scheffler-like circumstances may nevertheless experience an internal conflict. By definition, though, he does not face a conflict of duties: according to the moral theory he accepts, his duty is clear. Still, he may feel a tension between his moral obligation and other values. His obligation not to *x*, that is, may sit uneasily with the value he places on a world with less *x*-ing. There is no reason, though, why the deontologist cannot simply accept this as a fact of the moral life. He need maintain neither that our moral lives are simpler than they are nor that the right necessarily coincides with all the things we value.

Thus, although a deontological system disvalues all violations of restriction *C*, it can have sound reasons for requiring agents to respect *C* even when they believe they are in Scheffler-like circumstances. Far from being a failure of rationality, as Scheffler implies, the theory's insistence that *C* not be violated prevents the worse results that will follow from allowing agents to adopt a directly maximizing perspective. Does this line of reasoning turn the deontologist into a covert consequentialist? I think not. What makes his theory deontological in the first place is that it has nonconsequentialist reasons (whatever these may be) for introducing its particular moral restrictions. Those reasons explain the wrongness of violating *C*. Considerations of consequences are then introduced only as a dialectical move in order to help dissolve the paradox and rebut the charge of irrationality. That charge reflects the maximizing perspective characteristic of consequentialism. By advancing some considerations that meet the consequentialist on his own ground, the deontologist has not forsaken his nonconsequentialism.

If my argument is correct, then the deontologist can escape the charge of irrationality, but he is still left with the deeper task of explaining the grounds on which his theory justifiably maintains that my doing x is wrong both in principle and in that precise circumstance when doing x would minimize x-ing. This is the second of the Scheffler's two questions quoted above (p. 99), the one that I put aside. If his theory is otherwise plausible, I have argued, then the deontologist can rationally maintain restriction C despite the paradox of deontology. But while that paradox need not require the abandonment of deontology, it does point to foundational questions about rightness, about agency and responsibility, and about the nature of morality to which deontologists still need to attend.

7

New-Wave Moral Realism Meets
Moral Twin Earth[*]

Terence Horgan and Mark Timmons

There have been times in the history of ethical theory, especially in this century, when moral realism was down, but it was never out. The appeal of this doctrine for many moral philosophers is apparently so strong that there are always supporters in its corner who seek to resuscitate the view. The attraction is obvious: moral realism purports to provide a precious philosophical good, viz., objectivity and all that this involves, including right answers to (most) moral questions, and the possibility of knowing those answers. In the last decade, moral realism has reentered the philosophical ring in powerful-looking naturalistic form. Developments in other areas of philosophical inquiry have helped rejuvenate this position, by apparently providing for a strain of naturalism which is immune to the blows that decked older versions of moral realism, including traditional versions of ethical naturalism. This new-wave moral realism has come to dominate recent work in metaethics.

However, despite any advantages this new strain of naturalistic moral realism enjoys over previous versions of realism, we maintain that it is destined to travel the same road as its predecessors. In a series of papers (Horgan and Timmons 1992a, 1992b; Timmons 1990) we have made our case for this pessimistic prediction, investigating at some length the difficulties faced by new-wave moral realism. In this paper we provide a dialectical overview: we situate the new-wave position itself, and also our objections to it, in the context of the evolving program of philosophical naturalism in twentieth-century analytic philosophy. We seek to show that

---

* This paper is fully collaborative; order of authorship is alphabetical. It is a slightly revised version of a paper by the same title that appeared in the *Journal of Philosophical Research* 16 (1991: 447–65). We benefited from the discussion of Horgan and Timmons 1992b at the Mark Overvold Memorial Conference, and from Eric Kraemer's commentary on that paper.

although this new contender might initially look like championship material, it succumbs to punches surprisingly similar to those that knocked out the old-fashioned versions of naturalist moral realism. New-wave realism too has a glass jaw.

1. PHILOSOPHICAL NATURALISM

Moral realism faces well-known, serious philosophical obstacles—obstacles that seem particularly difficult given a thoroughgoing philosophical naturalism. So we begin the saga of ethical naturalism with some remarks about philosophical naturalism.

We take the naturalist outlook in philosophy to be at bottom a metaphysical view about the nature of what exists. The vague, pretheoretic idea that this view attempts to articulate and defend is simply the idea that all that exists—including any particulars, events, properties, etc.—is part of the natural physical world that science investigates. This core idea can be made precise in various ways, but common to most variants is what we shall call the *thesis of physical ontic primacy*:

> N1 The ontologically primary or fundamental entities (particulars, properties, facts, etc.) in the world are all part of the subject matter of physics.

There is more to metaphysical naturalism than thesis N1, however. Common sense, and ordinary discourse, recognize all sorts of entities that seem, at least prima facie, not to be literally identical with entities that are *narrowly physical*, i.e., explicitly countenanced by physics. And this fact generates a broad project for the philosophical naturalist: viz., somehow to accommodate, within a broadly naturalistic metaphysical/epistemological framework, *all* particulars, properties, facts, etc. as part of the "natural order." The operative notion of accommodation is itself vague and pretheoretic. It too can be made more precise in various ways, but the leading idea is what we'll call the thesis of *explainability*:

> N2 All truths are ultimately explainable on the basis of facts involving ontologically primary entities.

It is this second thesis that mainly drives the naturalist's program. And as views have changed about the kind of explainability that constitutes ontological accommodation, so has the entire program of metaphysical naturalism.

Additionally, the metaphysical viewpoint embodied in N1 and N2 has typically been accompanied by a nonskeptical outlook in epistemology, according to which we have access to—and can come to have knowledge of—the phenomena that make up the natural order. If one combines this nonskeptical outlook with metaphysical naturalism, then one has an overall philosophical package—call it *philosophical naturalism*—that imposes the following metaphysical and epistemological constraints on any nonskeptical version of moral realism:

C1 If there are any moral properties or facts, they must be naturalistically accommodated.

C2 If moral knowledge is possible, our access to and knowledge of moral properties and facts must be explainable according to epistemological principles we use to explain our knowledge of the natural world generally.

Failure of the moral realist to meet these constraints would evidently have quite a high price tag. The price for nonaccommodation is metaphysical queerness of moral properties and facts, plus all the epistemological problems that come with trying to plausibly explain how we have epistemic access to such oddball entities. Certainly these constraints on an acceptable version of moral realism impose quite demanding burdens on the moral realist, but ones well worth shouldering in light of the consequences of failure to do so.

Of course, this particular problematic for metaethics is driven by philosophical naturalism, and there have been those who do not buy that picture and so do not feel constrained by C1 and C2. But despite one's global metaphysical and epistemological proclivities, wouldn't it be nice if moral realism could meet these constraints? It would remove most of the metaphysical and epistemological worries about ethics.

2. REMEMBRANCE OF THINGS PAST

Those who take their philosophical naturalism seriously either have to go the eliminativist route and argue against the presumption that there are moral properties and facts to be somehow naturalistically accommodated, or get down to business and do some accommodating. How might the latter approach be implemented? That is, if there are indeed objective moral truths, then how might these truths be explainable on the basis of lower-order, nonmoral, facts?

Traditionally, this underwriting project was shaped by a certain, quite narrow, conception of philosophical naturalism—a strongly reductive version that took identity to be the proper relation between members of successive ontological levels and took some sort of reductive analysis of higher-level terms and concepts to be the only available strategy for securing the needed identities. Furthermore, it certainly appeared—at first, anyway—that about the only way to approach the reductive task was by way of showing that higher-level terms and expressions had the same meaning as lower-level terms and expressions. So, for instance, a synonymy criterion of property identity was thought to undergird legitimate reductions of one property to another.

The particular reductivist program, applied to moral phenomena, meant that moral properties and facts were to be reductively identified with more basic properties and facts, perhaps psychological or even biological ones. Moreover, the reduction was to proceed by way of analytic meaning connections between moral terms and expressions on the one hand, and nonmoral terms and expressions on the other. In short, moral terms were supposed to have analytic naturalistic definitions, and these were to provide the ultimate basis of the ontological accommodation of the moral to the natural. Call this version of ethical naturalism *analytic ethical naturalism.*

Of course, if the analytic ethical naturalist could provide the desired meaning reductions, then the two naturalist constraints would be satisfied and moral realism would be in good shape. But we all know what happened: in the early part of this century, G. E. Moore's "open question argument" lowered the boom on analytical ethical naturalism. Consider any proposed analytic definition of a moral term M by means of a nonmoral term or expression N, and consider a corresponding question of the form "Entity x is N, but is x M?" If the putative definition is correct, then the answer to this question should be knowable simply by reflection on its meaning, and in this sense closed; but invariably, such questions are open.

In light of the open question argument, it appeared that analytic naturalism was simply false. This, in turn, seemed to show that the philosophical naturalist's constraints could not be satisfied vis-à-vis moral properties and facts. So the available alternatives, apparently, were (i) non-naturalist moral realism (Moore's position), or (ii) irrealism about matters moral. Since nonnaturalism seemed so philosophically unpalatable, irrealism—in the form of noncognitivist accounts of moral language—proliferated in the decades following Moore. Moore's open question argument had evidently put ethical naturalism down for the count, and things looked bleak for moral realism.

3. THAT WAS THEN, THIS IS NOW

Times have certainly changed, even in philosophy. A number of recent developments have considerably altered the program of philosophical naturalism, and consequently made possible the reemergence of a new and improved version of ethical naturalism. Although the naturalistic outlook still reigns supreme, philosophers have lightened up about the constraints a respectable philosophical naturalism must satisfy. In particular, those wedded to the naturalist program no longer view N2 as requiring *reduction* of higher-order terms, concepts, theories, or properties to lower-order ones—not in the narrow sense involving inter-level analytic meaning equivalences between terms and expressions of different ontological levels, and also not in the somewhat wider sense involving type/type "bridge laws" involving interlevel *nomic* equivalences. This relaxing of constraints has emerged in the wake of a number of interrelated developments in metaphysics, epistemology, philosophy of language, and philosophy of mind in the 1960s and 1970s.

First, there has been a widespread rejection of a synonymy criterion of property identity, in light of numerous apparent counterexamples. For instance, the (sortal) property *being water* is identical with the property *being composed of H_2O molecules*; heat is identical with molecular motion; temperature is identical with mean molecular kinetic energy; and so on. But no one supposes that "being water" is synonymous with "being composed of H_2O molecules," or that "temperature" is synonymous with "mean molecular kinetic energy," and so forth for many other scientific identities.

Second, ever since the pioneering work of Kripke (1972) and Putnam (1975), there has been articulation and widespread acceptance of the idea that names and natural kind terms are *rigid designators*; i.e., such expressions designate the same entity with respect to every possible world in which that entity exists. Two important consequences result: (i) identity statements involving rigid designators flanking the identity sign, as in "Water = H_2O," are necessarily true without being analytic; and (ii) such statements constitute *definitions*—not the kind that express meaning connections and are thus analytic, but rather *synthetic* definitions that give the real essence of the particular, property, or kind designated by a certain term. Thus, if true, "Water = H_2O" is a nonanalytic necessary truth that expresses the real, underlying essence of water and thus provides a (synthetically true) definition of "water."

Third, ever since the pioneering work of Putnam (1967a, 1967b), there has been articulation and widespread acceptance of the idea that mental state types (properties), except perhaps phenomenal properties ("qualia"), are *functional* properties—i.e., their essence consists not in any intrinsic features, but rather in a certain syndrome of *typical causal relations* to other state types, in particular to sensory states, actions, and other mental states which themselves are also functional properties.[1] Functional properties are

---

1. Nowadays it is commonly conceded that an adequate functionalist approach must take account of the so-called "wide content" of propositional attitudes, as partially

potentially "physically realizable" quite differently from one occasion of instantiation to another—depending, perhaps, upon the specific physical composition of the cognizer in which they are instantiated.

Fourth, largely because of the influence of functionalism in philosophy of mind, philosophers have increasingly repudiated their earlier tendency to regard constraint $C2$ of philosophical naturalism as requiring that the entities (particulars, properties, kinds, facts, etc.) cited by higher-order forms of discourse be *identical* to entities posited by natural science, and ultimately by physics. A more relaxed, California-style attitude has emerged that counts certain higher-order, multiply realizable entities as naturalistically respectable—functional properties being the paradigm case. "Naturalness"—i.e., naturalistic respectability—of these higher-order properties and facts consists of (i) *supervenience* upon lower-order properties and facts, and (ii) the *explainability* of specific psychophysical supervenience relations.[2]

Fifth, in recent philosophy of language there has been widespread acceptance of so-called "causal" theories of reference for names and natural kind terms. In the simplest versions, such theories assert that the semantical property of reference is to be understood as essentially involving appropriate causal connections between speakers' uses of a term and the entity to which the term refers. Such theories propose to explain (i) how the reference of a term is originally determined (e.g., there being some sort of baptism or dubbing ceremony through which speakers in causal contact with an item acquire the ability to refer to that item by means of some expression used in the ceremony), and (ii) how the capacity to refer is spread throughout a linguistic community (again, by speakers' causally interacting with one another and with the item). This rather simple sketch can be elaborated in a number of ways, but the basic idea is clear: for some terms at least, reference is "grounded" by relevant causal hookups between speakers and the world.

Sixth, in epistemology there has been a move away from the idea that there are a priori constraints, of the sort associated with the traditional foundationalist program, on acceptable methods of knowledge gathering. Instead, philosophers have begun to move in the direction of "naturalized"

---

determined by one's physical and social environment. See Burge 1979, 1986; Loar 1982; White 1982; and Fodor 1986.

2. Philosophers have been rather slow to recognize that supervenience facts must be explainable, rather than sui generis, in order to fit smoothly into a broadly naturalistic metaphysics. For elaboration of the point, and discussion of how functionalism provides for the explainability of psychophysical supervenience relations, see Horgan and Timmons 1992a.

epistemology, which recognizes the radical contingency of our methods and procedures of inquiry, especially in science. Accounts of knowledge in terms of such causal notions as the reliability of belief-generating processes have begun to displace former views that rested heavily upon a priori epistemic principles. Moreover, essentially coherentist holistic frameworks of inquiry have largely displaced the more traditional foundationalist frameworks.

The various philosophical themes and developments just outlined all came together, in a manner highly relevant to the subsequent emergence of new-wave moral realism, in one of the two major species of functionalism in philosophy of mind: so-called *psychofunctionalism*. On this view, mental properties are multiply realizable functional properties whose relational essences are fully capturable not by the generalizations of commonsense mentalistic psychology ("folk psychology"), but instead by the generalizations of the (ideally complete) *empirical* psychological theory T that happens to be true of human beings.[3] According to psychofunctionalism, mental terms refer rigidly to these properties; and this rigid reference underwrites certain synthetic definitions of mental properties—where the definitive causal role of each such property is specified by means of the empirical theory T.[4] The reason our mental terms refer to *these* properties is that there are suitable reference-subserving causal relations linking (instantiations of) these specific functional properties to people's uses of mental terms and concepts; i.e., the mental terms and concepts "track" the relevant functional properties, in something like the way that radar systems track flying objects, or that traces in a bubble chamber track electrons. Accordingly, it is quite possible to know that certain mental properties are instantiated by certain individuals, even if one does not know the functional essences of the attributed properties, and indeed even if one has numerous false beliefs about those properties. The true nature and essence of mental properties, says the psychofunctionalist, is a thoroughly *empirical* question, to be answered not by a priori reflection but by scientific inquiry.

So although Moore's open question argument at first made betting on ethical naturalism a sucker's bet, and turned some form of irrealism into an

---

3. On psychofunctionalism, see Fodor 1968; Block 1978; Field 1978; and Lycan 1981. The other major species of functionalism, so-called *analytic functionalism*, asserts that the mental properties countenanced by folk psychology are functional properties whose relational essence is capturable by the generalizations of folk psychology itself; cf. Block 1978.

4. For discussions of how functional properties whose essence is captured by a theory are explicitly characterizable by means of (the Ramsey sentence of) that theory, see Block 1978 and Horgan 1984; these papers adapt a format originally proposed by Lewis 1972.

odds on metaethical favorite, with the emergence on the philosophical scene of an easygoing, nonreductive naturalism, all bets were off.

4. ETHICAL NATURALISM REVIVED

The various trends noted above, and jointly embodied in psychofunctionalism, are evident in the recent revival of ethical naturalism of the 1980s. To begin with, David Brink, one of most prominent of the new-wavers, has suggested that moral properties are functional properties of a certain kind:

> The moral realist might claim that moral properties are functional properties. He might claim that what is essential to moral properties is the causal role which they play in the characteristic activities of human organisms. In particular, the realist might claim that moral properties are those which bear upon the maintenance and flourishing of human organisms. Maintenance and flourishing presumably consist in necessary conditions for survival, other needs associated with basic well-being, wants of various sorts, and distinctively human capacities. People, actions, policies, states of affairs, etc. will bear good-making properties just insofar as they contribute to the satisfaction of these needs, wants, and capacities...[and] will bear bad-making moral properties just insofar as they fail to promote or interfere with the satisfaction of these needs, wants, and capacities. The physical states which contribute to or interfere with these needs, wants, and capacities are the physical states upon which, on this functionalist theory, moral properties ultimately supervene. (Brink 1984, pp. 121–22)

Brink also maintains that moral inquiry is a matter of seeking a normative theory that *coheres* best with both moral and nonmoral beliefs (Brink 1984, 1989). This coherentist methodology, usually called "reflective equilibrium," rejects any appeal to a priori moral truths or a priori constraints on moral inquiry: in ethics, as in science, our methods of knowledge gathering are radically contingent. For Brink, moral properties are functional properties whose relational essences are captured by whatever specific normative moral theory would emerge, for human beings, as the outcome of correctly applied coherentist methodology:

> The details of the way in which moral properties supervene upon other natural properties are worked out differently by different moral theories. Determination of which account of moral supervenience is best will depend upon determination of which moral theory provided the best account of all our beliefs, both moral and nonmoral. (Brink 1984, p. 121; cf. Brink 1989, p. 175)

One finds the clearest statement of the *semantic* component of new-wave moral realism in the work of Richard Boyd (1988), whose position has three key ingredients. First, Boyd proposes to construe moral terms like "good" and "right" (and the concepts they express) as being semantically like natural kind (and other scientific) terms, in having natural "synthetic" definitions that reveal the essence of the property the term expresses. This means, of course, that moral terms need not have analytic definitions of the sort central to more traditional versions of ethical naturalism. Second, the claim that moral terms function this way evidently requires that they are rigid. Like natural kind terms, moral terms allegedly rigidly designate the properties to which they refer. Third, Boyd maintains that for moral terms, just as for names and natural kind terms, reference is a matter of there being certain causal connections between people's uses of such terms and the relevant natural properties.

According to Boyd's own version of the causal theory of reference, reference is essentially an epistemic notion; so the relevant causal relations constituting reference are just those causal connections involved in knowledge-gathering activities:

> Roughly, and for nondegenerate cases, a term *t* refers to a kind (property, relation, etc.) *k* just in case there exist causal mechanisms whose tendency is to bring it about, over time, that what is predicated of the term *t* will be approximately true of *k* (excuse the blurring of the use-mention distinction). Such mechanisms will typically include the existence of procedures which are approximately accurate for recognizing members or instances of *k* (at least for easy cases) and which relevantly govern the use of *t*, the social transmission of certain relevantly approximately true beliefs regarding *k*, formulated as claims about *t* (again excuse the slight to the use-mention distinction), a pattern of deference to experts on *k* with respect to the use of *t*, etc....When relations of this sort obtain, we may think of the properties of *k* as *regulating* the use of *t* (via such causal relations).... (1988, p. 195)

Extending this version of the causal theory to moral terms, as Boyd proposes to do, commits him to what we shall call the *causal regulation thesis*:

> CRT *Causal regulation thesis*: For each moral term *t* (e.g., "good"), there is a natural property *N* such that *N* alone, and no other property, causally regulates the use of *t* by human beings.

On Boyd's view, then, the fact that humankind's uses of moral terms are regulated in the way described by *CRT* is what allows one to conclude that moral terms like "good" behave semantically like natural kind terms: they rigidly refer to certain natural properties and hence possess synthetic definitions. So we can summarize what we call new-wave moral semantics (as developed by Boyd) as the following thesis:

> CSN *Causal semantic naturalism*: Each moral term *t* rigidly designates the natural property *N* that uniquely casually regulates the use of *t* by human beings.

A corollary of *CSN* is that each moral term *t* has a synthetically true natural definition whose definiens characterizes, in purely natural terms, the unique natural property that supposedly casually regulates the use of *t* by human beings. (*CRT* too is a corollary of *CSN*, since *CSN* cannot be true unless each moral term *t* is indeed causally regulated by some unique natural property *N*.)

Boyd's views and Brink's are evidently quite compatible, and in fact are nicely complementary. Brink is explicit in claiming that moral properties are functional properties whose essence is captured by a specific normative moral theory, but says rather little about the semantics of moral terms. Boyd, on the other hand, explicitly claims that moral terms work like natural kind terms in science and that they designate natural properties, but says rather little about the nature of these properties. So the currently most plausible form of ethical naturalism is an amalgam—the Brink/Boyd view, as we shall call it. Boyd's thesis *CRT* and *CSN*, together with Brink's moral functionalism, combine to yield a thesis we shall call *causal semantic functionalism*:

> *CSF* Each moral term *t* is causally regulated (for human beings generally) by a unique functional property, and rigidly designates that property.

Also an integral part of the Brink/Boyd view is their holistic moral epistemology, involving a coherentist methodology of moral inquiry. In light of *CSF*, this commitment to epistemological coherentism in ethics is evidently quite compatible with Brink's and Boyd's moral realism. For, if indeed the normative theory *T* that best coheres with humankind's moral and nonmoral beliefs is true, then *T* will qualify as true not *by virtue* of this coherence—that would be an irrealist, "constructivist," conception of moral truth—but rather because coherentist methodology is likely, as a matter of *contingent fact*, to converge upon the very normative theory whose generalizations capture the essence of the functional properties that causally regulate the uses of moral terms by humankind, properties that are thus (according to *CSF*) the referents of moral terms.

This constellation of views—moral functionalism, a holistic moral epistemology, and causal semantic naturalism—together make up what we take to be the most plausible and complete version of new-wave moral realism to date. It is a species of what we call *synthetic ethical naturalism*, to be distinguished from its predecessor, analytic ethical naturalism. And certainly (this version of) synthetic ethical naturalism, with its many similarities to psychofunctionalism in philosophy of mind, has a lot going for it.

Recall the naturalistically inspired metaphysical and epistemological constraints on moral realism. The Brink/Boyd view seems to satisfy them quite well. Take the metaphysical constraint *C1*, requiring that any moral properties and moral facts must be naturalistically accommodated. According to the Brink/Boyd view, moral properties are perfectly respectable natural properties, viz., multiply realizable functional properties. If so, then contrary to J. L. Mackie (1977), there is nothing metaphysically "queer" about the supervenience relation that obtains between certain lower-order properties and moral properties. The supervenience of moral properties is no more queer than is the supervenience of mental properties, given a functionalist position in philosophy of mind: in either case, specific supervenience connections are naturalistically explainable on the basis of (i) the correct synthetic definitions of the higher-order properties, together with (ii) relevant lower-order naturalistic facts (see Horgan and Timmons 1992a).

The Brink/Boyd view also appears to hold the key for answering an epistemological worry about moral realism, thus satisfying the epistemological constraint C2. In answer to the question "If there are objective moral properties, what access do we have to them?" the ethical naturalist simply replies that we have access to—and hence come to have knowledge of—such properties in much the way we come to have access to, and come to have knowledge of, other sorts of objective properties. Just as scientific inquiry relies ultimately upon observations (often informed by theoretical assumptions, when it comes to matters highly theoretical in nature), so in moral inquiry we make moral "observations"—viz., spontaneous moral judgments—that provide cognitive access to moral properties and facts, thereby providing the basis for developing an overall coherent system of moral and nonmoral beliefs constituting moral knowledge. Of course, philosophical critics (e.g., Mackie 1977) have frequently argued that facts about disagreement in moral belief, and diversity in people's moral codes, make the idea of moral observations highly suspect. But if people's spontaneous moral judgments are *causally regulated* by the very properties to which moral terms refer, as new-wave naturalism asserts, then these judgments thereby possess an epistemic status roughly comparable to that of observational judgments in science. That is, spontaneous moral judgments provide human beings with a (defeasible) form of cognitive access to objective moral truth—access that can then become substantially refined, deepened, systematized, and (as need be) corrected by means of coherentist methods of moral inquiry. Although people sometimes disagree in their specific moral judgments, in the moral codes to which they subscribe, and in their conceptions of the properties expressed by moral terms, these facts do not seriously call into question our access to, or knowledge of, moral properties and facts. For moral terms (as for scientific terms), Boyd's semantic thesis *CSN* explains (i) how, despite interpersonal variations in moral beliefs (or scientific beliefs), there is indeed some single objective property that is the referent of a given moral (or scientific) term; and (ii) how, by virtue of the causal-regulatory nature of this reference relation, human beings have socially coordinated cognitive access to these properties and thus can acquire moral knowledge. (For elaboration of these points, see Timmons 1990.)

So, the Brink/Boyd version of synthetic ethical naturalism evidently meets both the metaphysical and the epistemological constraints imposed by philosophical naturalism. In doing so, this form of moral realism relies fundamentally on a certain semantic view about moral terms. Notice that this fact reveals a parallel between analytic and synthetic ethical naturalism: each species involves a particular moral semantics that plays an absolutely fundamental role in defending the view's naturalistic moral ontology and the associated epistemology. But synthetic ethical naturalism, besides comporting nicely with the antireductivist trends in the naturalist's program, also (and as a result) entirely sidesteps Moore's open question argument: who cares if moral terms do not have analytic naturalistic definitions? It appears that new-wave moral realism, having entered vigorously into the metaethical ring, has everything going for it. But so it seemed with Mike Tyson. The semantic thesis *CSN*, the linchpin of the Brink/Boyd view, is also its glass jaw.

5. ENTER: MORAL TWIN EARTH

Suppose someone grants that the use of "water" by human beings is causally regulated by some specific physico-chemical natural kind, but then questions the claim that "water" *rigidly designates* the natural kind (viz., H_2O) which happens to fill this role. (This skeptic might believe, for instance, that "water" designates a more general physical natural kind—a genus which has H_2O as only one of its various actual or physically possible species.) What sort of evidence can be put forth to support the contention that "water" really does rigidly designate the sortal kind property H_2O?

When philosophers defend such semantic theses with respect to, e.g., names and physical natural kind terms, a particular type of thought experiment looms very large: the Putnam-style Twin Earth scenario. Recall how those go. In one of Putnam's stories, we are to imagine Twin Earth—a planet pretty much like Earth except that the oceans, lakes, and streams are filled with a liquid whose outward, easily observable, properties are just like those of water, but whose underlying physico-chemical nature is not H_2O, but some other molecular structure XYZ. Despite outward similarities and the fact that speakers of Twin English apply the word "water" to this liquid composed of XYZ, reflection on this scenario yields a very strong intuition that Twin Earthlings don't mean by their Twin English term "water" what we mean by "water," and that their term is not translatable by our orthographically identical term. And along with this judgment come two further intuitive judgments: (i) that the English term rigidly designates H_2O, whereas the Twin English term rigidly designates XYZ; and (ii) that this fact explains why the terms differ in meaning.

Competent speakers have a strong intuitive mastery of both the syntactic and the semantic norms governing their language. Consequently, the intuitive judgments just described concerning the Twin Earth scenario constitute important (though of course defeasible) empirical evidence for the hypothesis that "water" rigidly designates the specific physico-chemical physical kind that happens to causally regulate the use of this term by human beings, viz., the kind H_2O.[5]

The form of argument just canvassed can be called a *semantic competence argument*.[6] Presumably, competent speakers have a comparable intuitive mastery of the semantic workings of "good" and other fundamental moral terms. So if the Brink/Boyd thesis *CSN* is correct, then things should go the same way they go with "water." That is, if indeed the term "good" purports to designate rigidly the unique natural property (if there is one) that causally regulates the use of "good" by humankind in general, then it should be possible to construct a suitable Twin Earth scenario with these features: (i) reflection on this scenario generates intuitive judgments that are comparable to those concerning Putnam's original scenario; and (ii) these judgments are accompanied by the more general intuitive judgment that "good" does indeed work semantically as *CSN* says it does. Conversely, if the appropriate Twin Earth scenario does *not* have these features—i.e., if the semantic intuitions of competent speakers turn out not to be what they should be if *CSN* is true—then this will mean that in all probability, *CSN* is false.

---

5. Some philosophers who espouse causal theories of reference, and who hold that statements like "Water = H_2O" constitute synthetic definitions, tend to regard the use of thought experiments and appeals to intuition as part of an outmoded, unduly aprioristic, philosophical methodology. This tendency is both ironic and misplaced: ironic, because of the key role that Twin Earth thought experiments have played in convincing the philosophical community that names and natural kind terms are rigid designators; and misplaced, because thought experiments and speakers' intuitions about them often constitute an important kind of *empirical* evidence concerning philosophical theses about language and about language/world relations.

6. This label is intended to suggest a relevant analogy between such arguments and a common form of reasoning within empirical linguistics: viz., the appeal to speakers' intuitions about the grammaticality and/or syntactic ambiguity of certain sentence-like strings of words, as evidence for or against various empirical hypotheses about natural language syntax. The latter kind of argument rests on the (empirically plausible) background assumption that syntactic intuitions normally reflect what Noam Chomsky has called speakers' "linguistic competence." For further discussion of semantic competence arguments and their relation to the methodology of linguistics, see Horgan and Graham 1991.

We maintain that things go the latter way—i.e., one's intuitive judgments concerning a suitable Twin Earth scenario go contrary to *CSN*. What is wanted is a Twin Earth where things are as similar to Earth as possible, consistent with the hypothesis that twin moral terms are causally regulated, for twin human beings in general, by certain natural properties *distinct from* those natural properties which (as we are here granting for argument's sake) regulate the use of moral terms by human beings in general.

So let us begin by supposing that, as the Brink/Boyd view maintains, human uses of "good" and "right" are regulated by certain *functional* properties; and that, as a matter of empirical fact, these are consequentialist properties whose functional essence is captured by some specific consequentialist normative theory; call this theory T^c. We further suppose that there is some reliable method of moral inquiry which, if properly and thoroughly employed, would lead us to discover this fact about our uses of moral terms.

(Of course, even if one grants causal regulation of moral terms by natural properties, it is still quite contentious whether any *single* natural property causally regulates the use of "good" for humankind in general; likewise for other moral terms. We are here granting this highly optimistic assumption because we want to show that even if it is true, *CSN* is incorrect anyway. We are also granting for argument's sake that the posited causally regulating properties are indeed *functional* properties whose essence is capturable by some normative moral theory; and this assumption will be built into the specific Twin Earth thought experiment we shall now set forth. But if one were to take a different view about the putative causally regulating properties—say, the view that moral terms (nonrigidly) designate, in a given socio-cultural situation, whatever first-order physical properties (or property clusters) happen to collectively satisfy T^c (in that situation)—then our Twin Earth story could be modified appropriately. This would not change the moral we shall draw from the story.)

Now consider Moral Twin Earth, which, as you might expect, is just about like good old Earth: same geography and natural surroundings, people who live in the twin United States by and large speak Twin English; there is a state they call "Tennessee" that is situated directly south of a state they call "Kentucky"; and every year a fairly large number of Twin Earthlings make a pilgrimage to Twin Memphis to visit the grave site of Twin Elvis. You get the idea. Of particular importance here is the fact that Moral Twin Earthlings have a vocabulary that works much like human moral vocabulary; they use the terms "good" and "bad," "right" and "wrong" to evaluate actions, persons, institutions and so forth (at least those who speak Twin English use these terms, whereas those who speak some other twin language use terms orthographically identical to the terms "good," "right," etc. in the corresponding Earthian dialects). In fact, were a group of explorers from Earth ever to visit Moral Twin Earth they would be strongly inclined to translate Moral Twin Earth terms "good," "right" and the rest as identical in meaning to our orthographically identical English terms. After all, the uses of these terms on Moral Twin Earth bear all of the "formal" marks that we take to characterize moral vocabulary and moral practice. In particular, the terms are used to reason about considerations bearing on Moral Twin Earthling well-being; Moral Twin Earthlings are normally disposed to act in certain ways corresponding to judgments about what is "good" and "right"; they normally take considerations about what is "good" and "right" to be especially important, even of overriding importance in most cases, in deciding what to do, and so on.

Let us suppose that investigation into Twin English moral discourse and associated practice reveals that their uses of twin moral terms are causally regulated by certain natural properties distinct from those that (as we are already supposing) regulate English moral discourse. The properties tracked by Twin English moral terms are also functional properties, whose essence is functionally characterizable by means of a normative moral theory. But these are *nonconsequentialist* moral properties, whose functional essence is captured by some specific deontological theory; call this theory T^d. These functional properties are similar enough to those characterizable via T^c to account for the fact that twin moral discourse operates in Twin Earth society and culture in much the manner that moral discourse operates on Earth. (We have already noted that if explorers ever visit Moral Twin Earth, they will be inclined, at least initially, to construe Moral Twin Earthlings as having beliefs about good and right, and to translate Twin English uses of twin moral terms into our orthographically identical terms.) The differences in causal regulation, we may suppose, are due at least in part to certain species-wide differences in psychological temperament that distinguish Twin Earthlings from Earthlings. For instance, perhaps Twin Earthlings tend to experience the sentiment of *guilt* more readily and more intensively, and tend to experience *sympathy* less readily and less intensively, than do Earthlings. (Those who were raised Catholic, as we both were, should have little difficulty envisioning this kind of psychological temperament vis-à-vis matters moral. Indeed, we doubt that there is really any single characteristic temperament—any single profile of sentiments—that operates, for Earthlings generally, in matters of morals. But for present purposes one can suppose there is. This supposition fits naturally with the optimistic (though implausible) empirical assumption, we are already granting for argument's sake, that there is some single set of natural properties that causally regulate the use of moral terms by Earthlings generally.)

In addition, suppose that if Twin Earthlings were to employ in a proper and thorough manner the same reliable method of moral inquiry which (as we are already supposing) would lead Earthlings to discover that Earthling uses of moral terms are causally regulated by functional properties whose essence is captured by the consequentialist normative theory T^c, then this method would lead the Twin Earthlings to discover that their own uses of moral terms are causally regulated by functional properties whose essence is captured by the deontological theory T^d.

Given all these assumptions and stipulations about Earth and Moral Twin Earth, what is the appropriate way to describe the differences between moral and twin moral uses of "good" and "right"? Two hermeneutic options are available. On the one hand, we could say that the differences are analogous to those between Earth and Twin Earth in Putnam's original example, to wit: the moral terms used by Earthlings rigidly designate the natural properties that causally regulate their use on Earth, whereas the twin moral terms used by Twin Earthlings rigidly designate the *distinct* natural properties that causally regulate their use on Twin Earth; hence, moral and twin moral terms *differ in meaning*, and are not intertranslatable. On the other hand, we could say instead that moral and twin moral terms do *not* differ in meaning or reference, and hence that any apparent moral disagreements that might arise between Earthlings and Twin Earthlings would be *genuine* disagreements—i.e., disagreements in moral belief and in normative moral theory, rather than disagreements in meaning.[7]

We submit that by far the more natural mode of description, when one considers the Moral Twin Earth scenario, is the second. Reflection on the scenario just does not generate hermeneutical pressure to construe Moral Twin Earthling uses of "good" and "right" as not translatable by our orthographically identical terms. But if *CSN* were true, and the moral terms in question rigidly designated those natural properties that causally regulate their use, then reflection on this scenario ought to generate intuitions

---

7. It should be stressed that differences in normative moral theory, between Earthlings and Twin Earthlings, do not constitute different claims about which property is identical to goodness, or to rightness, etc. For normative theories do not make such property identity claims. Rather, they make claims, for instance, about which natural property is the fundamental good-making property, which is the fundamental right-making natural property, etc. Normative theories per se are neutral between the metaethical claims (i) that moral properties are identical with natural properties; (ii) that moral properties are non-natural properties that supervene upon natural ones without being identical to them; or (iii) that moral properties do not exist at all.

analogous to those generated in Putnam's original Twin Earth scenario. That is, it should seem intuitively natural to say that here we have a difference in meaning, and that Twin English "moral" terms are not translatable by English moral terms. Yet when it comes to characterizing the differences between Earthlings and twin Earthlings on this matter, the natural-seeming thing to say is that the differences involve belief and theory, not meaning.

One's intuitions work the same way if, instead of considering the Moral Twin Earth scenario from the outside looking in, one considers how things would strike Earthlings and Twin Earthlings who have encountered each other. Suppose that Earthlings visit Twin Earth (or vice versa), and both groups come to realize that different natural properties causally regulate their respective uses of "good," "right," and other moral terms. If *CSN* were true, then recognition of these differences ought to result in its seeming rather silly, to members of each group, to engage in inter-group debate about goodness—about whether it conforms to normative theory T^c or to T^d. (If, in Putnam's original scenario, the two groups learn that their respective uses of "water" are causally regulated by different physical kind properties, it would be silly for them to think they have differing views about the real nature of water.) But such inter-group debate would surely strike both groups not as silly but as quite appropriate, because they would regard one another as differing in moral beliefs and moral theory, not in meaning.[8]

---

8. Sometime after we thought up the Moral Twin Earth story, we discovered that Hare uses a similar story to criticize ethical naturalism (though, of course, his target is analytic ethical naturalism). He has his readers imagine a group of missionaries landing on a cannibal island and discovering that by sheer coincidence "good" in Cannibalese is apparently a correct translation of "good" in English. However, whereas the missionaries apply the English term to people of genteel spirit, the cannibals use their term "good" to commend people who, among other things, collect more scalps than the average. Hare finds it natural to interpret disagreements between missionaries and cannibals as disagreements in the standards used by these different groups in evaluation rather than as mere disagreements in the meanings of the English and cannibal uses of "good." He writes:

> Even if the qualities in people which the missionary commended had nothing in common with the qualities which the cannibals commended, yet they would both know what the word "good" meant. If "good" were like "red," this would be impossible; for then the cannibals' word and the English word would not be synonymous. If this were so, then when the missionary said that people who collected no scalps were good (English), and the cannibals said that people who collected a lot of scalps were good (cannibal), they would not be disagreeing, because in English (at any rate missionary English), "good" would mean among other things "doing no mur-

(At any rate, this is how they would regard the matter insofar as they rely on their *pretheoretic* semantic intuitions. Intuitions can become skewed for those who are sufficiently in the grip of a philosophical theory. Some new-wave moral realists, for instance, may by now have become so strongly gripped by the Boydian conception of moral reference as causal regulation by natural properties that their own intuitions about Moral Twin Earth actually fall into line with their intuitions about Putnam's original case. For them some philosophical therapy may be necessary, to get them back into touch with their semantically true selves.)

Since semantic norms are tapped by human linguistic competence, and since the relevant linguistic competence is presumably reflected in one's intuitive judgments concerning Twin Earth scenarios, this outcome constitutes strong empirical evidence against *CSN*.

The outcome also underwrites the following "open question argument," a version directed not against analytic semantic naturalism (as was Moore's original open question argument) but instead against *CSN*. First premise: If *CSN* is true, then questions of the following form are *closed*, in the sense that any competent speaker who properly exercises his competence will judge—solely on the basis of his understanding of how the relevant terms work semantically—that the answer to each question is trivially and obviously "yes":

Q1   Given that the use of "good" by human beings is causally regulated by natural property N, is entity e, which has N, good?

and

Q2   Given that the use of "good" by human beings is causally regulated by natural property N, does entity e, which is good, have N?

Second premise: Questions of the form Q1 and Q2 are *not* closed, as evidenced by one's intuitions concerning the Moral Twin Earth scenario. Conclusion: *CSN* is false. (For a considerably more extensive articulation of this form of open question argument, see Horgan and Timmons 1992b.)

6. DOWN FOR THE COUNT—AGAIN

Moral Twin Earth packs a mean punch. Moral realism, having returned to the philosophical ring in newly lean and mean naturalistic shape, has been decked again. Furthermore, Moral Twin Earth is more than a specific thought experiment directed at the specific semantic thesis *CSN*. It is, in

---

der," whereas in the cannibals' language "good" would mean something quite different, among other things "productive of maximum scalps." (Hare 1952, pp. 148–49)

addition, a *recipe* for thought experiments. For any potential version of synthetic naturalism that might be proposed, according to which (i) moral terms bear some relation *R* to certain natural properties that collectively satisfy some specific normative moral theory *T*, and (ii) moral terms supposedly *refer* to the natural properties to which they bear this relation R, it should be possible to construct a Moral Twin Earth scenario suitably analogous to the one constructed above—i.e., a scenario in which twin moral terms bear the same relation *R* to certain natural properties that collectively satisfy some specific normative theory *T'*, incompatible with *T*. The above reasoning against *CSN* should apply, mutatis mutandis, against the envisioned alternative version of semantic naturalism.

No doubt various attempts at resuscitation might be made, now that new-wave moral realism is flat on the canvas. But in the end, we suspect, all such attempts will prove futile. Moral realism can be squared with the constraints imposed by philosophical naturalism only if *CSN*, or some similar form of semantic naturalism, is a viable approach to moral semantics. But synthetic semantic naturalism is down for the count.

8

A Man by Nothing Is So Well Betrayed as by His Manners[*]

Felicia Ackerman

Julie often thought that the second-worst thing about an unhappy life was that you couldn't talk about it. It annoyed people; she wasn't sure why. Maybe it had to do with the idea that you made your own happiness, as if failure to do so were a character flaw.

As she walked into her building now, she could feel the shakiness coming on and knew she wouldn't make it up the stairs. There were no Life Savers in her handbag. No instant glucose—she had never forgotten it before. And there was no one else in the hall but the disagreeable-looking man who lived below her, Nick Pinault. He was unlocking his mailbox and muttering to himself, looking irritable and exhausted.

"Do you have any orange juice or candy?" Julie asked.

He gave her a startled glance, but she was hardly embarrassed—just another example of that wonderful mature perspective illness is supposed to bring you, she thought dizzily. In the dim light, his face seemed blurred and distorted, as if it were underwater.

"Diabetic," she managed to get out. "I need...."

"Yeah." He pulled her into his apartment, kicked the door shut behind him, propelled her over to a sofa with two springs protruding like snakes about to strike, and left the room. In a moment, he returned with a grimy box of sugar and a spoon. At least he knows what to do, was her last coherent thought as she spooned sugar into her mouth.

Ten minutes later, she became aware that she was sitting in a dusty, curtainless room with piles of books and journals everywhere: on the floor,

* Lightly revised from original version published in *Mid-American Review* 6 (1986: 1–12). I thank Zelda Ackerman, Katrina Avery, Eve Barak, Eugene Davidson, Beverly Greenspan, Donna Harvey, Jincy Kornhauser, Claudia Strauss, and James Van Cleve for helpful discussions of the revisions.

on the chairs, even stacked precariously on a windowsill. Near her were issues of *Car and Driver* and *American Historical Review*. Nick was sitting at a rickety table, and unpleasant popping sounds, like the breaking of small bones, were coming from his direction.

"Thanks for the sugar," Julie said, standing up. "I could say I'm sorry I had to bother you, but my diabetes bothers me a lot more, if you see what I mean."

Nick grunted, rubbing his eyes with the backs of his hands. He was a large man of around forty, with a heavy face and coarse black hair. Julie thought he looked like a reject for the part of an aging tough guy in a movie, where even aging toughs had to be attractive. "There was this diabetic kid in my high school, and he always apologized for passing out. I couldn't stand the twerp. Sick people ought to resent it," he said, cracking a knuckle with another ugly little pop.

Julie smiled. "Haven't you heard that even if you're dying of cancer nowadays, anger is supposed to be only a stage?"

"Yeah, and if you get turned down for tenure at a crummy state college like I did, that's a big opportunity for a midlife career change."

She started giggling and found it surprisingly hard to stop. "I have a Ph.D. in philosophy from Stanford, and I never got a teaching job at all," she said.

"Yeah? Sit back down if you want. I went to Berkeley in history. They don't give me the time of day there now. Ever wish all the hotshots would go drown in the Pacific?"

Julie sat down, crossed her legs, and put her hands on her knee. Nick was regarding her expectantly, cracking several knuckles in succession. No one else she knew cracked his knuckles. It looked even worse than it sounded, as though Nick were slowly pulling his fingers out of their sockets. She looked away.

"One of them did drown," she said. "She was an assistant professor at Stanford when I was on the job market. I told her I was only getting interviews at third-rate schools with ferocious teaching loads. She said I should be glad to be getting any interviews at all, with the market so bad, and that I was too concerned with prestige. When she drowned in a canoeing accident," Julie took a deep breath, "well, I know any good psychology disciple would say it was normal for me to feel ambivalent, only I wasn't ambivalent; I was...."

"Thrilled."

"That's right." Julie closed her eyes and could see the woman's serene, lovely face. She'd had glossy red hair and long-lashed green eyes, and everything had come to her as readily as a Christmas present, and now she was dead. And Julie was alive. "I broke my diet to celebrate," Julie said, opening her eyes. "I never told anyone this before."

"Why the hell not?"

"Well, it sounds pretty awful, doesn't it?"

"No," said Nick.

"I met a sort of interesting man yesterday," Julie told Donna in the bakery the next morning.

Donna glanced up from a tray of iced cinnamon buns. She was a comfortable-looking woman, overweight but attractive, with rosy cheeks, a round face and an almost perfect widow's peak. "What do you want to do first, tell me about him or frost some chocolate cakes in the kitchen?" she asked.

"Oh, he wasn't *that* interesting," Julie said. She walked into the kitchen and inhaled deeply. The air was rich with chocolate. Feed a blindfolded man an apple while having him smell a pear and he'll think he's eating a pear, she had once read, and she'd tried sniffing chocolate while eating cottage cheese. It hadn't worked. Still, frosting chocolate cakes was better than having them out of her life entirely. She made a large bowl of mocha buttercream and swirled it slowly over the cakes, hardly raising her eyes until Donna came in.

"So let's hear about this fascinating man," Donna said, dipping a spoon into the frosting bowl.

"He looks like a slob, and he acts like a slob, and he hates the world."

"Sounds irresistible." Donna was licking the spoon daintily.

"He's refreshing—no, that's a stupid word." It was the kind of word diet book writers used in order to make something sound better than it tasted. "Have a refreshing piece of fruit for dessert," they liked to say. They never called ice cream sodas refreshing. "He's just not like the people at Stanford," Julie went on. "He eats junk food. His idea of outdoor exercise is driving, and he has a red Corvette. He resents academic big shots as much as I do."

"I thought you were getting over that."

Julie didn't answer. She reached for the last of the cakes.

"It doesn't sound like he's going to be good for you," Donna said.

"So I won't keep him in my medicine chest," said Julie. "Do you want me to work late today?"

"Could you?"

"No problem." Julie was swirling the frosting into little peaks. "This is practically my favorite place in Palo Alto."

Over the following month, Julie fell into the habit of going to Nick's apartment several times a week after her stint at the bakery. He was almost always there, reading, watching television, or working on one of his history papers, which seemed about as likely to be read as bottled messages sent out to sea. His virulence about journal editors was endless: "all those academic liberals who have academic liberal ideas about women and blacks and saving the whales, and who won't give your paper the time of day unless you've got a hotshot job." He was the only person she knew who didn't think resentment was a vice.

"That's the real taboo subject, you know?" he said once as they were driving to Modesto in the Corvette. "Not sex or death or any of that trendy junk it's practically taboo *not* to talk about, these days. What you really can't say is that you hate and resent people who have what you want and don't deserve it any more than you do."

"You can't even say you're unhappy," said Julie. "It's supposed to be your own fault for having the wrong attitude. Maybe I wouldn't hate the people on top if they weren't so smug."

Nick said of course people on top were smug, and if they weren't, he'd hate them anyway. Julie began to laugh.

"What the hell's so funny?"

"Nothing. It's just that I couldn't have this conversation with anyone else." She gazed out the window at the parched fields, faded and dusty as Nick's living room. "You know, I'm not crazy about healthy people, either," she said.

He nodded. "Want to go to Stockton Saturday?"

Julie would have preferred to drive along the coast, but she realized there was no point in mentioning it. Nick despised the ocean. In his mind it was bound up with the glossy side of California and the people he loathed. "Okay," she said. "It'll be my turn to drive."

"I drive better." He was enormously proud of his driving skills, which included the ability to take sharp curves at sixty miles an hour, as he often demonstrated on deserted roads.

"We agreed we'd take turns," Julie said.

"I didn't agree. Your driving stinks. Like your car."

"Well, I can't afford a Corvette," Julie said, not adding that she considered it a car for nineteen-year-olds who played football and weren't very bright.

"So go into the civil service."

"I don't want a job like yours." He was a demographics analyst, a stupid job, he said, but the pay wasn't bad. Julie leaned against the seat and could feel the car rushing forward. She had to admit it gave an exciting ride. But she liked any kind of car, any kind of driving. "The philosophy job I came closest to getting was at a former teachers' college where the chairman's favorite word was 'community' and he wanted to know all about my personal values. That was his second-favorite word, 'values'," she said.

"When they start talking about community, you can kiss your privacy good-bye," said Nick.

"Exactly. I would have taken it, though. I would have taken anything." She glanced at her watch. "It's time for my shot. You'll have to stop for a minute."

Nick grunted, pulling over to the breakdown lane. Julie hiked up her skirt and gave herself the injection in the thigh, something she would not have done in front of anyone else.

"That hurt?" Nick asked when she winced as the needle went in. She did not reply. He asked again.

Julie put the used syringe away, took out an empty one, and jabbed it into Nick's bare forearm.

"Ow! What the hell?" He jerked his arm away.

"Does that answer your question?"

"Jesus. You do that every day?"

"I do it three times a day and in more sensitive places than the forearm. It doesn't always hurt that much, though. It's partly a matter of luck."

"Christ," Nick muttered, starting the car. He cut ahead of a blue Toyota with a University of California sticker. The driver gave him a venomous look. "You can drive to Stockton," Nick said to Julie.

"I...can't believe I stuck you," Julie said. Her face was throbbing. "Nick?"

He shrugged, rubbing his puffy red eyes.

She met Warren three weeks later. It was at the first party she had been invited to all year; a friend from graduate school was having a housewarming. Standing in a living room with the color scheme of a chocolate cream pie (beige carpet, rich brown furniture, white walls, lampshades and ceiling), Julie wondered whether she had forgotten how to talk with the kind of people she used to know. Then a woman made a remark about her sister's obsession with food.

"An obsession is a strong interest someone disapproves of," Julie said. It was the sort of thing she said when she hoped to be noticed.

"That's great. I'll have to remember it next time someone starts in about my smoking," said a man's voice behind her. She turned around.

Her first thought was that he was too good-looking. Good-looking people rarely bothered with her. He had ruddy skin, regular features and large blue eyes. Smoke from his cigarette wafted in her direction as unerringly as a cat heading for the most allergic person in a room. She fanned with her hand.

"I admire the moral courage of people who smoke, nowadays," she said. "I'd just rather not have their moral courage go up my nose, if you see what I mean."

The man smiled, showing reassuringly uneven teeth. He lowered his cigarette and introduced himself.

His name was Warren Hendrickson. He smoked because he liked it. He taught music history at Stanford and he liked that, too. Before Stanford, he had taught at the University of California at Santa Cruz. He had not liked that at all. The school was a holdover from the sixties, with students who expected academic credit for understanding themselves.

"And a faculty whose favorite word was 'community,' I bet," Julie said.

He grimaced and rolled his eyes.

"When they start talking about community, you can kiss your privacy good-bye," Julie said.

∾ ∾ ∾

"I met someone nice at that party, after all," she told Donna the following morning.

Donna was nibbling on some gingerbread. "Nicer than Nick, I hope."

"Well, naturally," Julie said. "Being nice is hardly Nick's strong point."

Donna turned her attention to a thin woman who wanted detailed descriptions of every cake in the display case. Julie rested her elbows on the counter and beamed. She liked hearing the descriptions. She liked everything today.

"He's like Nick after a makeover," she continued as soon as the woman left. "He's just as interesting to talk to, but he isn't in a permanent bad mood and he doesn't look and act like a lout. Nick acts as if being civilized is against his principles or something."

"Everything you say about Nick makes him sound awfully immature."

Julie gazed across the room at the framed photograph of Donna's little girl. "Ever notice how people who get sentimental about kids are the ones who are always calling stuff they don't like 'immature'?" Nick had once said.

I ought to stick up for him, Julie thought, but two teenagers walked into the bakery before she could decide what to say.

∾ ∾ ∾

The next months were the best Julie had ever known. She saw Warren every weekend. Early Saturday evening, she would drive to his San Francisco duplex and sit in the kitchen, talking with him and playing with his cat while he prepared dinner. She always brought him something from the bakery. She enjoyed watching him eat dessert.

Once she arrived early and heard music inside. It was a violin solo, elegant and precise, making her think of ladies and gentlemen in powdered wigs. She rang the bell and the music stopped.

"What was that record you had on?" she asked when she was seated in the kitchen with the cat in her lap and a newspaper clipping on the table in front of her. "More diabetics switching to insulin infusion pump," was the headline.

He was standing at the stove. She could not see his face. "That wasn't a record. It was me," he said.

"It was? You sounded like a concert violinist."

He had tried to be, Warren said, coming to sit beside her in one of the oak-and-rattan chairs that were less comfortable than they looked. He had trained for years. Finally he'd given up and gone to graduate school in musicology.

His voice was even. She stared at him. "Didn't you mind?"

"Yes." A muscle twitched at his temple.

"But what about now?" Julie hesitated. "Don't you, uh, resent the people who actually got to be concert violinists and aren't any better than you are? Don't you ever, even for a minute, wish they'd all go drown in the Pacific?"

"What good would that do?" He smiled with a corner of his mouth. "I'm not like your friend Nick."

"You're … not like me, either," she said, and told him about the Stanford woman who had drowned. As she talked, Julie kept her eyes on the cat, now sleeping in a circle in her lap. "And I'm still glad she drowned," she finished, rubbing the cat's ears gently. "It wasn't just an immediate reaction. Do you think that's awful?"

Warren lit a cigarette and held it away from her. "You didn't kill her, did you?"

"What?" It came out almost squeaky.

"Didn't I ever tell you about the feminist fantasy group at Santa Cruz? Some women students decided they had to stop having reactionary daydreams about love and marriage; so they set out to re-educate themselves to have proper feminist fantasies. They kept journals of their daydreams and made progress reports to the group." He blew three smoke rings, not in her direction.

She giggled. "A Girl Scout is pure in thought, word and deed." Warren burst out laughing, making her realize how seldom Nick laughed.

The telephone began ringing, and Warren reached to answer it. "Hello?" He blew another smoke ring. "What number do you want?... That's the right number, but there's no Roger Gunderson here." He stubbed out his cigarette. "No, I've had it for two years. Are you calling San Francisco?" He thumbed through the telephone directory. "Well, he's not in the phone book....That's okay."

Julie was watching him mistily, her vision momentarily blurred. He's so nice, she was thinking, nice to everyone. Whether she entirely liked that, she wasn't sure. Maybe each person had a limited supply of niceness; what a waste to use up any on strangers. But this seemed unlikely of Warren. She glanced at the clipping he had saved for her, and felt her spirits rise, although her own experience with the pump had given her continual insulin reactions, and the bulky apparatus bobbing below her waist had made her feel like a kangaroo.

"Anyway," Warren said as he hung up the phone and her vision cleared, "so long as you don't go around killing people, why shouldn't you be glad they're dead if you want?"

"You have to understand," Julie said. "I always thought anyone who knew what I was really like and how I really felt about people like that woman who drowned would think I was dreadful. And then I met Nick, who's the same way, and I was so relieved to have someone I could talk to." She shifted her legs. The cat was so heavy it had made them fall asleep. "Do you remember when I said that when people start talking about community, you can kiss your privacy good-bye?"

"Of course." He touched her cheek. "That was the kind of thing that attracted me in the first place."

"Well," said Julie, "I got that one from Nick. It was his remark, and I used it to attract you, and you're someone he hates."

"But he's never even met me." Warren got up and took the casserole out of the oven. "Why does he hate me? Because of you?"

"Of course not," said Julie. "What have I been telling you? Nick isn't jealous that way. It's just that he'd hate anyone, *anyone* who had tenure at a good school. No matter how nice that person was, even if he was nothing like that woman who drowned, Nick would hate him."

"Amazing," Warren said, and for a moment, Nick's viewpoint did strike Julie as amazing. She felt disoriented, as if the room had suddenly tilted, but before she could decide whether she liked the feeling, it was gone.

≈ ≈ ≈

"So you're moving in with that hotshot," Nick said a month later, leaning forward and cracking all his knuckles against one another with a particularly loud and disagreeable pop. "Where'd you say he lives, Frisco?"

No, I said San Francisco. "Yes," said Julie. She was sitting between the protruding springs of Nick's sofa.

"So you still have to come to Palo Alto for the bakery. You could come see me afterwards." He rubbed his eyes and regarded her belligerently. "What's the matter, you think he'd be jealous? You know I don't care about having sex."

"I know," said Julie, who had slept with Nick once, five days before meeting Warren. It had been her idea (she'd had no one to sleep with in years), and he had done it as quickly and unceremoniously as if he had never heard about satisfying his partner. Afterwards, he told her sex didn't interest him much, especially since it had become something there was a right and a wrong way of doing. He'd rather talk. Well, so would Warren, but Warren enjoyed sex, too. She smiled dreamily, then forced her mind back to Nick. "Of course, I still want to see you. I'll come over as often as I can."

"You mean as often as you want to, which won't be much." Nick was rubbing his eyes again. They looked swollen, the way they invariably did, as if he never got enough sleep. But he slept ten hours a night, he had told her. He liked sleeping. "Soon as he gets a girl who's prettier and slicker, that hotshot's going to dump you. You can't count on people like that," he said.

"You don't know anything about him." There was no point in mentioning that Warren seemed uninterested in women's appearances. He didn't even try to tell Julie she was beautiful to him. He said that would be as silly as saying she was rich to him; if you really cared for someone, her looks didn't matter.

"He'll dump you so fast you won't know what hit you, and when he does, don't think you'll get the time of day here." Nick hit the top of the desk with his fist. Several sheets of lined yellow paper drifted to the floor, joining the books, dog-eared journals and empty potato-chip bags that would probably stay in the apartment as long as he did.

Julie looked at the floor, then at him. "Nick," she said, "why don't you do something about this place? Why don't you, uh, do something about yourself?"

"You see? You're getting no good already." Nick picked up two journals and hurled them to the floor. "Now get the hell out of here, you little creep. I never want to see you again."

"I didn't mean...."

"Get out."

"All right," said Julie and walked out.

∾ ∾ ∾

One day nearly two months later, Julie left the bakery early. The afternoon stretched in front of her like an easy obstacle course: buy a copy of the latest P. D. James mystery, get vegetables for the stew she and Warren would be having for dinner, go for her eye examination. The ophthalmologist, a small round man with a swooping mustache like a nineteenth-century villain's, would subject her to complicated procedures that included scrutinizing her eyes with a glass that reflected her retinal vessels before her like tiny, twisted worms. Not too bad, he always said, not bad for such long-standing diabetes, and wasn't she lucky? Julie always replied that lucky people didn't get diabetes in the first place. But this time she just might say yes. She turned on the car radio to a rock music station and pressed her foot on the accelerator, thinking how Nick's driving had ruined ordinary speeds for her. They seemed almost unnatural now, like driving in slow motion.

The bookstore and the supermarket both were crowded, and she reached the eye doctor's office barely in time for her appointment. He had shaved off his mustache, but the change seemed surprisingly trivial. His face wasn't transformed. It was just minus the mustache. As the testing progressed and the familiar masses of vessels appeared before her, Julie thought about mustaches and beards. Warren and Nick had neither, Nick because he associated them, beards especially, with in-groupy academic people, Warren because...he just didn't. He wouldn't consider beards and mustaches worth having opinions about. And they weren't, were they? Julie swallowed a yawn. It was oddly tiring to sit still and stare straight ahead. Her thoughts seemed flattened and slowed. Finally the doctor switched off his tiny flashlight and lowered the glass. "Well," Julie said, "are you going to tell me how lucky I am?"

"I'm afraid not," said the doctor. "I'm sorry."

∾ ∾ ∾

Fifteen minutes later, fleeing the doctor's office as if it had become radioactive, Julie collided with a man on the sidewalk. One of his shopping bags tore, spilling packages of frozen food onto the pavement, but she did not stop to help. The man wore glasses, didn't he? That meant he could see. He looked about twenty-five and aggressively healthy.

Julie dashed into her car, drove as viciously as she had ever known Nick to, and it was not until she saw his inflamed eyes in the pale light of her old building's hallway that she realized she had come to the wrong place.

"I told you not to come here," he said harshly.

"Oh, did you? Since when do you own the building? I still have an apartment here, in case you've forgotten. I...came to pick up some things."

"That hotshot throw you out?"

His face, surly and dispirited as ever, made her want to scream. "Who do you think I am, *you*?" she screamed. "Some jerk people only bother with as long as there's no one else around? Warren would never throw me out." Nick turned to go out; he was holding a large, thin book under his arm. "Don't worry, I've got a consolation for you!" Julie yelled after him. "Something you can gloat over. I'm going blind."

"What?" He turned around.

"Don't you understand English? I said I'm going blind. It can happen to diabetics, even obedient ones like me, who break their diets maybe once a year and shoot up three times a day; that's over twenty thousand injections I've had in my life...."

Soon she was in his apartment, seated between the protruding springs. He sat in the desk chair turned around to face her. Nothing in the room had altered. Even the stains on the floor were familiar.

"Well, obviously, I'm not blind yet," she was saying. "Don't you know anything? My vision's even still good enough for me to drive; how do you think I got here? It's...." But she couldn't bear to repeat the medical details; she had hardly been able to bear hearing them. "Just take my word for it," she said.

"Jesus." He was cracking his knuckles slowly, one by one. It seemed almost magically repellent.

"What a brilliant comment. No wonder you're such a professional success." He looked away. "Oh, what's the matter, am I upsetting you?" she said.

"You're going blind; you're not supposed to act like Rebecca of Sunnybrook Farm."

"I'm—" Julie glanced at the book he had been carrying in the hall. "Beginner's Flight Instruction Manual," was on the cover. "Are you learning to fly?" she asked.

"Yeah." He cracked another knuckle.

"Is that supposed to make you some kind of big adventurer? *You*? You've barely got the energy to get up in the morning!"

"Christ, anyone can fly a plane."

"Including people who can't see? Even a diabetic who isn't blind can't fly a plane. You can't get a pilot's license if you take insulin. You wouldn't understand, but for the first time in my life I was happy. I was so happy with Warren. You wouldn't know anything about that kind of thing. Oh, why couldn't this have happened to you instead? I've been through enough with twenty years of diabetes, and you've never really been sick, and…." She was crying now, harder than she had ever cried before, harder than she had realized it was possible to cry.

"Julie," said Nick, "you want to go for a drive? You can drive. You can drive the Corvette, if you want."

She got up abruptly, and Nick rose, too, as if they were about to leave together. "I wouldn't be caught dead driving your stupid Corvette!" she shrieked. "You look like an idiot in it, do you know that? People probably split their sides laughing at this middle-aged lout trying to drive a flashy car as if he were some sharp teenager. And that's all you'll ever be, a dumb lout. You'll never have another teaching job, do you know that?"

"Yeah." Nick sat down again, slouched, and stared at the floor.

"And no journal's ever going to publish any of those pathetic papers you keep writing, do you know that?"

"Yeah, Julie, I know that." His voice was dull and thick, as if he were talking in his sleep.

Julie sat back down between the springs. "And no one's ever going to like you or want to spend time with you, and you'll spend the rest of your life by yourself in this miserable room, do you know that, too?"

He didn't answer.

"What's the matter," Julie said, "am I making you feel bad?"

He shrugged.

"Well, it's not as bad as going blind, is it? And it's about time someone told you what a complete and permanent loser you are, and I like telling you. I like it, do you understand, and I'm going blind and you're not; so you can just put up with it. Or maybe you think I'm being unfair. *Unfair*?" She began laughing wildly.

"It's okay," Nick said. "It's like income taxes. Evens things up a little."

"Exactly," said Julie. "So now I'm going back to Warren. He doesn't know yet and I'm going to tell him, but you can be sure I won't treat him like this. I think too much of him. And anyway, I've gotten it out of my system on you. On you!" she flung out again and nearly toppled over when she got up to leave.

≈ ≈ ≈

Driving home to Warren, she felt guilty and exhausted. She longed to have him hold her and say he would make it all up to her. At the same time, she could hardly face telling him. It seemed like torturous, interminable labor, the whole account her mind and mouth would have to slog through before she could be comforted. Maybe I won't do it today, she said to herself as she swung off the main highway, but then, just as she had known she would, she told him as soon as she walked into the house.

"Warren, I'm going blind."

"*What?*"

She repeated it. For a long while, he was just the way she wanted. Then he began talking about seeing-eye dogs and cassettes and how blind people could do almost anything.

Except see. Julie pulled away from him. "Warren," she said, "I do not want to adjust to this."

"Adjust's a disgusting word, but in the long run, what else can you do?"

"I don't know. I'm so tired." She leaned back against him. "Are you going to feel differently about me...afterwards?"

"What?" He didn't sound offended, just bewildered. She almost smiled. For a moment.

"I want to go out to dinner," she said restlessly. "Remember I told you about Farley's?"

"Do you think that's a good idea?"

"I'm not expecting it to save my vision," Julie said. "What do you mean, is it a good idea?"

～ ～ ～

Farley's, where Julie had gone for special meals as a graduate student, turned out to be unchanged. The waitresses even still wore white blouses and black dirndl skirts. "Nice evening, isn't it?" their waitress said brightly, as she gave them each a menu.

Julie had been staring at the white tablecloth. She looked up. Through the plate-glass window she could see the sun, red-gold on the horizon, sending pink streaks across the sky. The waitress, who looked about twenty, had a smile that was also pink, and her hair was as yellow as lemons. Warren's eyes were the blue of the ocean Nick hated.

When you were blind, you couldn't *see.*

Julie slammed down the menu, "No," she said, "it's a lousy evening. And you sound like a stupid wind-up doll, anyone ever tell you that?"

The waitress gasped and disappeared from Julie's line of vision almost as if she had been vacuumed away.

Julie glanced at Warren, who was always nice to her. Who was always nice to everyone. "Why did you do that?" he said.

"I'm going blind."

"It's not her fault."

"It's not my fault, either. I did everything I was supposed to, but I'm going blind. If I can stand that, I'm sure she'll survive a five-second insult from a stranger."

"You really upset her."

Julie looked back down at the tablecloth, smooth and pearly as the inside of a seashell. She stared at the cloth for a long time. Then she raised her eyes, and everything briefly blurred. Have you noticed intermittent blurring of your vision, Julie? Yes, but I've always had that. I thought it was because I was tired.

"Warren," she said, "can't we please...." She broke off. The waitress, approaching from the side with a wary glance at Julie, turned to face him.

"Are you ready to order?" the waitress asked.

They ordered. "I hope you'll excuse what my friend said before," Warren added. "She's had a big shock today."

"I can imagine." The waitress looked at Julie curiously and walked away.

Julie was gripping the leg of the table. "I can't believe you said that," she said.

"There's no point in having you both upset."

"Both upset? You mean on a par?"

"Look," Warren said, "maybe we should talk about this later, after you've calmed down a bit."

She closed her eyes loosely. The darkness wasn't really black. It was no color she could name. Just because you're losing your vision is no excuse for losing your manners. The handicapped can be an inspiration to us all.

Her eyes snapped open. She was trembling. "Warren—"

He emptied two sugar packets into her water glass and pushed it into her hand. "You'd better drink this."

"I'm not having an insulin reaction. I'm having a reaction to you. I...." She drank the water.

"Julie," Warren was saying, "I know it's awful for you now, but—"

"It's going to get better when I'm blind?" Her voice, unexpectedly loud, gave her goose pimples.

"Are you planning to act like this from now on?" he asked very quietly.

"I'm not *planning* anything. That's not what I'm thinking about right now!"

"I don't want to spend the rest of my life listening to you abuse people whenever you feel like it," Warren said.

"The rest of your life? Don't worry." Her fingers made tiny pleats in her napkin. "How many juvenile diabetics do you think even make it into their fifties?"

"I don't want to spend another fifteen years this way, then."

Julie was silent. Her mind seemed paralyzed. "I was wrong," she said finally.

Warren put his hand on hers. "Of course, it's terrible. But I'll do anything I can...."

As long as I'm a good girl and never forget what they taught us in high school. A man by nothing is so well betrayed as by his manners.

Julie pulled her hand away. "That's not what—" She picked up a roll, its crust hard against her fingers. Hard rolls meant a restaurant was trying to be sophisticated, she had read.

"We'll be lucky if there isn't a nuclear war before we can get into our fifties, anyway," he was saying.

Julie bit into the roll.

"If I had ignored what you said to the waitress, it would have been condescension, as if you were some pathetic little creature who couldn't be expected to act like a decent person."

"No," Julie said, "it would have been justice. Can't you understand? If you just found out you're going blind, at least you ought to be exempt from the usual rules of etiquette, for Christ's sake!"

"But—"

"It evens thing up a little. It's like income taxes."

"That's ridiculous," said Warren. "It sounds like something you would have gotten from Nick."

"I did," Julie said.

"Well, I'm not Nick."

"You aren't," Julie said.

9

A Man by Nothing Is So Well Betrayed as by His Manners? Politeness as a Virtue*

Felicia Ackerman

Politeness and rudeness are important dimensions in social life and in day-to-day evaluations of people's behavior and character. But these concepts have received little philosophical attention. This essay aims at remedying that lack by explicating the concept of politeness and discussing the status of politeness as a virtue and its relation to other virtues.

I

Politeness is one of a family of concepts whose members include such notions as civility, good manners, courtesy, and etiquette, along with their opposites of rudeness, incivility, bad manners, and discourtesy. Within each group are concepts that have subtle differences of nuance. This essay concentrates on politeness/good manners as the central notion and uses the terms "politeness" and "good manners" interchangeably.

For attempts at general characterizations of good manners, it seems natural to consult etiquette books. As a sample, consider *Debrett's Etiquette and Modern Manners*, which describes good manners as follows:

> The object [of manners] is to put everybody at ease, whatever their [sic] age or rank. (Donald 1981, p. 7)

> Good manners mean showing consideration for others—a sensibility that is innate in some people and has to be carefully cultivated in others.

* "The gentle mind by gentle deeds is known / For a man by nothing is so well bewrayed / As by his manners." (Edmund Spenser, *The Faerie Queene*, Book VI, Canto 3, Stanza 1.) A version of this essay was originally published in *Midwest Studies in Philosophy* 13 (1988): 250–58. I am deeply grateful to Marilyn McCord Adams, Katrina Avery, Sara Ann Ketchum, Jincy Kornhauser, and James Van Cleve for graciously discussing various issues in this essay with me.

Whatever its sources, however, its purpose is to enable people to come together with ease, stay together for a time without friction or discord, and leave one another in the same fashion. This is the role of custom and of courtesy: the first stimulates personal confidence and reduces misunderstandings, the latter reassures us that our associates mean to be friendly (Donald 1981, p. 10).

This account has a number of strengths. It recognizes that manners inherently involve some notion of consideration for others and of helping social encounters flow smoothly. It also recognizes that manners have both a conventional aspect (as can be illustrated by the fact that handshaking is a customary greeting in American but not in Indian society), which seems to be what *Debrett's* means by "custom," and a non-conventional aspect, which seems to be what *Debrett's* means by "courtesy" and which sets down limits on the aims and functions a rule can have in order to count as a rule of good manners at all. Thus, regardless of which society one is considering, a system of rules for eating will not count as a system of table manners unless it has certain ends (preventing sudden death from choking or food poisoning would not qualify, for example), but how these appropriate ends are to be implemented will, of course, vary from society to society.

The term "custom" is actually a bit misleading here. What counts as polite behavior in a given society is less a matter of how people in that society customarily behave than of how whatever authorities the society recognizes on the subject of manners say good manners require people to behave. (Note the parallel here with rules of correct usage of a language. Whether "ain't" counts as correct English is not a matter of whether English speakers customarily use it, but of whether it would be accepted by the sources English speakers recognize as authorities on correct usage.)

An important weakness of *Debrett's* account is that the purposes specified for good manners are too broad. Rules of good manners do not aim to enable people to avoid just any kind of discord when staying together for a time; for example, they do not aim to enable Congress to meet without political discord. Similarly, they do not always aim to enable people to "come together with ease"; for example, they may aim to make it difficult to approach the Queen. *Debrett's* itself notes that rules of good manners may be designed partly to exclude and confuse "*arrivistes*" (Donald 1981, p. 9; see also Martin 1982, p. 7; Martin 1984, pp. 327–28). Moreover, good manners can be used on specific occasions to make someone feel guilty or otherwise uncomfortable, a practice often advocated by etiquette writer Judith Martin (a.k.a. Miss Manners), who delights in recommending "faultlessly polite and cheerful ways to drive others into the madhouse" (1984, p. 288; see also pp. xviii and 178; and 1982, pp. 7, 195, and 215; as well as Bracken 1964, p. 72).

Social scientists have suggested somewhat more sophisticated accounts. Thus, Goffman characterizes ceremonial rules (as opposed to substantial rules) as follows:

> A ceremonial rule is one which guides conduct in matters felt to have secondary or even no significance in their own right, having their primary importance—officially, anyway—as a conventionalized means of communication by which the individual expresses his character or conveys his appreciation of other participants in the situation...in our society, the code which governs ceremonial rules and ceremonial expressions is incorporated into what we call etiquette. (Goffman 1967, pp. 54–55)

This overlooks the cases where violating rules for conventional expressions of aspects of one's character would not constitute a breach of manners or etiquette. For example, it is conventional (at least on college campuses) to wear buttons with slogans expressing one's political (or other) views, but it is not a breach of manners or etiquette to wear a button proclaiming views one opposes instead. Similarly, during an election campaign, it is conventional to wear a button bearing the name of one's favored candidate, but it is not a breach of manners or etiquette to attempt to mislead by wearing a button for a candidate one opposes. Also, there are rules of good manners or etiquette that originally had (and sometimes still have) important "substantial" purposes beyond the ceremonial ones Goffman allows. The rule about not talking with one's mouth full has an aesthetic purpose. Rules of manners or etiquette regarding asking permission to smoke in social gatherings seem as much concerned with people's physical comfort as with their sensibilities. But there are limits. It may be impolite to smoke and make a mildly allergic person cough or to smell up a room with a cigar, but where the expected physical consequences are drastic enough (for example, in a case where one knows someone would drop dead instantly upon being exposed to one's cigar smoke), speaking of rudeness and politeness seems ridiculous.[1]

How might an improved account go? The following conditions seem relevant to whether a rule is a rule for polite behavior.

1. The rule concerns social behavior, i.e., behavior among people or other sentient beings normally capable of grasping rules of the system.[2]

---

1. See Bracken's (1964, p. 41) facetious remark about "Good Manners for the Smoker": "He mustn't smoke where there are NO SMOKING signs, for these usually mean business. It is bad form to explode a planeload of people or to blow a hospital sky-high."

2. Thus, Martin (1982, p. 202) seems right in holding that "the whole concept of proper and improper behavior does not apply between people and machines" and that it is preposterous to speak of politeness towards one's dog (p. 191). But simply someone's status as a living human being seems adequate to make him a suitable object of polite behavior, even if his particular cognitive capacities are not up to understanding or

2. The rule is extra-legal and is not enforced by legal penalties.

3. The rule is part of a system of rules (or may be the whole system as a limiting case) having the original purpose and/or current function for the intended beneficiaries of making social life orderly, predictable, comfortable, and pleasant, over and above considerations of survival, health, safety, economy, religious edicts, or playing a game,[3] and doing this by such means as:

   a. making social life aesthetically appealing and avoiding situations perceived as aesthetically repellent.

   b. minimizing embarrassment, hurt feelings, and unpleasant surprises.

   c. showing consideration for others, defining and maintaining people's privacy and autonomy.

   d. providing the security of conventional forms and rituals.

   e. reflecting distinctions of rank and privilege considered important.

4. It is socially sanctioned to take a violation of the rule by other people in situations involving oneself as an affront to oneself.

Note that rules of polite behavior help define as well as reflect what counts as aesthetically repellent, embarrassing, intrusive, etc. I suggest that being a rule of polite behavior is a concept that has what Alston calls combination of conditions vagueness (see Alston 1964, pp. 87–89); i.e., in order for something to fall under the concept, "enough" of a series of conditions must be satisfied, where it is unclear in principle how many are enough, and they may be unequally weighted. Thus, the rules relating to American eating habits that concern which utensils to use, who is served in what order, as well as such matters as chewing with closed mouth, not pressing others to violate their diets, not grabbing food from others' plates, etc., are clearly rules of good manners. Laws against murder and rules for playing solitaire clearly are not.

Matters can be less clear when only some of the conditions are satisfied. Conditions 1, 3a, 3b, 3c, 3e, and 4 seem particularly important, the others less so. For example, rules of polite behavior in medieval Japan violated condition 2. They were enforced by law (see Waldo 1965, pp. 53–54), as are contemporary rules against loud night parties in some cities (which does not prevent annoying one's neighbors by having such parties from being rude).

---

reciprocation. (For example, see Martin 1984, pp 336–37, on polite behavior towards "senile" people.)

3. The qualifier here reflects the insight behind Goffman's view about the limitations on the "substantial" function of ceremonial rules of etiquette, although the above counterexamples show that his account needs modification.

But the reason rules of grammar or rules for playing a musical instrument, unlike rules restricting the use of obscene language, do not count as rules of polite behavior seems to lie in conditions 3b, 3c, and 4. Rules of grammar or musical performance do not seem rooted in consideration for the feelings of others, and it is not generally socially sanctioned to take violation by others of these rules in social interaction with oneself as an affront. There is some social sanction, however, for feeling affronted by one's dinner companion's poor table manners, although the sanction for this decreases as the manners in question become more esoteric (using the wrong fish fork, for example). Note that condition 1 does not commit us to Martin's extreme view of the social nature of manners, that "In manners, as distinct from morals...the only [act that counts] is one that has been witnessed [by someone else]" (Martin 1982, p. 249). Such a view seems excessive, as it precludes attributing rudeness to someone who says to his deaf grandfather in no one else's hearing when the grandfather's back is turned, "Hurry up and croak, you old idiot, so I can inherit your money."

Some of the most interesting problems in characterizing rules as rules of polite behavior have to do with the qualification in condition 3 that mentions the intended beneficiaries of the rules. This, along with condition 3e, allows for the possibility that a system of manners may not only be hierarchical, but may not benefit or even be intended to benefit all the categories of people to which it applies. Several types of cases can be distinguished here. First are such cases as the rules of manners for showing respect for women or old people. While it can be argued that this sort of respect is actually a form of condescension whose function is to reinforce the subordinate role of its recipients, as long as there is a professed rationale that these rules benefit and show respect for the recipients, the rules clearly count as rules of good manners, although not necessarily desirable rules. But what about such cases as the practice that a lord is to walk through the door ahead of a commoner, or the elaborate "Jim Crow" set of rules of social segregation in the pre-1960s American South? "Jim Crow" rules had components that were legally enforced (such as blacks having to sit in the back of buses) and components that were not (such as blacks not entering the homes of whites through the front door or being entertained as guests in the living room). Limiting consideration to the cases that did not involve legal enforcement, we can distinguish three sorts of cases. The first would involve a rationale (however preposterous) that the rules in some sense benefited subordinates as well as superiors, for example, by making for a more orderly society[4] or one where people would not be embarrassed by being strained beyond their "true capacities." This still seems to count as a system of politeness, and one where there are politeness-obligations from the members of the superior class to those of the subordinate class, as well as vice versa. An even more debased case would involve no claim that the rules benefit the commoners or blacks, but would claim that members of the subordinate class are natural inferiors who accordingly owe deference to their natural superiors. At most, this seems to be a one-way system of politeness, where members of the subordinate class have politeness-obligations to members of the superior class, but not vice versa. A final case involves inegalitarian rules with no rationale at all beyond the power of the superior class to enforce them. It seems doubtful that this would count as a system of rules of politeness, which suggests that condition 3 should be amended to require that an appropriate rationale (of one of the sorts mentioned above) for the social distinctions in question be part of the system.

My account, like *Debrett's*, allows for both conventional and non-conventional aspects of politeness. There are actually three levels here. At the most general level are conditions 1–4 that can be used cross-culturally to decide whether a given rule is to count as a rule of politeness at all. Second is the room for cross-cultural variations in the specifics of the aims and functions in condition 3. For example, societies may differ as to what distinctions of rank and privilege are to be respected. Finally, there are a particular society's conventional polite social gestures, as illustrated by the above example that a handshake is a common greeting in the United States but not in India (which does not preclude the two societies' having similar cultural values about the importance of greeting someone with friendliness and respect).

These distinctions allow for the possibility of some polite behavior even from a person who does not know the conventions of a society he is visiting; he can at least stay off any topic that he has reason to believe his listener will find embarrassing or unpleasant and that there is no overriding need to discuss. Someone who is largely ignorant of the conventions of another society may still happen to know of a topic some particular person in that society would find embarrassing or unpleasant.

---

4. "When Dr. Johnson declared that it makes things much simpler to know that a lord goes through a door ahead of a commoner, he was no more striking a blow against individualism than against equality: he was only interested in saving everybody time" (Louis Kronenberger, quoted in Bracken 1964, p. 17). The obvious objections to this rationale (why not have the commoner or the taller man go first?), like the obvious objections to claims that "Jim Crow" was good for blacks, need not concern us here.

These distinctions also point to a way there can be a split between what one might call the letter and the spirit of good manners, as in the classic anecdote about a host who drinks the water in his fingerbowl to set at ease a guest who has made a similar move out of ignorance. Another, more interesting split of this sort involves flaunting one's pleasantness, professed interest, and professed considerateness as a means of making another person uncomfortable. As I have mentioned, Martin gives cases where one can (and on her view should) use politeness in this way, for example, by frustrating unsolicited advice-givers by repeatedly requesting ever-more-detailed suggestions, listening quietly, and then ignoring the advice ("one of Miss Manners' favorite faultlessly polite and cheerful ways to drive others into the madhouse" [Martin 1984, p. 288]) or by making a friend who did not invite one to her birthday party "feel terrible and remorseful—and all by behaving like a perfect lady!" (p. 178) (in this case by telling her one hopes she had a wonderful birthday and inviting her to one's own birthday party). Is this genuinely polite behavior? Consider another case. Normally, greeting one's colleagues is polite, but suppose someone knows that one of his colleagues would resent being subjected to his greeting, perhaps because she knows he was instrumental in denying her tenure. It seems clear that it would be kinder for him not to greet her, but would it also be more polite? In both cases, the answer seems to hinge on what, if anything, the society's rules of politeness have to say about what to do when the usual forms of politeness appear to defeat some of their own ends. Martin seems right that our society's concept of politeness allows unkindness in the sorts of cases she presents. For my question about the case involving the colleagues, the answer seems less clear.

II

Is politeness a virtue? If so, how is it related to other virtues? It may seem that if politeness is a virtue, it differs from the usual cases of moral virtues in a way illustrated by Foot's remark that "moral judgment concerns itself with a man's reasons for acting as well as with what he does. Law and etiquette require only that certain things are done or left undone, but no one is counted as charitable if he gives alms 'for the praise of men', and one who is honest only because it pays him to be honest does not have the virtue of honesty" (Foot 1972, pp. 312–13). This is certainly oversimplified for the case of law, which takes into account someone's intentions as well as what he does. It may be oversimplified for politeness as well. A person's actions may count as polite provided they accord with his society's rules of polite behavior, but it seems at least questionable whether generally acting politely is enough to make him count as a polite person. Suppose he aims at being rude but generally ends up doing what counts as polite through misinformation about a society's conventions. Is he a polite person? "In a sense, yes; in a sense, no?" Someone who follows the conventions of politeness "for the praise of men," on the other hand, clearly does count as a polite person. As long as he habitually acts with deliberate politeness, ulterior motives seem irrelevant to the question of whether he is a polite person. Thus, it is politeness that is not ulteriorly motivated whose status as a virtue should be examined. I will call this "intrinsic politeness."

Precisely what is the connection between intrinsic politeness and morality? Valberg has pointed out that "it is obvious that statements of etiquette are not in and of themselves moral statements" (Valberg 1977, p. 388). But, of course, there can still be moral grounds for obeying the rules of polite behavior, insofar as there are moral grounds for such ends as those in conditions 3a–e and for avoiding actions that will give other people social sanction for feeling affronted (condition 4). The diversity of these ends shows some of the complexity of this issue. For example, it is obvious that both moral defenses and moral objections can be made concerning the distinctions of rank and privilege embodied in a given system of manners. What is less obvious is that these distinctions may involve priorities that are a matter of gradations less standard than distinctions of age, gender, social class, or social caste. Martin, for example, is a staunch believer that good manners require unhappy people, even those who "have had a genuine tragedy in their lives,"[5] to put on a "false face" in order to avoid blighting the day of anyone who might be better off—a position that might be criticized as the equivalent of taxing the poor to support the rich. A related objection can be raised to the stricture that requires the bereaved to write personal replies to (possibly hundreds of) sympathy notes. But it might also be claimed that the pressure to maintain conventional forms and rituals is diverting and beneficial to the sufferer.

To the extent that intrinsic politeness is a virtue, it is presumably so because either the distinctions embodied in condition 3e, the forms of consideration embodied in 3a–c, the security embodied in 3d, or the avoidance of making people feel affronted (condition 4) are things that are intrinsically good. Thus, it seems doubtful that there is much virtue in intrinsic politeness that involves obeying the letter of conventionally polite forms that defeat the spirit of politeness in other conditions, except insofar as there is some virtue in upholding the system of rules itself (for example, to discourage defections by others or to provide the security of convention,

---

5. Martin 1982, pp. 243–44. For a slight qualification, see Martin 1984, pp. 319–20. A similar rule is supported by Emily Post (1965, p. 41).

as indicated in condition 3d, which cannot be defeated when the letter of conventionally polite forms is followed).

Common sense suggests that insofar as it serves the aims of conditions 3a–d, intrinsic politeness is a virtue, but not one of the most important ones.[6] It seems ludicrous, for example, to attach weight to whether someone who successively and painlessly murdered six wives in their sleep was an intrinsically polite person (let alone whether he was intrinsically polite to his wives!). But apparently not everyone finds this sort of consideration ludicrous. Newspaper stories from the 1950s and 1960s frequently quoted neighbors of a newly discovered ex-Nazi murderer as objecting to his extradition or prosecution on the grounds that he had rehabilitated himself as a decent person living a decent life, as witnessed by his good manners, neat appearance and well-tended lawn.

Thus, the limited importance of intrinsic politeness as a virtue leads to moral dangers in giving it undue weight, and one way this can happen is by giving someone's manners undue weight in judging him as a person. Even Martin (1984, p. 186) grants that "there is a ridiculous emphasis on the superficial [in the fact that people] will be judged more on their manners...than their character" and quotes Somerset Maugham's remark that

> few can suffer manners different from their own without distaste. It is seldom that a man is shocked by the thought that someone has seduced another's wife, and it may be that he preserves his equanimity when he knows that another has cheated at cards or forged a check...but it is hard for him to make a bosom friend of one who drops his aitches and almost impossible if he scoops up gravy with his knife.[7]

There are other ways in which intrinsic politeness can be overrated in judging a person. For example, someone may be overvalued for his good manners, when his intrinsic desire to maintain pleasant surfaces and avoid embarrassing others keeps him from speaking out against injustice. Similarly, politeness can be overvalued in making one's own decisions about how to behave. Another virtue that can conflict with intrinsic politeness is honesty, although it is often unclear how this conflict should be resolved. Martin, in explaining why one should answer a grandmother's question about the merit of her granddaughter's unmeritorious performance with insincere praise, holds that "Hypocrisy is not generally a social sin, but a

---

6. "Think of situations like 'I *know* Emily Post wouldn't approve, but etiquette hasn't got anything to do with this. This is *serious*'" (Becker 1973, p. 369; italics in original). Even using the less trivial-sounding terms "good manners" or "courtesy" does not militate against the view that "For all practical purposes, we may ignore considerations of [good manners] in life-or-death situations" (Becker 1973, p. 369).

7. Martin 1984, pp. 185–86, quoted from Somerset Maugham, *The Narrow Corner*.

virtue".[8] But an obvious objection to this sort of tact is that once it becomes a social practice, it undermines trust about the relevant situation. If politeness requires an affirmative answer to "Did you like my flute solo?" an affirmative answer will not be a reliable guide to the speaker's opinion. This problem is inherent in the nature of tact as a social practice, rather than being an avoidable result of taking polite conventions too literally, for example, by giving a literal answer to "How are you?" The greeting "How are you?" (as opposed to "Tell me, how have you really been?") is not intended to be taken literally (see Martin 1982, p. 170). Tactful praise, however, is intended not only to be polite, but to be believed. That is what makes it reassuring. And tact also requires a polite lie in response to "Tell me, what did you really think of my flute solo? I really want to know." It might also be argued that it is condescending to assume someone "really" wants or needs reassurance when he appears to be asking for an opinion.

Any virtue (other than loyalty itself) seems able to conflict with loyalty, since its requirements may conflict with the interests or desires of someone to whom one is or should be loyal. But politeness, with its usual stress on widespread impersonal agreeability, provides an especially fertile field for such conflicts. Suppose a man's wife wants him to "cut" (i.e., snub) an acquaintance she dislikes. The spirit of politeness may require that the husband greet this person pleasantly (and even the letter of politeness may afford no means for a snub in a particular situation)[9], but the wife may reasonably see such politeness as a breach of loyalty—and, of course, it may be a breach of loyalty even if she is not there to witness it. Politeness can also conflict with loyalty when there is no prior dislike to be given its due(?) by a snub. Consider the following case (see chap. 8, this volume). A woman is emotionally devastated by the unexpected discovery that she is going blind and a few hours later is impetuously rude and insulting to a waitress in a restaurant. Her lover is far more upset by her behavior than by her fear of impending blindness and in her presence apologizes to the waitress for this behavior—a move that the first woman considers a betrayal. "A man by

---

8. Martin 1984, p. 85. Compare Chafets' (1980, p. 201) affectionate description of manners in Israel: "Excessive displays of…good manners are considered suspect, manifestations of superficiality or worse. If you are in a good mood, you show it; and if your feet hurt, you show it that too."

9. In discussing cuts, Martin says (1989, pp. 418–19), "Etiquette recognizes the category of 'enemy' (although only among equals; someone for whom you can routinely make life miserable, such as an employee, cannot be treated as an enemy)." This makes it unclear whether it is the inequality or the possibility of routinely making someone's life miserable that is supposed to be the crucial factor (the two conditions are obviously not equivalent). And the "killing with kindness" sort of maneuver discussed on p. 157 above may not even be applicable in a situation that calls for only a brief, pleasant greeting.

nothing is so well betrayed as by his manners" here can have, not its original import that one can betray his boorishness and crudeness by his bad manners, but the import that one can also betray his superficiality, small-mindedness, and disloyalty by his overemphasis on good manners where their display is incompatible with deeper values.[10]

---

10. Martin apparently endorses apologizing for the rudeness of one's loved ones if they are "directly hurtful to someone" (1989, p. 212). She does not limit this to apologizing for one's small children; the example she discusses involves an adult's chronically ill mother.

10

Contractarianism and Bargaining Theory*

Paul Weirich

The contractarian theory of morality relies upon principles of rational agreement. So developments concerning principles of rational agreement may affect the principles of morality supported by contractarianism. I will argue for some revisions in the classical theory of bargaining and show that they lead to contractarian support for a utilitarian form of social cooperation.

1. CONTRACTARIANISM

The contractarian theory of morality has many forms. The central idea is that certain moral principles depend upon the agreements that people would reach in an "original position," sometimes conceived of as a state of nature. The main differences between the various versions of the theory concern the moral principles treated, the nature of their alleged dependence upon agreements, and the features of the original position.

I will consider a modest form of contractarianism that treats only principles of distributive justice and claims only that they are explained by deriving them from agreements. It does not attempt to derive rights to life and liberty from agreements. And it does not attempt to reduce principles of morality to principles of rationality. In particular, it does not try to show that being moral is in one's self-interest. As a result, it can allow some basic moral ideals to be built into the original position.

The version of the theory that I advance concerns forms of social cooperation, that is, assignments of tasks and compensations to members of society. It proposes a moral principle in the following pattern: the form of social cooperation should be one that people would agree upon in the

* A version of this paper was originally published in the *Journal of Philosophical Research* 16 (1991: 369–85). I received helpful comments from Craig Ihara, Dan Ihara, and Peter Markie. The discussion of my paper at the Overvold Conference provided many useful suggestions.

original position. Then it shows that people in the original position would agree upon a form of social cooperation that satisfies a utilitarian principle of distribution. It concludes that a form of social cooperation satisfying the utilitarian principle ought to be adopted. The main claim of the theory is that the utilitarian principle is explained by being derived from the contractarian principle about agreements in the original position.

Notice that the contractarian principle does not specify personal moral obligations. It merely specifies what ought to be the case, and not who should take steps to bring it about. Thus the utilitarian principle it yields does not specify the obligations of any individual. It expresses a moral ideal and not a principle of practical morality. There may be reasons why an individual ought not to take steps to bring about a utilitarian form of social cooperation.

Also, the contractarian principle does not say that the principles agreed upon in the original position are to be used publicly in settling disputes and the like. Thus the principles agreed upon need not compromise between ideals of distribution and practical concerns about the side effects of efforts to implement those ideals. This is another reason why the principle of distribution that emerges articulates a moral ideal rather than a rule of practical morality.

To flesh out our contractarian principle, we have to specify the features of the original position. These features are designed to make people represent their interests and resolve conflicts fairly so that an agreement in the original position constitutes a fair adjudication of their conflicting interests. Most contemporary versions of contractarianism assume that people in the original position are in realistic circumstances insofar as goods are scarce, and people are self-interested, so that competition arises. They also assume that social cooperation produces a net gain of benefits over burdens for each person so that all have an incentive to cooperate.[1] But the original position is usually taken to incorporate some idealizations as well. People are taken to be fully rational, free, equal, and impartial. Conditions for negotiation are taken to be perfect, in particular, communication is effortless and compliance with agreements is assured.[2] Self-interest and rationality motivate a person in the original position to pursue what is in his

---

1. Some forms of social cooperation produce net losses for some people. For example, cooperation for national defense results in the death of some members of society. So this assumption constitutes a restriction of contractarianism to forms of social cooperation that produce a net gain for all.

2. The general idea is that the original position is the closest possible world in which the conditions are met.

interest. Freedom and equality make his bargaining position fair. Perfect conditions for negotiation allow a fair settlement with others to emerge.

I will depart from the common specification of the original position in two respects. A contrarian explanation of principles of distributive justice is deeper going the fewer the moral qualities built into the original position. I will therefore exclude impartiality. The principle of distributive justice that I obtain is nonetheless impartial. But its impartiality is derived from principles of rational agreement and not built into the conditions of agreement.[3]

Secondly, I will suppose that agents in the original position are fully informed about the consequences of their agreement. Thus they choose in ways that are guided by the facts about their interests, and not just beliefs about them. Note that given full information, choosing a principle of distribution and choosing the distribution it yields amount to the same thing. There is no uncertainty about how the principle will apply.

Putting the preceding points together, and taking background points about competition and the like to go without saying, we obtain the following moral principle: the form of social cooperation should be one that people would agree upon if they were rational, fully informed, free, and equal. This principle is the moral foundation of our contractarianism. The other main component is a principle of rational agreement. I will present it in the following section.

2. BARGAINING THEORY

The members of a group of people can often cooperate in ways that benefit all. For cooperation to occur, however, they typically must agree upon a division of the benefits of cooperation. In such cases I say that the group has a bargaining problem. For example, the rules for an academic prize might stipulate that corecipients must agree upon a division of the prize money in order to receive any of it. Then corecipients face a bargaining problem.

Bargaining theory looks for the agreement it is rational to reach. If one person has a bargaining advantage, the rational agreement will favor him— and unfairly favor him if the bargaining advantage is unfair. The concern with rationality makes bargaining theory normative and part of philosophy. But bargaining theory is not part of ethics. It is only indirectly connected to

---

3. Many contractarians, e.g., John Rawls (1971, pp. 139–40), assume that impartiality or an equivalent is needed in order to assure that an agreement is reached in the original position. Without such a condition, they suppose that people would jockey for advantages endlessly, and never settle on any form of cooperation. This view may be justified given the classical analysis of problems of agreement. But in the following section I will present an alternative method of analysis that makes impartiality an unnecessary condition of agreement.

ethics via contractarianism's attempt to derive moral principles from rational agreement in the original position.

For simplicity, I will focus on bargaining problems for two people. My main claims about these cases generalize to cases involving any number of people. I also limit myself to bargaining problems where conditions for negotiation are ideal and all the agents are fully informed. These conditions are substantive, and not made just for the sake of simplicity. But results reached using these conditions carry over to the original position, since the same conditions obtain there.

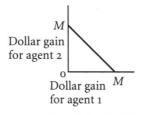

Figure 1. A Bargaining Problem

Consider a two-person bargaining problem about the division of a sum of money, say a million dollar prize. A diagram of the possible divisions of the money has the form given in Figure 1. The classical approach to a bargaining problem begins with a representation of the problem in utility space. Our two-person bargaining problem might have the representation in Figure 2. The line representing possible divisions of money might be curved in utility space because of the diminishing marginal utility of money. And it might be skewed because of differences in the rate of diminishing marginal utility. For simplicity, we will focus on bargaining problems whose utility representations have this sort of curved shape.

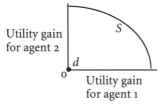

Figure 2. The Classical Representation of a Bargaining Problem

In Figure 2, S stands for the set of possible outcomes, and d stands for the outcome if bargaining breaks down, i.e., the disagreement point. For simplicity, we adopt the convention of setting the zero point for utility gains so that the origin represents the disagreement point.

Figure 3. Nash's Solution

The best known method of resolving bargaining problems is due to John Nash (1950). It says to adopt the intersection of the problem with the highest intersecting regular hyperbola ($x_1 x_2 = k$). (See Figure 3.) Ehud Kalai and Meir Smorodinsky (1975), and David Gauthier (1986, chapter 5) advance a rival proposal. It says to adopt the outcome of least equal relative concession from the ideal or "claim" point, i.e., the point at which each person obtains the maximum he can obtain in the problem (generally not a feasible outcome). (See Figure 4.)

The ideal point

Figure 4. Kalai and Smordinsky's, and Gauthier's Solution

The diagonal is a line of equal relative concession from the ideal point, and its intersection with the frontier of the bargaining problem is the outcome of least equal relative concession. In two-person cases, but not in general, the outcome of least equal relative concession is the same as the outcome of minimax relative concession. Gauthier proposes the latter as the solution to n-person bargaining problems.

These classical solutions to bargaining problems do not assume that utility scales are the same for each agent. They are insensitive to changes in an agent's utility scale. Although the utilities of outcomes for agents are depicted in the same diagrams, they are not taken to be interpersonally comparable in classical representations of bargaining problems.

Many attractive solutions to classical bargaining problems have been proposed. But there are objections to each.[4] And it is hard to choose among them. It appears that the classical representation of a bargaining problem underdetermines a solution. It leaves out features of bargaining problems that are important in resolving them. It is as if the classical representation of a problem presents the equation $x + y = 4$, and a classical solution proposes

---

4. For example, see Duncan Luce and Howard Raiffa (1957, pp. 128–34) for some criticisms of Nash's solution.

that x and y both equal 2—an attractive solution, but one underdetermined by the facts presented.[5]

Some writers suggest that solutions to bargaining problems should be obtained by taking account of features of bargaining problems that are not captured by their classical utility representations. Alvin Roth (1979, part 1) and Ariel Rubinstein (1982), for instance, suggest taking account of differences in bargaining power not depicted in the classical representation of a bargaining problem, e.g., differences in bargaining power arising from differences in sensitivity to the risk of negotiations breaking down, or to time pressure for reaching an agreement. And Philip Barnett (1983) argues that interpersonal utilities are needed to solve bargaining problems. He is led to this claim by bargaining phenomena such as the following. A shopper at a bazaar walks away from a stall where he has been haggling over an item. He wants the stall keeper to think he does not want the item very much. He hopes that the stall keeper will try to lure him back with a lower price. Some stall keepers have counterstrategies. They watch the eyes of a shopper. The greater the dilation of the pupils, the more the shopper wants an item, and the less the stall keeper will reduce its price. These strategies and counter-strategies suggest that interpersonal comparisons of utility play an important role in the way that rational people strike bargains.[6]

I adopt both suggestions about solving bargaining problems. I enrich their representations by including interpersonal comparisons of utility. And I introduce an explicit measure of the bargaining power of the individuals involved. Taking account of these additional features, a certain solution to bargaining problems clearly emerges.

The representation of interpersonal utilities is an easy addition. It requires only that the unit of utility be the same for each individual. The representation of bargaining power, on the other hand, requires some new

---

5. To make up for the deficiency of support for classical solutions, some authors, e.g., Lloyd Shapley (1969), introduce considerations of morality in addition to considerations of rationality. But given our contractarian objectives, we want the solutions to bargaining problems to rest exclusively on considerations of rationality.

6. A common objection claims that interpersonal utility has no influence on solutions to bargaining problems because rational agents act according to their personal utility assignments. But rational agents have beliefs about interpersonal utilities, and these beliefs influence their personal utility assignments, and hence influence their actions. For instance, consider the following case. A haggler walks away from a stall where he has made an unsuccessful pitch for an item. The stall keeper compares the haggler's intensity of desire for the item to the expected intensity of desire of other shoppers. He concludes that the haggler wants the item only a little in comparison to other shoppers. So he wants to offer a lower price to lure the haggler back, and acts on this desire. His beliefs about the interpersonal utilities of shoppers influence his personal utilities. And his personal utilities influence his behavior.

technical apparatus. For simplicity, I take bargaining power as the ability to obtain bargaining concessions. And I suppose that bargaining concessions are obtained by paying for them. Thus I take bargaining power as the ability to offer side payments for concessions. Also for simplicity, I assume that power is constant in a particular bargaining problem.[7] Power relations between agents can then be represented by lines in utility space indicating possible transfers of utility. (See Figure 5.) The slope of a power line represents the rate of utility transfers between agents 1 and 2. The steeper the slope, the more power agent 1 has with respect to agent 2, since the less it costs him to motivate agent 2. As indicated in Figure 5, by giving up one unit of utility, agent 1 can produce a two unit gain for agent 2. In this case agent 1 is twice as powerful as agent 2.

Figure 5. A Power Line

A power line runs through each point in the utility representation of a bargaining problem. It depicts the transfers of utility that could take place if the agents were to settle on the outcome represented by that point. The power lines all have the same slope. If agent 1 is twice as powerful as agent 2, as in our example, their slope is −2.

As the solution of a bargaining problem enriched by interpersonal utilities and a power structure, I propose the intersection of the set of possible outcomes S with the highest intersecting power line.[8] (See Figure 6.) Notice that as the power of agent 1 increases, the power line becomes steeper, and the intersection point moves along the boundary of the bargaining problem closer to the horizontal or x_1 axis so that the outcome is more favorable to agent 1, exactly as we would expect.

---

7. What happens when the simplifying assumptions about power are relaxed is an open question. Perhaps there are ways of generalizing the results obtained below. Or perhaps these results depend in an essential way upon the simplifying assumptions. In the latter case the assumptions must be justified as features of the original position, or else be treated as restrictions.

8. This solution, unlike the classical solutions, requires interpersonal utilities. First, the representation of power requires interpersonal utilities. Otherwise the transfer rates for utility would depend upon an arbitrary choice of utility scales. Second, the representation of the bargaining problem requires interpersonal utilities. Otherwise the location of the intersection point would depend upon an arbitrary choice of utility scales.

Figure 6. The Intersection Point

The argument for this solution is powerful. The intersection point is the only outcome of the bargaining problem that is Pareto optimal in light of the possibilities for side payments. In other words, it is the only outcome such that there are no alternatives that dominate it, i.e., the only outcome for which there are no alternatives where some agents do better and none do worse. Clearly, rational agents would agree upon this outcome.

To see that the intersection point is the unique Pareto optimal outcome of the bargaining problem, note that every bargaining outcome other than the intersection point is dominated by outcomes reached by moving to the point of intersection and having the gainer compensate the loser. In Figure 7, for example, the intersection point is u. Consider another outcome of the bargaining problem u'. Agent 1 loses in the move from u' to u, but agent 2 can compensate him by transferring utility so that after side payments the net result is u'', a result better than u' for both agents. This method of obtaining improvements for both agents is available given every bargaining outcome except u. Hence the intersection point u is the unique Pareto optimal outcome of the bargaining problem.[9]

Figure 7. Dominance via the Intersection Point

Given the overall bargaining situation, i.e., the bargaining problem and the power structure in which it is embedded, the intersection point is the unique Pareto optimal outcome of the bargaining problem. Rational people settle on it as the solution to the bargaining problem. But what is the final outcome of the entire bargaining situation? Are there any side payments after the intersection point is adopted as the solution of the bargaining problem? In particular, are side payments needed in order to provide incentives for the adoption of the intersection point? I have shown that the intersection point is the immediate outcome of the bargaining problem. But

---

9. In an n-person bargaining problem, the Pareto optimal outcome is the intersection of S with the highest intersecting hyperplane whose slope with respect to the axes for a pair of agents is the slope of a power line for that pair.

I have not shown that it is the final outcome of the bargaining situation after all side payments for bargaining concessions have been made. I have not shown that the final outcome is not some other point along the highest intersecting power line. To determine the final outcome, I need a principle of rational agreement in addition to Pareto optimality. I will appeal to a principle of symmetry.

In classical bargaining theory a common principle of symmetry says that if interchanging the agents does not change the representation of the bargaining problem, then the solution gives each the same amount of utility. In geometric terms, this principle says that if the representation of the bargaining problem is symmetrical about the 45-degree line through the origin, then the solution lies on the 45-degree line. (See Figure 8.)

Figure 8. Outcomes Permitted by the Principle of Symmetry

This principle stems from a general principle of symmetry that says that every advantage given an agent by the solution to a bargaining problem is justified by some advantage he has in his bargaining position. The general principle does not specify the type of justification required, but general principles of justification are assumed. So, for instance, if a certain advantage in bargaining position is taken account of by a certain advantage in the outcome, then any further advantage in the outcome is justified by some additional advantage in bargaining position. A corollary of the general principle of symmetry says that the solution to a bargaining problem does not give any agent an advantage if all agents have the same bargaining position. This corollary yields the classical principle of symmetry if it is granted that the classical representation of a bargaining problem is a complete representation of the bargaining positions of the agents so that symmetry about the 45-degree line implies equality of bargaining positions.

The general principle of symmetry is a principle of rational agreement that furnishes a link between rationality and morality. According to it, rationality imposes equity in certain circumstances. The main challenge for contractarianism is to obtain as much as possible from this link. I will use the general principle to derive a special principle of symmetry for our enriched bargaining problems. This special principle plays an important role in the argument for our utilitarian principle of distribution.

In one of our enriched bargaining problems, the agent with greater bargaining power gains an advantage in the immediate outcome of the problem. We showed that above. Should the final outcome accord other advantages? That is, should any agent receive an advantage in the final outcome that is not justified by bargaining power? Should the final outcome be more in his favor than the intersection point? Given Pareto optimality, this amounts to asking whether any agent should receive a side payment that moves him along the power line through the intersection point.

The general principle of symmetry says that any such additional advantage must be justified by some advantage in bargaining position besides bargaining power. But greater bargaining power is the only advantage in bargaining position that any agent has in our problems. There are no advantages in information since each is fully informed. And there are no advantages stemming from asymmetries in the utility representation of the problem. These asymmetries just do not provide any leverage, which is why classical bargaining problems are underdetermined.

Given equality in bargaining position apart from bargaining power, the general principle of symmetry requires that there be no advantages in the final outcome apart from advantages justified by differences in bargaining power. This means no advantages beyond what the intersection point gives, in other words, no side payments. Suppose, for instance, that in the situation depicted in Figure 7, agent 1 claims a side payment that would move the final outcome from the intersection point u to u''. He claims this side payment as compensation for having agreed to u rather than u' as the resolution of the bargaining problem. Agent 2 would then object that there is no reason to presume that negotiations start with u', and if they start with a point along the frontier of the bargaining problem above and to the left of u, they would end with u as the resolution of the bargaining problem and a side payment for him. In general, every argument that agent 1 should receive a side payment is countered by an analogous argument that agent 2 should receive a side payment.

The special principle of symmetry for our bargaining problems therefore says that if there is equality in bargaining position apart from bargaining power, then there are no side payments. This is a principle of limited symmetry, symmetry bargaining power aside. It follows from the general principle of symmetry given standard principles of justification and our claim that the absence of side payments constitutes equality aside from advantages justified by bargaining power. It rules out side payments in our bargaining problems given our claim that there is equality in bargaining position except for differences in bargaining power.[10]

---

10. We must be careful about what counts as equality in bargaining position and what counts as equality in bargaining outcome. Suppose, for instance, that someone proposes

Pareto optimality and symmetry therefore yield the intersection point as both the immediate outcome of the bargaining problem and the final outcome of the bargaining situation. Pareto optimality requires that the final outcome be on the highest intersecting power line. And symmetry requires that there be no side payments, so that the immediate outcome is also the final outcome. Since the only immediate outcome of the bargaining problem that is on the highest intersecting power line is the intersection point, it is the overall solution.

Now I shall show that the intersection point is a weighted utilitarian solution of the bargaining problem. Consider the following. In our bargaining problems the slope of a power line is the negative of the ratio of agent 1's power to agent 2's, that is, $-p_1/p_2$. Hence the equation of a power line is $x_2 = (-p_1/p_2)x_1 + k$, or $p_1x_1 + p_2x_2 = p_2k$, where p_2k is a constant. In other words, a power line is a locus of points having the same power-weighted sum of utilities, p_2k. Since p_2k is at a maximum for the highest intersecting power line, the intersection point maximizes the power-weighted sum of interpersonal utilities. That is, the intersection point maximizes the sum of utilities after weighting them according to power.

Weighted utilitarianism therefore solves our enriched bargaining problems. It provides a principle of rationality, not a principle of morality, since the solution it yields is unjust in cases where differences in bargaining power are unjust. Nonetheless, when it is applied in the original position, the solution it yields constitutes an ideal of morality. This is established in the next section. Weighted utilitarianism resembles other approaches to bargaining problems that introduce measures of bargaining power. For example, it resembles the asymmetric Nash solution and the risk sensitivity solution discussed by Alvin Roth (1979, part 1). And it resembles the time discounting solution presented by Ariel Rubinstein (1982). But unlike these solutions, weighted utilitarianism uses interpersonal comparisons of utility.

Weighted utilitarianism also resembles Lloyd Shapley's (1969) approach to cooperative games with transferable utility. The rates for transferring utility that he uses correspond to our ratios of bargaining power. The main differences are that he does not take interpersonal utility to be defined independently of a game's solution, and that he supports his solution with an equity condition, or principle of morality, as well as with an efficiency condition. John Harsanyi's (1955) proposal for social choice is similar to weighted utilitarianism. His proposal also uses sums of weighted utilities

---

equal relative concessions as equality in bargaining outcome. This would lead us to the Kalai-Smorodinsky solution in classical bargaining problems. Our characterizations of equality in bargaining position and outcome must be better supported than such rivals.

and is supported chiefly by efficiency. But Harsanyi's proposal does not involve interpersonal utilities or bargaining power. It involves personal utilities and envisages using the weights for utilities to put personal utilities on the same scale, and so obtain interpersonal utilities and standard utilitarianism. Finally, weighted utilitarianism closely resembles the method of resolving trading problems developed in general equilibrium theory. Power structures and interpersonal utilities in weighted utilitarianism have roughly the same function as initial endowments and prices in general equilibrium theory. The salient difference between the two theories is the type of problem addressed.

To extend weighted utilitarianism beyond the cases treated here and to increase the support for it, a number of things need to be done. For instance, when there are several outcomes that are Pareto optimal, as when the boundary of S is a straight line with the same slope as a power line, we have to say which Pareto optimal outcomes are solutions. I hold that they all are solutions, i.e., each is a rational outcome of the problem, although I will not defend this view here.

Also, we have to deal with cases where a splinter group or coalition can obtain benefits for its members without the cooperation of others. In such cases it might turn out that a coalition can do better on its own than under some Pareto optimal outcome. Then it has an incentive to block that outcome by withholding consent. It is even possible that for each Pareto optimal outcome some coalition has an incentive to block that outcome. Then it appears that no Pareto optimal outcome is stable, in particular, not the Pareto optimal outcome provided by weighted utilitarianism.

I propose to handle these cases by introducing a definition of stability according to which every bargaining problem has at least one stable outcome. Roughly, the definition says that an outcome is stable if and only if the opposition, if any, is itself opposed. This approach to stability is similar to the approach of Robert Aumann and Michael Maschler (1964). Under the new definition of stability, it turns out that the intersection point is a stable outcome of a bargaining problem even taking coalitions into account. See Weirich (1990) for further details.

Lastly, the method of argumentation we have used should be strengthened. We have supported weighted utilitarianism by principles of Pareto optimality and symmetry. The justification for these principles is the assumption that rational people will achieve Pareto optimality and symmetry given ideal conditions for negotiation. But the ultimate demonstration of the rationality of the weighted utilitarian outcome is a proof that this outcome follows from rational actions on the part of the individual bargainers. See Weirich (1991) for some progress in this direction.

3. UTILITARIANISM

Let us apply our contractarian principle in the light of our results about bargaining. First we reconstruct the original position, where bargaining about the form of social cooperation is imagined to take place. This position is hypothetical. All the ideal conditions of our bargaining problems are met in it. In particular, people are rational and fully informed, and conditions are perfect for negotiation. Also some moral desiderata are built in. People are free and equal, more specifically, equal in bargaining power. It follows from the previous section that people in the original position resolve bargaining problems by weighted utilitarianism, and given their equal bargaining power, that they resolve bargaining problems by standard utilitarianism. Hence they agree upon a form of social cooperation, an assignment of tasks and compensations, that produces a utilitarian distribution of net social benefits. According to our contractarian principle, the utilitarian form of social cooperation is the one that ought to obtain. It constitutes an ideal of distributive justice.

Our contractarianism has some advantages over alternatives found in the literature. John Rawls (1971, pp. 150–61) presents a contractarian argument for the difference and maximin principles of distribution. But his argument uses an original position that contains the veil of ignorance. This builds a form of impartiality into the original position and so weakens the explanatory value of the contractarian argument. And it rules out information to guide the selection of a form of social cooperation, so that without any particular justification risk becomes an important factor in its selection.

John Harsanyi (1953) presents a contractarian argument for rule utilitarianism. His argument also uses a veil of ignorance in the original position and thus introduces a form of impartiality that weakens the argument's explanatory value. Moreover, his argument for rule utilitarianism is weak since it relies upon a dubious principle of indifference or insufficient reason for obtaining probabilities, and since it assumes indifference to the source of one's satisfaction.

David Gauthier (1986, chapters 5 and 8) offers two contractarian arguments for a minimax relative concession principle of distribution. In the first he assumes a minimax relative concession solution to bargaining problems, a solution that is insufficiently supported. And in the second he adopts an impartiality condition for the original position, which weakens the explanatory value of his argument.

Robert Nozick (1974, part 1) offers a contractarian argument for a free-market form of social cooperation. He does not assume a veil of ignorance for the original position. But he does not assume full information either.

Hence people in the original position may agree upon a form of cooperation that turns out to have consequences that they would repudiate. Since their agreement rests on ignorance, it has dubious moral force. It does not represent a just adjudication of their conflicting interests.

I anticipate a number of objections to the utilitarian form of social cooperation. The first objection is that it exploits some members of society—it takes from the poor in order to give to the rich, or it takes from the rich in order to give to the poor. However, since the form of cooperation is agreed upon in the original position, it is not exploitative. Exploitation is an unfair suppression of someone's interest. The original position is a fair initial bargaining position, and the people in it are rational, self-interested, and fully informed. Since they agree upon a utilitarian form of cooperation, that form of cooperation does not exploit them. It gives due consideration to the interest of each.

The second objection is that utilitarianism makes supererogatory acts obligatory. This objection does not apply to our principle of cooperation, however, since it specifies what ought to be the case. It does not specify the obligations of any individual. It expresses a moral ideal rather than a standard of right action for individuals.

The third objection is that the quantitative interpersonal utilities that utilitarianism demands usually do not exist. This is clearly a problem for the application of our principle to actual societies. The principle cannot be applied with precision unless the quantities it requires exist—and, we concede, they often do not. However, even when the quantities the principle requires are missing, it serves as a guide to distributive justice. It generates comparative principles that place limits on the permissible forms of social cooperation, just as the classical utilitarianism of Bentham generates comparative principles that place limits on the permissible forms of punishment.

The last objection is that utilitarianism violates moral rights. The reply to this objection depends upon the moral rights alleged to be violated. Let us first consider the claim that a utilitarian form of social cooperation violates moral rights to the benefits of social cooperation. To begin a rebuttal, we point out that the only moral rights to social benefits are rights obtained under a form of social cooperation. None is independent of the form of social cooperation, as, for instance, a person's moral right to his tax refund is not independent of the tax laws. There are moral rights that are independent of the form of social cooperation, for example, the right to subsistence. And in virtue of such moral rights members of society may be obligated to use a portion of the benefits of social cooperation to assist an outsider in need. But the needy outsider does not then have a right to a share of the benefits of social cooperation. If he did, he would have a right to a share even when his needs can be met with natural resources rather than the benefits of social cooperation—and this is counterintuitive.

Since rights to social benefits depend upon the form of social cooperation, and since our utilitarian principle recommends a form of social cooperation, the principle does not violate rights to social benefits; it helps to lay them down. Given a utilitarian form of cooperation, a member of a society who performs an assigned task has a moral right to the compensation assigned to its performance. But the utilitarian principle in no way conflicts with this right.

One complication is the possibility that a society adopts a nonutilitarian form of cooperation. Then under that form of cooperation people will have entitlements that do not produce a utilitarian distribution. It may seem that our utilitarian principle says that those entitlements ought to be disregarded. But it does not. It only expresses an ideal for social cooperation. It does not say how conflicts between the ideal and entitlements under another form of cooperation should be resolved. In particular, it does not say that they should be resolved in favor of the ideal. So the principle does not violate the moral rights to social benefits that people have in virtue of such entitlements.

Next let us consider cases where the moral rights alleged to be violated are ones that obtain independently of the form of social cooperation, say, rights to subsistence. Suppose, for instance, that some outsider will die unless given some of the benefits of social cooperation. Does our utilitarian principle deny him the benefits he ought to receive? No, for two reasons. First, although the utilitarian form of social cooperation leads to a particular distribution of net social benefits in the original position, that distribution need not be the end result of that form of cooperation in the real world. Since people are differently motivated in the real world and in the original position (where they are assumed to be completely self-interested), the distribution achieved in the original position is unstable in the real world. Although the distribution is final in the original position, it is only an initial distribution in the real world. Our utilitarian principle says what the form of social cooperation should be. But it does not say that people may not exercise the entitlements they have under that form of cooperation in ways that change the distribution of net social benefits. In particular, there is nothing in the principle that discourages their using the goods to which they are entitled to fulfill obligations to help the needy.

Secondly, as already mentioned, our utilitarian principle of distribution expresses an ideal, not a principle of practical morality. When the ideal conflicts with moral rights, practical morality requires the ideal to give way.

Thus when an outsider's right to subsistance is in conflict with the utilitarian form of social cooperation, our principle does not lead to a violation of the outsider's right.

Part III

Self-Interest

11

The Reconciliation Project[*]

Gregory S. Kavka

Clarifying the nature of the relationship between ethical and self-interested conduct is one of the oldest problems of moral philosophy. As far back as Plato's *Republic*, philosophers have approached it with the aim of reconciling morality and self-interest by showing that moral behavior is required by, or at least is consistent with, rational prudence. Let us call this undertaking the Reconciliation Project. In modern times this project is generally viewed as doomed to failure (see, e.g., Sidgwick 1907; Prichard 1928, pp. 4–25; Phillips 1968; and Narveson 1967, pp. 263–65). It is believed that unless we make an outdated and implausible appeal to divine sanctions, we cannot expect to find agreement between moral and prudential requirements.

Can this negative verdict on the Reconciliation Project be avoided? Before we can deal with this question, we must distinguish among versions of the project along four dimensions. The *audience* dimension concerns to whom our arguments about coincidence of duty and interest are addressed. Sometimes it is supposed that a successful version of the Reconciliation Project must be capable of converting to virtue a hardened cynic or immoralist such as Thrasymacus. This is too much to ask. Immoralists are not likely to understand or appreciate the benefits of living morally, nor are they usually the sort of people who will listen to, or be swayed by, abstract rational arguments (cf. Nozick 1981, pp. 406–11). A more modest aim is to speak convincingly to the puzzled ordinary person, such as Glaucon, who fears that in following the path of morality he is being irrational and is harming himself, but who is willing to listen to and ponder arguments to the contrary. We shall here be concerned with versions of the Reconciliation Project having this more modest aim.

* This paper originally appeared in D. Copp and D. Zimmerman, eds., *Morality, Reason, and Truth: New Essays in the Foundations of Ethics,* © Rowman and Allanheld, 1984, and is used by permission.

A second dimension concerns the sort of *agent* for whom morality and self-interest are supposed to coincide. Versions of the Reconciliation Project that are ambitious along this dimension might attempt to demonstrate such coincidence in the case of all actual human beings, or even all possible human beings. More restrained versions would concentrate on more limited classes, such as persons without severe emotional disturbances or persons capable of self-assessment and love for others. The audience and agent dimensions of the Reconciliation Project are related. If one's aim in pursuing the project is to create or strengthen moral motivation, one would normally choose an agent class that just encompasses one's audience, so as to convince one's listeners that it pays them (promotes their own interests) to be moral, while at the same time exposing one's argument to the fewest possible objections. But if one aims at promoting theoretical understanding, one's agent class may be broader or narrower than one's audience. One may, for example, seek to convince reflective persons of goodwill that it pays everyone to be moral. Agent and audience classes need not even overlap; one might argue to sophisticated theorists that morality pays for the unsophisticated, who could not be expected successfully to disguise their immoralities.

The third dimension of the Reconciliation Project is the social one. Whether morality pays is partly a function of others' responses to one's immoralities. Are morality and prudence supposed to coincide, then, in all imaginable social environments, all feasible ones, all (or most) actual ones, some feasible ones, or some imaginable ones? Different answers to this question yield importantly different versions of the Reconciliation Project.

Fourth and finally, if we say that morality and prudence coincide, does this mean that (i) each individual ethical act is prudent or (ii) that there are sufficient prudential reasons for adopting a moral way of life and acting in accordance with moral rules? This question concerns the nature of the objects or entities to be reconciled and calls attention to the object dimension of the Reconciliation Project. Reconciling all particular acts of duty with prudence is so unpromising a task as to have been largely shunned by the major philosophical exponents of the project. (Although, as we shall see below, much depends on whether prudential evaluations of acts are undertaken prospectively or retrospectively.) Thus Plato argues the prudential advantages of moral dispositions or ways of life, while Hobbes focuses on providing a prudential grounding for moral rules.

Taking note of the object dimension allows us to clarify the Reconciliation Project by answering a preliminary objection to it. According to this objection, the project must fail because supposedly moral actions are not really moral if they are motivated by prudential concerns. We may, however, accept this observation about motivation and moral action without damaging the Reconciliation Project properly construed. For that project is not committed to morality and prudence being identical, or to moral and prudential motives or reasons for action being the same. Rather, prudence and morality are supposed to be reconcilable in two senses. They recommend the same courses of conduct (where conduct is described in some motive-neutral way). Further, it is consistent with the requirements of prudence to adopt and live a moral way of life, even though this involves developing a pattern of motivation in which nonprudential considerations play an important role.[1] Thus the Reconciliation Project survives the preliminary objection because it concerns, along its object dimension, acts or rules of action or ways of life, rather than motives or reasons for action.

Still, the Reconciliation Project is hopeless if we adopt very stringent interpretations of it along most or all of its four dimensions. We cannot expect to convince a clever immoralist that it pays everyone to act morally on every specific occasion in any sort of society. But why should we consider only such extreme versions of the project? Taking account of the dimensions of variation of the Reconciliation Project, I propose instead to discuss some less extreme versions (and modifications) of it to see to what extent they can be carried out and why they fail when they do. In the course of this investigation, I hope partly to vindicate the rationality of being moral and to clarify further the relationship between morality, prudence, and rationality.

I begin by sketching a Hobbesian version of the Reconciliation Project that presupposes psychological egoism and relies exclusively on external sanctions (social rewards and punishments) to reconcile obligations and interest. This Hobbesian approach provides considerable illumination, but it suffers from serious defects. To correct some of these, I consider the significance of internal (self-imposed psychological) sanctions.[2] Next, I take up the two most intractable objections to all forms of the project. These concern the obligation to die for others, and those duties owed by members of strong groups to members of weak groups who are apparently not in a position to reciprocate benefits bestowed on them. Finally, I note how the recognition of nonegoistic motives transforms the Reconciliation Project. Throughout, my remarks are largely programmatic. I sketch alternatives, problems and general strategies for solving problems and leave much detail to be filled in later. I hope nonetheless to say enough to show that the Reconciliation Project is still philosophically interesting and important.

---

1. See the discussion of the paradox of self-interest in § 11.
2. I borrow the internal/external sanction terminology from Sidgwick.

I. THE HOBBESIAN STRATEGY[3]

As a starting point, let us consider Hobbes's version of the Reconciliation Project. In seeking to reconcile duty and interest, Hobbes is limited by two self-imposed restrictions: He rules out appeal to religious sanctions, and he leaves no place for internal sanctions (such as guilt feelings) in his account of human psychology. Hence, Hobbes is reduced to arguing his case solely in terms of external sanctions; that is, social rewards and punishments. He does, however, marshal these relatively meager resources to good advantage.

The core of Hobbes's view is that the general rules of conduct that a farsighted prudent man concerned with his own survival, security, and well-being would follow are essentially the rules of traditional morality. The function of these rules is to promote peace, cooperation, and mutual restraint for the benefit of all parties. The rules therefore forbid killing, assault, and robbery, and they require keeping one's agreements, settling disputes by arbitration, providing aid to others when the cost to one is small and the benefit to them is large,[4] and so on. The self-interested individual, if sufficiently rational and farsighted, will follow these rules because doing so is the best (and only reliable) way to ensure peaceful and cooperative relations with others. The person, for example, who wastes on luxuries what others need to survive is not likely to be helped by others if he later falls into want; nor will his person and property ever be safe from the desperate acts of the needy. The dangers of hostile reactions by others that confront the habitual assailant, thief, or contract-breaker are even more obvious. And while people may try to conceal their violations of moral rules, the long-run dangers of exposure and retaliation by others are great.[5] Thus, argues Hobbes, morality is superior to immorality as a general policy, from the viewpoint of rational prudence.

One may agree that normally morality is a more prudent general policy than immorality but raise doubts about its prudential rationality in two special circumstances: when one is confident that a violation would go undiscovered and unpunished, and when others are not willing to reciprocate restraint. In the first case, it appears that one would benefit by offensively violating moral rules; that is, by not complying with them when others are complying. In the second case, prudence seems to call for a defensive violation—for noncompliance motivated by the belief that others

---

3. I further discuss some of the issues raised in this section in Kavka 1983a.

4. This aid principle is inferred from Hobbes's explanation of his fifth law of nature requiring mutual accommodation; see 1651/1958, p. 125. On Hobbes's belief in the welfare state, see also p. 271.

5. See Silberman 1978, pp. 75–78, where it is argued that virtually all career criminals end up in prison at some time.

are not complying and the desire not to put oneself at a disadvantage. Hobbes recognizes and attempts to deal with both cases.

Hobbes's argument against offensive violations of moral rules is presented in his famous reply to the Fool (1651/1958, pp. 120–22). He acknowledges that such violations will in some cases turn out, in retrospect, to best serve the agent's interests. But because they risk serious external sanctions (such as the withdrawal of all future cooperation by others[6]), they are never prospectively rational. Since the consequences of failure are horrible and the chances of failure are not precisely calculable, it is not a rational gamble to offensively violate moral rules. Underlying this Hobbesian argument is an intuition about rational prudence that is reflected in the usual connotation of the word "prudence." To be prudent is to play it safe and not take large, uncontrollable risks. It is not implausible to suppose that rational pursuit of one's own interests requires being prudent in this sense when one's vital interests are at stake.

To develop this point, let us follow decision theorists in drawing a distinction between choices under risk and under uncertainty. In the former cases, one has reliable knowledge of the probabilities that the various possible outcomes would follow the different available courses of action. In choices under uncertainty, one lacks such knowledge. Rawls contends that rationality requires that, when making vitally important choices under uncertainty, one follow a Maximin Strategy—choose the act with the best worst outcome (1971, pp. 152–58). I have argued elsewhere for using a Disaster Avoidance Strategy in such circumstances—choosing the alternative that maximizes one's chances of avoiding all unacceptable outcomes.[7] Both strategies favor playing it safe in the sense of aiming at avoidance (or minimization) of the risk of unacceptable outcomes.

Now suppose we view choices among actions in the real world as made under uncertainty. (This is plausible for the most part, given our limited understanding of the complex factors that determine the consequences of our actions.[8]) If, as Hobbes suggests, offensive violators risk the application of serious external sanctions, offensive violations would be irrational according to both the Maximin and Disaster Avoidance viewpoints. For the offensive violator accepts, under uncertainty, an unnecessary (or greater

---

6. By treating the loss of the primary social reward of morality—the goodwill and cooperation of others—as the main punishment for immorality, Hobbes implicitly takes account of both the positive and the negative external sanctions of morality.

7. Kavka 1980; a similar view is hinted at in Fishkin 1979, pp. 34 and 149 (n. 17). To employ the Disaster Avoidance Strategy, ordinal knowledge of the relevant probabilities is required.

8. See, however, the second objection discussed at the end of this section.

than necessary) risk of suffering disastrous consequences. So if either Rawls's analysis of rational prudential choice under uncertainty or my own is correct, Hobbes's argument against offensive violations under uncertainty is largely vindicated.

The considerations just presented attempt in effect to reconcile the requirements of morality and prudence as applied to (a certain class of) particular actions. They may serve, that is, as part of a Reconciliation Project focusing along the object dimension on acts. They function ever more effectively as part of an argument for the coincidence of rules of morality and prudence. We can imagine someone claiming that living by some rule such as the following would better serve one's interests than following moral rules: "Follow the moral rules except when you believe (or confidently believe) you can get away with violating them." But if one lives by this sort of rule, one is likely to undergo the risks inherent in offensive violations on a good number of occasions. And even if one is cautious in selecting the occasions, the risk of getting caught and suffering serious sanctions on one or more occasions will be substantial and much greater than the chance of getting caught on one particular occasion. Hence, insofar as rational prudence requires avoiding or minimizing risks of suffering serious sanctions, it would not recommend a policy of clever "compromise" between moral and immoral conduct as exemplified in this rule.

We have seen that Hobbes tries to reconcile duty and prudence in the case of offensive violations by denying that such violations are prudential. The opposite tack is adopted for defensive violations. These, Hobbes claims, are not contrary to moral duty. Agents are not obligated to follow the constraints of traditional morality unless others are reciprocating their restraint. To comply with moral rules unilaterally is to render oneself prey to others, and this, Hobbes urges, one is not required to do (1651/1958, pp. 110, 130).

The governing principle of Hobbesian morality, then, is what I call the Copper Rule: "Do unto others as they do unto you." This principle enunciates a less glittering moral ideal than the familiar Golden Rule, which requires us to treat others well regardless of whether they treat us well in return. In thus opting for a reciprocal rather than unilateral interpretation of moral requirements, is Hobbes abandoning traditional morality?

To answer this question, we must distinguish between two aspects of morality—practice morality and ideal morality. Practice morality encompasses the standards of conduct actually expected of, and generally practiced by, persons living within a given moral tradition. It is roughly the part of morality concerned with requirements, those standards for which people are blamed, criticized, or punished for failing to live up to. Ideal morality refers to standards of moral excellence that a tradition sets up as models to aspire to and admire. Praise, honor, and respect are the rewards of those who live by its higher, more demanding standards. But, in general, people are not blamed for falling short of such ideals, or even for not aiming at them.

Now there surely are important strands of unilateralism in the ideal morality of the Western tradition. The Golden Rule, the admonition to love thine enemy, and the principle of turning the other cheek, all concern treating well even those who do not reciprocate. But if we turn to practice, and the standards of conduct that are actually treated as moral requirements, we find Copper Rule reciprocity to be a reasonable summary of much of what we observe. For practice morality allows us considerable leeway to engage in otherwise forbidden conduct toward those who violate moral constraints, especially when this is necessary for protection. Thus individuals may kill in self-defense, society may deprive criminals of their liberty, contracts may be broken when reciprocal fulfillment cannot be expected, and so forth.

We may then, without committing Hobbes to absurdity, attribute to him the claim that, in practice, traditional moral rules contain exception clauses allowing for defensive "violations" of the main clauses of the rule, if these are aimed at other violators.[9] In adopting this pruned-down conception of moral requirements, Hobbes has abandoned the ambitious dream of achieving a reconciliation between ideal morality and prudence. But he has avoided one telling objection to the Reconciliation Project: that morality requires us (as prudence does not) to sacrifice our interests to the immoral, who will be all too ready to take advantage of such a sacrifice. Note, however, that the companion objection that morality sometimes requires us to sacrifice our interests for others who are moral is not dealt with by the Copper Rule interpretation of morality. Forms of this objection will be considered later (§§ III and IV).

As we have seen, Hobbes treats offensive and defensive violations of moral rules quite differently. In the former case, he reconciles prudence to morality by altering cynical interpretations of what prudence demands, while in the latter case he reconciles morality to prudence by offering a nonstandard interpretation of morality. Yet in each case he draws our attention to the oft-neglected social dimension of the Reconciliation Project. His discussion of defensive violations suggests that under certain conditions—anarchy or general noncompliance with traditional moral rules—moral and prudential requirements coincide, but only as a result of the effective loosening or disappearance of the former. Hence, how duty and interest are reconciled is a function of the social environment. In arguing for

---

9. For application of this idea, see Kavka 1983b.

the imprudence of offensive violations of moral rules, Hobbes presupposes threats of external sanctions that are serious enough to make such violations a bad gamble. Therefore, his argument does not apply to imaginary situations in which society rewards immoral actions, or even certain real ones in which it ignores serious immoralities when they are committed by members of some privileged groups.

Suppose, then, that our aim is to reconcile prudence with traditional moral requirements (without the exception clauses); that is, do not kill or steal, aid the needy when the costs are small, and so on. Hobbes suggests that this reconciliation is possible only in a certain sort of social environment—one we may call punitive. In a punitive environment, serious violations of moral norms are sought out, apprehended, and given stiff punishments frequently enough to make immorality a bad prudential risk. As a result, there is general compliance with moral rules and little need for one to undertake defensive violations. In a punitive social environment, offensive violations of moral rules are irrational and defensive ones are unnecessary. If an actual social environment is punitive, the Reconciliation Project seems to have succeeded with respect to it. And if such an environment is feasible but nonactual, those who wish people to act morally but fear the distracting influence of self-interest will have some reason to create it.

Let us now briefly summarize the Hobbesian approach to the Reconciliation Project, which is based on external sanctions. It consists first of proposing specific interpretations of that project along two of the four dimensions. With respect to the object dimension, it focuses on rules or policies rather than on individual acts (although the reply to the Fool fits within an act version of the project as well). And it presupposes a punitive social environment, avoiding the dubious claim that duty and interest coincide in any social context. Further, it provides a novel interpretation of moral requirements—the Copper Rule or reciprocal interpretation—and it rests on a "playing it safe" theory of rational prudential choice under uncertainty. All of these aspects of the Hobbesian strategy make contributions to the interpretation and development of the Reconciliation Project. None is without plausibility. However, there are two fatal objections that the Hobbesian Strategy cannot adequately answer.

The first concerns punitive social environments. These are beneficial in discouraging immoral conduct, but they have costs. To render immorality a bad risk solely via threats of punishments, such punishments must be made very heavy and/or very probable. In a society of significant size, doing the latter would normally require a massive policing establishment with large monetary costs (borne by the citizens), interferences with personal liberty and privacy (searches, eavesdropping, surveillance), and dangers of police power and influence over the political and economic institutions of society. Heavy penalties also have social costs—monetary costs of supporting prisons, lessened chances of reconciliation between offenders and society, dangers of gross injustice if the innocent might sometimes be punished, and so on. In short, we must accept trade-offs between various things that we value and the deterrence of serious immorality. And it may not always be possible for society, by use of external sanctions alone, to ensure that "crime does not pay" without sacrificing too much in the way of individual liberty, privacy, and protection from excessive state and police power.

Our second objection concedes that immorality generally does not pay, and even allows, that immorality is prudentially irrational under genuine uncertainty. However, some opportunities for immoral gain may present themselves under risk; that is, the probabilities of detection and punishment may be reliably known. In these situations, maximizing expected personal utility is arguably the most rational course, and this may imply engaging in an offensive violation. A slumlord, for example, may have relatively precise statistical data that allow him to estimate reliably the odds of his getting caught and punished if he hires a professional arsonist to burn one of his buildings so that the can collect the insurance. If the chances of arrest and conviction are low and the return is high, the crime may have positive expected value for him, and it will be prudentially rational for him to undertake it. The rules of a system of rational self-interest will be formulated to allow agents to take advantage of such situations.

These two objections reveal that while external sanctions alone can take us, via the Hobbesian Strategy, some considerable way toward reconciling duty and interest, they cannot take us far enough. We at least need some device other than a punitive social environment that can alter the calculations or dispositions of the slumlord and other potential criminals. The obvious candidates here are internal sanctions, psychic structures that punish immorality and reward virtue. Unlike external sanctions, these are relatively free of problems concerning evasion and detection, since one's conscience follows one everywhere,[10] and they do not threaten privacy and democracy as do secret police forces. In the next section, I will explore how their inclusion may extend and strengthen the Hobbesian arguments for the coincidence for morality and prudence.

---

10. This claim may be qualified to take account of self-deception and related phenomena without greatly affecting my argument.

II. INTERNAL SANCTIONS

Internal sanctions come in two varieties, negative and positive. The negative sanctions are guilt feelings and related forms of psychic distress that most of us are subject to feel when we believe we have done wrong. We develop the tendency to experience such feelings under such circumstances as part of the socialization process we undergo in growing up. It is no mystery why society nurtures and encourages the development of this tendency; it benefits others to the extent that it inhibits or deters misconduct by the individual. And once one possesses the tendency, it imposes extra—and relatively certain[11]— costs on immorality, costs which may tip the prudential balance in favor of restraint. Arson may not be the most rational option for our slumlord, for example, if in addition to prison he risks, with high probability, significant guilt feelings over endangering the lives of tenants or over cheating his insurance company. With internal sanctions operating along with external sanctions in this way, the social environment need not be so punitive to keep serious immorality within tolerable limits.

There is no entirely satisfactory label for the positive internal sanctions, the agreeable feelings that typically accompany moral action and the realization that one has acted rightly, justly, or benevolently. So let us opt for the vague term "the satisfactions of morality."[12] Moral people have long testified as to the strength and value of such satisfactions, often claiming that they are the most agreeable satisfactions we can attain. This last claim goes beyond what is necessary for our purposes. All we need to assert is that there are special significant pleasures or satisfactions that accompany regular moral action and the practice of a moral way of life that are not available to (unreformed) immoralists and others of their ilk.[13] For if this is so, then the forgoing of these potential satisfactions must be charged as a significant opportunity cost of choosing an immoral way of life.

---

11 This is important because experts say that in achieving deterrence, the certainty of a sanction is generally more important than its severity; see e.g. Von Hirsch 1976, pp. 61–63.

12. There may be other satisfactions that are incompatible with the psychological structure of the immoralist's mind. For example, Richmond Campbell (1979) argues that immoral egoism is incompatible with self-respect and genuine love of oneself. If this is so, these satisfactions (or the chance to obtain them) may be included as "satisfactions of morality," and their loss may be regarded as an opportunity cost of living an immoral life.

13. Are there compensating special satisfactions of the immoral life that are not available to the moral individual? Without discussing cases of obvious psychopathology, we might consider the pleasures of, for example, being strong and independent or outsmarting others. It seems, however, that all of these pleasures are available within the context of various moral lives, since being moral does not rule out being strong and independent, outsmarting others, and so on.

Can an individual have it both ways, enjoying the psychic benefits of morality while living an immoral life? He could, perhaps, if he lived immorally while sincerely believing he was not. Certain fanatics who selflessly devote themselves to false moral ideals, such as purifying the human race by eugenics or pleasing God by destroying nonbelievers, might fall in this category. Of more concern in the present context, however, is the individual who adopts morality as a provisional way of life or policy while planning to abandon it if a chance to gain much by immorality should arise later. This person, we would say, is not truly moral, and it is hard to believe that he would perceive himself to be, so long as his motives are purely prudential and his commitment to morality is only conditional. In any case, we would not expect him to experience the satisfactions of morality in the same way, or to the same degree, as the genuinely moral individual who is aware of the (relative) purity of his motives and the nature and depth of his commitment.

Note that if this is so we have arrived at a paradox of self-interest: being purely self-interested will not always best serve one's interests. For there may be certain substantial personal advantages that accrue only to those who are not purely self-interested, such as moral people. Thus it may be rational for you, as a purely self-interested person, to cease being one if you can, to transform yourself into a genuinely moral person.[14] And once you are such a person, you will not be disposed to act immorally, under risk, whenever so doing promises to maximize personal expected utility.

The lesson of this paradox, and the opportunity cost of being immoral, does not apply, though, to those (if any) who are no longer capable of learning to enjoy the satisfactions of living a moral life. Further, some people may still be capable of developing an appreciation of these satisfactions, but the transition costs of moving to this state from their present immoral condition may outweigh the advantages gained. For people such as these, especially those who are immune from guilt feelings, the prudential argument for being moral must essentially rest on external sanctions. And with respect to some individuals, such as hardened but cautious immoralists or clever psychopaths, the argument may fail.

Thus we must acknowledge a restriction of the Reconciliation Project along its agent dimension. It is too much to claim that it pays one to be moral, irrespective of one's psychological characteristics. Rather, the argument from internal sanctions supports the prudential rationality of

---

14. Moralists should not be too comforted by this argument. For somewhat analogous arguments suggest that the abandonment of morality may be called for in certain imaginable circumstances; see Kavka 1978b.

living a moral life for the two classes of people constituting the vast majority of humankind: First, those who are already endowed with conscience and moral motivations, so that they experience the satisfactions of living morally and are liable to suffering guilt feelings when they do wrong. Second, those who are capable of developing into moral persons without excessive cost—immoralists who are not fully committed to that way of life, and children.

Should we be dismayed that the Reconciliation Project may not encompass, along its agent dimension, those incapable of enjoying the satisfactions of morality? This depends upon our aims in pursuing the project and the audience to whom its arguments are addressed. Insofar as our aim is to reassure the ordinary good man that he is not harming himself by being moral, or to encourage parents who want to do the best for their children to give them moral education, we need not worry. And if we seek theoretical illumination, we achieve more by recognizing the variations along the agent dimension than by denying it. Only if our aim were the hopeless one of convincing dedicated immoralists to be moral, by using rational arguments, would we be in difficulty. Am I confessing, then, that we are helpless in the face of the immoralist? No, we are not helpless in the practical sense, for we can use external sanctions to restrain immoralists. Nor should we perceive an immoralist's gloating that it does not pay him to be moral (because the satisfactions of morality are not for him) as a victory over us. It is more like the pathetic boast of a deaf person that he saves money because it does not pay him to buy opera records.

III. THE ULTIMATE SACRIFICE

We have seen how the recognition of internal sanctions allows us to deal with two objections that undermine the Hobbesian external-sanctions approach to the Reconciliation Project. Two difficult objections remain, however, even when internal sanctions are taken into account. The first is that morality sometimes requires the sacrifice of one's life, and this cannot be in one's interests. The second is that morality requires powerful groups to treat weak groups fairly and decently, while it better serves the interests of the powerful group's members not to do so.

The objection concerning death runs as follows. In certain circumstances, morality requires of us that we give up our lives to protect others. We are bound by obligations of fair play, gratitude, and perhaps consent to fight in just wars of national defense. Fulfilling these obligations costs many people their lives. Extreme situations can also arise in civilian life in which morality requires one to accept one's own death. If gangsters credibly threaten to kill me unless I kill an innocent person, I must refrain. If I am a loser in a fair and necessary lifeboat lottery, I am morally bound to abide by the outcome. If half of the expedition's necessary food supply is lost as a result of my recklessness, I must be the first to agree to go without food on the long return trip so that others may survive. And so on. In each of these cases, however, self-interest seems to counsel taking the opposite course. Where there is life there is hope, and even if the likely cost of saving my life is to suffer severe internal and external sanctions (such as imprisonment, depression, and guilt for the military deserter) that cost must be less than the premature loss of my life, since such loss would deprive me of all future enjoyments and frustrate all of my main plans and desires.

In response to this objection, let us first note that there are fates worse than death. And for some people, living with the knowledge that one has preserved one's life at the cost of the lives of others, the sacrifice of one's principles, or the desertion of a cause one loves may be such a fate. In addition, society is aware of the heavy value that people place on the continuation of their own lives and typically responds by using heavy sanctions to encourage appropriate life-risking behavior in defense of society. Thus infantry officers may stand behind their own lines and shoot those who retreat, thereby rendering advance a safer course than retreat (see Brennan and Tullock 1981). (Even if advance is virtually suicidal, death with honor at the hands of the enemy may be a lesser evil than death with dishonor at the hands of one's own officers.) On the positive side, those who risk or lose their lives in battle are often offered significant rewards by fellow citizens—medals, honors, praise, and material compensation for themselves or their families.

The upshot of this is that in a substantial number of cases the sacrifice of one's life for moral ends may be consistent with the requirements of prudence because it constitutes the lesser of two extreme personal evils. It would, however, be disingenuous to suggest that this is so in most, much less all, cases. Officers cannot shoot all deserters or retreaters, nor are courts likely to sentence to death those who cheat in lifeboat lotteries.[15] And relatively few are so committed to morality that they could not eventually recover, at least partially, from the negative psychic effects of abandoning principle to preserve their lives. So we must concede that self-interest and morality will frequently, or usually, recommend divergent courses of action when there is a stark choice between immoral action and certain death.

Does this concession destroy the Reconciliation Project? Only if we have in mind a version of the project that focuses, along the object dimension, on acts. If instead we consider, as we have been, whether adopting the moral

---

15. See the report on the United States v. Holmes lifeboat case of 1842 in Davis 1966, pp. 102–18.

way of life is consistent with prudence, the answer may well be different. In adopting or pursuing a moral way of life, we are, it is true, running a risk of sacrificing our lives imprudently. For the requirements of morality may sometimes call for us to give up (or risk) our lives. And if we do develop the habits and dispositions appropriate to moral life, we are likely (or at least more likely than otherwise) to live up to these requirements at the cost of our lives, if we find ourselves in appropriate circumstances. Notice, however, that in assessing this risk and weighing it against the advantages of the moral life, we must consider how likely we are to find ourselves in such circumstances.

Now this depends, in turn, on our view of what the substantive rules of morality require of us. If they demand that one right all wrongs and fight all injustices anywhere at any time with all the means one possesses and regardless of the personal cost, the likelihood that one would be morally obligated to lay down (or seriously risk) one's life at some time or another is obviously large. But surely on any reasonable conception they require much less than this. Perhaps you are obligated to give up your life (i) to protect your country in a just war; (ii) to protect those to whom you owe special duties of protection (your children, or your passengers if you are a ship's captain); (iii) to protect those you owe immense debts of gratitude (your parents); (iv) to avoid seriously violating the rights of innocent others (as in the gangster threat situation); (v) to save others from dangers that your misconduct, recklessness, or negligence has created; (vi) to keep important agreements you have made (such as accepting employment as a bodyguard); or (vii) to save the lives of large numbers of innocent people when you are the only one who can do so. And perhaps there are other specific duties of sacrifice that I have left off this list. But as a whole, the duties are limited to special and quite unlikely circumstances. (Military service is the only seriously life-endangering required activity that is at all likely to confront a significant segment of the population. Presumably such service is morally obligatory only if the war is just, which frequently is not the case. Further, in most wars the percentage of those serving who are killed is rather low.)

Now if the chances are small that you will ever confront a situation in which you are morally obligated to surrender your life it may well pay you to adopt a moral way of life, even if doing so increases the likelihood that you would sacrifice your life in such a situation. For the relatively certain external and internal benefits of the moral life should far outweigh the very unlikely loss of one's life. Further, it is worth noting that many immoral lifestyles—crime, debauchery, deception of all those around you—may have much higher premature death rates than the moral life. Insofar as adoption of a moral way of life ensures that you will not lapse into one of these alternatives, it may even on balance increase your life expectancy.[16]

The argument, then, is that adopting a moral way of life carries at most a very small net risk to one's life. Since it provides significant benefits with high probability, it is a reasonable prudential choice.[17] It is useful in understanding this argument to compare adopting a moral way of life with two other activities that are not generally thought to be imprudent: joining the military and entering into a long-term love relationship, such as by marrying or having children. These undertakings are like becoming moral in the main respect relevant to our argument. They are likely to involve or produce changes in one's motivational structure that would render one more likely to risk or sacrifice one's life in certain circumstances, such as when your loved ones or comrades in arms are in danger. (In addition, military service carries a nonnegligible risk of finding yourself in precisely these circumstances.) But this feature of these undertakings is not usually thought to render them ineligible choices from a prudential perspective. Why, then, should the same feature render becoming moral a generally imprudent course of conduct? This activity, like entering a long-term love relationship, promises very large external and internal rewards while involving a relatively tiny risk of loss of life. The gamble is hardly more foolish in the case of virtue than in the case of love.

IV. GROUP MORALITY

Human beings, as has often been remarked, are social creatures. We need one another for a variety of practical and emotional reasons—for help in securing satisfaction of our material needs, for physical protection, for companionship, for love, and so on. The above arguments that duty and interest coincide all rest on this fact. Individuals need the help rather than the hostility of society to prosper, and in the process of social learning they internalize norms of conscience that further fuse their interests with those of the social group. However, one does not require the aid or cooperation of all others, only of a sufficient number of those with whom one is likely to come in contact. This fact generates the most telling objection to the

---

16. If it does not, then the decrease in life expectancy, together with the other costs of the moral life (such as lost opportunities to cheat), must be added together and compared to the benefits of the moral life. The decrease, if any, in life expectancy seems unlikely to be great enough to tip the prudential balance against the moral way of life.

17. This follows from the expected value principle if we treat the choice as one under risk. If we regard the choice as under uncertainty, we can obtain the same result by applying the Disaster Avoidance Principle. For rejecting, rather than adopting, the moral life is more likely to lead to an unacceptable outcome, such as imprisonment or ostracism.

Reconciliation Project: That it is not in the interests of powerful groups and their members to treat decently and to help, as morality demands, the members of weak groups, who are apparently not in a position to return good for good and evil for evil (see Boxill 1980).

It is clear that when we consider relations among groups, our earlier tools for reconciling interest and obligation cannot be used in the same way. External sanctions operate effectively, to the extent they do, because it is in the general interest of society and its members to restrain individuals from harming others. But if there is a split between groups in society, there may be no effective sanction against members of a dominant group harming members of a powerless group. For the others in the dominant group may condone, or even approve, such conduct, while members of the powerless group are too weak to punish the offenders. And if the norms of the dominant group allow, or even encourage, mistreatment of the powerless group—as throughout history they often have—even well-socialized members of the dominant group may carry out such mistreatment without suffering substantial guilt feelings.

This objection shows that there cannot be a satisfactory solution to the Reconciliation Project if the project is strictly interpreted along the social and degree dimensions. That is, we cannot hope to show that in all historically actual (much less all conceivable) social circumstances it has been (or would be) in the interests of all groups and their members to act morally toward members of other groups.[18] Instead, particular cases of supposed divergence of group duty and interest must be considered on an ad hoc basis, and the most we can reasonably aspire to is the presentation of arguments that make it plausible that obligation and interest coincide in actual present circumstances. This will not ease the anxiety of moralists who seek a noncontingent guarantee that interest and duty will never diverge. But it could suffice to convince the attentive moral individual, or group leader, that he or she is not being foolish in acting morally, or in leading his or her group in a moral direction.

Before discussing the three most important specific instances of the objection before us, it should be pointed out that whether there is hope of reconciling group interest and duty depends on what we take the demands of duty to be. In the case of individuals, we saw that a unilateralist-idealistic interpretation of moral requirements might render the Reconciliation

---

18. In certain cases immoral conduct might conceivably be in the interest of an oppressed group; for example, if terrorism is the only way of ending the oppression. These cases raise special problems about the morality of revolutionary violence and will not be discussed here.

Project impossible. Similarly, if we interpret morality as requiring rich and powerful groups to share so much with the poor and weak as to create absolute equality, there is very little prospect that duty and interest can be reconciled. But it is far from obvious that morality demands this much. What morality does clearly require is that the rich and powerful refrain from actively harming the poor and the weak, and that the former aid the latter when the costs of giving are small and the benefits of receiving are large. We shall see that with this modest interpretation of the obligations of the powerful, reconciling their obligations with their interests may be possible.

Let us turn to our examples, the first concerning justice within a society. Why should rich and powerful groups in a nation allow the poor opportunities for education, employment, and advancement and provide social-welfare programs that benefit the poor as morality requires? Why shouldn't they simply oppress and exploit the poor? There are several reasons why, in modern times, it is most probably in the long-term interest of the rich and powerful to treat the domestic poor well. First, some rich individuals, and more likely some of their children, may be poor at some time in the future and thus benefit from programs to help the poor. Second, offering opportunities to members of all groups widens the pool of talent available to fill socially useful jobs, which should provide long-run economic benefits to members of all groups.[19] Third, and most important, there is the reason that has impressed social theorists from Hobbes to Rawls: decent treatment of all promotes social stability and cohesion and discourages revolution.[20] This reason is especially important in contemporary times, when ideals of human dignity, equality, and justice are known and espoused virtually everywhere, and when revolution is frequently proposed as a legitimate means of attaining such ideals.

Taken together, these reasons constitute a strong case, on prudential grounds, for decent treatment of the domestic poor by a nation's dominant groups. In fact, if we apply Disaster Avoidance reasoning, it turns out that the third reason alone shows that good treatment of the poor is prudentially rational. For if the poor find the status quo unacceptable and apply such reasoning, they will revolt. Thus Hobbes writes, "Needy men and hardy, not contented with their present condition,…are inclined to…stir up trouble and sedition; for there is no… such hope to mend an ill game as by causing a new shuffle" (1651/1958, p. 87). The rich, being aware of this, will (if they

---

19. This argument is the liberal counterpart of the conservative "trickle-down" theory, which claims that direct benefits to the rich will indirectly benefit the poor.

20. Rawls 1971, § 29; Hobbes 1651/1958, p. 87 (quoted in text below), and p. 126. Psychological and statistical evidence supports this traditional view, with some qualifications (for example, rapid progress for poor groups can produce instability); see Gurr 1970.

follow a Disaster Avoidance strategy) seek to prevent the poor from falling into such unacceptable circumstances. For the rich thereby maximize their chances of obtaining an outcome acceptable to them: preservation of something resembling the status quo.

What about a wealthy and powerful nation aiding poor, weak nations? Is this in the long-run interest of the former as well as the latter? In a world of advanced technology, international markets, ideological conflicts among powerful nations, and nuclear weapons, it most probably is. In competition with other powerful nations, allies—even poor nations—are useful for political, economic, and military reasons. And economic development of poor nations should, in the long run, produce economic benefits for richer nations, such as by providing markets and reliable supplies of various raw and finished goods.[21] Most important, continued poverty in the Third World is likely to produce continued political turmoil, civil wars, and regional wars between nations. In a world armed to the teeth with nuclear weapons, and with more and more nations acquiring such weapons, the long-run danger of rich developed countries being drawn into a devastating military conflict started by a desperately poor nation, or some desperate group within such a nation, is far from negligible.

The above arguments about domestic and international justice suggest there is, after all, a form of reciprocity between powerful and weak groups because of interdependencies between the two in economic and security matters. The poor cannot return the aid of the rich in kind, but they can offer their talents, their purchasing power, and so on. If not treated well, they cannot directly punish the rich and powerful, but they can stir up serious trouble for them if they are willing to experience such trouble themselves. Thus they are able, and likely, to return good for good and evil for evil to the rich in the long run, and it will be rational for the rich to act accordingly.

Even this form of reciprocity is not available, however, to deal with our third and most puzzling example—the treatment of future generations.[22] Future generations (beyond the next few) are powerless to act upon us, since they will not exist until after we are dead. Yet we have substantial power to determine the quality of their lives by influencing their numbers and the nature of the social and natural environment into which they will be born. Given this absolute asymmetry in power to affect one another, how can it be in our interest to act morally toward future generations? Morality

---

21. This claim should be qualified by noting that worldwide development without environmental safeguards might be disastrous; see Meadows et al. 1972.

22. As is pointed out in Barry 1978.

requires us, at a minimum, to leave our descendants with enough resources to allow future people to live decent lives. But this would necessitate having a lower material standard of living than we could obtain by depleting resources and contaminating the environment whenever it is convenient to do so. If future generations cannot punish us for ruthlessly exploiting the earth in this way, doesn't rational prudence require it of us?

The supporter of the Reconciliation Project can come some considerable way toward answering even this objection. He might point out first that misuse of resources and damage to the environment will often produce substantial negative effects within our own lifetimes. So, for the most part, it is in our own interests to follow conservation policies that will turn out to benefit future generations. This reply will take us only so far, however. For there are policies whose benefits are experienced now and most of whose costs will be borne generations later (such as building nuclear power plants without having solved the long-term waste storage problem). Also, optimal rates of use of scarce nonrenewable resources will vary greatly depending upon how long we care about the resources lasting. Hence, there is a far from perfect overlap between the resource and environmental policies likely to most benefit present people and those likely to ensure a decent life for future generations.

A more promising argument begins from the fact that most people care very deeply about the happiness of their own children and grandchildren, and hence their own happiness would be diminished by contemplating the prospect of these descendants having to live in a resource-depleted world. Further, they realize that their children's and grandchildren's happiness will in turn be affected by the prospects for happiness of their children and grandchildren, and so forth. Hence, the happiness of present people is linked, generation by generation, to the prospects for happiness of some likely members of distant future generations. This "chain-connection" argument has considerable force, but it falls short of constituting a full solution to the problem before us. This is because the perceived happiness of one's children and grandchildren is only one component of the well-being or happiness of the typical parent. And the perceived happiness of their children and grandchildren is, in turn, only one component of the happiness of one's children and grandchildren. So there is a multiplier effect over generations that quickly diminishes the influence on a present person's happiness of the prospects for happiness of his later descendants.[23] And we

---

23. We can illustrate this point using arbitrarily chosen and artificially precise numbers. Suppose that my happiness is half dependent upon my perception of my children's well-being and half dependent on other independent things, and that I assume

must seek some other device to link living peoples' interests firmly with those of distant future generations.

The most promising such device is an appeal to our need to give meaning to our lives and endeavors. I have suggested elsewhere that one strong reason we have for providing future people with the means to survive and prosper is that this is our best hope for the successful continuation of certain human enterprises that we value (and may have contributed to)— science, the arts and humanities, morality, religion, and democratic government.[24] Similarly, Ernest Partridge (1981) has argued that human beings have a psychological need for "self-transcendence"; that is, a need to contribute to projects that are outside themselves and that will continue after their deaths. Those without such goals are unlikely to find meaning in their lives, especially during the middle and later stages of life, when people typically reflect on their own mortality. Thus Partridge says, "We need the future, now" (1981, p. 217).

There is a great deal of truth in this argument, but there are some limits to what it can show. It cannot reconcile the interests and obligations to posterity of the narcissist who has no self-transcending goals and is incapable of developing them. However, this need not worry us anymore than did the corresponding remark made earlier about the person no longer capable of becoming moral. The self-transcending life may be the happier life for the vast majority who still can live it, and these people have good prudential reasons for doing so. The more important problem is that not all self-transcending concerns need be directed toward the distant future. They may involve goals that do not extend much beyond one's lifetime (such as the prosperity of one's children, or the eventual rise to power of one's favorite political movement). Such goals may give meaning to one's life without supplying reasons to provide for the welfare of distant generations. Perhaps, though, it is a psychological fact that enterprises that promise to continue into the indefinite future are better able to provide meaning in our lives, or to provide consolation for our mortality.[25] If so, there would be powerful prudential reasons for one's adopting self-transcending concerns of unlimited temporal scope, and for protecting the social and natural environments for future generations.

---

the same will be true of them and their children, and so on. Then one-quarter of my happiness will be determined by the prospects of my grandchildren, one-eighth by the prospects of my great grandchildren, and so forth.

24. See Kavka 1978a, § IV, where I discuss reasons for wanting the continuation of the species, but some of the same points apply to assuring future people decent lives.

25. The fact that most of us do care a good deal about the future survival and prosperity of humankind may constitute evidence that this is so.

These are the best arguments I can think of for a coincidence of self-interest and our obligations to posterity. Many (including myself at times) will find them only partly convincing. Does this lack of complete conviction indicate that we should abandon the Reconciliation Project? No. Instead, we may broaden our interpretation of that project.

V. THE WIDER PROJECT

The general strategy I have followed in outlining a defense of the Reconciliation Project has been to restrain the project's ambitions where necessary. Thus the scope of the project has been narrowed in several ways. It applies to ways of life rather than particular actions and to practice morality rather than ideal morality. It succeeds with respect to most people and groups in actual social circumstances, but not with respect to all people and groups in all actual or possible circumstances. It may not convince the skeptical immoralist to change his ways, but it provides good reasons for moral people not to regret (or abandon) their way of life and for loving parents to raise their children to be moral.

However, to understand better the relationship between morality, rationality, and self-interest, we must briefly consider an important widening of the Reconciliation Project. For that project may be viewed as but a specific instance of a more general project: reconciling morality with the requirements of practical rationality. Given two special assumptions—the truth of psychological egoism and the interpretation of practical rationality as the efficient pursuit of the agent's ends (whatever they may be)[26]—this Wider Reconciliation Project would collapse into our original version concerning morality and self-interest. But the first of these assumptions is surely false; on any construal that does not render all motives self-interested by definition, people do sometimes have unselfish aims and possess and act upon non-self-interested motives. As a result, the question of whether moral requirements are consistent with the rational pursuit of the actual ends that people have is both distinct from and more important than the question of whether these requirements cohere with the demands of prudence.

---

26. This is a standard conception adopted by economists, social scientists, and philosophers such as Rawls 1971, pp. 142–46, and Richards 1971, p. 28. One could follow Richard Brandt (1979) in rejecting some ends as irrational and still maintain the links described below between the original project and the Wider Reconciliation Project, given the plausible assumption that many of our self-interested ends (such as security and material well-being) are rational in the relevant sense. These links would be severed, however, and the Wider Reconciliation Project trivialized, if we adopted Thomas Nagel's (1970) view that practical reasons are by nature general and not agent-relative.

Would shifting our focus to the Wider Reconciliation Project render irrelevant all we have said about the original project? If self-interested concerns played only an insignificant role in human motivation, it would. But clearly this is not the case. In fact, while psychological egoism is false, I would venture to propose that a milder doctrine, which I call predominant egoism, is probably true. Predominant egoism says that human beings are, as a matter of fact, predominantly self-interested in the following sense. At least until they have achieved a satisfactory level of security and well-being, people's self-interested concerns tend to override their other-regarding, idealistic, and altruistic motives in determining their actions. Further, those nonselfish concerns that are sufficiently powerful to move people to acts that seriously conflict with self-interest tend to be limited in scope, such as to the well-being of family and friends and the advancement of specific favored projects or institutions.[27]

Now if it is true that people are predominantly self-interested, in this sense, many or most of their strongest motives and dearest ends are self-interested ones. And the above arguments about reconciling duty and interest will be highly relevant to the task of reconciling duty and the rational pursuit of people's actual ends. But in carrying out this Wider Reconciliation Project, there would be a new resource to appeal to—the altruistic and nonselfish ends that most everyone actually has to some degree. The presence of these ends may extend the range of cases in which the requirements of reason and morality coincide beyond those in which prudence and morality coincide.

Consider again our relationship to future generations. Most of us do have significant nonselfish concerns about the well-being of our children and grandchildren and the survival and prospering of the human species.[28] So we have reason to provide for these things over and above the contribution that our awareness of such provision makes to our own psychic well-being.[29] This further strengthens both the chain-connection

---

27. For historical antecedents of predominant egoism, see Hume 1739/1968, III, 2, ii (pp. 488–89, 494–95); and Mill 1869, p. 225.

28. This is acknowledged even by Thomas Schwartz (1978, § 4), who argues that we have no obligations to distant future generations to promote their welfare.

29. I am here relying on a distinction, noted by critics of psychological hedonism, between desiring that X occur and experiencing pleasure at the thought X will occur. To take an example, I purchase life insurance because I desire that my family be provided for after my death, not because I seek the peace of mind of now knowing that they will be provided for, although the latter is also a predictable and expected result of my action. This action contributes to the fulfillment of two of my ends: the safeguarding of my family's future after my demise and the attainment of peace of mind for me now. It is thus more likely to be rational for me (that is, worth the cost in terms of foregoing fulfillment

and self-transcendence arguments for reconciling practical rationality with our duties to posterity. For it shows that in carrying out such duties we are fulfilling ends of ours not previously considered (that is, nonselfish ends) in addition to contributing to our own happiness.

The recognition of nonselfish ends also provides a fresh perspective on the sustenance of moral motivation over generations. We suggested earlier that parents seeking to promote their children's interest would have good reasons to raise their children to be moral. This suggestion would have little significance if we were operating upon an assumption of the truth of psychological egoism. (For then the only relevant question would be whether it is in a parent's interest to raise his or her children to be moral.) Since, however, concern for the well-being of one's children is among the strongest and most universal of non-self-interested human concerns, the suggestion is crucial to our understanding of how morality is rationally passed on from generation to generation. Typical parents who care strongly for the well-being of their children and care somewhat for the well-being of others have three significant reasons for raising those children to be moral: This will likely benefit the children (in accordance with our earlier arguments that being moral usually pays), it will likely benefit others who are affected by the children, and it will likely benefit the parents themselves (because their children will treat them better). And when children grow up as moral beings possessing consciences and the potential to experience the satisfactions of morality, it is, we have argued, almost always in their interest to continue to live a moral life. Further, they, as parents, will have the same reasons for raising their children to be moral as their parents had for raising them in this manner. Thus morality can be seen to be potentially self-sustaining from generation to generation, without even taking into account socializing influences on the child from outside the family.[30]

In raising children to be moral, and in providing for future generations, some of the ends that we seek to achieve are non-self-interested ones. Given the content of moral rules and their connection with protecting the interests of others, many morally required actions will satisfy ends of this kind. As a result, the Wider Reconciliation Project should be successful in more cases than the original project. We may restate this crucial point: While it is normally prudent to be moral, it is sometimes rational to be moral even if it is not prudent.

---

of other ends I could use the insurance premium money to forward) than if peace of mind were the only of my ends achieved thereby.

30. These outside influences may be necessary, however, because many parents do not know how to raise their children to be moral, or they are unwilling to make the necessary sacrifices to do so, or they are unconvinced that being moral is in their children's interests.

12

A Breakthrough in the Desire Theory of Welfare*

Brad Hooker

Mark Overvold's main publications make a profound contribution to moral thought.[1] They improve the prevailing philosophical theory of a central concept in ethics. Overvold's publications did three things: (i) they showed that the prevailing philosophical theory of self-interest (or personal welfare, or individual utility) needed serious revision; (ii) they supplied the needed revision; and (iii) they explained the implications of all this for attempts to answer the question "Why should I be moral?"

The theory of welfare or utility that has been dominant among philosophers and economists in the second half of the twentieth century has been the *desire-fulfillment theory* (the desire theory, for short). According to the desire theory, our lives go well in self-interested terms, our own utility is maximized, to the extent that our desires are fulfilled. Such a theory takes into account the *number* of our desires that get fulfilled, *how long* they last, and their *relative importance to us*. Further, some variants of the theory focus on our *actual* desires, while other—to my mind superior—variants instead focus on what we would desire if we were reasoning soundly and vividly aware of all relevant empirical facts. But these and other complications can be ignored here. Most contemporary utilitarians—e.g., J. J. C.

* A version of this paper appeared as "Mark Overvold's Contribution to Philosophy" in the *Journal of Philosophical Research* 16 (1991: 333–44). I am grateful to John Heil, Penelope Mackie, Frederick Stoutland, and Thomas Carson for helpful suggestions.

1. His personal life was equally admirable. Sublimely good natured, he enjoyed a great number of close friendships. Furthermore, although his discovery at age forty that he had inoperable cancer must have brought with it a considerable temptation to become self-absorbed, he was astoundingly unselfish and courageous throughout the nine weeks between diagnosis and death. Keeping that up must have been a struggle—even for him. The way he dealt with his own tragedy was thus an outstanding moral achievement.

Smart (1973), R. M. Hare (1981), John Harsanyi (1977), James Griffin (1986), Peter Railton (1986), and Shelly Kagan (1989)—have embraced the desire theory in one or another of its incarnations. So have leading contemporary contractualists—e.g. John Rawls (1971) and Gregory Kavka (1986). Indeed it is the "received view" among welfare economists (see Brandt 1982, p. 170).

For utilitarian theories, getting straight the nature of utility is of obvious theoretical importance. How can we set out to maximize utility until we know what utility is? Likewise, any theory committed to equality of welfare will need an account of welfare, or utility. Moreover, any theory (like W. D. Ross's) that lists a number of fundamental moral principles among which is a principle of beneficence will need an account of utility, because we cannot know what doing good for others is until we know what would constitute a benefit to them. And even many libertarian theories, which do not require us to do good for others, may need an account of welfare. For many of these theories include a principle of reparation requiring us to compensate those we harm by making them no worse off than they were before we harmed them. Clearly, proponents of such theories need an account of additions to, and diminutions of, someone's welfare.

There is a further advantage in getting straight what the best account of utility or welfare is. Getting this straight can also help us to figure out which moral theory is most plausible. Utilitarianism in particular can seem more or less plausible depending on what conception of utility is in play.

So, given the importance of obtaining the best possible account of personal utility or welfare, what is the problem Overvold found with the prevailing account, the desire theory? The problem is that it does not leave enough room for self-sacrifice. Overvold's (1980) argument is as follows.

P_1 On the desire theory of individual welfare, an act maximizes an agent's welfare if and only if it fulfills the agent's strongest desires.

P_2 An act can be an act of self-sacrifice only if it does *not* maximize the agent's welfare.

C_1 Thus, on the desire theory of individual welfare, an act can be an act of self-sacrifice only if it does *not* fulfill the agent's strongest desires.

P_3 An act is not an act of self-sacrifice unless it is voluntary.

P_4 An act is not voluntary unless it is caused by the agent's desires.

C_2 Thus, an act is not an act of self-sacrifice unless it is caused by the agent's desires.

P_5 An act is not caused by an agent's desires unless it is caused by the agent's strongest desires. (How could it be the case that the agent's weaker desires overpower his or her stronger desires?)

C_3 Given C_2 and P_5, an act is not an act of self-sacrifice unless it is caused by the agent's strongest desires.

C_4 Given P_3, C_3, and C_1, the only way, on the desire theory, for an act to be an act of self-sacrifice is for it (i) to be voluntary, (ii) to be caused by the agent's strongest desires, and yet (iii) fail to fulfill the agent's strongest desires.

P_6 The only way for an act to have that combination of features is if the agent is mistaken about which act will best fulfill his or her strongest desires.

P_7 The concept of self-sacrifice is such that if the agent fails to maximize her or his welfare *by mistake*, the act is not an act of self-sacrifice.

C_5 Thus, on the desire theory, there cannot be any acts of self-sacrifice.

P_8 Any theory of individual welfare ruling out the very possibility of self-sacrifice cannot be the correct theory.

C_6 Given C_5 and P_8, the desire theory cannot be correct.[2]

The target of Overvold's objection is a version of the desire theory that holds that your welfare or self-interest is a function of only your *present* desires: if your present desires get fulfilled, your welfare is maximized, no matter how much the fulfillment of your present desires frustrates your future desires. We might call this version *the present desire theory of welfare*. Overvold's objection goes through against this kind of desire theory.

There is another version of the desire theory, however, that does not discount future desires merely because of their futurity. This version holds that future desires that will be stronger or last longer than your present desires count for more than the present desires. Let me call this version *the atemporal desire theory of welfare*.[3] Because this theory gives direct weight to future desires, it makes room for self-sacrifice in cases in which your strongest present desires conflict with even stronger or longer lasting desires you will have later. Acting on your strongest present desires in such a case will be against your long-term self-interest.

Now, as theories of self-interest or individual welfare, the atemporal desire theory is much more plausible than the present desire theory.

---

2. A. K. Sen (1976, § 2) puts forward a similar argument against "revealed preference theory."

3. Does the atemporal theory count the fulfillment of *past* desires? Distinguish between desires about the future that are conditional on their own persistence and desires about the future that are not conditional on their own persistence. An example of a desire that is conditional on its own persistence is my desire in the morning to have dessert at dinner. A desire that is not conditional on its own persistence is my desire that I never try to advance my career by treachery. Arguably, we should count the fulfillment of past desires that were not conditional on their own persistence. (This distinction and the example about the desire for dessert appear in Bricker 1980; see pp. 389–90.)

Suppose Elaine is a seventeen-year-old who cares not one bit about what happens to her after thirty. And suppose that she at seventeen most wants the immediate thrills of some drug, even though she knows it will have debilitating and even lethal side-effects and that she will later greatly regret her decision to take the drug. To say that Elaine's further future has no place in the calculation of her self-interest or welfare unless she now cares about it is highly counterintuitive. If people are temporally extended beings, to fix the welfare of a temporally extended being by reference to the desires of only one time-slice of the person is deeply misguided. Therefore, I will set aside the present desire theory in favor of the atemporal desire theory.

Although the target of Overvold's objection was actually the present desire theory, his objection can be easily amended so that its target is the atemporal desire theory. As I indicated, the atemporal desire theory allows that self-sacrifice can occur when you act on your present desires even though you see that this act will cause other desires you will have later to go unfulfilled. Overvold's argument against the atemporal desire theory would be that it too does not make enough conceptual room for self-sacrifice. For an act might be one of self-sacrifice even when the agent acts on his or her strongest desires and does *not* have stronger or longer lasting later desires that oppose his or her present desires.

To make room for this possibility, we must modify or abandon the desire theory. Overvold argues we should modify it by restricting the desires counted by the desire theory in the following way: the only desires the fulfillment of which directly benefits me are my desires for states of affairs in which I am an essential constituent (see Overvold 1982). Examples of desires for states of affairs in which I *am* an essential constituent are my desires that I have pleasant experiences, that I have certain kinds of relationships with people, that I know the truth about important matters, that I have a good reputation, that I have a certain kind of character, and that I triumph over my rivals. The fulfillment of any of these desires would constitute a benefit to me, on Overvold's revised desire theory. Examples of desires for states of affairs in which I am *not* an essential constituent are my desires that a stranger on the train recover from her illness, that democracies work better, that Michigan's team beat Michigan State's, that suffering be minimized, that justice be done, and that the Loire valley never be turned into a parking lot. The fulfillment of any of these would not directly benefit me, according to Overvold's revised desire theory.

Overvold pointed out, however, that the fulfillment of such desires might nevertheless benefit the agent *indirectly.* The clearest way in which this can happen is as follows. One of my desires is that I experience pleasure. This is a desire for a state of affairs in which I am an essential constituent.

So, on Overvold's revised desire theory, the fulfillment of my desire that I get pleasure does directly benefit me. Suppose that another of my desires is that a certain social campaign succeed. This is a desire for a state of affairs in which I am not an essential constituent. So the fulfillment of my desire that that social campaign succeed would not benefit me *directly*. But it could benefit me *indirectly*, in that its fulfillment could bring me pleasure.

Consider now some attractions of Overvold's proposal. The first attraction is that it solves the problem Overvold identified with the desire theory. The problem was that the desire theory did not leave conceptual room for self-sacrifice other than in cases in which the agent sees that her or his future desires will conflict with her or his present ones. Overvold's theory leaves plenty of room for self-sacrifice even when the agent's desires do not change over time: only a subset of the agent's desires are directly relevant to his or her self-interest.[4] So there is the possibility of self-sacrifice whenever what would best fulfill *all* the agent's desires added together is not what would best fulfill the *subset* made up of the agent's desires for states of affairs in which she or he is an essential constituent. Here is one of Overvold's own examples. There is a father whose strongest desire is that his children have the education needed to lead rewarding lives. The only way this father can get his hands on the money for the needed education is to kill himself so that the children will have his life insurance money. He acts on his strongest desire and kills himself. His children then use the money wisely and acquire the education they need to lead rewarding lives. The man got what he wanted, but what he wanted was not in his self-interest. And Overvold's theory accounts for this possibility. The man's desire that his children get the education needed to live rewarding lives was not a desire for a state of affairs in which the man himself was an essential constituent. So the fulfillment of that desire did not directly benefit him.

A second attraction Overvold claimed for his revision of the desire theory concerns psychological egoism. One would have thought the psychological egoist's claim that one always does what is best for oneself is an empirical claim about human motivation, a claim that in fact we always act on desires for things *for ourselves*. And that is just what Overvold's revised desire theory would suggest the psychological egoist would say. The revised desire theory claims that the desires directly relevant to self-interest are ones for states of affairs in which the agent is an essential constituent. We would expect a psychological egoist to claim that every agent always acts

---

4. Again, Overvold's own theory actually points to a subset of the agent's *present* desires, but suppose it is amended so as not to discount future desires.

on desires for his or her own happiness, knowledge, achievement, etc., (i.e., on desires for states of affairs in which the agent is an essential constituent).

A third attraction of Overvold's theory is that it can explain how acting on unselfish motives can be in one's self-interest. Recall my earlier example about deriving pleasure from the fulfillment of one's desire that a certain social campaign be successful. Suppose that, acting on your strong altruistic desire that this campaign be successful, you devote much of your free time and energy to it, and that your contribution to the campaign turned out to be the deciding factor in its success. Now your motivation was unselfish—you did what you did for the sake of the cause. Nevertheless, you later derived so much satisfaction from seeing the success of the campaign that in fact your having acted so as to bring about its success maximized your own welfare. For you got more satisfaction from seeing the campaign succeed than you would have if you had instead devoted your time and energy to some other activity.

A fourth attraction of the revised desire theory is that it dovetails nicely with recent arguments that the implications of utilitarianism are much more attractive if what are called "external preferences," that is, preferences about things other than one's own life, are ignored in calculations of utility. A perennial problem with utilitarianism is that, because some people have preferences about how other people's lives go, total preference satisfaction might be maximized by rules withholding rights we think everyone should have. This problem can be sidestepped if utilitarians take the position that such external preferences are to be given no direct weight.[5] But some people might think that this position lends little credibility to utilitarianism, if the utilitarians' only reason for taking it is that it enables utilitarianism to avoid counterintuitive implications about right and wrong. Further, utilitarians should feel very uncomfortable if they are identifying utility (welfare) with the net fulfillment of all desires and then distinguishing between that and what is to be maximized (the net fulfillment of some more limited set of desires). Can one turn one's back on the maximization of utility and still be a utilitarian? But neither Overvold's objection to the desire theory of utility nor his proposed revision of that theory is derived from *moral* intuitions. He comes up with the objection and proposed revision by thinking about self-interest, individual welfare, utility—not morality. And if he is right about how the desire theory should be revised, utilitarians have a principled rationale for giving no direct weight to desires about how others' lives go,

---

5. For some general discussion of this matter, see Mill 1859/1956, § 4; Smart 1973; Harsanyi 1977; see also Dworkin 1977, pp. 234, 275, 357; Dworkin 1981; Gibbard 1988; Harsanyi 1988; and Vallentyne 1991.

the rationale being that the fulfillment of those desires is not part of self-interest, or utility. And this conclusion allows utilitarians to maintain the connection between utility and what is to be maximized.

I want now to take up some objections to Overvold's proposal. Overvold's proposal was that the only desires fulfillment of which directly counts for the agent's self-interest are ones for states of affairs in which the agent is an essential constituent, in the sense that the agent's existing at time t is a logically necessary condition of the state of affair's obtaining at t. Richard Brandt (1979, p. 330) and Gregory Kavka (1986, p. 41) have objected that this makes irrelevant to self-interest such desires as the desire for posthumous fame. The state of affairs of my being famous after I die can obtain without my existing at that time. Overvold rejected this objection about the desire for posthumous fame. His view was that "it is hard to see how anything which happens after one no longer exists can contribute to one's self-interest" (1980, p. 108). Even if while alive I have a desire that I be remembered and respected after my death, how can the coming about of the desired posthumous state of affairs benefit me? How can something benefit me after I am gone?

Many people share the intuition that, unless there is life after death, one's welfare is impervious to events after one's death; but not everyone is convinced of this. Consider Derek Parfit's discussion.[6] First he gives us the case of the exile.

> Suppose that I try to give my children a good start in life. I try to give them the right education, good habits, and psychological strength....I am now in exile, and I shall never be able to learn what happens to my children. Suppose that, unknown to me, my children's lives go badly. One finds that the education I gave him makes him unemployable, another has a mental breakdown, another becomes a petty thief. If my children's lives fail in these ways, and these failures are in part the result of mistakes I made as their parent, these failures in my children's lives would [by the desire theory] be judged to be bad for me. One of my strongest desires was to be a successful parent. What is now happening to my children, though it is unknown to me, shows that this desire is not fulfilled. My life failed in one of the ways in which I most wanted it to succeed. Though I do not know this fact, it is bad for me, and makes it true that I have had a worse life.

Then Parfit suggests that the desires of the dead are like those of the exile. He says that, if, because of mistakes he made as a parent, his children have wretched lives *after he is dead*, his life turns out to have been a failure in one of the ways he cared about most. He wants it to be true, even after he is dead, that he was a successful parent. He writes:

---

6. Parfit 1984, p. 495; but see also Feinberg 1980, pp. 173–76.

It is irrelevant to my desire whether it is fulfilled before or after I am dead. [Desire theorists] count it as bad for me that my attempts fail, even if, because I am in exile, I never find out they fail. How then can it matter whether, when my attempts fail, I am dead? All that my death does is to *ensure* that I will never know this. If we think it irrelevant [in the case of the exile] that I never know about the non-fulfillment of my desires, we cannot defensibly claim that my death makes a difference.

I cannot add anything new to the debate about whether fulfilling people's desires after they are dead benefits them. But I can point out that a small modification of Overvold's revised desire theory of welfare will enable it to countenance posthumous benefits. Overvold said that the desires directly relevant to self-interest are the ones for states of affairs in which the agent is an essential constituent in the sense that the states of affairs *logically cannot exist at time* t *without the agent's also existing at* t. We might modify this so that the relevant desires are the ones in whose propositional content the agent is an essential constituent in the sense that the state of affairs *is desired under a description that makes essential reference to the agent.* By this criterion, desires such as the desire that *I* be influential (or posthumously famous) or the desire that *I* have been a good parent count, though events after my death can determine whether or not such desires will be fulfilled.

Let me pause here to stress the significance of Overvold's published work. The desire theory is the prevailing theory of self-interest, or welfare. Overvold laid out a devastating objection to that theory, and then advanced a plausible and sophisticated way of modifying the theory so that it could avoid the objection. For reasons untouched upon here, some philosophers suspect that even the best version of the desire theory of welfare will turn out to be inferior to some other kind of theory. I have such a suspicion. I am not *certain*, however, that some kind of desire theory will not turn out to be the best theory of welfare. I am certain that Overvold's work constituted an enormous breakthrough in the development of desire theories of welfare, and that everyone now working on desire theories of welfare should take Overvold's ideas as their point of departure.

Let us turn to Overvold's discussion of the rational adjudication of conflicts between self-interest and morality. The revised desire theory shows how self-interest and morality can conflict even for someone whose strongest desires are that others prosper and that justice be done. If these are your strongest desires, then your acting on these desires can conflict with your self-interest, since the fulfillment of these desires does not count as benefiting you, and you sacrificed the fulfillment of other desires that would have benefited you. Overvold's (1984) paper "Morality, Self-interest, and Reasons for Being Moral" goes on to explain how standard deliberative rationality can adjudicate between morality and self-interest in cases of conflict. According to this theory of rationality, roughly the rational act is the one the agent would choose as a result of carefully weighing up all his or her present rational desires (i.e., desires he or she would have if he or she were aware of all relevant *available* empirical facts and were reasoning logically). On this view, obeying the demands of morality is rational if and only if that is what is best from the point of view of the *totality* of your present desires informed by available empirical information. Particularly if you have strong *moral* desires, sacrificing self-interest in order to act morally can maximally fulfill the totality of your present informed desires and thus can be rational. On the other hand, refusing to sacrifice self-interest *is rational* if that is what is best from the point of view of the totality of your present informed desires.

Overvold went on to argue that it can be rational even for purely self-interested people to cultivate in themselves moral sentiments and desires. Here we have the paradox of self-interest: my long-run welfare might be maximized by my coming to care deeply about some things other than self-interest, and even to care about those things so deeply that I might sacrifice at least some of my own welfare for the sake of those other things. Then, once the enriching moral sentiments and dispositions are developed in me, my acting on these moral motivations can be rational even when it involves self-sacrifice.

This is a fashionable line of argument. Furthermore, Overvold's version of it is appealingly restrained: he argued that it *can* be the case that a purely self-interested person would maximize his or her long-run self-interest were he or she to develop a full set of strong moral sentiments and dispositions. I accept that conclusion but want to ask: of what percentage of people is this true? Overvold himself was a good example of someone whose highly moral motivational makeup seemed more rewarding to him than any less virtuous alternative. But, because Overvold was in so many ways an atypical human being, I worry about over-generalizing from his case.[7]

---

7. There are two lines of thought that might be invoked in support of the view that being morally virtuous maximizes the agent's own welfare. One of these lines of thought starts from the claim that the agent needs to have moral dispositions in order to get others' cooperation. For a persuasive rebuttal of this line of thought, see Sayre-McCord 1989. The other line of thought involves the claim that being morally virtuous itself constitutes a benefit to the agent. The case for this claim is explored in Hooker 1994.

13

Posthumous Satisfactions and the Concept of Individual Welfare[*]

Alan E. Fuchs

Can events that take place after an individual's death affect that person's well-being? Aristotle apparently thought that they could (*Nicomachean Ethics*, book 1, chapter 10, 1100ª18–30), and Richard Brandt (1979, p. 330), Joel Feinberg (1984, pp. 79–84), Derek Parfit (1984, p. 495), Gregory Kavka (1986, p. 41), and Brad Hooker (this volume, pp. 211–12) all agree. Mark Overvold did *not*, and I believe that his account of why such posthumous effects are impossible constitutes one of his most significant philosophical contributions (see Overvold 1980, p. 108). Overvold, like many other contemporary moral theorists, analyzes the notion of a person's utility or welfare in terms of the fulfillment of the agent's desires, but he adds the important qualification that the desires must be for states of affairs in which the agent is an essential constituent. The clear implication of such a view is that our welfare *cannot* be affected by the post-mortem satisfaction of any of the interests which we had while alive. I shall defend Overvold against his critics on this point, since I believe that his

---

* A version of this paper appeared in the *Journal of Philosophical Research* 16 (1991: 345–51). It was originally presented as a comment on Brad Hooker's "Mark Overvold's Contribution to Philosophy," which appeared in the same issue (pp. 333–44), and a version of which appears in this volume as "A Breakthrough in the Desire Theory of Welfare"(pp. 205–13). In his paper, Hooker eloquently and effectively attested both to the significance of Mark Overvold's philosophical contributions and to the nobility of his personal character. I could not agree more with Hooker's expressed esteem for Overvold's philosophical contributions nor with his admiration for Overvold's many personal virtues. Therefore, in this brief paper I focus on the only issue on which Hooker and I disagree: the extent to which a person's well-being can or cannot be affected by post-mortem events and the significance of this consideration for the proper analysis of the concept of individual welfare.

version of the desire-fulfillment theory of utility, and not theirs, is the most defensible one available to moral philosophy today.[1]

Brad Hooker notes that Derek Parfit, Richard Brandt, and Gregory Kavka all object to Overvold's account of personal utility (or any similar analysis) by arguing that it is, in effect, too narrow. Since, according to Overvold's analysis, the living individual must be an essential constituent of the states of affairs that are desired (insofar as the satisfaction of such desires is to contribute to his or her self-interest), one's welfare obviously cannot be advanced (or set back) by any desires that are satisfied (or frustrated) after one's death. Parfit and the other critics contend, however, that when individuals have desires for states of affairs that may be realized after their deaths, the objective post-mortem satisfaction of those desires *does* contribute to their welfare and the posthumous objective failure of such personal interests harms them. In support of this claim, Kavka and Brandt simply cite the case of a possible desire for posthumous fame, the achievement of which, Kavka suggests, "surely" contributes to one's self-interest (Kavka 1986, p. 41; and Brandt 1979, p. 330). Parfit's argument, as quoted by Hooker, is more subtle, for it starts with a seemingly indubitable intuition, that the exiled father in the quoted story is clearly harmed *while alive* by the failure of his parental interests (even though he does not know that to be the case), and it then slides quickly to the apparently inescapable conclusion that the father is likewise made worse off by an equally unknown failure that just happens to take place after his death. Joel Feinberg contributes a similar story. In it, a woman devotes thirty years of her life to a worthy cause. She lives quite happily seeing her project flourish, pleased at the good that it does for others while also relishing her own personal repute. Unfortunately, shortly before her death, the entire enterprise is ruined and its benefactor disgraced. The woman never learns of these events, however, due to the misrepresentations of her associates. Feinberg assumes that we will all grant that the woman has been harmed, albeit unknowingly. But what would be the difference, he goes on to ask, if the scandal took place

---

1. I do not myself, however, wish to endorse the desire-fulfillment theory. It seems to me that a sophisticated hedonic (or "happiness") account, such as that defended by Brandt (1979, chapter 13), provides a more plausible account of individual welfare. Though the defense of such a claim must obviously be left for another paper, I would point out for the present that the happiness theory, any appearances to the contrary notwithstanding, also has each of four features which constitute, according to Hooker, the major attractions of Overvold's version of the desire-fulfillment theory (this volume, pp. 209–11). Considering these criteria alone, therefore, the two views are at least equally viable, and we can turn to other considerations to tip the scales in favor of the hedonic account.

shortly *after* rather than before her death? Are not her interests equally set back and her welfare thereby diminished? (Feinberg 1984, p. 88)

How can we defend Overvold's analysis against these purported counter-examples? First of all, I believe that we can marshal *other* examples that clearly support Overvold's intuitions and thereby weaken the plausibility of his critics' accounts. Recall, for one such case, Overvold's own story of the self-sacrificing father whose suicide leads to successful lives for his children. The father's desires have clearly been fulfilled after his death, but *he* is clearly not any better off as a consequence. Consider, too, some of the following cases: Has Alexander Hamilton's welfare been enhanced by the increasing power assumed by American presidents in the twentieth century, thus satisfying one of *his* most significant lifelong interests? Has Queen Victoria been harmed recently by the dissolution of the empire that she valued so much, and would she, on the other hand, have had a personally better life if Gandhi had never been born? And, is Vincent Van Gogh finally living well given the recent fulfillment of his fervent desire that his paintings sell well? Now, I grant that in these examples it is quite odd to speak of the posthumous events as influencing the subjects' utility mainly because the future conditions that satisfy or frustrate their desires take place so long after their respective deaths.[2] But if the objective satisfaction of people's desires can affect their well-being at all, why should it matter for the determination of their self-interest when the desire-satisfying (or frustrating) states of affairs come into being?[3]

How is it, then, that in some cases, such as the ones offered by Parfit and the other critics, our intuitions do seem to give some support to their views, while in others, such as the ones I have offered, the implications of their arguments appear so odd? Here is one suggestion. When successful, the suggested stories play upon the connection that frequently and typically does exist between our personal welfare and the objective satisfaction of our desires. Parents who desire the well-being of their children do get

---

2. Even Aristotle granted the strangeness of counting events that take place well after a person's death as contributing to that individual's happiness; *Nicomachean Ethics*, book 1, chapter 10, 1100^{a}26-30.

3. It might not be inappropriate while we consider how to respond to examples offered on both sides of this issue to remind ourselves continually that all of the parties to the dispute assume that there is no actual afterlife that is being affected for better or worse by possible postmortem conditions. We do, I concede, often talk about the dead "turning over in their graves" as they supposedly react to present conditions that frustrate interests which they had while alive. But such discourse counterfactually assumes, I take it, that the disquieted dead do indeed become aware of current events, and since we have agreed that they cannot really do so, we should also conclude that they cannot be harmed by any such news either.

satisfaction from knowing that their children are flourishing, and advocates of social causes derive pleasure from observing the advancement of their projects. This correlation suggests that there must be some possible manner in which the agent can become aware of a condition for that state of affairs to affect his or her well-being. In the critics' examples, the narratives start in conformity with this criterion, that is, with a situation in which knowledge of the satisfaction or setback of one's interests is at least possible. We do tend to agree, for example, that the father in Parfit's story has been harmed by the currently unknown failure of his parenting, but only, I suggest, because there is at least the possibility that he may become aware of his true situation. Exiles can, after all, eventually discover what has transpired in their homeland. We react similarly to the case of Feinberg's matron. We feel that her deathbed welfare *has* been diminished because she has become vulnerable to the shattering truth that her life's major endeavors have been fruitless. And likewise for all of the familiar, related arguments, such as the ones which claim that we are harmed by having a bad reputation even if we are perfectly deceived into thinking that others regard us well, or that our well-being would be diminished by having an unfaithful spouse even if he or she (and the rest of the world) completely succeeded in hiding the truth from us (see, for example, Griffin 1986, p. 9). But ignorance is not perfect bliss, for it is always liable to the cracks that let in damaging truths. It is simply false, for example, that someone with a really poor professional reputation could live an entire life oblivious to that fact. Would she still, one wonders, receive competitive research grants, receive invitations to speak at major universities, have hoards of groupies attend all of her lectures, have APA sessions devoted to analyzing every nuance of each of her many publications, and so on? Isn't it likewise almost certainly false that a life lived with a philandering spouse could be completely indistinguishable from one shared with a loving and devoted one? The cases we are considering, I suggest, play on our implicit knowledge of these truths, but they subtly ask us to forget them, thereby undermining the conditions upon which our intuitive reactions are based.[4]

This last observation leads to a related suggestion for explaining the prima facie appeal of some of the postmortem satisfaction examples. Part of

---

4. These examples therefore resemble the classic philosophical puzzles that result from the undetected violation of some key criterion for the proper use of a concept. E.g., could not the world have been created only two minutes ago along with all of the historical records, fossils, and memories that suggest to us a more ancient origin? Or couldn't my entire life be but a dream and I am in fact the only existent soul, though I do of course experience—in my life-long dream—appearances of others, waking vs. dreamlike sensations, and so on?

the apparent plausibility of the claim that the posthumous fulfillment of people's desires is relevant to their well-being is, I believe, traceable to the obvious and often-noted ambiguity of the word "satisfaction." One obtains satisfaction of one's desires in one sense of the term—the one that I have been using so far—whenever that which one desires to be the case actually obtains. For a desire to be satisfied in this sense it clearly does not matter when the valued condition is achieved, nor whether the agent who desired it is aware that it has been, or even that he or she is alive at the moment of ultimate fulfillment. So it may be the case that President Bush (along with countless others) keenly desires that the federal government balance its budget and eradicate its enormous deficit. This desire may eventually be "satisfied" (in this first sense), perhaps at the end of the next century. But I can see absolutely no connection between that desired state of affairs obtaining, say in the year 2090, and the augmentation of *George Bush's* welfare.5 The second sense of "satisfaction" obviously connotes a pleasant feeling of enjoyment or contentment, one which we often get when our desires are satisfied in the first sense. We characteristically enjoy or get satisfaction (in this second sense) from the various things in life which we have pursued, saved for, or wanted.6 Can it be that the extremely intimate connection in most of our ordinary experiences between these two quite different notions has led our critics (and *our* intuitions in so far as we tend to be swayed by their arguments) to confuse the one with the other, to think that the objective instantiation of a state of affairs that an individual wanted to bring about is the same thing as the personal satisfaction that *is* an obvious component of his or her well-being?

Since Brad Hooker agrees with Parfit that at least some posthumous satisfactions *can* affect a person's well-being, he does not defend Overvold, as I have done, by rejecting the alleged counterexamples. Rather, Hooker proposes a modification of Overvold's theory that enables it to embrace

---

5. If twenty-second-century historians show that the country's economic recovery in 2090 was attributable to actions which Bush had taken as president, they might legitimately use this posthumous success of his policies to reevaluate the influence of his presidency, to revise current judgments of his wisdom, or even to reassess his personal character. But since he, George Bush, will be dead, neither they nor events can retroactively make him personally any better or less well off than he actually was when alive.

6. But we might *not* receive satisfaction (in the second sense) from every satisfaction (in the first). Mick Jagger, a rock musician, complained in a popular song that he could not get any "satisfaction," even though he was presumably more than able to satisfy almost all of his desires. And the phenomenon of not enjoying the actual realization of one's desires (for wealth, fame, power, etc.) is alas by no means confined to rock-music stars.

such cases. Hooker suggests that we revise Overvold's limitation on the range of relevant desires to include only those "in whose propositional content the agent is an essential constituent in the sense that the state of affairs is desired under a description that makes essential reference to the agent" (this volume, p. 212). This, he observes, will allow the relevance of desires such as the one that *I* be influential or that *I* will have been a successful parent, while it will presumably rule out some of the more far-fetched cases that I have offered. For example, the revised criterion would distinguish Bush's desire that *he* will be thought to have been a good president from his interest in the eventual elimination of the U.S. government's budget deficit. Therefore, insofar as this move would allow some posthumous events to affect a person's welfare without sliding us completely down the slippery slope that I have tried to grease, I grant that it is a valuable suggestion.

Hooker's interesting proposal still fails, however, to overcome the general objection to admitting *any* posthumous influence on the well-being of a deceased person. Consider the life of Camille Claudel, who was for a time Rodin's student and then his colleague and mistress. Claudel not only wanted to produce great art and to have it appreciated, she also very much desired that her work be admired as *her* work, that *her* influence on Rodin be known, and that *she* become as personally famous as he. Each of these desires, I take it, therefore meets Hooker's revised criterion. But Claudel's interests were unfortunately not fulfilled during her lifetime, and she died in wretched misery. Only now can we say that her desires have been (at least partially) satisfied, but it is unfortunately too late for us *now* to cause her to have lived a personally more rewarding existence. Nor is it the case, more fortunately, that those who continue to disparage her art and to deny that she influenced Rodin (or anyone else for that matter)—thereby frustrating her desires—are now making her life any worse than it actually was. The soundness of Overvold's denial of the influence of postmortem events on personal utility is augmented, I believe, if we recall that what is at issue is the proper analysis of individual utility, personal well-being, or one's own good, and *not* some of the other closely related notions such as that which a person most wants (all things considered), or what it would be rational for an agent to desire, or what constitutes an excellent or a morally superior life. One of Mark Overvold's most important philosophical contributions was the demonstration of the consequences of failing to make careful distinctions among these importantly different ideas.

Mark Overvold had it right: to be helped or harmed, one has to exist. There must be an existent self for self-interest, a living being for personal well-being.

14

Overvold on Self-Interest and Self-Sacrifice[*]

Richard B. Brandt

In the period between 1980 and 1984 Mark Overvold published three papers on the subjects, roughly, of self-interest and self-sacrifice (Overvold 1980, 1982, 1984). These papers are uniformly learned, acute, careful, and original. Some of them criticized a view I expressed in 1972 (and earlier) and on this the main points of his critique are clearly correct, although I have rejected that view on other grounds, which I shall explain shortly. However, the main points of his critique are well-taken, and what I have to say here can be regarded as mostly a footnote on his views. I shall, however, discuss his view broadly, and at some points contrast it with the views of Parfit, an exercise which may be enlightening. The major aim of Overvold's articles is to clarify, in a wide-ranging way, the concepts of "self-sacrifice" and "self-interest," and to determine whether the demands of morality (or altruism) necessarily conflict with self-interest.

Let me begin by making a point about the usage of the terms "self-interest" and "self-sacrifice." Both of these terms have a dual usage: one we might call the "objective" sense, the other the "motivational" sense. In the objective sense, we might say that an action diminished the well-being of the agent. But to say that an act is "self-sacrificing" is to say something more,about the agent's motivation, although one might say—as Overvold seems to—that a self-sacrificing act is always *both* one that diminishes the agent's well-being and also has a certain motivation. Again, in the objective sense a person might do something which enhanced his welfare, but it would not follow that the agent had acted in a "self-interested" way—that, again, is a partly matter of what motivated him.

---

* A version of this paper appeared in the *Journal of Philosophical Research* 16 (1991: 353–63). It is a good deal more cogent than it would have been without careful criticisms proposed by Thomas Carson, in correspondence.

In order to get all these concepts straight, we must get clear what is to be meant by a person's "well-being." Overvold rightly says that some views of this get us into trouble. He points out (1980, p. 117 n.) that we might just identify a person's "well-being" with his long-run pleasure, so that to enhance a person's well-being is to increase his long-term pleasure; this view allows a clear and simple conception of self-sacrifice, but Overvold holds it is not plausible. A second possibility for a definition of "well-being," some form of which has recently been a favorite, is that well-being consists in satisfaction of a person's actual present desires, or the total set of his desires over his lifetime, or at least his "rational" desires (in the sense of ones informed at least about the nature of their object), where "satisfaction" just means the *occurrence* of the events wanted. (Parfit has suggested that this view is more plausible if we consider only "holistic" desires, ones that concern not just an immediate state of affairs, but the impact of something over one's whole life). A third possibility, which Overvold considers, is the occurrence in the agent of any one of a number of qualities we think it advantageous for him to have—Overvold lists knowledge, power, and achievements. He says "it is natural to suppose that attaining them enhances an individual's welfare...." Here he comes close to a view to which Parfit seems to be sympathetic (see Parfit 1984, pp. 501–2).

Now it is the second of these views which, at least if we take it in its *simpler* and currently popular form, gets us into trouble about self-sacrifice, for if we conjoin this view with the psychological thesis that what a person *does* is always to maximize his expectable desire-satisfaction, then it follows, according to the second thesis, that there *could not be* an action (mistaken expectations aside) which diminishes one's well-being and hence is self-sacrificial, at least in the objective sense. Overvold wants to explain what modifications need to be made, to avoid this result. This consequence *might* be avoided, of course, if we took this thesis in the form of desires over a lifetime, or holistic desires, or desires fully rational in an extended sense. Let us ignore these latter possibilities.

This result of the second theory, which Overvold rejects, is patently contrary to commonsense convictions, since it has the implication that persons never (rationally) *do* what they think to be to the self-interest of others, but not their own. For, if they are maximizing expectable utility, that act conceptually enhances their welfare. It might be replied that what apparently unselfish actions show is merely that the welfare of other people should be considered a part of the agent's "utility," if he really wants nice things to happen to them. And it is not implausible to say that an event which benefits my daughter is a *benefit* to me. But would it be, if I got no pleasure from this? Well-being in the ordinary sense seems to include long-term *pleasures/displeasures* of my mental state and if we take these substantially into account the total sum may show that I do *not* always come out ahead, even when I did maximize my expectable "utility" in the sense of desire satisfaction. If we look at matters this way, it seems that we need a conception of "well-being" different from the simple desire-satisfaction theory. So what is to be a more satisfactory definition of a person's "well-being" in the objective sense?

Overvold's answer, *as a first approximation*, is to go along and say that some state of affairs is part of a person's well-being, if, with full knowledge of it and its consequences, he *rationally* desires it. (He seems to use "rational" in the sense of being consistent with vivid awareness of available information, but it is not clear whether Overvold uses "rationally" in the rather extended sense in which the present writer has used it—roughly in the sense of having desires purified by "cognitive psychotherapy." He also does not recognize a further requirement that Parfit does, that certain desires are rationally *required* independently of how our *deliberations* might come out.) So Overvold holds *some* kind of desire-satisfaction theory after all. As a result, it looks as if he is saddled with much of the conclusion mentioned, that anything an agent actually does, at least, perhaps, in the presence of full information, enhances his benefit or well-being, given an agent's actions are motivated to maximize expectable desire satisfaction. Overvold wants to avoid this repugnant consequence, and does so by introducing an important restriction. A state of affairs is said to be part of, or conducive to, an agent's well-being, *only* if the *desires* for it, motivating action, cannot be satisfied without the *existence, alive,* of the agent at the time the state of affairs occurs. So, since satisfaction of the desire for justice to be done or for other persons to be well off does not count as contributing to one's well-being in this sense—however motivating they may be—there can be a clear distinction between what objectively contributes to one's well-being, and what does not. He adds to this requirement, for good reasons I ignore, that the agent's self must be *essentially* involved, for the act to enhance his well-being. Overvold does not explain "essentially involved" very clearly, but I think he means that the *thought* of some future state of *himself* is that which engages the relevant (rational) desire for the state of affairs which involves it (1982, 189–90). As he puts it a few lines later, a state of affairs which is the object of choice is part of one's objective well-being if choice of it is "motivated as it would be if he did not have any desires or aversions for features or outcomes of the act in which he is not an essential constituent."

Now my own view is that *all* pure desire-satisfaction theories are unsatisfactory as accounts of the agent's well-being, irrespective of whether the description of the wanted state of affairs entails that the agent is necessarily alive at the time the desired states obtain. I think it too simple that self-interest or benefit be defined in this general way, partly because it seems common sense to hold that some event, however desired beforehand, is not to one's benefit if it is boring or repugnant in the fact—a consequence which *pure* desire-satisfaction theories have to swallow; and I think the theory too simple partly for a somewhat more technical reason—that a person's desires can and often do *change*. As to the second point, suppose one person A wants to contribute to the well-being of person B, and acts at the time t so as to satisfy some of B's desires at t, perhaps to get a Greek lexicon, by an event to occur at t + k, but in the meantime B's desires change, perhaps for reasons of more information, but perhaps also in that his original desire was just a passing fancy. (There can be changes even if one takes a "holistic" view of an action, its consequences over a lifetime; for presumably, if a person's values change, his preferences among different prospective life histories will also change.) So if B rationally desires one thing more than another at an earlier time t but in the reverse order at a later time t + k, what is decisive about his benefit? Is it the relevant desires at the time the action is initiated, or when the wanted event occurs, or later? Or, again, if I am planning for my old age, is it just the desires I have at the moment of planning, or desires I know I shall have later, that are decisive? Or, to take a more concrete example, a woman might *want* a big wedding, *enjoy* it thoroughly (wanting it to go on) while it was occurring, but afterwards regret the whole thing as an expensive piece of foolishness. Which desires (or regrets) fix whether the event enhanced the person's welfare? Some writers think that desires at an earlier date are relevant to an action's contribution to benefit, say the desires one had as a boy. Or, as I have indicated others suggest, we might take into account a person's desires over a lifetime, saying that whether an act is to his benefit must involve both the intensity and duration of all these desires—perhaps not a bad suggestion, as I shall point out later, if we include retrospective desires about a particular event and take account of the desires I shall have when I am older. But this last view also runs into difficulties. To borrow an example from Griffin and Parfit, suppose a priest undergoes conversion to atheism and is an atheist for thirty years, during all that time expressing the desire that no priest be called when he is on his deathbed. Then, when he is on his deathbed, he asks for a priest to be called. Do we maximize his welfare by calling the priest, or not? The desire-satisfaction theory does not seem helpful at this point. I do not think a pure, simple desire-satisfaction theory is satisfactory, although possibly it could be amended to be so.

Now I admit that fully informed or "rational" desires may *not* change. Indeed, I rather hope they don't, for in this case it would be easier to accept a desire-satisfaction theory of the "informed" or "rational" variety. A claim that this is so does seem a bit speculative, but if it is correct this part of my objection to pure desire-satisfaction theories would be undermined. The earlier part of my argument, however, would still stand.

With a good deal of doubt whether it will do the job, I would like to offer a theory which I think has had the substantial support of various philosophers of this century: that an act contributes to an agent's well-being if it enhances his gratifications. We might call it a *gratification-enhancement* theory. Ordinary sensory pleasures, of course, count as forms of gratification; and we do desire them at the time—indeed, that is part of the definition of "pleasure." The theory, however, is not hedonistic in the sense of saying that gratifications are the only good; various sorts of thing can be gratifying, just as many sorts of thing can be desired. Desire satisfaction also is gratifying, in so far as the satisfaction of a desire is pleasant. This brings the gratification enhancement theory close to the desire satisfaction theory, if we assume that the pleasure at a desire satisfaction is roughly correlated with the strength of the desire being satisfied at the time. However, the insistence on a person's *liking* an outcome is a significant addition. But the proposal adds a further feature: that we must include the pleasures of *recollection* of some past desire satisfactions (or sensory pleasures). Since the proposal is that an event adds to the well-being of the person only in accordance with the *total* gratification of these several sorts, of course it has implications which desire-satisfaction theories reject but which I find highly intuitive: that events after a person's death do not count as adding to his welfare, and the to him unknown slander by his friends is not harmful to his well-being; and his false beliefs about important achievements, if pleasant, are benefits to him even if in fact there was no achievement.

How do gratifications from *recollection* differ from straight sensory pleasure, or from the pleasure of desire satisfaction? Retrospective gratification is *gladness*—which is pleasant in itself—at the thought of an event; it seems to involve a specific emotion along with the wish that the event happened as it did—a wish in the sense of a disposition to bring about the past event, if this were possible. Retrospective gratification arises from the conjunction of recall with the desires/aversions present *at the time of recall*. I offer no explanation of this, but point out that obviously it is a fact.

How does this proposal avoid the problem of change of desires? The answer is that it identifies the contribution of an event to a person's well-being with the set of gratifications to which this event leads—or to which it contributes in the sense that the gratifications would not have occurred had it not taken place—over a lifetime, beginning at the time of the event. So, in case a person's desires change over his lifetime, there may be retrospective regret about the initially pleasant event, so that the total impact of that event may be negative rather than positive. This view also avoids the counter-intuitive consequence of counting the desires a person had well *before* the event as increasing his well-being, say desires he had as a child. It also enables us to give a sensible answer to the proposal that it is satisfaction—in the sense merely that what is/was desired occurs—of a person's desires over his lifetime, estimated in terms of intensity and duration, that determine the value of an event for him; on my present suggestion, what is relevant to the total contribution to well-being is the total *gratification* a person will have after the event, perhaps as a consequence of later changes in desire. The answer to the example of the dying priest/atheist is that it would be more gratifying if a priest were called, unless the retrospective regret at the time would outweigh it, if it occurred. This example suggests, however, that we should perhaps take a *dispositional* form of the theory, thus avoiding the conclusion that a pleasure, say, adds to a person's welfare even if he *would* regret it retrospectively, provided the pleasant episode was never brought to mind again. So, in the case of the atheist/priest, what we might say is that calling a priest would do more for the well-being of the person, if the pleasure bringing a priest would give him is stronger than the retrospective regret the priest would have, if he thought about the matter, letting his then-existing desires/aversions play a role.

This complication of the theory, however, has serious difficulties, for are we to say that we are to count all the gratifications a person would have had if he had often, or continuously, reflected on an event? This problem, however, has a parallel for the over-a-lifetime desire-satisfaction theory; for are we to count the desires a person has over his whole lifetime, irrespective of whether they ever become conscious or motivating? I propose to leave this matter open.

On my proposal, how do we sum up, if an initially pleasant event is retrospectively regretted? I think we have to give greater weight (along with the intensity and duration of the pleasure of the gratification) to the attitude which is better informed about the event in its total context, so that a more intense retrospective regret has more weight unless, for instance, it involves a failure to recall what the event was like, say, how pleasant it was. I have no proposal exactly how to weigh these factors.

It seems we might require of a gratification the same as what we require of desires (according to a view possibly like Overvold's), that the gratification be *fully informed or rational* in the sense that it occurs in a person even if he possesses, vividly, available information about knowable facts which, if he knew of them, would change the reaction. For instance, information that a gratification would not have occurred if the person were not satiated or in a state of deprivation, or exhilarated or depressed, or drunk or tired, and so on. Again, suppose one feels retrospective regret about enjoying oneself because of having been taught that God disapproves (and believing it). Or suppose one dislikes being in a nonprestigiuos occupation, or married to a person of "inferior" race, on account of parental expressions of dismay, or things said by one's classmates. The trouble with such attitudes is that they prevent a person from responding to the full awareness of the state of affairs in question. We know how these likes/dislikes come about, through contiguity conditioning and stimulus generalization. When such causes have been in play, it seems a thoughtful person would make exceptions in his counting up how much gratifications add to his welfare, although I do not claim to show that being rational in this sense adds more to the felicity of the agent.

This proposal is obviously very different from the view that what adds to well-being is just the occurrence of events desired, irrespective of whether they are liked or boring. I concede that it is complicated, and I have no proposal for how *exactly* one is to go about deciding which of two actions would maximize gratifications—so, doubtless, economists would not like it.

But what has this proposal to say to the view that states of affairs like having power, or achieving, or contributing to the well-being of other persons add to one's well-being, apart from enjoyments therefrom? It seems to me that it leaves this issue open; for a person might be *glad* that such events occurred. What is implied is that if events desired do not produce gratification, then they do not add to the agent's well-being. And that is a different matter. Indeed, it is not obvious that the occurrence of pleasures will always be gratifying in retrospect—I think they often might not be. Obviously it is a long story whether achievement or knowledge does add to a person's well-being or totality of gratifications. I have discussed elsewhere whether these are desired *just for themselves*, with a negative conclusion (Brandt 1989). But the issues must be kept separate: whether gladness is a *test* of well-being, and whether the only good thing is pleasure.

This conception seems to meet Overvold's point about the distinction between objectively self-interested and objectively self-sacrificing action, just as he suggests a pleasure theory of benefit would do. For if a person does something such that his total gratification (rectified in the various ways mentioned) would be smaller than if he had not done so, he has diminished his objective well-being.

Let us turn now to the motivational sense of "self-interested" and "self-sacrificing." Manifestly it does not follow from the fact that an action enhanced an agent's welfare that it was self-interested, or from the fact that it diminished the agent's well-being that it was self-sacrificing.

A major aim of Overvold is to define motivationally "self-sacrificing" action, and to contrast it with motivationally self-interested action. His official definition of a motivationally self-sacrificial act seems to be the following (1980, p. 113): "Our discussion has produced the following account of self-sacrifice. An act is a genuine act of self-sacrifice only if:

I.   the loss of welfare is expected or anticipated (this is a condition on belief and not an epistemic condition);

II. the act is voluntary; and

III. there is at least one other alternative open to the agent at the time of the act which is such that (a) if the consequences of the alternative act had been as the agent expected them to be, then the alternative would have been more in the agent's self-interest than the act he actually did perform, and (b) if the agent had chosen to perform the alternative act, then his act would have been more in his self-interest, objectively, than the act which he actually did perform."

Now I believe that as an account of *motivational* self-interest or self-sacrifice, this *may* not sufficiently take into account the agent's beliefs about impact on his own well-being, although the first clause may be intended to do this. Overvold takes into account the agent's beliefs about the *consequences* of alternative actions, but (possibly) not his belief about the impact of these on his own well-being, although I should think that a thoughtful person would, on reflection, be quite aware of a loss of welfare in his self-sacrificing act. Overvold seems to hold that an action is motivationally self-sacrificing only if it would, on the basis of the agent's *expectations* about consequences, *objectively* have diminished his objective well-being.

This explanation seems to leave room for some questions, *if* it is supposed (as we shall see it is *not*, by Overvold) that an act which is not *self-interested* in this sense is *self-sacrificing*. A person might perform an action (say, just to speak bluntly to one's chairman), clearly believing that an alternative action would be, in some sense, better for him in the long run, more to his self-interest. Suppose the agent is right about this. Would we say that the act was a sacrifice, or, more, that his act was "self-sacrificing?" (Of course, one might say such an action is not self-interested because it would be irrational!) What I think we most naturally call a "self-sacrifice" is an act which is, and perhaps also is expected to be, the giving up of some benefit to one's self, for the benefit of *someone else*, or of some cause. So an addition seems called for, that the agent actually believed, at least on reflection, his action to be the choice of an alternative such as to benefit someone else in preference to himself.

Moreover, I have questions about the satisfactoriness of Overvold's definition of "self-interested" action as action motivated by desire for an event which essentially involves the agent's being alive at the time of the event. Suppose a person acts because of a strong desire for posthumous fame—to be remembered after his death to the extent Aristotle is. According to the definition, this is not a self-interested desire, even if it were a rational one, because the agent will not be alive at the time it comes about. But we should certainly say that this was a self-interested desire. (Possibly a better definition for Overvold would be to say that an act is self-interested if the statement of what is wanted necessarily involves an egocentric reference; this is weaker than saying it involves he must be alive at the time.[1]) Again, a person might commit suicide because he thinks his life has been a complete failure; on the definition it is not clear whether his act is self-interested or not. Part of the consequence of the action is that he not be alive, but the action does seem to concern him in an essential way. (One might say that the act made his life go better than otherwise; but this involves the notion of life going better when one is dead. Perhaps counterfactual proposals might help here.) Again, a person might wish to be punished in view of some regretted crime he had committed in the past. Would this be a self-interested action, unless he just wanted to escape guilt-feelings? (We shall see that it *could* be, on Overvold's view.)

What would I count as cases of genuinely self-sacrificing actions? Suppose I contribute my whole fortune in order to provide the best possible treatment for my daughter suffering from a serious illness. There are many things I would like to do and would enjoy which now cannot be done. Or suppose a person postpones work toward a graduate degree for some years, in order to stay home and care for an ailing mother. Are these self-sacrifices or not? They seem to be. One might say they are self-interested because of the aversive pangs that *would* follow if one did not take this course, and that the agent *could* have done what he did in order to avoid aversive pangs during the years involved. Gratifications are foregone, all right, but unpleasant regrets are avoided. I think that *we* would *say*, however, that these are cases of self-sacrifice if the agent was not *actually* motivated by thought of these possible results in himself. Of course, such self-sacrificing action might be perfectly *rational*.

Overvold rightly says that a "rational" action is not necessarily one that is self-interested (1984, p. 502), but, by his definition, a self-interested one

---

1. This possibility was suggested to me by Stephen Darwall.

must be rational. But he is much concerned with whether it is possible to act (rationally) in a self-interested way (according to his above definition) and in so doing also always be doing the moral thing, however much it costs by ordinary standards. Overvold maybe (roughly) thinks it is. Overvold says: "The benefits [of acting morally] follow from being a person who trusts others, who is genuinely concerned about the welfare of others, and who wants to see justice done....[If he is to get these benefits,] then a person cannot expect the rewards if he continues to keep his options open, refusing to commit himself genuinely....If he is to benefit, then he must allow himself to change, at least to the extent that he develops the appropriate interests" (1984, p. 505). So, in view of the prospective gains, the rational person will be motivated to change *himself*, so that he may not be one who is exclusively motivated by what are normally thought to be prudential considerations.

If I understand Overvold rightly, his proposal is that, in view of the probable self-interested benefits of living a genuinely moral life, it is rational for a person to develop interests in *his* acting morally. If he succeeds in this, since he is essentially involved in the target of his new desires, his desire to act morally is essentially *self-interested*, in the sense of Overvold's definition of "self-interest." Thus, given the evidence at his disposal, a rational person will develop himself either to care supremely for *his* acting morally (and thus implies that he will be alive at the time), or the motivating force of other self-interested considerations will always be inferior to the desire to act morally. So the morally committed man does not sacrifice himself— indeed adds to his well-being—in doing the moral thing from his motivation about being a certain kind of person.

This view differs markedly from that of Parfit, who is only wanting to show that altruistic or moral action is *rational* in his sense of "rational."

Parfit rejects the idea that an act is rational if it is one that would be undertaken in full vivid view of knowable facts, about oneself and other things. He does so because he thinks such deliberation might overlook some important things. (Unfortunately, he never explains what *he* means by "rational.") For instance, it might overlook the fact that achievement is a rational goal, or that it is irrational to discount the future, or that it is irrational to prefer a greater pain on a future Tuesday to a lesser one on a Wednesday, or that one should desire only what is in some respect worthwhile—and most important, that the equal well-being of oneself is not to be preferred to the well-being of other persons—as a matter of straight rationality. Now to this I have two objections, both in favor of Overvold's view. First, Overvold's view of rational action is simpler, and although it is possible that vivid deliberation might overlook some facts, there is no reason why it should. How could it be "full" deliberation if there were these omissions? Parfit asserts that there could be such omissions, but does not explain how or why. And how does Parfit know that achievement is a rational goal, or that time discounting is irrational, except by deliberating about it? Parfit himself says that if discounting the future arises from defective imagination, the bias "would never survive the process of ideal deliberation" (Parfit 1984, p. 133). In fact, I think the "fully informed deliberation" theory can handle all the counterexamples Parfit cites, except the one that it is irrational to prefer one's own good to that of others. This last example, however, seems to me absurd, although it has some backing from Sidgwick. But it seems to me ridiculous to suppose that it is irrational for me not to prefer that someone else suffer rather than my daughter (or me). In the second place, Parfit wants to show only that it is irrational in his sense to act immorally. Here it seems to me Overvold gives a much more realistic account: that one can see the long-range benefits of being moral, and as a result become changed so that one actually *wants* to be a moral person, with all that this entails. Viewed in this way, morality is not contrary to self-interest, in Overvold's sense, and it can be perfectly rational in the sense of surviving all knowable facts which, if vividly represented, might change it. On both these points, it seems to me Overvold has a more defensible view.

But will Overvold's view stand up, about acting morally being to one's self-interest when one has rationally changed so as to want to be a moral person? Well, it is a very ingenious completion of his conception of self-interest. If you accept his theory of self-interest, then you'll be able to say that acting morally is to your self-interest, which I think we philosophers would all want to say. Overvold's proposal strikes me as neater than all the attempts to show that morality is to your self-interest because of possible cooperation (etc.) with others (which Overvold of course recognizes). So I feel inclination to accept his proposal. But I think we shall continue to say that the man who gives up satisfaction of a major ambition, say of achievement, for a moral cause, has sacrificed himself—perhaps because we cannot take the point of view of the person who has made the change. Or, perhaps it is that we know that the old self-interested desires are there and pulling the agent in their direction, and although he follows his moral committment, he cannot but regret what he has given up. However this may be, Overvold's suggestion is a very ingenious one.

15

The Desire-Satisfaction Theory of Welfare: Overvold's Critique and Reformulation*

Thomas Carson

In a series of important and influential papers Mark Overvold presented a powerful objection to earlier formulations of the desire-satisfaction theory of personal welfare and proposed an alternative formulation of the theory (see Overvold 1980, 1982, 1984). In the first part of this paper I will explain his objection to earlier versions of the theory. Then, in part two, I shall argue that Overvold's revised version of the theory (while a great improvement over earlier versions) does not entirely escape from the objections that he himself raises. I formulate an alternative version of the desire-satisfaction theory. My version of the theory answers the objections that I raise against Overvold, but it is open to other serious objections. I do not know of any formulation of the theory that provides a fully adequate solution to the problem which Overvold raises. Overvold's own reformulation of the desire-satisfaction theory represents a substantial improvement on earlier versions and is a necessary point of departure for anyone who wishes to defend the theory. In the final section of the paper I shall state two general objections to Overvold's theory (and any other version of the desire-satisfaction theory) and briefly sketch possible lines of defense.

I

Standard versions of the desire-satisfaction theory of welfare are formulated in terms of the satisfaction of rational desires or desires that would persist in

* This paper evolved from my "Comments on Brandt's Paper" [*Journal of Philosophical Research* 16 (1991: 365–68)], presented at the Overvold Memorial Conference at Saint Olaf College, Northfield, Minnesota, October 1990. I am indebted for the criticisms I received on that occasion. I thank Brad Hooker for his helpful criticisms of an earlier version of this paper. I would also like to express my extraordinary personal and intellectual debts to Mark Overvold.

the light of full information, rather than the satisfaction of one's *actual desires*. Richard Brandt claims that the actions that are in a person's self-interest are the same as those that the person

> *actually would* perform at that time if (a) his desires and aversions at the time were what they would be if he had been fully exposed to available information, and if (b) the agent had firmly and vividly in mind, and equally at the center of his attention, all those knowable facts which, if he thought about them, would make a difference to his tendency to act, given his "cleaned-up" desires (as in (a)). (Brandt 1972, p. 682)

Overvold objects to Brandt's theory on the grounds that it makes self-sacrifice logically impossible, unless the agent acts on the basis of incomplete information or irrational desires. In order to be a genuine case of self-sacrifice an act must be (1) voluntary, (2) informed (one must be aware of the loss to one's welfare and one must be aware of alternatives more favorable to one's own interests), and (3) contrary to one's self-interest. But, according to Brandt's theory, any act that fully satisfies conditions (1) and (2) ipso facto maximizes one's self-interest and thus cannot be an act of self-sacrifice. On Brandt's theory, it is logically impossible for a rational and fully informed person to perform an act of self-sacrifice.[1] Brandt's theory makes the thesis of psychological egoism trivially true (Overvold 1984, p. 499). Brandt now concedes this objection and has abandoned the desire-satisfaction theory of welfare for other reasons (see Brandt 1982, p. 173).

Von Wright (1963, chapter 5) defends an analysis of personal welfare in terms of the satisfaction of one's informed preferences. With appropriate modifications Overvold's objection can be generalized to apply to von Wright's theory. I believe that Overvold's objections apply to the desire satisfaction theories of John Rawls (1971) and James Griffin (1986), but I shall not attempt to show this here.

Thomas Schwartz (1982, 1990) independently hit upon a similar criticism. Schwartz attacks von Wright's theory on the grounds that it makes psychological egoism true by definition. "If whatever I prefer is good for me then I only prefer what is good for me" (1982, p. 199). Von Wright (1990, p. 776) now concedes this criticism. Schwartz strongly opposes desire-satisfaction theories of welfare. He briefly considers the possibility of defining welfare in terms of the satisfaction of "strictly self-interested" preferences, but dismisses this possibility: "An analysis of human welfare in terms of strictly *self-interested* preferences would avoid the commitment to

---

1. This greatly oversimplifies the argument. For needed qualifications see Overvold 1980. Overvold refines the argument to make the even stronger objection that Brandt's view makes it logically impossible for there to be *any* genuine acts of self-sacrifice.

psychological egoism. But it would hardly be subjectivist. And it would be circular or nearly so" (1982, p. 200).

Overvold proposes a modified version of the desire-satisfaction theory that he thinks avoids the objections he raises against earlier versions of the theory. His general strategy is to restrict the kinds of desires that can count as logically relevant to the determination of a person's welfare or self-interest. A person's welfare is determined only by his desires for states of affairs of which he is an essential constituent, i.e., only those states of affairs such that the person's existing at t is a logically necessary condition of the state of affairs occurring at t. Overvold's modified formulation of the desire-satisfaction theory reads as follows:

> An act maximizes S's self-interest if it is the act (or one of them) that S would most want performed if he were fully informed of all the relevant facts, but choosing only on the basis of his rational desires and aversions for features and outcomes of the act that are such that S's existence at t is a logically necessary condition of the proposition asserting that the outcome or feature obtains at t. (1982, p. 188)

The idea is to exclude one's other-regarding desires and one's desires for things that happen after one dies as logically relevant to one's self-interest. This restriction enables us to speak meaningfully of self-sacrifice. Suppose that acting on the basis of full information and rational desires a woman willingly gives up her life or most of her money to save another person's life. Earlier formulations of the desire-satisfaction theory make it a conceptual truth that this act promotes her self-interest. Overvold's theory avoids this absurd consequence. On the basis of the totality of her desires, the woman preferred to give up her life. But if she had chosen solely on the basis of those desires which meet Overvold's restriction (this excludes her desires for the welfare of others), she might have preferred not to give up her life. In that case, we could say that giving up her life was not in her self-interest and that it might have been an act of self-sacrifice.

Overvold's formulation of the desire-satisfaction theory implies that things that happen after one's death *cannot* effect one's self-interest. In defense of this Overvold writes "it is hard to see how anything which happens after one no longer exists can contribute to one's self-interest" (1980, p. 108). Richard Brandt (1979, p. 30) and Gregory Kavka (1986, p. 41) have criticized Overvold's theory on the grounds that it makes a person's desire for posthumous fame irrelevant to her self-interest. This is a difficult question about which people have conflicting intuitions; I cannot hope to settle it here. However, we should note that Overvold's theory can easily be modified to accommodate this criticism. Very roughly, we can say that the desires that are logically relevant to the determination of S's self-interest are those whose objects are such that they cannot exist (occur) at *t* unless *S* exists *at some time or other*. (See the papers by Brad Hooker and Alan Fuchs in this volume.)

Parfit examines the desire-satisfaction theory of welfare in an appendix to *Reasons and Persons* (1984). Although he does not endorse the theory, he makes some illuminating suggestions as to how the theory is most plausibly construed. Like Overvold, Parfit realizes that we should not count *all* of a person's desires as logically relevant to his self-interest or welfare. Parfit holds that our welfare is determined by the satisfaction (or nonsatisfaction) of "our preferences about our own lives" (1984, p. 494). This seems plausible as far as it goes, but he provides no explanation or elaboration of this restriction. He needs to explain what he means by preferences which are and are not "about our own lives." To date, Overvold's theory is the only serious attempt to make out this distinction.

II

Overvold's reformulation represents a major improvement on earlier versions of the desire-satisfaction theory. But Overvold (1982, p. 189) raises the following difficulty for his own theory. Any desire that is excluded by the restriction can reappear under a different description. Any state of affairs of which I am not an essential constituent can be part of a larger state of affairs in which I am an essential constituent. Consider any state of affairs, *x*, of which I am not an essential constituent—*x* could be the happiness of the child who lives down the street, or peace and prosperity in distant lands. Desires for *x* are excluded as logically relevant to the determination of my welfare. But for *any* such state of affairs, we can imagine that I desire that *I* bring it about. My desire that *I* bring about *x* (whatever *x* is) satisfies Overvold's restriction. My existing at *t* is a logically necessary condition of my acting at *t* so as to bring about *x*.

Overvold tries to deal with this problem by introducing the notion of the *reason* someone desires a particular state of affairs.

> In determining an individual's self-interest, we are not interested in states of affairs where the individual only happens to be an essential constituent, that is, where one's essential involvement plays no role in one's desire that the state of affairs obtain. For the desire to be relevant to one's welfare, the reason that one wants the state of affairs to obtain must be due to one's essential involvement in that state of affairs. (1982, p. 189)

He illustrates this notion in the following example. If a man desires that he bring about his wife's happiness simply because he has an independent desire that she be happy, then his desire that *he* bring about her happiness is not logically relevant to his self-interest.

> Conversely, if the primary reason for his desire is his essential involvement in that state of affairs, so that he has virtually no interest in his wife's happiness apart from his being the one to bring it about, then it does not seem strange to include this desire as logically relevant to the determination of his self-interest. (1982, p. 190)

All of the foregoing is plausible, but a serious problem remains. In many cases, perhaps most, a person desires that he do certain things for others, both because he has an independent desire for their welfare *and* because of his own essential involvement in bringing it about. There are often cases in which: (1) a person desires that he bring about some good for others, (2) he has an independent desire that others enjoy that good regardless of his involvement in bringing it about, and (3) his desire that *he* bring about the good outweighs his desire that the good come about by other means. (Much the same holds for our desires and aversions with respect to harming others. I not only desire that my wife not be harmed, I desire that *I* not harm her.) In such cases Overvold wants to say that the person's desire that *she* bring about something for others has to count as relevant to her welfare but that its full strength cannot count. Speaking with respect to the man who desires the happiness of his wife, Overvold says the following:

> Surely, it is only insofar as a person's wanting the state of affairs to obtain is due to or a product of one's essential involvement in that state of affairs that the desire is relevant to the determination of one's self-interest. Insofar as the person wants the state of affairs to obtain for reasons other than one's essential involvement, the desire is not logically relevant to the determination of one's welfare. Thus, in cases in which a person's essential involvement is only part of the reason one wants the state of affairs to obtain, only part of one's desire for that state of affairs will be relevant. But how is this to be determined? (1982, p. 190)

We need, as it were, to subtract the purely other-regarding element from such desires. How much should the husband's desire that *he* help his wife count in terms of his self-interest? Overvold's answer is that we must ask the following counterfactual question: "how strongly would the man desire that he help others if he didn't have any independent desire for their welfare?" This yields the final formulation of his theory:

> The act (or one of the acts) that maximizes an individual's self-interest is the act that he would most want to perform if (1) he were fully informed, and (2) had only those desires or aversions for features or outcomes of the act in which the individual is an essential constituent. (1982, p. 190)

Overvold's final formulation of the desire-satisfaction theory leads to consequences that he regards as objectionable. Many (most?) people would have *no desire* that *they* benefit others unless they had some independent desire for the welfare of the other people in question. This is a contingent fact about human psychology, but it is crucial in the present context. I desire that *I* bring about (or help bring about) my wife's happiness. I prefer that it be the case that *I* promote her happiness to its being the case that her happiness is promoted in some other way. This desire seems to be logically relevant to the determination of my welfare. Overvold *wants* to say that it is. But if we ask Overvold's counterfactual question—"what would my desires be if I had *no* other-regarding desires?"—then the answer seems to be that I would have no desire whatever that *I* contribute to my wife's happiness. This desire is (causally) dependent on my purely other-regarding desire that she be happy. If I did not have any independent desire that she be happy, then I would not have any desire that I bring it about myself. Overvold's view implies that my desire that I help contribute to my wife's happiness does not count as logically relevant to my self-interest. This seems wrong and it is contrary to Overvold's stated intentions. He thinks that this desire is relevant to the determination of my self-interest, but that "only part of" the strength of my "desire for that state of affairs" is "relevant"—in other words, the full strength of my present desire should not count.

The objection I have just raised is generated by cases in which a person desires that *she* bring about states of affairs of which she is not an essential constituent. My reformulation of Overvold's theory will be guided by the following principles. First, a person's desires or aversions with respect to *her* bringing about a state of affairs, *x*, of which she is not an essential constituent, are not relevant to her welfare unless she has a preference between (1) her bringing about *x*, and (2) *x* occurring by other means. Second, if a person has a preference between her bringing about *x* and *x* occurring by other means, then her desire that she bring about *x* is logically relevant to the determination of her welfare or self-interest. Overvold *wants* to hold both principles, but his final formulation of the theory is inconsistent with the second principle.

The problem in question arises from Overvold's attempt to determine *how much* a person's desire that *she* bring about *x* should count in determining her self-interest. Consider the following alternative account of how much such desires should count towards the determination of one's self-interest:

> F Let *S* be any person and *x* be any state of affairs such that: (a) *S* is not an essential constituent of *x* and (b) *S* has a (rational) preference between *S*'s bringing about *x* and *x*'s occurring for other reasons. *S*'s desire that *S* bring about *x* (or not bring about *x*) counts as logically relevant to the determination of *S*'s self-interest, but the full strength of *S*'s desire does not necessarily count. For purposes of

determining S's welfare, this desire (or aversion) should be assigned a degree of strength equal to the *actual strength* of S's desire or aversion for a state of affairs y such that S is indifferent between: (1) S's bringing it about that x, and (2) x and y both occurring by means other than S's agency.

Let me illustrate this principle with an example. Let x be my wife's getting a new piano. I have a desire that I bring about my wife's getting a piano. I prefer my giving her a piano to her getting a piano in some other way. F allows us to determine *how much* my desire that I give her a piano should count towards the determination of my welfare. We need to find a state of affairs y such that I desire y and I am indifferent between: (1) my giving my wife the piano (my bringing about x) and (2) x and y. Suppose that my desire that my father win the contest in his garden club satisfies this condition. I am indifferent between: (1) my giving my wife a new piano, and (2) her getting a new piano in some other way and my father winning the contest. My desire that I give my wife a new piano is assigned the same strength as my desire that my father win the contest.

Suppose that we modify Overvold's theory in accordance with F. On this modified theory, a person's self-interest is determined by the overall preferences she would have provided that: (1) she were choosing solely on the basis of her rational desires and aversions for states of affairs of which she is an essential constituent and (2) the strength of her desires and aversions with respect to her bringing about states of affairs of which she is not an essential constituent were discounted in accordance with formula F.

The modified theory can be stated formally as follows: An act maximizes S's self-interest if it is the act (or one of the acts) that S would most want performed were S fully informed of all the relevant facts, but choosing only on the basis of S's rational desires and aversions for features and outcomes of the act that are such that S's existence at t is a logically necessary condition of the proposition asserting that the outcome or feature obtains at t. (Thus far my wording is identical with Overvold's first reformulation of the desire-satisfaction theory.) In this hypothetical choice situation, S's desires and aversions for features and outcomes of which S is an essential constituent are assumed to have a strength equal to that of the desires and aversions for those features that S would have were S fully rational, *unless* the desires or aversions are desires or aversions for S's bringing about features and outcomes, x, of which S is not an essential constituent. Such desires are assigned a strength in accordance with the following formula:

1. If (when fully rational) S would be indifferent between x occurring as a result of S's own agency and its occurring as a result of something else, then S's desire that S bring about x *is not relevant* to the determination of S's welfare. (Such desires are assigned a strength of zero.)

2. If (when fully rational) S would not be indifferent between x occurring as a result of S's own agency and its occurring for other reasons and would lack any independent desire that x occur or not occur (i.e., S would be indifferent between x occurring or not occurring unless S has something to do with bringing it about), then S's desire for or aversion to S's bringing about x is assigned its full strength. (It has the same strength that it would have were S fully rational and everything else were equal.)

3. If (when fully rational) S would not be indifferent between x occurring as a result of S's own agency and its occurring for other reasons and would have an independent desire or aversion that x occur, then S's desire or aversion to S's bringing it about that x is assigned a degree of strength in accordance with formula F.

F invokes the idea of adding and subtracting the strength of individual desires. This in turn assumes first that one's individual desires have a determinate strength or intensity apart from their place in one's entire system of desires, and second that one's overall welfare is a "sum" of the satisfaction of one's individual desires. My solution is highly problematic on both counts. My desire for a state of affairs cannot be assigned a determinate strength in isolation from my other desires. Often the strength of my desire or aversion for a feature or outcome depends on the larger context in which it occurs. My overall preferences exhibit what Moore calls "organic unity." My overall preferences about my life as a whole are not a sum of my individual preferences. Parfit (1984, pp. 496–99) thinks that it is much more plausible to view welfare as a function of the satisfaction of one's "global" preferences (preferences for one's life as whole) rather than as a sum of the satisfaction of one's individual preferences. I am persuaded by Parfit's arguments, but I cannot defend them here. In any case, it *is clear* that the re-formulation of the desire-satisfaction theory I have presented is a "summa-tive" (as opposed to "global") version of the theory. Any objections to sum-mative versions of desire-satisfaction theories apply to my reformulation.

Michael Slote (1983) offers other objections to summative versions of desire-satisfaction and hedonistic theories of value (welfare). Slote argues that the temporal order of the goods and evils one enjoys in one's life is an important consideration in determining the value of one's life as a whole. Other things equal, successes and failures in adulthood and the latter part of one's life are more important than successes and failures which occur in one's youth. Slote attacks both hedonism and desire-satisfaction theories of the good on this ground. However, "global versions" of the desire-satisfaction theory can be defended against Slote's arguments. If, on the one hand, I would prefer to enjoy success as an adult rather than as a youth if I were fully rational, a desire-satisfaction theory can permit us to say that my success as an adult is of greater value. On the other hand, if the ideally rational me would not prefer success later in life, then there is no reason to accept Slote's claim that it would be preferable for me to succeed as an adult rather than as a youth. Moore's arguments about the organic unity of value can be modified to generate objections to summative versions of the desire-satisfaction theory. But, inasmuch as our global desires are not a sum of our individual desires, global versions of the desire-satisfaction theory are able to account for much of what Moore says about the "organic unity" of value.

Overvold attempts to modify the desire-satisfaction theory so as to allow for the (logical) possibility of self-sacrifice. He tries to do this by restricting the determination of one's self-interest to some subset of one's desires—one's desires for states of affairs of which one is an essential constituent. We have examined two strategies for using such a restriction to modify the desire-satisfaction theory. Overvold's strategy in his final formulation of the desire-satisfaction theory involves a counterfactual condition. On this view, a person's self-interest depends on what he would (rationally) prefer if he had *no* desires for states of affairs of which he was not an essential constituent. I formulated an alternative strategy: take a subset of one's actual preferences, determine their strength in isolation from one's other preferences, and sum them. One's self-interest is determined by the sum of this subset. Both of these strategies lead to serious problems. I am unable to formulate a fully satisfactory version of the desire-satisfaction theory. But, future development and refinement of the theory must take Overvold's work as a point of departure.

III

There are two general objections one might make to desire-satisfaction theories of welfare. First, the theory clashes with our intuitions about what kinds of lives are better than others and our intuitions about what sorts of things are most beneficial to individuals. The objection is that some people, even if they were fully rational and fully informed, would just prefer "the wrong things." The problem is that some people (even if they were fully rational) would prefer x to y, when y is better for them than x. This objection is reminiscent of standard objections to the hedonistic theory of value. In the case of the desire-satisfaction theory, the worry is that some people might prefer a "subhuman" life to lives in which they more fully develop their "higher" capacities. Rawls (1971, p. 432) presents the strange case of a person who possesses the capacity to do important work in applied mathematics, but instead chooses to devote himself to counting blades of grass. Some contend that this person would be better off if he became a mathematician, even though he prefers to count blades of grass.

The preferred formulation of the desire-satisfaction theory does not hold that welfare consists in the satisfaction of actual desires—actual desires are often irrational and ill-informed. Rather, welfare consists in the satisfaction of ideal desires—desires or preferences we would have were we fully rational. This requirement is very demanding. In order to be fully informed a person's preference for being a grass counter rather than a mathematician would have to involve a vivid understanding of what it would be like to live (and enjoy the satisfactions characteristic of) these two kinds of lives. It is very unlikely that anyone who possessed this knowledge would prefer counting grass to other vocations which more fully utilize his "higher" potentials. I would appeal to what Rawls calls the "Aristotelian Principle." The Aristotelian Principle says that "other things equal, human beings enjoy the exercise of their realized capacities (their innate or trained abilities), and this enjoyment increases the more the capacity is realized, or the greater its complexity" (1971, p. 426). A fully informed person would be aware of the truth of this principle and would also be aware the many plausible arguments hedonists have given for the *extrinsic* value of developing one's "higher capacities."

Still, there are likely to be some cases in which the ideal preferences of people conflict with our intuitions about welfare or about what sorts of lives are better than others. Perhaps we could imagine a case in which it would be rational for someone to prefer not to develop his higher capacities. Someone might have such a painful and traumatic past that the best way for him to cope with it would be to devote himself to mindless, repetitive activities. I conjecture that it would be rational to fail to develop one's higher capacities only in very unusual cases. In such cases our intuitions about how people best promote their own welfare should not carry much weight. At most, our intuitions carry weight in common or ordinary cases.[2] There are other reasons to impugn the intuitions to which critics of desire-satisfaction theories appeal. First, not everyone shares those intuitions. If our intuitions clash and you claim that yours are correct and mine mistaken, you need to be able show that my intuitions are mistaken for some reason other than that they conflict with yours.

> Since it is implied in the very notion of Truth that it is essentially the same for all minds, the denial by another of a proposition that I have affirmed has a tendency to impair my confidence in its validity....The absence of such disagreement must remain

---

2. Here, I make much the same kind of argument Hare (1981) makes in response to intuitive objections to utilitarianism. Very roughly, Hare argues that: (1) act utilitarianism conflicts with our moral intuitions only in unusual cases, and (2) our moral intuitions are unreliable in unusual cases.

an indispensable negative condition of the certainty of our beliefs. For if I find any of my judgments, intuitive or inferential, in direct conflict with a judgment of some other mind, there must be error somewhere: and I have no more reason to suspect error in the other mind than in my own. (Sidgwick 1907, pp. 341–42)

To find a difference of opinion between ourselves and others, or between our own age and previous ages, should weaken perhaps our confidence in our own opinions, but not weaken our confidence that there is some opinion that would be true. (Ross 1939, p. 19)

The philosopher who appeals to intuitions in attacking the desire-satisfaction theory owes us an explanation of conflicting intuitions and an explanation of why her intuitions are correct.

Second, the intuitionist critic needs to claim that her intuitions are more than just projections of her own preferences. She needs to claim that her intuitions are reports of things that she *knows*. But that is plausible only given the truth of some version of axiological realism (or realism about welfare) and axiological realism is a very dubious position (for much the same reason that moral realism is a dubious position).

It would be useful to contrast moral realism with metaphysical realism. A special case of metaphysical realism is realism about the physical world. Realism about the physical world is the view that physical world exists *independently* of human (or other) minds; it exists independently of being the actual or possible object of knowledge or perception. The notion of "mind independence" is what distinguishes metaphysical realism from the idealism of philosophers such as Berkeley. Berkeley grants the existence of physical objects. He is a nonrealist because he denies that physical objects are mind independent. To be a realist about a certain kind of entity or fact x is to (i) the believe that x exists or that there are facts of type x, and (ii) believe that those facts are (in some appropriate sense) *mind independent*. The main difficulty in defining a particular species of realism consists in the difficulty of appropriately characterizing "mind independence."

By "axiological realism" I mean the view that there are *facts* about what things are good and bad *for* people (facts about what things do and do not promote their welfare) and these facts are independent of (and not constituted by) facts about the beliefs, attitudes, emotions, or actions of human beings (or facts about the beliefs, attitudes, emotions, or actions of human beings under "ideal conditions").[3] On this view, we would say that it is rational for me to pursue certain ends *because they are good for me* (cf.

---

3. David Brink (1989, p. 17) gives a different charterization of "mind independence" in his definition of moral realism: (1) There are moral facts, or truths, and (2) these facts or truths are independent of the evidence for them.

Perry 1926, p. 4: "the theory of value...must locate the seat or *root* of value...is a thing valuable because it is valued?...Or, is a thing valued because it is valuable?") I am not offering an argument against axiological realism. I am only trying to show that one sort of objection to the desire satisfaction theory is plausible only given the truth of axiological realism. To say that some things *just are* good or bad for one—independently of whether one desires them or would desire them under ideal conditions—is to assume the truth of axiological realism. To the extent that axiological realism is a contentious and problematic view, this objection is also contentious and problematic. We need to answer certain metaethical questions before we can fully determine the plausibility of the desire-satisfaction theory of human welfare. In particular, we need to (1) determine the status of intuitions about welfare, and (2) determine the plausibility of axiological realism. Certain forms of axiological realism, e.g., Moore's theory of value and hedonistic versions of realism, are inconsistent with the desire-satisfaction theory of welfare.

Further support for my contentions about the connection between the desire-satisfaction theory and metaethical or metanormative issues can be found by looking at the argument against hedonism which Overvold presents in a long footnote at the end of "Self-Interest and the Concept of Self-Sacrifice" (1980). In this footnote Overvold formulates his own modified desire-satisfaction theory. But before doing this he first asks why not accept a hedonistic theory of self-interest instead? A hedonistic theory of self-interest can easily account for the possibility of self-sacrifice. But Overvold claims that we should reject such a theory because of the implausibility of hedonism as a theory of value. The key passage reads as follows.

> Insofar as there are things other than pleasure which have intrinsic value (knowledge, power, and achievements, etc.) it is natural to suppose that attaining them enhances an individual's welfare or self-interest. Thus a hedonistic account of self-interest will be no more plausible than hedonism as a general theory of value (p. 117).

Overvold is assuming the truth of something like Moore's theory of multiple intrinsic goods. Given this, it is plausible to suppose that some of these goods can be possessed by individuals and that when someone possesses them they are constitutive of his welfare. This is a very interesting argument, but it is not an argument that a desire-satisfaction theorist can make. If the argument works against a hedonistic theory of self-interest then it also works against a desire-satisfaction theory of self-interest. If knowledge is intrinsically good and if my possessing this good contributes to my welfare, then my possessing knowledge is good for me regardless of whether I desire it, or would desire it if I were rational. Acceptance of a desire-satisfaction theory of personal welfare would seem to presuppose the rejection of realist theories of multiple intrinsic goods such as Moore's.

Brandt raises a second sort of objection to desire-satisfaction theories of welfare, one that stems from the problem of changing desires. Indeed, Brandt's worries about this problem led him to abandon the desire-satisfaction theory (Brandt 1982). Let me present a very simple example in order to show the seriousness of the problem. I now have to make a decision whether to cause x or y. This decision will have a very important influence on the rest of my life. I know all the facts; my preference is ideally rational. Let us also stipulate that only self-regarding considerations enter into the decision. I now prefer x to y. But I know that when I turn 60 my preferences will change and I will prefer y to x and I will regret that I chose x when I was 40. On balance, am I better off choosing x or y?

Let us see how Overvold's theory would handle this sort of case. According to Overvold, what is in my self-interest depends on what my ideal preferences would be at the time of the choice—in this case it depends on my present ideal preferences. It seems to me that Overvold's theory gives undue weight to preferences that I have at the time that I act. Why don't my preferences at other times count? Why should the perspective of my present preferences be decisive in this example? Granted, that is when I make the choice, but I will have to live with the consequences of this choice for the rest of my life. (To add force to this example let us suppose that the choice that I am making today concerns financial planning for my retirement.)

The following seems to be at least a conceptual possibility on Overvold's theory. Every act that I perform maximizes my own welfare. But because my desires are constantly changing I have an utterly wretched life on account of regret over the past. At every moment in my life I am doing what I most want to do in light of my present desires, but I bitterly regret my entire past life and am profoundly dissatisfied with my life as a whole (see McFall 1988, p. 72).

This is a serious problem for the desire-satisfaction theory. I believe that it requires substantial reformulation of the theory. I will not hazard a proposal as to how the theory should be revised to deal with the problem of changing desires. I will conclude with some brief remarks that may serve to mitigate the force of this objection.

In real life actual preferences often change. They often change as a result of changes in what we know or believe. A person may have preferred a certain kind of career and then later discovered that he found it boring, or that he was not very good at it, or that there was some other career that he liked more. Our ideal preferences involve full information. Our ideal desires might not change very much through time. They might not change at all. Further, unless we are completely indifferent to our own future happiness, we all have a strong interest in avoiding regret. We can try to minimize regret by giving weight now to our future preferences.

The desire-satisfaction theory of welfare has been subjected to a number of powerful criticisms. It remains to be seen whether the theory can be modified so as to answer these objections. In any case, Overvold's project of refining the theory (rather than abandoning it) in light of these objections is a viable endeavor worthy of being continued at the present stage of philosophical debate.

16

The Relation of Pleasure to Desire in Butler's Moral Psychology*

Mark Carl Overvold

Philosophers have often credited Joseph Butler with having refuted egoism, the thesis that all human actions are motivated by self-interest. C. D. Broad puts it this way:

> It was...fashionable in Butler's time to deny the possibility of disinterested action....One of Butler's great merits is to have pointed out clearly and conclusively the ambiguities of language which make it plausible. As a psychological theory it was killed by Butler; ...he killed the theory so thoroughly that he sometimes seems to the modern reader to be flogging a dead horse. Still, all good fallacies go to America when they die, and rise again as the latest discoveries of the local professors. So it will be useful to have Butler's refutation at hand. (Broad 1930, pp. 54–55)

Despite Broad's high praise, Butler's argument is not without ambiguities of its own which need to be untangled if we are to understand Butler and, for those of us who are Americans, arm ourselves against our natural tendencies. In what follows, I will argue that Butler's "refutation" rests on a conceptual proposal about how we should talk about pleasure, happiness and interest and their relation to desire. The examination of Butler's proposal takes us to the heart of some of the thorniest puzzles about the relations between pleasure, desire and interest, so that even if Butler cannot be credited with having refuted egoism, his discussion serves to point the way to the most fertile ground for discussion.[1]

---

* This paper, which appears here for the first time, began life as a commentary on Richard G. Henson's "Understanding Butler: An Argument from Sermon xi" (which was presented at the American Philosophical Association Eastern Division meeting, December, 1984). I benefitted from discussing these issues with him as well as from comments by John Heil, Brad Hooker, and members of the Department of Philosophy at the University of Florida to whom an ancestor of this paper was presented.

1. Indeed one might wonder whether anyone could ever hope to refute egoism *tout court* given its protean character (or perhaps we should say its phoenix-like character). No

The essence of Butler's case against the egoist consists in arguing first that happiness, interest, and pleasure all require the existence of desires that are not themselves aimed at happiness, interest, or pleasure. Thus the egoist is wrong to claim that the only thing we desire is happiness or personal welfare. Second, Butler might also be taken to have shown that the benevolent passions provide as good a source of happiness as the particular passions, so there is no reason to disparage the benevolent passions even on the egoist's terms.

Butler makes the first point succinctly in a passage from sermon XI.

> That all particular appetites and passions are towards *external things themselves,* distinct from the *pleasure arising from them,* is manifested from hence; that there could not be this pleasure, were it not for that prior suitableness between the object and the passion.[2]

In the paragraph immediately preceding this one, Butler contrasts the "particular passions" with the desire for happiness, which differs by being general, not particular, and by its object being "somewhat internal." He offers the following as examples of particular passions: hunger, ambition, revenge, resentment, benevolence and love of the arts—a motley collection by any standard. What these seem to have in common is that they all have as their objects things of a determinate sort. Thus, revenge aims at bringing about some misfortune for one's enemy and will not be gratified by the misfortunes suffered by those not on the list of one's enemies, even if one were responsible for their misfortune. Hunger aims at getting and eating suitable foods and will not be satisfied by swallowing stones. What will gratify a particular passion is determined by the object or aim of that passion, and the important point is that for the particular passions this must be something of a determinate sort. Furthermore, a particular passion will be gratified when it achieves its object whether it conduces to the overall happiness of the agent or not. That is what makes it the particular passion that it is. The relationship involved is logical. This helps us to understand what Butler has in mind when he talks of "that prior suitableness between the object and the passion." The prior suitableness consists in the passion being a passion for that object.

The general desire for happiness, in contrast, does not, according to Butler, have this determinate character. He points out that someone can

---

sooner is one version refuted than another rises to take its place. Broad shows himself to be well aware of this in his "Egoism as a Theory of Human Motives" (1950/1952) where he distinguishes a variety of theories and discusses the extent to which they may be true.

2. Butler 1726/1950, sermon XI, ¶ 6, p. 51. Hereafter, references to passages in sermon XI will be parenthetical.

desire happiness without having any idea of, or concern for, the particular character of what will produce happiness. Anything that brings happiness or gratification will do, so far as self-love is concerned. Even here, however, not everything will do. There is a sense in which even self-love has a somewhat determinate character. It will be gratified only by those things which produce happiness, and this does exclude a number of possible pursuits and experiences.

So the distinction between a general desire like self-love and the particular passions is not as sharp as we might suppose. This is even clearer once we recognize the "general" character of some of the particular passions. A person seeking revenge, for example, may want and be gratified by *anything* bad that happens to his enemy. Similarly a person's ambition may be gratified by *any* pursuit that will yield success. Even hunger is general insofar as it can be satisfied by a range of things. When I want dessert in a restuarant, often any of the things on the menu would satisfy me. Waiters usually demand a more specific choice, but the prompting that leads me to express a desire for the chocolate mousse produces a desire that will be satisfied by any good dish of mousse, so even here there is a sense in which the desire might be said to be general. Thus the difference between the particular passions and the one general desire of self-love must be one of degree.

If we turn to the distinction between desires whose objects are internal and those whose objects are external, the problems are more serious. The only examples of internal objects that Butler provides are the agent's happiness, enjoyment, and satisfaction. Self-love, he tells us, is concerned with objects that are "somewhat internal." By contrast, the particular passions are aimed at external objects, for example, the happiness of another, the esteem of another, or food. This suggests a spatial analogy or perhaps a distinction between the psychological states of the agent and everything else. Unfortunately, this will not work for the examples of particular passions that Butler provides. Consider hunger, for instance, a desire for a piece of cake. Butler could point out that the piece of cake is something external. But this is too quick. Typically, a desire for a piece of cake is a desire to eat a piece of cake or to taste a piece of cake, and this is arguably something internal, whether the internal is understood to be something spatial or psychological. Thus while some particular passions have external objects as their objects (a desire that my neighbor be happy), others have apparently internal objects (a desire to be warm), and yet others have objects that are both somewhat internal and somewhat external (the desire to know that you trust me). The only sharp distinction we can be confident Butler wants to promote would be that the category of external objects is meant to exclude pleasure, happiness, and satisfaction.

With these distinctions in mind, we can understand Butler to be offering the following argument in the passage quoted earlier:

> *Premise*: The pleasures arising from any particular passion could not exist unless the object of that particular passion were something other than pleasure, happiness, or interest.
>
> *Conclusion*: All particular passions are desires for things other than pleasure, happiness, or interest.

The conclusion of the argument appears to give Butler what he needs to refute the egoist's claim that all desires are desires for happiness, interest, or pleasure, provided we add the assumption that there are pleasures arising from particular passions.

Two things about this argument, however, are troubling. First, how, we might wonder, can Butler hope to establish the connection claimed in the premise? Second, what justifies the universal form of the conclusion, the claim that all particular passions must have as their objects something other than pleasure, happiness, or interest?

How does Butler conceive the connection between the existence of a particular passion and the pleasure associated with it? As it stands, the premise implies a necessary connection between a pleasure and the particular passion that gives rise to that pleasure. How could Butler hope to establish such a sweeping claim? If it is an empirical issue, Butler's admirers cannot help but be troubled by the absence of any empirical evidence in the *Sermons* for the truth of this crucial premise. Butler might be content to have his readers consult their own experience for support of his claim, but even here it is hard to see how a universal connection might be established on the basis of introspection alone.[3]

The problem is serious. If Butler regards pleasure as an introspectively distinctive sensation, class of sensations, or even as an introspectively discernable feature of sensations (à la Duncker or Broad) the connection

---

3. Does Butler take himself to have shown that there is a contingent (presumably causal) connection between the existence of any pleasure and the (prior?) existence of a particular passion whose object is something other than pleasure? This, we might note, is an empirical issue. For a long time I took it for granted that this was Butler's view. If it were not, Butler would appear to be guilty of the very thing to which he objects in Hobbes and other egoists of making their claims true by definition and thereby robbing them of their significance. In what follows we shall see whether Butler is vulnerable to this criticism.

between the particular passions and the pleasures associated with them will have to be contingent, leading to the problems we have been discussing.

In sermon XI, Butler insists that the very idea of happiness "consists in this, that an appetite or affection enjoys its object." This remark occurs in a longer passage:

> Happiness or satisfaction consists only in the enjoyment of those objects, which are by nature suited to our several particular appetites, passions and affections. So that if self-love wholly engrosses us and leaves no room for any other principle, there can be absolutely no such thing at all as happiness, or enjoyment of any kind whatever; since happiness consists in the gratification of particular passions, which supposes the having of them. (¶ 9, p. 53)[4]

He repeats that claim in the summary of the argument in sermon XI appearing in the preface and goes on to say: "the very idea of interest or happiness, other than the absence of pain, implies particular appetites or passions; these being necessary to constitute that interest or happiness"(preface, ¶ 37, p. 14).

What these passages suggest is that Butler might be thinking that the connection between pleasure and the existence of particular passions (not themselves directed at that pleasure) is conceptual, that the idea of pleasure consists in the gratification of particular passions.[5]

This would explain Butler's acceptance of the crucial premise in the argument that "there could not be this pleasure, were it not for that prior suitableness between the object and the passion," for it would be true by definition that one could not get pleasure without an affection enjoying its object. It would also explain why the existence of pleasure, any pleasure, will entail the existence of a particular passion, and why the particular passions would have to be other than desires for pleasure to avoid the circularity of defining "pleasure" in terms of the desire for pleasure. The trouble with this solution is that the underlying assumption appears to be much too strong. What might Butler have in mind when he speaks of an appetite "enjoying" its object?

Perhaps he is referring to the *experience* of pleasure associated with the fulfillment of any desire in the sense that it naturally follows the fulfillment of a desire, perhaps the characteristic feeling of having a desire satisfied. But

---

4. See also Butler's remark on happiness at the beginning of ¶ 16, p. 60 and the observation (¶ 19, p. 63, emphasis added) that "the object of every particular affection is equally somewhat external to ourselves; and whether it be the good of another person, or whether it be any other external thing, makes no alteration with regard to its being one's own affection, and *the gratification of it one's own private enjoyment.*"

5. Strictly, these passages speak only of happiness and interest, not pleasure. But Butler often identifies pleasure with happiness.

talk of the characteristic feeling of having a desire satisfied leaves open the logical possibility of feelings that are introspectively indistinguishable from the feeling "characteristic of having a desire satisfied" (assuming there is such a feeling) without a corresponding appetite being satisfied. Why, then, restrict the term "pleasure" to cases where there was a particular passion to satisfy?

There is another reason to resist this suggestion. Recall our earlier discussion of the distinction between general desires and the particular passions. We concluded then that the contrast would have to be one of degree rather than kind. Butler would be on the firmest ground if he could point to a sense in which the desire for happiness must always be more general than the particular passions. If, on the one hand, happiness consists of the gratification of particular passions, the desire for happiness will always be more general than the particular passions, because it is understood to be a second-order desire requiring first-order desires (the particular passions) for its object. Whereas particular passions are directed at specifically characterizable objects, the object of self-love is always parasitic on the particular passions. If, on the other hand, Butler treats pleasure as a characteristic feeling, it will not be clear that one could not have such an experience as the object of a desire—why couldn't one desire an experience of precisely that sort?—and if that is all pleasure is, it will be hard to see the desire for pleasure as anything other than a particular passion.

If instead of talking of the "characteristic feeling" associated with the fulfillment of a desire we think of pleasure as the fulfillment of a desire, Butler's underlying assumption would be that the fulfillment of a particular passion is necessary (and perhaps sufficient) for having pleasure. There is much to be said for the claim that desire fulfillment is necessary for pleasure, but it seems mad to think that it is sufficient, unless the class of desires is severely restricted. To see this, we need only consider Othello's desire that Desdemona be faithful to him. Despite the fact that one of his strongest desires is fulfilled, Othello gets no pleasure from it.[6]

Suppose, however, "pleasure" were defined as "desired experience." The fulfillment of Othello's desire that Desdemona be faithful would not be a

---

6. While the claim is too broad, there is some reason to think that Butler may have been using it, unless Butler accepts an account of benevolent passions that limits them to desires to experience helping others, or to see others be happy, or otherwise to experience interacting with others, a view to be discussed below. Recall his readiness in ¶ 19, p. 62 (quoted above, note 4) to jump from the observation that pleasure requires particular passions to the claim that benevolent passions are as good a source of pleasure as any others, on the grounds that like any other particular passion, their object is external.

pleasure, on this view, since the object of the desire is not one of Othello's experiences.[7] It would also be advisable to limit the relevant class of desires to intrinsic desires for contemporaneous experiences (a subclass of Hare's now-for-now and then-for-then desires; see Hare 1981, pp. 101–6). The limitation to intrinsic desires rules out counterexamples like that of the person who desires to experience hardship to know what poverty is like. There is no reason to suppose that the experience must be pleasurable. The restriction to desires for contemporaneous experiences would allow Butler to rule out the familiar case of the teenager who looks forward to being with his girlfriend, only to be miserable the whole time because of his shyness.[8]

Should Butler welcome this suggestion? It might be objected that it saddles Butler with an implausible view of pleasure. If one reflects, however, on the wide range of experiences regarded as pleasurable, it is hard not to be impressed by their variety. Compare the pleasures of watching a beautiful sunset, eating a hearty meal, taking a fast-paced run through the city, or discussing a philosophical issue. If we look for something these have in common, the best suggestion may well be that they are all such that when they occur, the person wants them to continue.[9] This also serves as a reply to the complaint that the proposed definition would rob Butler's claim that the particular passions are necessary for pleasure of any significance by making it tautological. Butler, or his defender, can argue that there are good theoretical grounds for adopting the proposed definition of "pleasure." It would be significant to learn that the best (or only plausible) concept of pleasure entailed that whenever pleasure was experienced, there had to be distinct particular passions whose object was something other than pleasure.

Accepting this suggestion would provide Butler with a necessary connection between pleasure and desire. How would it affect the rest of Butler's case against the egoist? Butler's main achievement was to undercut a familiar strategy of the egoist. For every putative case of someone helping another "with no ulterior motive," the egoist finds a pleasure and claims that this must be the reason for the act. It is such arguments that Butler is thought to have silenced. On the account suggested, Butler's reply would be

---

7. For examples of recent discussions of pleasure of the sort I have in mind here, see Parfit 1984, appendix I; and Brandt 1979, pp. 253–57.

8. One might also, following the suggestions of Brandt (1979, pp. 253–57), limit it to desires that present experiences continue and insist further that the experience be causing the desire that the experience continue. But we have already run well beyond the text and what could plausibly be attributed to Butler.

9. It might be suggested that it is vacuous to use the existence of pleasure as the sole ground for saying there must be a corresponding appetite or suitability. I am not sure that we have any means of identifying our experiences as pleasures apart from noting when they occur that we desire them to continue.

that it is impossible that the only desire operative in these situations is a desire for pleasure. At least one other desire must be present. The person's pleasure will consist in the fact that the experiences had while helping the other person (and perhaps those of reflecting on it later) were such that, as they occurred, the person desired that the experiences (characterized as experiences of particular, distinctive kinds, for instance the experience of seeing the smile on the other person's face, thinking how one would feel if one were in that person's shoes, accepting the person's thanks, remembering how happy the person looked) continue.

At this point the egoist might reply: "Still, all the person wants is *the experience* of helping another, and that is just *that person's experience*, so the act really is selfish, as I claim." What the egoist has done is to point to an important difference between a desire *that one experience making others happy* and a desire *that others be happy*. Which does Butler have in mind when he speaks of the benevolent passions and which does he need in order to refute the egoist?

Butler might be willing to settle for only the first, that is, for a view that sees the benevolent passions as desires to experience the various aspects of helping and interacting with others. This would make it easiest for him to establish what he says in the preface is his chief aim in sermon XI, "to state the notion of self-love and disinterestedness, in order to show that benevolence is not more unfriendly to self-love, than any other particular affection whatever" (¶ 35, p. 12). Provided that benevolent passions are restricted to those whose objects are experiences of the agent, fulfilling them will yield pleasure, and the benevolent passions will not differ in their relation to pleasure from any other particular passion whose object is an experience of the agent. Butler could use this account "to obviate the scorn, which one sees rising upon the faces of people who are said to know the world, when mention is made of a disinterested, generous, or public-spirited action" (¶ 38, pp. 14–15), for, he might say, it is enough that people genuinely enjoy helping others. The egoist may call that selfish if he wishes, but then we still need some distinction to mark the difference between those who enjoy helping others and those who get no intrinsic enjoyment from helping others or seeing them do well. So on this alternative, much of Butler's program can be retained.

I suspect, however, that Butler would have wanted to claim more than this. At least, many have thought that Butler established the existence of desires that were much more benevolent in character than those we have just been discussing. This suggests Butler would have preferred the second alternative according to which the benevolent passions are understood to be desires *for the good of another* rather than merely desires *to experience another person's doing well,* or *to experience bringing it about that others do well.* How does this affect his claim that the benevolent passions are as good a source of happiness and pleasure as any other? If Butler conceives of pleasure as desired experience, he will not have shown anything like that in the argument we have been considering. The most the argument has shown is that pleasure requires particular passions whose objects are experiences of the agent, and benevolent passions, in the sense we are now considering, are not desires of that sort. If Butler has arguments, they must lie elsewhere.

How then could Butler make the case for the benevolent passions if they are understood to be desires for the well-being of others? Two matters are important.

First, Butler says over and over again that his dispute with the egoist should be seen as an empirical dispute, and he thinks the verdict should be obvious to anyone. Perhaps he is thinking that if he can just get people to focus on the diverse character of their desires, they will see immediately that they do have many desires simply for the good or well-being of others. Extensive empirical argument may not be necessary.

That, however, raises a second issue, since it leaves open the question of whether the benevolent passions are as good a source of happiness as any other. Here I think it is instructive to recall that elsewhere in sermon XI, Butler moves back and forth between recommending the benevolent passions as sources of happiness and talk of a love of the arts. Behind both of these lies the commonsense suggestion that, as one extends the range of things one cares about, one extends the range of experiences that give one pleasure. It must be remembered, however, that the fulfillment of a benevolent passion or even the knowledge that it has been fulfilled in a latent or dispositional sense does not guarantee that the person gets pleasure, given the view of pleasure with which we have been working. If a very strong benevolent passion is fulfilled, even if the agent knows this is the case, he may get very little pleasure if distracted from thinking about or watching, or revelling in, the state of affairs that constitutes the fulfillment of the benevolent passion.

We sometimes talk of people who fail to take the time to enjoy their successes. Surely they know they have had success. But if they never take the time to reflect on their accomplishments, they may get very little pleasure, despite the fact that they have intense desires for success and these have been fulfilled. This is essentially Butler's point about the importance of disengagement: "a person may have so steady and fixed an eye upon his own interest whatever he places it in, as may hinder him from attending to many gratifications within his reach, which others have their minds free and open to" (§ 9, p. 54). The same thing applies to benevolent passions. In most cases, the individual will have some time to watch or think about the fulfillment of his benevolent passion, and these experiences will be pleasant in that, when they occur, he will desire that the experience (for instance the watching or the thinking about) continue. Presumably, if the original benevolent passion had not been present, if the agent were quite indifferent to the state of affairs, this would not happen.

On the second alternative, Butler will have to qualify his praise of the benevolent passions. He will not be able to say that they always lead to pleasure. He can, and does, argue, however, that a bold, wide-ranging strategy that involves cultivating the benevolent passions (as one might cultivate an interest in the arts), is more likely, or at least *as* likely, to lead to pleasure or happiness, as would a narrow strategy of pursuing and cultivating the more private passions and appetites.

17

Sidgwick's *Methods of Ethics,* Edition 7, Page 92, Note 1[*]

William K. Frankena

In conversation before a seminar, A. N. Whitehead said one day, in answer to a question from me, that Sidgwick's *Methods of Ethics* was the dullest book ever written, and that this was one of the reasons why he himself had not written about ethics. Having just read Sidgwick's book during a hot summer in Iowa, I was somewhat inclined to share Whitehead's sentiments at the time, but I have long since come to find it most interesting, including even or especially its footnotes. It is one of those footnotes about which I propose to write now. The topic involved would have been of interest to Mark Overvold, one of my best and favorite students, for it relates to the history of the discussion of his problem about whether or not the rationality of one's actions depends on one's experiencing the results oneself. In my opinion, no one had posed the terms of this question as well as he did, not even Sidgwick.

The footnote in question reads as follows:

> I shall afterwards try to explain how it comes about that, in modern thought, the proposition "My own Good is my only reasonable ultimate end" is not a mere tautology, even though we define "Good" as that at which it is ultimately reasonable to aim. (Cf. *post*, chapter IX and Book III, chapters XIII, XIV.)

The context is a short preliminary chapter on "Egoism and Self-Love" in which Sidgwick discusses several "interpretations" of ethical egoism in order to set them aside before proceeding further. The main one is that in which self-realization is represented as the only reasonable ultimate end. Having discarded this view as too indefinite to provide a distinct method of ethics, he then writes,

---

[*] This paper appears here for the first time.

for a similar reason we must discard a common account of Egoism which describes its ultimate end as the "good" of the individual; for the term "good" may cover all possible views of the ultimate end of rational conduct. Indeed it may be said that Egoism in this sense was assumed in the whole ethical controversy of ancient Greece; that is, it was assumed on all sides that a rational individual* would make the pursuit of his own good his supreme aim: the controverted question was whether this Good was rightly conceived as Pleasure or Virtue, or any *tertium quid*. (pp. 91–92)[1]

The footnote is attached to the last sentence at the point indicated by my asterisk. Incidentally, it is one of six footnotes in which Sidgwick refers ahead to what he is going to do in chapter IX, mostly on different topics.

I

These two passages make it clear that Sidgwick holds the following views: (1) that the ancient Greeks were egoists in the sense of taking for granted that the ultimate end is the good of the individual, not just in the psychological sense that one's own good is what one does ultimately aim at, but also in the more normative sense that it is what one will aim at if and insofar as one is rational; (2) that we moderns define "good" as that at which it is ultimately reasonable to aim; and (3) that the statement "my own good is my only reasonable ultimate end" is not a mere tautology for us, even though we define "good" in this way. It may be that Sidgwick thought the Greeks also defined "good" as we do, but he does not say or imply that this is so, at least not in these passages. He must also be holding (4) that modern ethical theory is not all egoistic in the sense indicated in (1), though he does not say so here. Now, (4) is obviously true; Hobbes and Spinoza were egoists, according to Sidgwick, but the intuitionists and utilitarians were not. It follows that (3) is true; said statement (hereafter *IT*) cannot even be true for intuitionists and utilitarians, let alone be a tautology.[2] For the purposes of this paper, I shall also assume (1) and (2) to be true, even though I doubt that (2) is true for all modern moral philosophers (it is I think true for Sidgwick himself). What interests me here is his saying in the footnote that

---

1. Numbers in parentheses in text refer to pages in *ME* or *OHE*, as the case may be. *ME* = *The Methods of Ethics*, 7th ed. (Sidgwick 1907); *OHE* = *Outlines of the History of Ethics*, 6th ed. (Sidgwick 1931).

2. Actually, an intuitionist in Sidgwick's sense *might* accept *IT*, though he is not likely to. For he can hold that what is right is not determined in whole or even in part by a consideration of what is good or of what is conducive to an end (*ME*, p. 3; *OHE*, p. 6). Even if he holds that there is an end to be pursued, viz., to do the right or to be morally good, he will not use this end in determining what is right or morally good. Thus, he can accept *IT* as part of the truth but will deny that it is the whole truth or even that it is an important element in the truth.

he will "try to explain how it comes about that [*IT*] is not a mere tautology" in modern thought. *What* does he mean to try to explain there and *how?*

Before going on to see, I must discuss another point. It is natural for a reader of our footnote to think that Sidgwick also held the view, (5) that *IT was* a mere tautology for the Greeks.[3] And it is true that, for all his respect for them, he is inclined to charge them with circularity and tautology, as we shall see. But I am not sure he means to do so here. He is, of course, implying that for the Greeks it was a mere truism—something they all took for granted, almost as going without saying—that a rational individual will make his own good his supreme aim. But this does not mean that *IT* was a mere tautology for them, certainly not that it was consciously so. In chapter IX to which he refers, Sidgwick argues that hedonists "who affirm—as a significant proposition and not as a mere tautology—that the Pleasure or Happiness of human beings is their Good or Ultimate Good" (p. 109) cannot be understood as thinking that "the good" just *means* "pleasure" or "happiness"; for, if it did, then "Pleasure (or happiness) is the good" would come to the same thing as "Pleasure is pleasure (or happiness is happiness)." The Greeks must similarly have affirmed or assumed their truism as a significant proposition and not as a mere tautology, and, if Sidgwick thought otherwise, he was simply mistaken.[4] That is why I say he may not have meant to imply that (5) is true, even though it is hard to see why he is interested in explaining how *IT* is not a tautology for us moderns if he is not thinking it was one for the ancients.

Now, suppose that the Greeks had (also) defined the good as that at which it is ultimately reasonable to aim. Then, by Sidgwick's logic in chapter IX, their common assumption would seem to be tantamount to "a rational individual will take what it is ultimately reasonable to aim at as his supreme end." But it still would not be a mere tautology, and they might not have regarded it as one even if they took it for granted. Even if they understood their truism as meaning that what it is ultimately reasonable for me to aim at is my only reasonable ultimate end—in which case it would seem to be a mere tautology—it still would not follow that they were egoists. That would depend on what they thought it is ultimately rational for one to aim at.

It is therefore somewhat unclear what Sidgwick can be thinking he is going to try to explain in the chapters he refers to. Is it how it comes about that we moderns no longer assume egoism in the sense indicated in my

---

3. One cannot help but wonder if "once a tautology, always a tautology" is not necessarily true, but I shall ignore this question.

4. Even if they did regard *IT* as a tautology, it does not follow that they did not define "good" as Sidgwick says we moderns do. See below.

second quotation to be true, or even think it to be; or is it how it comes about that *IT* is not a mere tautology (in the strict logical sense) for us? There is also another problem: What kind of an explanation is Sidgwick going to try to give? His words "how it comes about that" are somewhat ambiguous. They most naturally suggest that he will try to give a historical account of the rise of our modern ethical ethos or way of thinking. But such an account would be out of place in *ME,* even though it does contain many historical passages, and would rather belong in *OHE,* which we shall look at later. It could be, however, that Sidgwick has in mind to give a merely conceptual or logical explanation of how *IT* can be nontautological for us moderns *even though* we define "good" in the way indicated in our footnote. Such an explanation could be briefer and would also be more in place in *ME.* I emphasize the words "even though" because I am assuming that Sidgwick does not mean "even if," which would not commit him to what I called view (2). But actually I think he means to try to explain how it comes about that *IT* is not a mere tautology for us, *whether or not* we define "good" in the manner in question. I also think he means to explain why we regard *IT* as false, and not just as neither a tautology nor a truism.

II

With all of this in mind, let us look at what Sidgwick actually does in the three chapters he refers to and how. He himself gives us no help in this, for he nowhere refers back to our footnote or indicates that he is doing what he said there he would try to do. We simply have to see what we find that may be relevant, if anything. I may add that it is even harder to see where and how Sidgwick does what he says in some other footnotes he is going to do afterwards; he may not hang out red herring, but he does let loose threads dangle. My feeling is that he first wrote out those three chapters and then later put in the footnotes referring ahead to them, without checking to see how aptly they fitted. He did, after all, see *ME* through six editions![5]

The first chapter Sidgwick refers to in our footnote is ix of Book i, entitled simply "Good" and apparently intended as a preliminary discussion of that topic. Most of it deals with the meaning of "good," as adjective and substantive, "in the whole range of its application," but with an emphasis on "good" as applied to "ultimate ends" and on the expression "good in itself," and with some attention to the differences between "good" and "right." Before that, however, there is an interesting historical paragraph about the differences between ancient and modern ethics. Its main point is that the Greeks emphasized the "attractive" and nonjural notion of "good" while the

---

5. Our footnote first appears in the 3rd edition (1889).

moderns stress the "imperative" and "quasijural" notions of "right," "duty," and "law," with the Stoics forming a "transitional link" through their conception of natural law. This at least suggests a historical explanation of the sort mentioned earlier, but actually the paragraph does nothing more specific to show how it came about that *IT* is not a tautology for us or even that we are no longer egoists. Everything in it is compatible with ethical egoism as Sidgwick defines it (pp. 95, 119).

As for Sidgwick's treatment of the meaning of "good": given our concerns here, one wonders whether he thinks he is discussing (only) modern views about this or means to cover ancient ones as well. The relevant sections (2 and 3) contain nothing bearing on this question, though the paragraph just reviewed suggests he has ancient usage in mind as well as modern. However, he certainly means at least to be explicating the latter, and we may therefore expect him to say something relating to view (2). To proceed then, Sidgwick first argues that "good" does not mean "pleasant" or "actually desired;" rather, it means "desirable," either in the sense of what one *ought* to desire or in the sense of what one *would* desire *if* one possessed "a perfect forecast, emotional as well as intellectual, of the state of attainment or fruition." Then he concentrates on the notion of a person's "good on the whole," and considers the following definition of the would-if kind: "A man's good on the whole is what he would now desire and seek on the whole if all the consequences of all the different lines of conduct open to him were accurately foreseen and adequately realised in imagination at the present point of time" (pp. 111–12). He says he cannot deny that this definition "supplies an intelligible and admissible interpretation" of the terms "good" and "desirable," but notes that it is made out entirely "in terms of *fact,* actual or hypothetical," and does not introduce any "judgement of value" or any "dictate of Reason." He then argues that for (modern?) common sense the notion of my "good on the whole" is "*authoritative,* and therefore carries with it implicitly a rational dictate to aim at this end, if in any case a conflicting desire urges the will in an opposite direction." One might take this to mean that he thinks "my good on the whole" can be defined only by reference to what I *ought* to desire and seek on the whole; C. D. Broad draws precisely this conclusion. I now doubt, however, that it is what Sidgwick means to be concluding himself.[6] For he goes on to say, "Still we may keep the notion of 'dictate' or 'imperative' merely implicit and latent—as it seems to be in ordinary judgements as to 'my good' and its opposite"; and I take this to mean that

---

6. See his 1930, p. 176. I mistakenly followed Broad in my article on Sidgwick in Ferm 1956, p. 541.

we need not make it explicit by using "ought" in our definition. He then seems to give us the following two definitions (my italics):

(a)   "My ultimate good on the whole" means "what I should practically desire if my desires were *in harmony with reason*, assuming my own existence alone to be considered."

(b)   "Ultimate good on the whole," unqualified by reference to a particular subject, means "what as a *rational* being I should desire and seek to realize, assuming myself to have an equal concern for *all* existence." (p. 112)

As I read what Sidgwick does here, I take him to mean that, in accordance with modern common sense, we may define "good" and "desirable" in terms, not of "ought" or "right," but in terms of what it is *rational* to desire and seek. Broad is inexplicably misled by Sidgwick's use of "should" in (a) and (b) ; but surely the rules of grammar require us to take his "should" to mean "would if," not "ought to."[7]

Coming back to our footnote, I think we can conclude at least that Sidgwick is arguing here that we moderns, including himself, do define the good as that at which it is ultimately reasonable to aim, as view (2) says. But does his discussion explain how it comes about that *IT* is not a tautology for us, whether we so define the good or not? The answer is not at all clear. Obviously his discussion thus far does not give a historical explanation of anything, but it still may provide a conceptual or logical explanation of how it can be that *IT* is not a tautology for us moderns, since it offers us an analysis of what we mean by "my good on the whole," which forms *IT*'s subject term. If we use this analysis, and substitute "would" for "should" so as to avoid misleading readers like Broad, then *IT* will be equivalent to the following: "What I would desire or seek to realize if I were rational and considered only my own existence is my only rational ultimate end." Now, this certainly looks like a tautology, and it may be that the Greeks would have thought it to be one. Is it not one for us and if not, why not? Sidgwick does not say, but clearly thinks that (b) is part of our modern conceptual scheme as well as (a)—which may not have been true of the Greeks—and, if it is, then for us *IT*, as just reformulated, will not necessarily be true, for then it may be that I will not consider my own existence only but *all* existence, and, if rational, take as my ultimate end the ultimate good on the whole, unqualified by any reference to myself. Then Sidgwick would in effect be thinking that we moderns have another conception of what is rational besides or instead of that of the ancients, and that this is why *IT* is

---

7. In connection with my discussion, see Schneewind 1977, pp. 221–29.

not a tautology for us, or even necessarily true, even if or though we define the good à la view (2).[8]

Another way of representing Sidgwick's thinking here might be to say that defining "good" as what it is ultimately reasonable to aim at leaves it open for one not be an ethical egoist. One can then be an egoist, but one can equally well be either an intuitionist or a utilitarian, depending on what one regards as ultimately reasonable to aim at. Thus one can define "good" in the manner indicated and yet deny that *IT* is a mere tautology and even that it is true.

Then Sidgwick does in chapter IX furnish us with the materials for constructing a conceptual explanation of how it can be that *IT* is not a tautology for us, though he does not actually spell out such an explanation himself. But he still has not offered us a historical explanation of this fact or of how it came about that we have the conceptual scheme he thinks we have. Let us therefore go on. Section 4 of chapter IX does nothing for our purposes, but perhaps chapters XIII and XIV of Book III will. The former is on "Philosophical Intuitionism" and again contains nothing that is explicitly relevant to our footnote. In section 2 Sidgwick does, as I indicated earlier, charge the Greeks with depending on a number of circular or tautological "sham-axioms," but, interestingly, *IT* is not among them (pp. 374–79). Most of the rest of the chapter is given to a search for "self-evident moral principles of real significance," and, as is well known, he thinks he finds three that are either self-evident or rest on "self-evident elements": the principle of rational egoism, that of rational benevolence or utilitarianism, and a principle of equity or just distribution. He does not relate these findings to our problem, but, since the last two principles are nonegoistic, it follows that at least for him *IT* cannot be a mere tautology. In fact, even the first of these principles is for him a synthetic one of real significance. And, since he finds these principles by way of a reflection on Samuel Clarke, Kant, and other modern moral philosophers, we may suppose he thinks he has shown that *IT* is also not a tautology in modern thought generally.

Chapter XIV is on the good again; entitled "Ultimate Good," it is concerned, not with the meaning of "good," or of "the good," but with the question what is ultimately good, to which, as is also well known, Sidgwick gives a hedonistic answer. Only the opening paragraph is possibly relevant here. Its main point is that his previous discussion shows that "the practical determination of Right Conduct depends on the determination of Ultimate Good" as the ancients thought, and that we are therefore "brought round

---

8. Here see *OHE*, p. 198; also Frankena 1983. Actually, Sidgwick regarded all three of the principles mentioned in the next paragraph as synthetic, though necessary.

again to the old question with which ethical speculation in Europe began, 'What is the Ultimate Good for man?'—though not in the egoistic form in which the old question was raised." His adding the last clause is a bit misleading, since he believes that the principle of rational egoism is true, but the whole paragraph reflects his own belief—and that of much modern thought—that ethical egoism is in any case not the whole truth. It thus shows again that *IT* is not a tautology for us moderns, though it has nothing to add to the explanation of how this can be or came to be.

III

The above completes our review of the later chapters to which Sidgwick refers us for an explanation of "how it comes about that" *IT* is not a mere tautology for modern thought, whether or not it was one for the Greeks. We have found nothing like an explicit statement of an explanation, but we have found the makings of one kind of explanation, viz., a logical or conceptual one, mainly in chapter IX of Book I. Sidgwick's words suggest, however, that he may also have a historical explanation in mind—a historical story that explains how the modern ethos, so different from the ancient one, came about. I propose now to look at *OHE*, which was written as an encyclopedia article in 1878 and expanded into a book in 1886, i.e., after the first edition of *ME* and before some of the later ones. Since he was working on various editions of the two books at the same time, we may be able to find in *OHE* at least the outlines of a story that will complete the explanation promised in that footnote in *ME*. I must of course be brief and sketchy—and consequently most unjust to his profound, rich, judicious, and altogether remarkable little history. I shall also pick and choose from his larger scenario only what is relevant to our footnote, which Sidgwick may not have had in mind at all as he wrote *OHE*.

We have already noted that in *ME*, Sidgwick sees the following differences between ancient and modern ethics: (1) the former is egoistic, as *IT* is, but modern ethics is generally nonegoistic, and (2) in the former attractive nonjural notions like "good" and "virtue" are basic and primary, while in the latter jural or quasijural imperative notions are typically either of more central or of at least equal importance. He does also say there that another difference, which he seems to regard as the most basic, is that the former uses a "generic notion" and the latter a "specific one in expressing the common moral judgments on actions" (pp. 105–6), but his thinking on this point and its relevance to our concerns are not clear to me, and so I shall ignore it here. Toward the end of *OHE*, however, Sidgwick finds another difference, which he also calls "the most fundamental," and which is more relevant, viz., (3) ancient ethics recognizes but one regulative and governing faculty in human nature, egoistic reason or self-love, while modern ethics finds another in addition—universal reason or conscience (pp. 197–98); in this sense, the former is monistic, the latter dualistic. What we want then is his story about how these three differences came about.

In the introduction to *OHE*, Sidgwick gives a "brief conspectus" of what is to follow, but says nothing to our purposes. Chapter I is a general account of the subject of ethics, partly systematic and partly historical. As in *ME* he sees the ancient conception of ethics as asking, not what is right or duty or law, but "what is ultimately good or desirable for man," and adds that there is another conception of ethics "in which it is thought to be concerned primarily with the general rules of Duty or Right Action...viewed as absolutely binding on every man...." He also says, "it has a close affinity to abstract jurisprudence, so far as this is conceived to treat of rules of Law cognisable by reason as naturally and universally valid...," and may be regarded as "a modern view of ethics," the transition from the ancient view to the modern one "being due chiefly to the influence of Christianity, but partly also to that of Roman jurisprudence"—and to that of Stoicism. Through these influences "the subject matter of Ethics defined itself afresh as Moral Law, a body of rules absolutely prescribed, and supplying a complete guidance for human conduct, though not claiming to contain an exhaustive statement of human good." This moral law, he goes on, came to be thought of in Christianity as known either wholly by revelation or else partly by reason, and usually as consisting of revealed law and natural law. Along with "this jural view of morality" came the view of "conscience" as the moral faculty, "a faculty cognisant of rules absolutely binding," either via a special revelation or via a general revelation through human reason. Thus egoistic reason came to be regarded as no longer our only or primary regulative faculty, even if egoism was not explicitly rejected. The way was then open for at least one kind of ethical dualism—the view that there are two regulative faculties, egoistic reason and nonegoistic conscience.

Here then we have the germ of an answer to our question. Now let us see what chapter II on "Greek and Greco-Roman Ethics" has to add. Surprisingly, Sidgwick does not here play up the egoism he regards as characteristic of Greek ethics, though he does emphasize its concern with the achievement of human good. In connection with the Sophists he speaks only of a "fusion of the moral view of life with the prudential view" (p. 20), and in connection with Socrates of "an inseparable union of the conception of Virtue and Interest in the single notion of Good" (26). Most interesting for our purposes is his writing (pp. 24–25) that "if we would understand the position, not of Socrates only, but of ancient ethical philosophy generally" we must realize that it goes "from a pair of apparent truisms," viz., (a) that "every one wishes for his own good, and would get it if he could," and (b) "that justice and virtue [are] goods, and of all goods the finest," to the "nearly unanswerable deduction[s]," (c) that those who know what are just and righteous acts will prefer nothing else, and (d) "that justice and all other virtues [are] summed up in wisdom or knowledge of good." Sidgwick does not use or mention *IT* here but he is ascribing to Socrates and the other Greeks the egoism with which he associates it. Still, he does not make much of this in dealing with Plato and Aristotle, though he notes that Socrates and Plato "frequently assume" that "the ultimate good for any individual man is his own 'welfare' or 'wellbeing'" (p. 48). And he does, of course, describe the Epicureans as "egoistic hedonists" (p. 89).

This brings us to Stoicism. Just how, according to Sidgwick, does it help make the transition to the modern point of view? Well, the Stoics stressed the idea of a number of "duties" to be performed in life, and they tied this to the further ideas of conformity to nature and to universal laws of nature and reason and God (which they in effect equated), laws "binding upon a man as a rational being and a member of the great cosmic commonwealth of all rational beings."

> In giving prominence to this conception, Stoicism furnished the transition from the old Greek view of ethics, in which the notions of Good and Virtue were taken as fundamental, to the modern view in which ethics is conceived as primarily a study of the "moral code."

Through Cicero and Roman jurisprudence Stoicism made current "the conception of Natural Law...[which] became, as we shall see, the leading or cardinal conception of modern ethical speculation in its first stage" (pp. 97–98).

This brings us to chapter III on "Christianity and Medieval Ethics." Here Sidgwick, like many others, speaks of the rise of a "new moral consciousness." As its first feature he identifies "the conception of morality as the positive law of a theocratic community," writing that

> even if the notion of law had been more prominent than it was in ancient ethical thought, it could never have led to a juridical, as distinct from a philosophical, treatment of morality. In Christianity, on the other hand, we early find that the method of moralists determining right conduct is to a great extent analogous to that of jurists interpreting a code....This juridical method descended naturally from the Jewish theocracy, which was universalized in Christendom. (pp. 111–13)

Sidgwick also identifies other familiar and counterbalancing features of the new moral consciousness, especially its "inwardness," its theological virtues of faith, hope, and love, and its insistence on obedience, patience, benevolence, purity, humility, and alienation from the world and the flesh.

He particularly observes that love and benevolence were stressed by Christianity in ways that go well beyond anything in ancient ethics, thus preparing the way for the rejection of egoism and the development of utilitarianism in modern times. He also notices that Aquinas, for all his use of Aristotle, cast his ethics at least partly in terms of law, "divine" or specially revealed law, and "natural" law (which he also conceived of as God's law). This jural conception of ethics was much sharpened by the voluntarism of many of Aquinas's successors and came out most sharply in the casuistry that arose later in both Catholic and Protestant circles.

We now have most of the historical story we were looking for. In chapter IV on "Modern, Chiefly English, Ethics," Sidgwick first mentions the seventeenth century concern to replace this theological quasijural conception with a more independently philosophical one that still centers around such concepts as "right," "duty," "obligation," and "law," and shows how it emphasized the doctrine of natural law for some time and kept the concept of moral law for even longer (e.g., in the intuitionists, the theological utilitarians, and Kant). He also highlights the clear and explicit rejection of both psychological and ethical egoism in Shaftesbury, Hutcheson, and Butler, not so much in opposition to the ancients as to Hobbes; this he says first really made the philosophical development of nonegoistic ethics possible (pp. 183–84). In this way, Sidgwick traces the rise, out of Stoicism, Roman jurisprudence, and Christianity, of the two new characteristically modern "methods of ethics"—intuitionism and utilitarianism—which, along with egoism, he is mainly interested in discussing in *ME*.

What stands out in my impoverished sketch of Sidgwicks's story is this rise in modern ethics of deontological intuitionism, in which quasi-jural notions are basic and central and that of the good secondary, and of universalistic utilitarianism, which makes the pursuit of the good central, as ancient ethics did, but in a nonegoistic way. Even in the latter, as Sidgwick sees it, the notions of the right and of duty are also central, not just secondary or derivative, since it thinks of conduciveness to the greatest general good as the criterion for determining what it is right or duty to do; it is still a "method of ethics" in his sense, viz., a "rational procedure by which we determine what individual human beings '*ought*'—or what it is '*right*' for them to do, or to seek to realise by voluntary action" (p. 1, my italics). That, for Sidgwick, is what *we* want to know; "the controverted question" for us is whether or not a consideration of the good is needed to know what we ought to do, and, if so, in just what way. In any case, given his picture of modern ethics, we can see in this story at least roughly how it came about that *IT* is not now a tautology and egoism no longer a truism. Both intuitionism and utilitarianism, at least as Sidgwick sees them, in some sense or other deny that my own good is my only reasonable ultimate end, and we have traced his explanation of how they came about historically.[9]

IV

One thing more. I cannot forbear pointing out that there is an aspect of modern ethical thought to which Sidgwick is largely blind, due especially to his predilection to identify the morally or ethically right with the ultimately or practically rational. Actually, very few modern British moral philosophers make this identification in anything like the way he does. It is more characteristic of modern ethical writers to think that it must be shown (or postulated) that being moral, being virtuous, and doing right are ultimately rational for one to be or do. Sidgwick probably took his cue here from the Greek philosophers, even though Plato spent much of his *Republic* trying to show that justice is profitable in terms of happiness or self-interest and therefore rational. But both intuitionists and utilitarians reject the view that one's own good or interest is or can be the basic criterion of what is right or virtuous, even if they agree, in Butler's words, that "when we sit down in a cool hour, we can neither justify to ourselves this [pursuit of what is right] or any other pursuit, till we are convinced that it will be for our happiness, or at least not contrary to it" (quoted in *OHE*, p. 196). In this sense they not only disown the old view in which *IT* can be taken as a tautology, a truism, or at least a truth; they *also* disown Sidgwick's equation, borrowed from that view, of the moral or ethical with the practical or rational. Like him, they reject *IT*, but they do so from a *very* different perspective, since they do not conceive of ethics as simply the determination of what it is ultimately rational to be or do, as he and the Greek philosophers do. Even if he and they are right about this, Sidgwick is nevertheless mistaken in assuming that his view of ethics is that of all or even most modern moral philosophers.

Perhaps I can make my last point clearer. There are two ways of conceiving of ethics (or moral philosophy), different from and more fundamental than those distinguished by Sidgwick in *OHE*, chapter 1, and mentioned earlier. The first is to think of it as having only *one* task, viz., to determine or help us to determine what it is morally (or ethically) right or good to do or be, together of course with everything else that goes with doing this. Those who take this line have two alternatives. One is to identify the morally right or good with whatever it is finally *rational* to do or be. The other is to define the moral in some *other* way, e.g., in terms of respecting or loving others, or being concerned about their welfare. Either way, it would be held to be no part of ethics to ask or try to answer the questions, "Why

---

9. Here see again note 2, above.

should one be moral?" or "Is it rational to be moral?" Sidgwick, as I understand him, conceives of ethics in this first way and chooses the former alternative. The other way of conceiving of ethics is to think of it as having *two* tasks: one is to determine or help determine what is morally right or good, where this is defined, say, in terms of respect or love or concern for the welfare of others; the second is to try to show that we should, or that it is rational for us to, be moral in that way. My point, then, was to suggest that Sidgwick ignores this second way of conceiving of ethics and that it is more typical of modern moral philosophy than his is.[10]

---

10. In connection with this section, see *ME*, pp. 25, 119; also Schneewind 1977, p. 228; Frankena 1974, esp. 449–52; as well as Frankena 1992; Nagel 1986, chapter 10; and Williams 1985, chapter 1.

18

Egoism and Morality in the Theological Teleology of Thomas Aquinas[*]

John Langan, S. J.

At the beginning of the *Prima Secundae*, which is the part of the *Summa Theologiae* that deals with general questions of moral theory, Thomas places the questions concerning the ultimate purpose of human life and happiness or beatitude; for, as he says, "all our plans get their meanings from their final purpose" (*S.T.* I–II, *prologus*). Thomas adopts from Aristotle a teleological account of human activity in general (see Aristotle, *Nicomachean Ethics*, book i, chapter 1, 1094ª1–5). For Thomas, all human acts, that is, those acts which are proper to human agents and over which they exercise control by intellect and will "must be for the sake of an end" (*S.T.* I–II, 1, 1c). It is the intellect in its practical function that directs or orders things to an end or good which is desired by the will. Thomas writes: "Now the object of will is being an end and good, and so it is clear that this is the determining principle[1] of human acts as such" (*S.T.* I–II, 1, 3c).

Starting from this teleological notion of human action, Thomas then sets out to show that there is one ultimate end that all human beings seek in all their actions. The first step that he takes in arguing for this controversial conclusion is to observe that in the double pattern of intention and execution that is characteristic of final causality there must always be something first. In the order of intention this must be a *finis ultimus*, which is "that which originally moves desire" (*S.T.* I–II, 1, 4c) and which is not desired for the sake of something further. Anthony Kenny comments: "It does seem to be a necessary truth that one cannot choose everything for the

---

[*] A version of this paper appeared in the *Journal of Philosophical Research* 16 (1991: 411–26).

1. The Latin text here does not commit Thomas to the view that the end determines the will in any way incompatible with free choice.

sake of something else: chains of reasoning about means and ends must come to a halt somewhere" (Kenny 1966/1970, p. 44) In *S.T.* I–II, 1, 4, Thomas does not think that he has shown that there is only one ultimate end, but rather that he has shown that there is no infinite series of final causes and so that any series of things ordered for the sake of something else must have an ultimate member. Any series of means must have an ultimate end. From this it does not follow that *every* series of means must have one and the same ultimate end. Thomas does not suggest that such a conclusion follows; indeed, he admits that where things are only accidentally connected there can be an infinity of ends and means.

It is only in the following article that Thomas maintains that there is for each human agent a unique final end. He offers three arguments for this view, of which the first is the clearest and most important. Thomas writes:

> First, because in all things whatsoever there is an appetite for completion, the final end to which each move marks its own perfect and fulfilling good. Augustine says, "In speaking of the culminating good, we mean, not that it passes away so as to be no more, but that is so brought to completion as to be fulfilled." The ultimate end ought so to fulfill a man's whole desire. Now this would not be the case were something else outside it still wanted. Hence it cannot be that desire should go out to two things as though each were its fulfillment. (*S.T.* I–II, 1, 5c)

It is not clear just how close a connection Thomas intends between his claim in article 4 that there must be an ultimate end or thing desired for itself and not for the sake of another and his argument here that the ultimate end for an individual must be unique. But it is clear that in article 5, he uses a much stronger notion of ultimate end than in article 4. In article 4 an end is ultimate if it is desired for itself; in article 5, an end can only be ultimate if it is completely satisfying to an individual so that "nothing is left beside for him to desire." In understanding what Thomas has in mind in this stronger notion of the *finis ultimus*, we should realize that in article 5 he speaks of "those who include various objects in their final end and take them as collectively comprising the ideal of one perfect good" (*S.T.* I–II, 1, 5 *ad* 1), thus allowing an inclusive notion of the end.

Thomas's stronger notion of an ultimate end does not presuppose either that there is one thing that completely satisfies all desires or that human agents believe that there is such a thing. Rather, it is the first step in his linking of the ultimate end with good in general or the object of the will. This stronger notion of ultimate end can be taken in one of two ways:

(a) as a definite thing or condition or activity the attainment and realization of which is completely satisfactory;

(b) as the complete satisfaction of one's desires.

The first alternative is ruled out as an interpretation of the notion of ultimate end in question 1 both because it is only in question 2 that Thomas considers the various objects that might be said to satisfy human desires and to constitute human happiness and because he allows that the last end can be taken in an inclusive sense so that the last end can include a number of heterogeneous goods. Thomas himself says somewhat later: "All desire their complete fulfillment, which, as we have noted, is what final end means (*est ratio ultimi finis*)" (*S.T.* I–II, 1, 7c). The view that Thomas is adopting in *S.T.* I–II, 1, 5, is that beyond those things that count as ultimate ends because they are chosen for their own sake there is an ultimate end that is the condition of complete fulfillment or satisfaction of a person's desires. This, of course, confuses the notion of ultimate end; and it is not clear from the texts that Thomas himself realizes that he is working with two significantly different notions of ultimate end. It is well to remember, however, that things in the class of things chosen for their own sakes are chosen as instances of or participations in good in general, which is the object of the will as such; and so they need not be regarded as means and therefore as *eo ipso* not ultimate ends. But his use of two different notions of ultimate end creates the likelihood of equivocation in argument.

In the following article, Thomas maintains that everything that a human being wills is for the sake of the unique ultimate end. His primary line of argument is the following:

> First, whatever a man desires is because of its evidence of good (*sub ratione boni*). If not desired as the perfect good, that is, the ultimate end, then it is desired as tending to that, for a start is made in order to come to a finish, as appears in the products of nature and art alike. And so every initial perfection anticipates (*ordinatur*) the consummate perfection which comes with the final end. (*S.T.* I–II, 1, 6c)

Any good that is aimed at in a human act falls under the notion of good in general and is somehow directed to perfect good as to the final end. Thomas here is assuming the truth of the psychological thesis ultimately derived from Socrates that choice is always of good and is now going on to argue that all goods chosen are means to perfect and complete good. But such a conclusion does not follow, even if we adopt Thomas's views on the participation of particulars in universals, and even if we accept the truth of the psychological thesis. In the first place, the fact that a particular good is an instance of good in general does not show that it is a means that is causally conducive to an all-encompassing good. The relation of particular to universal and the relation of means to end cannot be regarded as the same relationship.

In this connection it is instructive to recall the way in which John Stuart Mill recognizes the diversity of satisfactions that agents can aim at and the possibility of regarding them as parts of happiness rather than merely as means. He writes in the fourth chapter of *Utilitarianism*:

> The ingredients of happiness are very various, and each of them is desirable in itself, and not merely when considered as swelling an aggregate. The principle of utility does not mean that any given pleasure, as music, for instance, or any given exemption from pain, as for example health, are to be looked upon as means to a collective something termed happiness, and to be desired on that account. They are desired and desirable in and for themselves; besides being means, they are part of the end. (Mill 1861/1957, p. 46)

Mill wants to make the further claim that some things, for instance, virtue, can pass from the category of means to the category of part or ingredient. Thomas does not draw this distinction between means and part clearly; but, as in the passage under review, he uses the language of development and fulfillment to indicate the relationship of the intermediate to the ultimate end. This would allow the intermediate object of choice to be more than a mere means, even though the movement of desire would pass beyond it towards something perfect. In fact, as his replies to the objections in the present question show, Thomas adopts an instrumentalist attitude toward both play and science (*S.T.* I–II, 1, 6, *ad* 1; *ad* 2).

Secondly, as Thomas's doctrine of sin makes clear, it is possible for human agents to choose goods that are incompatible with their last end. Sin for Thomas is not merely a conversion to a mutable good; it is also an aversion from the supreme and final good. It is not merely a matter of a human agent's choosing a good that is in fact not causally conducive to the last end (although, because of the psychological thesis, it must somehow be included in the extension of the notion of good in general), but of the agent's knowing in some sense that the good chosen in the sinful act is incompatible with the last end. That which is chosen in the sinful act must, then, be good if it is to be chosen; but it must not be causally conducive to or even compatible with the last end if it is to be sinful. If every object of choice had to be a means to the last end, then Thomas would have to maintain either that sinful objects of choice are means to the last end or that since all objects of choice are chosen as means to the last end, there cannot be a sinful object of choice. Neither alternative would be acceptable to Thomas as a Christian theologian or as an acute observer of human moral activity.

One possible line of defense for Thomas against this argument would be to maintain that the notion of sin as aversion from the last end is only applicable when it has been determined what that is in which the notion of the last end is actually realized. Thomas himself observes:

> We can speak of the ultimate end in two senses, namely to signify first what it means, and second that in which it is realized. As for the first all are at one here, because all desire their complete fulfillment which, as we have noted, is what final end means (*quae est ratio ultimi finis*). As for the second, however, all are not unanimous, for some want riches, others a life of pleasure, others something else. (*S.T.* I–II, 1, 7c)

Using this distinction between the notion of last end and that in which the notion is realized, one could maintain that human agents will everything for the sake of the satisfaction of their desires which is the last end considered in its *ratio* or meaning, even though they do not will everything for the sake of seeing God, which is that in which the last end actually consists according to Thomas. Sin, then, occurs when a human agent turns away from God, the last end, and chooses a lesser good; even though the agent still chooses for the sake of satisfying his desires. Thus Thomas concludes: "When men sin they turn away from that in which the idea of the ultimate end is truly realized, not from the intention of reaching it, which mistakenly they seek elsewhere" (*S.T.* I–II, 1, 7 *ad* 1). What Thomas does not advert to is that this defense reduces sins of malice to sins of ignorance and fails to deal with situations in which the agent believes that the object chosen is incompatible with his last end.

Anthony Kenny inquires whether the claim that there is a unique final end that a human agent pursues in all his choices is to be regarded as logically necessary or empirically true. He argues that the claim is neither; for, even though in voluntary action the agent acts as he desires to and aims at the satisfaction of his desire, this does not establish that he is aiming at the unique ultimate end of satisfying his desires. Kenny writes:

> If all that is being said is that when I act out of desire for *x*, then I am pursuing the satisfaction of my desire for *x*, it has not been established that I am pursuing a single end in all my actions; for there are as many different satisfactions as there are desires to satisfy. (1966/1970, p. 45)

Kenny's argument here shows that the claim that satisfaction of the agent's wants is a unique last end is not a logically necessary consequence of the thesis that the agent's voluntary activity always aims at the satisfaction of a desire of the agent. But Kenny's claim that "there are as many different satisfactions as there are desires to satisfy" requires some modification if we are to understand what Thomas is proposing in his account of beatitude. For the possibility must be left open that one thing or condition may simultaneously satisfy a number of different desires. Working this out in detail would require an account of how desires and satisfactions are to be individuated. But it is reasonably clear that if we are to understand what Thomas has in mind when he says that God alone "can satisfy our will" (*S.T.* I–II, 2, 8c) and is therefore our happiness and our last end, we must think of the desires that God satisfies as desires for classes of goods, and not for individually named goods. It is desirable to avoid an approach to this issue which insists that my desire for *x* can only be satisfied by *y* when *x* and *y* are identical.

Kenny then argues that the claim that a human agent always aims at a good "which consists in the satisfaction of *all* his desires," is "not even empirically true" (1966/1970, p. 45). Here his line of argument allows the possibility that there may be a unique end, but Kenny uses counter-examples to show that the end is not actually present in all one's choices. He writes:

> For it is perfectly possible not to have as a goal the satisfaction of all one's desires and indeed positively to hope that not all one's desires will be satisfied. Russell, for instance, in *The Conquest of Happiness*, says 'to be without some of the things you want is an indispensable part of happiness.' In so far as Russell wants to be happy, he must, in conformity with his dictum, want to be without some of the things he wants....Similarly, patience seems to demand that we should have inconsistent desires: at least that we should be willing that some of our desires should be dissatisfied. But whether or not such inconsistency in desires is desirable, it is certainly possible. If so, it cannot be a logical truth that in everything we do we seek a single aim of total satisfaction. (Kenny 1966/1970, p. 45)

We can grant that Kenny's contention that it is logically possible for a human agent to aim at goals and to make choices that require the non-satisfaction of some of his desires. In addition we can point out that at least on the level of desires for individual objects at specified times it is possible for persons to have desires for incompatible and even contradictory things, e.g., a person may desire to eat at a certain time because he is hungry and may desire not to eat at that time because he is busy or angry or worried. This again suggests the importance of understanding desire and the satisfaction of desire in a sufficiently general way that the hypothesis of total satisfaction of one's desires does not become trivially false.

Kenny's treatment of this problem, however, misses two important considerations that can illuminate Thomas's position. First, when Thomas speaks of happiness as the ultimate end of human beings, he is not thinking of something that is attainable in the circumstances of this present life. Thomas writes: "The general notion of happiness, of goodness perfect and sufficient, implies that every ill is banished, and every desire fulfilled. Neither is possible in this life" (*S.T.* I–II, 5, 3c). In the present order of things, we must make do with activities and results that fall far short of total satisfaction; and it is part of the task of the reasonable and virtuous human person to develop right and appropriate responses to this situation. Hence, the necessity of patience and of the moral virtues generally. But when the final end is attained, there is, according to Thomas, no need for such virtues except in their formal element, which is the order of reason (*S.T.* i–ii, 67, 1c). Thomas specifically quotes Augustine on the absence of patience in the situation of perfect beatitude when the human mind sees God directly.

> The act of patience in heaven will not be endurance of hardships, but the enjoyment of the blessings which we sought to reach by patience. So Augustine says that "in heaven, patience itself will not exist, for it is needed only when hardships are to be borne. But what we attain by patience will endure forever" [Augustine, *City of God*, bk. xiv, chap. 9]. (*S.T.* i–ii, 136, 1 *ad* 1)

So virtues that presuppose the existence of evils and conflicting desires have a fundamentally provisional character for Thomas. The virtue that provides a moral continuity between the imperfections of this life and the perfection of beatitude is the virtue of charity, which has for its primary object God himself (*S.T.* i–ii, 67, 6c).

Second, Kenny's easy acceptance of a situation in which a human agent adopts the attitude of wanting "to be without some of the things he wants" or in which he is "willing that some of our desires should be dissatisfied" obscures the paradoxical character of such situations. For the human agent to adopt such attitudes is only rational when he is doing so for the sake of some good that he values more than the goods he is willing to be without or than the desires he is willing to leave unsatisfied. Thus one might, as William James proposed, renounce the satisfactions of the genial mood and accept "the ethics of infinite and mysterious obligation" with a view to "getting out of the game of existence its keenest possibility of zest" (James 1891/1962, p. 213). The point is that such attitudes of renunciation require explanation and justification. Given the ordinary circumstances of life, in which the total satisfaction of all desires is an implausible goal, the weighting of desires according to the feasibility and importance and worth of satisfying them is rational and necessary and is indeed a central feature of most systems of morality and of prudence. So the justification of attitudes of partial renunciation is not particularly difficult; but it is needed if such attitudes are not to be regarded as evidence of failure to understand the notion of desire on the one hand or as signs of masochistic tendencies or willful perversity or insensitivity on the other.

We should add that justifying the partial renunciation of desires can apply not only to acts of choice but also to long-term policies and attitudes, e.g., acquiring and exercising the virtue of patience. The agent who adopts such policies and attitudes is in effect committing himself to a plan of life which does not aim at the total satisfaction of all his desires. In fact, Thomas himself, as a Dominican friar, adopted such a plan of life, in which he committed himself to the renunciations implied by the religious vows of poverty, chastity, and obedience. In his treatment of the religious life in *S.T.* I–II, 186, Thomas is particularly anxious to stress the incompatibility between satisfying certain kinds of desires and achieving the perfection of charity. "Regarding future happiness, one is directed to it by charity....But the possession of riches by its very nature impedes the perfection of charity, especially by alluring and distracting the soul" (*S.T.* I–II, 186, 3 *ad* 4).

The point here is that Thomas as a Christian theologian insists on the importance and value of policies of renunciation in a way that is surprising, given what he says about the complete fulfillment of human desire as the ultimate end of the human agent. It seems that when he considers the particular moral virtues and the institution of religious life, far from affirming that it is logically necessary that the human agent aim at the satisfaction of all his desires, he does not even think such a goal desirable.

One way to defend Thomas's position would be to hold that such renunciations are merely instrumental to the attainment of the last end. In fact, Thomas himself proposes such a view in his consideration of the religious life in *S.T.* I–II, 186, 1c and 3c. The situation, simply put, is that Thomas commends a life of renunciation in a religious order as a means to perfection, while at the same time proposing a goal of total satisfaction of desire beyond this life. Taken together, these recommendations do not constitute a self-contradictory program, though they do form a paradox.

Thomas's situation is parallel to the utilitarian difficulty in incorporating "the morality of self-devotion." Mill contends:

> A sacrifice which does not increase, or tend to increase, the sum total of happiness, it [utilitarianism] considers as wasted. The only self-renunciation which it applauds is devotion to the happiness, or to some of the means of happiness, of others; either of mankind collectively, or of individuals within the limits imposed by the collective interests of mankind. (Mill 1861/1957, p. 22)

Mill resolves the tension between sacrifice and the pursuit of happiness by making sacrifice instrumental to the welfare of others; Thomas does it by making sacrifice instrumental to one's own long-range good and by making sacrifice temporary and satisfaction permanent.

But since in Thomas's approach the goal to which renunciation is instrumental is not within our experience in this world, the relation between earthly renunciation as means and heavenly goal as end requires some further explanation. It is important to see that Thomas is not proposing a teleological theory in which the total satisfaction of desire is the unique goal of the agent and every instance of satisfaction in this life then counts as either a means to the goal or a partial realization of it. It is simply not the case that Thomas endorses every instance of satisfaction of desire, since some instances of satisfaction of desire are wrong and sinful and since he recommends a plan of life which involves the systematic renunciation of desires for certain classes of goods. So what, in some ways, might readily appear as an affirmation of a universal psychological egoism, in which all human persons aim at the goal of the total satisfaction of desire, and which would lead them to adopt a purely prudential plan of life, is also the basis for an austere ethics of renunciation.

Resolution of this paradox requires that we consider not simply Thomas's notion of the last end, but also his view on "that in which it is realized" (S.T. I–II, 1, 7). This, as we know, is God. But God for Thomas is not simply Yahweh, the God of Biblical revelation, who is a personal being guiding Israel and calling his people to union with himself. He is also a being of all-encompassing perfection who "necessarily contains within himself the full perfection of being" (S.T. I, 4, 2c) and who alone "possesses every kind of perfection by nature" (S.T. I, 6, 3c), and who "causes in all other things their being, their goodness, and whatever other perfection they have" (S.T. I, 2, 3c). God is not simply a being among other beings which individual agents might desire or not, depending on their own preferences. Rather, he is the first cause of the existence and goodness of other beings, the source in which they participate. Thus, Thomas maintains, "all things are said to be good by divine goodness, which is the pattern, source, and goal of all goodness" (S.T. I, 6, 4c). It is not to our purpose to assess Thomas's general account of the connection between God's attributes and those of creatures; but it is very important to see that Thomas can regard God as the unique last end of every human person only because he regards God as the source of goodness and universal good. His argument in S.T. I–II, 2, 8c makes this plain:

> The object of the will, that is the human appetite, is the Good without reserve, (*universale bonum*), just as the object of the mind is the True without reserve. Clearly, then, nothing can satisfy man's will except such goodness, which is found, not in anything created, but in God alone. Everything created is a derivative good (*habet bonitatem participatam*). He alone…can satisfy our will. (*S.T.* I–II, 2, 8c)

This conception of God as universal good is of pivotal importance to Thomas; for it enables him to maintain that a policy of renunciation of desires can lead to the attainment of an end that is the total satisfaction of desires, to maintain that all human persons share a unique end no matter what their actual desires are, and to propose a last end that is both inclusive and dominant. Our interest in this notion of God as universal good is not in the problems that it involves with regard to the distinction between particulars and universals[2] or with regard to God's relation to the world and its possible pantheistic implications, but rather with regard to its consequences for Thomas's ethical theory and his account of human action.

Now according to Thomas, the human will has a necessary movement to good in general as its proper object and last end, but it does not have such a necessary movement to God, who is the universal good. This position is an application of Thomas's distinction between the notion of the last end as complete fulfillment of desire and that end in which such fulfillment is found (S.T. I–II, 1, 7c). This distinction enables Thomas to run his arguments about the last end of man on two different levels. On the one hand, the human agent has a necessary direction to good in general, since this is the proper object of the will and since, according to the psychological thesis, nothing can be chosen that falls outside it. This orientation of the will does not involve any necessary movement of the will to specific goods and is intended to be compatible with any choices that the agent may make. Also, it does not entail the existence of any one thing that would be universal good or would be the source in which all lesser goods participate.

On the other hand, the human agent is supposed to direct her actions voluntarily to God as so many means to her complete good and last end. Not every action and object that is chosen can serve as a means to this last end; and so sin is possible (S.T. I–II, 1, 7 ad 1), even though what is chosen still must count as a good. It is clear that not all human beings consciously seek God as their last end, and it is obvious that it would be irrational for them to do so if they believed that He did not exist. It would indeed be logically impossible for atheists to take God as the last end of their activity.[3] Directing one's action to God as last end then entails that the agent believe in the existence of God. But it does not entail that the agent accept Thomas's account of God as the original good in which all others participate. For it is possible for a non-Thomistic religious believer to direct his actions to God as a determinate last end without regarding Him as an all-inclusive good. All that seems required for such a policy to be rational is

---

2. Thus D. J. O'Connor (1968, p. 27) singles out this passage (S.T. I–II, 2, 8c) as showing an ambiguous use of *bonum universale* as "(1) good in general which is the object of the will, end (2) the universal good which is identical with God."

3. See Hampshire 1960, p. 206: "But there is a sense in which I could not set myself to do what he is doing, namely, to ask God's forgiveness for my sins, unless I believe that God exists and that a sense can be attached to the notion of God's forgiveness and of human sin. The 'cannot' here represents a logical impossibility."

that the religious believer regard God as supremely good or good in the highest possible degree.

When these two levels of argument are distinguished and when it is seen that Thomas is using both a necessary movement of the will to good in general and a free movement of the will to God as universal good in his account of last end of the human agent, it is possible for us to explain a number of puzzling features of his position.

We can see the importance of distinguishing these two levels of argument when we compare Aquinas's position on the last end of man with that of Thomas Hobbes. Thus Hobbes, who rejects the notion of a last end, at the same time accepts the view that the human agent aims at the complete satisfaction of his desires. He writes in Leviathan:

> The Felicity of this life consisteth not in the repose of a mind satisfied. For there is no such finis ultimus (utmost ayme) nor Summum Bonum (greatest Good), as is spoken of in the Books of the old Moral Philosophers. Nor can a man any more live, whose Desires are at an end, than he, whose Senses and Imagination are at a stand. Felicity is a continuall progress from one object to another; the attaining of the former, being still but the way to the latter. The cause whereof is, That the object of mans desire is not to enjoy once onely, and for one instant of time: but to assure forever, the way of his future desire. And therefore the voluntary actions, and inclinations of all men, tend not only to the procuring, but also to the assuring of a contented life; and differ only in the way: which ariseth partly from the diversity of passions, in divers men and partly from the difference of the knowledge, or opinion each one has of the cause, which produce the effect desired. (Hobbes 1651/1968, pp. 160–61)

We note that Hobbes and Aquinas both hold that all human persons, while differing in their passions and beliefs, desire the satisfaction of their desires and a life of sure contentment. The crucial difference between them is about whether or not there is an object which, when possessed, can bring about the satisfaction of all human desires. Both would agree that if there is such an object, it is reasonable for a human agent to organize life with a view to attaining the object and to treat her activities as means to the end of possessing or enjoying that object. Since Hobbes holds that there is no such object, he interprets the human desire for complete satisfaction of one's desire as the basis for continual striving and acquisitiveness: "a perpetuall and restlesse desire of Power after power, that ceaseth onely in Death" (Hobbes 1651/1968, p. 161).

In Hobbes, the desire for the complete satisfaction of one's desires produces a progressive and insatiable egoism and is the source of conflict between persons. In Aquinas, by contrast, the desire for complete satisfaction of one's desires is an orientation to an uncreated perfect good, God, who alone "can satisfy our will" and in whom alone "our happiness lies" (*S.T.* I–II, 2, 8c). Aquinas holds that this orientation to perfect good ensures rightness of will in the agent, since "the will is rightful when duly bent on its ultimate end" (*S.T.* I–II, 4, 4c). It also produces a charitable and harmonious relationship with other persons, for "our loving choice of them results from our full loving of God" (*S.T.* I–II, 4, 8c).

When we look at Aquinas and Hobbes in this comparative fashion, we see that the difference between them about whether or not there is a finis ultimus is not a simple difference in factual belief about whether or not there is in the universe a being that completely satisfies human desires but that this difference has profound consequences for the character of the resulting ethical theories. For Hobbes, like Aquinas, regards good as "the object of any man's appetite or desire" (Hobbes 1651/1968, p. 120). Each person's interest in the satisfaction of his desires, in the absence of a single good that is capable of satisfying all desires, leads to an inherently limitless pursuit of objects that the agent thinks will satisfy his desires. The effective measure of the goodness of things is their capacity to satisfy the agent's desires. In Aquinas, on the other hand, although he shares Hobbes's understanding of good as the object of appetite or desire, affirmation of the existence of a particular object capable of satisfying all desires produces a transformation of the egoism of Hobbes. For attainment of this object becomes the effective norm for action. Thus not every satisfaction of a specific desire is ultimately good or forms part of a good or rational plan of life for the agent. It will, of course, be good from some standpoint or in some regard; otherwise, according to the psychological thesis, it would not be chosen; but, if it is not compatible with or lacks proper order to the ultimate end, it is also evil and lacks the goodness appropriate to it as a voluntary act. Aquinas writes (*S.T.* I–II, 19, 9c): "An act of will's goodness depends on the end intended. Now the human will's ultimate end is the supreme good, and this is God, as we have shown. For an act of human will to be good, then, it must be ordered to the supreme good." For Aquinas, sin is not a turning away from all desire of pursuing or reaching the last end, but is a turning away from that in which the last end is actually realized. The possibility of evil in voluntary actions or of sin requires then that the ultimate good be particular and not simply good in general; for, given Aquinas's psychological thesis, no object that could be chosen would fall outside the scope of good in general.

The last end must also be a particular and determinate good, if it is to serve in some way as a norm and first principle for the particular choices of human beings. Aquinas maintains that the last end provides the fundamental principle of moral and practical activity. He affirms: "Now the principle of the whole moral order is the ultimate goal, which relates to the realm of activity in the same way that self-evident principles are related to the realm of speculation" (*S.T.* I–II, 72, 5c). One might be tempted to think that "the principle of the whole moral order" is equivalent to the first precept of the natural law "that good is to be sought and done, evil to be avoided" (*S.T.* I–II, 94, 4c), which Aquinas also compares to the Aristotelian principle of noncontradiction in its fundamental function and which he explicates in such a way that it clearly refers to good in general. But such a formal and general reading of the fundamental principle, when combined with the psychological thesis, will authorize the choice of anything that can actually be chosen and will not provide normative guidance that will enable us to discriminate between courses of action that lead to or are compatible with a particular last end and those that lead away from it or are incompatible with it. God as the particular last end, to which (presumably) every action does not lead and to which there is not, in Aquinas's view, a natural and necessary movement of the will (as there is to good in general), can serve a normative and discriminatory function with regard to particular human actions and objects of desire. God as a particular last end can give a distinctive shape and direction to a human agent's plan of life, which an orientation to good in general cannot do precisely because of its all-inclusive character.

The agent's intention of God as last end and the subsequent evaluation of particular actions and of desires in relationship to the last end effectively differentiates Aquinas's moral world from Hobbes's and makes it theocentric rather than anthropocentric. While agents in both these moral worlds desire the complete and lasting satisfaction of all their desires, agents in Aquinas's world are committed to evaluating and choosing particular objects and actions on the basis of their relationship to the last end, which is itself a particular being, union with which brings complete and lasting satisfaction of their desires. If particular objects of desire are incompatible with this last end, then, though they fall within the extension of good in general, they cannot serve as means to the last end; and choice of them is sinful. On the other side, the renunciation of specific objects of desire is intelligible and rational if it leads to union with God as the particular last end; whereas, if one's last end is simply the satisfaction of all one's desires, then renunciation is incompatible with a last end conceived in such general terms.

God as particular last end serves as a reference point outside the system of the agent's desires and their objects, even though he is at the same time the object that completely satisfies all desires. He can serve as an independent teleological norm for desires, actions, objects, and plans of life, some of which may lead to him and some of which may not. If this independent reference point is removed by the denial of the existence of God or by putting him beyond the realm of human striving and attainment, then it is easy to see how agents with the general psychology described by Aquinas could be taken for egoists and could adopt a plan of life aimed at maximizing the satisfaction of desires. It would, however, be a mistake to regard such nontheistic Thomistic agents as Hobbesian egoists, since they would still have natural inclinations to act according to virtue and to live together harmoniously in society (*S.T.* I–II, 94, 2c; I–II, 94, 3c). The notion of God as last end introduces an independent constraint on the agent's pursuit of his own desires so that the damaging social consequences normally thought to result from egoistic attitudes can be avoided; and it provides an independent basis for evaluations such that courses of action contrary to the agent's conception of his own interest can be commended and even regarded as obligatory.

Furthermore, the object that is to be aimed at because attainment of it satisfies all of the agent's desires is not itself an economic good or a good that can be possessed by some to the exclusion of others. For, according to Aquinas, external goods are in no way "needed for the perfect happiness of seeing God" (*S.T.* I–II, 4, 7c). Human happiness does not consist in riches, honors, fame, power, or pleasure, or indeed in anything created (*S.T.* I–II, 2). So the human striving for happiness does not produce in Aquinas's world the "perpetuall and restless desire of Power after power that ceaseth onely in Death" and the "contention of Riches, Honour, Command, or other power" which "enclineth to Contention, Enmity, and War" that Hobbes saw as disruptive consequences of the human search for happiness (Hobbes 1651/1968, p. 161).

God as the object of the human striving for happiness and as the particular last end of human activity is unlimited good containing all perfections (*S.T.* I, 4, 2) and exceeding the finite capacity of any of his creatures (*S.T.* I, 12, 7). The person who attains the vision of God has no desire to abandon it for some lesser good and possesses it in eternal security (*S.T.* I–II, 5, 4). Aquinas writes of the situation of those who attain God as their last end in the following terms (*S.T.* I 12, 7c): "But the blessed have this triple gift in God, for they see him and seeing him they possess him, holding him for ever in their sight, and holding him they enjoy him as their ultimate goal fulfilling all their desires." Clearly there is no need and no place for either conflict or anxiety in such a situation; and so the striving to achieve such a situation has to be recognized as different from the effort to satisfy all one's desires under the conditions of this life, an effort that usually involves a person in conflicts of claims with others in ways that require moral and legal regulation.

In short, the blessed or those who have attained beatitude are no longer in the objective circumstances of justice, which Hume briefly characterized as the "easy change" of external objects, "joined to their scarcity in comparison of the wants and desires of men" (*A Treatise of Human Nature*, bk. iii, pt. ii, § ii). The blessed are in some sense beyond not merely justice but even the life of moral virtue itself. Aquinas writes:

> So then it must be admitted that these moral virtues as regards their material element do not remain in the future life. For then desires and pleasures in matters of food and sex will have no place, nor will fear and daring about dangers of death, nor distributions and exchanges of things employed in this present life. (*S.T.* i–ii, 67, 1c)[4]

The situation involved in attainment of the final end does not then require the exercise of acts of the moral virtues. The "material element," by which Aquinas means "a certain bent of the appetitive part to a certain manner of feelings and deeds" therefore lapses; all that remains is the formal element, the "order of reason" (*S.T.* i–ii, 67, 1c). The moral institution of life is appropriate and required in the conditions of this present life; but it is preparatory for and instrumental to the enjoyment of beatitude.

In this respect, Aquinas's teleological account of human action treats morality as a means to attaining an ultimate good that, since it includes all perfections, includes both moral and nonmoral good in itself. This instrumental aspect of Aquinas's ethical theory, despite certain affinities with utilitarianism, does not commit him to a utilitarian account of the derivation of moral rules or of the rightness and wrongness of particular acts. In contrast to egoism, there is a considerable similarity between Aquinas's ethical theory and utilitarianism. The point of comparison here is that, even if one takes Aquinas to be a long-range supernatural egoist who holds that actions are right because they are conducive to the agent's eternal happiness, the structure of his theory is such that it allows for and even requires restrictions on the individual's pursuit of his interest in this life in much the same way that utilitarianism requires such restrictions for the sake of promoting the good of all. A supernatural egoism based on traditional Christian beliefs about the afterlife and divine rewards and punishments still leaves a space between the egoistic motives and desires of the individual and the attainment of the object that satisfies them, a space which allows for the development of a morality and an asceticism even by egoistic agents. This leaves the question of whether Thomas holds a form of psychological egoism still unsettled; for there are moves available to Thomas and his defenders that would open the way to a nonegoistic interpretation of his

---

4. Here Aquinas echoes what Aristotle says about the happiness of the gods in the *Nicomachean Ethics* book 10, chapter 8, 1178^{b}7–23.

views. It also leaves open the possibility that, when the framework of supernatural orientation and fulfillment that gives content to the natural and necessary movement of the agent's will to the ultimate end of complete satisfaction is removed, the morality developed in "the space between" may be independent of psychological egoism and may actually be shaped by other considerations that may be of interest even to those who would find the supernatural framework implausible or unacceptable.

References

Alston, W. P. 1964. *Philosophy of Language.* Englewood Cliffs: Prentice-Hall.

Alston, W. 1989. *Epistemic Justification: Essays in the Theory of Knowledge.* Ithaca: Cornell University Press.

Archambault, E., and O. Arkhipoff, eds. 1990. *La Compatibilité Nationale Face au Défi International.* Paris: Economica.

Aristotle. *Nicomachean Ethics.* In W. D. Ross, ed., *The Works of Aristotle*, vol. 9. Oxford: Clarendon Press, 1915.

Audi, R. 1982. Believing and Affirming. *Mind* 91: 115–20.

Audi, R. 1986. Belief, Reason, and Inference. *Philosophical Topics* 14: 27–65.

Audi, R. 1988. *Belief, Justification, and Knowledge.* Belmont: Wadsworth Publishing Co.

Audi, R. 1989a. Causalist Internalism. *American Philosophical Quarterly* 26: 309–20.

Audi, R. 1989b. *Practical Reasoning.* London: Routledge.

Audi, R. 1991. Justification, Deductive Closure, and Reasons to Believe. *Dialogue* 30: 77–84.

Augustine, St. *The City of God.* In W. J. Oates, ed., Basic Writings of St. Augustine, vol. 2. New York: Random House.

Aumann, R., and M. Maschler. 1964. The Bargaining Set for Cooperative Games. In Dresher, Shapley, and Tucker 1964: 443–76.

Austin, D., ed. 1988. *Philosophical Analysis: A Defense by Example.* Dordrecht: Kluwer Academic Publishers.

Barnett, P. 1983. Rational Behavior in Bargaining Situations. *Noûs* 17: 621–35.

Barry, B. 1978. Circumstances of Justice and Future Generations. In Sikora and Barry 1978: 204–48.

Becker, L. 1973. The Finality of Moral Judgement: A Reply to Mrs. Foot. *Philosophical Review* 82: 364–70.

Block, N. 1978. Troubles with Functionalism. In Savage 1978: 261–325.

BonJour, L. 1985. *The Structure of Empirical Knowledge.* Cambridge: Harvard University Press.

Boxill, B. 1980. How Injustice Pays. *Philosophy and Public Affairs* 9: 359–71.

Boyd, R. 1988. How to Be a Moral Realist. In Sayre-McCord 1988: 181–228.

Bracken, P. 1964. *I Try to Behave Myself: Peg Bracken's Etiquette Book.* New York: Fawcett.

Brand, M. 1984. *Intending and Acting.* Cambridge: MIT Press.

Brandt, R. 1972. Rationality, Egoism, and Morality. *Journal of Philosophy* 69: 681–97.

Brandt, R. 1979. *A Theory of the Good and the Right*. Oxford: Clarendon Press.

Brandt, R. 1982. Two Concepts of Utility. In Miller and Williams 1982: 169–85.

Brandt, R. 1989. Fairness to Happiness. *Social Theory and Practice* 15: 33–58.

Brandt, R. 1991. Overvold on Self-Interest and Self-Sacrifice. *Journal of Philosophical Research* 16: 353–63.

Bratman, M. 1985. Davidson's Theory of Intention. In LePore and McLaughlin 1985: 14–28.

Bratman, M. 1987. *Intention, Plans, and Practical Reason*. Cambridge: Harvard University Press.

Brennan, G., and G. Tullock. 1981. *An Economic Theory of Military Tactics: Methodological Individualism at War*. Blacksburg: Public Choice Center, Virginia Polytechnic Institute and State University.

Bricker, P. 1980. Prudence. *Journal of Philosophy* 77: 381–401.

Brink, D. 1984. Moral Realism and Skeptical Arguments from Disagreement and Queerness. *Australasian Journal of Philosophy* 62: 111–25.

Brink, D. 1989. *Moral Realism and the Foundations of Ethics*. Cambridge: Cambridge University Press.

Broad, C. D. 1930. *Five Types of Ethical Theory*. London: Harcourt Brace and Co.

Broad, C. D. 1950/52. Egoism as a Theory of Human Motives. *Hibbert Journal* 48: 105–14. Reprinted in Broad 1952: 218–31.

Broad, C. D. 1952. *Ethics and the History of Philosophy: Selected Essays*. London: Routledge and Kegan Paul.

Broad, C. D. 1965. *Five Types of Ethical Theory*. Totowa: Littlefield Adams.

Burge, T. 1979. Individualism and the Mental. *Midwest Studies in Philosophy* 4: 73–121.

Burge, T. 1986. Individualism and Psychology. *Philosophical Review* 95: 3–45.

Butler, J. 1726/1950. *Five Sermons*. Indianapolis: Bobbs-Merrill.

Campbell, R. 1979. *Self-Love and Self-Respect: A Philosophical Study of Egoism*. Ottawa: Canadian Library of Philosophy.

Campbell, R. 1988. Gauthier's Theory of Morals by Agreement. *Philosophical Quarterly* 38: 343–64.

Capitan, W., and D. Merrill, eds. 1967. *Art, Mind, and Religion*. Pittsburgh: University of Pittsburgh Press.

Carson, T. 1991. Comments on Brandt's Paper. *Journal of Philosophical Research* 16: 365–68.

Castañeda, H. 1975. *Thinking and Doing*. Dordrecht: Reidel.

Castañeda, H., ed. 1967. *Intentionality, Minds, and Perception*. Detroit: Wayne State University Press.

Chafets, Ze'ev. 1980. *Heroes and Hustlers, Hard Hats and Holy Men: Inside the New Israel*. New York: Morrow.

Chisholm, R. 1977. *Theory of Knowledge*. 2d ed. Englewood Cliffs: Prentice-Hall.

Code, L. 1987. *Epistemic Responsibility*. Hanover: University Press of New England.

Copp, D. 1991. Contractarianism and Moral Skepticism. In Vallentyne 1991: 196–228.

Copp, D., and D. Zimmerman, eds. 1984. *Morality, Reason, and Truth: New Essays in the Foundations of Ethics*. Totowa: Rowman and Allanheld.

Crisp, R., ed. 1994. *How Should One Live?* Oxford: Clarendon Press.

Danielson, P. 1991. Closing the Compliance Dilemma: How It's Rational to be Moral in a Lamarckian World. In Vallentyne 1991: 291–322.

Darwall, S. 1986. Agent-Centered Restrictions from the Inside Out. *Philosophical Studies* 50: 291–319.

Davidson, D. 1970/1980. How is Weakness of the Will Possible? In Feinberg 1970: 93–113. Reprinted in Davidson 1980.

Davidson, D. 1980. *Essays on Actions and Events*. Oxford: Clarendon Press.

Davidson, D. 1985. Replies to Essays I–IX. In Vermazen and Hintikka 1985: 195–229.

Davidson D., and G. Harman, eds. 1972. *Semantics of Natural Language*. Dordrecht: Reidel.

Davis, P. 1966. *Moral Duty and Legal Responsibility*. New York: Appleton-Century-Crofts.

Donagan, A. 1978. *The Theory of Morality*. Chicago: University of Chicago Press.

Donagan, A. 1984. Consistency in Rationalist Moral Systems. *Journal of Philosophy* 81: 291–309.

Donald, E. B., ed. 1981. *Debrett's Etiquette and Modern Manners*. New York: Viking Press.

Dresher, M., L. Shapley, and A. Tucker, eds. 1964. *Advances in Game Theory*. Princeton: Princeton University Press.

Dretske, F. 1970. Epistemic Operators. *Journal of Philosophy* 67: 1007–23.

Dworkin, R. 1977. *Taking Rights Seriously*. London: Duckworth.

Dworkin, R. 1981. What is Equality? Part I: Equality of Welfare? *Philosophy and Public Affairs* 10: 185–246.

Feinberg, J., ed. 1970. *Moral Concepts*. Oxford: Clarendon Press.

Feinberg, J. 1980. *Rights, Justice, and the Bounds of Liberty*. Princeton: Princeton University Press.

Feinberg, J. 1984. *Harm to Others*. New York: Oxford University Press.

Feldman, R. 1988. Having Evidence. In Austin 1988: 83–104.

Ferm, V., ed. 1956. *Encyclopedia of Morals*. New York: Philosophical Library.

Field, H. 1978. Mental Representation. *Erkenntnis* 13: 9–61.

Firth, R. 1978. Are Epistemic Concepts Reducible to Ethical Concepts? In Goldman and Kim: 1978: 215–29.

Fishkin, J. 1979. *Tyranny and Legitimacy*. Baltimore: The Johns Hopkins University Press.

Fodor, J. 1968. Propositional Attitudes. *The Monist* 61: 501–23.

Fodor, J. 1986. *Psychosemantics*. Cambridge: MIT Press.

Foley, R. 1987. *The Theory of Epistemic Rationality*. Cambridge: Harvard University Press.

Foley, R. 1989. Reply to Alston, Feldman, and Swain. *Philosophy and Phenomenological Research* 50: 169–88.

Foot, P. 1972. Morality as a System of Hypothetical Imperatives. *Philosophical Review* 83: 305–16.

Foot, P. 1985. Utilitarianism and the Virtues. *Mind* 94: 196–209. Reprinted in Scheffler 1988.

Frankena, W. K. 1956. Sidgwick. In Ferm 1956: 541.

Frankena, W. K. 1974. Sidgwick and the Dualism of Practical Reason. *Monist* 58: 449–467.

Frankena, W. K. 1983. Concepts of Rational Action in the History of Ethics. *Social Theory and Practice* 9: 165–97.

Frankena, W. K. 1992. Sidgwick and the History of Ethical Dualism. In Schultz 1992: 175–98.

Freeman, N., and M. Cox, eds. 1985. *Visual Order*. Cambridge: Cambridge University Press.

Gauthier, D. 1984a. Afterthoughts. In MacLean 1984: 159–61.

Gauthier, D. 1984b. Deterrence, Maximization, and Rationality. *Ethics* 94: 474–95. Reprinted in MacLean 1984: 474–95.

Gauthier, D. 1986. *Morals by Agreement*. Oxford: Clarendon Press.

Gibbard, A. 1988. Hare's Analysis of "Ought" and its Implications. In Seanor and Fotion 1988: 57–72.

Goldman, A. I. 1986. *Epistemology and Cognition*. Cambridge: Harvard University Press.

Goldman, A. I., and J. Kim, eds. 1978. *Values and Morals: Essays in Honor of William Frankena, Charles Stephenson, and Richard Brandt*. Dordrecht: Reidel.

Goffman, E. 1967. Deference and Demeanor. *Interaction Ritual*. Garden City: Aldine.

Griffin, J. 1986. *Well-Being: Its Meaning, Measurement, and Moral Importance*. Oxford: Clarendon Press.

Gunderson, K., ed. 1975. *Minnesota Studies in the Philosophy of Science 7.* Minneapolis: University of Minnesota Press.

Gurr, T. 1970. *Why Men Rebel.* Princeton: Princeton University Press.

Hampshire, S. 1960. *Thought and Action.* New York: Viking Press.

Hardin, R. 1988. *Morality Within the Limits of Reason.* Chicago: University of Chicago Press.

Hare, R. M. 1952. *The Language of Morals.* Oxford: Clarendon Press.

Hare, R. M. 1963. *Freedom and Reason.* Oxford: Clarendon Press.

Hare, R. M. 1981. *Moral Thinking: Its Levels, Method and Point.* Oxford: Clarendon Press.

Harsanyi, J. 1953. Cardinal Utility in Welfare Economics and in the Theory of Risk-Taking. *Journal of Political Economy* 61: 434–35.

Harsanyi, J. 1955. Cardinal Welfare, Individual Ethics, and Interpersonal Comparisons of Utility. *Journal of Political Economy* 63: 309–21.

Harsanyi, J. 1977. Morality and the Theory of Rational Behavior. *Social Research* 44: 623–56. Reprinted in Sen and Williams 1982: 39–62.

Harsanyi, J. 1988. Problems with Act-Utilitarianism and with Malevolent Preferences. In Seanor and Fotion 1988: 89–99.

Hobbes, T. 1651/1958. *Leviathan.* Indianapolis: Bobbs-Merrill.

Hobbes, T. 1651/1968. *Leviathan.* Edited by C. D. Macpherson. Harmondsworth: Penguin.

Hooker, B. 1991. Mark Overvold's Contribution to Philosophy. *Journal of Philosophical Research* 16: 327–37.

Hooker, B. 1994. Does Moral Virtue Constitute a Benefit to the Agent? In Crisp 1994.

Horgan, T. 1984. Functionalism and Token Physicalism. *Synthese* 59: 321–38.

Horgan, T., and G. Graham. 1991. In Defense of Southern Fundamentalism. *Philosophical Studies* 62: 107–34.

Horgan, T., and M. Timmons. 1992a. Troubles on Moral Twin Earth: Moral Queerness Revived. *Synthese* 92: 221–60.

Horgan, T., and M. Timmons. 1992b. Troubles for New-Wave Moral Semantics: The "Open Question Argument" Revived. *Philosophical Papers* 21: 151–73.

Hume, D. 1739/1964. *A Treatise of Human Nature.* Edited by L. A. Selby-Bigge. Oxford: Clarendon Press.

James, W. 1891/1962. The Moral Philosopher and the Moral Life. *International Journal of Ethics* 1: 330–54. Reprinted in Perry 1962: 184–215.

Kagan, S. 1989. *The Limits of Morality.* Oxford: Clarendon Press.

Kalai, E., and M. Smorodinsky. 1975. Other Solutions to Nash's Bargaining Problem. *Econometrica* 43: 513–18.

Kavka, G. 1978a The Futurity Problem. In Sikora and Barry 1978: 186–203.

Kavka, G. 1978b. Some Paradoxes of Deterrence. *Journal of Philosophy* 75: 285–302.

Kavka, G. 1980. Deterrence, Utility, and Rational Choice. *Theory and Decision* 12: 41–60.

Kavka, G. 1983a. Right Reason and Natural Law in Hobbes's Ethics. *The Monist* 66: 120–33.

Kavka, G. 1983b. When Two 'Wrongs' Make a Right: An Essay on Business Ethics. *Journal of Business Ethics* 2: 61–66.

Kavka, G. 1984. Responses to the Paradox of Deterrence. In MacLean 1984: 155–59.

Kavka, G. 1986. *Hobbesean Moral and Political Theory.* Princeton: Princeton University Press.

Kenny, A. 1966/1970. Happiness. *Proceedings of the Aristotelian Society* 66: 330–54. Reprinted in Feinberg 1970: 43–52.

Klein, P. 1981. *Certainty: A Refutation of Scepticism.* Minneapolis: University of Minnesota Press.

Kornblith, H. 1983. Justified Belief and Epistemically Responsible Action. *Philosophical Review* 92: 33–48.

Kripke, S. 1972. Naming and Necessity. In Davidson and Harman 1972: 253–355.

Lehrer, K. 1990. *Theory of Knowledge.* Boulder: Westview Press.

LePore, E., and B. McLaughlin, eds. 1985. *Actions and Events: Perspectives on the Philosophy of Donald Davidson.* Oxford: Basil Blackwell.

Lewis, D. 1972. Psychophysical and Theoretical Identifications. *Australasian Journal of Philosophy* 50: 249–58.

Loar, B. 1982. *Mind and Meaning.* Cambridge: Cambridge University Press.

Luce, R., and H. Raiffa. 1957. *Games and Decisions.* New York: Wiley.

Lycan, W. 1981. Toward a Homuncular Theory of Believing. *Cognition and Brain Theory* 4: 139–60.

McFall, L. 1988. *Happiness.* New York: Peter Lang.

Mackie, J. L. 1977. *Ethics: Inventing Right and Wrong.* Harmondsworth: Penguin Books.

MacLean, D., ed. 1984. *The Security Gamble: Deterrence Dilemmas in the Nuclear Age.* Totowa: Rowman & Allanheld.

Martin, J. 1982. *Miss Manners' Guide to Excruciatingly Correct Behavior.* New York: Atheneum.

Martin, J. 1984. *Miss Manners' Guide to Rearing Perfect Children.* New York: Pharos.

Martin, J. 1989. *Miss Manners' Guide for the Turn-of-the-Millenium.* New York: Atheneum.

Meadows, D., D. L. Meadows, J. Randers, and W. Behrens. 1972. *The Limits to Growth.* New York: Universe Books.

Mele, A. 1987. *Irrationality: An Essay on Akrasia, Self-Deception, and Self-Control.* New York: Oxford University Press.

Mele, A. 1989. Intention, Belief, and Intentional Action. *American Philosophical Quarterly* 26: 19–30.

Mele, A. 1990. Exciting Intentions. *Philosophical Studies* 59: 289–312.

Mele, A. 1992 *Springs of Action: Understanding Intentional Behavior.* New York: Oxford University Press.

Michael Bratman, M. 1987. *Intention, Plans, and Practical Reason.* Cambridge: Harvard University Press.

Mill, J. S. 1859/1956. *On Liberty.* Indianapolis: Bobbs-Merrill.

Mill, J. S. 1861/1957. *Utilitarianism.* Indianaopolis: Bobbs-Merrill.

Mill, J. S. 1869/1970. The Subjugation of Women. In Mill and Taylor 1970: 123–242.

Mill, J. S., and H. Taylor. 1970. *Essays on Sex Equality.* A. S. Rossi, ed. Chicago: University of Chicago Press.

Miller, H., and W. Williams, eds. 1982. *The Limits of Utilitarianism.* Minneapolis: University of Minncsota Press.

Morton, A. 1987. The Explanatory Depth of Propositional Attitudes: Perceptual Development as a Test Case. In Russell 1987: 67–80.

Moser, P. 1989. *Knowledge and Evidence.* Cambridge : Cambridge University Press.

Nagel, T. 1970. *The Possibility of Altruism.* Oxford: Clarendon Press.

Nagel, T. 1986. *The View from Nowhere.* New York: Oxford University Press.

Narveson, J. 1967. *Morality and Utility.* Baltimore: The Johns Hopkins University Press.

Nash, J. 1950. The Bargaining Problem. *Econometrica* 18: 155–62.

Nisbett, R., and T. Wilson 1977. Telling More Than We Can Know: Verbal Reports on Mental Processes. *Psychological Review* 84: 231–59.

Nozick, R. 1974. *Anarchy, State, and Utopia.* New York: Basic Books.

Nozick, R. 1981. *Philosophical Explanations.* Cambridge: Harvard University Press.

O'Conner, D. 1968. *Aquinas and Natural Law.* New York: Macmillan.

Overvold, M. 1980. Self-Interest and the Concept of Self-Sacrifice. *Canadian Journal of Philosophy* 10: 105–118.

Overvold, M. 1982. Self-Interest and Getting What You Want. In Miller and Williams 1982: 186–94.

Overvold, M. 1984. Morality, Self-interest, and Reasons for Being Moral. *Philosophy and Phenomenological Research* 44: pp. 493–507.

Partridge, E. 1981a. *Responsibilities to Future Generations.* Buffalo: Prometheus Books.

Partridge, E. 1981b. Why Care About the Future? In Partridge 1981a: 203–20.

Parfit, D. 1984. *Reasons and Persons.* Oxford: Clarendon Press.

Peden, C., and D. Speak, eds. 1991. *The American Constitutional Experiment.* Lewiston: Edwin Mellen Press.

Perry, R. B. 1926. *General Theory of Value.* Cambridge: Harvard University Press.

Perry, R. B., ed. 1962. *Essays on Faith and Morals: William James.* Cleveland: World Publishing Company.

Phillips, D. Z. 1968. Does it Pay to be Good? In Thompson and Dworkin 1968: 261–78.

Pollock, J. 1986. *Contemporary Theories of Knowledge.* Totowa: Rowman and Littlefield.

Post, E. 1965. *Emily Post's Etiquette: The Blue Book of Social Usage.* Revised by Elizabeth L. Post. New York: Funk and Wagnalls.

Prichard, H. A. 1928. *Duty and Interest.* Oxford: Clarendon Press.

Putnam, 1975. The Meaning of "Meaning". In Gunderson 1975: 131–93.

Putnam, H. 1967a. The Mental Life of Some Machines. In Castañeda 1967: 177–200.

Putnam, H. 1967b. Psychological Predicates. In Capitan and Merrill 1967: 37–48.

Railton, P. 1986. Moral Realism. *Philosophical Review* 95: 163–207.

Rawls, J. 1971. *A Theory of Justice.* Cambridge: Harvard University Press.

Regan, D. 1980. *Utilitarianism and Co-operation.* Oxford: Clarendon Press.

Richards, D. 1971. *A Theory of Reasons for Actions.* Oxford: Clarendon Press.

Ross, W. D. 1939. *The Foundations of Ethics.* Oxford: Clarendon Press.

Roth, A. 1979. *Axiomatic Models of Bargaining.* Berlin: Springer-Verlag.

Rubinstein, A. 1982. Perfect Equilibrium in a Bargaining Model. *Econometrica* 50: 97–109.

Russell, J., ed. 1987. *A Philosophical Perspective on Developmental Psychology.* Oxford: Basil Blackwell.

Savage, C., ed. 1978. *Minnesota Studies in the Philosophy of Science* 9. Minneapolis: University of Minnesota Press.

Sayre-McCord, G. 1989. Deception and Reasons to be Moral. *American Philosophical Quarterly* 26: 113–22.

Sayre-McCord, G., ed. 1988. *Essays on Moral Realism.* Ithaca: Cornell University Press.

Scheffler, S. 1982. *The Rejection of Consequentialism: A Philosophical Investigation of the Considerations Underlying Rival Moral Conceptions.* Oxford: Clarendon Press.

Scheffler, S. 1985/1988. Agent-Centred Restrictions, Rationality, and the Virtues. *Mind* 94: 409–19. Reprinted in Scheffler 1988.

Scheffler, S., ed. 1988. *Consequentialism and Its Critics.* Oxford: Oxford University Press.

Schilpp, P., and L. Hahn, eds. 1990. *The Philosophy of Georg Henrick von Wright.* La Salle: Open Court.

Schmitt, F. 1992. *Knowledge and Belief.* London: Routledge.

Schneewind, J. B. 1977. *Sidgwick's Ethics and Victorian Moral Philosophy.* Oxford: Clarendon Press.

Schultz, B., ed. *Essays on Henry Sidgwick.* Cambridge: Cambridge University Press.

Schwartz, T. 1978. Obligations to Posterity. In Sikora and Barry: 3–13.

Schwartz, T. 1982. Human Welfare: What it is Not. In Miller and Williams 1982: 195–206.

Schwartz, T. 1990. Von Wright's Theory of Human Welfare: A Critique. In Schilpp and Hahn 1990: 217–32.

Seanor, D., and N. Fotion, eds. 1988. *Hare and Critics.* Oxford: Clarendon Press.

Sen, A. K. 1976. Rational Fools: A Critique of the Behavioral Foundations of Economic Theory. *Philosophy and Public Affairs* 6: 317–44.

Sen, A. K., and Williams, B., eds. 1982. *Utilitarianism and Beyond.* Cambridge: Cambridge University Press.

Shapley, L. 1969. Utility Comparisons and the Theory of Games. In *La Decision.* Paris: CNRS.

Shaw, W. 1980. Elementary Lifesaving. *Southern Journal of Philosophy* 16: 87–97.

Sidgwick, H. 1907. *The Methods of Ethics,* 7th ed. London: Macmillan.

Sidgwick, H. 1931. *Outlines of the History of Ethics,* 6th ed. London: Macmillan.

Sikora, R., and B. Barry, eds. 1978. *Obligations to Future Generations.* Philadelphia: Temple University Press.

Silberman, C. 1978. *Criminal Violence, Criminal Justice.* New York: Random House.

Skyrms, B. 1990. *The Dynamics of Rational Deliberation.* Cambridge: Harvard University Press.

Slote, M. 1983. *Goods and Virtues.* Oxford: Clarendon Press.

Smart, J. J. C. 1973. An Outline of a System of Utilitarian Ethics. In Smart and Williams 1973: 3–74.

Smart, J. J. C., and B. Williams. 1973. *Utilitarianism: For and Against.* Cambridge: Cambridge University Press.

Sosa, E. 1991. *Knowledge in Perspective.* Cambridge: Cambridge University Press.

Stich, S. 1990. *The Fragmentation of Reason.* Cambridge: MIT Press.

Thompson, J., and G. Dworkin, eds. 1968. *Ethics.* New York: Harper and Row.

Timmons, M. 1990. On the Epistemic Status of Considered Moral Judgments. *Southern Journal of Philosophy* 29 (Spindel Conference Supplement): 97–129.

Ullmann-Margalit, E., and S. Morgenbesser. 1977. Picking and Choosing. *Social Research* 44: 757–85.

Valberg, E. 1977. Phillipa Foot on Etiquette and Morality. *Southern Journal of Philosophy* 15: 387–91.

Vallentyne, P. 1991. The Problem of Unauthorized Preferences. *Noûs* 25: 295–321.

Vallentyne, P., ed. 1991. *Contractarianism and Rational Choice: Essays on David Gauthier's* Morals by Agreement. Cambridge: Cambridge University Press.

Vermazen B., and M. Hintikka, eds. 1985. *Essays on Davidson: Actions and Events.* Oxford: Clarendon Press.

von Hirsch, A. 1976. *Doing Justice: The Choice of Punishments.* New York: Hill and Wang.

von Neumann, J., and O. Morgenstern. 1953. *Theory of Games and Economic Behavior.* Princeton: Princeton University Press.

von Wright, G. 1963. *The Varieties of Goodness.* London: Routledge & Kegan Paul.

von Wright, G. 1990. A Reply to my Critics. In Schilpp and Hahn 1990: 731–887.

Waldo, M. 1965. *Myra Waldo's Travel Guide: Orient and Asia.* New York: Macmillan.

Weirich, P. 1990. L'Utilité Collective. In Archambault and Arkhipoff 1990: 411–20.

Weirich, P. 1991. The General Welfare as a Constitutional Goal. In Peden and Speak 1991: 411–32.

White, S. 1982. Partial Character and the Language of Thought. *Pacific Philosophical Quarterly* 63: 347–65.

Willats, J. 1985. Drawing Systems Revisited: The Role of Denotation Systems in Children's Figure Drawings. In Freeman and Cox 1985: 78–100.

Williams, B. 1973. A Critique of Utilitarianism. In Smart and Williams 1973: 77–150.

Williams, B. 1985. *Ethics and the Limits of Philosophy.* Cambridge: Harvard University Press.

Wilson, T., and Nisbett, R. 1978. The Accuracy of Verbal Reports About the Effects of Stimuli on Evaluations and Behavior. *Social Psychology* 41: 118–31.

Index

Contributors

FELICIA ACKERMAN is professor of philosophy at Brown University. Her philosophy articles have appeared in various journals and anthologies, including the *Midwest Studies* and *Philosophical Perspectives* book series, and her short stories have appeared in *Prize Stories 1990: The O. Henry Awards*, *Commentary*, *Playgirl*, and elsewhere.

FREDERICK ADAMS is professor and chair of philosophy at Central Michigan University. He writes on epistemology and the philosophy of mind and is editor, with Leemon McHenry, of *Reflections on Philosophy*.

ROBERT AUDI is professor of philosophy at the University of Nebraska. He is author of *Belief, Justification and Knowledge* and *Practical Reasoning*.

RICHARD BRANDT is emeritus professor of philosophy at the University of Michigan. He is author of a number of books including *The Philosophy of Schliermacher; Hopi Ethics: A Theoretical Analysis; Ethical Theory; A Theory of the Good and the Right;* and *Morality, Utilitarianism, and Rights*.

THOMAS CARSON is associate professor of philosophy at Loyola University of Chicago. He is author of *The Status of Morality* and various papers on moral philosophy.

WILLIAM K. FRANKENA is emeritus professor of philosophy at the University of Michigan. He is author of *Ethics, Perspectives on Morality* (edited by K. E. Goodpaster), *Three Historical Philosophies of Education, Thinking About Morality*, and many articles.

ALAN E. FUCHS is professor of philosophy at the College of William and Mary. He is the author of several articles on ethical theory and the philosophy of law.

JOHN HEIL is professor of philosophy at Davidson College. He is author of *Perception and Cognition* and *The Nature of True Minds*.

BRAD HOOKER is associate professor of philosophy at Virginia Commonwealth University. He is editor of *Rationality, Rules, and Utility*.

TERENCE HORGAN is professor of philosophy at Memphis State University. He has published articles in metaphysics, the philosophy of mind, and the philosophy of language; has edited (with John Tienson)

Connectionism and the Philosophy of Mind; and is currently completing (with John Tienson) *Connectionism and the Philosophy of Psychology: Representational Realism Without Rules.*

GREGORY S. KAVKA teaches moral and political philosophy at the University of California, Irvine. He is author of *Hobbesian Moral Theory* and *Moral Paradoxes of Nuclear Deterrence.*

JOHN LANGAN, S. J., is Rose Kennedy Professor of Christian Ethics at Georgetown University. He is editor of *Human Rights in the Americas* and *The American Search for Peace.*

ALFRED R. MELE is professor of philosophy at Davidson College. He is author of *Irrationality* and of *Springs of Action,* and editor, with John Heil, of *Mental Causation.*

FREDERICK SCHMITT is professor of philosophy at the University of Illinois at Urbana-Champaign. He is the author of *Knowledge and Belief* and the editor of *Knowledge and the Social.*

WILLIAM H. SHAW teaches philosophy at San Jose State University. He has edited several books, including *Social and Personal Ethics* and (with John Arthur) *Justice and Economic Distribution.* He is author of *Marx's Theory of History* and *Business Ethics.*

HOLLY M. SMITH is professor of philosophy and Vice Provost for Academic Affairs at the University of Arizona. She has published widely on normative ethics, metaethics, and issues in applied ethics. She is presently working on a book manuscript examining the role of human cognitive shortcomings in moral theory.

MARK TIMMONS is associate professor of philosophy at Memphis State University. He has published articles in the areas of ethics and epistemology; is editor of *Moral Epistemology* (1990 Spindel Conference Supplement, *Southern Journal of Philosophy* 29); and is currently writing a book, *Morality Without Foundations.*

PAUL WEIRICH is associate professor of philosophy at the University of Missouri-Columbia. He is the author of articles on decision theory in *Philosophy of Science, Theory and Decision,* and other journals.

Standard Book Number: 226–03712–6
Library of Congress Catalog Card Number: 78–101359

THE UNIVERSITY OF CHICAGO PRESS, CHICAGO 60637
THE UNIVERSITY OF CHICAGO PRESS, LTD., LONDON

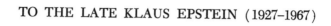

TO THE LATE KLAUS EPSTEIN (1927–1967)

Contents

Acknowledgments

I want to express my appreciation to the librarians and archivists of the Bundesarchiv in Koblenz and the Deutsche Staatsbibliothek in East Berlin, whose helpful assistance was invaluable. I am especially grateful to Udo Dräger of the Deutsches Zentralarchiv and Professor Constantin von Dietze, who permitted me to work in the Seminar für Agrarpolitik in Freiburg im/B, and who made available to me the personal library of Max Sering. To the late Klaus Epstein, both my mentor and my friend, whose untimely death was a terrible tragedy as well as an irrevocable loss to the historical profession, I am indebted for his personal kindness and for his guidance of my development as a historian. Among the scholars whose critical comments on the manuscript aided me in making revisions, I wish to thank Eugene Black and Paul Kecskemeti of Brandeis University, Donald Rohr of Brown University, and Forrest MacDonald of Wayne State University. I want to thank my wife Elizabeth, whose patience was extraordinary, especially in view of her observation that every chapter sounded the same to her.

ABBREVIATIONS   DZA   Deutsches Zentralarchiv,
                             Abteilung II, Merseburg

                     BA   Bundesarchiv, Koblenz

                     DSB   Deutsche Staatsbibliothek,
                             East Berlin

                     DSB II Deutsche Staatsbibliothek,
                             Marburg/L

Introduction

The 1906 edition of the *Wörterbuch der Volkswirtschaft* and the 1909 edition of the *Handwörterbuch der Staatswissenschaften* both contain articles entitled *Agrar- und Industriestaat*. Significantly, earlier editions of the two encyclopedias have no such headings. The new heading was but one sign of the recognition by Germans around the turn of the century that a conflict existed between a society based on agriculture and one based on manufacturing. The articles sharply contrast the patriarchal gentry exercising power on the local level and the steadfast landed peasantry of an earlier day, with the small body of affluent capitalist entrepreneurs and the massive, impoverished proletariat arising in an industrial civilization. The *Industriestaat* was characterized by the profit motive and a tendency toward accumulation as against the cooperation and concern with a just division of wealth prevalent in the *Agrarstaat*. Social cohesion was replaced by violent conflict when a society began to industrialize. One fostered familial and local self-sufficiency while the other led to a growing involvement in the world economy. Because the German states, unlike England or France, did not experience a gradual transition from a rural, noncapitalist society to a mature industrial power, there was a marked tendency in the encyclopedia articles (and in all late nineteenth-century German thought) to present agriculture and industry as holistic and completely contrasting economic and social systems. That a society could combine elements of both was either overlooked or ignored.

Although German industrialization began in the 1830s and gained momentum after unification, it was not until the 1890s that the scions of the old order felt themselves seriously threatened by the new phenomenon. During this decade, in which social radicalism of the right manifested its enormous potential, there was prosperity in all economic spheres except agriculture, and continuous urban migration reached the point at which a majority of Germans resided in towns of 2,000 or more.[1] Furthermore, the social and economic policies of the empire became more responsive to the changes; a development distressing to agrarians, who had been accustomed to look upon government as the prime benefactor of agriculture. These events were compounded by the accession to the throne of Wilhelm II, who evinced more pride in the industrial achievements of Germany than in its rural past. Staunch agrarians now came to believe that their primacy in society and politics stood in jeopardy. Almost all economic legislation and many proposals in other areas were weighed by agrarians solely on the basis of which type of society they appeared to promote. Organizations were founded, newspapers published, and rallies held, to resist the permeation of Germany by industrialism and its accompanying rationalist spirit. Not to be outdone, industrialists and merchants

1. Rural dwellers declined from 57 percent to 45 percent. It was not only the Junkers who turned to anticapitalism in the nineties. The combination of a depression in agriculture and industry in the early nineties led many thinkers to question the long-term viability of industrial capitalism. The large anti-Semitic vote in the Reichstag and the Saxon election in 1893 also demonstrated the growth of social radicalism among the peasants and *petits bourgeois*. America also witnessed the growth of anticapitalism in this period. Cf. Frederic Jaher, *Doubters and Dissenters* (Glencoe, 1964); and the novel of cataclysm by Ignatius Donnelly, *Caesar's Column* (Chicago, 1891).

used the resources at their disposal to counter this assault on their position.

The conflict was set in motion in 1891 during Reichstag debates over a tariff treaty with Austria-Hungary. Today, when tariff discussions are tedious and a matter for specialists in international trade, it is difficult to conceive of their ever serving as the catalyst for a controversy of major proportions. But in Germany, as in any nation in the midst of industrialization, tariffs are an important yardstick by which to judge whether the forces of change or of the status quo are determining government policy. Both in fin de siècle Germany and in Britain during the anti–corn law campaign, the level of tariffs were considered a guide to the type of society desired by those in authority; that is, which segments of society were to be encouraged to grow and prosper and which were to be left to fall by the wayside.[2] In 1891 the interests of agriculture and industry were irreconcilable, and the novice chancellor, Caprivi, took the part of the latter. Because of Caprivi's unprecedented decision, the Junkers sought to consolidate the cultivators of the soil into one agrarian movement under their auspices to combat the chancellor's policy and to thwart the impending triumph of industrialism. The next decade was devoted to winning back the economic primacy thought to be lost between 1891 and 1894, when the Austrian treaty was augmented by agreements with Romania and Russia.

Another consequence of Caprivi's policy was the launching of a controversy in the academic world about the desirability of an agricultural as against an industrial, capitalist economy. Throughout the course of the nineteenth century there had been a strong, conservative antipathy to capitalism, based on Christian and patriarchal grounds. With the onslaught of an agricultural depression in the nineties and the apparent decline of Junker power, the critique intensified and led several major political economists to espouse comprehensive theories about the danger to German security and

2. Tariff rates have become a focal point of conflict in almost every nation when industrialization is progressing but the preindustrial forces are still quite powerful. This occurred in America during the 1890s, Russia in the early twentieth century, and France in the 1880s.

Volkstum inherent in industrial capitalism. The passing of the old Germany of estates was held to be a national disaster. Industrialism was thus subjected to two distinct but related attacks that owed their origins to the same change in the direction of tariff policy. This caused liberals to rush to the defense of the rising economic order. The controversy began with an acrid dialogue between Karl Oldenberg, an instructor from Berlin, and Max Weber, an advocate of rapid industrialization, after the former's Cassandra-like speech "Deutschland als Industriestaat" at the Protestant Social Congress in 1897.[3] Four years later the dispute had created such divisions among economists that the Verein für Sozialpolitik devoted its convention to the theme "Agrar- und Industriestaat." At the turn of the century, books and pamphlets dealing with the subject multiplied rapidly as each author hoped that his work would influence the crucial tariff rates for grain and thereby the future character of Germany.

By 1901 the theoretical and pragmatic strands in the anti-industrial movement had converged. Conservative professors spoke at meetings of the Bund der Landwirte and the Vereinigung der Steuer- und Wirtschaftsreformer and wrote for agrarian publications.[4] Junker politicians, ministers, and academics together discussed the plight of agriculture at the government-convened *Agrarkonferenz*.[5] Conversely, it was not uncommon for agrarians in the various right-of-center parties to cite the theories of their learned supporters. Chancellor von Bülow's decision to raise the grain duties was in part determined by his "personal friend" and the "greatest influence on his economic thought," Adolf Wagner, who was the leading professor in sympathy with the agrarian cause.[6]

The controversy entered the practical sphere again in 1901, when the government headed by von Bülow introduced the new tariff schedule. During the subsequent year, Reichstag delegates, influ-

3. *Verhandlungen des 8. Evangelisch-Sozialen Kongresses*, 1897.
4. In 1894 Adolf Wagner told the leaders of the *Farmers' League* that he agreed with their program in all its essentials. It became common in the nineties for professors to receive invitations from all sorts of interest groups.
5. *Landwirtschaftliche Jahrbücher*, supp. 23, pt. 2 (1894).
6. Bernhard von Bülow, *Denkwürdigkeiten*, 4 vols. (Berlin, 1926) 2:383, 4:118.

4

enced by the economic interests of their constituencies and the plethora of literature appearing, debated the pros and cons of industrialism. In December 1902, a settlement was achieved whereby the interests of agriculture received priority, although not quite to the degree wished for by agrarians. The controversy then waned because the leaders of heavy industry were willing to accept the primacy of the Junkers in return for economic privileges. In effect, the German house was to have an agricultural frame but to be well stocked with industrial furniture.

Strangely, the years 1890–1902 have never before been viewed as a unitary period centering on the conflict between *Agrar- und Industriestaat.* Excellent studies of these twelve years by Eckart Kehr and Pauline Anderson have related politics to foreign policy, but the economic controversies themselves and their resolutions have not received the attention they merit.[7] Nor has proper consideration been given to the appreciable influence of contemporary thought, particularly that of the anti-industrial economists, on the politics of this era. Studies of Heinrich von Treitschke have tackled this problem for the Bismarckian period, and Klaus Schwabe has done admirable work on the professoriat during World War I, but the intervening years have been neglected.[8] In *The Politics of Cultural Despair,* Fritz Stern refers to the paucity of our knowledge about antimodernism in nineteenth-century thought. Although much has been written about this trend in the 1920s, its antecedents, particularly in the 1890s, have received little attention. Stern himself has made a great contribution here, but has found few followers.

In the present work I have tried to bring the significant antimod-

7. Eckart Kehr, *Schlachtflottenbau und Parteipolitik* (Berlin, 1930); Pauline Anderson, *The Background of Anti-English Feeling in Germany, 1890–1902* (Washington, 1939).

8. Schwabe, "Zur politischen Haltung der deutschen Professoren im ersten Weltkrieg," *Historische Zeitschrift* 193, no. 3, (December, 1961). The recent study of the *Verein für Sozialpolitik* by Dieter Lindenlaub is mainly concerned with conflicts in thought among the members. Cf. *Richtungskämpfe im Verein für Sozialpolitik* (Wiesbaden, 1967). Also see F. Ringer, *The Decline of the Mandarins* (Cambridge, Mass. 1969).

ern currents to bear on the controversy over industrialization. Their role in influencing political decision making is often underestimated despite considerable evidence that the ideas of numerous scholars turned publicists played a part in determining the outcome of the conflict. Even more than exerting a direct influence, these professors were responsible for the rhetoric and theories proffered by politicians. By increasingly propagating their views to the general public they built up a large reservoir of anti-industrial sentiment. I would further suggest that their influence on public attitudes and state policy far exceeded that of the cultural critics of the Bismarckian and Wilhelmian empire, Paul de Lagarde, Julius Langbehn, and Friedrich Nietzsche. Despite their fervent attachment to the empire and the absence of any alienation, these professors condemned the changes engulfing Germany as vigorously as the cultural critics. They provided a rational critique of industrial civilization that took the peculiarities of German history into account, which had great appeal to patriotic Germans who lacked even the capacity to be culturally alienated.[9] And they were in a better position to influence the immediate course of events than aesthetes who lived in a state approaching complete isolation. The agrarians spoke to interest groups, served on government commissions, and were in personal contact with the leading decision makers in the government. Few of the politicians who voted to restore agricultural primacy in 1902 had read or heard Julius Langbehn, but their speeches evidenced a familiarity with the ideas of Adolf Wagner and Max Sering.

9. This is not to deny that the cultural critics had a significant, long-term influence and that their thought gradually found an increasingly responsive audience. The point is that antimodernism was not confined to these men in the 1890s, and the political economists demonstrated the possibility of anti-industrialism's influencing the political course of events in 1902. It seems to me that their ideas and willingness to suggest immediate remedies to prevent the further decline of rural civilization had a more significant effect than that of any other group disillusioned with industrial society. It should be pointed out also that apart from the political economists and cultural critics, sociologists displayed a growing hostility to the modern world. Cf. Arthur Mitzman's dissertation, "Sociology and Discontent in Imperial Germany" (Brandeis University, 1963). I would disagree with Mitzman's belief that the disillusionment was bound up with the sociologists' personal lives. The phenomenon of antimodernism was too widespread to be anything less than a social development.

Therefore, I have considered the theoretical as well as the practical campaigns against industrialism, although they do not fully overlap. I believe that an artificial distinction is drawn if the relationship between the political economists and the agrarians is ignored because the reasons for their antipathy to industrial capitalism diverged on occasion. Certainly the leading professor, Adolf Wagner, did not make the distinction. When he was insultingly called an "agrarian reactionary" by an opponent, he proudly announced that it was an honor to be so classified.[10]

Before introducing the anti-industrial economists I have chosen to discuss the opportunities of the Wilhelmian professoriat for influencing public opinion and state policy deserve some attention. A small number of professors joined parties and sat in the Reichstag. Treitschke held a seat for thirteen years, and Hermann Paasche and Graf Hertling both had successful academic careers before shifting to politics. Hans Delbrück was an active member of the Free Conservative delegation in the Reichstag while editing the *Preussische Jahrbücher* and occupying a chair in history at Berlin. Nevertheless, it has been frequently observed that professors, on the whole, hesitated to join parties and viewed a career in partisan politics as a threat to the objectivity indispensable for excellence in scholarship.[11] While the professoriat as a whole failed to take sides on important contemporary issues and has justifiably been regarded as apolitical, it does not necessarily follow that academics were apolitical, except in the narrowest sense of the word. If apolitical connotes a lack of interest in, or an unwillingness to express opinions on, controversial topical issues, the German professor was definitely political. It is worth recalling here a passage written around the turn of the century by Delbrück, a professor at home both in a smoke-filled room and in the more rarified atmosphere of the university.

> Almost all of the younger generation coming to
> the fore are mediocre. For many years no
> scholar has sat among the representatives of the

10. *Korrespondenz des Handelsvertragsverein,* 15 November 1901.
11. This was true, for instance, of Lujo Brentano. See James J. Sheehan, *The Career of Lujo Brentano* (Chicago, 1966).

> people of poets and philosophers. Nor in this epoch of dazzling economic prosperity is there a single leader of industry, trade, or finance. The great aristocrats too, the dukes, princes, ambassadors, that formerly sat in the Reichstag have almost disappeared. Elections no longer appeal to such men, and if they did receive a mandate, they would not accept it. Instead of estate owners we see the directors of the Farmers League; instead of industrialists, the secretaries of chambers of commerce, and instead of scholars, honorary professors.[12]

Delbrück was groping toward an important point in understanding the Wilhelmian political scene. The parties and the legislature were simply not at the center of German political life in any meaningful sense. One of the results of Bismarck's pseudoconstitutionalism was that power lay in the hands of a small oligarchy of officials and the emperor. As the Reichstag's impotence became evident, the Bambergers, Laskers, and Windthorsts of the seventies found no worthy successors to replace them. By the nineties, men of talent and conviction sought more meaningful ways of influencing decision making than the hollow honor of a Reichstag seat.

Thus, we must look elsewhere before we judge the professors apolitical. It is interesting to note that contemporaries did not share historians' subsequent generalizations. Frederic Wile, a British journalist, writing about his prewar experiences as a correspondent in Berlin, noted, "The ascendency of no single other caste excels their [the professors'] influence on affairs of state."[13] Rudolf Martin, the legal advisor to the Ministry of the Interior, wrote the fol-

12. Delbrück, *Vor und nach dem Weltkrieg* (Berlin, 1927), p. 173; In 1907 he said, "The parties are unimportant and have no power of attraction. Many have withdrawn from direct political life not because of indolence or lack of interest but because practical party politics has no appeal. That there is no lack of interest is shown in crises, when these circles emerge to show unexpected strength." Also see H. Kaelble, *Industrielle Interessenpolitik in der Wilhelminischen Gesellschaft* (Berlin, 1967), pp. 115–16. The number of industrialists in the Reichstag fell by one-half between 1870 and 1900.

13. Wile, *Men around the Kaiser* (Indianapolis, 1914), p. 107.

lowing words as evidence of Adolf Wagner's and Gustav Schmoller's effect on Bülow's domestic policy:

> The time is past when German professors have nothing to say. Public opinion is not far removed from the views of our best professors of economics and history. The *Geheimräte* and ministers study their opinions carefully before they begin planning legislation, and the parliamentarians and editors peruse . . . the books and articles of professors.[14]

Three methods emerged by which academics and industrialists as well sought to have an effect on policy—personal contact, university lectures and writings, and public speaking.

In Imperial Germany, with its small oligarchy in power and a relatively narrow *Bildungsbürgertum*, it was not uncommon for an elite group like university faculty members to be acquainted with ministers and even chancellors. Martin observed, "Gustav Schmoller was well acquainted with Bismarck but stood much closer to Prince Bülow. . . . Through Bülow, he was often invited to meet the emperor."[15] Schmoller listed the following ministers among his personal friends: Berlepsch, Lohmann, Delbrück, Miquel, Bötticher, and Falck.[16] At the informal gatherings of the Berlin Staatswissenschaftliche Gesellschaft, professors met and discussed current issues with the capital's leading civil servants. Both the historian Theodor Schiemann and the theologian Adolf Harnack dined with Wilhelm II at regular intervals and even accompanied him on vacation trips.[17] Schiemann was used by the foreign office to translate decoded Russian messages. Wagner knew Bismarck and Bülow personally and consulted with the Ministry of Finance. After his dismissal in 1909, Bülow used Schmoller and Harnack as intermediaries to communicate with Wilhelm II.

14. Martin, *Deutsche Machthaber* (Berlin, 1910) p. 534.
15. Ibid., p. 535.
16. Schmoller, *Zwanzig Jahre deutscher Politik, 1897–1917* (Munich, 1920), p. 189.
17. On Schiemann, see Klaus Meyer, *Theodor Schiemann als politischer Publizist* (Frankfurt, 1956); and on Harnack see Agnes von Zahn-Harnack, *Adolf von Harnack* (Berlin, 1936).

In the normal course of lecturing and writing, professors exerted an enormous influence, which is often underestimated. Admiral Tirpitz, who had learned of Germany's need for a navy from Treitschke's lectures, used their talents as propagandists in the campaign for the fleet because of the respect accorded their opinions. Despite their hesitancy about joining parties, Schmoller, Brentano, Sering, and Wagner hastened to do the admiral's bidding.[18] The Verein deutscher Studenten was founded as a result of Treitschke's inspiring lectures. Helmuth von Gerlach notes in his autobiography that he remained a Conservative for years despite grave reservations because of Wagner's expressed sympathy for the party.[19] Popular lecturers such as Treitschke and Wagner drew thousands including state officials, generals, and Reichstag members. An article by Karl Oldenberg of Berlin led to the first regulation of adult male working hours in Prussia. Each generation of civil servants in Germany usually espoused the ideas imbibed during their university studies. This was as true of the Prussian free traders under Friedrich Wilhelm III as of the social reformers under Wilhelm II.

Around the turn of the century it became increasingly common for professors to abandon their lecterns for appearances before nonacademic audiences. Many Berlin professors held weekly lectures open to the public on matters of current interest. Schmoller and Sering led the faculty at Berlin in a series of meetings in 1907 to increase support for German colonization policies; in 1900 they had debated all comers in support of a powerful navy. Speeches to farm and labor organizations became a routine practice. Sering spoke at least once a year to agrarian groups between 1894 and 1909. At meetings of the Verein für Sozialpolitik and of the Evangelisch-Soziale Kongress, the hundreds of laymen attending heard the latest views of the academic elite.

After unification was achieved in 1871, political economists gradually replaced historians as the leading professorial publicists.

18. See Alfred von Tirpitz, *My Memoirs* (New York, 1919), p. 143; and Wolfgang Marienfeld, *Wissenschaft und Schlachtflottenbau in Deutschland, 1897–1906.*

19. Von Gerlach, *Von Rechts nach Links* (Zurich, 1937), p. 69.

Writing in 1903, Otto Hintze pointed to the rise of economics:

> The discipline of economics, neither at this time [1848–1870] nor earlier, had a leading position at German universities, and until the calling of Adolf Wagner in 1870, only a small place at Berlin. Immediately after this date, economic and social problems moved to the center of public life. . . . This epoch of our national history called economics to the forefront.[20]

While at the Ministry of the Interior, Theodor Lohmann relied on the ideas of economists in framing social legislation. According to his biographer, "his concrete outlook was deepened by his attending countless lectures on economics, history, *Sozialpolitik,* and technology."[21] Berlepsch, the minister of trade under Caprivi and Hohenlohe, founded his own Gesellschaft für soziale Reform, where officials and economists could keep abreast of one another's ideas. Bülow's minister of the interior, Graf Posadowsky, regularly attended these meetings. Karl Erich Born recently wrote of the growing influence of economists:

> Schmoller's and Wagner's *Handbuch der Volkswissenschaftslehre* was the standard work of the period. . . . In the economic and social-political departments of the empire and the states, the number of councillors who had been through the school of Schmoller and Wagner was steadily rising.[22]

Thus, as the center of national concern shifted from unity to the social problem, the age of the political economist dawned.

Of the numerous professors supporting the agrarian cause I have chosen to write about three—Karl Oldenberg, Adolf Wagner, and

---

20. Hintze, "Gustav Schmoller; Ein Gedenkblatt," in *Soziologie und Geschichte,* ed. G. Oestreich (Göttingen, 1964), p. 520.

21. Hans Rothfels, *Theodor Lohmann und die Kampfjahre der staatlichen Sozialpolitik* (Berlin, 1927), p. 35.

22. Born, *Staat und Sozialpolitik seit Bismarcks Sturz* (Wiesbaden, 1957), pp. 44ff.

11

Max Sering. They demonstrate the breadth as well as the depth of antimodernism among political economists. Wagner was a deductive thinker rooted in the classical tradition; the others were of the historical school. All three devoted their energies in the nineties to the *Agrar- und Industriestaat* question. More than their likeminded colleagues, they took on the role of publicists in order to influence politicians and the popular mind about the crisis that Germany faced. Associated with the University of Berlin, Wagner and Sering were in a particularly good geographical location to accomplish this task. Yet it should not be forgotten that a host of other major economists, including Karl Diehl, Ludwig Pohle, and Adolf Buchenberger, were writing in a similar vein.[23]

Seeking to integrate the intellectual currents with the political disputes and economic developments around one theme creates obvious problems of organization. After considerable experimentation I have chosen to present the controversy in three parts and to treat the interaction between the economic, political, and intellectual aspects wherever it is relevant. This choice merits some explanation. If the three had been combined, the result would have been chaotic. Every time a professor's speech to an agrarian group were being reported, the narrative would have been interrupted by an analysis of the speech. By presenting the ideas in a separate section, the inner unity of their thought is preserved. The logic and appeal of the anticapitalist current of thought are also more evident.

---

23. See Buchenberger, *Agrarwesen und Agrarpolitik* (Leipzig, 1892); Pohle, *Deutschland am Scheidewege* (Leipzig, 1902); Diehl, *Zur Frage der Getreidezölle* (Jena, 1911). Sartorius von Waltershausen and Adalbert Wahl were also sympathetic to the agrarians, as was Gustav Schmoller.

PART ONE

Und der König absolut
wenn er unsern Willen tut

Old satirical couplet

1

The Legacy of the Nineteenth Century

THE POLITICAL SYSTEM OF THE EMPIRE

From its founding in 1871 until its demise in 1918, the second German empire was governed under the constitution designed by Bismarck for the North German Confederation. When the constitution was drafted in 1867, northern Germany comprised thirty-three independent states, whose economic base almost without exception was agricultural. Two-thirds of the empire's forty million inhabitants resided in rural villages. While industrialization was leading to urbanization in England and France, this process was retarded in Germany by political disunity. During the half-century from the Congress of Vienna to the Austrian war of 1866 the number of Prussians dwelling in urban areas had increased by a mere eight percent. Had Madame de Staël revisited Germany in the 1860s, she probably would have modified her earlier, idyllic descriptions of rural life, but the continuity with the past would have struck her more than the change.

Although Germany, like the United

States, was composed of numerous states, an essential difference lay in the dominant position held by Prussia.[1] After annexing Hanover, Hesse-Kassel, Nassau, and the free city of Frankfurt, as spoils of the "Seven Weeks War," Prussia's territory amounted to 75 percent of the North German Confederation and approximately 60 percent of the later German empire. In population as in area, Prussia was superior to all the other states combined. By its possession of the Rhineland and Silesia it also ruled over the only regions where industrialization had made serious inroads. Every conceivable criterion pointed to the ascendancy of Prussian power in Germany.

The constitution formulated by Bismarck reflected the essentially rural nature of society and the importance of Prussia, although both were concealed within an elaborate network of political relationships. Following the pattern of the stillborn 1848 constitution, Bismarck provided for two legislative bodies; one to represent the people and the other the state governments. The lower house or Reichstag was to be composed of 397 members elected by universal manhood suffrage in single-member constituencies. To preserve the essence of his work, Bismarck later conceded the secret ballot, although Prussia itself continued to use the open ballot until 1918. In theory the Reichstag's ability to reject by a simple majority any bills introduced by the government seemed to make it an important reservoir of power; however, its practical powers were circumscribed by the tendency of the government toward indirect taxes and long-term military bills, both of which required approval only once or twice in a decade. Assent to the budget, of course, could be repeatedly denied in any conflict with the Chancellor, but the failure of this tactic in the Prussian constitutional dispute was still fresh in most memories. Although Bismarck admitted that his actions had been arbitrary in an indemnity bill, he never foreswore a repetition if the liberals should

1. The books I have drawn upon for this section are: Huber, *Verfassungsgeschichte* (Stuttgart, 1963), vol. 3; A. Rosenberg, *Die Entstehung der deutschen Republik* (Berlin, 1928); Fritz Hartung, *Deutsche Verfassungsgeschichte* (Leipzig, 1914); and Johannes Ziekursch, *Politische Geschichte des neuen deutschen Kaiserreichs,* 3 vols. (Frankfurt/M, 1928–30.)

seek another test of strength. The lower house's power was further limited by an article declaring that all legislative proposals were to be submitted first to the upper house or Bundesrat and could be sent to the Reichstag only after the approval of the Bundesrat.

The power of the legislature was severely circumscribed in foreign affairs also. In an age of secret diplomacy, deputies were rarely informed of the existence, much less the terms, of international agreements. Particularly during Bismarck's rule, the representatives were made to feel that international politics constituted a recondite sphere beyond the comprehension of mere elected delegates. Thus, the Reichstag was subject to restrictions in all spheres considered pivotal by western parliamentary thinkers. Its negative powers precluded its devolution into a debating society similar to the later Russian Duma, but in comparison with the lower houses of the western democracies, the Reichstag was a comparatively impotent body.

Each of the thirty-three state governments possessed at least one vote in the Bundesrat. Voting in the upper house was by state, but unlike the American system the votes of a state could not be divided. Prussia with seventeen of the fifty-eight ballots was vastly underrepresented if population and territory are taken into account; however, since only fourteen negative votes were necessary to defeat a constitutional amendment, the system could not be altered against Prussia's wishes. In practice government proposals rarely succeeded in getting to the Reichstag if the Prussian delegates expressed disapproval. Indeed, the situation would have been anomalous if Prussia's material preponderance in the empire had not been reflected by its domination of the Bundesrat. As power in the empire lay in Prussia, its governmental system is deserving of some scrutiny.

A written constitution had been introduced in Prussia after the events of 1848 convinced Friedrich Wilhelm IV that some concession to the liberal spirit was necessary. As formulated in 1850, the document provided for two houses and a minister president responsible only to the king. The rights of the Crown to declare war, conclude treaties, and exercise unrestricted control over the army were confirmed, and remained in effect until the monarchy's

17

collapse. Election to the House of Deputies (Abgeordnetenhaus) was based on the three-class franchise, whereby each constituency was divided into three groups according to the amount of direct taxes paid by the inhabitants. The taxes collected in each district were divided into three equal parts, and those, beginning with the highest taxpayer on down, whose payments constituted one-third of the total formed the first group. Each group was entitled to cast one-third of the votes in the district. This system of representing wealth in the form of land rather than inhabitants meant that the choice of two-thirds of the lower house's members was limited to less than 15 percent of the population. In combination with the open ballot and the overrepresentation of rural constituencies, the three-class suffrage led to an almost perpetual domination of the House of Deputies by conservative agrarian interests.[2] All attempts to make the house reflect the changing social reality shattered because of the inflexibility of the privileged conservative majorities. The House of Lords (*Herrenhaus*) was even more hopelessly out of touch with the Prussian population. Its composition of princes, agricultural magnates, elderly professors, and retired military men, was no more than a cross section of Conservative party members.

Ministerial responsibility as it was understood in England was adapted in neither the Prussian nor the German constitution. Bismarck and his successors owed their allegiance as minister president of Prussia to the king, who, if he chose, could arbitrarily dismiss them despite their control of a parliamentary majority. While parliamentary defeats could weaken a minister's position, in the final analysis only loss of the king's confidence could be fatal. Among the most important duties of the minister president were: presiding over the cabinet, formulation of government policy, and the task of finding majorities for his program. Prussia was, then, ruled by a land-based gentry, whose traditional predominance had

2. Discussing the gains made by the Social Democrats in the 1903 Imperial elections, the Center historian Karl Bachem observed the advantage of the Prussian electoral system to be in the predictability of its results, for while the Social Democrats had increased by thirty seats in the Reichstag, they had yet to gain their first mandate in the Prussian house.

merely been codified by the constitution granted by Friedrich Wilhelm IV.

The sovereignty of Prussia in Germany was enhanced by the provision for the union of the Prussian Crown with the German, and the tendency of the Prussian and German chancellors to be identical. In his capacity as German emperor, the Prussian king dispensed nearly all the powers in the empire that he was accustomed to doing in Prussia, including the prerogative to dismiss imperial chancellors. The position of the imperial chancellor was strange indeed; he presided over the Bundesrat officially, but was in reality always seeking minorities from two lower houses based on entirely different franchises. A conservative majority was always assured in Prussia by the operation of the three-class voting system, but the democratic franchise in Reichstag elections might well produce a majority of the middle or left-oriented parties. If the chancellor should work with the parties of the left in the Reichstag, he was bound to face defiance from the Prussian Conservative party. It was inherent within the system that a chancellor should seek support in the conservative parties in the Reichstag. After manipulating right-oriented majorities for twelve years, Bismarck realized in 1890 that the waxing socialist movement was endangering his entire governmental system, because conservative majorities were increasingly difficult to achieve within the empire. Recognizing the near impossibility of ruling with the left in Germany and the right in Prussia, Bismarck came to the conclusion that a coup d'état was the only method of preserving a conservative-oriented policy in Germany.[3] Caprivi's later failure to do the impossible only confirmed Bismarck's foresight. In trying to base his majorities on the Center and the Radicals, he witnessed the growing hostility of the right in the Prussian and imperial lower houses. Caprivi's failure to reconcile the Conservatives to his policy was instrumental in bringing about his dismissal only four years after he assumed the chancellorship.

As urbanization gained momentum in the decades following unification, the Reichstag became an ever more imperfect reflec-

3. Egmont Zechlin, *Staatsstreichspläne Bismarcks und Wilhelms II, 1890–1894* (Stuttgart and Berlin, 1929).

tion of the political outlook of the German people. Because constituencies were never rearranged to mirror shifts in population, the parties whose strength lay in urban areas were grossly underrepresented. The Social Democrats polled approximately as many votes in 1903 as the two next largest parties together; yet they received only half as many seats. Bülow claimed a victory over socialism in the 1907 election when the Socialist party lost twenty-six seats, but those who cared to observe the returns more carefully found that Bebel's party had gained several hundred thousand supporters. The constituencies were so grossly out of date by 1907 that each Conservative deputy required an average of 18,000 votes for election while a Socialist needed approximately 70,000.[4] Thus the conservative landowners of Prussia managed through a series of intricate constitutional maneuvers and intentional omissions to extend their domination of Prussia to all Germany after unification. The fears expressed by many Prussian conservatives that their power would diminish in a German state proved groundless, for Bismarck's constitution established the gentry's mastery over Germany as the Prussian franchise had confirmed their dominion in Prussia. It is impossible to understand the industrialization controversy of the 1890s without a firm grasp of the gentry's extraordinary political power, for the result of the dispute hinged on the ability of these landowners to force the dismissal of a hostile chancellor and sway national policy by the ready use of power on the state level.

The loyal cartel of conservative parties and National Liberals that had formed a secure majority for Bismarck disintegrated in the 1890 election without hope of revival. By 1903, the three so-called *Reichsfeinde* commanded over 200 seats in the Reichstag, and were always theoretically capable thereafter of coalescing to defeat government proposals. Caprivi, then, arrived on the political scene at a moment when the traditional government coalition of the right had ceased to exist. Choosing to work with a majority from the left and center in tariff policy, Caprivi faced rising Conservative intransigence in Prussia and difficulty in passing military

4. *Jahrbuch des Hansa-Bundes* (Berlin, 1912), p. 153.

bills through the imperial legislature. After Caprivi's dismissal in 1894, chancellors abandoned all hope of ruling with the left-of-center parties, and endeavored rather to win the Radicals or Center for government-sponsored bills by quid pro quo's. In this system the parties devolved even further into interest groups clamoring for petty concessions without expectation of ever formulating basic policy. Perhaps the most serious criticism that can be brought against the Bismarckian constitution as it evolved in practice was its failure to allow the parties to mature into responsible institutions through the wielding of real power. It is no wonder that under these conditions the great party leaders of the *Reichsgründungszeit* found no successors other than mediocre party politicians.

THE ECONOMIC STRUCTURE OF THE EMPIRE

The present political division of Germany reflects an economic division existing since the Black Death of the fifteenth century. When the plague decimated the serf population of Europe, the lands east of the Elbe were organized into large agricultural estates in contrast to the small holdings that gradually evolved in western Germany. As serfdom step by step declined in the old German lands, it began to strengthen its hold on the peasants in the conquered territories between the Elbe and the Vistula. Into the age of "Enlightened Despotism" serfdom remained so firmly entrenched in Prussia that Friedrich II could do no more than loosen the bonds of those toilers on his personal domains. Only defeat in the Napoleonic wars caused the Prussian government to review the state's economic and social foundations, which Stein and other bureaucrats regarded as too narrow for success against the French emperor. The embarrassing failure of the Prussian nobility at Jena precluded any immediate determined stand against reform of property relations, but the landowners were certainly not psychically prepared to sacrifice their hitherto privileged position.[5] Even before Napoleon was defeated at Leipzig there arose among the

5. See W. H. Simon, *Failure of the Prussian Reform Movement* (Cambridge, 1955). On the Junkers cf. Hans Rosenberg, "The Rise of the Junkers in Brandenburg-Prussia, 1410–1653," *American Historical Review* 49, nos. 1 and 2 (October 1943 and January 1944).

Prussian Junkers an organized opposition to the break with Prussia's social heritage which the implementation of Stein's reforms would entail.

First in a series of edicts between 1807 and 1821 was that of October 9, 1807, abolishing the caste system, whereby commoners had been prevented from owning estates and nobles forbidden to participate in trade.[6] The free choice of professions introduced by this law terminated the age-old noble monopoly of the land. Even the lowliest serf became a citizen of the Prussian state with the theoretical possibility of eventually becoming an ennobled estate owner. A clarification edict of 1809 prohibited the payment of monetary compensation to the lord for personal freedom, and terminated the free labor service formerly provided by serfs' children. The property rights of the domain peasants were confirmed in 1808 at the same time as the obligatory services were converted into a money fee. Three-quarters of the indemnity had to be settled by 1832 while the last quarter became a perpetual land tax. For the future of Prussia the ordinances of 1811 and 1816 regulating the peasants' relation to the lands he cultivated were of crucial importance. According to the first edict, those peasants having inheritable rights to their land received full possession of two-thirds of their land upon alienation of the other third; those without rights to inheritance had to give the lord one-half of what they cultivated to receive the other half. In the years following this declaration, some estate owners, guided by von der Marwitz, launched a vociferous attack upon the liberal principles guiding the land reforms. Old, time-tested ways were being sacrificed, in their eyes, to the hated ideas arising from the French revolution. Nothing proved the unpreparedness of the Prussian aristocracy for the abolition of serfdom more than the bitterness of their diatribes against any minister seeking to model Prussian land relations after

6. For the reforms I relied on: Theodore von der Goltz, *Agrarwesen und Agrarpolitik* (Jena, 1914), and *Geschichte der deutschen Landwirtschaft*, vol. 2 (Stuttgart, 1902); Heinz Haushofer, *Die deutsche Landwirtschaft im technischen Zeitalter* (Stuttgart, 1963); Friedrich Lütge, *Deutsche Sozial- und Wirtschaftsgeschichte* (Berlin, 1960); Sigmund von Frauendorfer, *Ideengeschichte der Agrarwirtschaft und Agrarpolitik* (Munich, 1957); R. Krzymonski, *Geschichte der deutschen Landwirtschaft* (Berlin, 1961).

the western patterns. The fruit of the noble reaction was the second edict regulating agricultural property.

By the 1816 declaration, all peasants not owning enough land to support their family lost their house, land, and several years later their commons rights. Peasants who could not prove that the same parcel of land had been cultivated by their family before the Seven Years War were categorized with the above-mentioned smallholders. Those peasants who were not *spannfähig* (capable of hitching a team to work in the fields) were similarly denied regulation under the 1811 ordinance. Through the new regulations the landowners had succeeded in limiting the number of peasants empowered to gain full possession of a piece of their former land. A proclamation of 1821 aimed at removing hindrances to the introduction of new agricultural techniques abrogated all peasant usufruct on the commons. The peasants fared even worse in Mecklenburg-Schwerin, where an edict of 1820 allowed the lords to take possession of the serfs' holdings in exchange for personal freedom and the termination of labor services. All the social problems confronting German statesmen in the post-Bismarckian period could be directly or indirectly traced back to the manner in which the reform legislation was finally executed in the East Elbian lands.

Although estimates about the amount of land accruing to the estate owners through indemnity payments vary from 400,000 to 500,000 hectares, it is generally agreed that when the acquisition of small holdings and property purchases are considered, the estates gained not less than one million hectares by mid-century. Loss of commons privileges proved to be a particularly severe blow to peasants accustomed to graze a cow or gather firewood in the forests. Unable to eke out a living under the new regulations, many smallholders sold their land to the former lord rather than cultivate with insufficient means. The result of the reform legislation was not a stable independent peasantry as Stein had intended, but the creation of a large propertyless class of day laborers. Since money wages were rare in rural areas, the day laborers received payment in kind in return for the work pledged in yearly contracts. Apart from a cottage with garden attached and fuel for heating, the laborers were given a fixed percentage of the grain harvest. Social mobility was practically impossible, as the members of the new class owned no land and could save nothing from their wages. When opportunities for emigration to America later developed, the contractual workers formed the bulk of those Germans forsaking their fatherland for the chance to own a piece of land.

Before the reform decrees had been thoroughly executed, a worldwide agricultural depression broke out, which lasted with varying degrees of severity until the 1830s. The average price of Prussian rye dropped precipitously from a profitable 206 marks a ton in the years following the Congress of Vienna to 121 marks in the 1820s. As in later German agricultural crises, the grain farmers bore the brunt. Thus the large eastern estates, which often produced a single crop for export, suffered considerably more than the diversified western farms, where the market price was not so crucial to prosperity.[7] Particularly hard hit were those Junkers in the process of investing in tools and workers' dwellings when the decline commenced. Both the credit institutions founded by Friedrich II and direct government subsidies combined to prevent many old families from losing their estates to urban financiers. Many noble landowners faced with ruin began to manage their estates personally. Gradually the situation improved at the decade's close as new factors arose to influence grain price formation.

What initially appeared to be merely a price recovery was in fact the harbinger of a golden age that was about to dawn on German agriculture. The research of both von Thünen and Justis von Liebig began to find successful application on the large- and middle-sized farms, causing the yield per acre to double by 1870. Greatly expanded railroad mileage brought hitherto inaccessible markets within the realm of eastern producers. By reducing grain duties in numerous west German states, the Zollverein enabled eastern farmers to find new markets within the German confederation. Rye prices in Koenigsberg rose seventeen marks during the

7. The cause of the price decline was to be found in the expanded cultivation of rye during the continental blockade. Each nation sought by increasing the acreage tilled to lessen its dependence on grain imports, because war had dislocated the established trade routes. When peaceful conditions returned, these nations attempted to keep the marginal lands under cultivation by the imposition of high grain duties. Thus, vast surpluses flooded the European market.

1830s and another thirty in the *Vormärz* period. From 1851 to 1870 the five-year average market price never fell below the highly favorable 200 level.[8] If the average prices of the 1820s were taken as 100, by mid-century the index numbers for wheat, rye, barley, and oats were respectively 174, 189, 129, and 196.[9] Meat prices also showed a steady rise from the post-Napoleonic decade until the founding of the empire.

The introduction of two new sources of revenue requiring extensive acreage permitted the larger estates to derive particular benefit from the flourishing agricultural situation. To offset their losses from grain cultivation, many Junkers had adopted sheep raising in the 1820s because of an increased demand for wool. During the following decades the receipts from wool exports became a necessity for many estates, and the main income for a small number.[10] After the introduction of protective tariffs for sugar in the 1830s, Prussian farmers expanded their production of sugar beet tenfold in the succeeding years. As taxes on refined sugar climbed and consumption fell off, the growers turned to the lucrative export market, which the government encouraged by an 1861 law rebating all sugar beet taxes when the refined product was exported.[11] In view of the grain prices and sugar kickbacks it is not to be wondered that this era was described by an economic historian as "the happiest that German agriculture ever experienced at any time."[12]

An entire generation of farmers grew up having only experienced prosperity, and by their speculations in land demonstrated a belief in the continuance of high prices. It was to be expected that land

---

8. O. Schmitz, *Die Bewegung der Warenpreise* (Berlin, 1903).

9. Ibid., table at end.

10. Goltz, *Agrarwesen . . .* , p. 350.

11. Friedrich Aereboe, *Agrarpolitik* (Berlin, 1928), pp. 328–30. The ratio of beet to sugar was estimated at 11½ *Zentner* for every *Zentner* of sugar sent abroad. As sugar production underwent considerable mechanization in the years after the 1861 law, the actual ratio declined to 8:1; however, the government continued to refund 11½ *Zentners'* tax for each *Zentner* of sugar. During the thirty years of the law's validity, sugar beet growers were induced by the large export premiums to sell at a lower price in Great Britain than domestically. German preserve manufacturers were hard pressed in these years by British competitors who purchased German sugar at lower prices than they themselves could.

12. Goltz, *Geschichte der deutschen Landwirtschaft*, 2:350–52.

prices would rise as agriculture flourished, but the extent of the increase indicated that land was becoming an object of speculation. According to a study by Rodbertus, the changes in land ownership per one hundred Knight's estates between 1835 and 1864 in Silesia, Posen, and Pomerania were 229, 222, and 204 respectively.[13] The 4771 estates investigated underwent 23,654 changes in proprietorship, 61 percent of which were due to sales on the open market. Based on an index of 100 for the years 1770–89, the price of feudal estates in Mecklenburg rose to 331 during the twenty-year period preceding the revolution of 1848, and then jumped to 605 in the next ten years. Nor was the situation different with allodial estates, where the average purchase price rose by 400 percent in the 1830–70 period. Potential earnings of the land were lost sight of, as was the possibility of a price decline, in the rush to acquire land on credit in order to sell in the future profitably. Like all speculative booms, the vast majority of purchases were on credit with a 25 percent down payment sufficient for the transfer of ownership. While independent farmers and estate owners reaped the fruits of universally high prices, the contracts of the rural working class underwent considerable change, but whether the improvement in their standard of living corresponded to the general prosperity is dubious.

The introduction of money wages in rural areas often denoted an attempt by the lord to lower the real income of his workers, who otherwise would have gained handsomely from the increased yeld per acre. As grain cultivation became more profitable, the custom of granting each laborer an acre or two for vegetables fell into disuse, because the proprietor could now most beneficially bring them under cultivation.[14] Traveling through Prussia in 1840 Ernst Moritz Arndt moaned:

13. Johann K. Rodbertus, *Zur Erklärung und Abhülfe der heutigen Kreditnot des Grundbesitzes* (Jena, 1876), table at end.

14. Aereboe, *Agrarpolitik*, pp. 156–60. By 1850 the payment in kind for harvest work had declined from $\frac{1}{10}$ to $\frac{1}{15}$, and, where machinery had been introduced, reached $\frac{1}{20}$ of the grain threshed by the laborer. On the estates where the percentage was done away with in favor of steady money wages, the worker was prevented from sharing the gains from new techniques and higher prices.

The man who knows what the majesty of a
state is, travels with an uncomfortable feeling
through the sleepy, noble estates, which are
erected out of destroyed peasant villages, and
on which hordes of wandering day laborers
and wage servants live squeezed together in
wretched hovels. Oh beautiful land that is my
home, who will re-create the destroyed
peasantry, where shall the restorer come
from?[15]

The last quarter of the nineteenth century demonstrated that competition for labor from urban factories rather than rural prosperity
was necessary to raise the standard of living on Junker estates.

After forty years of steadily rising grain prices the trend changed
in the decade in which political unity was achieved. As Germany
for the first time in its history began to import grain (see below),
the prices began to descend by degrees until, just before Bismarck's
dismissal, they had reached the level of the 1830s. Whereas in industry a definite week could be designated as the beginning of the
crash, in agriculture, no one year could be singled out, so gradual
was the reversal of the trend. The decline was severer by the bread
grains, rye and wheat, than by barley and oats.

TABLE 1   GRAIN PRICES (Per 1,000 kilograms)

	WHEAT	RYE	BARLEY	OATS
1879/82	210	166	137	138
1882/85	178	144	133	131
1885/88	162	131	120	120

SOURCE: Kaiserliche statistische Amt, *Deutsche Landwirtschaft* (Berlin, 1902).

Since Germany could no longer supply its own grain needs after
unification, the root of the problem was diagnosed to be in the supply rather than the demand. The benefits of railroads, which had
enlarged the markets of domestic grain producers from the 1830s
onward, were now enabling other continents to export their sur-

15. Quoted in Friedrich Naumann, *Demokratie und Kaisertum* (Berlin,
1900), p. 91.

27

pluses to Europe at minimal prices. Between 1868 and 1880 the cost of sending a ton of wheat from Chicago to New York had fallen by 35 percent; by the century's end it was only one fifth of what it had been in 1868.[16] Similarly, steamships lowered their rates to attract a greater volume of business, so that the cost of shipping grain from Chicago via New York to Liverpool decreased by 75 percent within twenty years. As virgin lands came under the plow through the Homestead Act, America began exporting huge quantities of wheat to Europe, depressing the prices from their former favorable levels. Simultaneously with the American expansion, Argentina, Australia, and India began to compete for the British market, which had formerly been the preserve of eastern Germany.

The years of speculation had forced land prices so high that German producers did not have the requisite capital to compete with the low production costs of the New World. It was not uncommon for eastern estates to be indebted for more than half of their estimated value. Those Junkers depending on further price rises to liquidate their debts were caught shorthanded. Capital investment in machinery and new techniques came to a halt as all spare money was needed for discharging mortgages. After doubling in forty years, the yield per acre remained stable at 13.5 *Doppelzentner* per hectare for the entirety of Bismarck's reign as chancellor. Because the population was growing with unprecedented speed, Germany's dependence on foreign grain increased enormously in the years following the empire's founding.

Apart from low prices the most serious problem confronting grain growers was the labor shortage resulting from the unexpected exodus to America. Emigration began to reach grave proportions toward the end of the 1870s, when the number leaving German ports exceeded 50,000 per year. The succeeding years were even more ominous as the average reached 170,000 in the early 1880s and leveled out to 100,000 by 1892.[17] In terms of the population, the

16. Lujo Brentano, *Die deutschen Getreidezölle* (Stuttgart, 1910), p. 43.
17. *Statistisches Jahrbuch für das deutsche Reich* (1893, 1914).

number per 100,000 inhabitants departing approached 390 in 1881, but dropped to a still substantial 202 by 1886. There was never any doubt that the bulk of the emigrants were day laborers on the large eastern estates. Emigration from Pomerania was three times as great as from the thickly populated Rhineland, and scarcely a district with a predominance of estates gained in population between 1870 and the war.

In 1892 the Verein für Sozialpolitik published a comprehensive study of the emigration, in which the causes were attributed to the social and economic discontent prevalent on Junker estates.[18] Lacking the opportunity to gain land, the laborers sought to reach America, where their relatives wrote of the extensive availability of homesteads. The editor, a noted expert on population, concluded that there were no signs of a letup in the exodus, which he prophesied would probably continue unabated for another decade. Actually the social dissatisfaction of the laborers was of long standing and could not have triggered the emigration if other factors had not combined to offset the tribulations of crossing the ocean. Undoubtedly the Homestead Act of 1862 provided more security for migrating farmers, but the primary spurs to leave Germany are to be found in the removal of previous administrative hindrances. Only in 1861 did Prussia grant complete freedom of movement within and without its borders to all inhabitants. Before unification, the crossing of state borders often required time-consuming applications to the pertinent state authorities.[19] Lastly, the cost of transatlantic crossings decreased noticeably as steamships took the place of sailing ships. The claims of Junkers that the agricultural depression caused the migration does not correspond to the effects of the crisis on the working population. Facing labor shortages, the employers were continually raising wages in attempts to compete with the lure of America.

Bad as the laborers' conditions were in Prussia toward the cen-

18. Eugen von Philipovich, ed., *Auswanderung und Auswanderungspolitik in Deutschland* (Leipzig, 1892), pp. xxiii–xxv.
19. J. H. Clapham, *Economic Development of France and Germany* (Cambridge, 1921), pp. 204–5.

TABLE 2   DAY WAGES (in marks)

	SILESIA	EAST PRUSSIA	SAXONY	POM-ER-ANIA	BADEN	MECKLEN-BURG
1873	.90	1.14	1.46	1.62	1.84	1.60
1892	1.60	1.50	1.83	1.83	2.14	1.88

SOURCE: Karl Steinbrück, ed., *Die deutsche Landwirtschaft* in the series Handbücher der Wirtschaftskunde Deutschlands (Berlin, 1902), p. 41.

tury's end, the Junkers were correct in pointing out that they had never been so favorable. The roots of the German exodus, unlike an earlier one from Ireland, were not to be found in mounting poverty but in a combination of lingering social dissatisfaction and improved possibilities of forsaking the homeland.

For a variety of reasons the small and medium holdings withstood the decline much better than the estates. The peasants had not speculated during the good years; thus their financial obligations never approached those of the larger farms. Above all, the economy of small farms was diversified, enabling the farmer to shift to those crops whose prices had remained stable or had risen. The favorable trend in meat, butter, and egg prices, concurrent with the declining profitability of grain cultivation, contradicted the frequently expressed claim of the estate owners that the depression embraced all agriculture. Table 3 shows the price direc-

TABLE 3   MEAT AND DAIRY PRICES (pennies per Kg.)

	BEEF	CALF	LAMB	PORK	BUTTER	EGGS
1851–66	70	—	—	92	147	—
1861–70	87	—	—	104	178	—
1875	113	94	106	131	245	354
1880	114	98	109	122	220	322
1885	119	102	111	120	212	327

SOURCE: *Statistisches Jahrbuch für Preussen* (Berlin, 1914), p. 263.

tion of a number of items crucial to the prosperity of small farms. The slump in butter and egg prices in the 1880s was only temporary as they reached new highs in the next decade.

A survey of the agricultural scene before 1890 would not be complete without a look at the size of farms and the acreage in various categories. Table 4 shows the amount of farmers in each category

TABLE 4   SIZE OF FARMS

ACREAGE	NUMBER OF FARMS	% OF LAND IN GROUP
0–5	3,276,000	5.6
5–12	1,016,000	10.1
12–50	998,000	29.9
50–250	281,000	30.3
250 and over	25,061	24.1
Total	5,558,000	100

SOURCE: *Statistisches Jahrbuch für das deutsche Reich,* 1909.

of land holding from those owning from two to more than one hundred hectares in the census year 1895. Listed next to the number of farmers is the percentage of arable land tilled in each size category. The 25,061 estate owners amounted to one-half of 1 percent of the empire's cultivators, but owned almost one quarter of the arable land. In the industrialization controversy of the 1890s it was this small numerical group that proved most vocal while the vast majority remained relatively inarticulate.

When Caprivi accepted the unenviable task of succeeding Bismarck, agriculture was suffering from two distinct maladies. Indebtedness ensuing from unwise investments plagued both peasant and Junker. The situation of the latter, however, was more acute because large estates had often become essentially speculative ventures. The declining profitability of grain farming aggravated the debt problem for estate owners because grain was their principle source of revenue. Many south German wheat and barley growers were also hard hit by the slump, but moderate debts and a willingness to adapt prevented the situation from reaching desperate proportions. Beginning in the 1870s, the estates were faced with serious labor shortages resulting from the emigration of day laborers weary of the lack of opportunity in the east. Thus, the depression primarily threatened the existence of the fraction of farmers possessing one hundred hectares or more, whose property, however, comprised a significant percentage of the land under cultivation. The long years of high prices had conditioned the Junkers to view prosperity as a natural state of affairs. When prices fell, their reaction, similar to that of American and French farmers, was an attempt to buoy up their sagging economic position by the utilization of political power. Accurately diagnosing their plight in the eighties and nineties to be caused by foreign competition, the gentry tried to re-create their previous prosperity by simply isolating Germany from the world grain trade, thereby banishing the interloper that had disturbed their serenity.

BISMARCK'S SHIFT TO PROTECTION

Throughout the eighteenth century the spirit of mercantilism in its cameralistic form pervaded the economic policy of all the major German states. Despite his foresight in other spheres, Friedrich II followed his ruling compatriots in hoarding gold, erecting barriers, and attempting to isolate his state economically. As the century drew to a close, the teachings of Adam Smith began to be disseminated in Prussia, especially from Königsberg University, where Christian Jakob Krauss' lectures influenced the economic outlook of a generation of Prussian bureaucrats. Krauss' work bore fruit in 1818, when all hindrances to free internal trade were removed. The Zollverein denoted the victory of the free traders led by Maassen over the defenders of Friedrich II's policy, who looked askance at the egotism inherent in the liberal economic philosophy.

From its founding until the French trade treaty of 1863, the Zollverein maintained a moderate tariff wall that was regularly adjusted to the needs of the current economic situation. Since the grain duty was too low in the prosperous postwar years to affect the domestic price seriously, it was more than doubled when prices collapsed in the 1820s. As agriculture began to flourish, the duties were gradually reduced until they were negligible by 1856, and completely abolished by 1865. Protection of manufactured goods had been set at approximately 10 percent ad valorem in 1818, but were boosted considerably in the crisis-ridden 1840s when Georg Friedrich List's ideas came into vogue. List's *System of National Economy* was not an assault on the principles of free trade, as German economists later maintained, but merely an attempt to modify certain liberal tenets. Struck by the difficulties a new business faced in competing with an established firm, List advocated temporary tariffs until the firms could compete fairly. Nowhere did he abandon free trade as the desirable goal, nor did agricultural tariffs ever win his favor. List's recommendations were designed, in fact, to remove hindrances that a doctrinaire free trade policy put in the path of rapid industrialization. Far from seeking to preserve agriculture, he found "Raw agriculture is dominated by mental sluggishness, physical awkwardness; a clinging to old concepts, customs, practices, and procedures; a lack of culture, well-being, and freedom." In comparison, industrial work engendered "greater diversity and a higher quality of mental characteristics and skills."[20]

One of Bismarck's first independent moves upon taking office was to conclude a trade treaty with France, which was accepted by the Zollverein members in 1865 after behind-the-scenes pressure was exerted by the Prussian minister president. All the increases of the 1840s were removed, in addition to drastic reductions in 161 tariffs, many of which were reduced below the moderate level of 1818. The trend toward free trade was confirmed in the Austrian agreement of 1868, whereby the duties on iron, cotton cloth, linen, chemicals, and wine were reduced. Bismarck's faith in the future of liberal economics was never greater than in 1871, when he incorporated a "most favored nation" clause in the Peace of Paris. Although their political principles were antagonistic, Junker and merchant shared the chancellor's conviction that the empire should follow the path of free trade.

So widespread was the belief in the beneficence of free trade that the unexpected outbreak of a European depression in 1873 did not at first engender disillusionment with the empire's economic policy. Radical free traders and large farmers succeeded, while the depression raged, in abolishing the duties on raw iron and in providing for the termination of all tariffs on iron products by 1877. Only the hesitation of industrialists, who viewed the declining prices with alarm, prevented Germany from achieving complete

20. List, *Das nationale System der politischen Ökonomie* (1841), p. 111.

free trade in 1873. When industrial prices continued to remain at low levels, the heavy industries led by iron and steel formed an association to convince the public of Germany's desperate need for tariffs. Founded in 1876, the Centralverband deutscher Industrieller sought to counter the prevalent free trade theories by sponsoring lectures and distributing literature that advocated protection as the only method of shaking the paralysis engulfing the German economy.[21] Declining prices did not initially dampen the enthusiasm for free trade in agricultural circles. The majority of estate owners as late as 1876 were convinced free traders, who viewed high iron prices as the gravest problem facing agriculture.[22] When in 1876 an organization of landowners was formed to consider the crisis in agriculture, the gold currency rather than the absence of tariffs was diagnosed to be the root of the trouble. Grain tariffs began to gain support among the Junkers only when Bismarck's pronounced opposition to bimetallism became evident.

For Bismarck, the renunciation of gold a few years after its adoption presented obvious political perils. Such a move would incur determined resistance from industry, commerce, and possibly even the emerging Social Democratic party. The resulting isolation of the Junkers and the monarchy from the new social forces arising from industrialization would recreate the dangerous situation of Vormärz, when the monarchy found itself facing the combined hostility of artisans, workers, and the urban middle class. Bismarck had recognized in 1848 that the state had to win allies among the bourgeoisie to forestall a new revolutionary coalescence of forces. A confrontation between agriculture and industry, as had occurred in Britain during the anti–corn law campaign, could lead to serious instability at best and the triumph of the latter at worst.

Tariffs offered the ideal solution to Bismarck's dilemma of buoying up agriculture without alienating industry. When industrialists in the Reichstag gained enough Conservative support to submit a

21. On the Centralverband see Hartmut Kaelble, *Industrielle Interessenpolitik in der wilhelminischen Gesellschaft, Centralverband deutscher Industrieller 1895–1914* (Berlin, 1967).

22. Ivo Lambie, *Free Trade and Protection in Germany* (Wiesbaden, 1963), pp. 54–69.

petition signed by a majority of delegates requesting the restoration of high tariffs, the chancellor responded quickly. Bismarck, who was certainly no doctrinaire in economic matters, abandoned free trade because he perceived both political and financial advantages to be derived from protection. Politically, the union of the industrial barons and conservative Junkers formed a sound basis for opposing the Progressive and Social Democratic enemies of the empire. Furthermore, the Center Party could be expected to support a government that rejected the egocentric individualism inherent in the liberal Weltanschauung. In view of the growing strength of the snowballing socialist movement, a secure majority from the *staatserhaltenden* parties was a pressing need. A nationalistic economic policy seemed a small price to pay for such a coalition. However attractive free trade was in theory, it could no longer unite merchant and Junker as it had in the fifties and sixties, nor fill the imperial coffers as well as could a comprehensive system of tariffs.[23]

Bismarck's shift to protection, while of great consequence, is not the watershed in modern German history pictured by some historians. The maintenance of free trade in spite of the superior competitive ability of American farmers would have constituted a sharp break with tradition. The Prussian state had pursued a laissez-faire commercial policy because it coincided with the interests of the Junker squirearchy.[24] With the onslaught of an agricultural depression in the seventies, state aid became more expedient for the attainment of rural prosperity. The "marriage of iron and rye" that emerged in 1879 was the result of Bismarck's casting aside the liberal commercial bourgeoisie for an alliance with protectionist-minded heavy industry; changed circumstances called for new methods to preserve traditional goals. It is a tribute to Bismarck's

23. On the shift to protection, see, in addition to Lambie, Hans Rosenberg, *Grosse Depression und Bismarckzeit* (Berlin, 1967), chap. 5; M. Nitzsche, *Die handelspolitische Reaktion in Deutschland* (Stuttgart and Berlin, 1905); and Helmut Böhme, *Deutschlands Weg zur Grossmacht* (Cologne and Berlin, 1966).

24. See Böhme, p. 309. This is not to deny that free traders tended to be more liberal politically than protectionists. However, it is unlikely that they would have been able to change the constitution in a democratic direction.

genius that the direction of tariff policy could be altered without isolating the Junkers both from the merchants and from their traditional adversaries, the industrialists. In politics, the alliance of 1879 heralded no drastic departure from the recent past. Bismarck's intention was to insure the continued economic and political ascendancy of the Junkers in a Germany in which commercial and industrial capitalism could flourish as long as the bourgeoisie accepted their junior partner status. But this aim was already apparent in the constitution of the North German Confederation and Bismarck's retention of the three-class suffrage in Prussia. To be sure, conservative Junkers were skeptical (and in the end justifiably so) about the durability of Bismarck's vision; however, no other viable alternative existed for them. After 1879, as before, the Junkers and a segment of the bourgeoisie formed the main bulwarks of the German empire. For Bismarck to have resisted the mounting pressure for state intervention would have required a denial of his own vision of Germany's future.

On 12 December 1878 the Bundesrat selected a committee to revise the existing tariff treaties. Five months later, the government placed before the Reichstag its plan to restore iron duties and to introduce a one mark levy on wheat and oats. Bismarck struggled in committee to impose the one mark on all grains, but finally accepted half a mark for grains other than those mentioned above. He vehemently denied that his departure from free trade would cause substantial harm to the impoverished urban population. In a letter to Prussian ambassadors at German courts he predicted that all consumers would suffer equally from higher prices, while only pensioners might not benefit from the anticipated industrial boom.[25] As loyal citizens of the empire, Bismarck emphasized, farmers had refrained from complaining, but the time had arrived for the export profits of foreign cultivators to be nullified by tariffs. Writing to the Barmen city council, he stressed the similar needs of agriculture and industry. By mutual support they could survive the de-

25. H. von Poschinger, *Aktenstücke zur Wirtschaftspolitik des Fürsten Bismarck* I (Berlin, 1890), pp. 260.

pression, but neither sector by itself had the strength to get the necessary state support.[26]

When finally adopted on 12 July 1879 by a vote of 186 to 160, the plan had undergone only moderate alterations, the most significant being the doubling of the rye duty. The portentous warning of Eduard Lasker, "Do you not see that you are opening a struggle between agriculture on the one hand and industry and the cities on the other?" passed unnoticed in a Reichstag that believed that the common welfare advanced simultaneously with the prices of industrial and agricultural goods.[27] Although Lasker's prediction seemed the converse of the truth to contemporaries, eleven years later his prescience became evident. For the alliance of 1879 did not uninterruptedly determine the course of the empire until its demise, as is often presumed, but scarcely survived Bismarck's dismissal from office. Bismarck's victory lay not so much in initiating extremely moderate tariffs as in establishing state support for powerful interest groups as a norm and free trade as an aberration. This also engendered a shift in public opinion. After 1879 liberal economists were regarded as the outcasts whose vague theoretical solutions were no longer in tune with the problem of a developing nation.

Throughout the remaining years of Bismarck's chancellorship, Germany continued to enjoy the low tariffs of its liberal western neighbors. Although free trade had lost its unassailable reputation in western Europe, protectionist thought had not gained a sufficient hold to motivate retaliatory tariffs. In eastern Europe, however, where mercantilism had never lost its grip, the German move initiated a spiraling of duties that continued into the next decade. In 1883 and again in 1887 Austria-Hungary raised its tariffs on German imports to such heights that German industry was hard pressed to maintain its dominant trade position. Between 1879 and

26. Poschinger, *Fürst Bismarck als Volkswirt* (Berlin, 1890). Bismarck himself had invested most of the money he received from the Reichstag after unification in land. Thus, he personally felt the decline in land prices in the mid-seventies. Cf. Hans Rosenberg, p. 176.

27. Quoted in Lambie, p. 215.

1890 the tsar elevated Russia's already high import duties four times, so as almost to exclude Germany from the vast Russian market. Italy joined the eastern powers in retaliation after its trade treaty expired in 1887.

Meanwhile, Bismarck used the protectionist cartel to raise the wheat and rye duties to three marks and the other grains to one and one-half in 1885. Undeterred by the repeated warnings of the Chamber of Commerce (*Handelstag*), he proposed an unprecedented duty of six marks in 1887, but accepted Windthorst's plan allowing five marks for wheat and rye, four marks for oats, and two and one-quarter for barley. It became increasingly evident during the eighties that commercial agriculture required much greater protection than industry to meet foreign competition. The Junkers could not form cartels, share markets, or cut costs in the manner that became common in heavy industry. With many thousands of suppliers, farmers were at a natural disadvantage when bargaining with the limited number of merchants dealing in grain. To maintain duties on manufactured products, the Centralverband deutscher Industrieller acceded to the rises, although Bismarck made no further concessions to industry. Recognizing the threat to international trade posed by the chancellor's policy, the Handelstag voted unanimously in 1885 and 1887 that the grain duties constituted "a serious danger to the prosperity of the nation."[28]

Upon introducing his protectionist program, Bismarck had boasted of the economic prosperity that tariffs would produce. A perusal of statistics of the 1880s will shed light on the reliability of the chancellor's foresight, as well as outlining the situation faced by Bismarck's successor when he succeeded to the chancellorship. Tables 5 and 6 illustrate the progress of Germany's international trade during the decade of Bismarck's duties. Even when the 10 percent deflation in prices is taken into account, it is evident that the tariffs did not aid Germany in overcoming the commercial stagnation accompanying the depression of 1873. Imports increased moderately because of the growth in population and larger purchasing power of the working class, but the rise in exports was

28. *Der deutsche Handelstag* 2 (Berlin, 1913): 438.

TABLE 5   IMPORTS AND EXPORTS (In 100,000s of marks)

	1881		1885		1890	
	IM-PORTS	EX-PORTS	IM-PORTS	EX-PORTS	IM-PORTS	EX-PORTS
Chemicals	144	241	129	226	141	272
Glass	36	98	33	89	42	105
Textiles	867	1,300	821	1,177	853	1,355
Machines	75	139	92	169	143	213
Manufactures	1,973	3,029	1,827	2,966	2,159	3,439

SOURCE: *Statistisches Jahrbuch für das deutsche Reich,* 1890.

TABLE 6   IMPORTS AND EXPORTS (in 100,000s of marks)

NATION	1883		1890	
	IMPORTS	EXPORTS	IMPORTS	EXPORTS
Russia	411	190	541	206
Austria	488	355	598	351
Switzerland	183	182	174	179
France	248	315	267	231
Great Britain	479	552	640	705
Italy	62	87	140	94
U.S.A.	136	179	405	416
Total	3,290	3,335	4,272	3,409

SOURCE: *Statistisches Jahrbuch für das deutsche Reich,* 1890.

infinitesimal. Foreign trade per head of the population declined from 1879 until 1886, when it began to rise, so that the graph of the trend is a parabola with both ends of the decade on approximately the same level. Another indication of stagnation was the absolute decline in the number of ships entering and leaving German ports from European harbors.

Unlike exports, industrial productivity steadily increased throughout the decade, although value did not keep pace as the price index just as steadily declined. Prices of the major industrial goods averaged between 10 and 15 percent lower than they had in 1880. "Profitless prosperity" was an apt term to describe the plight of many manufacturers.[29] The Junkers experienced even greater

29. For the effects of the tariffs on heavy industry cf. R. Sonnemann, *Die Auswirkungen des Schutzzolles auf die Monopolisierung der deutschen Eisen- und Stahlindustrie, 1879–1892* (Berlin, 1960).

hardships. Tariffs cannot alter basic economic trends; at best they can cushion the harmful effects for protected groups. Despite the quintupling of grain duties, the prices of rye and wheat fell by approximately 20 percent in the 1880s. Barley and oat prices declined somewhat less precipitously, but the trend was nevertheless the same.

It would be entirely unfair to blame Bismarck's tariffs for causing the depression they were intended to cure. However, they can be justifiably criticized for introducing a mercantilist spirit into economic policy without showing the much-vaunted practical results that protectionists continually ascribed to their proposals. Later assertions that the tariffs prevented an already bad situation from degenerating ignore the fact that German industrial productivity during the period did not rise as rapidly as the average of developed nations.[30]

Thus, Caprivi inherited a series of protective tariffs, whose overall economic consequences had been negligible apart from injuring trade with eastern Europe. Three courses of action lay open to him after he assumed the chancellorship. From the point of view of domestic politics, the maintenance of the autonomous tariff system was the safest, and, according to informed contemporaries, the path that Bismarck would have trodden. Continuity would at once retain Bismarck's vision of Germany's future and confirm the alliance between the Junkers and industrial barons. Such a policy promised to arouse the opposition of only the impotent Social Democrats and Progressives. However, the implications for the economy and for Germany's foreign policy were more ominous. Unenviable as Bismarck's economic legacy was, Caprivi had to consider the possibility of further deterioration when a complex of trade treaties expired in February 1892. Fifteen major agreements, many of them based on "most favored nation" clauses, were up for renewal, and the exacerbation of many governments with Germany's presumed benefits from an autonomous tariff policy indicated that retaliatory duties were in the offing. Looming on the horizon,

30. R. Wagenfuhr, "Das Geheimnis der Gegenseitigkeit im Wirtschaftsleben," *Vierteljahrsheft zur Konjunkturforschung* 2, pt. A (1936): 16–18.

should western Europe follow Russia in erecting barriers against German exports, was a series of tariff wars with several of Germany's main trading partners. The inertia distinguishing the economy could easily degenerate into full-scale depression if Austria-Hungary, Switzerland, Italy, Belgium, Spain, Romania, and Russia all started to spiral their tariffs simultaneously. Such a war had already occurred on a limited scale between France and Italy, causing not inconsiderable damage to both economies. Caprivi had also to consider the political ill will that would be aroused by a tariff war just when Russia's diplomatic friendship had been spurned in favor of a rapprochement with England.[31] Lastly, the alliance of the Conservatives, Free Conservatives, and National Liberals that had prevailed in the Reichstag since 1879 lost its majority on the eve of Bismarck's dismissal, greatly enhancing the difficulty of a chancellor seeking parliamentary approval for the continuation of the *Sammlung* policy in tariff questions.[32]

A policy fraught with even greater perils was the sacrifice of industry to provide further support for agriculture. Such a move, while the Junkers suffered from a prolonged slump, was certainly in accord with Prussian traditions and by no means out of the question. Von Kardorff of the Free Conservatives had already begun clamoring for higher grain tariffs and the introduction of bimetallism, and in view of the price decline of the late eighties, these measures were rapidly winning new adherents. The adoption of an agrarian program had two major drawbacks. First, tariff wars were a certainty and likely to be even more prolonged than if Bismarck's duties were continued. (A precipitous fall in the exports of manufacturers appeared unavoidable.) Second, higher grain duties would create the very split that Bismarck had sought to prevent. Industrialists, already chafing under the barren results of the autonomous system, were likely to abandon the *Sammlung* in order

31. In 1890 the Reinsurance Treaty with Russia was not renewed by Germany.

32. The *Sammlung* parties lost 87 seats in the 1890 election. According to J. C. G. Röhl, Bismarck himself wanted to destroy the *Sammlung* majority because the crisis created thereby would make him indispensable to the emperor. See Röhl, *Germany without Bismarck* (Berkeley, 1967) chaps. 1 and 2.

to join the Progressives in opposition to the government. (This alignment occurred briefly in 1909, when the Hansabund was founded.) All the forces for industrial change would stand arrayed against a state which seemed to represent the narrow interests of agriculture. Not only would Reichstag majorities be difficult to come by, but the unemployment and slump in trade arising from the tariff wars might generate a dangerous, possibly even revolutionary, disaffection from the government.

The third alternative offered the best hope for renewed prosperity and was unlikely to face tough sledding in the Reichstag. This entailed the initiation of discussions with Germany's trading partners for the purpose of arriving at agreements establishing tariff rates for an extended period of time. The success of such a maneuver would at once preclude the mutually harmful escalation of tariffs and stimulate exports by providing German manufacturers with guarantees against sudden changes in foreign import duties. Socialists, Progressives, and National Liberals could all be expected to join in applauding this policy, which would foster greater industrial productivity. The problem in this course lay in the concessions that other nations would require of Germany before the conclusion of treaties. Clearly, Russia, Austria-Hungary, and Romania would demand reductions in grain duties as a quid pro quo for modifying and fixing their prohibitive industrial duties. Opening Germany's frontiers to increased competition in grain at a time when the large commercial estates stood in critical straits would boldly challenge the Junkers' traditional primacy. It would entail a radical break, far greater than that of 1879, with Prussia's and Germany's past. For to spur an industrial capitalist economy at the expense of agriculture meant, in effect, that the state no longer viewed the squirearchy as indispensable to its welfare. No matter how many palliatives the government conceded to the Junkers' wrath, a new vision of Germany's future based on the supremacy of the commercial and industrial sectors would have replaced Bismarck's. As Lasker had predicted, a battle between agriculture and industry was to commence, but—as no one had foreseen—with the state, at least temporarily, on the side of the latter.

The task of Bismarck's successor was not an enviable one. Two of his options augured the possibility of economic disaster while the third promised to rock the traditional foundations of the Prussian and German state. Ultimately, the choice hinged on whether the new chancellor looked to the past or the future for his vision of the German empire in the twentieth century.

2

The Novelty of the "New Course"

DEPARTURE FROM BISMARCK'S ORTHODOXY

According to an old tale that has found its way into the textbooks, Caprivi and a companion were strolling past the imperial chancellory one afternoon, when the former mused aloud, after considering the building intently, Who would be fool enough to succeed the Iron Chancellor? Fools with this ambition were not lacking, but Caprivi cannot be counted among them. Having passed his entire adult life in the military, the general was aware of his inadequate qualifications for as demanding a position as the chancellorship; nor did he have the desire at fifty-eight to assume a post at once unfamiliar and uncongenial to him. When the emperor designated him to succeed Bismarck, Caprivi accepted the call dutifully as the command of his military superior, but he could not still his inner forebodings about the criticisms he would be subjected to. The weakness of the constitution was never more apparent than in 1890, when a novice in politics was asked to deal with problems that Bismarck himself had considered insoluble except by

a coup d'état. Several years later, Caprivi described his initial difficulties in the following manner. "In 1890, I entered a totally strange
territory, which required a considerable amount of work to orient
myself and develop a point of view."[1]

Caprivi's task was not simplified by the election results of 1890,
which precluded his manipulating the parties in imitation of Bismarck. The loss of eighty-five mandates by the government coalition, and the left's gain of seventy-six, signified that Bismarck's
conservative-oriented policy had failed to retain popular support.
In order to get legislation through such a Reichstag, the demands
of the left would have to receive more attention than previously.

Not many months after Caprivi assumed office, he was faced
with his first serious domestic problem in the form of an extraordinary rise in grain prices. An unusually small harvest in Europe,
combined with gloomy forecasts about the American crop, caused
grain prices to surge to heights unknown for thirty years. Berliners
rioted in front of bakeries as bread prices reflected the scarcity of
grain. Whereas the five mark duty had prevented German prices
from falling too steeply since 1887, it worked during an inflationary
period to maintain the German price well above the already high
world price. As American suppliers held back their exports in hope
of even higher prices, unrest broke into violence in the German
capital. Grain prices were the highest in Europe although Germany
was a leading grain producer.[2]

The obvious measure to alleviate distress was a temporary sus-

TABLE 7   GRAIN PRICES (1891) (in marks per kilogram)

	RYE	WHEAT
Budapest	150	175
Amsterdam	170	169
New York	—	166
Berlin	211	224

SOURCE: W. H. Dawson, *Protection in Germany* (London, 1904), p. 10.

1. Max Schneidewin, "Briefe des Reichskanzler Caprivi," *Deutsche Revue*
1 (1922): 255.
2. Helen Farnsworth, "The Decline and Recovery of Wheat Prices in the
Nineties," *Wheat Studies* 10 (1934).

pension of grain tariffs, but Caprivi repeatedly rejected such a move to the dismay of Radicals and some Conservatives. The public, he believed, would never allow the reintroduction of the tariffs. A five-month suspension was proposed by Bötticher, vice-president of the Ministry, at a Crown Council in May 1891 in order to discourage support for the Auer-Richter plan to abolish grain, wood, and sugar duties altogether.[3] The Conservative expert on agriculture, Graf Kanitz, expressed his willingness to support a temporary measure if the rates were fully restored within a short time. In his reply to Bötticher, the minister president explained his rejection in terms of his decision to seek trade treaties rather than continue the autonomous tariff system. If Germany should lower its duties unilaterally, he reasoned, what concession could be offered to grain-exporting nations in trade discussions?[4] Having chosen to treat the chronic export deficit by long-term trade agreements, Caprivi could not prejudice his bargaining position by yielding to the public clamor for lower bread prices. He felt sure, in any case, that grain supplies were adequate until the next harvest. Thus, the dropping of the five mark excise would not cause a corresponding decline in domestic grain prices.

For a variety of reasons the chancellor had rejected alternative methods of preventing a European tariff war in 1892. The adoption of an approach hostile to reductions, as Bismarck was thought to have favored, would have led to tariff wars just at the time German exporters were suffering from the new American McKinley tariff. A hard line presupposed that Germany could maintain its political allies while warring against them in the economic sphere, a policy which Caprivi found senseless and felt incapable of pursuing.[5] The mild industrial depression of the early 1890s and the exorbitant grain prices also militated against a policy favoring agriculture at the expense of industry. Another suggestion was advanced by Graf Berchem of the Foreign Ministry, who hoped to strengthen the empire's foreign policy by a carefully executed series of economic

3. DZA, "Minutes of Ministry Meeting," 28 May 1891, Rep 90a B III 2b Nr. 6 CV 290. DZA, Rep. 90a, "Ministry Meeting," 9 December 1890.
4. Ibid.
5. Ibid.

agreements. In a sixty-page memorandum to the chancellor, Berchem admitted that an autonomous tariff no longer concurred with the national interests, and proposed a manner of common market among four European powers.[6] This proposal resulted from a series of conversations Berchem held with the Munich free trade economist, Lujo Brentano. Germany was to aim for an agreement with Austria-Hungary, France, and Italy respectively, calling for a gradual reduction of their mutual excise levies in contrast to a high tariff wall to be erected against the nonparticipants. Such an internal market, Berchem stressed, would provide an enormous outlet for industrial goods without injuring agriculture, since, of the four, only Austria-Hungary could compete in the German grain market. France's adhesion could be expected to hamper Russian attempts to escape the isolation that the nonrenewal of the Reinsurance Treaty had brought about. Should the plan prove incapable of realization, Berchem recommended that Italy and the Habsburg monarchy be given precedence over France and Russia in tariff negotiations.[7] Caprivi's marginal notations indicated that he believed the time unpropitious for a European customs union, and that he opposed exceptional tariffs against Russia and America. The proposal to double grain rates if no agreements were reached by the chancellor—a suggestion submitted by Berchem in the event his other plan did not materialize—was flatly rejected by Caprivi on the ground that protection was already too prevalent.[8]

The road finally taken was the one expounded in a memorandum of the chief of the imperial chancellory and former school comrade of the chancellor, Karl Goering. He urged the negotiation of trade treaties on the basis of mutual concessions—Germany would demand low industrial tariffs in return for reducing those on agriculture.[9] Only large farms on which grain was the primary crop would suffer, Goering emphasized, rightly drawing a distinction between the interests of the western smallholders and the East Elbian es-

6. DZA, "Denkschrift des Grafen Berchem," 25 May 1890, Reichskanzlei (Akta betr. Handelsverträge), 414, 3, 4.
7. Ibid.
8. Ibid.
9. DZA, "Denkschrift von Goering," 12 May 1891.

tates. Peasants seeking tariff protection did not realize that their interests as consumers conflicted with their desires as producers. Goering admitted that the estates had not prospered recently, but he attributed this to mismanagement and luxurious living. Enhancing state support would perpetuate this undesirable situation as well as contribute to the growing Junker belief that aid was a prerogative rather than a temporary expedient. The benefits to industry and all consumers, he predicted, would far outweigh the damage inflicted on grain cultivators. Economic reasoning prescribed agreements based on moderate grain rates, but Goering wisely cautioned the chancellor of possible political repercussions if the wishes of the Junkers were opposed.[10]

Caprivi was aware that Italy's desire for a trade pact was motivated as much by the need to strengthen the Triple Alliance as by economic necessity. After meeting Italian Prime Minister Crispi in November 1890, Caprivi noted, "He looks upon it as a vital question of the Triple Alliance that we succeed in founding a commercial league between Italy, Austria, and ourselves.[11] Graf Kálnoky of Austria-Hungary had also expressed interest in settling the chronic tariff disputes that periodically raised tempers in Berlin and Vienna.

Dictates of foreign policy confirmed the need for a halt in protection, which Caprivi had already submitted for discussion at a Crown Council meeting in September 1890. At this session, the ministers voted unanimously for the initiation of parleys to prevent the expiring agreements from paralyzing the German export industries. The minister of agriculture, Lucius von Ballhausen, later declared that only political necessity could justify a cut in grain tariffs, and that even then such a step was to be taken with extreme regret.[12] Caprivi, however, was convinced that the empire's economic well-being could best be served by a nexus of pacts securing important European markets for German exporters. The election results of 1890 were interpreted by him to mean that free trade was on the rebound. He considered it both wise and expedient to mod-

10. Ibid.
11. *Die Grosse Politik* 7, no. 1394, p. 53.
12. DZA, Rep. 90a, Crown Council.

ify agricultural protection in accord with the public wishes; however, free trade was to be resisted even if a Reichstag majority could be procured for its execution.

Because of his inexperience, Caprivi recognized neither the novelty of his aims nor the difficulties to be faced in realizing them. Since the reform legislation of the Stein era had failed to weaken the commanding role of the Junkers in society, no minister had dared to deny them primary consideration in economic matters. Export premiums for sugar and brandy attested to the privileged position the Junkers had acquired during the course of the century. Germany had pursued a free trade policy as long as agriculture found it profitable. When falling grain prices caused protectionist sentiment to wax, the empire had abandoned free trade. Not industrialists' demands for tariffs but the conversion of the Junkers to the view that they were needed sealed the fate of free trade in Germany. Basing his coalition on the Junker-dominated conservative party after 1878, Bismarck had never failed to meet the economic needs of this class, of which he himself was a member. In his trade policy Caprivi thus undertook rather ingenuously to combat the protectionist developments that had taken on the aura of sacredness to agrarians in the years after unity was achieved. Moreover, the landowners who were expected to assume the role of sacrificial lambs were, as described in the previous chapter, firmly ensconced in critical centers of power. As the leading social class in the empire, the noble landowners could use their access to the emperor, as they had done in the reform period, subtly to undermine the ruler's confidence in his chancellor. Seldom in history has a ruling class been persuaded that its interests are in conflict with those of the totality; yet this was the task that Caprivi unconsciously set for himself. Naïvely, he believed that the horizons of the aristocracy were wider than their own purses and that their support could be won by stressing the benefits to the commonweal expected from long-term pacts. It was evident from his sanguine aspirations that Caprivi had not been a student of German politics before accepting its most demanding post.

Furthermore, in seeking to foster industrialization and encourage German involvement in the world economy, Caprivi was pitting himself against a strong anti-industrial current among academic intellectuals. This attitude could be traced back to Adam Müller and had taken on new intensity after the *Krach* of 1873 destroyed so many illusions about unity. It should not be forgotten that Bismarck's social legislation was in part a response to the concern of conservative thinkers about unregulated industrialism. Popular professors like Adolf Wagner and Heinrich von Treitschke were warning large audiences in the 1880s of the greedy commercial spirit accompanying industrialization. As far back as 1871, Wagner had warned an overflow church audience, "The situation in the free competition system whereby work is treated as a commodity, and wages the price for it, is not merely unchristian but inhuman in the worst sense of the word."[13] Thus Caprivi could not count upon much backing from the influential German professoriat. Indeed, as the controversy evolved, he was to face severe criticism from academics.

THE AUSTRO-HUNGARIAN TREATY

Because he had successfully resisted the Richter motion to abolish all grain levies, Caprivi was able to introduce the terms of the Austro-Hungarian, Italian, and Belgian agreements in the Reichstag on 10 December 1891. The moment was particularly propitious for the plan's success for grain prices still stood at immoderately high levels, and the recent parleys of the Triple Alliance powers had underscored the need for closer collaboration in the economic sphere. By far the most important treaty, whether measured by volume of trade or concessions granted, was concluded with the Dual monarchy. If accepted, the treaty would bring to an end eleven years of spiraling tariffs that had wrought not inconsiderable damage to the economy of both alliance partners. As an importer of grain and an exporter of industrial goods, Germany consented to lower its agricultural barriers to gain stable markets for its manufactured surplus. Wheat and rye rates were reduced from 50 to 35 marks per *Doppelzentner*, leaving them still slightly higher than those in effect before the 1887 increase, and consider-

13. Adolf Wagner, *Rede über die sociale Frage* (Berlin, 1872), p. 9.

ably above the level that Bismarck had believed (in 1879) any reasonable man could demand. Austrian barley, a necessity for several varieties of beer, was to be admitted at 20 marks instead of the 22.5 mark duty. Some minor reductions made in meat products and luxury goods were of little value to Austria-Hungary as long as Germany prohibited livestock imports for health reasons and continued to satisfy its need for the designated luxury wares. The Austrian negotiators had obviously striven for and achieved a special position for Hungarian grain surpluses as against those of Russia in the German market.

Of the 340 million marks annually imported by the Dual monarchy from its German neighbor, the rates on 198 million were fixed for twelve years, and those on one-third of the latter amount were reduced.[14] Returning to the levels of 1887 and, in a few cases, of 1879, Austrian concessions like those of Germany denoted a retreat from immoderate protection rather than a rehabilitation of the recently abandoned free trade. In addition to the lowering of textile duties by 20 percent, the 1887 increases on iron, machines, glassware, and toys were erased. Germany could also expect to benefit from the clause providing that each nation, in inland transportation, should accord similar treatment to the other nation as it would to its own nationals. The prohibitive transportation costs hindering exports into the Balkans would be considerably diminished with this measure. The criticism frequently directed at the negotiators by contemporaries and later writers for not having extracted greater advantages fails to take into account that by Austrian standards the German concessions were meager, amounting not even to a full abolition of the 1887 boost.[15]

Changes were imperceptible in the Belgian Treaty, wherein Germany continued to enjoy Belgium's modified free trade policy as it had done in the past. To bolster Italy's economy at the expense of France, German negotiators granted favored treatment to Italian wines, with the hope that they would drive French wines from the

14. Werner Sombart, "Die neuen Handelsverträge," *Schmollers Jahrbuch* 16 (1892): 92.

15. Tirrell claimed that the German negotiators did not receive as much as they could have.

market. Since wine consumption was minute in comparison with beer, Germany's concession was not expected to disturb the beverage industry. Italy correspondingly bound only 60 million marks of the 90 million it imported yearly from Germany, 23 million of which were at lower levels than in 1887. Reductions were not prominent in heavy industrial wares such as steel, chemicals, and mechanical instruments. The difficulties each side encountered in extracting concessions indicated that the mystique of protection had not lost its vitality. Rather, it had come to be recognized as a two-edged sword that closed foreign markets simultaneously with the exclusion of imports. The sluggish state of the economy that was in part responsible for the renaissance in protection had, by its persistence, forced Caprivi to experiment with long-term moderate tariff agreements to revitalize German industry.

In stepping before the Reichstag on 10 December 1891 to defend his program, the chancellor carefully chose to emphasize the chronic ills that the treaties were designed to cure. Germany was in the unpleasant situation, he stated, of having to export men every year because industrial expansion lagged far behind the growth in population.[16] Unable to procure employment in cities, the surplus land population emigrated to America, where opportunity existed in the cities and on the land. The root of the evil Caprivi diagnosed to be Germany's attempt to lock itself out of the world market in imitation of Russia and America. The inner market vaunted by protectionists and anti-capitalist thinkers as more desirable than mercurial foreign outlets had miserably failed to stimulate the nation's dormant economy. "The more," he pointed out, "industry limited itself to the inner market, the more the shady sides of the system were evident; namely, the market was overfilled, and overproduction had set in."[17] Another "shady side" was the ever increasing trade deficit, which had already passed the 800 million mark level annually. Rather than rely on insufficient domestic consumption, German industry needed to expand its old markets and seek new areas for the sale of goods. By negotiating long-term pacts, the government, said Caprivi, sought to remedy

16. Caprivi, *Die Reden des Grafen von Caprivi*, ed. Rudolf Arndt, p. 176.
17. Ibid., p. 166.

the abiding instability in German trade relations that prevented the growth of exports and thereby restricted employment opportunities. As long as industrialists could not be assured that their markets would not disappear overnight because of newly erected tariff walls, they could not gear their production to satisfy the long-run needs of foreign consumers.[18] Germany had, for instance, been hard pressed to maintain the Russian market during the 1880s, when British manufacturers used every discriminatory tariff spiral to displace the empire as Russia's supplier. The government's program, Caprivi predicted, would provide the prerequisites for economic growth by terminating the commercial insecurity.

Shifting to the anticipated effects on agriculture, the chancellor vigorously denied that the farmers were being treated as stepchildren. Grain farmers were not being sacrificed, he maintained, but were merely being asked to forego certain of their recently gained privileges that had burdened the entire consuming population. In a rhetorical question bound to stir up the anger of Junkers, Caprivi asked whether tariffs were not, after all, a sacrifice imposed on all buyers to bolster a particular sphere of production. In any case, the decline in protection would not engender severe hardships as the landowners forecast, since preceding duties had not had the desired effect on price formation. The government, he reminded agrarians, also had a duty, with regard to the two-thirds of the population earning less than 900 marks a year, to supply grain as cheaply as possible without endangering the existence of farmers. Conceding that religiosity, family bonds, and patriotism seemed to be more firmly entrenched in rural areas, Caprivi expressed his disbelief that these qualities, which he valued highly, would degenerate as a result of a moderate reduction in grain rates.

Unlike interest groups, the government, emphasized the chancellor, had to consider the foreign political implications of its economic policy. As German agriculture had demonstrated its inability to meet the nation's grain needs, it was imperative to establish good relations with grain-exporting nations so that Germany need not fear starvation in a future war.[19] The chancellor also expressed his

18. Ibid., p. 393.
19. Ibid., p. 178.

disapproval of waging economic war against a political ally. Intentionally to weaken a nation whose help would be required in critical situations, he considered an anomalous strategy. Marschall von Bieberstein, secretary for foreign affairs, who defended the government's economic policies in the Reichstag because of his previous experience in this sphere, confirmed the chancellor's utterances.

In view of the departure of the treaties from Bismarck's orthodoxy, it may appear surprising that support was forthcoming both from the Socialists and from many Conservatives. The favorable reception that the treaties received from nearly all the parties was a result of the different aspects emphasized by each party rather than a consensus about anticipated economic prosperity. According to the Socialist Paul Singer, the government's plan would break the Junkers' domination of tariff policy that had forced the working class to pay exorbitant bread prices.[20] The Junkers were accused of not producing at full capacity in order to spur imports, which they could then levy with excise duties to insure high grain prices. Although the Socialists believed that only free trade benefited the worker, they wisely supported the treaties as a step in the right direction instead of adhering to sterile dogmas.

Different as the political outlooks of the Socialist and Radical parties were, the prospect of weakening the agrarian hold over tariff policy united them in backing Caprivi's trade policy. Rickert of the Radicals joined the Socialists in vilifying the Junkers, who, he claimed, were wealthy enough to dispense with the contributions they received from the working class.[21] Repeating the classical arguments in favor of free trade, the party leaders acclaimed the proposed end of the tariff spiral begun by Bismarck. Peace and prosperity, Deputy Broemel assured the Reichstag, had always been the product of free trade, just as unequal distribution of wealth accompanied protection. In a parting blow at the less doctrinaire liberals, the Radicals averred that duties on necessities were irreconcilable with any truly liberal party program.

20. *Verhandlungen des Reichstages* . . . *Stenographische Berichte* (Berlin, 1871–1938), 1890–92, vol. 5, 3349. Hereafter cited as *Sten. Ber.*
21. Ibid., 3200.

The National Liberals harbored no intention, however, of opposing the reduction in excise rates, even if their eleven-year coalition with agrarian protectionists should thereby be threatened. Trade wars were not kindly thought of by industrialists suffering from stagnating exports and a mild depression. Ochselhauser expressed the views of the party's rapidly expanding industrial wing when he forecast an expansion of German economic influence throughout Europe if the chancellor's plans were realized.[22] The bait of twelve years of tariff stability was too enticing for the party's businessmen to reject because of grain reductions. Not desiring to create the impression that agriculture was being left in the lurch, National Liberal spokesmen urged the government to compensate farmers in other areas for their presumed revenue losses. Unable to contain their glee at the prospect of secure markets, party members urged approval before Christmas recess so that industry could begin to reap the anticipated advantages.

The Center party determined to follow the National Liberals in abandoning the sterile Bismarckian economic policy. After Bismarck's dismissal, their venerable leader Ludwig Windthorst told party members that enduring coalitions were a thing of the past; the party in the future must weigh each issue before voting to ascertain whether it coincided with the interests of the Catholic population.[23] As Bismarck's approach to the social problem had proved barren, he predicted that the alienation of the workers from the state would occupy the politics of the 1890s. When Windthorst died in 1891, Lieber was elected as his successor. The new leader had formulated his economic views during the free trade era, and only grudgingly had followed the party in its protectionist course. Even more important reasons for the Center's support of the new chancellor than Windthorst's injunctions or Lieber's personal opinions were Caprivi's Polish policy and his plans for educational reform. By abandoning Bismarck's attempt to Germanize the Catholic Poles, Caprivi won the respect and gratitude of the Center. His preparation of a plan requiring religious instruction in Prussian

22. Ibid., 3326.
23. Karl Bachem, *Vorgeschichte, Geschichte, und Politik der deutschen Zentrumspartei 1815–1914* (Cologne, 1927–32), 5:122.

schools was fully endorsed by all Christian parties, and particularly by the Center, which considered atheistic socialism a threat to the Catholic working population in the Ruhr. A small minority led by Dr. Orterer refused to follow the party lead and declared that any policy favoring industry over agriculture would spur rural depopulation as well as weaken the patriotism of the peasants.[24] Most party members, however, considered the high grain prices and declining interest rates sufficient evidence that agriculture must for the moment take a back seat to consumer needs. Moreover, rejection would alienate the chancellor, who had shown greater consideration for Catholic wishes than had Bismarck. It was also imperative for the party to prevent the growing Catholic proletariat from being won over to socialism.

Two divergent schools of thought developed within the conservative parties. The faction in favor led by Manteuffel did not put much stock in tariffs as a means to aid agriculture, and therefore refused to believe that the government had abandoned the farmers by moderately reducing rates. Accustomed to support the government as a symbol of authority, the Manteuffel group chose to emphasize the patriotic sacrifice they were making to strengthen the foreign policy of Germany. This view was represented by the notoriously reactionary president of Pomerania, Robert von Puttkamer, in his reply to the emperor's query about the anticipated reaction of the province's farmers to the treaty. The treaty was a sacrifice, said the president, but in view of the international situation and the political importance of good relations with Austria, the province's landowners were behind the government. They trusted, he continued, that the emperor would come immediately to their aid if the situation became intolerable.[25] Among proposals submitted by these "patriotic" conservatives to alleviate agriculture's chronic problems, bimetallism and the abolition of free internal movement were urged upon the chancellor with the greatest frequency. By achieving the former it was hoped that the debts of the estates would be quickly liquidated, and the latter's execution

24. *Sten. Ber.*, (1890–92) 5, 3376.
25. DZA, "Puttkamer an Wilhelm II," 12 December 1891, Rep 89H Abt. XXIV. vol. 1 Nr. 6 Akta betr. Massregeln zur Hebung der Landwirtschaft.

would solve the labor shortage plaguing nearly all large estates. Manteuffel's desire to prohibit youths under twenty-one from deserting the east for greater opportunity in industrial cities attested to the continuing vitality of the feudal spirit east of the Elbe.

Conservative opponents of the Austro-Hungarian treaty differed sharply from Manteuffel about the government's intentions. They accused Caprivi of seeking to replace the agricultural base of German society by an industrial one. Graf von Kanitz, the spokesman for the opposition, divided his vituperation between the government, which had foolishly veered from Bismarck's course, and the industrialists, who, he insisted, had split asunder the 1879 coalition of manufacturers and agrarians. Considering industrial support for the treaty outright treachery, he warned the National Liberals that Conservatives would be able to find few grounds for maintaining industrial duties. They had, in his view, commenced a struggle between city and land which could only be looked upon with satisfaction by the disruptive elements in society.[26] Industry was responsible only for following the new policy; the government had introduced it. Kanitz saved his greatest verbal assaults for the chancellor, who had ignored the sound economics of his predecessor to return to the errors of free trade. Under the Iron Chancellor, he reminisced, Germany had preserved its freedom to adjust tariffs to the changing economic realities, and the inner market had been wisely valued above the outer. With the new policy, the government would be unable to manipulate tariffs should the need arise; furthermore, the balance of payments could be expected to alter to Germany's disadvantage because of a flood of foreign grain imports. "Until then," Kanitz observed, "agriculture had been accustomed to see its best friend in the government." Now he feared that "in the future the case would be otherwise. . . . With the defeat of the agrarians, the tariff struggle will end, and the democratic camp will triumph."[27]

Even more pointed was Wilhelm von Kardorff of the Free Conservative party, who prophesied that the nation must yield its position as a great power if the English pattern of lopsided indus-

26. *Sten. Ber.* (1890–92), vol. 5, 3311.
27. Ibid.

trialism was imitated. Reducing agricultural protection would transform the grain-growing estates into hunting retreats for wealthy businessmen.[28] Only if the reductions were combined with the introduction of bimetallism, said Kardorff, would agriculture be capable of progressing side by side with industry. Both Kardorff and Kanitz were quick to perceive the dangers Caprivi's policy posed to the landed Junkers, especially if carried to its logical conclusion. Any step hinting that agriculture was not the primary economic concern threatened the entire social order, in their view, for the Junkers had come to depend on the government's assistance during hard times. Should the government fail to preserve the economic well-being of the Junkers, it would signify that industrialists were replacing them as the most influential political group. Kardorff, in particular, who was familiar with the writings of the conservative economist Adolf Wagner, having frequently cited his writings on bimetallism to the Reichstag, believed that such a development would destroy a system of values that had evolved over centuries. All proposals for industrial growth that did not foresee a similar development for agriculture were therefore suspect to these agrarians. The threat of the "New Course" to established power relations seemed so great to Kardorff that, a mere three days after the Austrian treaty was introduced, he expressed disappointment when the banker Bleichröder assured him that the emperor would not dismiss Caprivi. The Emperor's faith in the chancellor would not, he wrote to his wife, prevent him from aggressively criticizing Caprivi in the Reichstag.[29] Actually, the speeches attacking the chancellor were rather temperate, for the Conservatives were divided and the large agrarian wing was not yet certain whether the treaties were unique or the basis of a complete departure from the autonomous tariff policy.

Caprivi could view the parliamentary division over his treaties with some equanimity, and the mail received from interested parties was also encouraging. The *League for the Advancement of Trade Treaties* (Handelsvertragsverein) submitted for the chancellor's perusal a summary of the conclusions adopted by ninety-

28. Ibid., 3334.
29. Siegfried von Kardorff, *Wilhelm von Kardorff*, p. 247.

eight chambers of commerce in regard to the treaties. Without exception, the opinions were favorable; even those chambers accustomed to advocate protection expressed enthusiasm for the stability that treaties would inaugurate.[30] Wiesbaden and Cologne sent letters in addition congratulating the chancellor for the resolution with which he had pursued the course necessary to restore trade prosperity.[31] The German Agricultural Council (*Deutsche Landwirtschaftsrat*), an organization that contrary to its name represented mainly the large estate owners, displayed its displeasure with the "New Course" in the minutes of its annual meeting, which were forwarded to the Ministry of Trade. The Council's conclusions predicted a weakening of the forces loyal to the government, and the accompanying growth of socialism, if the treaties were approved.[32] Any action taken by the government to meet the legitimate grievances of the workers was suspect to the agrarians, who perceived merely the support of revolutionary elements. In its often expressed desire that agriculture and industry progress side by side, the Council, in effect, was trying to preserve the status quo, for all the factors combining to favor industrial development were entirely lacking in agriculture. The demand for parity increasingly became a mask to conceal the Junkers' desire to hamper industrialization.

Caprivi's most powerful opponent in 1891 lay not in the agricultural organizations or in the Reichstag but in the person of his predecessor. If Bismarck should decide to lead a movement against the treaties, the magic of his name was liable to draw enough support to forestall parliamentary approval. Foregoing several opportunities to return to public life, the former chancellor limited himself to criticizing government policy in the *Hamburger Nachrichten* and private interviews. Two days after the Reichstag received the Austrian Treaty, he attacked the new policy wherever it departed from his precedents. In conversation, Bismarck is reported to have designated any tariff reduction a national calamity.

30. DZA, Akta betr, Österreichische Verträge, Rep 120 C XIII 14 vols. vol. 3, p. 320.

31. Ibid.

32. Ibid., p. 302.

Twelve years was too long, he stressed, forgetting that he had concluded a treaty of similar length with France in 1863, and his fore-
runners had done likewise in an 1853 pact with Austria.[33] Inter-
viewed in early 1892 by the editor of the *Neue freie Presse,* Moritz
Benedikt, he condemned the idea of trading agricultural for industrial concessions as a policy of second-rate men that never would
have occurred under his chancellorship.[34] The unifier of Germany
realized that his constitution was not likely to withstand the social
and economic changes that Caprivi was fostering. When the treaty
was accepted on 18 December, after only eight days of discussion,
by a vote of 243 to 48, Bismarck did not cease to vilify the Reichstag for ignoring the issues involved. Still, he refused to play an
active role in organizing the treaties' opponents. His talent for per-
ceiving the realities of a situation moved him to warn Conservatives of the consequences if industry should succeed in replacing
agriculture as the favorite of the government. Conservative leaders
took heed of Bismarck's criticism less than a year after the treaty
had been approved.

THE REACTION—THE FARMERS' LEAGUE

The surge in grain prices did more than anything else to ease the
government's task of finding a majority for the Austrian treaty.
When bounteous harvests in every grain-exporting land caused a
sudden price decline in 1892, the reaction of agrarian representatives and their constituents was not slow in coming. On 21 December 1892 a Silesian tenant farmer named Ruprecht aus Ransern
published an article in a local stock-breeding journal denouncing
the government's farm policy. The article, entitled "Proposals for
Bettering Our Situation," suggested that farmers renounce their
traditional deference to the government in favor of a hostile attitude similar to that of the socialists.[35] Furthermore, the author
called upon farmers to organize, in order to convince Caprivi of
agriculture's determination to protect its interests, if assistance

33. Willy Andreas, *Bismarcks Gesammelte Werke* (Berlin, 1926), 9:147.
34. DZA, Rep. 120, "Gespräch mit Moritz Benedikt," 24 June 1892.
35. *Schulthess' europäischer Geschichtskalender,* vol. 24 (1893). Ransern's article was entitled, "Ein Vorschlag zur Besserung unserer Lage."

were not speedily forthcoming. "We must stop being and choosing liberals, ultramontaines, or conservatives," wrote the enraged farmer, and "we must join together in a great agrarian party and thereby seek to win by more influence in parliament and the legislature."[36]

Coming at a time when low prices were distressing grain farmers, and a severe epidemic of foot-and-mouth disease had erupted, the appeal found a large audience. Soon thereafter it became the basis of a rural counterattack against the chancellor's program. Less than two months later, on 18 February 1893, several agricultural organizations, the most prominent being the German Peasants League (*Deutsche Bauernbund*), banded together at a meeting in the Tivoli Hall in Berlin, to form the Farmers' League (*Bund der Landwirte*). With an initial membership of 180,000, which rose by the century's end to over 200,000, the league was never solely a spokesman for the East Elbian Junkers; nevertheless, as more than half of its members and 141 of 250 local committees originated from the eastern grain-growing areas, it scarcely constituted a representative cross-section of German farmers. The first chairman was a nobleman named von Plötz, who had formerly headed the German Peasants' League. The funds that allowed it to publish numerous pamphlets, a daily newspaper, and a weekly journal, and to employ 112 employees at the Berlin headquarters, indicate that the wealthier estate owners were interested in using the league to propagate their points of view. Precisely this point was emphasized in the rejoinder of the Bavarian Peasants' League to a Farmers' League invitation for amalgamation. "For the representation of peasant matters, we want no nobles, no intellectuals, no doctors, and no professors, but only peasants."[37] As we shall see, the League went out of its way to publicize the desires of smallholders in order to avoid the charge of Junker domination, but it did prove embarrassing when the members representing estates were continually more successful than the peasants in achieving their aims. A historian has characterized the role of the Junkers

36. Ibid.
37. Heinz Haushofer, *Die deutsche Landwirtschaft im technischen Zeitalter* (Stuttgart, 1963), p. 214.

in the Farmers' League in the following manner: "Prussian conservatism, which under Friedrich Wilhelm IV still had a political world view, and under Bismarck still embodied a spiritual tradition, became a mere interest group under Caprivi, which was manifested expressly in the Farmers' League."[38]

The program adopted at the Tivoli meeting showed that the League's origin was a response to Caprivi's new commercial policy rather than a response to the chronic problems of German agriculture. The first of eleven points insisted upon the tariff rates necessary for the maintenance of agriculture as a profitable enterprise. Seeking to reinforce this, the second point opposed the conclusion of any treaties, particularly with Russia, that necessitated lower grain duties. Another point, aimed at Austria and America, suggested that Germany continue to bar the import of diseased animals. Farmers were inclined to blame the recent outbreak of foot-and-mouth disease on Caprivi's Austrian treaty, although the disease had been on the rampage several months before the agreement went into effect. Among the remaining demands, the introduction of bimetallism, agricultural chambers, and state supervision of the stock exchange were all to play a significant role in agrarian politics during the succeeding years. The League showed a marked tendency to blame the Jews for the potpourri of rural ills, and one of its leading Polish members warned that the upsetting of the social structure that Caprivi's policy was leading to could only benefit "the Jewish gentlemen" (*die Herren Israeliten*).[39] The hostility to Jews seemed to be designed to rally the sentiment of patriots and the *Mittelstand* to the side of agriculture in its dispute with the government. Invariably, League deputies in the Reichstag supported, and were supported by, Liebermann von Sonnenberg and his anti-Semitic compatriots.

Concurrent with the rise of the German agrarian movement,

38. Rudolf Stadelman, "Der neue Kurs in Deutschland," *Geschichte in Wissenschaft und Unterricht* 4 (September 1953). The best work on the Farmers' League is Hans-Jürgen Puhle, *Agrarische Interessenpolitik und preussischer Konservatismus* (Hanover, 1966). Puhle argues convincingly that the league transformed the Conservatives into a modern demagogic party appealing to *Mittelstand* prejudices.
39. W. von Skarzrnski.

American farmers began to organize to express their grievances so that some observers drew a parallel. Because of the social disparity among German farmers, it would be incorrect to consider the Farmers' League as the German counterpart of the American populist movement. True, the decline in world prices was instrumental in coalescing rural discontent on both continents, but whereas the farmers in America could claim lack of political influence, this was hardly the case in Germany. In the previous chapter, the inordinate power of estate owners was outlined. The Farmers' League united within itself two groups whose aims were quite different despite some overlapping. All the members were interested in restoring the profitability of grain growing, irrespective of the size of their farms. For the small- and medium-sized farm owners, this aim took precedence and was the motivation behind their membership. With the Junkers, however, who filled the league's hierarchy, the goal was rather to restore agriculture to the privileged position that they believed had been lost with the introduction of the Austrian treaty. In 1894 Adolf Wagner told Chairman Plötz, "I am quite close to the gentlemen [leaders of the league] in their views, particularly in the tariff question, the currency question, and in a whole series of points in the Farmers' League program."[40] Wagner was especially pleased with the league's campaign to regulate the stock exchange—a policy he had advocated for years.

Responding to the dissemination of anti-industrial ideas by conservative economists, the league also began to attack the spirit engendered by industrial society. Honor, obedience, and other values associated with the land were now held up as foreign to the industrial mentality. Von Oldenburg-Januschau, a reactionary figure even among Junkers, held an important post in the league, and summarized its success in the following manner. "The historical service of the league is to have compelled the government to recognize the importance of agriculture to the state."[41] In succeeding chapters it will be shown that the league refused to cooperate with industrialists, whom it considered of minor importance for the empire's future, and was rarely in agreement with the Conservative

40. *Landwirtschaftliche Jahrbücher* 23, supp. 2 (1894), p. 309.
41. E. von Oldenburg-Januschau, *Erinnerungen* (Leipzig, 1936), p. 39.

party, which it believed tepid in putting forward agrarian demands. All attempts of the newspaper *Kreuzzeitung* to win the league's endorsement of the Conservatives failed because of the former's uncompromising attitude. While American populists had sought to break the monopoly of power held by finance and industry, the league envisioned its task to be the preservation of agriculture's cardinal place in a rapidly industrializing society. If success were to be achieved, the rapid spread of industry had to be impeded unless industrialists voluntarily accepted the primacy of agriculture and the values it engendered. As late as 1905 the league maintained, "There is no *staatserhaltende* policy that is not at once an anticapitalist policy."[42]

Even before the Farmers' League had been organized the Conservatives recognized that their division over the Austrian treaty reflected a more fundamental dichotomy of views among their members. The aggressive nationalism of men like Kanitz and Oldenburg-Januschau was in conflict with the moderate views of Chairman Helldorf, who viewed anti-Semitism and the ascendancy of narrow economic interests as incompatible with the party's tradition. When matters came to a head over Caprivi's withdrawal of the religiously oriented school bill, Helldorf was ousted as party chairman. Manteuffel's accession to Helldorf's post in May 1892 denoted a victory for the more nationalistic and anti-industrial wing of the party, despite the new leader's moderate background. The Conservative program (Tivoli program) drawn up in December 1892 confirmed the change of the party's mood to a more militant and demagogic one. Points 8–11 concerning agriculture and industry indicated that the party would henceforth take a united stand against Caprivi's economic policy. The party demanded the abolition of the privileges of finance capital and a strengthening of inheritance laws and family ties, especially in rural areas. Hoping to resurrect the Bismarckian cartel, the party, in point 11, stressed the necessity of industrial protection.[43] Five months later the party's electoral declaration spelled out the new course clearly, for the conclusion of treaties entailing agricultural sacrifices were fore-

42. Quoted in Puhle, *Agrarische Interessenpolitik*, p. 95.
43. *Schulthess'* 23 (1892): 193.

sworn, and the Farmers' League was given unqualified approval.[44]
The Free Conservative party of Kardorff and Stumm tried to cover
up the division Caprivi's policy had wrought within its ranks by
announcing its support for all economic sectors loyal to the monarchy and church.

In February of 1893 the most serious attack to date was launched
against Caprivi and his entire economic policy. Kardorff accused
the chancellor of being an adherent of the Manchester school,
whose doctrinnaire free trade ideas were far more radical than
those of Adam Smith.[45] To support industry while agriculture languished, he termed folly. The introduction of bimetallism would
solve agriculture's problems, he predicted, and such an idea was
not farfetched, for Adolf Wagner, a leading economist, supported
this reversal in monetary policy. Von Mirbach of the Conservatives
deplored the "dissonance" in economic matters between his party
and the government, but felt confident that it could be rectified if
all future chancellors were drilled in agrarian politics by his cohorts
in the party. Again he suggested that a bill be introduced to limit
the free movement of farm laborers under twenty-one years of age
in order to stop the exodus from the countryside.[46] Also desirable
would be a law forbidding laborers to emigrate to the city unless
they could give evidence of having a sanitary dwelling for which
they could afford the rent. Times had changed, lamented Manteuffel; one could not abolish freedom of movement, but severe restrictions were still possible. The shrewdest of the agrarians, Kanitz,
recognized that a principle was at stake, and therefore called for a
general change of policy rather than compensation for agriculture.

Facing mounting criticism for his tariff policy from the Conservatives and the newly founded Farmers' League, Caprivi felt compelled to answer his critics on the floor of the Reichstag. His speech
was unique in several respects. Deputies accustomed to the ha-
rangues of Bismarck were surprised to hear a chancellor speak
with modesty and forego a haughty admonition to the dissident
factions. Taking conservatism to mean more than petty economic

44. *Schulthess'* 24 (1893): 56.
45. *Sten. Ber.* (1892–93), col. 1088.
46. Ibid., pp. 1013–19.

interest, the chancellor spelled out the realities to the Junkers as Bismarck had never done and no succeeding chancellor would have the courage to do again. He indicated that conservatism must be adaptive to remain viable, and that attempts to preserve fading institutions led to stagnancy and decadence. Although not a keen intellect, nor a man given to theoretical reflection, Caprivi was aware that new problems must be met with new solutions. He warned that a devotion to once hallowed ways naturally led to inflexibility and eventually to decline.

Agrarians, he emphasized, had refused to accept the development of a world market in grain and misguidedly sought to balance the falling transportation rates by rising tariffs. Adjustment was necessary, he warned, for the conditions of 1860 had departed forever. According to the chancellor, the flight from the land was a natural development that governmental measures could not prevent; to expect agricultural relations to remain unchanged was fanciful. In a not very tactful statement, he added, "I believe further: every protective tariff is a sacrifice that the nation must bear."[47] Caprivi made it quite clear that he was not a free trader, but this did not deter him from considering tariff duties an unfortunate burden which circumstances made necessary.

Several days later, the chancellor returned to his theme when deputies of the right challenged his claim to be a conservative. His conservatism, he forthrightly replied, was based on the desire to preserve the Christian monarchical form of government in Germany. Caprivi had to admit that he was not an agrarian, nor did he possess "a piece of land or blade of grass" (*Ar und Strohhalm*), but he rhetorically questioned whether this was requisite for conservative beliefs.[48] Was it not preferable for men in government to be free of pecuniary motivations in deciding questions of national policy? If all chancellors were to be landowners as some Conservatives suggested, Caprivi expressed the foreboding that agriculture would become too privileged, with disastrous consequences for the nation's future. In concluding, he said that he had tried to rule in the interests of the common welfare rather than in the interests

47. Ibid., p. 1085.
48. Ibid., pp. 1113–16.

of a particular group, and if his policy did not promote the nation's well-being, or the emperor lost faith in him, his resignation would be immediate. Duty, not the lures of power, caused him to remain in office.

THE ROMANIAN TREATY

It was to be expected that the next series of trade agreements set before the Reichstag would experience more difficulties than the Austrian treaty. The formation of an agrarian interest group, and the replacement of Helldorf by Manteuffel as Conservative chairman, had measurably strengthened the opponents of Caprivi's policy. By the summer of 1893 all the resources at the disposal of the agrarians were being mobilized to bring the ministry down. The uncertainty and divisions of 1891 were a thing of the past.

At a Prussian ministerial council in early November of 1893, Caprivi announced his intention of bringing a new set of treaties before the Reichstag during the following month. According to the chancellor, the treaties with Romania, Serbia, and Spain were a continuation of the policy previously inaugurated. They were expected to enlarge German export markets in return for concessions on agricultural products.[49] The latter two treaties were of minor importance, the one with Spain never having gone into effect because the Spanish Cortez refused ratification. Romania, however, exported a sizable quantity of wheat annually and was a significant buyer of industrial goods. Caprivi admitted that diplomatic considerations had played some role in his decision to seek a trade agreement with Romania. He anticipated no damage to German agriculture as long as the tariff war with Russia endured.

Actually, the treaty would only confirm the provisional concession that the empire had made to Romania in July of 1892, in an attempt to weaken a tariff wall erected in 1891. Utilizing the power to make temporary tariff reductions granted to him by the Reichstag on 30 January 1892, Caprivi had allowed Romania the 35 mark duty until a long-term agreement was reached. When negotiations were successfully concluded in October 1893, the Balkan kingdom

49. DZA, Rep. 90a, "Minutes of Ministerial Council," 8 November 1893.

agreed to numerous reductions in its 1891 tariff. In return for the maintenance of the lower grain rate until the end of 1903, the duties on heavy industrial goods were substantially lowered. Although the government recognized the growing hostility to its policy, it was not prepared for the torrent of criticism unleashed by Conservative and Center deputies. Elections in June 1893 had returned a more conservative Reichstag, increasing the chancellor's difficulty of securing approval for the trade treaties. Since the elections were fought over the military bill, the results cannot justifiably be interpreted as evidence of dissatisfaction with the Austrian treaty. Further proof that the results did not denote a rejection of the chancellor's policy were the success of the Social Democrats and the maintenance of the Radicals' popular vote despite their loss of twenty-nine seats. However, the refusal of the Farmers' League to endorse candidates who did not promise to support their legislative demands caused many Center deputies from rural areas to modify their former economic views. (140 delegates elected in 1893 formally adhered to the league platform.) The striking gains of the anti-Semitic parties could only be interpreted as a strong anticapitalist reaction to the industrial and agricultural crisis of the early nineties by small towns and rural constituencies.

TABLE 8 REICHSTAG ELECTION RETURNS

	1890	1893
Conservatives	73	72
Imperialists	20	28
Anti-Semites	5	16
National Liberals	42	53
Center	106	96
Poles	13	19
Radicals	66	37
Social Democrats	35	44
Others	32	23

Marschall defended the Romanian treaty by projecting a comparison of the economy depending upon whether it passed or was rejected. Passage would mean increased employment and a boost to the sagging industrial sector, which would simultaneously aid agriculture by stimulating the consumption of foodstuffs.[50] Disapproval would cause the dismissal of 70,000 workers dependent on Romanian exports, with a concomitant reduction in their consumption. Agriculture could expect no price relief from the maintenance of the 50 mark duty, for Romania supplied only 10 percent of Germany's imported grain, and the effects of a 15 mark reduction would be negligible. Unlike Caprivi's presentation in 1891, Marschall's aimed at converting the agrarians. While no more pliable, the government was taking notice of the preceding year's events.

Socialists and Radicals repeated their desire for free trade and their willingness to accept Caprivi's moderate move in this direction. Richter took the opportunity to denounce Bismarck for arousing greed in all economic spheres and parties and for his responsibility in halting the international trend toward free trade. Unable to resist a final sally at the Junkers, he insisted that if they really desired to assist agriculture, the division of their estates among the peasants and the abolition of entails would be more successful than the rejection of a trade treaty.

Neither the National Liberals nor the Center party insisted upon party discipline in their vote. Thirty-four of the forty-seven National Liberal ballots favored the Romanian treaty, mainly because of the anticipated benefits to industry. Schulze-Henne summarized the majority view when he expressed doubt that rejection could alleviate the agricultural crisis. According to Paasche, the Romanian market could not be replaced, and dubious agricultural benefits did not justify sacrificing workers and industrialists. The minority disapproving of the treaty were influenced by their constituents, who were from rural Protestant areas of Baden and Württemberg. In agreement with the opinions of Paasche, were the majority of Center deputies, who were also favorably disposed to the government's education and Polish policies. The forty-four deputies opposing the treaty were mostly from Bavaria, where the Farmers' League had stirred up the population against candidates who could be denounced as hostile to agriculture.[51]

Like the parties of the middle, the Free Conservative party di-

50. *Sten. Ber.* (1892–93), vol. 1, col. 1103.
51. Bachem, *Vorgeschichte*, 5:335.

vided its vote—twenty members for rejection and six for approval. Baron von Stumm, the leading industrialist of the Saar, set himself an imposing task when he sought to defend the treaty without alienating his agrarian colleagues. The baron implored the representatives of agricultural and industrial interests not to dispute over a minor trade treaty, for in the long run "the interests of industry and agriculture are identical; our common opponent is free trade."[52] Why should rural representatives get worked up over Romania, he asked, when America had received the lower duty as a most favored nation without a word of objection. With its immense exports America was certainly a greater danger than a tiny Balkan state. Industry, Stumm emphasized, was undergoing difficult times, but agrarians were too self-concerned to notice. Joining the host of supporters, he predicted that agriculture would suffer no harm from the treaty. Kardorff merely asked the deputies to observe that the chancellor's support and applause came from the Socialists, whose policy was apparently in accord with his goals. Kardorff was more candid about Caprivi's treaties in a letter to Stumm. "It appears to me that we are stirring up a revolution, which will be more terrible than the one in 1848, and in such times it would be cowardly to leave my post, when I am convinced that we are moving toward a terrible catastrophe with no possibility of being saved."[53]

Conservative leaders chose to attack both the treaty and the general direction of policy. There was no possibility of a major split developing in the revitalized party; only six of sixty-four members favored the treaty. Graf zu Limburg Stirum began the assault by auguring the possibility that Russian grain might be sent to Germany at the reduced rate through Romania.[54] The treaty would be a hostile act against Russia, for every other exporting country would enjoy the 35 mark rate, while the Tsar's empire suffered under a 75 mark duty. A Russian treaty with all its suspected dangers to domestic agriculture was a logical necessity, he warned. Graf von Mirbach compared the 70,000 workers who would be

52. *Sten. Ber.* (1893–94), vol. 1, 54–60.
53. Fritz Hellwig, *Carl Freiherr von Stumm-Halberg, 1836–1901* (Heidelberg and Saarbrücken, 1936), pp. 462–63.
54. Ibid., p. 388.

unemployed with the 12,000,000 farmers dependent on a declining agriculture for a livelihood. Shifting to a more general point, he implored the chancellor to recognize that the state itself stood in great danger when agriculture was in difficult straits. The departure from Bismarck's economic policy was the sole cause of friction between the Conservatives and the government, and until this change was rectified there could be no harmony. Bismarck's son Herbert charged the government with fostering the growth of socialism by allowing rural distress to continue.[55] Rural day laborers, unable to find work, migrated to industrial cities, where they joined the Socialists and thereby were transformed from patriots into opponents of the empire's existence. This observation was confirmed by Kanitz, who also warned of the declining physical fitness of city dwellers. Healthy country lads, who were the mainstay of the army, deteriorated into unsuitable recruits after a decade of urban living. Rather than exclude Russia from the treaty's system, Kanitz advised, it would be wiser to enter negotiations to terminate the other treaties immediately.[56]

The views of the Farmers' League can be gauged from Freiherr von Wangenheim's (the leader of the League's later Reichstag faction) article in the *Kreuzzeitung*. "German agriculture," he stated, "would not allow itself to be ruined by a foreign bureaucracy. . . . The person of the chancellor was dispensable, German agriculture was not."[57] Contrary to this position was that of the Chamber of Commerce (Handelstag), which criticized farmers for their unwillingness to endure slumps as industry and trade frequently were obliged to do. The Chamber castigated agriculture's attempt to disrupt the economy because of their feud with industrialists.[58] By 189 to 165, a margin much narrower than anyone had anticipated, the treaty was approved on 13 December 1893. The Polish vote proved to be decisive, and the chancellor could thank his benevolent Polish policy for his victory.

When the manner of debate and voting are considered, the Ro-

55. Ibid., pp. 490–99.
56. Ibid., p. 481.
57. Kurt Burger, *Die Agrardemagogie in Deutschland* (Berlin, 1911), p. 47.
58. *Der deutsche Handelstag*, 2:460.

manian treaty proved to be the forerunner of the Russian treaty rather than a successor to the Austrian one. No Conservative was any longer heard to question the patriotism of members voting against the government, nor did the party show interest in the strengthening of Germany's foreign relations which the treaty was thought to have achieved. The party ignored Caprivi's contention that the treaty would tie Romania even more tightly to the Triple Alliance. Particular criticisms had blossomed into theoretical attacks on the direction of policy. Inconceivable under Bismarck's rule were the Conservative accusations that the chancellor abetted the growth of socialism and endangered the very fabric of the state. The attacks of the Farmers' League against Caprivi that mushroomed during the Russian debates had already begun with an acid article stressing the undesirability of the chancellor. Although less than a year old, the league had thrown a scare into Center and National Liberal deputies from rural areas, causing them to oppose the majority of their respective parties. The division of the Reichstag on the treaty depended more on the rural or urban character of the delegates' constituencies than on party affiliation.

Above all, there was the realization that the first round of treaties had set the stage for several more rounds instead of being a final settlement of the question. Faced with a decline in grain prices and insufficient exports, the government chose to devote its resources to the latter problem and to apply minor measures to relieve the former crisis. As the agrarians increasingly became aware of industry's preferential treatment, they began to discern in the tariff controversy a conflict between a rising industrial leviathan that threatened the social and political structure and the tillers of the soil, who were steadfast, religious, and loyal. Bismarck's skill had enabled him to smooth over the disputes between the land-owning gentry and the new industrial entrepreneurs. The cartel was the fruition of a policy aimed at emphasizing the mutual interests of the two groups. In the 1890s, with Bismarck gone and with the coincidence of rural and urban depression, hostility developed between the two economic sectors over the priority of needs. By the time the Russian treaty came up for discussion, the gulf separating agrarians from supporters of industrialism had gradually become unbridgeable. The issues were losing their concrete character as the more abstract and irreconcilable problem of the desirability of an industrial capitalist spirit permeating society increasingly occupied the disputants. This change was encouraged by economists who were developing an interest in the controversy. Evidence for this lay in the *Preussische Jahrbücher,* which published an article by Wagner in 1893 calling for the preservation of the *Landvolk* at any cost.[59]

THE RUSSIAN TREATY

Judged by every criterion, a treaty with Russia would be the most significant of the group concluded by Caprivi. Since Russia was the largest exporter of grain to Germany, a reduction in rates would have severe repercussions on German agriculture if agrarian claims about the effects of tariffs were valid. One of Germany's main markets before the tariff spiral of the 1880s, Russia could again become a major receiver of German industrial exports. The lines could not be more clearly drawn; farmers saw in Russia a vast fertile land waiting to pour reserves of grain into Germany, while industrialists saw a nation with a large population needing capital goods to industrialize. Although the Reinsurance Treaty and its nonrenewal had not been publicly disclosed, the cooling of Russo-German relations in the early 1890s was apparent to all. This development precluded Caprivi from defending the treaty as a tightening of friendly bonds; at best he could argue that the treaty would prevent a further deterioration of relations. The fear of a Russian treaty had been manifest since the introduction of the Austrian agreement. At that time, Kanitz had warned of the impossibility of discriminating against Russian grain, and his premonition was echoed by Conservatives during the Romanian debates. Both Caprivi and the emperor realized that all the resources at their disposal had to be utilized if the plan were to receive the assent of the Reichstag.

Already in December 1890, Shuvalov, the Russian ambassador,

59. Adolf Wagner, "Über englische und deutsche Nationalökonomie," *Preussische Jahrbücher* 1893, p. 73.

approached Marschall about initiating trade discussions similar to the much rumored ones with Austria.[60] The foreign secretary, skeptical about Russia's intentions, replied to the inquiry evasively. Marschall was most probably taken by surprise, for the tsar had never concluded a trade agreement with a western nation despite numerous entreaties. In February 1891, Caprivi learned from his Russian ambassador, von Schweinitz, that it was rumored Russia would grant industrial tariff concessions in return for reductions by Germany on grain, wood, and oil. Von Schweinitz added that the Russians were in no hurry, and the wisest course would be to wait for their next move.[61] This strategy proved sound, for Caprivi was told in April that trade proposals would be forthcoming, and Marschall was asked to submit a list of German demands. The foreign secretary complied by listing the wares that German exporters were most interested in, warning the Russians that the reduction would have to be greater than the 20 percent surtax they had imposed on German goods in 1890.[62] He was urged to stand firm by von Schweinitz, who reported heavy discrimination against German exports in favor of those from Great Britain. When the disastrous harvests of 1891 caused the tsar to forbid all exports of grain, foreign office officials advised the chancellor that there was nothing to be gained by pursuing trade talks while the Russian economy remained in a state of famine. To soften German demands, Witte, the minister of economics, initiated a discriminatory tariff in the spring of 1893 against countries not granting Russia the "most favored nation" clause. He promised to exclude Germany and even to grant the same concessions France had recently received, if the provisional reductions given to Romania in the preceding year were extended to Russia.[63] Upon receiving a refusal, Witte initiated a tariff war that lasted until new discussions were begun in October 1893. The fruit of these negotiations was embodied in the ten-year trade pact that Caprivi brought before the Reichstag in February 1894.

60. *Die Grosse Politik* 7:1626.
61. Ibid. 50:627.
62. Ibid., p. 1630.
63. Ibid., p. 1634.

Recognizing the need for industry's undivided support, the chancellor had wisely invited leading industrialists to advise German negotiators of their tariff wishes. The resulting tariff schedule was thus more generally praised by manufacturers than the Austrian or Romanian agreements had been. From table 9 the Russian reductions on German wares can be gauged. Germany allowed the 35 mark rate on rye and wheat, and lower duties on wood. The Ger-

TABLE 9   RUSSIAN TARIFF RATES (in rubles)

	1891 TARIFF	1893 WAR TARIFF	PROPOSED RATES
Hops	1.00	1.5	0.50
Machine parts	8.00	15.60	6.00
Leather	8.50	15.30	6.80
Cement	0.10	0.18	0.08
Chemicals	2.40	4.32	1.50
Iron	0.35	0.35	0.30
Rolled Iron	0.60	1.08	0.50
Steel	0.60	1.08	0.50
Iron products	1.70	3.31	1.40
Steel wire	9.00	17.55	3.20
Locomotives	2.82	3.90	1.80
Electrical goods	8.00	15.60	6.00

SOURCE: *Die Allgemeine Zeitung,* 9 February 1894.

man Chamber of Commerce applauded the reductions as unprecedented in Russia's trade relations with any country. On many exports, such as dynamoes, accumulators, and cables, they reported that the duties were lower than ever before.[64] This was in contrast to the views of the Kreuzzeitung, which wrote of the unbridgeable chasm that had developed between the chancellor and the Conservatives. Pursuing a policy beneficial to socialists and liberals, the chancellor had, according to the Conservative paper, "no longer any trust among the Conservatives."[65] Since Caprivi laid no value upon the importance of a strong Conservative party, nothing fruitful could derive from a close association.

64. *Der deutsche Handelstag* 2:478.
65. *Kreuzzeitung,* 20 December 1893.

Caprivi began his defense by anticipating the opponents who would attack the treaty on political grounds. Although the treaty was essentially economically motivated, he said, there were also political reasons to have closer ties with Russia. The conclusion of long-term trade treaties demonstrated Germany's desire to maintain the peace. In truth, the chancellor was somewhat concerned with improving Russian relations, for attempts to cement Anglo-German ties had stalled after the success of the Helgoland-Zanzibar treaty. "If the hand which Russia is stretching out toward the west is spurned," warned the chancellor, "then Russia will be left to her own resources, and she will become Pan-Slavic with all the dangers that we connect with that word."[66] Again Caprivi emphasized the unreality of the agrarians' refusal to admit Germany's need for foreign grain. The Farmers' League, he lamented, had stooped to demagoguery and anti-Semitism, and had not hesitated to call for his own dismissal. Their agitation had rent a cleft between agriculture and industry, without having gained a single advantage for farmers. In closing, Caprivi castigated the league for stirring up an atmosphere of hatred and recrimination.

Marschall took another approach. He pointed out that the Zollverein had succeeded because it negotiated a series of trade agreements.[67] Autonomous duties constituted an unsuccessful experiment introduced by Bismarck to remedy economic stagnation. Conservatives were asking the government to renounce the system that had brought Germany to a competitive position with Great Britain, in order to preserve a system that had failed to realize agrarian aims while ruining the export market for industrial goods. Russia, he noted, the land of an autonomous trade policy par excellence, had finally recognized its incompatibility with commercial prosperity; yet it was the Russian policy that Conservatives now advocated for Germany. Wooing the industrialists, Marschall recalled the undeclared tariff war that had existed for thirty years, and asked exporters to ponder the effect that ten years of trade security with Russia would have. If the treaty should be rejected, he reminded the deputies, the tariff war would continue, and ex-

66. *Sten. Ber.*, 1893–94, 1:1452.
67. Ibid., pp. 1430–32.

porters would have to renounce the large eastern market. Agrarians had brought forth no evidence, he contended, that a reduction would depress grain prices. In 1893 the duty against Russian rye had been 75 marks; yet rye prices were the lowest in years. The difference between the German and world grain prices remained 35 marks despite exorbitant rates against Russia. If agrarians had not been helped by a high Russian duty, he concluded, there was no reason why a lower duty would damage them.[68]

To convince dissident deputies of the right, Caprivi demanded that Miquel, the minister of finance, and a highly respected man in Conservative circles, speak for the treaty. The minister's speech was, however, so equivocating, that Barth asked the following day whether the minister was meant to defend or oppose the treaty. Although Miquel gave the chancellor complete support in council meetings, he obviously did not desire to court unpopularity on the right, especially as he was widely considered a possible successor to the chancellorship. To insure his position with the agrarians, he had already informed Kardorff of his desire to be rid of Caprivi.[69] His attempts to moderate agricultural fears were weak, therefore, whereas his portrayal of rural woes was comprehensive. Alienating the agrarians would not enhance his chances of succeeding Caprivi.

The Social Democrats demonstrated once more that they would support the government even more persuasively than its own ministers when policy eschewed class interest. Deputy Schultze criticized the tendency to neglect consumer interests in discussing tariffs.[70] As long as German workers continued to be underpaid, he said, bread prices had to remain cheap, or the survival of many poor families would be at stake. What the Conservatives desired, according to Schultze, was the return to a feudal golden age, in which the interests of the city population had no weight.

Rickert, a prominent leader of a new radical party that had broken with the Progressives over the military bill, lost no time in

---

68. Ibid., p. 1428.
69. Walter Bussmann, *Staatssekretär Herbert von Bismarck* (Göttingen, 1964), p. 577. Many other ministers apart from Miquel displayed greater loyalty to the Junkers than to Caprivi.
70. *Sten. Ber.*, 1893–94, I: 1485–91.

showing he could match Richter in vituperation. All Europe was lauding Germany for winning Russia over to the treaty system, he remarked, while Conservatives opposed this very step. Avoiding the treaty's specifics, he ridiculed the Conservatives as the party of reaction, which had objected to every forward step including the Stein-Hardenberg reforms. Bismarck had sought in vain to achieve what Caprivi presented to the Reichstag. Only the narrowness of vision and fear of change, Rickert said, prevented agrarians from seeing the multiple advantages that the treaty would bring. Barth, of the orthodox Radicals, questioned, as Caprivi had done, whether agriculture was being burdened or whether the sacrifices of the urban population were being moderated. Without a Russian treaty, he warned the Junkers, the rye prices would not be at a lower level than the wheat prices; thus wheat would replace rye as the main grain in bread.[71] Such a development would be disastrous for the northern estates, where weather and soil precluded the cultivation of wheat. In general, his expectation was for reduced consumer prices without a severe dislocation of agriculture.

The leadership of the Center party was again in conflict with the recalcitrant Bavarian delegates, who would not support any pro-industrial legislation because of the agricultural character of their constituencies. Bachem, the later party historian, spoke for the majority of his compatriots in denying that agriculture would be eclipsed by the Russian treaty. Should the party's prediction prove incorrect, Bachem believed the official position would be changed when the treaties came up for renewal. In his subsequent history, he admitted that the party had been moved to support Caprivi because of its desire for the abolition of the law forbidding Jesuits in Prussia.[72] Center forebodings were represented by Freiherr von Heeremann, who looked upon agriculture as the "foundation of all relations, and the securest protection for the strength, power, and order of the state."[73] It is the duty of the state, he said, to prevent the deterioration of agriculture to English conditions, even if class legislation should be necessary. Replying to Radical charges of re-

71. Ibid., p. 1527.
72. Bachem, *Vorgeschichte*, 5:347.
73. *Sten. Ber.*, 1893–94, III:1899.

juvenated feudalism, von Heeremann claimed, "In these so-called feudal limitations lay much more welfare and wisdom than in all the modern arrangements that we now seek to create." At the final vote, thirty-nine of eighty-five Center delegates voted against approval, the bulk of them being Bavarians.

Having played a decisive role in the passage of the Romanian treaty, the Poles with sixteen delegates were again expected to cast the deciding vote. Caprivi's policy of allowing Polish divisions in the army with German officers, and Polish as the language of Posen's elementary schools, was thought by Conservatives to be a bribe for the support of tariff treaties. The traditional Polish hostility to Russia was set aside by von Koscielski, as he emphasized his party's desire for peace. A Russo-German war meant civil war for his people.[74] Prince Radziwill confirmed the primacy of foreign policy in the Polish view by praising the good relations the treaty would initiate.

Hartmann of the Württemberg People's Party cast the nine votes at his disposal for the treaty, although it was common knowledge that farmers constituted the backbone of this small party. According to Hartmann, the smallholders of Württemberg depended upon the prosperity of neighboring cities to sell their products, and the amount of surplus grain that they could sell was not of sufficient value to justify high tariffs. Many Württemberg families sent their children to the city for a supplementary income; thus the interests of village and city were not antagonistic as the agrarians claimed. In Württemberg, Hartmann stressed, the diminution of the workers' real income was contrary to peasant interests.[75]

Hesitant to antagonize the agrarian leaders with whom they had formed a majority for so many years, most National Liberals tempered their praise for the treaties and urged compensation for farmers. Bennigsen, the venerable leader, lauded the direct benefits to the export industries, whose prospects, he forecast, would change considerably when the tariff war was terminated. More important than the present concessions, he prophesied, was the change in Russian policy, which might lead to more satisfactory

74. Ibid., II:1520.
75. Ibid., 1505.

treaties in the future. The National Liberal leader admonished the Farmers' League mildly for its demagogic agitation, but was willing to attribute its truculence to the organization's lack of experience. Its ultimate aim—to preserve the Junker aristocracy—Bennigsen approved of unequivocally. Retorting to jeers from the left, he said that he also had once thought the Junkers undesirable, but age had taught him that there was no group to replace them in the bureaucracy, army, or foreign service.[76] A small group of National Liberals insisted on rejecting the treaty because the agricultural crisis was so severe, in their opinion, that any further deterioration would ruin the peasantry. This group comprising sixteen of the party's fifty-three mandates voted in the negative to please their southern rural constituencies.

The attack mounted by the Conservatives against the government was unrivaled for its strength and the degree of hostility. For the first time the party threatened to use its power in the Prussian lower house against the government, and even to reject military appropriations. Kanitz once again questioned the wisdom of concluding long-term treaties when the price situation could change, so as to make the treaty bound rates inadequate. Eastern estate owners and peasants were bound to go bankrupt, he stated, when Russian grain began to compete in German markets. Apart from the damage to agriculture, the reduction in rates would cause the treasury to lose 40 million marks in revenue annually. The states would be asked to replace this loss from their matricular contributions, which would mean higher rural taxes to add to the farmers' burdens. In order to cut down expenditures, Kanitz disclosed that the Conservatives had decided in caucus to vote against the proposed increase in military spending asked for by the minister of war.[77] After considerable soul-searching, he said, the party had found no other way to pare down the budget, despite the departure from tradition that such a vote would entail. He personally would also vote against the proposal for a Prussian canal system in the

76. Ibid., 1460. National Liberal deputies from Hanover, Bavaria, Württemberg, and Hessen were forced to subscribe to the Farmers' League's program in order to prevent the desertion of peasant voters.
77. Ibid., III: 1923.

Landtag, although the party had not yet decided to follow his lead. Agriculture, he warned, had no intention of bearing the increased monetary burdens as well as the competition of all grain-growing lands.[78]

König of the Conservatives proposed two novel theories designed to convince the Reichstag of the faults of the treaty policy. According to him, Germany was experiencing the growth of two conflicting forces—the industrialists and the workers. If these groups continued to grow without forsaking their hostility, the nation would be shaken to its foundations by the battles between labor and capital. Fortunately there was a class in society that could prevent the polarization implied in industrialization. This class was the independent peasantry, which formed the backbone of the social structure, and which if maintained could ease the social tensions. König stated his other theory clearly to the deputies, "One must above all maintain the national strength and the economic strength of that part of the population which is in the first line called upon in the hour of danger to defend the fatherland; that is our old peasantry, gentlemen."[79] It was inconceivable that the government should seek to strengthen economically the very groups opposing the increase in the nation's military potential.

Another agrarian spokesman, von Mirbach, insisted that Caprivi was bringing about the socialization of Germany by fostering the growth of cities. His policy would first destroy agriculture and then cause the peasantry to flee to cities, where they would be won over to socialism. Patriarchal relations as they existed in the east would be destroyed. If an industrial depression occurred, the urban multitudes would stir up a revolution because they lacked the discipline of rural workers.[80] Von Mirbach did not hesitate to accuse Caprivi of following a revolutionary policy that ultimately would prove dangerous to the nation. Freiherr von Hammerstein, employing traditional protectionist arguments, criticized the chancellor for neglecting the inner market in favor of insecure foreign outlets. Agriculture, he maintained, could be the greatest buyer of indus-

78. Ibid., II:1511.
79. Ibid., 1453.
80. Ibid., 1426–28.

trial goods if the government strengthened the purchasing power of the rural population.[81] Should farming become unprofitable, industry might prosper a while, but in the end it would suffer the same fate, for without an inner market there could be no secure development.

Von Staudy, a doctrinaire Junker from Posen who was director of agriculture for the province, contended that the country could be self-sufficient in rye if the government gave up the erroneous idea that Germany was an industrial nation. Agriculture possessed the same potential as industry, but capital was lacking for investment. Since the nation could not prosper without agriculture, he advised that it be given primary economic consideration.[82] Liebermann von Sonnenberg, an anti-Semitic delegate with close ties to the Conservatives, began his attack by terming the treaty an inner Jena; he called for a Scharnhorst to save the situation. Caprivi, he said, received the support of the left because he was carrying out their aim of destroying the Junkers. To base a nation on trade and industry was dangerous, he maintained, for only an agriculturally based state could provide a strong army, a healthy populace, and spiritual contentment.[83] A state monopoly on grain imports was needed so that the Jews would be prevented from ruining agriculture. If the government would purchase the required grain at the world price and sell it at a profit, he prophesied, the rural problems would be solved.

Perhaps Junker fears found their best expression from the pen of General Waldersee, who was in close touch with Conservative leaders and harbored ambitions of succeeding to the chancellorship. Waldersee wrote, "Even if agriculture should not be harmed by the Russian treaty, as many now maintain, it certainly must suffer from the whole economic policy of the New Course.[84] The Conservatives, thought the general, would not hesitate one moment to vote for the treaty if Caprivi were dismissed and a chancellor with loyalty to agriculture was appointed. Waldersee correctly

81. Ibid.
82. Ibid., III: 1730.
83. Ibid., 1906.
84. Waldersee, *Denkwürdigkeiten II, 1888–1890* (Stuttgart, 1922), p. 307.

perceived that the Junkers' anger was caused by the general direction of policy rather than the particular treaty. They feared that their estates could not survive the crisis without government aid. Lamenting the division of many estates into numerous farms, Waldersee blamed the government for allowing the loyal, monarchically minded aristocracy to decline.[85] Nowhere in his diary were to be found statements about smallholders, for he probably recognized that this was a ruse by the Junkers to gain support in their battle against industry.

Prior to the Russian treaty, the Farmers' League had limited its assaults to Caprivi and his cabinet. When the emperor endorsed his chancellor's policy, the league declared in its weekly newspaper, that any German farmer who was honest must admit that the emperor was an enemy of German agriculture.[86] Heretofore, even the parties of the left had hesitated to attack the emperor, who was supposedly above factionalism. It was a decided novelty that a conservative, agrarian organization dared to do so. The old satirical couplet, "Und der König absolut, wenn er unsern Willen tut," never seemed more valid than in 1894. Abstract economic theory and *Interessenpolitik* were wedded at the league's annual meeting when Adolf Wagner delivered a blistering attack upon the industrial civilization that Caprivi was fostering. For a variety of reasons, some economic, some romantic (see chapter 4), he urged the membership to continue its campaign against the treaty. Plötz, the chairman, followed with an appeal to patriots, recalling the battles of liberation and unification in which peasants led by Junkers had triumphed. Were these two classes to be replaced by financiers and men who, if they were called into the army, "could not storm a house of cards"?[87] In the Reichstag, he said that the knell of the empire would sound when the peasants were not available to protect the country in time of danger. The Hohenzollerns, he hoped, would realize before it was too late that they were cutting off the

85. Ibid., p. 308.
86. *Korrespondenz des Bundes der Landwirte,* 27 March 1894.
87. *Die Allgemeine Zeitung,* 19 February 1894. Puhle, the historian of the Farmers' League, believes that anti-Semitism and anticapitalism were essential ingredients in the league's peculiar *Mittelstand* ideology.

branch on which they were sitting. As the Farmers' League judged a group's worthiness by its martial valor and monarchical patriotism, the workers received short shrift from its observers. Portrayed as a warrior caste, the peasants were deserving of state support, in Plötz's view, for their special value as guardians of the nation's security.

Kardorff of the Free Conservative party continued to display his distaste for the chancellor and his economic policy. He recorded in his diary that he had received several invitations from Caprivi but that he would not reply to them. Only if he were called to the chancellor in his official capacity, he wrote, would he be willing to speak to him.[88] In the Reichstag, Kardorff introduced a resolution, which he later withdrew, calling for high duties on goods imported from a nation with a silver currency. He accused Caprivi of bringing about the downfall of the Junkers, who were the pillars of the state, and for ruining the peasantry, whose existence was necessary as a counterpoise to the socialist working class. In agreement with Kardorff was von Moltke, a former General Staff officer from Schleswig, who questioned the right of western industrialists to destroy the eastern estate owners, whose sacrifices had been necessary to create a united Germany. Baron von Stumm again tried unsuccessfully to heal the split caused by the treaties. He implored agrarians not to exaggerate agriculture's plight, and to seek compensation in other areas rather than dissolve the coalition of industry and agriculture.[89] His attempts to minimize the conflict fell on deaf ears; nine Imperialists voted for the treaty and sixteen rejected it.

Although he was the single largest landowner, the emperor would have nothing to do with the economic objections raised by his fellow landowners. Intent on being a modern emperor, Wilhelm II desired to build up the industrial capacity of his country. He was proud of the entrepôt Hamburg and the waxing industrial cities of the Ruhr. Industrial magnates were welcome at the imperial court. Until Caprivi's resignation, he also wanted to show the working classes that the throne was not necessarily their foe. A system of

88. S. von Kardorff, *Wilhelm von Kardorff*, p. 292.
89. *Sten. Ber.*, 1893–94, III:1915.

trade treaties enabled him to pursue a policy beneficial at once to workers and capitalists, and eased a rapprochement with Russia. The disruption of Russian relations caused by the nonrenewal of the Reinsurance Treaty had been forced upon the emperor by Eulenberg and Holstein; his consistent aim after the Kronstadt visit of the French fleet was to restore "the wire to Saint Petersburg." Wilhelm made it quite clear to the Conservatives that Caprivi's policy had his support. Conservative leaders were purposely omitted from the invitation lists to dinners during the debates on the Russian treaty, and at one such dinner the emperor exclaimed, "I have no desire to go to war with Russia because of a hundred dumb Junkers."[90] He claimed subsequently that he had given his personal pledge to the tsar that the treaty would be passed within three months. At another dinner (in an obvious reference to the Conservatives), he admonished all parties to think of their fatherland before their pecuniary interests in the final vote. Not to appear hostile to agriculture, Wilhelm received a delegation from the Farmers' League after its founding, and promised to introduce agricultural chambers in a speech in January 1894. The emperor's belated attempts at reconciliation with Bismarck were probably motivated in part by his desire to win the former chancellor's endorsement for his policy. Bismarck did refrain from leading a campaign against the treaty, perhaps because he recognized the government's attempts to restore his pro-Russian policy, or perhaps because it would have placed the emperor in an embarrassing position. In the *Hamburger Nachrichten* he merely questioned the lack of time devoted to discussing the treaties, and claimed that it would be a misfortune if agriculture and industry should remain at loggerheads.[91]

The reaction outside the Reichstag to the proposed Russian treaty hinged entirely on whether the group was agricultural or industrial. Respectful of its past alliance with agriculture, the Centralverband der deutschen Industrieller declared publicly that it had no desire to gain at the expense of agriculture and would not seek to break the coalition of 1879. It did note, however, that many

90. Waldersee, *Denkwürdigkeiten II*, pp. 306ff.
91. *Hamburger Nachrichten*, 9 February 1894.

of its experts had aided the government in drawing up the treaty; thus the advantages to German industry would be manifold should the treaty pass.[92] At its 1894 meeting, the Centralverband, whose light industrialist members did not secede until the following year, abandoned its hesitancy when a resolution was approved greeting the Russian treaty as an aid to the growth of industry and trade. The losses to farmers were minimized, and it was concluded that the solidarity of economic interests need not be disturbed by the treaty.[93] The German Chamber of Commerce called a special convention which gave full endorsement to the Russian treaty. A resolution claimed, "The maintenance of a strong, growing population is only possible through measures which place industry and trade in a position to expand out of the inner market."[94] Without harming agriculture, the Chamber contended, security had been gained for Germany's export trade. The Society of Berlin Salesmen expressed their approval of the reductions in their trade bulletin. Among the numerous trade councils sending their approval to the ministry of trade were those of Kassel, Dortmund, and Breslau.[95] Petitions were received from heavy industry in particular—the Federation of Iron and Steel Industries submitted a document signed by 7400 firms approving the government's policy.[96] Nearly every industry producing finished goods had in some way given the government support for the Russian treaty.

Petitions also poured in from villages and organizations at odds with the proposed grain reductions. More than a thousand letters were received from Posen and East Prussia, often from humble peasants, pleading for the maintenance of the rye duty. The Saxon Agricultural Federation reproached the government for ignoring the parties that had supported the military bill. According to the Saxons, the sedentary ways (*Sessenhaftigkeit*) of the rural population were being threatened by the mushrooming of cities, and the government, instead of hampering this development, was fostering

92. H. A. Bueck, *Der Centralverband der deutschen Industrieller 1876–1901* (Berlin, 1902–5), p. 34.
93. *Die Allgemeine Zeitung*, 22 February 1894.
94. *Der deutsche Handelstag*, 2:470.
95. DZA Rep. 120.
96. Ibid.

it to the disadvantage of farmers. Farmers did not contest the workers' demand for low bread prices, but the stock exchange was to be blamed for extracting the profits of high bread costs, not the penurious peasant.[97] From west of the Elbe, where small holdings abounded, scarcely any petitions are to be found among the papers of the Ministry of Trade.

On 10 March 1894 the treaty was approved by a vote of 200 to 146. The breakdown of the vote is shown in Table 10. A plan to re-

TABLE 10 VOTE ON RUSSIAN TREATY

PARTIES	FOR	AGAINST
Conservatives	6	54
Free Conservatives	9	16
Center	45	39
Poles	15	0
National Liberals	34	16
Radical Union	12	0
Radical People's Party	22	0
Social Democrats	40	0
Other	17	21

store the duties to fifty marks was defeated three days later 205 to 151. Caprivi expressed relief that the ordeal was over and informed a friend of his expectation that agrarian hostility would now abate. Recalling the struggle, he wrote, "I had more difficulties to overcome and more hate to experience from people who earlier were closer to me than one may believe."[98] The emperor proudly proclaimed the treaty "as a fundamental work that all European states should look upon as a model for the conclusion of treaties with one another."[99] According to the *Allgemeine Zeitung*, Germany had left the ranks of the agricultural nations to join the industrial nations—a step forward economically, but a doubtful step insofar as national development was concerned.[100]

For no other legislative proposal after unification had the gov-

97. DZA, Rep. 120. December 1892.
98. Schneidewin, "Briefe," p. 139.
99. DZA, Rep. 90a Abt. B III Nr. 3 vol. 5.
100. *Die allgemeine Zeitung*, 15 February 1894.

ernment faced such heated opposition from the Conservatives as the Russian treaty. Although they were opposed to the Kultur-kampf, and to the reduction of military service to two years, the party had never previously threatened to go into opposition in the Prussian lower house, as Kanitz proposed during the treaty debate. Under the guise of austerity, the agrarian spokesman had voiced his opposition to military spending—something inconceivable before the Caprivi period. Kanitz was merely showing the government how much it depended upon the Conservatives in crucial issues, and how this support could be withdrawn if agrarian demands were disregarded. The Social Democrats were obviously not the only party that could launch attacks on the government when their class interests were scorned.

During the course of the Russian treaty debates it became clear, however, that class preservation was not the sole reason for the agrarian attitude. Gradually the agrarians had imbibed the ideas of numerous scholars who were sympathetic to their cause for more abstruse reasons. In 1894 Wagner advanced anti-industrial theories by speaking to the Farmers' League and the agricultural conference convened by the minister of agriculture, while Max Sering introduced them to the overwhelmingly Junker Landes-Ökonomie-Kollegium. Repeatedly they claimed that the Conservatives were fighting for the long-range interests of the nation and not for selfish aims. Both also wrote for widely read periodicals in 1894, Wagner penning "Agrar- und Industriestaat" for Harden's *Die Zukunft*, which endorsed his position.[101] The League of Tax and Economic Reformers, a Junker organization, heard Wagner declare agriculture "the largest and most important business in Germany . . . and the agricultural population the main strength of the entire nation." He ended with a warning: "We are surrounded by enemies and must strengthen the main support of the nation—agriculture—by tariffs, bimetallism, and in every way."[102] The tenor of these ideas was a romanticizing of agricultural society with its close primary relationships. The fear was frequently expressed in these lectures

101. Adolf Wagner, "Agrar- und Industriestaat," 8 September 1894.
102. *Verhandlungen des Vereins für Steuer- und Wirtschaftsreform*, 1894, p. 148.

that an industrial victory in the tariff controversy would connote the downfall of this kind of society. (For a full discussion of these ideas see chapter 4.) This trend of thought, which blended well with the virulent anticapitalism that emerged after the crash of 1873 and class interest, was quickly absorbed by the agrarians. Kanitz's speeches and the agrarian press increasingly emphasized the "agrarian myth" argument after 1894. What had begun as a slight modification in tariff rates had become, in the minds of many, a battle over the future character of Germany. The *Deutsche land-wirtschaftliche Presse* lamented, "Must we really depart from the old Prussia, from the old Germany? Is it definite that Germany will be compelled onto a path that departs from the way which all friends of the fatherland have hitherto judged right?"[103] The increase in such criticism and the persistence of hostility toward Caprivi and the emperor indicated that an agrarian offensive was in the offing.

THE KANITZ PROPOSALS

While the various treaties were being discussed in the Reichstag, one proposal was advanced from the right to alleviate the rural plight without prejudicing the trade agreements. Kardorff repeatedly suggested that Caprivi abandon the gold currency for bimetallism. As early as 1875, the Free Conservative leader had written in *Against the Stream* that nothing less than the adoption of a two standard system could solve the debt problem in agriculture.[104] Bismarck's one failing, in Kardorff's view, had been his inability to recognize the deficiencies of gold. Maintaining correspondence with protectionists of similar views in America, Kardorff was confident that gold would decline rapidly as the world's currency if the German government could be induced to assume leadership in the bimetallist movement. The bimetallist tide that was gaining strength in America even more than in Germany can be attributed to the increased use of gold in the expanding European economy at a time when no major gold strikes had occurred for forty years. When gold was simultaneously discovered at the century's end in

103. *Deutsche landwirtschaftliche Presse*, 23 November 1895.
104. Wilhelm von Kardorff, *Gegen den Strom* (Berlin, 1875).

Alaska, South Africa, and Australia, the agitation abated almost immediately.

Kardorff's repeated assertion that the treaties would be acceptable if a double currency was adopted drew a number of responses from Caprivi. During the course of the Austrian debate the chancellor disclosed that after discussing the currency question with a panel of experts, he was convinced that bimetallism was impractical and in any case could not be introduced without Great Britain's compliance, which appeared unlikely.[105] Lest the importance of the movement be exaggerated, Caprivi averred that Kardorff was the sole prominent spokesman for a double currency, and the few economists supporting him were not held in high esteem by the profession. Lastly, he deplored the tendency of bimetallists to ally themselves with the anti-Semites and use demagogic methods to win adherents. The following year Caprivi announced to an incredulous Reichstag that certain members had implied that their vote on the military bill would be contingent on the introduction of bimetallism.[106] He said that the bill had been proposed by the government because it was necessary, and he refused to be blackmailed by deceitful patriots whose love of their fatherland was secondary to their pecuniary interests. Again in 1893 Caprivi considered it necessary to call the bimetallists to order. "I see in the countryside," he observed, "the attempt that has been made to hitch anti-Semitism and bimetallism to the same wagon, and to drive with the means for agitation."[107] His government, he emphasized, would have nothing whatever to do with demagoguery. Observing no result from his previous rebukes, Caprivi again denounced anti-Semites and bimetallists during the Russian debates for their use of socialist procedures to stir up the peasantry. Although he was adamantly opposed to Kardorff's views, Caprivi was compelled, as we shall see, to make certain concessions to bimetallism because of the rising agrarian tide after the conclusion of the Russian treaty.

Refusing to despair at the inconsequential results of the bimetal-

105. Arndt, *Die Reden*, p. 184.
106. Ibid., p. 292.
107. *Sten. Ber.*, 1892–93, vol. I:273.

list agitation, Kanitz decided that the agrarians must present their own plans for the relief of agriculture, since the chancellor ignored their plight. In a pamphlet, Kanitz spelled out the contemporary dangers as follows: "The signs of the present times are very distinct; decline of agriculture and the small businessman, depopulation of the land, capital accumulation in the big cities, and the rise of the Social Democrats."[108] Only the reviving of agriculture could prevent the situation from worsening. If the state did not intervene to strengthen its most loyal supporter, anarchical developments would continue to grow. In the Reichstag, Kanitz warned that the state would lose its roots if it did not provide the care and trust needed by agriculture. Since Caprivi had expressed the desire to entertain proposals for the redress of agrarian grievances, he informed the members that he was introducing a bill to nationalize the importation of foreign grain needed for domestic consumption. This grain was to be purchased at world prices and resold in Germany at prescribed levels. He suggested minimum prices of 215 for wheat, 165 for rye, and 155 for barley and oats, to insure that all farmers received a profit from the cultivation of grain. Kanitz subsequently proposed that minimum prices be established by taking the average prices of the years 1850–80, and advised the government to store a part of each year's purchases for insurance in case of war. The plan was not socialistic, he maintained, but designed to replace the protection of agriculture that Caprivi had so lightly dropped. Any profits resulting from the sale of grain were to be divided between a fund to offset future losses and an attempt to make the peasantry more sedentary. The plan received immediate acclaim on the right, where deputy Will admonished the smallholders that they had better support Kanitz or the estates would take up cattle raising and drive the peasants out of business.[109] Limburg-Stirum regretted that the days of cooperation between the government and the Conservatives were past, and admitted the need for an aggressive agricultural program. Any man who was *königtreu* must shake his head at the direction of the "New

108. Graf von Kanitz, *Die Festsetzung von Mindestpreisen* (Preussisch-Holland, 1894).
109. *Sten. Ber.*, 1893–94, III: 2090–2100.

Course," said Werner, who believed that Caprivi was forcing the farm population to join the workers in hostile criticism.[110] Kanitz's plan, thought Werner, offered the last possibility to preserve the healthy segment of the population.

Caprivi countered that the execution of the plan would spoil Germany's good name, as well as arousing mutual recriminations among the states. According to the chancellor, the constitution did not provide for the federal government's right to establish a monopoly and set up warehouses on state territory. The various states, he assured the Reichstag, would battle for warehouses and points of entry, and in so doing would weaken the fabric of unity. Apart from this result, Germany's reputation for reliability would suffer throughout the world, for the treaty nations were certain to judge the plan a violation of good faith. Everything the treaty policy had aimed for—good foreign relations and expanding exports—was certain to be set back by the execution of the Conservative plan. To those critics who accused the government of a renegade policy, Caprivi retorted, "What you are now doing separates you much more than what was done earlier, not only from industry, but from all that is loyal to the state."[111]

Instead of gaining adherents from the middle parties, as he anticipated, Kanitz discovered that the factions supporting the trade treaties were vociferously opposed to his plan. Barth of the Radicals called it socialism applied to benefit the wealthy part of society rather than the poor. He insisted that the plan meant a duty of 100 marks, and therefore was prohibited by the recently approved treaties. Bennigsen refused to take the plan seriously. Approval, he said, would foster greed and vested interests on a scale previously unimaginable. Agriculture was indeed in a difficult situation, but such plans only forestalled any intelligent attempt to restore prosperity, said the National Liberal leader.[112] The Center party was solidly opposed to Kanitz, for, as Bachem said, the western farmers must necessarily suffer from such a proposal. Kanitz had overlooked the cost of transporting the wheat within Germany, and the

110. Ibid., 2139.
111. *Schulthess'* 25 (1894): 35.
112. *Sten. Ber.*, 1893–94, III:2130.

differences in prices between the south and the northeast. Furthermore, Bachem believed that the plan moved in the direction of socialism and antagonized the Catholic population, who were supporters of a free, private, economy. In a parting blow at Conservative greed, the Center historian asked why no maximum grain price had been suggested, should prices soar above necessary profit levels.[113]

Without the formality of a committee hearing, the plan was rejected by a vote of 205 to 46. The weight of the defeat did not deter Kanitz from vowing to introduce the plan annually until agriculture was restored to its proper position. In 1895 the persistence of slumping grain prices caused the Reichstag to establish a committee to consider the plan, despite the devastating attack of a respected Conservative economist. Gustav Schmoller, a mild-mannered Conservative who held the most distinguished chair of economics at the University of Berlin and served in the Prussian House of Lords, devoted a long article in his yearbook to Kanitz's proposals. Testing the effect that Kanitz's plan would have had if executed in 1894, Schmoller came to the conclusion that it was equal to a duty of 115 marks on wheat, 83 on rye, 78 on barley, and 58 on oats.[114] He estimated that 750 million marks would be taken from the pockets of bread consumers and simply given to grain-producing farmers. If applied in a period of unemployment, in his view, the plan would be an unjust burden on the working class, perhaps even a stimulant to revolution. Schmoller harbored no illusions that the socialism initiated by the plan would be without subsequent effect; he predicted that the government would have to nationalize the internal grain trade as well, and after a while mills and bakers would also experience government control. Most dangerous, in Schmoller's opinion, would be the resulting dissatisfaction of traders, workers, and even farmers, which, he believed, would be directed toward the state. The revolutionary implications of the plan were therefore enormous. The influx of foreign workers would never be ended while the weaker estates were cultivated.[115]

113. Ibid., 2108–14.
114. G. Schmoller, "Einige Worte zum Antrag Kanitz."
115. Ibid.

Schmoller was but one more case of a scholar torn from his ivory tower by the controversy and seeking to influence the outcome by his writings. In the years to come his example was to find numerous imitators.

In contrast to Schmoller, the Farmers' League foresaw the wane of German agriculture if Kanitz's bill were defeated. Abandoning its attack on the Socialists, the league paper averred that it was the duty of the state to aid agriculture and free it from the bonds of international capital. Not the law of supply and demand but the machinations of greedy capitalists, said the *Korrespondenz*, were responsible for the crisis in grain prices.[116] Forgotten was the fact that grain prices were lowest during 1892, when Germany scarcely needed to import grain. Although the debt problem was assailed, the league neglected to mention that most debts were incurred from unwise speculation in the 1870s. Despite the agrarians' agitation and threat to reject further military appropriations as they had done in 1894, Kanitz's plan gained only ninety-seven votes in 1895.

At least one observer has seen in Kanitz's proposal a harbinger of the post–World War II legislation in America designed to maintain the profitability of farming.[117] The differences, however, between mid-twentieth-century American farmers and late nineteenth-century German farmers are qualitatively so great that any comparison is bound to be superficial. The injustice of Kanitz's plan in comparison with American farm policy can in part be measured by examining the source of funds for agriculture. In America the money came from the federal government, whose income was mainly based on a highly graduated income tax. Consumers of bread were expected to bear the imposition in Germany. Because the penurious part of the population depended on bread as a staple, the burden increased as income declined, in the manner of a regressive tax.[118] Kanitz was hardly a champion of the right of a

116. *Korrespondenz*, 15 May 1895.
117. See Sarah Tirrell, *German Agrarian Politics after Bismarck's Fall* (New York, 1951), "Conclusion."
118. Kanitz hoped to insure a substantial profit to all sellers of grain, and, as every German knew, the Junkers were the principal sources of surplus grain. Caprivi's successor, Hohenlohe, calculated that 75 percent of German

poor, unacclaimed segment of the population to a share of the nation's wealth.

AGRICULTURAL GAINS UNDER CAPRIVI

From the preceding sections it may appear that agricultural claims for assistance during the four years of Caprivi's chancellorship were completely ignored. Although it is true that Caprivi expected his policy to benefit farmers by necessitating their adaptation to the changed market conditions of the last quarter of the century, he experimented also with other measures to relieve rural distress. Many of his attempts were on the state level, since he believed that the competence of the federal government to treat such matters was limited. Some of the most successful methods of assistance were adopted after Botho zu Eulenberg had assumed the Prussian minister presidency in 1892. Still, Caprivi should be accorded the credit, for they were introduced with his approval or at his behest.

Less than six months after he assumed office, the chancellor convened a cabinet session to discuss the problem of foreign agri-

---

farmers would receive no advantage from legislation to aid grain cultivators, and only a small portion of the remaining quarter would benefit significantly. Even Bavarian delegates realized that Kanitz had not designed his plan to benefit the more than three million farmers west of the Elbe. The group to receive a guaranteed income was not lacking in political influence as the American farmers were, but rather exercised a power disproportionate to their numbers. Despite their lamentations, there was no question of the poverty of the Junker estate owners, but rather a possible diminution in incomes of tens of thousands of marks, in a nation where 64 percent of wage earners received less than 900 marks annually. American legislation was aimed at preserving the existence of family farms, which were often at the mercy of large corporative enterprises. Lacking organization, they could not exert any power on the prices that they paid to farm machinery companies or to railroads which purchased their goods. Thus, the American farmer required government intervention to allow him to compete in a market dominated by giant concerns. On the other hand, Kanitz desired to maintain the declining position of a relatively wealthy aristocracy by freeing their income from the fluctuations of the market. No other single piece of legislation, aside from entail, so blatantly aimed at maintaining a class in power at the expense of the common welfare. While American farmers were being rewarded because they were too efficient, Kanitz's plan would have prevented the normal attrition rate of inefficient farms. By causing an artificial rise in land prices, it might also have set off another round of inflation, leading to a worsening of the debt problem.

cultural workers. The minister of the interior suggested the establishment of government-financed peasant holdings on bankrupt estates. Smaller holdings, he pointed out, did not require the number of migrant workers that estates did.[119] He also submitted for discussion the abolition of identity passes, which will be examined below, and stricter police regulations. Von Ballhausen, the minister of agriculture, opined that none of the proposals would stop the flow of migrants without damaging production. Finance minister Miquel contended that the proposal concerning identity passes might make agriculture more profitable and stop the flight of German laborers from the land. It was the chancellor's belief that a movement of population from east to west was a European phenomenon and that police regulations could not bring it to a halt. He desired no hindrances to the free immigration of Slav workers, but agreed to certain modifications in deference to the minister for religious affairs, who deplored the growing Catholic influence in the eastern provinces. The following year a bill was approved reversing a law of 1885 that had considerably restricted Slav migration. In easing the entry of migrant laborers Caprivi ignored the admonition of many observers, including Bismarck, who feared that the Slav influence in Posen and East Prussia would become dangerous in the future if Russia resuscitated a Pan-Slavic policy. Junkers were inclined to make light of the Slavic danger, for their estates could no longer be properly cultivated without the yearly influx of foreign workers. In his decision to relax border restrictions, Caprivi showed more willingness than the Iron Chancellor to sacrifice national interests for the immediate needs of agriculture.

Since 1837 the more efficient producers of sugar from beets had had an enormous advantage over other domestic producers because the export premium increased with the amount of sugar extracted from a given amount of beets. An 1891 law abrogated the inequalities of the old formula, and in establishing an equitable premium stimulated the growth of sugar refining on eastern estates.[120] Previously Saxony had enjoyed the benefits of sugar legis-

119. DZA, Crown Council, June 1891, Rep. 90a B III 2C Nr. 3 IV 288.
120. Friedrich Aereboe, *Agrarpolitik* (Berlin, 1928), pp. 330–40.

lation almost alone. As in the previous year, a Crown Council was called in June 1891 to suggest remedies for rural problems. Von Ballhausen proposed the treatment of overindebtedness, while Miquel advised the adoption of inner colonization whereby peasants would be settled in the east at government expense.[121] A bill was introduced by Caprivi a few months later providing government funds to peasants desirous of settling for a designated period of time in the sparsely populated provinces. Such a plan, it was hoped, would at once end the unequal distribution of land, diminish the need for migrant laborers, and Germanize predominantly Polish areas. Although the appropriation was small, it constituted a beginning that could have altered the complexion of later central European history if it had been augmented periodically.

In condemning Caprivi, agrarians omitted to mention the many millions of marks they saved by the introduction of Miquel's plan, supported by the chancellor, for reforming Prussia's tax structure. Quite naturally the system of taxation had been built around the agricultural nature of German society; thus the most lucrative tax was on land. As industrial wealth multiplied, the tax structure had not been reformed to take the new sources of wealth into account. Miquel's proposal for tax reform was designed to equalize the burden of taxes. The federal duties on land, houses, and certain businesses were handed over to the local communities, and were replaced by an all-embracing income tax, which graduated from zero to 4 percent. The Conservatives actually wanted a height of five percent. Miquel himself was quite clear about the aim of the tax reform. "The purpose of the transfer must be to unburden landed property in contrast to mobile property."[122] Apart from saving 28 million marks a year in land taxes, the Junkers also benefited from the clause allowing the deduction of debts from taxable income. As rulers of the local communities, many Junkers were able to prosper from the land tax, which they could now impose. Other changes in the estimation of taxes on farmers favored the holdings in direct proportion to their size. Aereboe, the agricultural histo-

---

121. DZA, Rep. 90a Crown Council.
122. Walter Geiger, *Miquel und die preussische Steuerreform 1890–93*, (Göppingen, 1934), p. 19.

rian, doubted if the reform was of value to any farmers having less than 125 acres.[123] It was realized by estate owners and agricultural experts that the changes had provided significant tax relief for estates over 250 acres.

To assist eastern farmers in their search for markets, the government had consented in September 1891 to establish a sliding-scale rate system for the Prussian railways. The purpose was to allow eastern farmers to win markets for their surplus grain in southern and western Germany by cutting their transportation costs to these areas. The plan was naturally opposed by the governments of Baden, Bavaria, and Württemberg, but as the measure was passed through the Prussian legislature, their complaints were ignored. During the next three years the southern states objected on many occasions to the lower rates on longer distances, until it was rumored in 1894 that they would make their vote on the Russian treaty in the Bundesrat contingent on the abolition of this concession to eastern farmers. Meanwhile, both exporters and farmers in the east were disappointed with the recently acquired western markets, and petitioned Caprivi to abolish identity passes. These passes had been initiated by Bismarck with his protectionist policy in 1879 in order to provide free transit for grain that was imported only to be reexported. Upon demand, a trader could receive an identity pass for the amount of grain he imported into the country, and if he exported the identical grain (not the amount) within a stated period of time, he would receive back the duty paid at the time of the grain's entry. This procedure was not uncommon, for many varieties of Russian rye were imported to be mixed with higher-quality German grain and then exported to Scandinavia. What the farmers desired was the dropping of the identity pass, so that for every ton they exported, they would receive a pass allowing them to import a ton of grain duty free (obviously not the identical grain). Such passes would prevent the tariffs from being a hindrance to exports, and in effect would work as an export premium. Whenever the difference between the world price and the German price was less than the amount of the tariff, it would be

123. Aereboe, *Agrarpolitik*, p. 386.

more rewarding for a farmer to sell his grain abroad than at home. In such a case he would receive the world price plus the pass, which he could sell to an importer for slightly less than the excise duty. As we have seen, the termination of identity passes was discussed in an 1890 Crown Council as a means to assist agriculture.

When eastern farmers began to agitate for abolition as a minimum compensation for the treaties, the government began to consider such a step. On 23 December 1893, the East Prussian Conservative League published a letter demanding bimetallism and an end to identity passes in compensation for the damage a treaty with Russia would entail. Caprivi replied, "I consider the abolishing of the identity pass useful for the eastern provinces without damaging the interests of the totality or another part of the empire."[124] He refused even to consider a double currency. The problem lay in the opposition of the east to the abolition of the sliding scale on railroad rates, and the antagonism of western farmers to the termination of identity passes without the concomitant end of cheaper railroad rates. To win the support of agrarians for the Russian treaty, Caprivi saw to it that the Prussian minister president, Eulenberg, terminated both the passes and the sliding scale. Western farmers thus lost an undesirable competitor, and the Junkers regained their Scandinavian markets. It will be demonstrated below that the new passes provided an immense stimulation to the export of German grain, although considered from a military point of view it necessitated a great risk. Should a war break out after Germany had exported its surplus grain, and before Russia exported its surpluses to replace it, the nation could be starved out within a short time. This was very nearly the case in 1914. Despite this concession to agriculture, rural representatives continued to claim that Caprivi was hostile to farmers. In his diary, Kardorff admitted that the new passes "were a very sufficient compensation for agriculture."[125] He would have voted for the Russian treaty because of the passes, had the currency question and his protectionist principles not forbidden it.

Because of an interpellation in the Prussian upper chamber, a

124. *Schulthess'* 35 (1894).
125. Siegfried von Kardorff, p. 292.

99

ministerial conference was convened on 17 January 1894 to draw up a reply to a deputy who had accused the government of ignoring agriculture.[126] In addition to the above-mentioned measures, the establishment of agricultural chambers in every district was suggested. This was long overdue, and at a cabinet meeting the only discussion was whether to make the chambers optional or compulsory. Caprivi also said that a committee was being formed at Kardorff's insistence to debate the issue of bimetallism. Although he personally placed little value in such an undertaking, the persistence of the agrarians had convinced him of the wisdom of allowing them to air their opinions.

Thus, in numerous ways Caprivi had sought to ease the rural distress. However, he avoided those measures that would merely have shifted the burden to another group in the population, or would seriously have endangered the defense of the nation. Perhaps it is not really surprising that all these measures were overlooked by agrarians, for they were so accustomed to government intervention in their behalf that only its cessation could make an impression.

CAPRIVI'S FALL

Most historians attribute Caprivi's resignation in October 1894 to his dispute with the emperor over a proposed antisocialist law; yet it is certain that the virulent hatred of the Conservatives aroused by the trade treaties had prepared the path. Actually, he resigned after the Kaiser received a delegation of agrarians whose hostility to him was well known. Caprivi paid dearly for his discovery that

126. DZA, Rep. 90a Crown Council, 17 January 1894. After Caprivi's fall, the Prussian government attempted to aid agriculture further by appropriating 3 million marks for the construction of grain storage warehouses. First adumbrated by O. Glass-Klanin in 1888 and later in *Kornhaus contra Kanitz* (Stettin, 1895), the warehouse plan was intended, as the American Populist subtreasury plan, to improve the farmers' position vis-à-vis the buyer. The former would be able to sell his grain gradually when prices were favorable instead of all at once after the harvest. Although Bavaria and Württemberg followed the Prussian example, the scheme failed within three years, because farmers stored only their poorest-quality grain and proved to be inexperienced and incompetent managers of the warehouses. For a detailed analysis cf. Ulrich Teichmann, *Die Politik der Agrarpreisstützung* (Cologne, 1955), pp. 227ff.

conservatism revolved around narrow vested interests and myths about the soil rather than embracing a theoretical Weltanschauung. He was subjected to insults from men of his own station and, although he bore it stoically, suffered untold anguish. A letter from Graf Hohenthal to State Minister von Metzsch described the Conservatives' attitudes toward Caprivi. "The hate with which he is followed from this side is so intensive that even his honesty and good will have been brought into question."[127] The Graf went on to attribute this hate to the arrogance with which Caprivi had carried out his trade policy. Kardorff described how Conservatives refused to speak with the chancellor at state dinners. He himself, according to his biographer, never showed personal malice toward his foes except in the case of Caprivi.[128] Eulenberg wrote to Bülow in November 1894 that "in four and a half years [Caprivi] has not managed to make a single friend at court."[129] Schmoller believed that the chancellor had simply been sacrificed to the agrarians. When an agrarian journal published an article about Caprivi entitled *Schweinhund*, Caprivi wrote that nothing would surprise him any longer.[130]

This animosity cannot be explained if the treaties are considered from a narrowly economic point of view. To the Junker agrarians they represented the first step in a transfer of power to the urban industrialists. In a conflict of interests between the city (many agrarians noted that the rancor between Social Democrats and industrialists abated during the treaty discussions) and the country, the government had responded more readily to the needs of the former. As a conservative nobleman and initiator of this policy, Caprivi was viewed with the particular venom reserved for heretics

127. Egmont Zechlin, *Staatsstreichpläne Bismarcks und Wilhelm II 1890–1894* (Stuttgart and Berlin), p. 223. Basing his conclusions on the Eulenberg Papers at the Bundesarchiv, J. C. G. Röhl has recently emphasized the importance of agrarian hostility in the events leading to Caprivi's fall. It is clear that Miquel and both Eulenburgs sought Caprivi's dismissal in large part because of the unbridgeable gulf that had developed between the government and the Conservatives over the tariff issue.

128. Siegfried von Kardorff, p. 301.

129. Johannes Haller, *Philip Eulenberg: The Kaiser's Friend* (New York, 1930), pp. 264–66.

130. Schneidewin, "Briefe," p. 146.

rather than opponents. His crime was class betrayal. The antipathy of conservatives might not have led to his de facto dismissal had he received hearty support from the Radical, National Liberal, and Center parties. But these parties were so accustomed to dealing with each issue on its own merits that endorsement of a chancellor, particularly a conservative general, was beyond their range of vision. In 1901 many liberals were to rebuke themselves publicly for not having recognized the merits of Caprivi seven years earlier.

In many respects Caprivi represented what was best in the Prussian conservative military tradition. Because he was a neophyte in politics, his ideals were not corrupted by a sensitivity to vested interests which was the hallmark of German conservatism in the 1890s. His tenure in office proved to be a continual process of disenchantment with what passed for German conservatism. Not many months after his resignation he wrote to a friend of his forebodings about the agrarians.

> In regard to the [agrarian movement] I see only evil, and it appears to me that a revolution by the agrarians is not impossible and for the moment more dangerous than a Social Democratic revolution. If the agrarian agitation continues—who will stop it? . . . When our Junkers begin to make their views dependent on their incomes, and when they make conditions for their patriotism which the state finds impossible to meet, then the best quality in our little nobility, their patriotism, is destroyed, and their value for the state so reduced that one can ask, Is it worth while for the state to make sacrifices for this class?[131]

No other imperial chancellor had the insight or perhaps the courage to recognize that the danger to Germany's future from the right could be greater than that from the left. But no other chancellor had seriously challenged the economic privileges of the Junkers.

131. Ibid.

3 Economic Trends under the Caprivi Treaties

In the preceding chapter the hopes and forebodings of the various parties concerning Caprivi's trade policy were spelled out in some detail. The task of the present chapter will be to examine the German economy during the thirteen years (1892–1905) of the treaties' duration, in order to determine to what extent the fears of the agrarians were borne out and whether an industrial upswing was inaugurated as many free traders had forecast. Such an investigation is necessary because the controversy arising around the turn of the century among professional economists and in the Reichstag centered on the effects of the liberal tariff policy. To understand the polarization of attitudes that developed, the changes in the economic structure have to be ascertained. Without such a perspective the rancor of the conflict over tariffs and industrial capitalism is inexplicable.

The relative position of the working class in these years will also be scrutinized to establish the correctness of the Social Democrats' contention that a tariff reduction increased the real income of the workers. It will be remembered that agrarians foresaw the decline in the profitability of agriculture, and believed that both the peasantry and the large estates would suffer equally from the new policy. Many spokesmen also claimed that industry could not prosper if agriculture remained in the doldrums. Industrialists minimized the harm to the agricultural sector and predicted that the period of tariff stability would usher in an age of expansion and prosperity. Preoccupied primarily with the class conflict, the Social Democrats believed that the treaties would prevent the economic position of the workers from declining to the advantage of the estate owners, who were thought to be the beneficiaries of a protectionist policy.

In the attempt to determine the effects of a tariff policy on the aforementioned sectors of the economy, several pitfalls must be avoided. First, it is difficult to distinguish tariff policy from other domestic measures that may cause an upswing in the economy. Thus, a boom might arise in spite of, rather than because of, a new tariff policy. It might also be erroneous to attribute an upswing to domestic factors if there is worldwide prosperity, which carries along most economies in its wake. Regarding the former danger, it can be said that Caprivi's treaties constituted the only significant change in economic policy from 1890 to 1906, so that there is small likelihood of another factor's having influenced the economy to any great extent. The latter possibility, however, presents several problems. During the efficacy of the treaties, the European economy revived from the stagnation persisting since the crash in 1873, and a period of expansion set in that lasted with some breaks until the First World War. The German upswing can be viewed as merely a by-product of the more general phenomenon. This approach avoids some very fundamental questions. It is theoretically conceivable that the German developments caused, rather than were caused by, a European revival. Since the treaties came into force just prior to the upswing, it is likely that they were of considerable importance in stimulating the continent's economy. This is not to deny a multiplicity of other factors such as the increase in the amount of gold, caused by discoveries in Alaska and South Africa. Comparisons must also be drawn to establish the progress of the various national economies during the boom period. If it can be shown that the tariff policy of certain nations allowed them to expand at a much faster rate than others, the tariff policy may merit praise for permitting the nation to utilize the boom period more successfully.

Although no clear line can be drawn to distinguish the effects of tariffs on a nation's economy from all the other causal factors at work, the attempt to evaluate tariffs need not therefore be abandoned. It must merely be kept in mind that tariffs are not the sole cause of prosperity or depression, and that the weight of their role varies from age to age and nation to nation. In trading nations such as Great Britain and Germany, the role has always been more direct than in nations with large domestic markets and abundant resources.

EMIGRATION

When Caprivi introduced the Austrian treaty, he emphasized his desire to bring the unusually high rate of emigration to a halt. Since the approval of Bismarck's protectionist legislation, the number deserting Germany, mainly for the United States, had risen to startling proportions. Judging by the statistics, economic opportunity in America appeared more attractive than the advantages of German unity for many less privileged Germans. A total of 33,000 emigrants left in 1870; the number jumped to 117,000 in the following year, and 220,000 during the year after that.[1] An increase of 600 percent in two years attested to the belief of most rural day laborers that conditions had not improved with unification. During the remainder of the decade the number fluctuated around the average of 125,000. The combination of high bread prices and industrial depression caused the amount to increase by 30,000 in the first two years of Caprivi's rule. Of every 100,000 of the population, emigrants averaged approximately 270 yearly during the 1880s, but fell to 197 in 1888, only to reach 241 in 1890.[2] During the first full

1. *Statistisches Jahrbuch für das deutsche Reich* (1913), p. 347; Mack Walker, *Germany and the Emigration, 1816–1885* (Cambridge, 1964); Jürgen Kuczynski, *Die Geschicte der Lage der Arbeiter unter dem Kapitalismus* (Berlin, 1962), 3:267–75.

2. W. H. Dawson, *The Evolution of Modern Germany* (London, 1908), p. 238.

year in which the Austrian treaty was in effect, only 87,600 Germans emigrated, the lowest number since 1879. As the other treaties came into force, the amount diminished to 41 at the decade's end.[3]

The decline is surprisingly large when one considers the growth of population. During the two decades after the achievement of unity, the population of the empire increased by an average of 400,000 per year, but in the period when emigration leveled off, the growth rose to 670,000 yearly. Clearly, the rate should have in-

TABLE 11   EMIGRATION

YEAR	NUMBER
1891	120,000
1892	116,000
1893	87,600
1894	41,000
1895	37,000
1896	34,000
1897	25,000
1898	22,000
1899	24,000

SOURCE: *Statistisches Jahrbuch für das deutsche Reich,* 1893, 1914.

creased had not some unforeseen factors begun to exert considerable influence. In *Auswanderung und Auswanderungspolitik in Deutschland,* a publication of the Verein für Sozialpolitik, the editors, writing in 1892, prognosticated a continuing high rate of emigration for the 1890s. Caprivi's supporters, of course, attributed the rapid diminution to the success of his trade policy, but were subject to criticism from agrarian apologists such as Adolf Wagner, who perceived the pertinent factor to be the sparsity of untilled land remaining in the United States.[4] According to this view, the desire to emigrate continued to prevail but the destination was no longer enticing. If this was true of the United States, it still fails to explain

3. *Statistisches Jahrbuch für das deutsche Reich,* 1893, 1914.
4. Adolf Wagner, *Grundlegung der politischen Ökonomie,* 2d ed., p. 557; "Volksmehrung und Auswanderung," *Münchener Allgemeine Zeitung,* Beilage, 10 June 1880.

why the destination did not change to Canada, Australia, or Argentina, where land remained plentiful. Even in the United States, opportunity was manifold in the cities, where two million Jews from Russia and a myriad of Italians found employment in the succeeding decade. In one respect Wagner's criticism was valid. The rural day laborers of the east had not suddenly become enamored of their surroundings, and the desire to leave the large estates had not abated. Actually, more laborers left the Junker estates in the 1890s than in any preceding or subsequent decade. The movement of population was unprecedented, but instead of forsaking Germany, the migrants poured into the western financial and industrial centers. Table 12 outlines the growth of Germany's important cities in the decade under examination and the percentage of the population born outside the urban areas.[5] From this table it

TABLE 12   URBAN GROWTH

CITY	1890	1900	PERCENT BORN OUT OF THE CITY
Königsberg	161,000	188,000	56
Danzig	120,000	140,000	49
Hanover	163,000	236,000	62
Frankfurt	180,000	288,000	61.7
Cologne	282,000	370,000	47
Munich	350,000	500,000	64
Dresden	276,000	395,000	61.8
Leipzig	295,000	455,000	59.8

SOURCE: *Vierteljahrsheft zur Statistik des deutschen Reiches*, 1901 p. 225.

can be assumed that the cities were able to accommodate a larger number of rural laborers than had been the case under Bismarck's rule. Emigration had been the result of the inability of cities to absorb the surplus farm labor in search of more lucrative and secure employment. A table of population migration in Prussia's provinces during the two five-year periods of the 1890s (table 13),

5. *Vierteljahrsheft zur Statistik des deutschen Reiches* (1901), p. 225. Karl E. Born, "Der soziale und wirtschaftliche Strukwandel Deutschlands am Ende des 19. Jahrhunderts," *Vierteljahrsschrift für Sozial- und Wirtschaftsgeschichte* 50 (1963): 362.

TABLE 13   POPULATION CHANGE

PROVINCE	1890/95	1895/1900
East Prussia	−87,000	−146,000
West Prussia	−67,000	− 69,000
Berlin	+16,000	+126,000
Pomerania	−54,000	− 54,000
Posen	−90,000	−127,000
Silesia	−77,000	− 73,000
Westphalia	+35,000	+178,000
Rhineland	+17,000	+181,000

SOURCE: *Vierteljahrsheft zur Statistik des deutschen Reiches,* 1901.

shows rising numbers leaving the east, with foreign migration simultaneously dwindling. The reason for the decline of emigration, then, must be sought in the cities. From 1890 to 1900 the urban population of the empire rose by 12 percent, and the rural population declined by a corresponding number. An urban migration of such proportions without force or famine as a stimulant is unknown in modern European history. Below, it will be shown how Caprivi's trade policy can be credited for the tremendous expansion of trade and industry that was necessary if the cities were to accommodate the discontented laborers of the east.

One of the reasons frequently proffered by Conservatives for their rejection of the lower grain duties had been their apprehension that total tariff revenue would thereby decline. If their fears were realized, they believed that the government would have to resort to taxing agriculture in order to compensate for the revenue

TABLE 14   TARIFF REVENUE

	AMOUNT COLLECTED IN 1,000 MARKS	PENNIES PER HEAD
1891	107,000	0
1895	108,000	208
1897	134,000	251
1899	128,000	231
1901	159,000	279
1903	162,000	277
1905	180,000	299

SOURCE: *Vierteljahrsheft zur Statistik des deutschen Reiches* 1897, 1901.

loss. In table 14 the inaccuracy of the pessimistic prediction can be seen. Assuming that Caprivi's treaties would not spur trade, the Conservatives made the error of simply deducting the amount of the reduction from the total income. In fact, trade increased as Caprivi had anticipated, and the lower rates were more than made up for by the expanding volume of imports. Not only did the total income rise, but, as the third column of the table indicates, the revenue per inhabitant increased measurably.

INDUSTRIAL GROWTH

When World War I began, Germany was the leading industrial nation on the European continent and in some respects even more advanced than Great Britain. The speed with which the empire overtook its British competitor has led many economic historians to designate 1870 as the takeoff point for German industrialization. There is some truth in this assertion; however, if one reviews the industrial gains made between 1870 and 1890, the tempo is disappointing. Germany certainly would have lacked the resources to endure a four-year war in 1914 if the rate of growth after 1890 had been similar to that of the two previous decades. In order to increase exports, a nation such as Germany at the close of the last century had to expand its industrial production. Caprivi had hoped that his policy would solve the problem of stagnating production

TABLE 15   INDEX OF INDUSTRIAL GROWTH

	1880	1890	1900	1910
Germany	25	40	65	89
Britain	53	62	79	85
France	43	56	66	89
Russia	17	27	61	89
U.S.A.	17	39	54	89
World	26	43	60	88

SOURCE: Wagenfuhr, "Das Geheimnis der Gegenseitigkeit im Wirtschaftsleben," *Vierteljahrsheft zur Konjunkturforschung* 2, pt. A (1936), pp. 16, 18. The volume of industrial production per head (1900 = 100) advanced from 62 in the years 1868–78, to 70 from 1879–86, to 82 from 1887–94, and to 102 in the Caprivi tariff period. Kuczynski, *Die Geschichte der Lage der Arbeiter unter dem Kapitalismus* (Berlin, 1962), 3:114. Also see W. G. Hoffmann, *Das Wachstum der deutschen Wirtschaft seit der Mitte des 19. Jahrhunderts* (Berlin, 1965), pp. 347–74.

and exports simultaneously with the problem of emigration. He realized that if production rose, the accompanying need for labor would alleviate the necessity to emigrate. Table 15 presents an index of industrial growth for the pertinent years with 100 equivalent to 1913.

A glance at the statistics of the steel industry will confirm the impression that the bulk of German industrialization took place during the tenure of Caprivi's treaties. From table 16 it can be seen that Germany outstripped all its competitors in the percentage gain of steel production. According to the index table, the German economy began a spurt the very year the Austrian treaty went into effect, which continued unabated until the treaty's termination in 1906. A recent study of Germany from 1870 to 1945 by an economist seems to verify the progress outlined on the index. Gerald Bry finds that there were eight boom years, three years of moderate growth, two years of recession, and one year of capital shortage in the period between 1893 and 1906.[6] No other period before Adenauer's administration compares favorably with the span of the trade treaties.

TABLE 16   STEEL PRODUCTION (In millions of tons)

	1880	1895	1898	1899
U.S.A.	1.3	6.3	9.0	10.7
Germany	.6	2.8	5.7	6.3
Britain	1.3	3.4	4.6	4.9
France	.4	.7	1.4	1.5

SOURCE: F. C. Huber, *Deutschland als Industriestaat* (Stuttgart, 1901) p. 299.

A substantial rise in productivity should be reflected in the proliferation of businesses and an increased need for labor. That this happened appears to be borne out by the statistical yearbooks and subsequent studies. Between 1896 and 1906, corporations with ten million marks in capital increased from 108 to 208, whereas in 1886 there had been only 74. The number of businesses employing less

6. Gerald Bry, *Wages in Germany* (Princeton, 1960), p. 475.

than 200 workers doubled between 1895 and 1907. In the same period those having between 200 and 1,000 workers rose from 1,781 to 3,000. Table 17, showing the number of factories and employees in the major German industries, attests to the stepped-up pace of industrialization. It thus appears incontrovertible that German industrialists utilized the stable period inaugurated by the trade pacts to increase their investment in capital equipment and thereby provide more employment. In the surplus rural population they found a source of cheap labor which would have been absorbed by the United States had the industrial outlook been unfavorable.

TABLE 17 NUMBER OF PLANTS AND EMPLOYEES IN GERMAN INDUSTRIES

INDUSTRY	1895		1907	
	PLANTS	EMPLOYEES	PLANTS	EMPLOYEES
Chemicals	10,385	115,231	10,562	172,441
Machines	87,879	582,672	94,492	1,120,282
Textiles	205,364	993,257	136,364	1,088,280
Paper	17,361	152,909	19,787	230,925
Trade	635,209	1,332,993	842,140	2,063,634
Construction	198,985	1,045,516	208,418	1,563,395

SOURCE: *Statistisches Jahrbuch für Preussen* (Berlin, 1913). More joint stock companies were founded in each of the years from 1897 to 1900 than in any year (apart from 1889) between 1872 and 1914. Kuczynski, *A Short History of Labour Conditions under Industrial Capitalism* (London, 1945), vol. 3, pt. 1, p. 122. Hoffmann, *Das Wachstum*, pp. 215–50.

"Either we export men or we export goods." In this fashion Caprivi had attempted to impress upon the deputies the need to end the stagnation in foreign trade. For over a decade the value of foreign trade per capita had remained at about 135 marks. Protective duties had failed to diminish the growth of imports, and exports had not risen. If the predictions of Bassermann of the National Liberals and Rickert of the Radicals about the waxing of exports as a result of tariff treaties had been true, Caprivi's aim would have been realized.

Judging by the foreign trade per head of the population, the treaties were a success, for the 144 marks of 1893 rose to 179 by

111

1900 and 219 in 1905.[7] The total value of exports and imports increased from 8,195 million marks in 1890 to 15,554 million in 1906. Although the treaties seemed to have been successful in activating foreign trade, an analysis of trade with the treaty countries shows that the general European economic recovery of the 1890s also played a major role.

TABLE 18   GERMAN TRADE WITH TREATY NATIONS
(In millions of marks)

	1893	1905
Austria		
Imports	580	773
Exports	420	594
Romania		
Imports	84	94
Exports	43	44
Italy		
Imports	249	215
Exports	85	175
Switzerland		
Imports	143	190
Exports	187	369
Russia		
Imports	353	1090
Exports	184	368

SOURCE: *Statistisches Jahrbuch für das deutsche Reich* 1894, 1906.

Trade with the nations listed in table 18 increased considerably but not as much as the total rise in the volume of trade would lead one to expect. This is to be explained by the direction of German trade. The nations with which Germany carried on the bulk of its trade were bound by "most favored nation" clauses. Thus, the volume of trade with the treaty nations was on the whole secondary to that with the U.S.A., Great Britain, and France. It would be incorrect, however, to minimize the direct effect of the treaties, and attribute

7. Ernst Wagemann, *Konjunkturlehre* (Berlin, 1928), p. 277. The percentage increase in exports doubled during the first eight years of the Caprivi treaties and was higher than during the succeeding eight-year period. Jürgen Kuczynski, *A Short History of Labour Conditions under Industrial Capitalism* (London, 1945), 1, pt. 1, p. 126.

the expansion of exports mainly to the flourishing trade with recipients of the "most favored nation" clauses. Table 19 outlines the percent increase in exports with the treaty countries in goods whose duties were lowered by treaty.

TABLE 19   PERCENTAGE OF INCREASE IN EXPORTS

Austria	75
Belgium	130
Switzerland	131
Italy	175
Russia	370

SOURCE: Handelvertragsverein, ed., *Die Wirkungen der Handelsverträge* (Berlin, 1901). Germany's share of world trade rose by 2 percent from 1890 to 1900; only America equalled this increase. Kuczynski, *Die Geschichte*, 3:124.

TABLE 20   EXPORTS (In millions of marks)

	1890	1900
Chemicals	130	238
Machines	68	206
Light industrial goods	70	153
Heavy industrial goods	167	329
Stone and glass	63	109
Toys and jewelry	60	136
Educational materials	61	114

SOURCE: Verein für Sozialpolitik ed., *Beiträge zur neuesten Handelspolitik Österreichs* vol. 90 (Berlin, 1901), appendix; Hoffmann, *Das Wachstum*, pp. 517–24.

The *Verein für Sozialpolitik* concluded after investigating the trade with treaty nations that German statisticians tended to underestimate the growth of exports. Using Austrian statistics, the editors found that the amount was much higher and seemed to accord with the estimations of industrialists. The tables showing the nature and amount of the exports were found to present a more accurate picture.

Apart from statistics, the success of Caprivi's policy was noticeable from the reaction of many industries when the treaties expired. As early as 1896, the Berlin Merchants' Association *Altesten der Kaufmannschaft von Berlin* reported, "It must be conceded that the treaties have certainly had those favorable consequences for Germany's export trade which impartial judges predicted would result from them."[8] A group of export-oriented industries banded together at that time to urge the government to continue Caprivi's policy. This organization, called the League for Trade Treaties (*Handelsvertragsverein*), published a series of pamphlets written by leading industrialists who believed that their industries could prosper only if the treaties were continued. One pamphlet, written by a prominent clothing manufacturer, claimed that the industry's export markets had been created since 1892 and would disappear if the treaties were not looked upon as a precedent.[9] The photography industry's representative recounted the tremendous expansion of Russian orders that had occurred within a short period.[10] Among the numerous other industrialists contributing pamphlets were the manufacturers of toys, jewelry, linen, grain meal, and chemicals. In a concluding piece, the editors praised Caprivi for his foresight and expressed their conviction that "the total development of foreign trade in the time of Caprivi's treaties far outweighed that in the years of Bismarck's protectionist policy."[11] Even Sartorius von Waltershausen, an economic historian critical of free trade, judged that the treaties with the exception of the Austrian had more or less fulfilled all reasonable expectations. In his opinion, the Russian treaty had produced more favorable results than any subsequent agreement.[12] A specialist on the metallurgical industry reported that the sudden growth of the Austrian, Russian, and Swiss markets had brought an unexpected wave of prosperity. Conservative economists such as Adolf Wagner admitted in unguarded moments that Germany had never witnessed a boom to compare with the one of the 1890s, though they believed

8. W. H. Dawson, *Protection in Germany* (London, 1904), p. 124.

9. Dr. Feitelberg, "Bekleidung," *Interesse an der neuen Handelsverträge* (Berlin, 1901).

10. Fritz Hansen, "Photographie," *Interesse an der neuen Handelsverträge* (Berlin, 1901).

11. G. von Siemens, *Rede über die Handelsverträge* (Berlin, 1901).

12. A. Sartorius von Walthershausen, *Deutsche Wirtschaftsgeschichte,* p. 425.

it augured evil for the future. Before he died in 1898, Caprivi wrote that his most important contribution had been the trade treaties and the augmentation of the military's manpower.[13] When the treaties lapsed, few critics claimed that the predictions made in 1891 about increased trade had been unduly optimistic.

In defending his policy, Caprivi had stressed the government's responsibility to the masses of urban workers. He hoped, no doubt, that his policy would lessen socialist hostility to his government and the empire. The Social Democrats chose to throw their full support behind the chancellor because they anticipated that the success of the treaties would cause industry to prosper and food prices to remain relatively stable. Such developments would enhance the relative position of the working class in the economy. To help evaluate the advantages or disadvantages of the treaties for the laboring and consuming population, tables 21–23 analyze costs and wages. It must be remembered that tariffs do not determine costs but merely add to the price of a commodity. Since Caprivi had lowered the rates on agricultural goods, German prices tended to be lower than they had previously been in years of inflationary rises and deflationary slumps. They would, in effect, approach the world price more nearly than the previous higher rates. Table 21 shows the results of numerous investigations into the average cost of food in the period under consideration. Under each analyst is listed the area or cities for which the research is valid—the year

TABLE 21   INDEX OF FOOD COSTS

	KU-CZYNSKI: EMPIRE	JUNGST: 4 CITIES	KRUPP: ESSEN	BRUTZER: BERLIN	ZAHN: BAVARIA
1888–90	95	96	98	101	100
1891–93	95	102	100	111	101
1894–96	95	98	96	98	98
1897–99	98	99	98	99	101
1900–02	101	101	102	102	102

SOURCE: Gerald Bry, *Wages in Germany* (Princeton, 1960), p. 354.

13. Max Schneidewin, "Briefe des Reichkanzler Caprivi," *Deutsche Revue* 1 (1922).

1900 equals 100 on the index.[14] The table indicates that food prices remained unusually stable over a fifteen-year period. This was due in part to the lack of fluctuation on the world market and in part to lower grain duties. If higher grain rates had been maintained, the price structure would have been stable but at a much higher level. A sampling of bread and meat prices in various cities will confirm the conclusions drawn from the table. Interviewing Berlin bakers, the *Zeitschrift für Agrarpolitik* found that after a temporary rise in 1891 and 1892, rye prices remained at about twenty-one pennies per kilogram for the next six years, and then increased moderately.[15] According to the Imperial Statistical Bureau, the price of beef varied less than four pennies per kilogram in the decade subsequent to the treaties' introduction. Similar studies of bread prices showed a remarkable uniformity marred only by a slight rise after the turn of the century. Although a number of treatises on general

TABLE 22   COST OF LIVING (1913 = 100)

YEAR	INDEX
1891	77
1892	76
1893	75
1894	74
1895	73
1896	72
1897	74
1898	76
1899	76
1900	77
1901	78
1902	77
1903	78
1904	79

SOURCE: Gerald Bry, *Wages in Germany*, p. 464; Kuczynski, *Die Geschichte*, 3:302; Hoffmann, *Das Wachstum*, pp. 630–31.

14. See Kuczynski, *Die Geschichte* 3:436; Hoffmann, *Das Wachstum der deutschen Wirtschaft seit der Mitte des 19. Jahrhunderts* (Berlin, 1965), pp. 617–58. The major works on wages, cost of living, etc. are those by Kuczynski, Bry, and Hoffmann. Although they disagree on details, the authors agree on trends. Where possible, references will be given from all three works.
15. Editors, *Zeitschrift für Agrarpolitik*, December 1903.

living costs were compiled by economists before World War I, they showed a marked tendency to reflect the biases of the writer. Gerald Bry's recent work is free from this objection.[16] Numerous very specialized studies all came to the conclusion that the German cost of living hardly rose from 1892 to 1904. The real income of the worker would not have undergone much change if the stability in prices had been matched by the same pattern in wages. This was not the case, however, as the expansion of industry caused employers to bid for reliable labor. The index of wages in some representative industries requiring skilled labor is shown in Table 23.

TABLE 23   WAGE INDEX (1913 = 100)

YEAR	METAL	CHEM-ICALS	BUILD-ING	CLOTH-ING	PRINT-ING
1890	62.1	67.5	62.2	61.7	93.9
1892	62.2	68.9	62.6	64.6	84.9
1894	63.0	68.8	62.1	65.9	79.5
1896	65.2	70.7	65.0	70.0	77.6
1898	69.1	73.7	69.1	71.3	87.6
1900	71.3	75.4	74.1	72.0	88.2
1902	72.7	75.4	74.1	74.9	85.4
1904	76.7	78.9	76.5	82.4	84.1

SOURCE: Gerald Bry, *Wages in Germany,* p. 472; Kuczynski, *Die Geschichte,* 3:295–319; Hoffmann, *Das Wachstum,* pp. 458–59.

Almost all industries show substantial wage increases in the designated period, and even printing did not fare poorly if the unrepresentative year 1890 is omitted. Daily average earnings for workers of the Krupp complex increased from 4 to 5.35 marks in the same time span. Miners in the Ruhr area earned approximately 976 marks in 1892, and about 1175 marks in 1901.[17] From these figures it would appear that income rose 15 percent in thirteen years, or slightly more than 1 percent per year.

Of the studies undertaken to determine the growth of real income in pre–World War I Germany, the work of Bry and an earlier German economist, Tyszka, agree about the rise, almost to the per-

16. *Wages in Germany.*
17. Wagemann, *Konjunkturlehre,* p. 297.

cent. Because of his Marxist bias, Kuczynski posits a somewhat smaller rise. A volume published by the German Statistical Bureau in 1932 shows a much smaller increase, but is suspect because in the years after 1906 the results depart significantly from all other studies. The latter work appears defective, especially as it shows an increase in the year 1906 when prices skyrocketed, and wages continued their moderate climb. Bry believes that from 1871 to 1890 the index rose from 74 to 87, and in the next decade, to 98.[18] Tyszka lists the real income as rising from 77 to 88 in a fifteen-year period.[19] If Bry's figures are continued for five more years, they show little relative change, so the rate of growth appears to have been 14 percent for the 1890s with little change thereafter.

Several other criteria suggest impressive improvements in the state of the working class in the era of Caprivi's agreements. For example, the number of Prussians having savings bank accounts had increased by three million in the fifteen years prior to the treaties, and by another two and a half million in the next eight years. Yearly deposits also showed unprecedented rises. In Bavaria the number of depositors rose by 60 percent in ten years, and savings climbed by 67 percent.[20] All of these rises were far greater than what could be expected from a normal response to population growth. The growing prosperity was evident in the fall of the death rate also. Between 1852 and 1891 the rate per thousand declined from 29.9 to 24.7, but only eleven years later it had dropped to 20.6. Perhaps the best evidence of the improvement in working-class conditions was the publication of *The Propositions of Socialism and the Problems of Social Democracy* by Eduard Bernstein in 1899.[21] Familiarity with German conditions led Bernstein to reject Marx's contention that the masses would become ever more impoverished. His comprehensive critique of Marxism was based

18. *Wages in Germany*, pp. 71–73; Kuczynski, *A Short History*, pp. 129–30.

19. Carl von Tyszka, "Löhne und Lebenskosten in Westeuropa im 19ten Jahrhundert," *Schriften des Vereins für Sozialpolitik 145* (1914): 281.

20. Editors, "Sparkassen," *Handwörterbuch der Staatswissenschaften*, 2d ed.

21. E. Bernstein, *Die Voraussetzungen des Sozialismus und die Aufgaben der Sozialdemokratie* (Stuttgart, 1899).

largely on his observations of the industrial boom and simultaneous improvement of the workers' real income. Caprivi's treaties must be conceded most of the credit for holding down prices, for an autonomous tariff policy never would have accomplished this objective. Certainly, a series of tariff wars in the 1890s would have severely retarded economic development. On the whole, Ricardo's dictum that the real conflict is not between worker and employer but between both of these and the landowner appears to hold true for the 1890s. Both manufacturer and laborer progressed as they had never done before. Now we must turn to the landowners, who had prognosticated a catastrophe if the treaties went into effect.

AGRICULTURE

Agriculture presents many more problems to the analyst than industry and labor do. Simple statistical charts about prices, production, and trade do not suffice for agriculture because of the diversity of crops cultivated and the size of farms. Unlike industrialists, farmers cannot determine the costs of production with accuracy, nor are these costs consistent from year to year. We shall therefore examine a number of guideposts usually considered to be indicators of agricultural prosperity. Prices are the first such indicator.

TABLE 24   GRAIN PRICES (Marks per 1,000 kilograms)

YEAR	WHEAT	RYE	BARLEY	OATS
1892	176	176	149	149
1893	151	133	131	157
1894	136	117	122	131
1895	142	114	110	121
1896	156	118	129	115
1897	173	130	130	131
1898	185	146	139	144
1899	155	146	128	123
1900	151	140	129	125
1901	163	100	132	138
1902	163	144	127	145
1903	161	132	128	122
1904	174	135	130	123

SOURCE: *Statistisches Jahrbuch für das deutsche Reich,* 1906; Hoffmann, *Das Wachstum,* pp. 552–56.

Declining prices in the mid-1890s were a direct result of bumper crops in all major grain exporting lands. After a brief recovery in 1898, wheat and rye prices remained at low levels until 1905. Barley and oat prices never declined as much as the bread grains, nor was their cultivation unprofitable in the 1890s. To place the price decline in the proper perspective, it must be pointed out that London wheat prices averaged thirty-three marks lower than the German in the 1890s, and thirty-six marks lower in the first five years of the twentieth century. A glance at a price graph would also show prices to have been at similar levels in the 1820s, 1830s, and for a time in the 1850s. Contemporary agricultural analysts have not followed the agrarians in viewing the prices as unprecedently low but, like Heinz Haushofer, have called it "the severest decline since the middle of the century."[22] Nevertheless, the eastern estates and numerous middle-sized western farms whose principal crop was grain were forced to endure a decade of prices that frequently fell below their production costs. Low prices were a worldwide phenomenon, and agrarian claims that higher duties meant higher prices were valid. The agrarians failed, however, to consider the handicaps industry and labor would have been saddled with, had a five mark duty been retained. Prospects were, in any event, not as gloomy as grain prices led them to appear. A table of meat and dairy prices shows that many western farmers could view the price levels with equanimity.

It is customary in most lands for farmers to abandon crops that

TABLE 25   PRICE INDEX, BAVARIA (1881 = 100)

YEAR	OX	CALF	PIG	MILK	BUTTER	EGGS
1881	100	100	100	100	100	100
1890	123	131	106	93	101	105
1895	125	137	104	106	100	100
1900	119	133	106	106	104	105
1905	133	150	124	106	111	118

SOURCE: *Statistisches Jahrbuch für Bayern* (Munich, 1911), p. 211. Also see W. Hoffmann, *Das Wachstum,* pp. 556–60.

22. Haushofer, *Die deutsche Landwirtschaft im technischen Zeitalter* (Stuttgart, 1963), p. 209.

bring in no return and give no promise of doing so. Certainly, few farmers would expand the acreage under the plow of a crop selling at extremely unfavorable prices. Yet this was the practice in Germany. Between 1891 and 1905, the number of acres devoted to rye rose by 1,700,000; to wheat, by 100,000; oats by 75,000; and only those devoted to barley dropped by 420,000. Conservative politicians and economists habitually criticized the reduced rates because they believed that such a policy seriously weakened the nation's capability of feeding itself in time of war. Economic nationalism was supposedly the only method of keeping the nation prepared for all contingencies. Surprisingly, the statistics do not bear out this argument. Although it is difficult to draw exact comparisons of harvests because the manner of estimation was changed in 1892, the general trend can be determined. In table 26 the statistics begin with 1893 to avoid the differing methods of estimating the harvests.

TABLE 26   HARVESTS (1879–1882 = 100)

YEAR	RYE	WHEAT	BARLEY	OATS
1893–96	116	114	108	109
1897–00	134	134	122	135
1901–04	159	148	143	155

SOURCE: *Statistisches Jahrbuch für das deutsche Reich,* 1899, 1906; Hoffmann, *Das Wachstum,* p. 288.

The harvests of the southern state Baden showed a 25 percent increase in bread grains during the eleven-year period. Several other studies confirm the immense rise in food production in a period of liberal trade policy. According to a graph in a recent work by Graf von Finckenstein, the production of grain in Prussia moved in the following pattern: 1879–82 = 100; 1891 = 99; 1895 = 116; 1900 = 122; 1905 = 140.[23] A chart in a postwar study by Johannes Conrad, a leading agricultural economist, showed a percent increase in the four grains of 59, 48, 43, and 55 respectively in the quarter-century following the introduction of protection,

23. H. W. Graf von Finckenstein, *Die Entwicklung der Landwirtschaft in Preussen und Deutschland* (Basle, 1959), vol 3, graph 3.

with by far the largest part of it falling in the period of Caprivi's treaties.[24] Yield-per-acre averages also showed substantial improvement. In a three-volume work on Prussian agriculture, von Finckenstein concluded that there were two turning points between the Congress of Vienna and the World War—1861 and 1891. He wrote that "after 1891 the development of great intensity was reached, in which grains showed a strong increase in yields."[25] Indeed, Eckart Kehr considered the Caprivi era the most successful in raising production figures of any between 1871 and the war. He claimed that Germany was able to hold out for so long only because of Caprivi's trade policy.[26] From the last years of Bismarck's autonomous policy to the lapse of Caprivi's treaties, grain yields per acre rose by 21 percent, or more than they had since mid-century. This period experienced large capital investments in agriculture to improve techniques and expand acreage.

A malady common to almost all German political economists is their uncritical belief that the Junkers were the most efficient farmers in the empire. This was not, however, the conclusion of a comprehensive work done at the century's end, in which 1100 communities and estates were put under observation. Except for rye, small farms demonstrated a much higher yield in grain per acre than the estates. The conclusion was emphatic: "The productivity of cultivation in small enterprises is with regard to the total arable area absolutely greater than in the estates."[27] Care, attention, and better use of fertilizers were found to be the cardinal reasons for the efficiency of the farms under fifty acres. These results imply that the Junkers did not show the flexibility and willingness to adapt that the independent farmers did. Apparently, a rigidity had set in among the Junkers that was not noticeable in the 1820s, when they led the way in efficiency. Yields improved on their estates, but

24. J. Conrad and A. Hesse, *Grundriss zum Studium der politischen Ökonomie*, 39th ed. pt. 4 (Jena, 1924), p. 197; Hoffmann, *Das Wachstum*, p. 277.

25. Finckenstein, *Die Entwicklung*, 3:18; Hoffmann, *Das Wachstum*, p. 271.

26. Eckart Kehr, *Schlachtflottenbau und Parteipolitik, 1894–1901* (Berlin, 1930), p. 252.

27. Erich Keup and Richard Mührer, *Die volkswirtschaftliche Bedeutung von Gross- und Kleinbetrieb in der Landwirtschaft* (Berlin, 1913) pp. 128–30.

the improvement was larger and intensive farming greater when estates were broken up into numerous farms.

In the previous chapter, the abolition of the identity passes was listed as one of the significant means by which Caprivi aided agriculture. How much their value was to the Junkers can be judged from the increase in grain exports from 1893, when the passes were not yet ended, and 1894, the first year of the new regulations.[28] Exports rose by several thousand tons for the four major grains between 1893 and 1894. According to the statistical yearbook, the growers of grain to be exported earned 211 million marks from the sale of the new passes. Germany began to export huge quantities of rye in the spring, and to meet domestic needs from the importation of Russian surpluses in the summer. The enticement of an export premium for grain was probably one cause of the expanded acreage and better yields in the east. Of the treaty nations that were expected to deluge Germany with grain, only Russia did so to any extent, and this was a result of the export passes. American grain exports increased by several hundred percent, but this was due to Germany's inability to meet its own needs. The empire's need for foreign grain varied according to the size of the harvest; however, the tendency in Caprivi's time, as it had been in Bismarck's, was for a yearly increase in dependence. Although the production of rye and oats kept pace with the increase in population, the percentage of wheat and barley imported steadily mounted. Despite the growing intensity of cultivation, it was apparent that German farmers could not keep pace with expanding grain consumption. To blame Caprivi for this is to ignore the continuation of this tendency under the later protectionist policy of Chancellor Bülow. It is more likely, as Kehr suggests, that without the treaties the need for imports would have risen more precipitously.

One indicator of rural conditions, often examined along with prices to determine the financial state of farmers, is land prices. The following figures represent the average number of marks per two and one-half acres paid by the Settlement Commission in each of the ten years after the Russian treaty: 503, 609, 539, 785, 727,

---

28. Lujo Brentano, *Die deutschen Getreidezölle,* chart at end; Hoffmann, *Das Wachstum,* p. 154.

869, 821, 753, 778, 968.[29] Contrary to expectations, the trend was irregularly higher. This is confirmed by W. Rothkegel, whose works on land prices are the most comprehensive ever done in Germany for the late nineteenth century. In his *Studies of Value,* he contended that land prices rose on the whole, but less so east of the Elbe, and hardly at all on large estates.[30] A companion study by Aereboe concluded that prices rose rapidly until 1889, when the trend became more moderate.[31] Only on estates over 1200 acres, it was found, had the prices begun to decline. The decline of the value of estates is also apparent from the statistics of their income from rents in the 1890s. A gradual decline set in at the time of the 1893 slump and worsened as grain prices failed to recover. Land price trends confirm the failure of the Junkers to adapt to their new competitors, and their decreased relative efficiency in comparison with western peasants. Where the farmers were flexible and sought to lower production costs, land prices rose in defiance of lower grain prices.

Indebtedness, however, waxed in both east and west Germany in a steady fashion. Whether this occurrence should be viewed as the result of healthy capital investment or last-ditch efforts to preserve farms is difficult to assess. In the eastern areas, where indebtedness had reached 50 percent of the estimated value of the estates, it was no doubt unhealthy and the cause of agrarian radicalism. Spokesmen for bimetallism, high tariffs, and Kanitz's plan were all concerned with wiping out the debt problem that had been created by unwise speculation in the 1870s. Having these burdens, eastern estate owners were much more sensitive to slumps than western peasants, whose debts rarely exceeded one-quarter of their property's value. Conditions were certainly bleak in the east, but not irredeemable, for the number of foreclosures was diminishing considerably. Agrarian observers tended to discount the bankruptcy statistics, and claimed that conditions were so bad that nobles simply abandoned their estates rather than go into bankruptcy. A

29. *Statistisches Jahrbuch für Preussen,* 1913.
30. W. Rothkegel, *Schätzungslehre* (Berlin, 1930), vol. 1, appendix.
31. Friedrich Aereboe, *Die Beurteilung von Landgütern und Grundstücken* (Berlin, 1921), appendix.

TABLE 27   FORECLOSURES IN PRUSSIA

YEAR	NUMBER
1888	2442
1890	2220
1892	2299
1894	1566
1898	1411
1900	1291
1902	1134
1904	1076

SOURCE: *Zeitschrift des Preussischen Statistischen Bureau,* vol. 6 (Berlin, 1901).

more realistic reason for bankruptcy would be the ability of the Junkers to sell their estates to the Settlement Commission or to wealthy businessmen bent on attaining the prestige associated with owning a rural retreat. As government spending on agriculture in Prussia rose from 11¼ million marks in 1890 to 20¼ in 1899, and 26½ in 1904, the situation was not as disastrous as the Conservatives portrayed. Caprivi's policy cannot be censured because of the continued debt problem, since debts multiplied later under the protectionist policy of Bülow also.

Caprivi's belief that more competition would stir agriculture to modernize and adapt was nowhere better substantiated than in the sphere of agricultural technology. Forced to compete with the virgin soils of America and low wages of Russia, German farmers adopted techniques that made them the most efficient intensive farmers in the world. The use of steam machinery more than doubled between 1895 and 1907, while in the same time span the use of potash increased by 700 percent. In twelve years, it is estimated, the number of machines on the farm doubled. The peasantry also showed its resilience by forming cooperatives to promote their mutual welfare. Table 28 shows the growth of peasant organizations. Bavarian peasants belonging to such organizations increased by 130 percent in these years. Another example of the peasant reaction to competition was the growing number of farms devoted to livestock. The number of cows and pigs listed in the periodic censuses grew astonishingly fast, and it is interesting to note that this

TABLE 28   GROWTH OF PEASANT COOPERATIVES

YEAR	CREDIT	PUR-CHASING	DAIRY	OTHER	TOTAL
1890	1,729	557	639	101	3,006
1895	4,872	869	1,222	207	7,170
1900	9,793	1,115	1,917	1,443	19,323

SOURCE: S. Korte, ed., *Deutschland unter Wilhelm II*, 3 vols. (Berlin, 1914), 2:473. Rapid formation of cooperatives was also a common response of American farmers beset by low prices in the 1890s. See R. H. Elsworth, "Agricultural Cooperative Associations," *United States Department of Agriculture Technical Bulletin*, no. 46 (1928).

growth ceased as soon as Bülow raised grain duties. Germans demonstrated during the 1890s their ability to knuckle down under pressure and produce more intensively with better machinery, or, when this was impossible, to change to more lucrative methods of agriculture. For these reasons the numbers of peasant farms did not diminish during the era of Caprivi's treaties, whereas the inflexibility of the Junkers was mirrored in their relative decline. The trend shown in table 29 is toward a decline in percentage proportional to the size of the farm. The sharpness of Junker attacks was no doubt caused by their realization that the government's course, and their opposition to adaptation, threatened their demise as a viable economic group.

On balance, Caprivi's policy allowed the German economy to

TABLE 29   NUMBER OF GERMAN FARMS

ACREAGE	1895	1907
0–5	3,236,367	3,378,509
5–13	1,016,318	1,006,277
13–50	998,804	1,065,539
50–125	239,643	225,697
125–250	42,124	36,494
250–500	11,250	10,679
500–1250	9,631	9,389
1250–2500	3,608	3,129
2500+	572	369

SOURCE: *Statistisches Jahrbuch für das deutsche Reich*, 1907, p. 212.

experience a period of general prosperity unmatched until the *Wirtschaftswunder* of recent years. Industrialists had nothing but praise for the treaties once their effects were obvious, and socialists proved their satisfaction by the acerbity of their tone when the course was abandoned. As to the question of whether the European economic boom or the trade treaties were responsible for the progress, it appears that the treaties provided the stability necessary for the German economy to take the greatest possible advantage from the revival. Apart from Russia, which began from a minute base, no country in the world progressed industrially as fast as Germany between 1890 and 1905. Even more than industrial development, the rise in real income of the working class was a result of the treaties. An autonomous tariff policy would certainly have resulted in a higher cost of living.

Agriculture, however, did not present as clear a picture as did the other sectors of the economy. Burdened with debts and receiving low returns for their labor, eastern estates owners experienced more hardships than other economic groups. In the west, where grain was not so prevalent and a market-oriented economy had not evolved, farmers did not fare badly. The reaction to the slump in prices was, on the whole, healthy; farmers' mutual help organizations were formed, livestock farming increased, and technology was introduced to make farming more intensive. It seems clear, nonetheless, that, in terms of wealth produced, agriculture was rapidly falling far behind the industrial sector. Western farmers did not prosper as well as workers or industrialists, but held their own in a time of unusually severe crisis. As conditions in the east are customarily exaggerated, it is well worth noting again that bankruptcies declined and land prices rose moderately during the years of the slump. Because the Junkers were relatively inflexible in the face of change, the crisis was probably harsher than necessary. Their expectations that the government would "bail them out" of their difficulties proved unjustified. Their actions seemed to attest to the traditional free trade argument that once a group becomes accustomed to protection, it loses the vitality to respond to competition. Frequently, agrarians claimed that climatic conditions prevented the east from transforming the grain economy of the area. But this belies the changes of the 1920s, when grain agriculture became exceedingly unprofitable. At that time the number of pigs in the east multiplied many times, showing that nature was not the only cause of the earlier inflexibility. A higher tariff in the 1890s would only have given sustenance to the Junkers' desire to resist change.

The combination of malaise in agriculture and rapid industrial expansion was viewed with uneasiness by Oldenberg, Wagner, and Sering. Accustomed to weighing the social and political implications of economic developments, they predicted a time of troubles for Germany. We now turn to the problems they foresaw and the solutions offered.

PART TWO

It is generally believed that the socialists were the first to criticize capitalism as a social system; in actual fact, however, there are many indications that this criticism was initiated by the right wing opposition and was then gradually taken over by the left opposition. . . . The abstractness of human relationships under capitalism which is constantly emphasized by Marx and his followers was originally the discovery of observers from the conservative camp.

Karl Mannheim

4

The Conservative Persuasion

Despite the progressive Stein-Hardenberg reforms, the spirit permeating Prussia in the early decades of the nineteenth century was still a corporate one. The power of the landed gentry over farm labor was essentially feudal in nature; money wages were not introduced until the 1840s and '50s. In neighboring Mecklenburg-Schwerin, representation in state government was by estates as in centuries past. The kind of patriarchal and organic thought that characterized cameralism was still a strong force in the eastern states of the German Confederation long after it had ceased to impress British and French economists.[1] It should not be surprising, therefore, that the earliest critiques of industrial capitalism were from the pens of conservatives enamored of the Prussian *Ständesstaat*. Even before factories dotted the Prussian landscape, Adam Müller and Johann Gottlieb Fichte lamented the commer-

1. When the University of Berlin was founded, one of the most important chairs was in "Cameralist Studies." Until mid-century, many German universities, including those in the South, entitled their chairs in economics in the above fashion.

cialization of British society. Socialist criticism of capitalism had to await the physical existence of industrial enterprise in the Ruhr.

In his *Agrarische Briefe,* Müller expressed his conviction that economics would always be subordinated to more fundamental values in a healthy society. Agriculture was of course the foundation of any worthy social order. He wrote, "I would like to speak of the exclusive and eternal marriage of a people [*Volk*] with a particular body of soil; upon this depends all prosperity and all growth, all inner organic development, and all strength."[2] If the bourgeoisie set the standards, society would take on a nomadic character. In 1801 Fichte published *Der geschlossene Handelsstaat,* in which he initiated a reaction to Adam Smith's theories not long after they were introduced in Germany. Self-sufficiency and inner harmony were portrayed as more desirable goals than increased wealth or expanded trade, both of which were held to lead to domestic discord. Fichte was against Germans even visiting other lands except for scholarly purposes.

By mid-century, liberal economic thought had gained wide support, but the patriarchal tradition advocated by Müller and Fichte was by no means submerged. Among its products, three stand out because of their impact on the thought of succeeding generations. Robert von Mohl, a professor at Heidelberg in the 1850s, inculcated in his students ethical reservations about industrial society despite his nominal liberalism. Distressed by the poor housing, alcoholism, and prostitution common to the new urban centers, he called for government intervention in behalf of the laboring class. Like Ruskin in England, von Mohl considered the absence of pride in work a product of a manufacturing economy. The second and perhaps greatest influence on young economists of a conservative bent was the estate owner and theoretician Karl Rodbertus. Similar to his contemporary in political thought, Friedrich Julius Stahl, he valued society or man in his collective state above the individual. "The interests of the masses and the individual are to be sacrificed

2. Friedrich Lenz, *Agrarlehre und Agrarpolitik der deutschen Romantik* (Berlin, 1912), pp. 96–97.

for the social totality, the progress of civilization."[3] Greatly influenced by Hegel, he wrote of the state in almost mystical terms, and ascribed miraculous powers to it. Thus, he believed: "The state is self justifying. . . . The state . . . is the central organization of the social body. . . . The state . . . precedes its relationship with associations and individuals."[4] To cope with the problems arising from industrialization, he prescribed a state capitalist economy in which capital was nationalized and free enterprise abolished.

The sway of laissez-faire thought was still great enough to cause Rodbertus' call for state operation of the economy to appear somewhat radical. Young conservative economists found a slightly milder alternative in the writings of Albert Schäffle, a professor and Austrian minister of commerce in the 1870s. Rather than a state-directed economy, Schäffle envisioned a state-regulated one, wherein power was exercised in all spheres but the decision-making process remained in private hands. Intervention would be fostered but not expropriation. With the exception of Müller, all of the aforementioned writers sought by a variety of means to curb the excesses of industrial capitalism. Their theories were generally expounded in huge tomes which made more of an impression on academicians than on the formulators of state economic policy.

The patriarchal tradition of criticism experienced radical changes in the 1890s. In contrast to their predecessors, economists such as Adolf Wagner, Karl Oldenberg, and Max Sering believed that Germany stood at a crossroad.[5] Karl Oldenberg expressed the central problem of his epoch in these words. "It depends on whether we look upon the individualistic period in which we stand

3. Heinrich Dietzel, *Karl Rodbertus* (Jena, 1888), p. 44. On von Mohl, see Erich Angermann, *Robert von Mohl, 1799–1875* (Neuwied, 1962); Donald Rohr, *The Origins of Social Liberalism in Germany* (Chicago, 1963).

4. Dietzel, *Karl Rodbertus*, pp. 47–51. Wagner felt a deep debt of gratitude to Rodbertus, and edited the unfinished work left at his death. See Wagner's article, "Lassalle und Rodbertus," *Allgemeine Zeitung*, 9 October 1878.

5. The titles of books published in these years are evidence of the sense of crisis. Apart from Oldenberg's *Deutschland als Industriestaat*, there was one with the same title by F. C. Huber, and Ludwig Pohle's *Deutschland am Scheidewege* and a series of articles by Wagner in *Die Zukunft* with a similar title.

as a conclusion or as an episode." Would Germany choose, "cosmopolitan export policy on the one hand or self-limitation based upon national independence on the other? Still more! Industrialism and extreme individualism or rural culture and the ancient conservative authority?"[6] A sense of crisis pervaded their writings and speeches throughout the 1890s, and on into the next century. The industrial tide that they and their forbears had criticized was becoming stronger. Whether the industrial leviathan would fully embrace Germany in its grasp, they believed, would be decided by their generation. Industrialism was no longer to be regulated as previous writers had proposed; now it had to be thwarted or relegated to a limited role in the economy. To do this they had to influence all legislation pertaining to the future character of Germany, particularly the renewal of tariffs in 1902. It was considered essential to join the Junkers in a concerted campaign against the growth of industrial capitalism and its political manifestations. Thus, to the practical assault on burgeoning industrial power the conservative economists added a theoretical attack.

The general reasons for the intensified hostility to industrialism and for the attempt to influence practical politics are not difficult to discern. When von Mohl and Rodbertus were writing, there were only industrial islands in a rural sea. The social evils accompanying industrialization were more apparent when the pace of development speeded up after unification and again after Caprivi's treaties had taken effect. In 1866 Treitschke expressed surprise on his first trip to Berlin at the, "new city hall, stock exchange, and what of course goes with it—the synagogue."[7] In later years the reaction of professors raised in tranquil university towns was even more extreme. Economists who set aside their books during the 1890s to view the urban and rural landscape perceived a change in emphasis. With the spread of electric lighting, multiple-story dwellings, and department stores, the cities were losing the aura of

6. Oldenberg, *Deutschland als Industriestaat* (Göttingen, 1897), p. 104.
7. Andreas Dorpalen, *Heinrich von Treitschke* (New Haven, 1957), p. 104. The reaction of Treitschke to industrial Berlin was not uncommon in the seventies and eighties. Similar quotations could be found in academic autobiographies of the period.

being rural appendages and were taking on a character of their own. It became increasingly difficult for a city dweller to demonstrate his country background by keeping up a vegetable garden or rearing some chickens. Because the Protestant church reacted slowly to the rapid urbanization, parishes in Berlin reached 100,000 in size. Especially after the introduction of lights for advertising, when nighttime in the city was no longer dark as in the countryside, the city became qualitatively as well as quantitatively an entity apart from the village. If this trend continued, the rural character of German society would pass, and men like Oldenberg, Wagner, and Sering were not sanguine enough to believe that it would ever return.

The issue of whether industrialization should be fostered or hampered smoldered beneath the surface of academic polemics during Caprivi's tenure as chancellor. Buried in a two-volume work of Wagner, the subject received considerable discussion but understandably did not emerge as a topic of public debate. Numerous lectures by Wagner and Sering to agrarian groups and the Prussian *Agrarkonferenz* (1894) similarly did not stir controversy. The issue became contentious in 1897, when Karl Oldenberg, a young economist at the University of Berlin, delivered a speech entitled *Deutschland als Industriestaat* to the Protestant Social Congress, an organization founded in 1890 to bring pastors and professors together to study social problems.[8] Beginning in the question period following the lecture, the controversy over the moral, social, and economic benefits attendant upon industrial development became the central concern of liberal and conservative theorists.

EARLY SOCIAL OBSERVATIONS

Born in 1864, Oldenberg was brought up in an atmosphere of stern Protestant religiosity. Those who remember him recall a frail, withdrawn man with a marked disposition toward pessimism. He wrote

8. Wagner, Max Weber, and Friedrich Naumann disagreed sharply over Oldenberg's thesis in the question period following the speech. On the Protestant Social Congress see the sketchy dissertation by Hans Eger, *Der Evangelisch-Soziale Kongress, ein Beitrag zu seiner Geschichte und Problemstellung* (Heidelberg, 1930).

his dissertation on Russian nihilism at Berlin under the tutelage of Gustav Schmoller, the leader of the historical school of economics. Perhaps because he began his studies in the faculties of theology and philosophy, Oldenberg's economic views always evidenced a profound concern with moral and ethical questions. He worked closely with Schmoller for eight years on the editorial staff of *Schmollers Jahrbuch* before accepting a post at Marburg—a call that resulted directly from his widely publicized critique of industrial society in 1897.

In the early nineties, Oldenberg investigated the employment procedures of several large Berlin manufacturers for some essays he planned to write on unemployment. These essays describe how impoverished rural workers come to cities out of desperation and find the opportunities for jobs limited because of periodic crises.[9] In letters to his friend Werner Sombart, Oldenberg despaired that the conditions of the impoverished urban proletariat would ever improve. He wrote of employer organizations that formed specifically to keep wages down and to forestall coalitions of workers.[10] Adherence to abstract economic theories prevented the government from interfering with the distribution of power. Whenever the workers in an industry succeeded in gaining better conditions, the employers inevitably responded by closing ranks to preclude any further concessions. Such was the case in the bakeries, in which, as a result of Oldenberg's scathing articles in *Soziale Praxis*, the Ministry of Trade had introduced the first limitation of working hours for adult males in Germany. Rather than taking heart at this measure, he emphasized the lack of real change in the workers' lives. Piecemeal regulations hardly scratched the surface of the inequities in the rising industrial order. Writing to a colleague in 1896, he described his efforts to aid the proletariat by working for the government-sponsored charitable organization, Die innere Mission der evangelischen Kirche, but closed on a pessimistic note be-

9. Oldenberg, "Die Konditorei Arbeiter," *Soziale Praxis* 2 (1893); "Die heutige Lage der Commis nach neuerer Literatur," *Schmollers Jahrbuch* 16 (1892).

10. DZA Oldenberg, "Letter to Sombart," 13 November 1889, *Nachlass Sombart*.

cause he did not see any countervailing power arising to challenge the industrialists.[11]

His investigation of the conditions of retail sales people led him to conclude that their lot was gradually deteriorating.[12] Before the appearance of department stores there had been an organic process whereby a young boy began as an apprentice and could work his way up to the ownership of an enterprise. At the initial step, the apprentice was aware that diligence would be rewarded by eventual independence. Oldenberg deplored the success of department stores because it destroyed the patriarchal bonds of the former system and fostered a worker-employer relationship similar to that of the factory. If department stores continued to increase in number, he warned, the small tradesmen would be driven out of business. Apart from the undesirable growth of large firms, such a development would mar the charm of the German cities. In his opinion, these stores interfered with the congeniality of urban life by their impersonal nature, and spoiled the consumers with their displays of luxury goods. Material covetousness was aroused in the working population by the advertising of these large enterprises.

Many talented young men who grew disenchanted with the evolving pattern of industrial society turned to socialism because it offered a comprehensive critique and a program for altering the existing economic relations. Although Oldenberg did not take this path, it was necessary for him to come to grips with Marx's analysis of industrial capitalism. In "The Aims of Social Democracy," published in 1891, he found that "the most serious objection to socialism is that its ideal society would be similar to a large prison; perhaps more accurately, a big army."[13] The remedies offered by Marxist socialism for working-class evils were considered worse than the malady. Instead of working for capitalists, the workers would be under the aegis of an amorphous bureaucracy, which would enforce a discipline more onerous than at present. Socialist

11. DSB II Oldenberg, "Letter to Diehls," 31 December 1896, *Darmstädter Sammlung.*

12. Oldenberg, "Die heutige Lage," p. 402.

13. Oldenberg, "Die Ziele der deutschen Sozialdemokratie," *Evangelische Soziale Zeitfragen* series 1, vols. 8/9 (1891).

thought was built on unstable assumptions and idealistic phantasies. Materialism, the most malevolent force of the age, was not combated by socialists but was lauded and made the basis of an interpretation of history. Especially in its treatment of religion, Oldenberg found the writings of Marx a wholly unsatisfactory basis for a future society. Apart from these reservations, the facile optimism of Marxism did not accord with the pessimistic temperament of Oldenberg. The real sin of the socialists was their belief in the progressive nature of industrial capitalism; a belief that belied all of Oldenberg's experience of rural and urban societies.

The few references to liberalism in Oldenberg's early letters imply that he had little faith in its providing a solution to the social problem. It was, after all, the proponents of liberalism who evinced the greatest faith in the benevolence of the industrial system. The cardinal principle of the liberal credo, the naturally functioning market economy, he found positively detrimental to the welfare of the workers. In one letter to Sombart he expressed bitter disapproval of Brentano and his liberal school.[14] Another time he used the term "rationalist" in a pejorative manner to describe the Austrian economist Böhm-Bawerk. The hesitancy of liberals to urge the control of cartels disabused him of any hope of finding an answer in their quarter. The germ of Oldenberg's future trend of thought is to be found in a letter of 2 February 1890 in which he mused about the natural qualities of an agricultural economy.[15] Family ties, he observed, suffered proportionately as a society became industrialized. In concluding, he wondered if the burdens on agriculture were not too great in an industrialized society.

Adolf Wagner, whose reputation as a political economist was second only to Schmoller's in the second empire, announced early in his career his intention of seeking a general audience for his views on industrial development. In 1872, at the age of thirty-seven, he wrote of his "hope to have an effect on circles which for

14. DZA Oldenberg, "Letter to Sombart," 5 August 1889, *Nachlass Sombart.*
15. DZA Oldenberg, "Letter to Sombart," 4 February 1890, *Nachlass Sombart.*

the most part remain beyond our [professorial] influence."[16] Two decades later he told members of the Protestant Social Congress, which he had helped to found, that propaganda through lectures and the press was necessary to enlighten public opinion about current social problems.[17] Wagner's importance in the industrialization controversy can be gauged from the comments of Helmuth von Gerlach, a free trader belonging to Friedrich Naumann's National Social party: "Adolf Wagner is the star of the agrarians. His scholarly importance, his honesty and objectivity, his social past, make him their most effective speaker. . . . If the new tariff for which he has spoken, passes . . . Wagner will and must be held in no small part responsible."[18]

As a young student at Göttingen and Heidelberg in the 1850s, Wagner could not help being profoundly influenced by the theories of the Manchester School. The 1850s were the heyday of Cobden and Bright, and economic liberalism was responsible for the successful union of the German states into a trading bloc. The leading organization of economists, the Kongress deutscher Volkswirte, subscribed wholeheartedly to the economics of Adam Smith and David Ricardo. Blithely ignorant of the effects a laissez-faire policy might engender on the traditional society in which he was reared, Wagner wrote a doctoral dissertation completely under the sway of Manchester thought. A generation later, when he emerged as the nation's leading proponent of state intervention, his earlier views struck him as a youthful escapade.

Both at Dorpat in Russian Estonia and at Freiburg in the sixties, Wagner acquired a reputation for his financial studies and his ardent Prussian patriotism. Two pamphlets written in the aftermath of the German victory over France encouraged the nation to

16. Wagner, *Offener Brief an Herrn H. B. Oppenheim* (Berlin, 1872), p. 19.

17. Wagner, *Verhandlungen des 7. Ev. Soz. Kong.* (1896), p. 139. Wagner never left any doubt that he meant to influence public opinion and governmental policy. This was one reason he helped to found the Evangelisch-Soziale Kongress.

18. Helmuth von Gerlach, "Die agrarische Bewegung," *Die Hilfe* 35, (1 September 1901).

develop a healthy egotism like that of the French and the British, and not to allow a moribund cosmopolitanism to weaken the nation at its inception.[19] In *Alsace-Lorraine and Its Recovery for Germany*, Wagner expressed those narrowly nationalistic opinions that were widely held by the succeeding generation of scholars, and were unlikely to encourage the peaceful integration of Germany into the European state system. Liberal tariff barriers and general disarmament became anathema to Wagner, who believed that such proposals were intended to weaken the recently achieved unity. The trends of thought in fin-de-siècle Germany can frequently be traced to a feeling of insecurity about Bismarck's creation. As we shall see, Wagner was preoccupied throughout his life with gaining acceptance for German unity and fighting those forces that threatened the Bismarckian solution to the German problem. Bismarck's epigoni looked upon themselves as the guardians of unity and destroyed it by excessive care, just as an overprotective mother might smother her child.

In 1870 Wagner joined the faculty of the University of Berlin, where he remained until his death in 1917. Apart from a brief stay in Hamburg, he had never resided in a major industrial city until 1870. His knowledge of the vast social changes generated by industrialization was primarily academic. The Germany he had experienced was comprised of idyllic university towns and rural landscapes. Berlin, already undergoing the changes that would transform it from a provincial north German city to the capital of a mighty industrial nation, provided a severe shock at first and then a challenge to Wagner's laissez-faire approach. The working-class squalor and shoddily built houses had no parallel in his experience. He had anticipated neither the predominance of Jews in

19. Wagner, *Elsass und Lothringen und ihre Wiedergewinnung für Deutschland* (Leipzig, 1870) pp. 68ff; and *Die Veränderungen der Karte von Europa* (Berlin, 1871) pp. 11ff. In the former he declared: "According to all historical experience only the sword decides, and it does not appear that it will soon be different. Still, the PRINCIPLE OF POWER, FORCE, THE RIGHT OF POWER, THE RIGHT OF CONQUEST DECIDE, AND MUST DECIDE. So will it be in Alsace-Lorraine, and with full justification. On Wagner's early studies see Anthony Oberschall, *Empirical Social Research in Germany 1848–1914* (The Hague, 1965).

Berlin's economic life nor the unbridled profit motive to be seen at work in the stock exchange and the dealings of real estate speculators. His Manchester views did not survive a year in this unrestrained atmosphere of Berlin during the *Gründerjahre*.

Invited to speak at the prestigious Versammlung evangelischer Männer in October of 1871, he stunned the distinguished audience with his candid analysis of the social problem. In language resembling Marx's he said, "The system of free competition which permits work to be treated as a commodity and wages as the price for it, is not merely unchristian, it is inhuman in the worst sense of the word."[20] He went on to denounce the paltry wages and insecurity characteristic of factory labor. Having no legitimate recourse for the redress of their grievances, the workers became prey to radicals and atheists. Should the Manchester philosophy continue its sway unimpeded, he warned, German society would increasingly become polarized between a few men of wealth and an impoverished, discontented mass. He now found that the successful entrepreneur under a free trade system was not the most talented but the most unscrupulous. Economic liberals expressed interest in the thorough application of their doctrines rather than the suffering of men under them. Wagner urged scholars to reexamine the sterile theories lacking in ethical content that emanated from England.

Unlike Marx, he foresaw no Armageddon; there was still time for countervailing forces to arrest the course of events. To stem the trend Wagner called for the restoration of ethical considerations in human affairs, and state intervention in the economy. "Let us not deceive ourselves," he admonished his listeners; "Far-reaching intervention through the law and the means of compulsion at the behest of the state is necessary to fulfill the simplest obligations of humanity and Christianity."[21] Nor was Wagner vague about the nature of the reforms. Toward the end of his speech he adumbrated a number of proposals for implementation, including state regula-

20. *Die Verhandlungen der kirchlichen Oktober-Versammlung in Berlin von 10. bis 12. Oktober, 1871* (Berlin, 1872). Wagner's speech was printed separately under the title, *Rede über die Sociale Frage* (Berlin, 1872). The audience expressed surprise at Wagner's sharp critique of the government.

21. Wagner, *Rede*, p. 30. Again and again after 1871 Wagner was to repeat that economics was an ethical science.

tion of hours and wages, accident and sickness insurance for industrial labor, factory safety legislation, and the introduction of a progressive income tax.

He did not fool himself about the difficulty of his task. Manchester ideas were still in the ascendant in 1871, as Bismarck's alliance with the National Liberals indicated. The Prussian civil service leaned toward liberalism in its economic if not in its political views. Few officials in positions of power were alive to the threat of further polarization. Several times during the speech Wagner pondered whether the social dislocation was not in fact irremediable. He stressed that "limitless freedom of movement and the end of all restrictions on the contracting of marriages . . . brought great advantages on the one hand, but on the other, considerable disadvantages, so that some regulation might appear advisable."[22] While not in favor of repealing such privileges, he did call for a discussion of their consequences. If his proposals failed to counteract the growing divisiveness of German society, he hoped at least to leave open the option of braking or even reversing the process.

For the succeeding twenty years, however, Wagner worked as assiduously as any socialist, and with more effect, to improve the squalid conditions of working-class life. Recognizing the peculiar sensitivity of the empire to strong pressure groups, Wagner and several like-minded young economists founded the Verein für Sozialpolitik in 1872.[23] These idealistic *Kathedersozialisten* (socialists of the lectern), as they were called, hoped to arouse the educated public to the growing divergence of the workers from the mainstream of German life. At its periodic meetings and through its widely read journal, the Verein encouraged scholars to discuss the harmful by-products of industrialization and to propose reforms. After a scant five years Wagner resigned in a fit of pique.

22. Wagner, *Rede*, p. 16. Actually, freedom of movement was not common in Prussia until the 1860s, so that Wagner's concern about its results is not as reactionary as it would appear.

23. A discussion of the Verein's origins is to be found in Hans Gehrig, *Die Begründung des Prinzips der Sozialreform* (Jena, 1914); Lujo Brentano, *Mein Leben im Kampfe um die soziale Entwicklung Deutschlands* (Jena, 1931); and Julius von Eckardt, *Lebenserinnerungen* (Leipzig, 1910).

His desire that the Verein adopt a unified program based on his recommendations proved unacceptable to the more catholic-minded leadership.[24] Wagner's abrasive personality and frequent posture of self-righteousness had resulted in continual friction, thereby hampering the organization's effectiveness. Unable to agree with his colleagues, he joined the small and conservative Zentralverein für Sozialreform, where his drive and scholarly credentials enabled him to determine social policy. In 1879 the Zentralverein merged with court pastor Adolf Stöcker's Christian Socialist movement to form a Protestant political party committed to basic social reforms. In 1881, the year in which Wagner became the party's president and editor of its journal, *Der Staatssozialist,* both he and Stöcker were invited to court for a discussion of current social problems with Wilhelm I.[25] The party's social and economic platform passed into Wagner's hands because Stöcker was more concerned with fostering a religious revival among the workers and combating the Jewish influence on German life.

In his scholarship, Wagner developed the ideas he had first adumbrated before the assembly of Protestant laymen into a theory he termed state socialism. He anticipated that it would eventually take its place alongside classical economics and collectivist socialism as a main current in European economic thought. Differentiating his thought from that of Marxist socialists, he contended that it was nationalist in flavor rather than international, and based on the legacy of history rather than revolutionary innovation. In a monarchy above parties and interests Wagner found the interme-

24. For Wagner's side in the controversy with the Verein members, see "Der Verein für Sozialpolitik und seine Verbindung mit dem volkswirtschaftlichen Kongress," *Die Communalsteuerfrage* (Leipzig and Heidelberg, 1878). Wagner was forever involved in petty professorial disputes because of slights or criticisms of his views. For many years he did not talk to Schmoller, and then he wrote a letter accusing Schmoller of ignoring him. The letter wound up by attacking Schmoller's views, while asking for greater personal recognition. DZA Wagner to Schmoller (3 February 1899), *Schmoller Nachlass.* Brentano reports many incidents in which Wagner's self-righteousness and pedantry shocked his colleagues. Brentano, *Mein Leben,* p. 72.

25. Paul Massing, *Rehearsal for Destruction* (New York, 1949), p. 44. On Stöcker see Walther Frank, *Hofprediger Adolf Stöcker und die christlichsoziale Bewegung* (Berlin, 1928).

diary that could allay the grievances of the workers within the existing governmental framework.[26] As head of the church and constitutional sovereign, the emperor had the power of moral suasion and political influence to improve the lot of the otherwise disinherited industrial masses. Perhaps the workers, like the liberal middle class earlier, would cast aside their revolutionary principles and embrace a monarchy sympathetic to their aspirations. The compassionate speech of Wilhelm I in 1881 stressing the state's responsibility to all citizens was an example of the role the monarch might play in rousing the nation to action. Germany was indeed fortunate, for its state remained the farthest removed from society. Bourgeois republics like France and the United States, where powerful economic cliques controlled the state, would have considerable difficulty in coping with their social problem.[27]

Despite Wagner's contention about the universal applicability of state socialism where the prerequisites existed, the system was a product of the particular German situation and certain national currents of thought. State socialism was a direct response to the Hohenzollerns' failure to face up to the pressing problems of a rapidly industrializing nation. Heretofore, the only response had emanated from the Social Democrats, whose internationalism and advocacy of revolution was anathema to patriotic Germans. Appealing to nationally minded conservatives in the Prussian Landtag, Wagner asserted that state socialism "is not merely a duty of humanity and Christendom . . . but the task of a policy bent on buttressing the present state."[28] His hopes for the future stability of Germany became stronger when Bismarck said, "It is possible that our work will go to pieces when I am dead. But state socialism will see it through."

As he himself recognized, Wagner had returned to the monarchical socialism of his early teacher, Rodbertus. He had become con-

26. For a full account of Wagner's state socialist views see his *Grundlegung der politischen Ökonomie*, 2 vols. (Leipzig, 1892–94), 1:24ff; *Sozialismus, Sozial Demokratie, Katheder Sozialismus und Staatssozialismus,* Speech in Barmen (Berlin, 1895), pp. 14–15.

27. Wagner, *Grundlegung*, vol. 1, pt. 1.

28. *Stenographische Berichte über die Verhandlungen des . . Landtages, Haus der Abgeordneten* (1882–83), II col. 806.

vinced, much as Friedrich II and Baron vom Stein before him, that when reform comes from above, the lesions in the body politic are healed most quickly and with the least disturbance to the organic character of the state. Change through opposition movements and by means of social conflict challenged the integral nature of the social order. Thus, pluralism struck him as a threat, and ideological conformity was judged the hallmark of a healthy society. Wagner could never free himself from the warped, Romantic notion of a holistic preindustrial Germany that lacked conflict. His ideal of the state as the neutral balancer of opposing and often unequal social forces appears to be a secularized version of the Romantic (particularly Adam Müller's) emphasis on Jesus as the indispensable intermediary between man and God. For Wagner and the Romantics, man is incapable of seeking his destiny without the aid of a benign conciliator or patriarch to smooth his path. According to Ralf Dahrendorf, this tendency to extol concord and condemn discord has marked German attitudes toward the social order for the past two centuries.[29] Dahrendorf's point, convincingly presented in *Society and Democracy in Germany,* helps to explain both the broad appeal of Wagner's state socialism in the eighties and his anti-industrial convictions of the nineties.

Orthodox Conservatives and industrialists regarded Wagner's somewhat unconventional ideas with great suspicion. He had anticipated the barbs of the capitalists but expressed dismay to Gustav Schmoller at the ire his financial proposals had aroused among Berlin Conservatives.[30] Conservatives certainly found it difficult to understand Wagner's attitude toward the Social Democrats. His speech before the Protestant Social Congress on the extremely radical Erfurt program, adopted by the Socialists in 1891, endorsed the party's specific economic goals. He described their proposals for the reform of German education, sanitation, justice, finance, and taxes as essentially sound and worthy of serious consideration.

For dogmatic Marxism he had nothing but contempt. Nevertheless, he devoted both time and effort to Marx's writings, perhaps

29. Ralf Dahrendorf, *Society and Democracy in Germany* (Garden City, N.Y., 1967).
30. DZA Wagner, "Letter to Schmoller," (1886), *Schmoller Nachlass.*

because there was an affinity between Marx's critique of industrial capitalism and Wagner's own. As Karl Mannheim has shown, mid-nineteenth-century German left-wing social critics borrowed freely from their Romantic elders on the right. Thus, Wagner could join Marx in viewing labor as a commodity, despising the bourgeoisie, and calling for social change. They separated when it came to economic determinism and religion.[31]

Wagner contended that statistical investigations had shown Marx's economics to be full of vague and unsubstantiated generalizations. Instead of a growing concentration in agriculture, peasant farms rose yearly in number at the expense of estates. Wagner mockingly pointed to backward Russia, where private property was rare in agriculture, as the model for a socialist utopia.[32] He dismissed as pure sophistry the theory of surplus value along with Marx's analysis of wages and capital. Here Wagner could utilize his training in statistics to dispute predictions that Marxists accepted without qualification.

His most serious reservations lay, however, on the religious or psychological plane. A pessimistic nature like Wagner's could not bear the undaunted optimism of Marx. Repeatedly he attacked the materialist conception of history because of its assumption that human nature was a malleable entity affected by changes in the productive forces. "The socialists," he wrote, "prophesy a heaven on earth. We deny it on the basis of all psychology and all human experience."[33] Rather than viewing Christianity as part of an outmoded superstructure, he emphasized that Christian social ethics offered the best hope for mitigating the inequalities of nascent industrial society. A well-integrated social order depended upon restricting man's capacity to do evil, not upon forlorn attempts to destroy it.

31. Mannheim's views are in "Conservative Thought," *Essays in Sociology and Social Psychology,* ed. Paul Kecskemeti (London, 1953). For Wagner's views on Marxism, see *Das neue Sozial-Demokratische Programme* (Berlin, 1891), and *Die akademische Nationalökonomie und der Sozialismus* (Berlin, 1895).

32. Wagner, *Die Abschaffung des privaten Grundeigentums* (Leipzig, 1870), p. 20.

33. Wagner, *Die akademische Nationalökonomie,* pp. 30–33.

Malthusian logic, a legacy of his Manchester days, also led Wagner to cast doubt upon Marx's sanguine predictions. The dour pessimism of the English parson appealed to Wagner's Lutheran sense of man's innate limitations.[34] Responding to socialist dreams of unimagined affluence, as Malthus had to Condorcet, he found the unchecked growth of population a substantial impediment to the realization of a corporeal utopia. In the end, what impressed Wagner about industrial capitalism was not the material benefits that Marx expected to open new vistas for humanity, but the disintegration it caused in a formerly cohesive society.

In some respects Max Sering does not belong to the same category as Oldenberg and Wagner. He showed little interest in socialism or any abstract theories and must be counted among the most inductive economists of the historical school. Among his numerous publications, there are scarcely any that do not treat the contemporary problems of agriculture. Nevertheless, he played an important role in the controversy. As the University of Berlin's expert on agriculture and the annual speaker at the Landes-Ökonomie-Kollegium, an institute founded by the Prussian government in 1842 to disseminate knowledge about agriculture, he was in a unique position to influence the views of the leading landowners of the east. (The membership of the institute included most major land holders, particularly those engaged in political activity.) Although his views were not wrapped in neat dogmatic theories, he too came to urge the subordination of industrialization to the maintenance of a healthy rural society. During the nineties, Sering also began to wonder how agriculture could survive in Germany when industrialization and the spread of capitalistic farming elsewhere made life on the land unprofitable and undesirable. Subsequent to Reichstag approval of the Russian treaty, he warned members of the *Agrarkonferenz* convened by Caprivi, "We must prevent the rape of the land by mobile capital."[35] Before the vote, he had told the Kollegium: "If the rural population is left in the lurch, then our

34. Wagner, *Grundlegung* 1:449. He believed that Malthus's theories had been confirmed by all studies on population since the latter's death.
35. *Landwirtschaftliche Jahrbücher* 23, supp. vol. 2 (1894): 193.

state will lose its support and go through violent shocks, perhaps to its demise."[36] Sering demonstrates the scope of the hostility to industrialism, showing that it was not tied to any particular school or methodology.

After receiving his doctorate in 1881 for a history of the Prussian iron tariffs, Sering wrote to Friedrich Althoff, the Prussian *Kultusminister*, of his growing concern with American grain competition. In 1883 he managed to accumulate sufficient funds to embark on a two-year journey to the American Midwest to study grain competition in the world market. He returned in 1885 to accept a position at Bonn, where he published his findings in 1887, and shortly thereafter moved on to Berlin.

When Sering's *The Agricultural Competition of North America in the Present and Future* appeared in 1887, it was accepted immediately as the authoritative work in the field; partly because of its great erudition and partly, perhaps, because of its sanguine attitude toward the future.[37] The decline in German grain prices beginning in the seventies was attributed to the rapid settlement of fertile areas in the United States and the completion of a transportation network from the American Midwest to Europe. After the American Civil War, a steady migration to the lands opened for settlement by the Homestead Act had developed. Fertile areas the size of Germany were extensively cultivated, with no concern for their future productivity. American farmers were thus able to export wheat at prices considerably below European levels.[38] At first there was no reaction on the part of German farmers, who had become so accustomed to prosperity that they continued to bid up the price of land despite falling prices. As it became clear that agriculture was faced with a long-term competitor, a clamor began for tariffs and a bimetallist currency. Sering was not pessimistic, however, for his research had shown that the fertile areas were almost all being cultivated, and there was little likelihood of further expansion.

36. Ibid., supp. vol. 1:8.
37. Max Sering, *Die landwirtschaftliche Konkurrenz Nord-Amerikas in Gegenwart und Zukunft* (Berlin, 1887). On Sering's life see the essay by his former student, Constantin von Dietze, in *Gedanken und Bekenntnisse eines Agrarpolitikers* (Göttingen, 1962).
38. Sering, *Die landwirtschaftliche Konkurrenz*, p. 571.

Moreover, many homesteads were coming into the hands of speculators whose primary interest lay in profits from soaring land values rather than from the fruits of farming. Sering also noticed the tendency of American farmers to change their crops rapidly when prices fell. He considered this practice a self-regulating mechanism that would, in time, limit competition to the most efficient farmers. He counseled German farmers to be patient for a few years until these trends had become even more obvious and world grain prices had risen again to profitable levels.[39]

Events did not follow Sering's predictions. Grain prices skyrocketed in 1890 and 1891, only to fall to extremely low levels in the succeeding three years. In 1894, Sering tried to analyze the causes of the erratic price patterns and prognosticate what farmers might expect in subsequent years. His treatise examined all the major grain-exporting nations with the purpose of projecting future trends as he had done in the case of America. Sering confirmed the prevalent idea that poor European harvests in combination with the Russian ban on exports had forced prices up. In his view, the higher prices had encouraged American farmers to capitalize by expanding their acreage under cultivation. When the increased acreage continued to be cultivated during good harvest years in Europe, prices had fallen drastically. Sering's optimism in face of American competition remained undaunted. Once the lower prices were apparent to American farmers, he felt sure they would be reflected in the abandonment of recently expanded acreage. The American population was growing so rapidly also that the predicted American surpluses would diminish because of domestic demand. Similarly, Sering did not find reason to worry about Indian exports, for the introduction of a sound currency and a growing domestic market in India were removing any danger of stepped-up competition from that country.[40] However, Argentina and Russia gave him cause for deep concern. In the former, Italian immigrants worked for extremely low wages on the estates of grandees whose lands had not even begun to come under the plow. A paper currency added to Argentina's ability to undercut the

39. Ibid., p. 587.
40. Sering, *Das Sinken der Getreidepreise* (Berlin, 1894), p. 44.

world price. The future did not look good for the German farmer, Sering thought, if immigration and the acreage under cultivation grew side by side in South America. Russia also presented a problem. The construction of railroads in central Russia had led to the cultivation of areas formerly isolated. Henceforth they would be capable of flooding European markets with cheap grain, and a weak currency abetted this development.

THE ECONOMIC CRITIQUE

Not until the mid-nineties did the conservative economists put forward a comprehensive critique of industrial capitalism. Their earlier letters and essays expressed a strong dislike of working-class conditions and an even stronger dislike for the solutions proposed by the socialists; but these opinions were strewn throughout their writings rather than brought together in any organized form. With the publication of *Deutschland als Industriestaat* by Oldenberg in 1897, a conservative ideology of anti-industrialism began to crystallize—one that quickly found its way into the speeches of Reichstag delegates as well as the writings of political economists. What distinguishes this ideology is its comprehensiveness and unrelieved pessimism. Not only does it bring to bear objections raised by earlier Romantics and orthodox Christians, but it forecasts eventual economic chaos and national disintegration if Germany should continue along the course laid out by Caprivi.

According to the conservative economists, every industrial nation imported raw materials and foodstuffs from undeveloped lands and in return exported manufactured goods or occasionally paid in gold. Since it was necessary for the developed areas to use many resources that were not available within their borders, they invested in the areas where these resources were abundant. By this procedure the industrial nation received the needed material and a return on its investment. The experiences of Great Britain and Germany had also shown that, as a nation industrialized, it became increasingly unable to meet its food requirements and grew dependent on the surpluses of agricultural nations. In this pattern of relations between industrial and farming lands, Oldenberg, Wagner, and Sering perceived the position of the latter as stable, and that of the former as so precarious that it must finally end in ruin.[41]

The essence of their criticism lay in the belief that the mutual dependence inherent in the industrial system was an insecure foundation upon which to build a society. Oldenberg emphasized: "The impossibility of founding a lasting export industry lies not only in the unreliability of its markets, but still more in the future of food imports. The heart of industrialism is the dependence of the export-industrial population upon food from foreign soil; otherwise it would not be necessary to seek markets abroad."[42] The conservative economists foresaw a day, not far off, when all the nations of the world would industrialize. Food would then be at a premium, and only those nations that had had the sagacity to remain agricultural would survive. There would be a scramble by the developed nations to go back to an agricultural economy, but this would prove technically impossible. As bread became dearer, the advanced nations would resort to "forcibly maintaining the undeveloped lands at the agricultural stage." To avoid the calamity that would ensue from the competition, the conservatives counselled the nation to remain a predominantly rural country and to resist the temptation to industrialize fully.

Apart from the food danger, the conservative economists expressed doubts about whether markets for industrial products would expand in the course of years. They saw the world being rapidly divided up into huge autarkic empires. First the Russians and the Americans had erected high protective tariffs, and Britain, with Joseph Chamberlain calling for imperial confederation, gave every evidence of following the same path. As this process evolved,

41. Oldenberg, *Deutschland* pp. 94–103; Wagner, *Agrar- und Industriestaat: Eine Auseinandersetzung mit den Nationalsozialen und mit Professor Lujo Brentano über die Kehrseiten des Industriestaats und zur Rechtfertigung agrarischen Zollschatzes* (Jena, 1901). This work is the crystallization of a critique that began with the 1894 article, "Agrar- und Industriestaat," *Die Zukunft* 5 (8 September 1894), and was further developed in "Zur Frage von Industriestaat und wirtschaftlicher Entwicklung," *Der Lotse* (17 and 24 November 1900), and "Bankbrüche und Bankkontrolle," *Deutsche Monatschrift* 1 (1901). Also see Sering, "Rede," *Archiv der Landwirtschaft* (1902), pp. 67ff; and "Agrar- und Industriestaat," *Wörterbuch der Volkswirtschaft,* 2d ed. vol. 1, col. 54.

42. Oldenberg, *Deutschland,* p. 94.

Germany, not having Britain's great empire or America's enormous reservoir of natural resources and large domestic market, would gradually be closed out of whole continents. They also pondered whether German goods would be competitive when Japan, whose workers earned one-fourth as much as their European counterparts did, offered its merchandise to buyers. As even more nations industrialized, they prognosticated a worldwide struggle for markets, which would force industrialists constantly to lower their costs of production to remain in the game.[43] Eventually, declining exports would spur violent class conflict by creating massive unemployment, and hamper the nation's capacity to pay for grain imports. Sering anticipated the outbreak of international conflict from the drive for markets, and when war erupted in 1914, he wrote, "But this imperialist spirit in modern times is not merely power hunger and not supported by the instincts of an agricultural people, but narrowly tied to large commercial, industrial, and capitalist interests."[44] Curiously, this interpretation of the war resembled that of Lenin more than those of Sering's colleagues; both the Berlin professor and the future Russian leader held modern industrial capitalism to be the culprit.

The conservatives lamented the hostility—encouraged by Marxists—between the workers and the nobility, for they both would suffer from an industrial-oriented society. The workers had to be taught that industrialism would lead to a degeneration of their standard of living, and that their natural allies were to be found in the villages, not in the radical intelligentsia. Once the urban popu-

43. Ibid., p. 103; also "Deutschland als Industriestaat," *Soziale Praxis* 8, no. 28 (13 April 1899). When the Conservative government took office in England in 1895, Chamberlain was appointed minister for colonies. He sought to bring the dominions and colonies closer to England, particularly in regard to tariff policy. Many German economists, along with Wagner and Oldenberg, feared that Germany would now be closed out of all British markets. This, it must be remembered, came only a few years after the very high American McKinley tariffs. The theory of the three major empires' closing out the newcomer, Germany, became so pervasive that Heinrich Dietzel, a liberal, wrote a series of articles seeking to undermine its foundation, "Die Theorie von den drei Weltreichen," *Die Nation* 17, nos. 30–34, (28 April to 26 May 1900).
44. Sering, "Rede," *Landwirtschaftliche Jahrbücher* 31, supp. vol. 2 (1902): 165.

lation realized "that the whole German proletariat must decline perhaps to the level of Japanese or Chinese workers," it was hoped they would seek alliance with the farmers to oppose contemporary economic changes. The decision whether Germany would follow the path of Britain was at hand, the conservatives emphasized, and all Germans had to take into consideration how their heirs would fare under a competitive international capitalist system.

In *Agrar- und Industriestaat,* published in 1901, Wagner took the economic critique of industrialism to its logical culmination.[45] He came to the conclusion that industrialism was a transitory stage that arose in response to rural overpopulation and would disappear with the recognition that the remedy created more problems than it solved. England, a paradigm for economic liberals, already appeared to him to have passed its peak. Faced with competition from continental Europe and America, British production and exports had slumped seriously in the seventies and eighties. Despite the advantages of technological know-how, England's primacy no longer seemed assured. And Germany did not have Britain's combination of natural and inherited advantages—a colonial empire, an incomparable fleet, and a coastline virtually impossible to blockade. Situated between France and Russia, and without a significant navy, Germany could not afford the luxury of dependence on foreign grain. Rather than boasting of German industrial progress in the nineties, Wagner asked: "Can one really believe that Germany or North America, even if they make further inroads upon British export trade, will in the long run have a better fate?" The answer was a resounding negative: "For Germany [industrialism] would be an insane, ruinous policy, which no patriot, no statesman, no reasonable man could contemplate in earnest."[46]

Among the conservatives, only Oldenberg admitted that his eco-

45. Wagner, *Agrar- und Industriestaat,* p. 173.
46. Ibid., p. 173ff. By using statistics from the year preceding the "Great Depression" and comparing them with the eighties and early nineties to the disadvantage of the latter, Wagner came to the conclusion that England had seen her best days. His hostility to England did not abate with age. At seventy-seven he wrote *Gegen England* (Berlin, 1912), which attacked the British in much the same way Werner Sombart and Max Scheler were to do during the war.

nomic reservations would be overcome if "we seek economic areas over which we have political power."[47] Thus, if Germany possessed a vast empire organized around a common currency with monopoly control of raw materials, and markets, and a cheap labor supply— very much the advantages Britain began with—the perilousness of industrialism diminished considerably. It is questionable whether Oldenberg was proposing this alternative seriously or merely conveying his musings. He did not go on to elaborate, because the likelihood of such a hypothesis' being realized seemed rather remote in 1897. Bismarck's colonies were for the most part considered worthless, and Caprivi, despite his years as an admiral, evinced more interest in Helgoland than in African empire. Moreover, Germany lacked the indispensable prerequisite for overseas expansion in 1897—a powerful navy—although such a navy was closer to being attained than anyone realized. Even after Tirpitz's fleet campaign began (from which Oldenberg remained aloof) and *Weltpolitik* suddenly became a reality, Oldenberg did not seize upon these developments to quell his former misgivings. Nor did Sering and Wagner moderate their hostility to industrialism after Tirpitz's navy and a colonial empire began to take shape around 1900. Despite their active efforts in behalf of the emperor's *Weltpolitik*, both Berlin professors continued, and in fact increased, the tempo and severity of their attacks upon industrial society.[48]

To many of their contemporaries (and to us today), the conservatives' predictions of economic disaster appeared unduly pessimistic. Ironically, they warned of impending famine when the spread of railroads and steamships were opening up the vast American and Canadian wheat harvests to European buyers. They failed to observe the sharply increased yields per acre that resulted from

47. Oldenberg, *Deutschland*, p. 124.
48. Because of their preoccupation with security, Wagner and Sering became leading advocates of a large navy around the turn of the century. Nevertheless, because of Germany's geography and late start in colonization, they insisted that industrial development would be disastrous. Wagner's views are in "Flottenverstärkung und unsere Finanzen," *Handels- und Machtpolitik* (Stuttgart, 1900); and Sering's are in "Die Handelspolitik der Grossstaaten und die Kriegsflotten," in the same book. Both belonged to the Deutsche Kolonialgesellschaft and worked actively for Tirpitz.

the application of technology to agriculture. Their belief in the imminent industrialization of all nations ignored the slow and ponderous development of Russia despite an enormous influx of French investment. The major industrial nations, as evidenced by contemporary yearbooks, found their most lucrative markets in trade with each other rather than with their colonies or with undeveloped nations. And industrialization is not a one-step process whereby equality with all advanced societies is attained when a nation passes some arbitrary standard, such as the majority of its inhabitants' being engaged in nonagricultural labor. While a developing land might be concentrating on the manufacture of rifles, the older industrial powers have usually advanced to more complicated weaponry. Thus, the conservatives' economic reasoning ignored certain trends and carried others to their seeming conclusion without regard for those unforeseen occurrences that often make a mockery of economic predictions. What Karl Mannheim wrote about Germans in general applies most aptly to Oldenberg, Wagner, and Sering. "In Germany there has always existed a tendency to go to extremes in pushing logical arguments to their ultimate conclusion—a tendency which has not existed in such a marked fashion in the European countries outside Germany."[49] Once the harmful implications of a trend in some distant future have been denoted, the trend must be totally discredited in the present.

THE MORAL AND ETHICAL CRITIQUE

Germany's strides into the world arena might have relieved conservative reservations about industrialism if their concerns had been solely economic in origin. However, their bitter hostility to industrial capitalism resulted from a series of perspectives of which the economic was but one. Their generation, it should not be forgotten, sharply criticized the absence of ethical considerations in classical economic thought. Both Oldenberg and Sering rejected the laissez-faire approach completely, while Wagner, although remaining a classical economist fundamentally, took the lead in attacking the amorality of the Manchester School's philosophy. The

49. Mannheim, "Conservative Thought," p. 79.

combination of stern religious upbringings, and the rapid departure from the relatively static and rural Germany that they took to be a model, led the conservatives to examine closely the moral atmosphere prevailing in the emerging urban-industrial society.

Like many contemporaries, both in Germany and in other industrial nations, the conservatives frowned upon the moral climate in the mushrooming cities of the nineties. They found that neither the spirit nor the body had room to grow in overcrowded tenements where children had few places to nourish their curiosity. Viewing the hulking, colorless, industrial structures beginning to stamp the Berlin landscape, Oldenberg concluded that the workers who spent twelve hours a day within their walls were bound to be deficient in health as well as in spiritual values. Factory inspectors continually deplored "the sitting life, lack of fresh air, and high temperatures of the workrooms."[50] A prisoner of the modern world, the worker had lost the pride in his work that was still noticeable in a self-employed craftsman. Work had come to take on a pejorative connotation. Sering wrote of Berlin: "In short, it is too far removed from connection with the natural creation. The metropolis with its barracks and the factory with its highly refined specialization of labor form terrible soil for the normal development of human beings."[51]

The very nature of urban life seemed to foster immorality. True individuality was stifled and incapable of blossoming. Like all sinful lures, they observed, the city had a certain superficial charm— an inexplicable attraction—that caused migrants to overlook the superior qualities of life on the land. Thus Wagner noted: "The Bible says, lead us not into temptation, but one walks now on the streets in the evening with the electrical lighting, where the immense displays and the elegant shops with their luxury articles of all kinds arouse attention. . . . This awakens envy and greed; it is

50. Oldenberg, "Konsumption," *Grundriss der Sozialökonomik* 2.1 (1923): 24.

51. Sering, *Archiv der Landwirtschaft*, pp. 52, 64. Critiques of urban life are common in industrializing lands, to be sure, but rarely have they been so all-embracing as with the conservatives, who, it should be added, continued to live in industrial Berlin.

unhealthy through and through."[52] He went on to warn Protestant Social Congress members that the contemporary evils were more deeply rooted than presumed; "You do not understand that people are no longer remaining loyal to the Bible, primer, and catechism. They hold the whole scriptures for a work of scholars and journalists."[53]

Concurring with Wagner's analysis, Oldenberg found the willingness to sacrifice and the sense of duty that characterized Germans on the land apparently replaced by egotism and immoderate ambition in industrial centers. Seeking a life guided by no other principle than pleasure, the city dweller avoided all personal sacrifices for the benefit of the group. The loss of authority resulted in naked individualism in which the "I" took precedence over all else. The most striking example of the new spirit rested in the attitude of the urban population toward the size of families. Whereas the spirit pervading the countryside caused parents to look upon a large family as a sign of divine favor, the worker sought to limit the size of his family for economic motives. Obligated to spend less of his income on children, he could determine where the greater portion of his disposable income went. More often than not, Oldenberg thought, such savings were wasted on the frivolous luxuries that abounded in cities.[54] The end result of rationalism was discernable in the two peoples whose ways of life had been most influenced by the spirit of capitalism; the French and the Jews. In both cases there was a decided drop in the birth rate after the 1789 revolution, and this trend had continued to a point where a decline in actual numbers had become a reality. Oldenberg considered the French and Jewish examples of immediate relevance to the German situation, for neo-Malthusian thought, birth control societies, and movements for legal abortion were spreading from the French capital to the German Rhineland.

52. Wagner, *Die sozialen und wirtschaftlichen Gesichtspünkte* A speech given before the Vereinigung der Steuer- und Wirtschaftsreformer (Berlin, 1901), p. 16.

53. Wippermann, ed., *Deutscher Geschichtskalender* (1897), 1:261.

54. Oldenberg, "Über den Rückgang der Geburten und Sterbeziffer," *Archiv für Sozialwissenschaft und Sozialpolitik* 33 (1911): 354.

In view of the dismal quality of urban life, Oldenberg was not surprised at the rise of alcoholism, and of deaths resulting therefrom, that characterized industrial cities. Even more than drinking, venereal diseases were found to be a product of cities. The incidence of these maladies, he noted, was seventeen times higher proportionately in Berlin than in the surrounding countryside. Unable to cope with his plight, the urban laborer also became prey to mental illness. Oldenberg quoted the findings of a doctor who claimed that the frequency of mental disorder was much higher in the cities. Pastors told him that urban parishioners tended to be nervous and unsure of themselves. This debit side of modern life, he wrote, did not appear in statistical yearbooks, but its effects were enormous. "The path led to the dissolution of the family, also to the weakening of other moral powers upon which the bonds of the nation were built."[55] The huge floating population of cities, which included derelicts, the unemployed, and hoboes, he viewed as the logical end product of a system that discarded those lacking in economic utility like industrial refuse.

Wagner took the ethical critique a step farther than his conservative compatriots. For him the many manifestations of urban decadence and the decline of spiritual values proceeded inevitably from the intrinsically immoral character of industrial capitalism. It clearly fostered a society in which egotism received rewards and a concern for the commonweal led to ruin. The process whereby a speculator could earn millions from astute buying and selling, while a farmer might barely cover his costs after a year's strenuous labor, caused him to condemn the functioning of the stock exchange and attribute its invention to the cunning of the Jews ten years before Werner Sombart expounded this thesis. He regarded the practice of trading in grain futures as positively immoral. Similarly, the speculation in land in the vicinity of industrial centers aroused his indignation. After the bank scandals of 1900, he added bankers to his list of villains who amassed wealth at the expense of

55. Oldenberg, "Der Rückgang der Geburten," *Archiv des Deutsche Landwirtschaftsrats* (1912), p. 537. Also see "Englische Agrarpolitik," *Die Zeit* 2 (1903): 647.

the general welfare.[56] When Wagner spoke out in the Prussian Landtag, he lumped together the stock exchange, land speculation, and lotteries as examples of the acquisitive spirit pervading industrial society. Already in the industrial metropolises of Britain he saw the tone being set by the rapacious capitalists. The frenzied reaction of the once virtuous English to the indefensible Boer War demonstrated how far a Christian people could be led astray by the trader spirit.[57] Germany itself stood threatened by the rise to power of "a true money aristocracy . . . a plutocracy of millionaires and billionaires as in North America." Wagner's observations were confirmed by the growing influence of the Jews in German life.[58] While he did not mount crude racial arguments against the Jews, he was incapable of considering them other than as the living incarnation of the egotistical spirit that threatened patriarchal Christianity. He took great delight in bringing the *Landtag's* attention to the arrest of Jews for economic crimes. To Progressive party criticism of Adolf Stöcker's anti-Semitism, he replied that he supported the court chaplain unreservedly, and believed 99 percent of Christian Socialist accusations against the Jews fully justified.

THE THREAT TO POWER AND SECURITY

The disillusionment with industrialism of the conservative economists is to be distinguished from that of cultural critics like Nietzsche and Julius Langbehn, who loathed the Bismarckian empire for its crass materialism. On the contrary, Oldenberg, Wagner,

56. Wagner, "Bankbrüche und Bankkontrolle," *Deutsche Monatschrift* 1 (1901).

57. Wagner delivered a sharp critique of the Boer War to the Alten Herren des Vereins deutscher Studenten on 6 November 1901. There is a synopsis of the speech in Wippermann, ed., *Deutscher Geschichtskalender* 3 (1901): 112. The Boer War confirmed the belief of conservatives that industrial capitalism inevitably led to war.

58. Wagner was given to tirades against Jews in his years in the Landtag. On one occasion he said, "The new economic conditions have allowed a foreign race to exploit our economic relations; a race whose motto 'Gain as much as possible' fits in well with the new economics." *Sten. Ber. Abgeordnetenhaus* (1884), 3, col. 1825. For his other anti-Semitic attacks see (1883), 1, col. 167; (1885), 1, col. 581. His anti-Semitism is also evident in *Agrar- und Industriestaat* pp. 31, 81.

and Sering never wavered in their admiration for the Iron Chancellor, and rather than rejecting the empire, they feared that it stood in danger of being undermined by rapid industrialization. Strongly nationalistic in sentiment, they weighed the effects of economic and social change on domestic solidarity and national security carefully. In contrast to their opponents in the industrialization controversy (treated in chapter 5), who professed similar concerns with German power, the conservatives forecast intensified inner discord and weakness in the international arena if Caprivi's policy of spurring change continued. Although their perspectives varied, and often appeared contradictory to one another, they were united in the pessimism of their conclusions.

Both Oldenberg and Sering concentrated primarily on certain demographic trends which seemed to forebode eventual disaster. Throughout his writings Oldenberg devoted inordinate attention to the decline in the birth rate; its causes and results were expounded in articles approaching the length of a small volume.[59] The decline heralded for him the beginning of an even more far-reaching one—that of German culture. After satisfying himself that the egocentric morality of the city was responsible for the lower birth rate, he sought to alert his colleagues to the danger. For the time being, he admitted that the corresponding fall in the death rate prevented the population from decreasing absolutely as in France. But the death rate could not continue to fall; this was particularly true because Oldenberg's studies convinced him that the chances for longevity were greater in rural areas. With progressive urbanization the death rate would reach a stable level while there was no end in sight for the drop in births. The situation appeared especially depressing because rural birth rates had begun to follow the urban pattern. Should the day approach when the German people could not replenish their numbers yearly, the Slavs would then become a threat to German culture. Already he found the increase in foreign workers had reached such proportions that in some districts Slavic traits predominated. He compared the Slavs to the

59. Oldenberg, "Über den Rückgang,"; "Der Rückgang,"; "Über Volksernährung im Industriestaat," *Die Zeit*, 9 July 1903; and "Landarbeitermangel und Abhilfe," *Zeitschrift für Agrarpolitik* 5, no. 2 (February 1907): 85.

barbarians who had first weakened Rome's defenses by intermarriage and mixing cultures in the border areas. "Thank God," he wrote, "that until now our farm lands could supply enough men to fill most industrial places without resorting to Poles."[60] The *Deutsche Landwirtschaftsrat* was warned that Polish migrant labor on the eastern estates connoted a setback for German civilization.[61] If Germany ceased to be autarkic in manpower he predicted a national catastrophe.

The low birth rate also meant that in the event of war with Russia the German armies would be vastly outnumbered. Power was not directly proportional to numbers but some correlation did exist. One of the reasons for Prussia's triumph over France in 1870 had been the startling growth of Prussia after the Napoleonic wars in contrast to French stagnation. France had been the dominant power in Europe from 1648 to 1815—a period in which her soldiers outnumbered the Germans, Austrians, or the British. What was the use, Oldenberg asked, of pursuing *Weltmachtpolitik* when Germany's position in the world was bound to wane in the next generation.

Sering's fears meshed neatly with Oldenberg's. He repeatedly warned the King's Agricultural Collegium that the deceptive charms of the city as well as higher wages were leading to the depopulation of Prussia's strategic eastern provinces. The nation faced two distinctive dangers in his view. First, echoing Oldenberg, he said: "It is to be regretted that the Polish migrants are organized against us in a hostile manner, and protect their character strongly. With rising Polish immigration the whole cultural level of eastern Germany will be reduced."[62] The second danger lay in the growing dependence of Germany on the willingness of Austria and Russia to allow free emigration in the harvest season. Strained relations with either nation could mean the cessation of such migration, and concomitantly the rotting of eastern crops for

60. Oldenberg, "Der Rückgang," p. 541.
61. Ibid., p. 542; Also see his piece during the war, "Die Slawische Gefähr," *Das neue Deutschland* 4, No. 17, (February 19, 1916); and "Aushungerung," *Schmollers Jahrbuch* 43, (1919), p. 874.
62. Sering, *Die Verteilung des Grundbesitzes und die Abwanderung vom Lande* (Berlin, 1910), p. 622.

want of harvesters. Depopulation in the east thus provided Germany's neighbors with leverage in international relations.

What troubled Sering even more were the consequences of urbanization on German military might and *Volkstum*. Ever wary of German strength vis-à-vis its enemies, Sering was also distressed by the falling birth rate. Germany would be placed at a disadvantage against Russia, whose birth rate remained high. The average age of the population would mount, causing military recruits to be both older and fewer.[63] A modern industrial economy apparently augured ill for the nation's ability to survive in the armed Europe of the day. He warned that the debilitating physical effects of urban living had already weakened Germany's military capacity. Statistical studies by the Prussian army showed that the percentage of physically fit recruits was much higher in East Prussia than in Berlin. Sering pointed to a Bavarian survey that had found the recruits coming from artisan families to be the healthiest, followed by those from agriculture, forestry, trade, and industry respectively. He went on to wonder whether national security did not dictate a reversal of the urbanization process.

All three conservatives saw in the city a solvent that worked to destroy the unique qualities that constituted German culture. Sering detected "a worsening of *Volkstum* and a worsening of *Rasse* [race]" in the cities.[64] Speaking to a conference of the landed gentry, Oldenberg observed: "What good will it do us to become more powerful today, if a following generation of aliens arrives to seize our inheritance and to introduce foreign customs into our house?"[65] A generation that failed to recognize the importance of duty and the necessity for a religious ethic was held to be a poor successor to the one that produced Bismarck. They adjudged the problem to be

63. Sering, "Die Bedeutung der landwirtschaftlichen Bevölkerung für die Wehrmacht des deutschen Reiches," *Archiv des deutschen Landwirtschaftsrats* 26 (1902): 50–61.

64. Sering, *Die innere Kolonization im östlichen Deutschland* (Leipzig, 1893), p. 98.

65. Oldenberg, "Der Rückgang," p. 538. The conservatives, perhaps, had too good a sense of history. Because Germany had been occupied and ruled by foreigners so often, they were paranoid about this issue and saw every change as heralding a new occupation.

the result of the increasing percentage of the urban population dependent on employers and the vagaries of the market for their livelihood. These workers, at the mercy of forces beyond their control, lacked the requisite independence to contribute to the formation of a resilient national character.

Wagner's gravest reservations about the future resulted from the ominous cleavage in wealth that seemed to accompany industrial development. He warned that the cohesive social fabric of the countryside broke down in the city, and the traditional hierarchical system characterized by stability and patriarchal relationships stood in danger of being undermined by one that stirred violent class conflict. Discord seemed to be the hallmark of industrialism in contrast to the concord that distinguished agricultural society. Whether the newly unified empire could survive the intensifying malintegration appeared uncertain. For Germany, with its tenuous bonds of unity—already divided between Catholics and Protestants and liberals and conservatives over fundamental questions—the social price required for industrial development struck him as prohibitively high. He warned *Verein für Sozialpolitik* members in 1897 that inner strife had always been the nemesis of the German people. A religious split in the sixteenth century prevented the evolution of a national state; now, social cleavage could lead to the undoing of Bismarck's greatest achievement. "We must remain together at any price . . . ," he exhorted his listeners, "to preserve the greatest goods for people and state. Only one thing can save us —UNITY. Our conflicts should not divide us."[66]

THE TURN TO THE PAST

During the mid 1890s the conservative economists came to doubt the compatibility of industrial capitalism with a reasonably holistic social order and national security; their earlier reservations had evolved into a far-ranging critique of the very essence of the emerging economic order. From a posture of conservative state socialism they moved rapidly in the direction of agrarian irrationalism.

---

66. By 1897, the height of the Stumm Era, Wagner clearly believed that centrifugal forces had never been stronger in the empire. See his comment from the floor, *Schriften des Vereins für Sozialpolitik* 76 (1897): 441ff.

While in industrialism they increasingly saw the Pandora's box from which all the evils of the modern world had arisen, they came to look upon the peasants as the healthy fountain of youth (*Jungbrunnen*) of the German people. In their writings and public speeches the importance of the preindustrial orders for the nation's future became a pervasive theme.

How is their lack of faith in industrial society to be explained? It is apparent that not long after Bismarck's dismissal, the conservatives, especially Wagner, gave up any hope of institutionalizing and, thereby, moderating the class conflicts following in the wake of industrialization. Their new emphasis on the strengths of preindustrial Germany is evidence of their desire to preserve what remained of a supposedly healthy social structure.

The key to their emerging anti-industrial ideology lies primarily in the combination of an agricultural and industrial depression in the early nineties and Caprivi's economic policy. When Rodbertus had deplored the social effects of industrialism in the 1850s, the factory system had yet to alter the German landscape, and agriculture had enjoyed a long period of prosperity that was not to end until the seventies. But by 1895, 50 percent of the population lived in towns (many cities had almost doubled in size within a decade) and fifteen mediocre years had been capped by the lowest prices agriculture had experienced in generations. In addition, German farmers, particularly the eastern estate owners, were deeply in debt and plagued by a severe labor shortage. Caprivi's decision to sacrifice agriculture by lowering tariffs at such a time in order to spur industrial exports astonished the conservatives. Under Bismarck, three tariff increases within eight years attested to the primacy of agriculture; for the first time the rural population could not look to the state in a time of crisis.

The tariff policy of the New Course led grain farmers to found the Farmers' League and the Conservative party to take on the character of an agrarian interest group in their Tivoli program of 1892. The conservatives responded to the state's seeming acquiescence in the decline of agriculture by becoming the leading agrarian publicists in the academic world. Before Caprivi they had not seriously contemplated the implications of rapid industrialization on agriculture.

Now they tended to view agriculture and industry as rival economic and social systems vying to determine the future character of Germany. (One result of the lack of transition from feudalism to industrial capitalism was the tendency in nineteenth-century Germany to think of agriculture and industry as integral and separate systems.) From their perspective the healthy fundament of society was being sacrificed in behalf of a system that led to social disintegration and might ultimately imperil unification. Sering defined his fears in a candid letter to Lujo Brentano in 1895. A crisis in agriculture in mid-century, he wrote, would not have had severe implications because the artisans were still a vital segment of the economy and an urban proletariat had not yet arisen.[67] But, he continued, if the depression persisted, and engulfed dairy farmers and cattle breeders, the social structure would be transformed beyond repair. Sering repeatedly criticized Caprivi before assemblies of Junkers for lowering Bismarck's duties to a point where they no longer assured a profit to the grain farmer. He found little sense in a tariff scale that did not mitigate the effects of the depression. Fearing that Caprivi would eventually move to abolish grain tariffs, Sering warned, "the free trade policy appears anachronistic in our times, since everywhere large closed economic empires arise, and even England is striving to erect one."[68]

At the 1893 meeting of the *Verein für Sozialpolitik,* Wagner expressed reservations about Caprivi's course. A year later, he accused the chancellor of naïveté and ignorance in economic affairs. His most stinging attack appeared in *Die Zukunft,* where he asked God to bless Germany with a statesman who would not lead the country down the path to an export-industrial state.[69] Speaking to the distinguished members of the Prussian *Agrarkonferenz,* he said: "To me, as to many theoreticians—not only agrarians—it is

67. BA Sering, "Letter to Brentano," (26 March 1895), *Nachlass Brentano.*
68. Sering, *Handels- und Machtpolitik,* p. 37. The effect of Chamberlain's idea of imperial federation on German economists was enormous.
69. Wagner, "Agrar- und Industriestaat," *Die Zukunft* p. 450.

inconceivable how one could fix grain tariffs for ten or twelve years at this moment, especially at such a moderate level. . . . I regret it."[70] It is not surprising that, as Kardorff wrote to his wife, Caprivi looks upon Wagner as one of his three "most terrible personal enemies."[71]

The conservatives' spirited criticism of the New Course also arose from their fear that class conflict was an unalterable accompaniment of industrial capitalism. Wagner, who was most concerned with the polarization of the classes, found that little had occurred in the preceding twenty years to modify his reservations. The years from 1873 to 1893 had been marked by industrial depressions—so much so that they struck him as inevitable occurrences every few years. Bismarck's social legislation had not succeeded in winning the workers away from political radicalism. With every election the Social Democrats gained hundreds of thousands of new voters, and their affiliated trade unions greatly surpassed their Christian and Hirsch-Duncker counterparts in size. The party's Erfurt program was considerably more Marxist and revolutionary in tone than the last one adopted at Gotha. And the near future did not promise any new attempts to mitigate the polarization occurring in the cities; in fact, governmental policy seemed designed to exacerbate the prevailing conflicts. After issuing a manifesto (February 1890) sympathetic to labor, Wilhelm II had gradually come under the influence of the notoriously reactionary Saar industrialist, Baron von Stumm.[72] Stumm accused Wagner and the other *Kathedersozialisten* in 1895 of sympathizing with socialism, and demanded their dismissal from the universities. Although the faculty expressed its support by electing him rector and the students held a day in his honor, Wagner knew the trend of the times favored his adversary. The Stumm Era, as the midnineties became known, produced no new social legislation to sup-

---

70. Wagner, comment from the floor, *Landwirtschaftliche Jahrbücher* 23, supp. vol. 2, p. 121.

71. Siegfried von Kardorff, *Wilhelm von Kardorff* (Berlin, 1936), p. 298.

72. Wagner and Stumm became bitter enemies after Stumm challenged Wagner to a duel. Although Max Weber offered to fight in place of Wagner, the duel never took place. On the controversy see Wagner, *Mein Konflikt mit dem Freiherrn von Stumm* (Berlin, 1895).

plement Bismarck's and Caprivi's.[73] Rather, attempts were made with the emperor's approval to shackle trade unions and to protect scab labor during strikes. Another distressing sign of the times were the resignations of Freiherr von Berlepsch, Theodor Lohmann, and Karl Heinrich von Bötticher from the imperial cabinet.[74] These architects of the progressive social welfare policies of Bismarck and Caprivi felt out of tune with the emperor's shift to a militant antilabor stance. The conservatives recognized the irrelevance of state socialism in an age in which the government, as in America and France, identified completely with the interests of big business. Strangely, they thought that this same state, which had ceased to aid the workers, could be the salvation of the preindustrial estates.

PEASANTRY AND MITTELSTAND

Given the conservatives' assumptions, which were widely shared by contemporaries, there was a peculiar logic in the sense of urgency they felt, and in the new themes that began to emerge in the nineties. The counterpart of their critique of industrial capitalism was a vigorous defense of the preindustrial orders. The reservations expressed earlier about social change hardened into dogma. Wagner could now say, "It has been an error to break with the restrictions and protective arrangements of the guild system, also the whole system of corporations, and to place the individual wholly on his own," and long for the days of Goethe and Fichte, when society had not been "profane and vulgar."[75] With great certitude, Sering warned the Junkers that the social structure of a nation must have a single base and not be an equilibrium of conflicting forces. As a peasant nation, Germany was obliged to preserve its traditional economy or witness the disappearance of that group which

73. There is an excellent chapter on the Stumm Era in K. E. Born, *Staat und Sozialpolitik seit Bismarcks Sturz* (Wiesbaden, 1957), chap. 4. In addition see Fritz Hellwig, *Carl Freiherr von Stumm-Halberg 1836–1901* (Heidelberg and Saarbrücken, 1936).

74. See Born, and J. C. G. Röhl, *Germany without Bismarck* (Berkeley, 1967).

75. Wagner, *Von Territorialstaat zur Weltmacht*, Rede am Geburtstage des Kaisers (Berlin, 1900).

had given the nation its character. The decline of the peasantry would set off a continuing chain reaction until all social groups experienced terrible convulsions.[76]

As scholars the conservatives were not inclined to wander among isolated villages or establish utopian rural communities in imitation of contemporary romantics, but rather to surround the peasants with a mystical halo that defied the stings of economic reasoning. They cavalierly dismissed reason as a fallacious guide in weighing the value of the land and its cultivators. The land was "an object with which no other good . . . is to be compared, and for which, therefore, another legal system has always existed, must always exist, and will always exist, an object that must be considered a special case."[77] The fate of Germany's peasantry could not be decided by the evaluation of abstract numbers. The discredited majority principle had no place in crucial social decisions; what had to be weighed in regard to the peasants was whether the weakening of *Wurzeln und Stamm* was in the long-run interests of the nation.

They did not doubt that the special qualities of those working the soil justified preferential treatment. Manifesting the neo-Romanticism of the nineties, they were wont to describe the peasantry in the vague and almost mystical manner of Rilke. "Rightly," Sering wrote, "we designate the people of the land as the source of eternal renewal of the physical strength of all classes. The fountain of youth of our national strength would be spent with the destruction of the peasantry."[78] Irreplaceable traits were attributed to the tillers of the soil by Wagner. In *Die Woche* he described them as "the strongest part of the domestic population, the reserve of national nerves, muscles, and brain power."[79] Oldenberg urged that the school years of city children be increased by one in order that they learn farming through actual experience. The proposal was designed at once to improve the physical and spiritual training of youth and to reverse the migration to the cities.

76. Sering, "Die Bauern," *Deutsche Monatschrift*, November 1901, p. 237.
77. Wagner, *Grundlegung*, 2:469. Wagner repeatedly urged that economic reason and logic be abandoned when they conflicted with healthy ethical and social ends.
78. Sering, *Handels- und Machtpolitik* pp. 38–39; *Die Verteilung*, p. 630.
79. Wagner, "Die Erhöhung der Getreidezölle," *Die Woche*, 2 March 1901, p. 389.

In the third edition of *Grundlegung der politischen Ökonomie*, Wagner compared the peasantry with the urban working class.[80] He found the former sturdier, more disciplined, and having a greater concern for moral values. Unlike the factory laborer, the peasant considered himself part of a larger community; therefore, he was capable of transcending selfish vested interests. The village churches were filled to capacity every Sunday while those in the cities languished. The peasants were physically tougher, more robust, and unlike socialist workers, ready to die if their country called upon them to do so. Overcrowded cities simply did not produce enough healthy young men with the sense of duty necessary for a reliable fighting force. The peasantry emerged from his analysis as a reservoir for the recruitment and renewal of the urban population. If the source dried up, the cities would quickly atrophy and die. Wagner did not hesitate to draw out the implications of his line of reasoning before a group of staunch agrarians in 1901. "Our future," he said, "has been and still is on the land, and so will it remain."[81]

Like Gustav Schmoller, the conservatives noticed the apparent wane of the *Mittelstand* with regret. In his earliest writings, Oldenberg had denounced the rise of department stores at the expense of small shops. In the late nineties, he called Wagner's attention to the decline of the independent entrepreneur. Wagner, who was old enough to reminisce about local statutes that permitted only one book shop in a town, saw a threat to the state's authority in the trend toward bigness.[82] With economic freedom a holding company in Berlin could establish a hundred branch stores in the provinces, driving the small shopkeepers out of business. The profits from the book trade, instead of being shared among numerous local store owners, amassed at the company's central headquarters, where they were often used to prevent the passage of social legislation. The often distorted guild system, he asserted, provided both for a more equitable distribution of wealth and a close relationship

80. Wagner, *Grundlegung*, 2:456ff. These pages contain a devastating critique of urban life and the values it fostered.
81. Wagner, *Die sozialen und wirtschaftlichen Gesichtspünkte*, pp. 8, 16. There can be no doubt then, that the building of the fleet and the acquisition of foreign territory did not moderate Wagner's hatred of industrialism.
82. Wagner, *Verh. d. 7. Ev. Soz. Kong.* (1896), p. 98.

between employer and apprentices. He warned that the state itself stood in danger from the enormous accumulations of property and capital possessed by the Krupps and the Stumms. Ruling over the lives of forty or fifty thousand workers, these titans had carved out large spheres of power free of state interference. "Here is room for contemplation," he mused, "in the medieval social order more protection was granted to the institution of property, even for the dependent, than in today's society of limitless expansion by the big entrepreneurs."[83]

Max Weber and Lujo Brentano irked the conservatives by viewing the trend toward concentration as inevitable and even beneficial. They were convinced, to the contrary, that the success of large retailers depended heavily on state subsidies. Without bulk mail rates for advertisements, a cardinal advantage of the department stores would disappear. Why, Wagner asked, does the state burden its mailmen and the public by subsidizing "junk mail" when the beneficiaries were socially undesirable? Advertising, he insisted, ought itself to be forbidden; "It is unaesthetic, against every *Volkssprichwort*, and thoroughly immoral."[84]

THE JUNKERS

The conservatives sensed in Caprivi's supporters among Progressives and Social Democrats a determination to bring to an end the extraordinarily privileged position of the Junkers. In taking up the cudgel for them, Wagner and Sering were no less spirited than in their defense of the peasantry. They refused to judge the Junkers by the criterion of economic utility; this, they insisted, was the worst vice of Manchester thought. Their social and political contributions to a stable German empire, which did not appear on statistical charts, were held to outweigh all of their faults. Sering articulated the social and ultimately national considerations that most clearly motivated the defense of the Junkers. "Not the prob-

83. Wagner, *Verh. d. 8. Ev. Soz. Kong.* (1897), p. 61.
84. Wagner decried the growth of specialization in all areas of life. He pondered whether technology had really accomplished that much. Generations earlier, he observed, a man purchased one high-quality suit and passed it on to his son. Now, each generation bought a poorly made suit which wore out quickly. *Verh. d. 7. Ev. Soz. Kong.* (1896), p. 96.

able enlargement or the decrease of domestic grain production, not the price movement as it is, is what causes unrest in public opinion, but the possibility of a social upheaval which could shake our national organism to its foundations."[85]

In harking back to Prussia's past, the conservatives never failed to refer to the Junkers' service to the German people. They were credited with the leadership that drove Napoleon from central Europe, with the acumen and military boldness that led to success in the wars of unification, and with the determination to preserve the victory of 1870. Appealing to patriotic sentiment, Wagner reminded his audiences in 1901, "Was it not the oft-maligned Junkers, who, along with the Hohenzollerns, over many years and through slow work— in war and peace—had molded the Prussian state and prepared the way for the new German empire?"[86] Ignoring the tight monopoly the squirearchy imposed on high state positions, he wondered which class possessed the qualifications to replace the Junkers in the military and diplomatic corps. Both Wagner and Sering were repelled by the vision of a Germany dominated by industrialists and bankers. These groups were held to be no more patriotic than the socialist workers and entirely lacking in the tradition of public service. The idea of Germany falling into the clutches of "mortgage banks, capitalists, and usurers" struck them as a possibility which "no prudent theoretician, reasonable statesman, or good patriot," could seriously entertain.[87]

Sering admitted and was troubled by the existence of absentee landlords, entails, and a tendency toward land speculation in the east. He attributed these developments to the influx of the bourgeoisie, who, as in England, purchased the estates of nobles for hunting retreats or on speculation. Recognizing that the growth of entails in the east prevented a middle-sized peasantry from de-

85. Sering, *Die landwirtschaftliche Konkurrenz*, p. 562.

86. Wagner, *Die sozialen und wirtschaftlichen Gesichtspünkte*, p. 10; *Grundlegung*, 2:461ff. Probably no professor in Wilhelmian Germany defended the Junkers so frequently and vociferously as Wagner.

87. Wagner, *Agrar- und Industriestaat*, p. 116; Sering, "Arbeiterfrage und Kolonization in den östlichen Provinzen Preussens," *Deutsche Landwirtschaftliche Presse* 19 (February 1892): 123; Sering, comment, *Schriften des Vereins für Sozialpolitik* 98, (1901): 238ff.

veloping, Sering, nevertheless, could not bring himself to condemn this archaic institution. He hedged about its effects on the German *Agrarverfassung* and finally came to the conclusion "that in our state a landed aristocracy truly independent and perpetually tied to the soil is necessary as a counterweight to the capitalistic powers and the bureaucracy, . . . and protection through the suitable legal institutions should not be denied them."[88] Avoiding judgments when the interests of the Junkers seemed to be in conflict with the commonweal, Sering preferred to commend the Junkers for providing the peasantry with examples of efficient cultivation. To the radicals desiring expropriation, he pointed to the advantages of farming on a large scale, which could not be duplicated in the dwarf-sized holdings that emerged from estate subdivision.

The conservatives came to believe that there could be no compromise between the estate system of an agricultural people and the more atomized society accompanying industrialization. In their view, the peasantry, *Mittelstand,* and Junkers had the common interest of preserving a social order in which they were a majority and their aims took precedence. By this maneuver the vastly different economic interests of peasant and noble were glossed over. The desire of the peasants to preserve the old order is presumed, albeit they never had a position of power in it. And the working class, for whom the conservatives professed great sympathy, are asked, ironically, to accept new burdens in behalf of a more rural and presumably a more cohesive society.

THE PROGRAM

The conservative economists differed from contemporary neo-Romantics in that they were not fatalistic and believed there was still time to reverse the social and economic trends. They had a program which centered around tariffs and involved them in the burning political issues of the day. For them, the level of tariffs, bimetallism, and incentives to return to the land—questions that bored most cultural critics of industrialism—were supremely important if

---

88. Sering, "Fideikommiss," *Wörterbuch der Volkswirtschaft,* 3d ed. (1911), p. 853. Sering harped upon this theme at his yearly meetings with leading Junkers at the Landes-Ökonomie-Kollegium.

their generation were to have an effect on the future course of German history. Thus they felt impelled in the nineties to take on the role of publicists to ensure that their ideas and policies reached a wide audience, particularly among those involved in the political process. In 1896 Wagner told members of the Protestant Social Congress that professors should actively seek to win public opinion around to their views.

The conservatives implemented their desire to influence policy in a variety of ways. Wagner's weekly public lectures on topical issues drew hundreds of Berliners, including the leading civil servants and army officers. Lujo Brentano wryly observed that Wagner's teachings were disseminated throughout the country by countless economists who had attended his lectures.[89] Treitschke decided to offer a course in socialism at Berlin because Wagner had led so many students astray with his ideas.[90] Sering and Wagner were personally acquainted with Berlepsch, the minister of trade, and Theodor Lohmann of the Ministry of Interior, both of whom listened to these economists' ideas at the informal gatherings of the Staatswissenschaftliche Gesellschaft. The conservatives also sat on the governing board of the Gesellschaft für Soziale Reform along with the leaders of the Center and National Liberal parties.[91] In 1894, they participated in Caprivi's *Agrarkonferenz*, where they discussed tariffs and bimetallism with Miquel, Plötz of the Farmers' League, and Minister von Puttkamer. Oldenberg and Wagner wrote for the widely read *Die Woche, Die Zukunft,* and *Schmollers Jahrbuch.* While Oldenberg frequently spoke to religious groups, Wagner sought a mass audience by accepting speaking engagements in Ruhr mining towns as well as from the Farmers' League. When the tariff controversy raged around 1901, Wagner embarked

89. Brentano, *Mein Leben,* p. 72.
90. Dorpalen, *Heinrich von Treitschke,* p. 203.
91. The Gesellschaft für Sozialreform was founded in 1901 by Freiherr von Berlepsch and included among its distinguished board of directors, Bassermann, Erzberger, Stegerwald, Paasche, and Trimborn of the Center party. On the Berlin society, see Hans Rothfels, *Theodor Lohmann und die Kampfjahre der staatlichen Sozialpolitik* (Berlin, 1927). Among those participating in the Agrarkonferenz were: von Puttkamer, Graf Zedlitz, Graf Kanitz, Johannes von Miquel, and the minister of agriculture, von Heyden.

on a tour of local agrarian assemblies despite his sixty-five years. Wagner's importance reached its height after 1900 when Bernhard von Bülow, who looked upon him as a friend and the greatest influence on his economic thought, ascended to the chancellorship. As the annual speaker at the *Landes-Ökonomie-Kollegium,* Sering was in an excellent position, at the time of the tariff debates, to influence the views of the most politically conscious Junkers.

Two proposals for reversing the tide toward industrial development repeatedly emerged in the speeches and writings of the conservatives—higher tariffs and bimetallism. In both areas they expected effective state action to prove the emptiness of liberal claims about the irrevocability of the rapid social and economic changes experienced by Germany. A half-century of economic freedom, the result of Prussian state policies, had lent an aura of inevitability to urbanization and increased involvement in the world economy. Now that the disastrous consequences of earlier decisions had become apparent, this myth could be shattered by returning to the comprehensive regulations of the cameralist era.

The most extreme demands among the conservatives came from Oldenberg, who called for a policy of complete autarky.[92] In a return to the mercantilistic aims of the eighteenth century, he saw a means of slowing down industrialization without concomitantly weakening German power. Although Germany imported approximately 25 percent of its food, he considered it within the realm of possibility for the nation to grow all its own food. If 30 million farmers produced sufficient food to feed a population of 40 million, then 10 million could safely be allowed to reside in cities; any further urbanization would imperil the nation's future.[93]

For Germany to achieve an autarkic state—one that freed it from the hazards of involvement in an international economy—farming had to be made more rewarding than urban labor. He centered his hopes around either the adoption of Kanitz's plan or a change in

92. Oldenberg, "Kann ein Industriestaat im Kriegsfalle ausgehungert werden?" *Zeitschrift für Agrarpolitik* 1, no. 7 (20 July 1903); "Über den Weizenpreis der bevorstehenden Handelsvertragsperiode," *Zeitschrift für Agrarpolitik* 1, no. 5 (30 May 1903).

93. Oldenberg, "Über den Rückgang," p. 868.

tariff policy. He accused Caprivi and Hohenlohe of dismissing Kanitz's ideas without comprehending the issues that made acceptance imperative. Should Kanitz's plan be repeatedly rejected, he urged the abolition of Caprivi's treaties and the initiation of the tariff rates demanded by the Farmers' League.[94] Such a step would gradually halt the flow from the countryside to the city. The advantages would be numerous, for rural emigration had depressed the wages of urban workers as well as necessitating the employment of migrant Slav labor. By slowing the exodus, urban labor, estate owners, and German civilization in the east would benefit simultaneously. To hasten the deurbanization of Germany, Oldenberg recommended compulsory farm labor for all young males, regulation of internal migration, and the location of military barracks in rural districts. Ultimately, he envisioned a Germany free from dependence on foreign nations and free from social strife in a Europe marked by industrial depression and internal disintegration.

Somewhat less grandiose in his aims, Wagner strongly recommended a five and six mark duty for rye and wheat respectively, but added that raises far higher were justified and even desirable.[95] He campaigned for the changes like a politician running for office. He spoke frequently at agrarian rallies, and at Liegnitz he declared that when liberals called him an "agrarian reactionary," he considered it an honorable name (*Ehrennamen*).[96] Liberal newspapers expressed shock at the sight of a professor stirring up crowds with somber warnings of Germany's imminent decline. Wagner sought to still Social Democratic qualms by offering hopes of a great internal market and a flight back to the land, lessening the labor supply. He urged that funds collected from higher tariffs be used to support the widows and orphans of deceased workers, a plan that was later adopted. The workers were exhorted to remember the pettiness of their concern for bread prices when the nation's destiny hung in the balance. That Wagner believed Germany stood

94. Oldenberg, "Über den Weizenpreis"; "Landarbeitermangel und Abhilfe," *Zeitschrift für Agrarpolitik* 5, no. 2 (February 1907).
95. Wagner, "Die Erhöhung," p. 388; *Agrar- und Industriestaat*, pp. 42ff.
96. *Korrespondenz des Handelvertragsvereins* (15 November 1901); also see *Korrespondenz* (21 March 1902).

at a crossroads cannot be doubted. In 1901 he encouraged the government to ignore Reichstag majorities if they opted for the wrong path; "And the cry will be silenced, as after 1879, and as after all the great changes (1834, 1862, 1866) when an established government had to compel—against a misled public mind—blessings for the German people."[97] After a five and one-half mark duty passed, Wagner admitted the necessity for compromise, but regretted that agrarian aims had not been fully achieved.

When Bismarck introduced the gold standard in 1873, Wagner supported the policy as an indication of Germany's financial solvency and the arrival of the new empire to major power status. He scoffed at the reasoning of bimetallists, claiming that Germany was "swimming in gold," and the supplies from Australia, Siberia, and California more than sufficed for the world's needs.[98] When the agricultural depression persisted into the eighties, he began to reexamine his position on the currency question. He became aware of a dwindling world supply and the manipulations used by silver-standard nations to negate the effects of Germany's tariff. His conversion to bimetallism, which became fully manifest in 1894, must be understood in terms of his loss of faith in tariffs alone as a means of resuscitating agricultural prosperity. By the mid-nineties it was evident to him that agriculture's problems were not the result of a temporary combination of factors. Many of the criticisms of gold made in 1894 had been equally valid in 1873, but at that time agriculture had not been in serious straits. In 1894 he could say what was unthinkable in 1873: "We cannot allow our landed, our peasants, also our Junkers to be ruined . . . as in England. We ought . . . not surrender the working class to the power of money capital, the dependence of the economy to the money powers of the stock exchange, which increases under the gold stan-

97. Wagner, *Agrar- und Industriestaat,* p. 85. This work, containing the most extreme statement of Wagner's views, went through several printings and two editions in the first year of publication. For the remainder of his life Wagner defended his active role as a publicist in the 1902 tariff campaign. See "Die Reichsfinanznot und die Pflichten des deutschen Volks wie seiner politischen Parteien," *Die Woche,* nos. 35–37 (29 August, 12 September 1908); and his essay in *Deutschland unter Wilhelm II* (Berlin, 1914).

98. Wagner, "Unsere Münzereform," *Deutsche Zeit- und Streitfrage* (Berlin, 1877), no. 6. Also see *Für bimetallistische Münzpolitik Deutschlands* (Berlin, 1881).

dard."[99] He warned the Farmers' League and ministers at the *Agrarkonferenz* of agriculture's bleak future if gold continued to be worshiped. Where England's gold standard had previously been admired, it was now considered a major cause of the decline of the island nation's agriculture. Although not as eloquent as William Jennings Bryan, Wagner came to believe that Germany was also being crucified on a "Cross of gold." He joined Kardorff in prodding Caprivi to establish an investigation of currency problems. Kardorff's pressure, with the support of Wagner and other financial experts, forced Caprivi to convene a currency committee in 1894, which managed to resist the bimetallist onslaught. Three years later, on the eve of new gold discoveries in Alaska, Kardorff claimed that a Reichstag majority for a double standard lay just around the corner.[100]

Although Wagner invested his greatest hopes in tariff and currency changes, occasionally he broached a third means of halting the industrial tide—emigration. Believing that overpopulation spurred industrialization, he wondered in the nineties if the process could not be brought to a halt by the state's adoption of a carefully designed population policy. France, with its low birth rate, had neither the leveling of culture Wagner observed in Germany, nor the hypertrophied urbanization. With great vigor, Wagner urged the *Agrarkonferenz* (1894) to set a goal of no more than 500,000 increase per year; that is, a reduction of some 300,000.[101] Disagree-

99. Wagner, *Die neueste Silberkrisis und unser Münzewesen* (Berlin, 1894), p. 4. At the Agrarkonferenz in 1894 Wagner told the members that he agreed fully with the Bund der Landwirte position on bimetallism. He was often quoted by Kardorff in the Reichstag as the leading academic supporter of a double currency.

100. Under Kardorff's prodding, the Prussian Landtag passed a resolution approving bimetallism by 188 to 92. Support for bimetallism was mushrooming in the Reichstag in the mid-nineties after the repeated defeats of Kanitz's plan. S. von Kardorff, *Wilhelm von Kardorff*, pp. 328ff.

101. Wagner, comment, *Landwirtschaftliche Jahrbücher* 23, supp. vol. 2, p. 252. For his views on population, see "Die Auswanderung," *Allgemeine Zeitung*, Beilage, 8 June 1880; *Grundlegung*, 1:650ff; *Agrar- und Industriestaat*, pp. 74ff. According to Wagner, a Spartan system of rigidly selecting marriage partners with regard to their health, intelligence, and character was lacking in virtue, "but it was not more terrible than the present reality." At times, he lamented new discoveries in medicine, which allowed weak and deformed children to live on and become a burden on the state.

177

ing sharply with Oldenberg, he demanded that emigration be encouraged and incentives be given for families to limit their size. Germany need not develop a two-child family as in France, he stated, but the eight- or ten-child family was positively harmful.

Along with the other conservatives, Sering emphasized the importance of the tariff. He considered it the simplest mechanism for increasing the cultivator's share of the national wealth. Dismissing the traditional arguments of economic liberals, he pointed out that the peasantry would not have survived the depression of the eighties had Bismarck been an adherent of the Manchester philosophy.[102] The ineptness of theory was once again demonstrated, Sering thought, by the inability of the doctrinaire free traders to save agriculture without sacrificing their precious dogma.

The level of the tariff was to depend upon the requirements of grain cultivators. Sering would have favored a sliding scale if the manipulation of speculators did not customarily prevent this system from functioning as ideally as on a drawing board. During his annual speeches before the *Landes-Ökonomie-Kollegium,* he repeatedly criticized Caprivi and encouraged the Junkers to fight Caprivi's policies. Unlike Oldenberg and Wagner, he did not deny the adverse effect of grain duties on bread prices. The sacrifices demanded of the working class seriously troubled him. To lighten the consumers' burden, he suggested the removal of coffee and petroleum taxes as a corollary to the rise in grain duties. To assuage his conscience further, Sering implored the Junkers to use their increased funds to improve the conditions of day laborers on their estates.

Sering had never placed all his faith in higher tariffs; nor did he have much confidence in the plans of Kanitz or the bimetallism of Kardorff. In 1896 he assured Brentano and Tippel that nationalization of the grain trade would be a disastrous move for all economic interests and would never receive his support.[103] He emphasized, however, that the crisis in agriculture was serious, and that liberal economists had not shown much initiative in dealing with it. Al-

102. Sering, *Handels- und Machtpolitik,* p. 37; "Die Bauern," p. 237.
103. BA Sering, "Letter to Brentano," (26 March 1896), *Nachlass Brentano.*

though an adherent of bimetallism, Sering was sufficiently realistic not to count upon its adoption by the German government. The external opposition of Great Britain and the domestic concerns of industrialists and bankers were, he presumed, of sufficient importance to prevent Hohenlohe or Bülow from abandoning gold.

Toward the mid-1890s Sering perceived that the root of agriculture's problem lay in the *Agrarverfassung* of the eastern provinces. Since the Stein-Hardenberg reforms, the Prussian government had actively encouraged the growth of estates to the detriment of the independent peasant farmer, who gradually fell into the impoverished group of contractual day laborers. In the inability of the day laborer to become an independent peasant Sering detected the cause of overindustrialization, the Polonization of the east, and the rural labor shortage. If the eastern agricultural areas could be populated by middle-sized farms, the crisis in agriculture and industry might abate.[104] The situation in the east would then parallel the west, where migration to the cities had never been substantial and the demand for Slavic labor had never reached the dimensions that it had in the east.

With the publication of *Die innere Kolonization im östlichen Deutschland* Sering began his campaign to change the *Agrarverfassung* in Prussia's eastern provinces. In his frequent speeches before agricultural groups he reiterated the necessity for a fresh approach to the division of the land. The east could support three times as many farmers if the land were more equitably divided. To realize this aim, Sering urged the government to allocate huge sums for the purchase of bankrupt estates and Polish farms. Actually, the much vilified Caprivi had recognized the importance of an eastern peasantry in 1890, and had set aside funds for the very purpose Sering was advancing. Sering pointed to the rapid increase in yields on peasant farms in the west. The future belonged to the intensive cultivator who required few laborers and knew every inch of land he owned. He predicted that with more education and easier sources of capital the peasantry would far outstrip the estates in yields per acre and profitability. In personal letters to Althoff he

104. Sering, "Arbeiterfrage," pp. 10–13.

was more outspoken, accusing the Junkers of having evolved into a privileged class.[105] France and the United States were lauded for encouraging the survival and even the growth of a rural middle class. Only in Great Britain, where agriculture had declined and industrialization triumphed, had the independent farmer largely disappeared. The lack of an independent peasantry was attributed to the government, whose policy throughout the century had favored the estates. Capital was easily acquired by the large cultivators since the time of Friedrich II, but not until the 1890s had it become accessible to the small entrepreneur. By the establishment of *Fideikommiss* and protective tariffs the Junkers had received the bulk of the benefits from the state's intervention in agriculture. Now, he claimed, "the settlement of a part of the estate territories by peasant homesteads is not only a social requirement but a requirement of technical and economic pragmatism. By its correct execution, inner colonization will increase rather than diminish agricultural yields.[106]

Sering praised the colonization law of Caprivi as a turning point in Prussia's agricultural history. The state, henceforth, would throw its weight behind the diligent peasant who could not finance his own holdings. Freely competing in the open market, the state would buy up land, which it would distribute in twenty- to fifty-acre parcels to deserving peasants. If the peasant agreed to till the homestead for a stipulated number of years, he would receive a long-term mortgage. No doubt Sering was favorably impressed by the example of the 1862 Homestead law in America, the execution of which he had witnessed. He urged the Hohenzollerns to follow up the Colonization Act by distributing their vast domains among their tenant farmers and establishing model peasant villages with the excess lands.[107] The paltry funds devoted to colonization were not enough if the German character of the east was to be preserved.

The agrarian magnates attending Sering's speeches were startled to hear that they had contributed to the Polonization of the east;

105. DSB Sering, "Letter to Althoff," (12 December 1897), *Nachlass Althoff*.
106. Sering, "Die Bodenbesitzverteilung und die Sicherung des Kleingrundbesitzes," *Schriften des Vereins für Sozialpolitik* 58 (1893): 141.
107. Sering, "Rede," *Landes-Ökonomie-Kollegium* (1911), p. 388.

that they were indirectly responsible for industrialization, and lastly that they had hindered progress in agriculture. Sering was bombarded with questions. Did he mean to destroy the Junkers as a class? Did he intend to do away with *Fideikommiss?* Was it his intention to deprive the squirearchy of its lands and livelihood? Were the Junkers not the class that had united Germany and guarded its independence? These were questions that Sering should have been prepared to answer. The Junkers were correct in sensing a social revolution in the plans of this conservative professor. Freiherr von Wangenheim, a leader of the Farmers' League, expressed doubt whether Sering's plans would strengthen the agricultural economy of the east and warrant support from the Junkers. Although phrased less militantly, these plans reminded von Wangenheim of socialist programs for agriculture.

The Junkers need not have feared. No professor in Wilhelmian Germany, especially no conservative economist, would have had the temerity to demand a social revolution. As far back as 1894 Sering had defended the Junkers from the attacks of the left. He pointed to the vital role of the landed aristocracy in the nation's economy, and attributed the criticism to traditional hatred.[108] If they had taken the trouble to read *Die innere Kolonization im östlichen Deutschland* carefully, the Junkers would have discovered that Sering believed them to be a social necessity, and that his plans were only designed for the inefficiently administered estates. There was no intention of depriving the Junkers of their power in local government, or for that matter, of weakening their power at all. In another piece he wrote: "I do believe that our nation would suffer a considerable loss through [the Junkers'] disappearance. The most intelligent and wealthiest landowners, who cultivate themselves, will not be lacking when the colonization plans are executed. After all is achieved, the large agricultural entrepreneur and the power position of the Junkers will not be damaged by inner colonization."[109] Continuing to modify his position, Sering asserted that only where the administration of an estate was dominated by a

108. Sering, "Preussische Agrarkonferenz," *Schmollers Jahrbuch* 18 (1894): 968. The same point was made at conferences of the Bund der Landwirte.
109. Sering, *Die Verteilung*, p. 630.

short-sighted capitalist spirit was it antisocial. Still later, Sering thought it unwise to appropriate more than one-seventh of the arable area in the east for the peasantry, and that would derive mainly from expropriated Polish estates.[110]

Sering's clear disavowal of any revolutionary plans did not prevent those landed Junkers influential in the Conservative party from supporting a bill which made inner colonization extremely difficult. The private parcelling of land became subject to bureaucratic machinations and the cost became prohibitive. Sering did not lose heart but pressed the government for greater allocations and urged local councils to supply funds for the division of bankrupt estates within their competence. Needless to say, his advice went unheeded.

By 1912 Sering was despondent about the accomplishments of inner colonization. Between 1890 and 1912 more land had come under entail than had been divided into peasant homesteads in Prussia. The bureaucracy had obviously worked against the success of the legislation. In the end, only 22,190 peasants had been resettled, and the vast majority of these originated in the west. Few day laborers had qualified for resettlement; therefore, the migration to the city had continued with its effects on the shortage in rural manpower. The number of Slavs working on estates rose with each year. Conceived with the hope that it might solve all Germany's economic and social problems, inner colonization expired without having been fully tried or having even minimized the particular crisis for which it was originally intended.

Despite significant differences in methodology, the agrarian thinkers discussed all reacted in similar fashion to the crisis of the 1890s. In this reaction the conservatives reflected three common experiences and attitudes not normally associated: their generation lived through the achievement of unity, all were disciples of Bismarck's *Realpolitik,* and all were products of the cameralist tradition. In addition, their works were marked by the contemporary nostalgia for the *Landvolk;* a sentiment not uncommon in rapidly

110. Sering, "Rede," *Landwirtschaftliche Jahrbücher* 36 (1906): 234.

industrializing nations. They could not divorce their romanticism from their economics. Without the confluence of these factors, it is unlikely that their fears about industrialization would have been so cataclysmic or their attempts to influence the political process so determined.

Those who grew up in the generation of unification appreciated the brilliance of Bismarck's work, and were all too aware that they might not be worthy of preserving his creation. They never took national unity for granted. For this reason the concepts of power and security played a large role in the thought and politics of Germany after 1890. Part of Oldenberg's, Wagner's, and Sering's hostility to industrialization arose from their fear that the diminishing of German power would ultimately lead to political fragmentation. Because unity had been achieved under the aegis of a land based aristocracy they were not inclined to witness the latter's demise. They came to associate patriotism with loyalty to a rural social order. Would the empire be more secure when led by industrialists and defended by workers? A negative response was common to all three, who had witnessed the rise of divisive social forces concomitant with industrial expansion. A healthy social fabric was possible only while the Junkers were the dominant class.

Bismarck's legacy was also apparent in the conservative economists' refusal to rely on other nations for necessities. The attempt to make the other nations dependent on German manufactures, and at the same time to make Germany independent of other nations' goods, was a policy stemming from the Iron Chancellor and his desire to keep illusions out of foreign policy. Because of this realism, sound economics were brushed aside. Free trade became a naïve program of visionaries instead of a dictate of good political economy. Selfish national interests took precedence over the possibility of creating more wealth among nations or distributing the wealth more fairly within a country. Because Bismarck believed Germany's great power status very precarious, a situation of war was considered the norm in formulating economic policy. This trend of thought impressed Bülow as hard-headed realism.[111] That autarky

111. Bülow, *Imperial Germany* pp. 266–67. Much of Wagner's and Sering's thought found its way into Bülow's speeches and writings.

might foster strained relations with friendly powers and arouse their suspicion was not seriously regarded. The sacrifice that autarky imposes on economic growth was deemed worthwhile in view of the supposed gains in national security.

The decade of the nineties was one of social protest in America and Great Britain as well as in Germany. Falling grain prices and industrial depression caused indebted farmers to seek governmental aid in all three countries. But only in Germany did the economic crisis result in intellectuals' seriously advocating a return to a less complicated and presumably more cohesive society.[112] The reason is to be found, I believe, in the vitality of the corporate tradition in German thought. An industrial economy was imposed on a society whose conceptual patterns had not yet been emancipated from the estate system prevalent in Prussia until 1807 (and in spirit and practice long after that date). The unrivaled speed with which Germany industrialized made adjustment all the more difficult. Oldenberg, Wagner, and Sering could not sanction the precedence of individual needs over those of the state. Their training, both economic and religious, led them to view the individual as a small part of a greater whole—whether estate or nation; to constitute society in his interests would result in chaos and the disintegration of the organism.

All three economists manifested a hostility to social conflict, recently characterized by Ralf Dahrendorf as the hallmark of modern German thought. After varying periods of seeking to regulate the strife between industry and labor, the three political economists gave up in the mid-nineties, when Freiherr von Stumm's growing influence on state policy became apparent and when the agricultural population stood with its back to the wall. All dreaded a dynamic society based on unlimited and perpetual social conflict, which they anticipated if industrialization progressed while agriculture languished. Would not such a development immeasurably

112. In America the populist movement had little intellectual support. See C. Vann Woodward's essay "The Populist Heritage and the Intellectual," in *The Burden of Southern History* (Baton Rouge, 1960). Although not fully adequate, the only introduction to German corporatist thought is R. H. Bowen, *German Theories of the Corporate State* (New York, 1947).

increase the strong centrifugal forces that had always characterized the German people, and thereby undermine the empire from within, scarcely a generation after its auspicious beginnings? From this point, it was only a short step farther to yearn for the simpler, and supposedly static society of an earlier age in which harmony rather than conflict was thought to be the rule, and to call upon the state to shift its focus from the working class to the preservation of those groups surviving from the earlier period. As Dahrendorf emphizizes, Germans have found it particularly difficult to recognize that discord is far more prevalent than concord in nature and society.

Raymond Williams points out in *Culture and Society* that organic conservative thought was impossible in England after Burke, because he was the last thinker to experience a preindustrial society. In America the absence of a patriarchal tradition precluded a longing for the past by serious thinkers. Since the golden age was not far in the past for Oldenberg, and his fellow conservatives, their reaction to the economic crisis of the nineties was to retreat from the seemingly insoluble problems arising from the new order. By this response they moved away from traditional conservative thought toward irrationalism and in the direction of a *völkisch* position. Industrialization was destroying the model, integrated social order that had characterized Prussia until the 1870s. England, where disintegration had advanced the farthest, struck them as immoral and past the point of possible redemption. They could not, like Social Democratic intellectuals, look beyond the social dislocation to the inevitable arrival of socialism and a new harmony, for their commitment to national security and the contemporary power structure was too great. According to Friedrich Naumann, Germany entered the twentieth century led by Junkers and bishops hand in hand. The conservative economists bear some responsibility (and would have been proud had they known it) for the continued leadership of the former.

5 The Liberal Response

The Germans have recently suffered, for
obvious reasons, from interpretations of
their history which exaggerate the role of
authoritarian thought in German historical
development. The liberals of 1848 have
been found to have been more nationalistic
than liberal, and the pre–World War I
socialists more bureaucratic than Marxist.
While recent history has enabled scholars to
unearth some of the weaknesses of these
left-wing movements in nineteenth-century
Germany, it has also unfortunately led to a
disproportionate emphasis on the strength
of movements whose aims were later
adopted and exploited by Hitler.

The patriarchal, anti-industrial economists already treated represented only one
trend in German social and economic
thought. In seeking to influence the government they had to compete with a
number of proindustrial economists who
were convinced that Caprivi's policy had to
be continued and augmented if possible.
Since the proindustrials did not recognize
the existence of a crisis, their writings were
responsive in nature, and therefore fewer
in number.

For the most part, the supporters of industrialization were adherents of the Manchester school of economics. Lujo Brentano, Wagner's frequent antagonist, was the leading German proponent of free trade. After two years of study at the University of London in the 1860s, he returned to Munich a crusader for free trade, but unlike the more dogmatic English economists, he recognized the necessity of government intervention in behalf of the working class. His earlier belief that trade unions would constitute a countervailing power to cartels faded in the 1880s. Friedrich Naumann, whose periodical *Die Hilfe* published numerous articles on the industrialization controversy, was a founder of the National Social Movement, which sought to win the Protestant church for the proletariat's cause. Eschewing the paternalism of Stöcker, Naumann wanted the church to support measures, such as the tariff reductions, which were of direct benefit to workers. A third economic liberal was Heinrich Dietzel of Bonn and Freiburg universities, who was noted for his work on tariffs and social reform.

Also subscribing to the proindustrial theme were several prominent economists whose works reflected an ambivalence about free trade or protection. Albert Schäffle was an ardent supporter of Caprivi and fought Bülow's policy of higher tariffs tooth and nail; yet previously he had received a reputation as a "state" socialist while serving as Austrian minister of commerce in the 1870s. Ironically, Wagner had always looked upon Schäffle's works as one of the significant influences on his thought. Similarly, the doyen of agricultural historians, Theodor von der Goltz, inclined more toward the liberals than in the 1880s, when he had approved of Bismarck's renunciation of free trade.

Although the approaches to the controversy by the pro-industrial economists differed, there was a unanimous rejection of the elaborate theories by which Oldenberg and Wagner justified their opposition to continued industrialization. By destroying the premises of the agrarians and demonstrating the impracticability of their aims, the proindustrial writers sought to discredit the agrarian position entirely. Max Weber began the counterattack immediately after Oldenberg's speech in 1897 by contemptuously denying the insecurity of the modern industrial state. According to Weber, the autarkic nation was far more insecure, for its productivity was entirely at the mercy of natural elements.[1] Should drought or early frost wipe out such a nation's crops, it would have to endure famine if adequate foreign exchange had not been earned. Schäffle criticized the agrarians for exaggerating the dependence of industrial nations on agricultural ones. His experience in Austria-Hungary had led him to believe that many industrial products were necessities, and interdependence more accurately described the trade relationship than the dependence of modern nations upon the undeveloped trading partners.[2] In his volume *The Terrors of the Predominantly Industrial State,* published in 1901, Brentano doubted the ability of a nation to export food surpluses if it refused to buy industrial goods.[3] Where would an industrial nation get the exchange to buy food, he asked, if the agricultural states did not provide markets? It was in their interest to have markets for their agricultural surpluses, and recent history had shown that their largest outlets were the industrial exporters with whom they traded.

The aim of deliberately seeking to make Germany autarkic came under particularly heavy fire. Weber warned Oldenberg that no rural idyll would follow the achievement of his goal, but the mass emigration of both capital and men. The restricted possibilities for economic growth would preclude foreign or domestic investment. Not being able to generate new jobs for the growing population, the autarkic state would see its talent siphoned off to countries with greater potential.[4] Adolf Weber, a theoretical economist at

1. Max Weber, "Critique of Oldenberg" *Verh. d. 8. Ev.-Soz. Kong.* (1897), p. 108. The best work on Weber is Wolfgang Mommsen, *Max Weber und die deutsche Politik, 1890–1920* (Tübingen, 1959). See also Weber's *Gesammelte politische Schriften.*

2. Albert Schäffle, *Ein Votum gegen den neuesten Zolltarif* (Tübingen, 1901) p. 198. Brief biographies of most of the liberal economists can be found in Dieter Lindenlaub, *Richtungskämpfe im Verein für Sozialpolitik,* (Wiesbaden, 1967), vol. 1.

3. *Die Schrecken des überwiegenden Industriestaats* (Berlin, 1901), p. 32. Also see the recent biography of James Sheehan, *The Career of Lujo Brentano* (Chicago, 1966). For Brentano's methodology cf. Lindenlaub, 1:123–30. Just before he died, Brentano wrote an autobiography, *Mein Leben im Kampfe um die soziale Entwicklung Deutschlands* (Jena, 1931),

4. Max Weber, "Critique of Oldenberg," p. 108.

Cologne, scoffed at the very idea of autarky. Asserting that the United States with all its natural resources and territory imported 13.1 percent of its consumer needs, he ridiculed a policy seeking self-sufficiency as self-defeating and bound to fail.[5] Fritz Huber, an economist teaching in Stuttgart, who devoted a book to the problem, considered Wagner's aims "fit today only for uncivilized, barbaric peoples."[6] Brentano did not question Germany's ability to achieve self-sufficiency in foodstuffs, but pointed out that this could only be accomplished with imported labor, fertilizers, and horses. Naumann confirmed Brentano's contention by accusing the very groups who desired autarky of cutting their costs through the importation of migrant Slavic labor.[7] Brentano also discerned a certain irony in the position of the agrarians. On the one hand they were repelled by the squalor produced by industrialism, but on the other, they advocated a policy bound to redistribute the national income to the disadvantage of the workers. In order to cultivate enough grain for the domestic market, tariff barriers would have to be high enough to make it profitable to farm even the least fertile lands. This procedure could not help but cause bread prices to soar. To strengthen the inner market Brentano thought it necessary to increase the disposable income of the working population (a theory later put into practice by Henry Ford), and free trade was the most expedient means to accomplish this task.[8]

Adolf Weber and Brentano were particularly critical of the deep pessimism of Wagner about the workers' future. At the annual conference of the Verein für Sozialpolitik in 1901, Ludwig Pohle, a theoretical economist from Leipzig, espoused the anti-industrial theories of the conservative economists. He was immediately challenged by Weber, who asked facetiously whether the speaker did

5. Adolf Weber, *Volkswirtschaftslehre* (Berlin, 1928), 3:465.
6. Huber, *Deutschland als Industriestaat* (Stuttgart, 1901), p. 191.
7. Friedrich Naumann, *Neue deutsche Wirtschaftspolitik* (Berlin-Schönberg, 1906), Cf. the biography of Theodor Heuss, *Friedrich Naumann: der Mann, das Werk, die Zeit* (Stuttgart, 1937); William O. Shanahan, "Friedrich Naumann: A Mirror of Wilhelminian Germany," *Review of Politics* 13 (1951); and W. Conze's essay on Naumann in *Schicksalswege deutscher Vergangenheit*, ed. W. Hubatsch (Düsseldorf, 1950), pp. 355–86.
8. Brentano, *Die Schrecken*, p. 34.

not know that in all the major export industries wages were rising and hours declining.[9] Only in the textile industry, which was not highly mechanized, were the workers faced with unemployment and misery. Brentano admitted the dark side of early industrialism. He perceived, however, in the mushrooming trade union movement a countervailing power to industry—a power that was succeeding in improving the workers' standard of living. In those industries in which unions had penetrated there had been marked progress, and it was attested to by the migration of rural laborers to those firms. Despite his Manchester background, Brentano supported public housing to remedy the unsanitary conditions caused by rapid urbanization. He counseled economists not to despair but to press for legislation to strengthen unions and deal with the distress arising from infant industrialism. There was no other choice, reasoned Brentano, for the evidence was overwhelming that industrialism was not a temporary phenomenon. Old maxims about everybody prospering when the peasant had money were no longer true. Not only did the majority of the population live in towns, but the tax statistics showed even more pointedly that the land had ceased to be the center of German life. The Prussian government collected two-thirds of its taxes from towns and cities. Forty-two percent of urban dwellers qualified to pay income tax in 1900 while only 26 percent on the land were in the same category. Brentano considered that the only alternative to the alleviation of proletarian distress was the disruption of the entire economy with disastrous effects on all classes. This, he claimed, would be the likely result of the implementation of Wagner's and Oldenberg's plans.[10]

Neither Naumann nor Brentano considered Wagner's concern with overpopulation serious enough to require a comprehensive critique. Although not a professional economist, Naumann pointed out the fallacies in Malthus' and Marx's prediction of increased misery. Even the layman in 1900 could see that the workers' stan-

9. Adolf Weber, speech reported in the *Schriften des Vereins für Sozialpolitik* 98 (Berlin, 1901): 292.

10. Brentano, *Die Schrecken*, pp. 30–40; cf. Brentano, "Wagner und die Getreidezölle," Die Hilfe 7 (1901): 5; *Die Getreidezölle als Mittel gegen die Not der Landwirte* (Berlin, 1903), p. 278.

dard of living had been edging upward for over three decades. Brentano believed that the best method of discrediting Wagner's population theories was to satirize his hopes for Germany: "Therefore the future of the German nation lies in the production of agricultural supermen in the midst of increased child mortality, and the doing away with superflous elderly people by means of poverty induced by dearer bread."[11] In a more serious vein, Brentano alluded to the trend toward reduced birth rates apparent in all western nations, which precluded any overpopulation problems in the immediate future.

Conservative fears of an adverse balance of payments were similarly not disturbing to proindustrial economists. Karl Helfferich, subsequently minister of finance, noted the tendency of the wealthiest countries to have trade deficits while poorer nations such as Austria-Hungary and Russia had export surpluses.[12] There seemed to be no correlation between affluence, standard of living, and economic growth, and the balance of payments. On the surface, America had a very favorable balance, but when tourism dividends and shipping costs were deducted the surplus dropped sharply.

Since most liberal economists looked upon England as the Mecca of economic theory, they were compelled to defend the repeal of the Corn Laws in 1846. (Wagner had criticized it.) According to Adolf Weber, the two and a half decades after 1846 were among the most prosperous in England's history. Grain prices had not sunk as low as farmers anticipated, and where costs were too high there was a transformation toward dairy and cattle farming.[13] Brentano noted that no parliamentary commission was appointed in these decades to investigate agriculture. Only in the 1880s, when farmers were in dire straits all over Europe, was a parliamentary committee necessary.[14] The decline of the independent peasant, so lamented by conservatives, was not a result of Peel's treachery,

11. *Die Schrecken*, p. 52; "Adolf Wagner über Agrarstaat und Industriestaat," *Die Hilfe* 7, nr. 23–28.
12. Helfferich, *Handelspolitik* (Leipzig, 1901), p. 53. Helfferich, who studied both with Wagner and Brentano, started as a disciple of the latter but became a nationalistic conservative after the war.
13. Adolf Weber, speech (see n. 9), p. 539.
14. *Die Getreidezölle als Mittel gegen die Not*, pp. 29–34.

Brentano emphasized, but an eighteenth-century occurrence related to enclosure and high grain prices. At that time the capitalist farmers had bought out the independent peasantry or enclosed their land in order to take greater advantage of the sellers' market. In 1846 those farmers who cultivated infertile soil at high costs and whose profits were dependent on inordinately high grain prices suffered. But, Brentano continued, these farmers had only entered the grain market because of the artificially high prices of the Napoleonic war period. Normally their cultivation of grain would have ceased in 1815 if their political influence had not caused grain to be kept at abnormally high prices until 1846. He summarized his defense of England's economy by calling it the soundest and wealthiest in the world, because it had carried the international division of labor farther than any other nation.[15]

Although proindustrial economists lightly dismissed the arguments advanced by their opponents, they never underestimated the pull of these ideas on educated Germans. In the growth of navalism and colonial demands, Brentano perceived the logical development of Wagner's thought. The next war, he warned, would begin not because there was a competition for markets but because Germany was seeking to insure supplies of raw materials and politically dominate markets, both of which derived from Wagner's dogma. Helfferich believed the danger of Sering's and Oldenberg's policies to lie in domestic affairs. At the Verein für Sozialpolitik conference in 1901 he said, "I see the greatest danger not in an industrial state per se, but in that we pursue an agrarian policy in an industrial state; a policy . . . which will destroy industry and the proletariat."[16] Max Weber did not predict the destruction of industry, but he did predict one ominous development—the feudalization of the German middle class. If Liberal economists were to convince legislators of the desirability of low tariffs, they had to present their views of agricultural distress, and their cures as well as reasoned critiques of the protectionists.

In the 1890s, few denied the existence of distress in agriculture.

15. *Das Freihandelsargument* (Berlin, 1901), p. 12.
16. Helfferich, speech reported in the *Schriften des Vereins für Sozialpolitik* 98 (Berlin, 1901): 259.

The causes, however, were very much in question. Oldenberg, Wagner, and the Junkers held low grain prices responsible for all the evils afflicting farmers. Shortages of labor and indebtedness were conceded to be disturbing, but not of great relevance to the crisis. Sering, as we have seen, placed the emphasis on the chronic problems, and men such as Brentano and Weber went farther than Sering in discounting the price decline.

Several economists, sought to put the farm crisis in perspective by investigating conditions in different states and among different types of farmers. Johannes Conrad, a rarity among liberal economists because of his former life as a West Prussian estate owner, claimed that advances in communication and transportation in the late nineteenth century enabled astute eastern farmers to find compensation for their loss of grain revenues.[17] With the coming of the railroad to Prussia's eastern provinces, bulky resources such as lumber, construction materials, and dung could be transported for the first time with considerable profit. Conversely, the railroad had cheapened the cost of many goods that were annually imported on the large estates. Von der Goltz sought to prove in his *History of Agriculture* that the depreciated price levels were primarily in the crops of the East Elbian estates. Schleswig-Holstein and Bavaria, where pigs and cattle were common, did not experience a crisis at all, he stated.[18] Walther Lotz, an economist at Leipzig, confirmed von der Goltz's work when he alluded to his studies of Bavaria. In this south German state he found that the income from grain amounted to 15.5 percent of the farmers' total, or 127,491 marks out of 824,407 marks in one area.[19] Finally, all these economists agreed with Max Weber's assertion in 1897 that Germany was not an economic entity, but consisted of two distinct agricultural halves about which there could be no common generalization.[20] According to these writers, there existed minor distress in the west and a seemingly severe crisis in the east.

17. Conrad, "Die Stellung der landwirtschaftlichen Zölle," *Schriften des Vereins für Sozialpolitik* 40 (1900).
18. Goltz, *Geschichte der deutschen Landwirtschaft* (Stuttgart, 1902), 2:395.
19. Walther Lotz, "Wirkungen der gegenwärtigen und Ziele der künftigen Handelspolitik," *Schriften des Vereins für Sozialpolitik* 92 (1901): 134.
20. "Critique of Oldenberg," p. 111.

Common to all liberal economists was the belief that the Junkers had "feathered their own nest" by amassing inordinately high debts in speculative ventures in the 1870s. The comparatively high indebtedness of the estates in contrast to the peasants has been discussed earlier. Schmoller, Brentano, and Von der Goltz believed that German agriculture would never be sound as long as the Junkers remained large debtors. To proposals of debt ceilings, they responded that the problem was one of already existing debts, not the anticipation of future speculation. Von der Goltz and Weber were alone in questioning the vitality of the Junkers as an economic group. In high indebtedness the former perceived a symbol of the growing incapability of the squirearchy to manage their farms. Educated to the military or the bureaucracy, they returned to their estates in middle age with little grasp of agronomy, and evinced more interest in land speculation than in the routine of farm management.[21]

However, the cause given greatest emphasis by proindustrial writers was not indebtedness but what Helfferich called the "incongruity between land value and land productivity."[22] Since 1770 the price of arable land had risen 800 percent, of which 300 percent had occurred since 1850. It was evident that neither productivity nor prices had warranted such an inflationary spiral. The result of the German experience was that two and a half acres in 1900 cost between 28 and 240 marks in Russia, 72 and 384 marks in America, and 648 and 824 marks in Germany, despite the fact that interest rates and taxes were less of a burden to the German farmer.[23] Brentano reasoned from these figures that the costs of German grain were growing less rather than more competitive because of the land prices and the fall in transportation rates enjoyed by Germany's competitors. Tariffs in the 1880s had prevented land prices from falling in response to the new competition, so that the noncompetitive state of agriculture was perpetuated. In a normal economy land prices would have declined in response to a less optimistic outlook and thereby reduced the costs of production. Both

21. Goltz, *Geschichte*, 2:404.
22. Helfferich, speech (see n. 16), p. 173.
23. Brentano, *Die deutschen Getreidezölle*, p. 27.

Weber and Brentano pointed to the inability of a farmer to invest in machinery, manure, and the like, when all his resources were necessary to pay for his rent or mortgage. Would tariffs alleviate the causes of distress? Over this question the bitterest dialogue took place between pro- and anti-industrial economists.

The controversy in the years 1900 and 1901 was not over free trade, as some protectionists proclaimed, but over the preservation of Caprivi's tariff levels. Not even the most dogmatic of free traders hoped to see a reduction of the duties. Attacked by agrarian organizations and Junker politicians, they were forced to defend Caprivi rather than press for further reforms. It could not be denied that grain prices had fallen during the course of the Caprivi treaties, but few economists attributed the drop solely to the reductions. Even Schmoller, who hedged about the entire tariff question, refused to sanction the agrarian claim that a fifteen mark reduction caused a fifty mark drop in price. At the Verein für Sozialpolitik convention of 1901, Schmoller praised the treaties for having provided a balance between the interests of agriculture and those of industry.[24] To von der Goltz, Caprivi was free of any blame for the depressed grain prices. Despite the reduction, the German price had remained well above the world price, and von der Goltz reminded his readers that the price of wheat in Munich was higher than in Paris notwithstanding the higher French duty.[25] There was no evidence, he thought, to presume that the continuation of Bismarck's duties would have moderated the decline. Helfferich pointed to the tariff wars engaged in by France against Switzerland and Italy because of its protection; wars Germany had avoided because of Caprivi.

Agriculture aside, it was difficult to deny that the German economy had enjoyed a prolonged boom period in the 1890s. In unguarded moments Wagner joined the chorus of economists who looked back on the 1890s with satisfaction. Schmoller also departed from his usual equivocation to say: "Let us not be deceived. We

24. Gustav Schmoller, speech reported in the *Verhandlungen des Vereins für Sozialpolitik* 98 (Berlin, 1901): 266.
25. Goltz, *Geschichte*, 2:9, 13.

have experienced from 1894 to 1900 such a dazzling upswing as not to be matched in the last fifty, sixty, or seventy years."[26] Adolf Weber called it "the period of the greatest technical and organizational progress."[27] Faced with the seeming challenge of anti-industrialists to the preconditions of prosperity, liberal economists let loose a vociferous attack on protection and its adherents. Scores of pamphlets were published. Brentano belabored the liberal outlook in numerous volumes until 1918, when he was seventy-seven years old.[28]

In 1901, many liberals perceived a unique departure from former protectionist campaigns. Previously tariffs had been defended by reference to Hamilton or List, both of whom had advocated educational duties until industries came of age to compete. Neither had been particularly well disposed to agricultural duties. These duties had always been considered temporary, to be kept in force only as long as a crisis persisted. But now, Schäffle said, the protectionists no longer looked upon tariffs as a necessary evil, but were speaking of the positive good they would do. Only a few still insisted on the temporary nature of the tariffs. Whereas prior duties might be rescinded immediately if prices rose, this was not the case under long-term treaties, which stipulated that tariffs could not be lowered unilaterally.[29] Appalled by the new tactics of the protectionists, Huber accused them "of gradually and unconsciously planting the antiquated mercantilistic idea deep in the national consciousness."[30] As tariffs were legislated in the Reichstag it was feared that they would buoy up only those groups with political influence. Once accustomed to support, the groups, whether small farmers or chemical manufacturers, would not agree to their removal. The danger of protection was that it might lead to the enrichment of en-

26. Schmoller, "Die wirtschaftliche Zukunft Deutschlands und die Flottenvorlage," *Handels- und Machtpolitik* (Stuttgart, 1900), p. 4.

27. Speech (see n. 9), pp. 488, 508, 546.

28. Brentano continued publishing works on the tariff controversy until 1918. Some of these works are: *Ist das System Brentano zusammengebrochen?* (Berlin, 1918); *The Industrial Organization of Germany under the Influence of Protection* (London, 1908); "Über Ausfuhrprämien," *Jahrbuch der Hilfe*, 1904.

29. Schäffle, *Ein Votum*, p. 90.

30. Huber, *Deutschland als Industriestaat*, p. 132.

trenched political groups at the expense of the general welfare.

Those economists who differentiated between the *Gutscherr-schaft* of the east and the *Grundherrschaft* of the west refused to see in the tariff controversy a struggle between the interests of the consumer and of agriculture. Although the small farmers frequently subscribed to the economic views of the Junkers, it was the opinion of Schäffle and Max Weber that this resulted from ignorance. Both could point to the active support given to the liberals by the peasant organizations of Franken and Oberpfalz.[31] Certain ministers in Baden and Württemberg also came out in favor of retaining Caprivi's tariffs. According to Schäffle, only farmers having more than thirteen acres could benefit from the duties, and as they did not constitute more than one-quarter of the total, no solid agricultural bloc with a uniform interest in higher tariffs existed.[32] Weber referred to the interest of the farmers situated near metropolitan areas in raising the disposable income of urban workers. Even if these farmers sold some grain, their income was more dependent on the ability of the urban population to buy vegetables, eggs, and meat. Quite often, Weber said, these farmers failed to see they shared the same economic aims as factory workers.[33] Schäffle similarly considered the tariff issue too complicated for the peasantry, and explained their frequent support of the Junkers in terms of the enormous investment in propaganda by the estate owners. While some economists tried to prove that the tariffs were not justified by the needs of the peasantry, others sought different reasons for discrediting them.

All the Anti-industrial economists were distressed by Germany's need to import one-quarter of its foodstuffs. Tariffs had been proposed as one method of achieving self-sufficiency. Robert Drill, one of Brentano's disciples, subjected this defense to a penetrating analysis. After weighing tomes of statistics, Drill found that Germany could theoretically reach a point where food imports might

31. Brentano, *Die deutschen Getreidezölle*, pp. 26–27. Farmers from Württemberg and Oldenburg also generally supported low grain tariffs because of their reliance on urban markets and cattle for income.

32. *Ein Votum*, p. 36.

33. "Critique of Oldenberg," p. 122.

be dispensed with. The increased production would have to come from a more intensive use of the soil under cultivation, since few fertile areas remained unplowed.[34] This could only be achieved, wrote Drill, if the government barred all further foreign grain competition. In effect, the market for grain would have to be guaranteed by the government irrespective of its price. As a result, the spiraling price of grain would induce farmers to invest heavily in machinery, hire more labor, and bring semifertile areas under cultivation. Once farmers were assured that the financial risks involved in expansion were small, grain production could be expected to rise until the nation's needs were covered. In the opinion of Drill and other liberals, however, the cost of such an enterprise was prohibitive. The goal of self-sufficiency in grain would necessarily be accompanied by rising production costs, and as a result the price of bread would rise a significant percentage. Farming would also begin to draw investment away from sectors where it was more needed and normally more profitable.[35] Thus, industry would want for capital and the consumers would devote ever larger percentages of their disposable income for food. The national income would suffer accordingly.

Max Weber and Brentano further feared the rise of an agricultural marketing cartel. Having a guaranteed domestic income, Junkers whose production costs were low might use their fat profits to undercut grain prices in foreign markets. It would be ironic, thought Weber, if the aim of protecting the German farmer from competition was realized in such a manner as to make him a menace on the international market because of the amount of the subvention. He termed "subvention of agriculture the only example of a real export premium that we in Germany know."[36] Concurring with Weber, Brentano viewed the tariffs as aggressive insofar as they were designed to enable the Junkers to compete in foreign markets. But the major concern revolved around the effects on the penurious working class.

34. Drill, *Soll Deutschland seinen ganzen Getreidebedarf selbst produzieren?* (Stuttgart, 1895), p. 117.
35. Ibid., pp. 22ff.
36. "Critique of Oldenberg," p. 106.

From Adam Smith to Gottfried Haberler, free-traders have abhorred tariffs primarily for their tendency to reduce real wealth. Agricultural duties have come under more fire than others because they work in a regressive manner, striking most severely the families who devote a large percentage of their income to food. Desiring to prevent any upward changes in 1902, liberal economists emphasized the irony of raising bread prices while pursuing an active social policy. Was the government not taking away from the worker with one hand what it was offering with the other, asked Lotz? Rather than being strengthened by higher duties, the empire, liberals feared, would be weakened by a resurgence of socialist militancy, supported by an enraged, bread-consuming populace. Dietzel warned that those seeking changes in rates would be responsible for an upsurge in the parliamentary representation of the socialists.[37] Schäffle, who was given to flights of the imagination and who had an elevated view of citizenship, warned of a German version of the anti–corn law movement and possibly even a boycott of German bread by consumer groups. Pensioners dependent on fixed incomes would suffer immeasurably and might be led into the radical camp. In his view a new tariff constituted an extremely radical piece of legislation.[38] Using the protectionist framework of thought, von der Goltz sought to establish that the military strength of the nation would be impaired. Recruits who had been raised on diets free of meat and vegetables because of high bread prices would not make rugged soldiers. To relegate a generation of workers' children to undernourishment, von der Goltz said, was no way to fortify the body politic.[39]

Dietzel devoted a pamphlet to disproving the inner-market theory propagated by Oldenberg. Opposing the view that the domestic economy was strengthened by tariffs, he showed how they harmed numerous economic groups. Utilizing the multiplier theory, Dietzel pointed out that industrialists and truck farmers would lose their domestic consumers because funds formerly spent on

37. H. Dietzel, Speech reported in the *Verhandlungen des Vereins für Sozialpolitik* 98 (Berlin, 1901): 247.

38. *Ein Votum*, p. 209.

39. Goltz, *Agrarwesen*, p. 25.

their products would now go to the purchase of bread. And so on, throughout the economy, consumption would decline, causing unemployment and wage reductions. Dietzel concluded that an economy cannot prosper on the basis of artificially raised prices and a depressed real income of the majority of the population.[40]

More practical arguments were also adduced to convince legislators of the tariff's deleterious effects. Lotz referred to the German villages in Switzerland and Holland, whose inhabitants considered it cheaper to live beyond Germany's borders while working in its factories. Drill sought to prove that the crime rate was dependent on the price of bread, by publishing graphs that showed a direct relationship.[41]

Paul Mombert, a statistical economist, undertook to substantiate the liberal allegations. He found that in the years of high tariffs (the 1880s) bread consumption declined by 14 percent while that of potatoes rose by 7 percent.[42] This change in diet he believed to be a prime cause of lung diseases in the cities. Wagner was accused of misleading the people because of his assertion that grain and bread prices are not necessarily directly proportional. There were numerous instances cited to prove that a change in the grain price was eventually absorbed by the consumer rather than the grower or middleman. Another economist, Arthur Schulz, wrote of the 1.5 million workers whose income was dependent on exports, and who would be directly harmed by any retaliation to higher German duties. Schulz emphasized that the prosperity of one group did not signify that other groups would be advantageously affected.[43]

Having destroyed the illusion of protection to their satisfaction, the liberals next turned to the real purpose of the protectionists. It was not to aid agriculture, or to make the nation self-sufficient, but to guarantee the Junkers a minimum income from their estates. According to Schäffle, they were the sole economic group that refused to adapt to the changing economy. Rather than seeking new prod-

40. Dietzel, *Kornzoll und Sozialreform*, (Berlin, 1901), pp. 35ff.
41. Drill, *Soll Deutschland*, p. 32.
42. *Die Belastung des Arbeitereinkommens durch die Kornzölle* (Jena, 1901), pp. 16, 21.
43. *Kornzoll, Kornpreis, und Arbeitslohn* (Königsberg, 1902), pp. 50–60.

ucts to remain competitive, they devoted their energies to isolating themselves from competition. Walther Lotz sought to put the situation in perspective for the Verein für Sozialpolitik members: "The leaders of agriculture, whose aims are the same today as at the time of the Kanitz plan, are striving through higher duties for a guaranteed profitable price for their wares; first by state intervention and second by sacrificing the public. The only analogy is with the demands of the workers for minimum wages and an eight-hour day."[44] Lotz emphasized the difference between demands for economic security by the leading social and political group and the impoverished masses of the empire. Conrad called upon his experience as a landowner to assure his readers that the Junkers could introduce new crops if they wanted to. Naumann explained the Junkers' lack of desire in terms of their inflexible opposition to change, whether economic, political, or social.[45] All the proindustrial writers agreed that prices would not be stabilized as the Junkers proclaimed, but would become more mercurial because of the reduced sources of grain. When free trade was in force, prices remained relatively stable because a poor crop in one area was usually contemporaneous with bumper crops elsewhere. In an autarkic nation, prices would skyrocket in bad years and fall precipitously in good ones. The most penetrating view was from the pen of Conrad. Taking cognizance of the frequent buying and selling of land in the east, he pointed out that a new owner did not receive any benefit from established duties because they were discounted in the purchase price of his lands. Thus, to increase the value of his property he had to seek higher duties, which would escalate land prices on the grain-growing estates.[46]

Both Max Weber and Naumann were among the most perceptive critics of the Hohenzollern empire. They knew that the *ultima ratio* for the tariffs was not to be found in economics, but in the social and political structure of the empire. It was from this controversy that Weber began to question Marx's premises, for he witnessed

44. "Wirkungen, der gegenwärtigen und Ziele der künftigen Handelspolitik," *Schriften des Vereins für Sozialpolitik* 92 (Berlin, 1901): 127.
45. *Neue deutsche Wirtschaftspolitik,* p. 192.
46. Conrad, "Die Stellung," p. 118.

the great industrialists sacrificing their economic interests to ally themselves with the sovereign class. Instead of seeking a lower cost of living for their employees, industrialists were concerned with commissions in the army, social prestige, and getting their sons into aristocratic fraternities; all of which were to be achieved only by recognition of the nobility's prerogatives. Weber explained these bourgeois values in terms of the "feudalization of bourgeois capital."[47] The result was the continued predominance of the Junkers in German political life. The tariffs were a tour de force, whereby the Junkers demonstrated their ability to use their political influence to fortify their source of wealth. The success of their attempt connoted the complete feudalization of the industrialists, who found it more congenial to oppose the impotent mass of Social Democrats than the determined grip of the Junker oligarchy.

Naumann, whose *Demokratie und Kaiserthum* remains with Arthur Rosenberg's *Entstehung der deutschen Republik* and Kehr's *Schlachtflottenbau und Parteipolitik* among the best analyses of power in the post-Bismarckian empire, refused to see the controversy as a dispute over a fifteen mark difference in duties. "All economic debate," he wrote, "is only the accompaniment of a bitter struggle for power in the state. The present leaders of the tariff movement were themselves free-traders thirty years ago. At that time free trade was the path to power. . . . The tariff is not to be conceived of as an economic measure; as such it is and must remain incomprehensible. It is a foray of political will into the economy. As an old, tested ruling class, the grain nobility knows the borders of its power, and would rather share it with the iron barons than give it up.[48] What Naumann did not himself understand was that a *Sammlungspolitik* of industry and agriculture entailed not the full sharing of political power but shadowy concessions by the Junkers to maintain the essence of power.

A key argument in the arsenal of Wagner and Sering was the weakness of an industrial nation in wartime. Particularly after the

47. "Critique of Oldenberg," p. 109. Also see Mommsen, *Max Weber und die deutsche Politik.*
48. *Neue deutsche Wirtschaftspolitik*, p. 192.

cementing of the Franco-Russian alliance and Fashoda, many Conservative thinkers considered war even more likely. A nation dependent on foreign food supplies and experiencing a growing rate of rejection, on medical grounds, of urban draftees, was not preparing for the eventuality of conflict. Wagner and Sering held industrialization responsible for the nation's seeming military weaknesses. Postwar writers looking back on the controversy often adjudged the protectionist arguments valid because they had foreseen the need to increase food supplies.

In fact, the shortage of food during World War I may well have been due to the execution of the protectionist program. During the tenure of the 35 mark duty, dairy and cattle farming increased at an unprecedented pace concurrently with the improvement of grain yields. Schäffle suggested that the government purchase grain on the open market for storage. Grain sellers would thus have an additional market, and the fear of scarcity in war would be reduced. But all this worry would prove unnecessary, he thought, if Germany recognized that it would never be self-sufficient, and fostered good relations with Great Britain—the only power capable of a blockade.[49] Brentano, of course, emphasized that no matter how much grain was cultivated on the eastern estates, Germany would never be self-sufficient because of the emigrant labor necessary for harvesting. During hostilities the labor shortage would grow even worse.

The one subject on which proponents of industrial development and agrarians shared common opinions was *Weltpolitik*. Brentano, Max Weber, and Naumann joined Sering's and Wagner's campaign in behalf of a large navy.[50] To a greater or lesser extent they all believed that Germany had no choice but to expand into Asia and

49. Schäffle, *Ein Votum*, p. 95, and "Zur wissenschaftlichen Orientierung über die neueste Handelspolitik," *Zeitschrift für Staatswissenschaften*, 1893, pp. 126, 133.

50. Tirpitz thanked Brentano for his efforts in behalf of the navy. Cf. Sheehan, *Lujo Brentano*, p. 180; Max Weber, "Der Nationalstaat und die Volkswirtschaft" *Gesammelte politische Schriften* (Tübingen, 1958); Mommsen, *Max Weber und die deutsche Politik*, p. 88; Max Weber, *Verhandlungen des 7, Ev.-Soz. Kong.* (1896); Naumann, *Neue deutsche Wirtschaftspolitik*, p. 19.

Africa or be strangled by the world empires of the British, Americans, and Russians.[51] Both in his 1895 Freiburg inaugural lecture and before the Protestant Social Congress in 1896, Max Weber anticipated the wave of imperialist sentiment that swept over Germany after Tirpitz's rise to prominence. He told the Protestant group: "We require foreign territory (*Raum nach aussen*), an increase in the possibilities for profit through expansion of the opportunities for markets; that means expansion of Germany's economic sphere of power, and this is absolutely necessary today through expansion of political power outwards."[52] More than a year later Oldenberg, Wagner, and Sering began to expound this theme.

Despite the agreement on aims, differences emerged almost immediately between the two groups of economists. For Weber and Brentano an autarkic trade policy and *Weltpolitik* were irreconcilable objectives. An agricultural society simply could not generate the wealth required to support a powerful navy and sizable commercial fleet. To substantiate this point, Brentano referred to the taxation statistics of Prussia, where, in 1900, of an assessed income of 7.8 billion marks, 5.4 originated in towns and cities and 2.3 in rural areas. Taxes per inhabitant in Saxony averaged 8.3 marks per annum within urban districts to 2.0 in the villages.[53] Weber's frequent and vitriolic attacks on the Junkers must be understood in the context of his belief that their continued political hegemony and the attainment of world power status for Germany were incompatible. Thus, the desire not to be left behind in the race for empire often motivated the drive for intensified industrialization.

Brentano also sought to show, with the aid of the Bavarian statistical survey, the exaggerated nature of protectionist claims about the physical fitness of peasants for military duty. First, he asked his readers to remember that the funds to support the army were collected predominantly in urbanized districts. Next, he pointed to the

51. Even Schmoller urged colonial expansion in Brazil. *Zwanzig Jahre deutscher Politik, 1897–1917* (Munich, 1920), pp. 3–9; *Handels- und Machtpolitik*, p. 12. On the attitude of professors toward the navy cf. Wolfgang Marienfeld, *Wissenschaft und Schlachtflottenbau in Deutschland, 1897–1906* (1957).
52. *Verhandlungen des 7. Ev.-Soz. Kong.* (1896), p. 123.
53. Brentano, *Die Schrecken*, p. 10.

large population growth made possible by an industrial economy. From 24 million people in 1815, the new economic base had provided employment for the support of 60 million in 1900. Emigration and famines had ceased with the triumph of industrialism. About physical fitness he wrote, "Certainly there exists a difference in the suitability of those born on the land and those in the cities, but it is neither universal, nor, where it exists, considerable."[54] In Bavaria, of every 1,000 recruits, about 10 percent more from the land than from the city were found to be eligible. If the occupation of the male parent was the criterion, the difference fell to 5 percent. In Brentano's opinion this did not even provide evidence of rural superiority; for with the workers were included students, professional men, and the *Lumpenproletariat* in the cities. Also, many laborers who worked in suburban factories and lived in villages were counted among the rural recruits. To draw a line between farmer and laborer obliterated these relevant distinctions. By occupation, artisans proved to be the most desirable recruits although they resided indiscriminately in towns or villages.[55] The rapidly growing navy was devoid of peasants. When everything was considered, Brentano found Germany a greater military power because of industrial and urban growth.

Free trade would actually ward off wars, he thought, by giving nations little cause for resentment. The alliance system was attributed rather naïvely to the resurrection of protection in 1879. During and after World War I, Brentano, Weber, and Dietzel blamed the protectionists for alienating Italy and Britain by their narrow and selfish economic views.[56]

The proindustrial cause enlisted the sympathies of economists with disparate motives and opposing methodologies. Younger men like Naumann and Max Weber were attracted to the battle against

54. Brentano, "Der Streit über die Grundlage der deutschen Wehrkraft," *Patria* (1906), pp. 66–70; and, with R. Kuczinsky, *Die heutige Grundlage der deutschen Wehrkraft* (Stuttgart, 1901).

55. Brentano, "Der Streit," pp. 56–58.

56. Brentano, *Ist das System Brentano zusammengebrochen?* p. 51; "Handel und Krieg," *Österreichischen Rundschau*, 15 February 1915, p. 18; *Über den Wahnsinn der Handelsfeindseligkeit* (Munich, 1916).

Junkerdom and agrarian romanticism by the lure of national power and the desire for "a place in the sun." As Weber never ceased to reiterate, the persistence of Germany's feudal past stood in the way of an expansive foreign policy and increased national security. For Brentano and his two students Dietzel and Lotz, the dictates of laissez-faire economics caused them to take up the cudgel against the seeming return to eighteenth-century mercantilism. To the conservative elders of the profession, von der Goltz and Schäffle, the Junker demand for protection beyond the levels granted by Bismarck smacked of a selfishness unworthy of a conservative force in society. Agrarian romanticism was alien to the thought of all three groups. The task of seeking common positive opinions holding this diverse group together is not an easy one. Perhaps the strongest unifying force was a common rejection of the patriarchal state. For them, Germany would be immeasurably stronger when state and society ceased to be rigidly separate entities. They denied Wagner's contention that unity could not withstand the decline of the Junker elite and saw no particular increment to German security in the state's devoting all its resources to support the class from which it allegedly derived its strength. Lastly, they were all free of the characteristic that Mannheim considered the bane of German thought: the assumption that the loathsome trends of early industrial society would proceed inexorably. They demonstrated faith in man's ability to cope with the difficulties of change, and they recognized that the task of resisting all change was not only an imposing one but ultimately self-defeating.

In terms of theory and logic the proindustrial group marshalled a good case; yet the chances of achieving their desired goals were decidedly slim. The ministers whose support Caprivi had relied on while pursuing his tariff reduction course, Marschall von Bieberstein and Freiherr von Berlepsch, either were forced out or resigned during the emperor's widespread purge of 1896–97.[57] Miquel, who in public had been ambivalent about Caprivi's policy, and in private, outright hostile, had since been promoted to the

---

57. See the excellent book by J. C. G. Röhl, *Germany without Bismarck* (Berkeley, 1967). Röhl convincingly shows how Wilhelm II ousted all ministers with independent minds by 1897. This prepared the way for his personal rule and that of his loyal follower Bülow.

vice-presidency of the Prussian Ministry, where his opinions carried considerably more weight than they had earlier. Graf von Posadowsky-Wehner, the scion of a Silesian noble family, had received the Ministry of the Interior primarily because of his antipathy to labor, but equally as strong was his adversion to anything that might undermine the agricultural base of German society.[58] Having served in the provincial administration of the East Elbian province Posen for twenty years, he showed little inclination to yield to arguments posed by liberal economists on behalf of urban consumers. Together, Miquel and Posadowsky selected the members of the all-important committee assigned to draw up new tariff rates. Similarly, Bernhard Bülow, an advocate of the *Sammlungspolitik* between agriculture and industry, had become heir apparent to Hohenlohe at the foreign ministry. Contrary to Weber, Bülow viewed the domestic peace that a successful *Sammlungspolitik* would initiate as an important prerequisite for an active *Weltpolitik.* This new and far more conservative ministry that came into being in the mid nineties dismissed the liberal economists as naïve and lacking in understanding of the peculiar German situation.[59] Also, not coincidentally, two of the three agrarian economists held professorships in Berlin, where their opinions might be politically influential, while Brentano, Max Weber, and Adolf Weber had appointments far from this seat of power.[60] Thus, Caprivi's supporters made little impression on the political scene and, moreover, they failed to rally the nation behind them. As we shall see in the next chapter, their pleas went unheeded by Bülow, who found Wagner's ideas extremely convincing.

58. Hohenlohe, *Denkwürdigkeiten der Reichskanzlerzeit* (Stuttgart, 1931), p. 156; also quoted in Karl E. Born, *Staat und Sozialpolitik Seit Bismarcks Sturz* (Wiesbaden, 1957), p. 143.

59. Theodor Lohmann of the Ministry of the Interior was familiar with Brentano's views and wrote, "Most of [the liberals] have studied the English situation and understand only with great difficulty that the same needs lead us on a different path from there, where there is a different conception of the state" Hans Rothfels, *Theodor Lohmann und die Kampfjahre der staatlichen Sozialpolitik*, (Berlin, 1927), p. 70.

60. That the conservatives were in Berlin was no accident but a product of *Kultusminister* Althoff's decisions. See Arnold Sachse, *Friedrich Althoff und sein Werk* (Berlin, 1928). Lindenlaub points out that the division in the Verein für Sozialpolitik often occurred between Prussian and non-Prussian professors. Of course the Prussians defended the conservative causes.

PART THREE

Es ist die tiefe Tragik des Deutschen
Kaiserreiches, dass sich die Entscheidungen,
die seine innen- wie aussenpolitische Lage
im Jahre 1914 bestimmten, auf die wenigen
Jahre 1897 bis 1902 zusammendrängten
und dass den Zeitgenossen diese ungeheure
Krisis in ihrer letzten Bedeutung nicht
bewusst geworden ist.

Eckart Kehr

6

Bernhard von Bülow: The Pragmatic Approach

The tariff legislation of 1902 has not been accorded the attention it merits. The scope and duration of the debates have been forgotten, as has the passion that a seemingly innocuous tariff proposal aroused. A few statistics will convey the importance contemporaries attached to the changes suggested by Bülow. During the course of the debates 112 speakers rose to make 697 speeches, which filled 1147 pages. Hopeful about the outcome, the right-of-center coalition took slightly less than one-third of the time, while the Social Democrats, whose energies and faith were increasingly put into parliamentary battles, used up nearly half of the total debating time. The latter denied accusations of filibustering by pointing up the immense number of items covered (946 compared with 387 in the previous schedule). The debates were also noteworthy because, for the first time in the history of the Reichstag, members had to be forcibly ejected, and they were consequently rebuked by the president for emulating the parliamentary practices of their Austrian counterparts. More important, however, the tariffs

211

adopted in 1902 were the basis for a system of long-term treaties negotiated with most of Germany's neighbors. And as will be shown in the next chapter, the standard of living of the various classes between 1906 and 1914 was significantly affected by the level of the duties. The controversy throws much light on the functioning of German political institutions, and on what kind of approach by a chancellor was most likely of success. Also, as Eckart Kehr has pointed out, the outcome conditioned German foreign policy for the next decade and put the seal on the ostracism of the Social Democrats from political life. Lastly, the discussions provided a forum at which the merits of industrial capitalism as well as of tariffs were weighed, often with reference to the theoretical controversy engaged in by scholars. As far back as 1810 the industrial revolution had come under criticism in Germany, but never were its characteristics and effects debated so heatedly and so publicly as in the Reichstag sessions of 1902.

To gain perspective on the tariff dispute one must return to certain developments of the 1890s. The fall of Caprivi had been greeted with glee by the Conservatives, who considered him personally responsible for the pro-industrial, pro-Polish, and pro-labor policies of his government. Despite the nobility of Prince von Hohenlohe-Schillingsfürst, his accession to the chancellorship was received with coolness by Caprivi's opponents. Their skepticism seemed confirmed a year later when the chancellor expressed the opinion held by economic liberals that only farmers owning more than twelve and a half acres profited from grain duties. However, Hohenlohe redeemed himself in 1896 by supporting a law long clamored for by Wagner and the Conservatives, which placed restrictions on the practices of the stock exchange. The new law limited and practically ended all trading in grain futures on the exchange, and initiated strict qualifications for all traders in futures. Actually, Caprivi had convened a committee of bankers, merchants, and financial experts in April 1892 to investigate demands by anti-industrial theorists for stringent regulation of the exchange. The committee report proposed the end of certain abuses but denied the need for comprehensive reform. What moved the Reichstag to action was the blatant attempt of the Cohn and Rosenberg brokerage house, in league with several banks, to corner the market in certain agricultural commodities. Occurring while the committee report was being debated in the Reichstag, the attempt led to an overwhelming outburst of passion against the exchange, and to the passage of a tough bill.[1]

Agrarians expected the legislation to end the huge profits made by speculators. No doubt, some regulation was needed in Germany, as in every other industrial country, but the extreme nature of Conservative wishes proved self-defeating, for along with their profits, speculators frequently absorbed losses in depressed years. When prices fell they often paid more than the market value for the grain, and unintentionally stabilized the prices paid to farmers. Within four years agrarian leaders recognized the folly of this attempt to isolate Germany from the world economy.

On 15 November 1897, Hohenlohe announced plans to form an economic committee for the preparation of trade treaties, with Graf Posadowsky, secretary of state for internal affairs, as chairman. There could be little question about Posadowsky's views. A year earlier, he had told the chancellor that trade treaties would strengthen "the part of the population on which the throne cannot rely—the people of the big cities and industrial districts. Only the land population offers support for the monarchy."[2] Of the thirty-six members chosen to serve on the committee, ten were estate owners, eleven came from chambers of commerce, five were from industry,

1. Ulrich Teichmann, *Die Politik der Agrarpreisstützung* (Cologne, 1955), pp. 215–17. Futures trading continued informally outside the exchange until 1900, when exchange leaders and agrarians worked out a compromise. Representatives of agriculture received a predetermined number of seats on the exchange's board of directors, and futures trading returned under a different name. American Populists sought to regulate futures trading also. The Hatch Act was introduced for this purpose in 1891 and actually passed both House and Senate before dying in committee when the congressional session ended. Several southern and western states thereafter prohibited trading in futures within their borders. See Cedric Cowing, *Populists, Plungers, and Progressives* (Princeton, 1965), pp. 5–29.

2. Hohenlohe, *Denkwürdigkeiten der Reichskanzlerzeit* (Stuttgart, 1931), p. 156. For Posadowsky's views cf. Karl E. Born, *Staat und Sozialpolitik seit Bismarcks Sturz* (Wiesbaden, 1957), chap. 6; also *Graf Posadowsky als Finanz-, Sozial-, und Handelspolitiker,* ed. J. Penzler, 4 vols., (Leipzig, 1907–11).

and the remainder were Reichstag members or state officials.³ Both
von Wangenheim and Kanitz were on the committee. The chancellory immediately began to receive complaints from trade organizations and chambers of commerce objecting to the manner of
selection. Posadowsky was soundly criticized for his failure to ask
organized interest groups for representatives. Instead, the members were chosen by the chairman without recourse to the groups
whose interests would be affected by the tariffs. A petition from
the Wiesbaden Chamber of Commerce questioned the appointment of representatives from heavy industry to the exclusion of
those from light industry, and deplored the decision to hold the
sessions behind closed doors.⁴ Along with the Centralverband
deutscher Industrieller, the Wiesbaden Chamber regretted that the
government had not seen fit to appoint a committee to advise the
negotiators subsequently in the bargaining sessions with the treaty
partners. To still hostile criticism, Caprivi had permitted industrialists to sit in on the talks with Russia in 1894. Trading groups,
of course, claimed that there was a noticeable dearth of free-traders. What was more evident and went unmentioned was the absence of a single delegate from the Social Democrats, small farmers, or consumer groups. It was but one more example of the
general lack of concern with the commonweal in post-Caprivi politics. Nearly all the members were concerned with how duties
would affect their particular economic interests, but few if any
were preoccupied with the effects of higher duties on the cost of
living of the 65 percent of Germans earning less than 900 marks per
year. The patriarchal system could not very well function when the
patriarchs themselves were in danger. In a history of the Centralverband deutscher Industrieller written in 1905, the president in
1897, H. A. Bueck, whose sympathies had been with agriculture,
wrote of the patronizing manner that industrialists encountered in
their discussions with agrarians on the committee.⁵ He did not

3. DZA, "Wirtschaftlicher Ausschuss," *Akta betr. Handelsverträge* Rep.
120 CXIII I 80.
4. DZA, "Handelskammer von Wiesbaden," ibid.
5. Bueck, *Der Centralverband deutscher Industrieller und seine 30-jährige
Arbeit* (Berlin, 1913).

doubt that the primary purpose of the committee was to redress Junker grievances against the tariff.

One further event in the 1890s was of supreme importance for an understanding of Bülow's policy. In the first chapter the complicated system by which the Junkers exercised inordinate power under the constitution was described. Their methods of influencing government programs were never more evident than after their defeat over the Russian trade agreement in 1894. Cut to the quick by the failure of their efforts, they determined to utilize the power accorded them in the three-class suffrage system to thwart the attempts of the Prussian government to link east and west Germany by a nexus of canals.[6] Wilhelm II was anxious to be recognized as an enlightened ruler of an industrialized country; unlike most Hohenzollerns his pride was aroused by the sight of Hamburg docks rather than Pomeranian estates. His particular interest in the navy was a symbol of his approval of modern technical developments. Especially in the early years of his reign, Wilhelm wanted to impress Europe with his modern ideas and sympathy with contemporary economic changes. For these reasons, he imparted his support to the ministry's plan for building the Dortmund-Ems branch of the Mittelland canal in 1894. Usually, the combined support of the emperor and the ministry was sufficient to get enough Conservative votes to pass a bill in Prussia. But, still smarting from their recent defeat, the Conservatives, in league with the Center, decided to prevent the canal bill's passage. The canal was correctly considered a means to lower the transportation costs of "coal barons" desirous of gaining eastern markets. While it would also enable the Junkers to compete in the western grain markets, von Schalscha, an East Elbian estate owner, summed up the agrarian view when he said that the primary interest of the party was to put a brake upon industrialization and to protect the customers of small farmers.[7] If the Ruhr basin continued to prosper while agriculture languished,

6. Hans Herzfeld, *Johannes von Miquel*, (Detmold, 1938), pp. 501–6. The best work on the subject is Hannelore Horn, "Die Rolle des Bundes der Landwirte im Kampf um den Bau des Mittellandkanals," *Jahrbuch für die Geschichte Mittlel- und Ostdeutschlands*, vol. 7 (1958).

7. *Stenographische Berichte der Verhandlungen des Preussischen Abgeordnetenhauses* (hereafter cited as Sten. Ber.), 54 Sitzung (1894).

the canal would serve merely to lower the cost of internal emigration for the sorely needed day laborers. Speaker after speaker rose to criticize the ministry for its coddling of industry when agriculture demanded attention. In a show of agricultural power, the canal proposal was soundly defeated.

Five years later the emperor took heart once more and asked Miquel, the Prussian minister of finance, to reintroduce the canal bill. In the meantime the government had sought to conciliate the Conservatives by agreeing to present the Reichstag with a list of recommendations on the labor shortage which included: extended admission of foreign workers, more inner colonization, strict punishment of contract breakers, and "measures to limit the growth of the right to freedom of movement."[8] The ministry was met with an even greater rebuff than in 1894. Von Wangenheim of the Farmers' League was blunt: "So long as we are not able to have a tariff unregulated by treaties . . . so long will nothing be left for us but to decide against extensions of the canal."[9] Kanitz also condemned the canal proposal as a continuation of the ill-conceived policy of disturbing the equilibrium between industry and agriculture.[10] He implied that the canal would never be built while the grain tariff remained at thirty-five marks. The Anti-Semites and Reichspartei lined up with the Conservatives, and thus doomed the bill to its second defeat. On the third reading in April 1899 a majority of eighty-eight votes were recorded against the canal. The emperor could not respond by dissolving the legislature and calling for elections because Conservative votes were needed for the imminent decision on the *Zuchthausvorlage*. He vented his rage at the defeat by dismissing eighteen *Landräte* and two *Regierungspräsidenten* for voting with agrarians.[11] Civil servants belonging to the Farmers' League were advised to resign their membership or suffer dismissal, and Conservatives who voted against the emperor's pet project found themselves excluded from court.

Still not dejected, Wilhelm refused to believe that the Conserva-

8. *Schulthess' europäischer Geschichtskalender*, 42 (1901):7.
9. *Sten. Ber.* 57 Sitzung (1899), 1851; Horn, 286.
10. *Sten. Ber.* 58 Sitzung, 1902.
11. Horn, p. 328; J. C. G. Röhl, "Higher Civil Servants in Germany, 1890–1900," *Journal of Contemporary History* 2, no. 3 (July 1967).

tives were serious in their attempt to force an agrarian tariff policy upon him. Bülow and Miquel were required to bring the bill before the Prussian House of Deputies another time in 1901. More wily than his predecessors, Bülow offered the Conservatives significant concessions. If the bill were accepted, the government would establish a shipping route between Berlin and Stettin, unite the Oder and Weichsel rivers by canal, and expand the Spree canal. Furthermore, Bülow announced, "The King's government has decided to work for a higher protective tariff for agricultural products, and see to its passage as quickly as possible."[12] Writing to his wife about the chancellor's speech, Kardorff said, "Bülow spoke very skillfully in the House of Deputies—he promised agriculture tariff protection, etc. We will not fall for promises any longer, but want the tariff introduced before we will allow the canal project to enter committee discussions."[13] When a favorable response was not forthcoming, the emperor declared that he would not sanction a higher duty unless the bill passed. However, the bluff was a vain one, for Wilhelm's power did not equal that of a determined and united Conservative party. Kanitz and von Wangenheim remained firm; the bill would not pass until a satisfactory grain tariff received Reichstag approval. In May the bill was withdrawn. Miquel resigned and died not long thereafter.

For Bülow the consequences were not as serious. The intransigence of the Conservatives only confirmed his earlier observation that Germany could be ruled with the Junkers and not at all against them. Coming in his first year of office, the canal bill's fate impressed upon him how simplified his task would be if he could establish good relations with the Junkers. Rarely during his nine years in office did he intentionally alienate the Conservatives from the government.

When Bülow was appointed Hohenlohe's successor in October 1900, two years remained before the tariff treaties expired. The

12. *Schulthess'* 42 (1901): 5. In view of Miquel's failure and the unresolved conflict between agrarians and industrialists over the Canal Bill, I am unconvinced that the *Sammlung* was reconstituted before 1902. Röhl puts the date at 1897.

13. S. von Kardorff, *Wilhelm von Kardorff* (Berlin, 1936), p. 345.

atmosphere was, however, extremely tense. Prices were above the low levels of the early nineties but still far below what grain cultivators considered satisfactory. Commerce and industry were thriving, and it was commonly held that the treaties were responsible. Both those who were interested in the renewal of the agreements and those seeking higher duties had begun to marshal their forces long before the 1902 deadline. Although the Farmers' League had been originally formed in 1892 to forestall a treaty with Russia, its failure only stiffened the determination of the leaders to be prepared for the next round of tariff discussions. For eight years the organization maintained an elaborate campaign of propaganda through its newspaper, journal, and publishing house. It has been estimated that seven million pieces of literature were distributed by the league in the crucial year 1902. League speakers toured villages and hamlets, intent upon stirring up passions for the next battle against the city. The Bavarian finance minister, Riedel, warned his legislature that the league was endangering the foundations of order.[14] Indeed, historians who view the Social Democrats as the only mass organization relying on demagoguery overlook the Farmers' League. The newspaper *Deutsche Tageszeitung* made it clear to Bülow before the tariff plan was published that his aim should not be to make agriculture's situation bearable, but to restore it to primacy in the economy.[15] In June 1901, the Kreuzzeitung assured its readers that the only question was how much higher the duties would be, not whether they would be raised.[16]

Anticipating the struggle ahead, many leaders in commerce and small industrialists formed the Commercial Treaties Association (*Handelsvertragsverein*) in 1897. A year later the Zentralstelle für Vorbereitung von Handelsverträge was established, whose purpose was to publish relevant material on the forthcoming tariff proposals. The parent organization campaigned for the continuation of Caprivi's tariffs by means of its newspaper. Thus, reams of litera-

14. Quoted in Wilhelm Gerloff, *Die Finanz- und Zollpolitik des deutschen Reiches nebst ihren Beziehungen zu Landes- und Gemeindefinanzen,* (Jena, 1913), p. 383.

15. *Deutsche Tageszeitung* 8, no. 290 (24 June 1901).

16. *Kreuzzeitung,* no. 274 (14 June 1901).

ture had already been vying for the attention of interested parties when Bülow came on the scene. All the aforementioned organizations looked nervously to the new chancellor for some indication of his trade policy in 1900.

Two chancellors could hardly differ more in background and attitude than Caprivi and Bülow. The former was educated from late adolescence to be a Prussian officer, and was inculcated with a Spartan sense of duty. Appointed to a post he did not desire and was ill prepared for, Caprivi had to rely on his integrity and capacity for hard work to master the problems of the chancellorship. In contrast, Bülow spent most of his early life in the penumbra of the Wilhelmstrasse, his father having served as secretary of state under Bismarck. During the Congress of Berlin, the young Bülow attracted attention because of his diplomatic skills and suave manner.[17] Apart from Bismarck, no chancellor of the empire was as well trained in foreign affairs, for he had served with distinction as ambassador to Romania and Italy, and in 1897 was promoted to secretary of state for foreign affairs. Although not a direct partici pant in party politics, Bülow was extremely sensitive to debates in the Reichstag. He came to office with an awareness of each party's position on most matters and had observed most carefully the successes and failures of his predecessors. Personally, Bülow impressed people with his charm, his turn of phrase, and his wit. Unlike his colleagues he was remarkably free of the heaviness characteristic of north Germans. Shrewd observers were not beguiled by Bülow's charm; they found him lacking in integrity and having a compulsive need to please those around him. He played notoriously upon the emperor's vanity, and chose the role of a fawning courtier rather than of a sincere friend. That was perhaps his most serious fault: he could not be genuine, and he played at politics with great cunning but without sufficient seriousness. His strongest interest seemed to be in furthering his own career, and he knew which people and what attitudes would get him the farthest.

While serving in Bucharest and Rome, Bülow was acquainted

---

17. Erich Eyck, *Das persönliche Regiment Wilhelms II,* (Erlenbach-Zurich, 1948), pp. 123–84.

with German contemporary politics through the correspondence of his friend Graf Monts. Not partial to agrarian wishes, Monts wrote of the covetousness of the Junkers and the difficulties experienced by Caprivi and Hohenlohe at their hands.[18] When Bülow was called from Hubertusstock to Bad Homburg in the fall of 1900, the emperor was still smarting from the defeat of his prized canal bill and the criticism he was subjected to by the Conservative press. He informed Bülow immediately that the Junkers' demands must be thwarted, for trade treaties were essential to the economy.[19] Wilhelm was in no mood to compromise with the Conservatives after their attempts to stall the modernization that he was bent upon. Bülow, who realized that ruling against the Conservatives was risky, and who was well versed in Wagner's ideas, demurred. Bülow had been questioned in economics by Wagner for his diplomatic examination in 1875, and had continued to read his works. He hinged his acceptance of the chancellorship on the emperor allowing him a free hand to raise the tariffs.[20] In words showing that he had readily absorbed Wagner's ideas, Bülow told Wilhelm: "I hold increased protection for agriculture absolutely necessary out of economic, and still more out of social, political, and national grounds. . . . The cities are swelling into a hypertrophied state, the land is being depopulated. Therein lies the great danger, not only from the standpoint of our military strength, for the land delivers, all in all, better soldiers than the cities, but for our whole social structure. . . . The emperor was visibly shocked by my refutation."[21] To the emperor's interjection of British power after Peel's repeal of the Corn Laws, Bülow calmly replied that the German urban masses were not as nationally minded as those of England, and a balance therefore had to be maintained between the land and the city. He added that with proper handling, the negotiating of trade treaties would be possible notwithstanding higher duties. Having no alternative prospect for the post and not prepared to counter these arguments, Wilhelm agreed to give Bülow a free hand if he

18. Bernhard von Bülow, *Denkwürdigkeiten*, (Berlin, 1930–31), 1:41.
19. Ibid., pp. 382–83.
20. Ibid.
21. Ibid.

sought to renew the treaties. The victory was important, for had the emperor held out, Bülow would not have become chancellor during those crucial early years of the twentieth century.

Upon taking office, the new chancellor found that memoranda from both the trade and foreign ministries urged the retention of the thirty-five mark duty, the former because of its economic results and the latter for fear of alienating Russia and Italy.[22] Bülow's mind, however, had been made up before assuming the chancellorship. As a student he had come under the influence of Wilhelm Roscher, an economist of the paternalist school. In his memoirs Bülow wrote of his debt to this professor. "Already as a young man I learned from Roscher that the aims of Social Democracy . . . were incompatible with the general welfare, national interests well understood, and the existence of a strong and happy empire." From his reading of scholarly journals in economics, Bülow learned, "The eternal poles around which national, social, and economic life turned and which was the center of domestic political struggles was not so much liberal and conservative as individualist and central."[23] Of course the second pair was much to be preferred. In the 1890s Bülow found that he "had passed beyond the teachings of Roscher to those of Adolf Wagner and Gustav Schmoller."[24] Thus his whole education was permeated with anti-industrial currents. In addition, he had witnessed Caprivi's vain attempt to survive without Conservative support despite the emperor's backing. The lessons of the canal bills were not lost on him. To have a quiescent Reichstag and a majority in Prussia he would have to pay with an increase in tariffs.

Once Bülow charted his course, his political maneuvering demonstrated a rare skill at handling the extremists on both sides. He was unusually adept at moving toward his goal in such a manner as to alienate as few politicians as possible. Indeed, one cannot fault Bülow's tactical abilities. On 3 November 1900, Bülow looked on approvingly at a cabinet meeting when Posadowsky said that industry should not be antagonized at a time when the lines were

22. Herzfeld, *Johannes von Miquel*, p. 616.
23. Bülow, *Denkwürdigkeiten*, 4:120.
24. Ibid., p. 118.

girding for the tariff battle. If hostility to the government were aroused at this point, little support for grain duties could be anticipated later.[25]

Bülow himself lost no time in enunciating his views. By assuming an agrarian posture in the House of Deputies, he hoped to begin his term with a major victory in the Mittelland canal issue. As has been shown, the Conservatives remained chary of the minister president's promises, and forced the bill to be withdrawn. Rather than take offense, Bülow set out in earnest to convince the agrarians of his sympathy with their aims. In March he told the Reichstag, "I am of the opinion that agriculture is the most important constituent of every state, . . . that it has a right to the most energetic care and advancement from the government."[26] In his *Nachlass*, Bülow left the preparations for many speeches on agriculture. One, which particularly gives evidence of his having been influenced by Wagner, whom he described in his memoirs as his "patron and friend," begins, "A land population tied to the soil for generations and patriotic [*auf ihrer eigener Scholle angesessen- und heimatsfroh*] is a state-preserving [*staatserhaltende*] element, it forms the fountain of youth (*Jungbrunnen*) of our people.[27] In another prepared speech he spoke of the blood sacrificed by the Junkers over centuries, and predicted military deterioration if agriculture and industry were not balanced. The German Agricultural Council was told that Bülow considered aid to agriculture not a duty but a dictate from his heart.[28] The emperor's apprehensions about foreign hostility to a high duty were stilled by Bülow, who expected Germany to continue to import the same quantity of goods at the same prices.[29] A decade later Bülow sought to explain his motives further in a book entitled *Imperial Germany*. Again the influence of Wagner, Sering, and Oldenberg is evident. "We are more inclined

25. DZA, *Ministry of State meeting*, 3 November, 1900 Rep. 90a B III 26, 6, 141.

26. *Schulthess'* 42 (1901): 62.

27. B. A. Bülow, "Entwürfe für parlimentarische Rede III Nr. 26," 1900–1909, *Nachlass*.

28. Karl Wippermann, *Deutsche Geschichtskalender* (1901) 1:127.

29. *Die Grosse Politik* 18, p. 5392.

than is good for us to make our arrangements with regard to economic matters as if this peace were to be permanent. . . . But every state department should be organized as if war were going to break out tomorrow. This applies to economic policy as well."[30] Having more time to write this section on the tariff controversy than he had in writing speeches in 1901, Bülow borrowed profusely from the agrarian economists. Their whole syndrome about the future of industrial states was taken over completely. Caprivi was criticized for not continuing the "agrarian bias" so indispensable to the general interests of the community. There can be little doubt that Bülow genuinely believed the dire predictions about the future of an industrial state. Pragmatism as well as abstract theory determined that he seek to raise the duties. For he no less than Wagner was tied to the Bismarckian constitution and the primacy of the Junkers, and furthermore his tenure as chancellor might be cut short if the Conservatives did not realize their aims.

Throughout the spring of 1901, newspapers were full of rumors about the impending tariff schedule. Articles and pamphlets on the benefits and disadvantages of change were vying for the attention of readers. All parties and organizations were optimistic. Bülow realized that in this atmosphere his proposals for minimum duties were likely to be pounced on by both sides in the Reichstag. Any change would arouse the liberals and only an extreme rise would satisfy the agrarians. Since he was wooing the agrarian-dominated Conservatives, he hoped to win their immediate support for his plan, for if they objected to the amount of the increase it would never be passed. With extraordinary cunning, Bülow leaked his proposals to the *Norddeutsche allgemeine Zeitung*, and confirmed the validity of the paper's charts.[31] By so doing, the Conservatives were forced to rush to the chancellor's support although their extreme demands had not been met, because liberal and socialist newspapers were vilifying Bülow. Even this astute maneuver failed to rally the Farmers' League to Bülow's side. The tariff changes are charted in Table 30.

30. Bülow, *Imperial Germany* (New York, 1914), pp. 266–67.
31. Ibid., p. 526.

TABLE 30   TARIFF RATES (in marks)

	CAPRIVI	BÜLOW
Rye	35	50
Wheat	35	55
Barley	20	30
Oats	28	50
Buckwheat	20	50
Potatoes	0	10
Horses	10–20	50–360
Cows	3–9	18–20
Meat	15	27–35
Bacon	20	36

The all-important grains were raised between 45 and 100 percent. Actually, they were raised even more, since Bülow introduced a double tariff, the minimum levels of which only have been listed. The maximum approached seventy-five marks, but it was only to be used if trade negotiations failed. Tariffs on live animals rose even higher.[32] The Bismarck duties of 1887 were superseded in every instance.

More than sixty raw materials and semifinished goods received higher duties. Chemicals and textiles were moderately higher while leather and clothing were subject to large raises. It is extremely difficult to calculate the increase in machinery duties; machines that had previously been classified together were now listed separately and the duties were adjudged by weight rather than number. The duty on sewing machines increased by 45 percent and locomotives by 37 percent. Paper goods received a 10 percent raise and leather rose between 30 and 40 percent. Liberals immediately recognized that agricultural machinery experienced little change. Bülow also extended the identity pass law so that most fruits and grains were covered, and the exporter of any one product would be given certificates valid for the duty-free importation of any item on the list. When this change was effected, the value of the certificates rose by 90 percent in one year.[33]

32. Stenographische Berichte der Verhandlungen des Reichstages (hereafter cited as Sten. Ber. Reichstages) (1900–1902), Anlage Band 4, 10.
33. Ibid., 6.

Only a masterful politician could have drawn up the schedule of tariffs. There was something for all parties concerned except the powerless consumer. The agrarians who wanted a seventy-five mark duty would have to settle for twenty marks less, but received compensation from the moderate duties on agricultural machinery and a more flexible interpretation of identity passes. Bülow considered the twenty mark difference necessary if the conclusion of treaties was to have any chance of success. Industrialists whose support was desirable might overlook grain tariff changes, for foreign competition was to be virtually excluded from the German domestic market by the higher industrial duties. The incentive to form cartels was now overwhelming. Centrists could be gratified that agrarian demands were not totally met, and the way was open to add an amendment providing for some compensation to consumers. If even half the Center party voted for the proposals, their success was assured. Of course, Bülow's plan seemed highly protectionist to liberals and socialists. It appeared that he was buying off the opposition by raising the duty on items that protectionists had not even deemed necessary. In dissecting the proclaimed moderate tariff they found that 33.2 percent of the goods experienced no change, 6.9 percent were in part lowered, 4.6 percent were fully lowered, 25.5 percent were fully raised, and 29.9 percent were partially raised. Viewing the tariff history of Prussia as being predominantly liberal with only the aberration of Bismarck's later years, they believed that Bülow was harping back to the mercantilism of the eighteenth century.

Newspaper reactions to the disclosure were more bitter than Bülow had anticipated. Neither side was in a mood to accept anything other than their oft-stated demands. The socialist paper claimed that their most pessimistic expectations had been superseded.[34] The liberal *Vossische Zeitung* urged a nationwide campaign to combat a tariff designed to ruin business and impoverish the workers. A National Liberal paper, the *Kölnische Zeitung,* predicted rejection by the Reichstag unless the grain duties were lowered substantially.[35] Most disheartening for the chancellor was the

34. *Schulthess'* 42 (1901): 5.
35. Ibid., p. 6.

editorial in the *Deutsche Tageszeitung*, in which compromise in the struggle between the land and the stock exchange was portrayed as immoral. "One who really strives for a national policy," said the editorial, "who desires to preserve the life strength of the nation, who will protect and strengthen creative labor, can only struggle against the exchange, trade, and the Manchester philosophy. The chancellor must take up this battle or renounce agricultural support."[36] Subsequently the paper chided Bülow for following in Caprivi's footsteps. Only some Conservatives and Reichspartei members welcomed the schedule, and even they were not terribly enthusiastic over its moderation. Bülow had not reckoned with the intransigence of the agrarians; he had considered his plan the best that could be granted them without seriously damaging the national economy.

On 2 December 1901, Bülow formally presented the schedule of minimum tariffs to the Reichstag. His accompanying speech was directed primarily at the National Liberals and Center delegates, whose votes were essential for passage. These two pivotal parties were assured that the proposals did not signify a departure from the policy of trade treaties. Bülow denied any intention of hindering exports, and expressed his belief that industry, trade, and agriculture would mutually prosper from the new duties. Since agriculture had not flourished equally with the other sectors of the economy, it had been necessary to increase its protection, but this had not been done without increasing industrial duties. The aim of the tariff was the protection of national labor, both in industry and on the farm, for the chancellor claimed, "A world policy which did not provide protection for domestic work . . . would be a fantastic, unhealthy, and chimerical policy."[37] Secretary of State Posadowsky criticized those advising the transformation of farming from grain to cattle. Without sufficient grain for fodder, he did not foresee any increase in the number of cattle in the empire; thus grain agriculture could not be ignored.[38]

36. *Deutsche Tageszeitung*, Nr. 360 (3 August, 1901).
37. *Sten. Ber. Reichstages* (1900–1903) II 4, 2930.
38. Ibid., 2905–12.

The reaction of the Reichstag was not easily predictable, except for the parties of the left. Although Bülow believed he had given the agrarians everything possible short of antagonizing the parties whose support was necessary, still the agrarian press had responded coolly to the publication of the tariffs, and scarcely any party newspaper was excited about the proposals. The Social Democrat, Molkenbuhr, left no doubt about his party's views by presenting a petition with 3½ million signatures against higher grain duties. He then accused the government of limiting free choice of vocation by legislating against natural developments. If industrialization were proceeding too quickly, he ascribed the blame to the Junkers, whose maltreatment of day laborers was responsible for urban immigration.[39] Bebel insisted that agriculture had not been the stepchild of the economy during the previous decade, and alluded to the increased pay for village teachers, the reduction in long distance railroad rates, silos built with state funds, the founding of *Zentralgenossenschaften* for credit, identity passes, and state-aided education of farmers in new techniques, all of which had been introduced after Caprivi's accession to office.[40] The socialist leader cited Mombert's study to prove the increased costs that the workers would have to bear. After castigating the Junkers for excessive greediness, he turned to the iron industrialists, whom he accused of desiring protection despite the 440 percent rise in production in less than three decades. All the Social Democrats saw in Bülow's proposals a hypocritical departure from the proclaimed *Sozialpolitik* of Wilhelm II, and were determined to cast their forty-four votes against the proposals.

The Progressive parties presented a coordinated front against Bülow in which three specific points were emphasized. Bräsicke and Pachnicke referred to the inefficient cultivation of the estates arising from the Junkers' inadequate training in farm management. In their view the tariff was designed solely to preserve the Junkers' estates notwithstanding their inability to compete with other grain-growing nations.[41] Assuming this interpretation to be valid, Richter

39. Ibid., 2980–88.
40. Ibid., 2990–93.
41. Ibid., 3051–56.

excoriated the emperor for allowing vested interests to determine the character of legislation. If the function of the monarchy was to stand above all parties, the Progressive leader said, how could it countenance such an obvious piece of class legislation? The emperor was accused of neglecting his role and of demeaning the concept of monarchy, and was warned that the next elections would show an increase in socialist votes.[42] Never having recovered from Bismarck's abandonment of free trade, the Progressives all claimed that the remarkable growth of the German economy was in spite of rather than a result of protection.

The difficulty in gauging the sentiments of the small independent farmer becomes evident from the attitude of two minor parties whose support came from the south German states. Payer, the leader of the Württemberger Volkspartei, announced that he and his supporters were opposed to the increase in duties. The high standard of living enjoyed by Germans was attributed to industrialization. Most small farmers in Württemberg had little interest in grain, but were concerned with the purchasing power of the urban workers. Agricultural workers had no more right than any other group to seek a guaranteed income, and, Payer warned, some day a generation would have to pay for the sins of protection if the proposals passed.[43] On the other hand, Dr. Heim of the Süddeutsche Partei criticized Bülow for appeasing the left. Along with the twenty thousand Junkers he foresaw two million peasants going into bankruptcy unless the tariff was raised to sixty marks, and, echoing the Conservatives, Heim concluded, "We are against developing into an industrial state at all costs."[44]

In the early 1890s National Liberal members had for the most part welcomed Caprivi's initiative in concluding trade treaties. After ten years of relative prosperity, the industrialists constituting the backbone of the party were seeking to expand their markets and enlarge their profits. The recessions of the 1880s and early 1890s had passed from their memory, and with it went the economic importance of the treaties. Expansion now necessitated col-

42. Ibid., 2920–28.
43. Ibid., 3017–26.
44. Ibid., 3140–46.

onies and a navy, and, perhaps even more important, the exclusion of competitors from the domestic markets. Since the Progressives and Social Democrats were inalterably opposed to the construction of a navy for imperial ventures, only the Conservatives might be won over for Tirpitz's plans by "log rolling." National Liberals well remembered the slogan of Conservatives who voted against four new cruisers in 1895—"Ohne Kanitz, keine Kähne." Similarly, the monopolization of the home market was dependent on Conservative approbation. To insure the realization of their economic aims, National Liberals recognized that they would have to bolster the sagging position of the Junkers, whose general primacy in society was at stake. Their readiness to do so proved once again that self-interest and fear of Social Democracy were the most marked characteristics of the industrial bourgeoisie. Dr. Paasche told the Reichstag of industry's and agriculture's common interest in cutting down ruinous foreign imports; this despite the most profitable decade for German industry in the nineteenth century.[45] Agriculture must be profitable, he continued, or the entire economy would founder; again despite the experience of the previous decade. Dr. Beumer, editor of *Eisen und Stahl,* hinged the acceptance of social legislation on higher tariffs. German industry could not maintain its profitability while absorbing the costs of social insurance, unless American and British competition were excluded. Cartels were the friends of the workers. Free trade, a principle of the party in the 1860s, was termed a reactionary philosophy unworthy of men with a modern outlook.[46] The *Sammlung* policy of the pre-Caprivi days was lauded in turn by each National Liberal speaker in the debates.[47]

Because of Lieber's free trade convictions and Caprivi's Polish policy, both Center and Poles had delivered the vast majority of their votes for reduced tariffs in the 1890s. With the colorless and extremely conservative Spahn in line for the party leadership, and

45. Ibid., 2934–42.
46. Ibid., 3070–74.
47. For a fuller treatment of the origins of the *Sammlungspolitik* see Kehr's essays "Klassenkämpfe und Rüstungspolitik im kaiserlichen Deutschland" and "Englandhass und Weltpolitik" in *Zeitschrift für Politik* 17 (1928).

dependent on Bülow's support for the return of the Jesuits to the empire, the Center had few practical reasons to remain loyal to its earlier policy. In addition, several local party branches had threatened to go over to the Farmers' League if the agrarian program were not fully supported.[48] Particularly in Silesia the party feared the defection of the landowners should Bülow's proposals fail. If this confluence of reasons was not sufficient, the Center was subjected to further agrarian pressures by the Volksverein für das katholische Deutschland, whose leaders were from the Centrist delegation in the Reichstag. In one of the Verein's pamphlets, Carl Herold, an estate owner from Münster whose influence had been growing in the party, argued that the maintenance of an agrarian state was necessary for moral and religious reasons. The rural population was described as "holding to the old morality, not easily won for political movements, loyal and dependent on their religion, and valuing morality."[49] Denying the effects of duties on the consumer, Herold closed by calling for a seventy-nine mark wheat duty—higher than even the Farmers' League dared ask. Other Verein pamphlets relied heavily on Wagner's belief that a protectionist policy could be combined with a progressive social policy. Wagner was frequently quoted as the scholarly authority on tariff issues.[50] During the first reading, Spahn demonstrated that the pressures had been unnecessary as his sympathy lay with agriculture. He called for a halt to further urbanization and the transformation of military barracks to the countryside (much as Oldenberg had done) in order to slow down the flight of rural boys to the city. His associate, Speck, claimed that the peasantry and Junkers were a necessary bulwark against the growth of atheistic socialism.[51]

48. Wippermann, *Geschichtskalender* (1896), I:288, 294.
49. Carl Herold, *Die wichtigsten Agrarfragen* (Munich, Volksverein für das katholische Deutschland, 1900). For further information cf. Emil Ritter, *Die katholische soziale Bewegung und der Volksverein für das katholische Deutschland* (Cologne, 1954).
50. Editors, *Ist eine Erhöhung der landwirtschaftlichen Schutzzölle notwendig?* (Munich: Volksverein für das katholische Deutschland, 1901).
51. *Sten. Ber. Reichstages* (1900–1903), II 4, 3011–16. The attitude of Center leaders toward the tariffs and industrialism would appear to undermine Hans Rosenberg's belief that the party accepted modernization and began to move in a democratic direction after 1896. Rosenberg, *Grosse Depression und Bismarckzeit*, pp. 255–56.

Herold and the Poles seconded the Centrist leader's concern for the "land people." In ten years the Center changed from a policy of concern about urban labor's plight to one of sympathy for the aristocracy and peasantry. This is not surprising when it is remembered that Catholic workers tended to vote Centrist and not Social Democrat despite the party's social policy or lack of one. The Centrists never violated their principles in the second empire— pragmatism and the maintenance of party unity were the prime ones.

The Reichspartei and the Conservatives can be treated together, for their reaction was similar. Both sought to resurrect the *Sammlung* that had enabled Bismarck to enact his economic program. Gamp of the Reichspartei and von Tiedemann of the Conservatives were gratified at the raises and forecast that the renewed vitality of agriculture would confirm the alliance of throne and altar.[52] Kanitz was as adamant as ever in denying the utility of treaties. Autonomous tariffs that could be changed according to the level of prices were his aim, but the *Sammlung* could not be reborn if the Conservatives adopted such a program.[53] Schwerin-Löwitz, chief of the German Agricultural Council, claimed that Caprivi had acted on the false assumption that agriculture's potential was limited in comparison with industry's. With adequate protection he did not doubt the ability of Germany to be self-sufficient in foodstuffs. Unfortunately, Bülow's proposals were not satisfactory, and he hoped the party would hold out for more accommodating changes.[54] Several spokesmen repeated Sering's analysis of the military weaknesses of an industrial state. The two parties were split over the acceptability of Bülow's rates, with perhaps a small majority for the chancellor.

Before it reached the Reichstag, the plan had been termed "totally unacceptable" by the Farmers' League. A memorandum distributed to members in November defended the ability of German agriculture to provide secure employment for a growing population. It opined that farmers could supply all national requirements without any industrial expansion or greater involvement in the

52. *Sten. Ber. Reichstages,* 2956–61.
53. Ibid., 3110–20.
54. Ibid., 2884–94.

world economy.[55] Wangenheim made clear the league's aims when he asked the government for a level of protection that would entice laborers back to the farm. He insisted that Kanitz's purchase plan of 1894 had been the most promising method of restoring rural prosperity. As Kanitz himself had lost hope of gaining adherents, Wangenheim considered the tariff as the only means to achieve league aims. Bülow was subjected to abuse by Wangenheim and other League speakers for daring to introduce such a moderate raise. They left the impression that they would vote against the chancellor.

Disturbed by the reaction in Conservative circles, Bülow undertook to speak at the German Agricultural Council and party meetings in order to win the agrarians for his plan. Quite earnestly he told his audience that he could go no farther, for any rise in prices would bring down the weight of consumer opinion on him, which could only result in the abolition of all protection.[56] He had to gauge what the public would tolerate. In effect, Bülow said that he had not compromised but had given all that the traffic would allow.

In February 1902, the government proposals were given over to a committee for study and recommendations. Not until the following autumn were the committee's suggestions presented to the Reichstag. In the interim period many organizations took a stand on the tariff, and pamphlets by Junkers, industrialists, and merchants continued to flood the market. A survey of the literature will indicate the divisions among economic interest groups toward the proposals and the hostility that Bülow had to endure because of his plan.

The previously mentioned Zentralstelle für Vorbereitung von Handelsverträge was established in August of 1897 by the German chamber of commerce and the Centralverband deutscher Industrieller, although the latter withdrew its support quickly when the Zentralstelle's views became apparent. The organization hoped to

---

55. Ibid., 3045–52. Also see G. Dieter von Tippelskirch, *Agrarhistorische Ausschnitte aus der Zeit von 1893 bis 1924 im Lichte des Wirkens von Dr. Gustav Roesicke* (Stollhamm, 1956), p. 100.

56. *Mitteilungen des Handelsvertragsvereins* (15 February 1902), p. 3.

coordinate the activities of all the groups seeking the extension of Caprivi's agreements, a gold currency, and increased canal building. At the 1900 and 1901 meeting, Vosberg-Rekow, the director, emphasized the extraordinary upswing that had taken place since the early 1890s and asked the membership to support the treaties' retention.[57] The Zentralstelle greeted the 1901 plan with derision, calling it a return to eighteenth-century mercantilism. Compensation was demanded for export industries whose markets would be lost. The Junkers were of course castigated for greed at the expense of the commonweal and as the purveyors of autarky.[58]

Similarly, the Deutsche Handelstag had voted for the retention of the treaties in spite of some minor defects. In the resolution was included the emperor's phrase that the treaties were "a saving act and of historical importance." When the new terms were announced, the Handelstag quickly held a vote on several resolutions in order to establish a common policy. By a vote of 219 to 79 a resolution declaring that higher duties were necessary for a prosperous agriculture was defeated. A heavy majority also termed the plan a severe hindrance to the negotiating of new agreements. Lastly, a majority of three was all that could be produced for a resolution against any rise in the tariff.[59]

The Handelsvertragsverein had come into being primarily because many light industrialists and merchants desired a strong organization to counter the propaganda of the agrarians. On 28 May 1902, a petition was sent to Bülow which began: "The duties agreed upon by a majority of the tariff commission for agricultural products, whose execution must hinder the conclusion of even unfavorable commercial treaties, proves that it is not possible to arrive at an understanding with the agrarian movement. The power

---

57. Dr. Vosberg-Rekow, *Die Zolltarifvorlage und ihre Begründung* (Berlin, 1902).

58. "Resolution of 1898 meeting," *Schriften der Zentralstelle für die Vorbereitung der Handelsverträge* 4 (Berlin, 1898).

59. *Der deutsche Handelstag* 2:544. On interest groups see Thomas Nipperdey, "Interessenverbände und Parteien in Deutschland vor dem ersten Weltkrieg" *Politische Vierteljahresschrift* 2 (1961); and Gerhard Schulz, "Über Entstehung und Formen von Interressengruppen in Deutschland seit Beginn der Industrialisierung," ibid.

and danger of the agrarians is increased through their union with the industrial protectionists, who demand duties on semi-finished goods."[60] This theme was repeated in newspapers and other literature published by the association. Industrialists were asked to write pamphlets on the presumed effects of the duties in their fields, which were published by the Handelsvertragsverein, and will be treated below.

Friedrich Naumann's National Social Party condemned the grain duties categorically at its party day in Frankfurt. Both cartel formation and a rise in land prices were predicted if the proposals were enacted into law.[61] At another party day the Christian Social Workers Association resolved that inordinate burdens had been laid upon the urban population without sufficient cause.[62] A similar resolve was voted by the mayors of seventy-seven cities meeting in Berlin in 1901. Lastly, the liberal position was unanimously endorsed by the Bund der Industriellen, an offshoot of the Centralverband representing light industry, which had found its interests unattended to in the larger organization. Viewing commercial treaties as the sine qua non of a healthy economy, the Bund desired the cessation of minimal duties as a concession in negotiating treaties.[63]

Assuming a position between the two extremes, the Centralverband deutscher Industrieller expressed sympathy for the agricultural situation, but rhetorically asked whether minimal duties were the wisest method of alleviating the crisis. The iron- and steel-oriented organization feared the duties would prevent the renewal of trade agreements, yet did not want to antagonize the Junkers because of their recent support for the navy and higher industrial duties. Although the Centralverband in the end adopted a position of mild support for the chancellor, it was subjected to abuse by the *Kreuzzeitung*, which threatened a Junker-labor alliance against industry if the industrialists did not show more con-

60. *Mitteilungen des Handelsvertragsvereins* (1 June 1902), p. 7.
61. Ibid., (25 October 1901), p. 4. Also cf. Peter Gilg, *Die Erneuerung des demokratischen Denkens im wilhelminischen Deutschland* (Wiesbaden, 1965).
62. *Mitteilungen des Handelsvertragsvereins* (1 November 1901), p. 6.
63. Ibid. (4 October, 1901), p. 5. The Bund der Industriellen represented primarily those industries concerned with exports.

cern for agriculture.[64] In effect, agrarians warned the heavy industrialists that their collaboration against Social Democracy depended on rural prosperity.

Clearly on the side of the agrarians was Stöcker's and Wagner's Christian Social Party. At their convention in 1902 they resolved to support the tariff proposals exactly as they had been introduced.[65] The Association of Tax and Economic Reformers lauded the government for returning to the national economics of Bismarck's time. While this was to be praised, the chancellor still was not cognizant of the seriousness of the agricultural crisis, as evidenced by his inadequate program of aid. Although not acceptable, Bülow's proposals could serve as the first step in a rehabilitation of the agricultural sector; bimetallism would be the next step.[66]

Since most state legislatures were dominated by the Conservatives and the Center, it is not surprising that Bülow received their support. The extremely agrarian-minded Prussian legislature forced through a bill against the chancellor's wishes calling upon the Reichstag to raise the duties beyond his suggested levels.[67] The Württemberg minister of the interior adopted an idealistic pose when he claimed that agriculture was the foundation of society and urged passage of the tariff despite the state's importation of one-third of its grain requirements. Upon being questioned, the minister admitted that every additional mark of tariff cost Württemberg inhabitants 2,300,000 marks.[68] The Bavarian situation was not very different from that of its northern neighbor, for higher barley duties would harm the breweries, and the state had come to depend on industrial taxation sources.[69] Nevertheless, the Center-dominated legislature backed the chancellor unequivocally.

The reaction of industries to Bülow's plan was extremely diverse. It has already been described how the iron and steel dominated Centralverband greeted the changes in industrial tariffs and ex-

64. *Schulthess'* 42 (1901): 147; Hartmut Kaelble, *Industrielle Interessenpolitik in der wilhelminischen Gesellschaft*, (Berlin, 1967), pp. 52–54.
65. *Mitteilungen des Handelsvertragsvereins* (1 November 1902), p. 10.
66. Ibid. (15 February 1902), p. 5.
67. Wippermann, *Geschichtskalender* (1902), 1:111.
68. *Schulthess'* 42 (1901): 27.
69. Ibid., p. 141.

pressed the hope that grain rates would not hinder the renewal of treaties. Brewers, however, were distraught over the raises in malt and barley duties, which affected their costs of production. Similarly, the director of the Organization of Chemical Manufacturers, Dr. Richter, pointed out that his industry supplied almost all Germany's needs and sought further growth by increasing exports, but expected tariff retaliation if the present plan were enacted.[70] Despite the lack of competition, the industry had been subjected to high protection. Leather industry representatives anticipated a rise in the costs of their raw materials that would amount to four million marks a year. They failed to understand why tariffs were placed on raw materials necessary for German manufacturers. These opinions were repeated by leaders in the paper and linen industries. After lauding Caprivi for introducing unrivaled prosperity, Eugen Hagen, a member of the tariff commission of the paper manufacturers, wrote, "Instead of the requested reductions, there have been increases, and, indeed, increases to many times the value of the wares; instead of the former free trade, new high duties."[71] Deriving their profits primarily from exports, linen manufacturers were less hopeful about their future than in the 1890s.[72]

Hjalmar Schacht, the subsequent architect of currency reform, wrote in defense of industrialists whose wares had been accorded protection despite their protests.[73] By no logic, he wrote, did the chemical industry require duties, since it had evolved to its worldwide dominance in a free trade economy. All industrial nations looked to Germany for rolled iron wire; yet duties had been introduced. Schacht listed industries that, despite export- import ratios of between 5 and 15 to 1, had been subjected to protection. He concluded that the purpose of the plan was to create cartels in semifinished product industries such as iron and steel, where minimal competition did exist.

Bülow was apparently trying to buy industrial support for his

70. *Schriften der Zentralstelle* 9 (1900): p. 92.
71. Hagen, "Die papierverarbeitende Industries und die Handelsverträge," *Deutsche Wirtschaftszeitung* 1, no. 22 (November 1905).
72. Heinz Potthoff, "Die Leinenindustrie und die Handelsverträge," ibid.
73. Schacht, "Inhalt und Kritik des Zolltarifentwurfs," *Schmollers Jahrbuch* 26 (1902): 330–53.

grain rates by raising industrial duties indiscriminately without concern for particular needs or wishes. Whereas Bismarck had made economic concessions to weaken the political radicalism of the industrialists, Bülow had to go further. He had to offer privileges, for his need of industrial support required an even greater abandonment of liberal principles than Bismarck had requested. Industries desiring to monopolize the home market and undersell competitors abroad went along with the chancellor. Where the domestic market was small and exports counted for most sales, the chancellor's plan was condemned. Industries requiring iron and steel in great quantities also did not view the decline in competition with equanimity. Thus, the success of the plan was by no means a foregone conclusion at the termination of the first reading.

When the Reichstag returned to the tariff proposals in early October of 1902, there began one of the most peculiar and complex chapters in German parliamentary history. The tariff committee had convened 112 times before an alternate proposal was agreed upon that could muster a majority. Before the report was read to the Reichstag, Bülow made another plea for support, a plea that was directed primarily at the Conservatives. He recounted the superiority of the inner market theory, the need for self-sufficiency, and pointed to the substantial raises in grain duties he had proposed to attest to his faith in the above ideals. As a chancellor, he told the Reichstag, he had to weigh all opinions and yet not introduce a schedule that would prevent new trade agreements. In closing, he told the agrarians, "It will be a long time, in my opinion, before an imperial chancellor does for agriculture what I have striven to do by introducing this tariff plan."[74]

The committee report then asked for a five mark increase over Bülow's plan for rye and wheat, twenty-five marks for barley, and fifteen marks for oats. Higher duties were suggested for other grains also. Most surprising was the committee's request that all surplus income from the tariffs be devoted to a widows' and orphans' insurance scheme. Apparently, the Center's committee

74. *Sten. Ber. Reichstages* (1900–1903), III 1, 5683–87.

members had pushed for the adoption of this amendment because of pressure from Catholic workers. The idea originated in an article by Wagner in which he had listed various means to alleviate the burden of more expensive bread on the working class. Bülow had dropped a hint in March 1901 that he would consider social uses for the increased tariff income. Not long after the insurance plan was put forth, Trimborn of the Center amended it so that only the income from meat, rye, and wheat duties would be used, and then only when the surplus was over and above the normal increase occurring from population growth.[75] Trimborn believed that his plan would bring fame to the session for its social concerns. Center members had felt pangs of conscience at the thought of funds derived from the higher price of necessities being used for military purposes; now the increased duties appeared paternal. Spahn termed Trimborn's plan pathfinding in its recognition of the government's responsibility for the care of those impoverished through no fault of their own.[76]

Only the National Liberals greeted the plan with the enthusiasm of the Center. Like the Center, they had some qualms about the social injustice of higher duties, and had supported Caprivi partly because of the cheaper bread that would result from lower duties. The Trimborn plan was ideally suited to relieve any doubts of unfairness to the working class population resulting from higher industrial tariffs. Ledebour, the subsequent ally of Ebert in 1918, explained why the Social Democrats grudgingly had decided to align themselves with the plan's exponents. The party was naturally against the tariff, but if it did pass, the Trimborn plan might moderate its effects.[77] Even if the funds for insurance were not likely to be sufficient, the problem was now in the forefront, whereas it would remain unnoticed for many years should both the committee's and Trimborn's plans be rejected. Molkenbuhr added that the workers would not be lulled into thinking that the plan was intended for their benefit; like Bismarck's social legislation, it was a drop in the bucket.

75. Ibid., 6486–88.
76. Ibid., 6517.
77. Ibid., 6511–12.

Richter detected a subtle attempt to tie widows' insurance to protection, so that the former could not exist without the latter. Not a friend of social legislation in any case, he advised that other financial problems were more pressing, and public funds should not be spent on private needs. Unlike the more scholarly liberals, Richter had not shed the dogmatic liberal principle of non-intervention in the economy.[78] Roesicke of the Progressives protested that 600,000,000 marks was being taken from the consumers while a maximum of 78,000,000 marks would be in the surplus fund. Logically, he continued, if the tariffs had the desired effect of warding off competition, the intake would diminish, and no surplus would develop.[79] The Progressives were not disposed to compromising their principles as the Socialists had done.

Kanitz no less than Richter was a man of principle. Having argued for years that the workers would not suffer from grain duties, he was not about to vote for the Center plan and thereby admit that there was a wrong to be redressed.[80] The other Conservatives agreed that social legislation was distinct from tariffs and should not be considered with them. Both the Reichspartei and the Farmers' League followed the Conservative lead on this issue. When the committee plan came to a vote on 21 November, it was soundly defeated 204 to 43, with only the Social Democrats for it. However, the Trimborn plan passed by 143 to 106, as the National Liberals, the Poles, and the Center joined the Socialists against the minority of Progressives, Conservatives, and Reichspartei.[81] A stranger coalition of majority parties probably never came together under the second empire.

When the second reading commenced, it became obvious to the parties of the right that the Social Democrats and Progressives were going to filibuster in order to lengthen the duration of the Caprivi duties. Progressive speakers such as Gothein read for three or four hours without adding anything new to the controversy. Many amendments having no chance of passage were introduced

78. Ibid., 6506.
79. Ibid., 6506–8.
80. Ibid., 6510–12.
81. Ibid., 6517.

by the Socialists because of their time-consuming quality. For instance, Molkenbuhr asked that all duties be abolished when the price levels reached the heights desired by the agrarians. It was defeated 191 to 41. Conservative and Centrist delegates began to fear that the Socialists were finding their model in the Irish practices in the British parliament or the Pan-Germans in the Austrian parliament.

Although both wings of the Progressives were more assiduous in preparing their speeches, the intention to stall was also evident. Barth expressed his fear that Socialist opposition to the state would grow. He asked for an election in which the people would be allowed to decide the tariff issue so that the divisions in the Reichstag did not become cemented.[82] Alluding to the Conservative contention that the duties would benefit the consumers, Dr. Pachnicke quoted from the works of Sering and Wagner to show that even the scholarly defenders of protection recognized that some compensation was justified.[83] Other speakers instructed the Reichstag in the virtues of free trade, of Caprivi, and of the economic developments of the previous decade.

Between the first and second reading there was a major transformation in the sentiment of the Center. Previously, the party had been a mild supporter of the agrarians but had not assented to the extreme demands of the Farmers' League. Probably a consensus of party opinion was for Bülow's plan. But in the interim, Lieber died, thus removing the strongest antiagrarian voice, and Herold, a militant agrarian, became the party's spokesman on economic matters. In addition, the acceptance of the widows' and orphans' insurance scheme assuaged many consciences about the injustices of the grain duty increases. In Herold's first speech, the trade treaties were demoted to a secondary concern of the party; adequate protection for agriculture was the major one.[84] Heim of Bavaria followed by denouncing export industrialism and introducing an amendment to make the tariff sixty marks on all four grains. According to Bachem, the amendment was a maneuver to unite the

82. Ibid., 5805–7.
83. Ibid., 5749.
84. Ibid., 5797.

parties for protection around one plan in order to cut short the stalling tactics of the left.[85] By this action, the Center adopted an agrarian position and gave expression to its previously latent hostility to industrialism.

The National Liberals found themselves in a predicament on the second reading. Supporting the government proposals turned out to be a lonely and unrewarding task. To their right there was common agreement on the inadequacy of Bülow's plan, and to their left all parties were opposed to higher rates. Uncomfortable in their role, the National Liberals dissociated themselves from all groups by asking the government to withdraw the plan, call an election solely on the tariff issue, and accept the electorate's decision as final. Sattler said that the obstruction of the left could not be terminated without agreement on duties by a strong majority; something that appeared extremely unlikely. The only sound alternative was abandonment of the issue until a coalition could be won for moderate proposals.[86]

Conservatives were agreed on two matters: first, they all considered Bülow a hypocrite who was selling out agriculture while claiming to be its friend, and second, they all applauded the changes in the Center's views. Both Kanitz and Schwerin-Löwitz demanded a seventy-five mark duty as agriculture's due, but both recognized that a majority was not likely to be achieved. Schwerin-Löwitz welcomed the Center plan as giving adequate if not ideal security for agriculture's future.[87] Kanitz, however, despised the National Liberals for yielding to their liberal qualms about agricultural protection, and warned that for every mark sacrificed by the Conservatives they would seek a corresponding drop in industrial tariffs. As for Bülow, he was becoming susceptible to the propaganda of international Jewry.[88]

Moving farther right, Dr. Roesicke of the Farmers' League told the Reichstag that only when the Junkers could pay their laborers

85. Karl Bachem, *Vorgeschichte, Geschichte, und Politik der deutschen Zentrumspartei* (Cologne, 1927–32), 4:134ff.
86. *Sten. Ber. Reichstages* (1900–1903), III 1, 5785–91.
87. Ibid., 5705.
88. Ibid., 5785.

wages comparable to industrialists and offer similar social benefits would agriculture be healthy again. By considering treaties his ultimate purpose Bülow had demonstrated his failure to understand agriculture's problems.[89] Von Wangenheim emphasized the need for higher grain duties by comparing the ability of industries to form cartels with the impossibility of this maneuver in agriculture. If Bülow's proposals were enacted, the federal government was "cutting off the branch upon which the monarchy sits."[90] Von Wangenheim, then, demonstrated his patriotism to the empire by introducing an amendment to raise the grain duties to seventy-five marks on the four major grains. After thirty-six sessions of the second reading, the Reichstag prepared to vote on four schedules. Von Wangenheim's rates were defeated 289 to 44 and 242 to 83, with Farmers' League members and some Conservatives in the minority. Heim's plan went down 242 to 83 and by a voice vote. The Reichstag committee proposals were accepted: 187 to 152, 194 to 145, 183 to 133, and 180 to 139.[91] The majority of Conservatives, the Reichspartei, nearly all Center deputies, and some National Liberals formed the majority.

TABLE 31   TARIFF SCHEDULES (In marks)

	RYE	WHEAT	BARLEY	OATS
Committee Plan	55	60	55	55
Heim Plan	60	60	60	60
Von Wangenheim Plan	75	75	75	75
Bülow Plan	50	55	30	50
Caprivi Rates	35	35	20	28

With the second reading over, only the Center could look back with pride at the results. All the parties on the left, the National Liberals, and the chancellor thought the duties too high, while the right had accepted the committee's report only as a minor improvement over Bülow's plan. Few were looking forward to the denouement in the third reading. The Progressives and the Social Demo-

89. Ibid., 5816–17.
90. Ibid., 5755.
91. Ibid., 5901–8.

crats hinted at going over every one of the 946 duties in detail, which might have taken years. On the right there was anxiety that the Caprivi duties might remain in effect until the left grew hoarse from speaking. Thus, the last reading began with increasing uncertainty about what the duties would be in the next decade.

While the second reading was still in progress, Kardorff of the Reichspartei wrote to a friend about his pessimism regarding the tariff.[92] The left and Farmers' League opposed it and were prolonging discussions, and Bülow had shown no initiative in quelling the obstruction of the Social Democrats. Kardorff concluded with the observation that only a change in the procedure of the Reichstag would facilitate the bill's enactment. Thereafter, he sought out the leaders of all the parties seeking higher rates in order to arrange a compromise plan that could be passed through the Reichstag in short order.

When the third reading opened on 27 November 1902, the parties of the left were shocked to learn that Kardorff was introducing a tariff plan with the backing of the Center, the National Liberals, the Reichspartei, and the Conservatives. He not only was calling for an amendment but wanted it voted upon quickly and then accepted in the third reading without discussion. Because of the obstruction of the left, he said, four parties had come together on terms rather than see Caprivi's duties continue, and he saw no need for much debate as the issues had already been clearly defined.[93] The four parties had agreed to accept the original Bülow plan for grain duties with the one exception of barley, which was raised to forty marks for brewers but abolished when used for foddering. Also, the duties on many industrial products, particularly plows, threshing machines, and sickles, and the like, which were used in agriculture, experienced significant reductions. Evidently the agrarians had lowered their demands in return for sacrifices by the industrialists which were of direct benefit to farmers. The compromise was not entered into willingly by either side, but was a result of the growing pessimism about the enactment of the bill after the government's failure to react to the tactics of the left.

92. S. von Kardorff, *Wilhelm von Kardorff*, p. 348.
93. *Sten. Ber. Reichstages* (1900–1903), III 2, 6655–75.

For four days the Reichstag debated the change in the business order necessitated by Kardorff's proposal. When the president of the Reichstag decided to accept the amendment, the majority parties allowed only one day for discussing the proposed changes. Bebel delivered a long speech on 11 December, calling the decision a travesty of procedure unique in German history. Progressive members denounced the unconstitutionality of the amendment and' the government for accepting changes it had hitherto opposed. With the knowledge that they were impotent before the coalition, the left unleashed a barrage of attacks on the Conservatives and on the government. The Social Democrat Singer had to be removed for disobeying the president's order to sit down. The outrage of the left knew no bounds. That same afternoon the amendment was adopted by 183 to 136 with the Farmers' League joining the left in the minority.[94] Although the third reading was still to be held, passage was now a foregone conclusion.

No more generous than on 11 December, the majority parties allotted 14 December for the last remarks and the vote on the treaty. Bülow was in a good humor, for a few weeks earlier his plan had appeared in great jeopardy. He praised both the insurance scheme and the new barley rates. His final words were already aimed at the foreign negotiators with whom he soon hoped to renew the trade treaties. Germany, he said, needed the agreements less than other nations, and would not make concessions to insure renewal.[95] The Socialists used their last opportunity to castigate industrialists and Junkers for ignoring the wishes of the workers and peasants. Richter claimed that the tragedy had begun in 1897 when a majority of agrarian sympathizers had been appointed to the economic committee preparing recommendations. Barth accused the government of inaugurating a rebirth of mercantilism that would cause trade treaties to be ever more difficult to negotiate. The Farmers' League was outraged at the compromise. Having campaigned for a seventy-five mark duty for ten years, they were not about to accept fifty-five marks.[96] Their abuse was directed at

94. Ibid., 7130–42.
95. Ibid., 7154–64.
96. Ibid., 7145.

the Conservatives for abandoning agriculture and insuring the growth of industry. Not until the proletariat ceased to multiply, said von Wangenheim, would agriculture be ensconced in the dominant position once again. The vote on 14 December appears in Table 32. The thirty absentees on the right betokened silent opposi-

TABLE 32 VOTE ON KARDORFF COMPROMISE

	NUMBER	YEA	NAY	ABSENT
Conservatives	52	30	13	9
Reichspartei	20	19	0	1
Deutsche Sozial	10	0	10	0
Center	105	88	0	16
Poles	14	5	0	9
National Liberals	53	48	1	4
Progressive Union	13	0	6	7
Progressive Volkspartei	26	0	17	9
German Volkspartei	7	0	4	3
Social Democrats	58	0	41	7
Unattached	35	12	8	15
	393	202	110	90

SOURCE: *Sten. Ber. Reichstages* (1900–1903), 3: pt. 2, 7170.

tion to the low level of the duties. Those on the left were a result of the obvious hopelessness of the situation. The Farmers' League voted nay, probably because the bill would pass in any case, and if its effects on prices were not significant the league would be the moral victor.

For the remainder of December and in early January the Reichstag was not in session and tempers seemed to quiet down. However, Kanitz, who had never been satisfied with the government proposal, wrote in the 8 January edition of the *Kreuzzeitung* that if the government were serious about helping agriculture, the recently concluded program should be considered the first in a series of steps.[97] At the Conservative party meeting in March, Kanitz's view was applauded by Graf von Mirbach. In September 1902, the party caucus had found Bülow's proposals wanting, and the party

97. *Kreuzzeitung*, 8 January 1903.

leader emphasized that there had been no subsequent change of opinion; rather, the continuation of Caprivi's rates had forced the acceptance of inadequate duties.[98] Many members thanked the Farmers' League for their useful educational work during the 1890s. Although still disgruntled, the Conservatives recognized the many pressures preventing Bülow from meeting their demands, and rewarded his sympathies by passing the Dortmund-Ems canal bill on its fourth time around in 1904. Even so, Bülow had to concede lower rates for agricultural goods and uniformly higher ones for all products shipped from west to east. Despite these concessions the Farmers' League and a majority of Conservatives voted with the defeated minority. According to the league press: "All such canal building was in conflict with railroad building, and was designed to promote and give privileges to the association of capital and heavy industry, and to damage agriculture and small business—and thereby to advance the transformation of Germany into an industrial and *Welthandelsstaat* dominated by international *Grosskapital*. The whole of German agriculture sees in such a development a danger not only for its existence but for the whole state [*Staatswesen*]."[99]

Incensed by the treachery of the Center and some Conservatives, the Farmers' League threatened to win away peasant support from the two parties because of their "Manchester policies."[100] Von Wangenheim addressed an agrarian rally in Berlin in which he termed the solution an economic misfortune and exhorted his audience against the sham monarchy of Great Britain and the corrupt republic of the United States, both of which were the result of industrialism. The league decided to remain in existence for as long as it was necessary to insure the supremacy of agriculture.[101]

Bülow's response to his agrarian foes was measured in tone. To defeat socialism, a healthy and expanding economy was necessary. If the demands of the Farmers' League were realized, industry

98. *Stenographische Berichte über die Verhandlungen des Delegiertentages der deutschen Konservativpartei* (Berlin, 1903).

99. Horn, p. 285.

100. *Schulthess'* 44 (1903):

101. Wippermann, *Geschichtskalender* (1903), 1:42.

would be paralyzed and socialism a growing force to contend with. He therefore urged the two agrarian parties to moderate their desires in order to form a *Sammlung* with the bourgeois parties that could withstand any leftist onslaught.[102]

The parties of the left saved their diatribes until the election in 1903. Both the Progressives and Social Democrats sought to attract consumer votes by playing up the protectionist sentiment of the other parties. Their efforts were not in vain. The only change of any significance in representation was the gain of twenty-six seats by the Social Democrats. As the two Progressive parties lost a total of twelve seats, the left gained only fourteen, but a brief résumé of the votes gives a more accurate picture. From 2,107,000 votes in 1898, the Social Democrats moved up to 3,087,000 in 1903—a gain of almost one million. Despite the loss in seats, the Progressives picked up 32,000 additional votes.

After his success in the Reichstag, the next problem on Bülow's agenda was the negotiation of the trade treaties. That it took two and a half years to arrive at agreements is some indication of the hostile international reaction to Germany's new protectionism. The treaties with Italy, Belgium, and Switzerland were concluded quickly because grain was not an issue with these countries. Of the troubles with Austria-Hungary, Bülow told the Reichstag, "I am betraying no diplomatic secrets when I say to you that only with difficulty, with great difficulty, have we succeeded in concluding commercial treaties with Austria at the rates stipulated by the Reichstag."[103] A Russian treaty was an even more arduous task. As far back as December 1901, German manufacturers in Russia had written to the Ministry of Trade of the determination of Russian industrialists not to renew the treaty in view of the German grain duties.[104] Moscow textile manufacturers met the disclosure of the duties in June 1901 with glee, for they anticipated large increases in Russian duties. In April of 1901 the German ambassador informed Bülow of unwished-for economic and political conse-

102. B. A. Bülow, "Entwurfe," *Nachlass.*
103. *Schulthess'* 46 (1906): 75.
104. DZA, "Bericht von deutschen Industriellen in Russland," *Akta betr. Handelsverträge Rep.* 120 CXIII 69 35 vol. 6.

quences if Witte's reform plans were upset by Germany's tariff policy.[105] Bülow's forebodings were realized when after fifteen months of negotiations no progress had been achieved. On 29 March 1904, Wilhelm sought to end the standstill by asking Tsar Nicholas II to send an emissary to negotiate with Bülow personally.[106] The tsar complied by sending Witte with instructions to be as accommodating as possible. The change in the Russian temper was caused by the need for German friendship after the unexpected outbreak of war with Japan. Desiring both a German loan and neutrality, the tsar was willing to be more agreeable on economic matters. Alvensleben, the German ambassador, asked Bülow if the loan should not be hinged upon acceptance of German terms on the treaty. The chancellor agreed that some pressure was warranted but warned of an excess that might divert Russia to French bankers.[107] Witte's attitude before and during the talks are to be found in his memoirs: "Upon the outbreak of hostilities, Emperor Wilhelm hastened to assure His Majesty of his devotion to Russia and of the security of our western frontiers. Nevertheless, as if in compensation for his promise not to attack us, the German emperor in a private letter to his Majesty requested his consent to a number of changes in the commercial treaty of 1894, which had just then expired. These changes were so ruinous to our industries that I resolutely opposed them and advocated the maintenance of the status quo . . . ; we had to yield. At a special conference it was decided we had to submit to Germany or suffer a break in relations. . . . I cannot say that I acted freely."[108] Bülow himself wrote the emperor that Witte only made the concessions "sur l'ordre formel de son Auguste Maître."[109] Right up until the war the "mailed fist" policy used by Germany in 1904 rankled the Russians. In 1913 a

105. Henry Jordan, "Der Einfluss der Schutzzollpolitik auf die Beziehungen zum Ausland," pp. 37–41.

106. *Die Grosse Politik* 19, 1, pp. 182–84.

107. Ibid., 18 entry I, 5404.

108. Sergei Witte, *The Memoirs of Count Witte* (London, 1921), pp. 412–13.

109. Spectator, *Prince Bülow and the Kaiser,* trans. Oakley Williams (London, 1931), p. 130.

Duma deputy, Shingaryov, called the treaty a worse defeat than the Japanese war. The following year Professor Mitranoff of Moscow said that Russia had been a "tributary to Germany for eight years because of the treaty concluded under duress."[110] It is difficult to gauge the effects of the treaty on Russo-German relations, but certainly the Russian industrialists and estate owners became antipathetic to closer ties with Germany. In an article written during the war Brentano blamed the whole catastrophe on the Russian trade treaty, as did Aeroboe in his 1925 volume *Agrarpolitik*. Writing in 1928, Kehr ascribed the growing hostility between Germany and Russia after 1902 solely to the economic policies of the Junkers. Neither in foreign policy nor in political ideology did he find any irreconcilable conflicts separating the two empires.[111]

The treaties presented to the Reichstag for approval on 5 February 1905 were on the whole favorable to Germany, although not to the extent of the earlier ones. The duties were raised on 37 percent of the value of German imports, lowered on 11 percent, and maintained on 52 percent. Treaty partners raised duties on 46 percent of the value of German exports, lowered it on 7 percent, and left unchanged 47 percent. The treaties were passed without much delay, for the Progressives were delighted that they had been negotiated at all. Only the Socialists and some agrarians demurred. Despite the compromises of the Conservatives in 1902, the Caprivi rates were not replaced until 1 March 1906.

Bülow never changed his attitude toward agriculture during his term of office and there is no reason to presume that he was insincere. He was deeply committed to the Wilhelmian state and recognized that its institutions rested on an agricultural foundation. For the successful conclusion of the treaty negotiations he was made a prince, and Posadowsky was given the order of the Black Eagle. In 1907, when the rancour of the controversy had passed, Bülow held out the olive branch to the Farmers' League and commended its actions against the Social Democrats. He concluded with the wish that his tombstone bear the inscription, "The deceased has been an

110. Jordan, "Der Einfluss der Schutzzollpolitik," p. 42.
111. Kehr, *Der Primat der Innenpolitik* (Berlin, 1965), p. 171.

agrarian imperial chancellor," and he continued, "Gentlemen, that
I was, that I am, and that I will remain."[112]

When all the passions and the disagreements over tariffs in 1901
are remembered, it would appear that the acceptance of the government's plan and the conclusion of trade treaties in 1905 were a
great victory not only for Bülow but also for those desiring a strong,
nationally oriented empire. The pressures on the novice chancellor
had been overwhelming. First, the emperor whose support was absolutely necessary had to be won over to higher duties and convinced that treaties were nevertheless possible. On the left were
two parties whose followers had reaped great benefits from the
Caprivi treaties. From their vantage point further reductions of
grain duties appeared to be the logical course. On the right the
Farmers' League and many Conservatives believed that the only
purpose of the tariff should be to restore agriculture to its lost
primacy. Some even hoped the proposals would allow agriculture
to surpass industry in generating wealth. In the middle were the
National Liberals, whose industrialists, like the emperor, were primarily interested in treaties, and who would doubtless oppose rates
that doomed negotiations to failure. In 1901 it was difficult to predict the attitude of the Center party, which comprised a variety of
economic interest groups within itself. Although a protectionist
group was gaining strength, Lieber, the leader, was an old adherent of free trade. Faced with the problem of fashioning a majority
from this multiplicity of views and renewing trade agreements,
Bülow succeeded against what appeared almost unsurmountable
odds.

Why did he succeed? Here three factors are relevant. First of all,
Bülow astutely recognized that the two seats of power were the
agrarian-dominated Conservatives and the emperor. The former
wanted the highest possible rates and the latter the renewal of
Caprivi's treaties. Rather than formulating a program on the basis
of academic theories or analyses of the previous treaties' results, he
suggested the highest rates that would not prejudice treaty discus-

112. *Schulthess'* 48 (1907): 87.

sions. By basing his policy on the existing distribution of power, his chances of success were enhanced. Second, Bülow's skill as an active politician must be accorded credit. From the outset he knew that whatever program was ultimately adopted would require the approval of the Conservatives. Therefore, he sought to win their favor immediately after his accession to the chancellorship by avowals of his agrarian bias in the *lower house* and at agrarian meetings. Also in this category is Bülow's ability to separate the fundamentals in his proposals from the trivia. Thus, he readily accepted the changes in barley tariffs and the widows' insurance scheme in order to win Center support, but would not tolerate even a five mark increase in major grain rates. His raising of industrial duties, while somewhat haphazard, was an intelligent maneuver to win National Liberal votes. Lastly, two factors beyond Bülow's control contributed significantly to his success. If the Social Democrats and Progressives had not annoyed the other parties by their delaying tactics, a compromise favorable to the government might have been more difficult to work out, especially as a majority of votes had already been cast for the committee proposals. The propitious outbreak of the Russo-Japanese war was an unforeseeable event that made a Russian treaty possible.

What were the chances of getting a thirty-five mark duty through the Reichstag? Assuming that Bülow had been of Caprivi's mind, there were numerous tactics that could have been tried; nevertheless the chances were bleak. The emperor might have been induced to put pressure on the Center and the National Liberals. In view of the tariffs' importance, concessions in other areas such as the return of the Jesuits, a lenient Polish policy, and social legislation might have won over the Center. An election in 1902 on the tariff issue would have increased the number of thirty-five mark duty supporters in the Reichstag. All these tactics were possible; yet the embarrassing position of having to rely on the left in the Reichstag while remaining dependent upon the right in the Prussian legislature would have put any chancellor in a difficult if not impossible position. In one sense, the chances of success were irrelevant. A chancellor with integrity, and with an understanding of the long-term interests of the German people, would have been compelled to try to continue Caprivi's rates, just as Stein had sought reforms in 1807 in spite of the hostility of the Junkers.

There are two reasons for Bülow's failure to act. The chancellor was swept up in the economic and social currents prevailing in Wilhelmian Germany. Accepting the theories of Wagner and Sering uncritically, as did many other men in powerful positions, he did not perceive the dangers inherent in the agrarian demands. Like most imperial statesmen, he was given to exaggerating the socialist danger and viewing a *Sammlung* of industry and agriculture as the best guarantee for a strong Germany. The blame in large part lies with the professors' dire predictions concerning the future of an industrialized Germany. The anti-industrial economists were spokesmen of a narrow, nationalistic approach. When these views were translated into policy, disaster became probable. Thus, Bülow could quite comfortably choose the expedient path believing it to be the wisest also; both short- and long-term goals seemed to be identical. A statesman must on occasion swim against the tide when his reason tells him that public opinion or those in powerful positions are misguided; Bülow clearly lacked the qualities necessary to recognize that the situation in 1902 called for this sort of action.

7

The German Economy under Bülow's Tariffs

How higher grain duties and the trade treaties negotiated in 1905 affected agriculture, industry, and the consumers, until the outbreak of World War I, will now be discussed. In tracing Bülow's agrarian course, it will be shown that Bülow's subventions enabled the large and inefficient estates to survive in a heavily industrialized country despite the continuation and, in fact, aggravation of East Elbian agriculture's traditional problems. Thus, the Prussian Junker, unlike his English counterpart, did not have to invest in urban real estate, take up stock breeding, or rely on income from coal mines, to maintain his privileged social and economic position.

AGRICULTURE

The immediate purpose of Bülow's duties was to force the prices of the four major grains to rise. None of his supporters or even the dissenters who had wanted further raises expressed disappointment with the results. On the other hand, the worst predictions of Brentano and of the exponents of industrialism appeared close to realization. Table 33 lists the Berlin prices for the three major grains; after 1906, barley prices were divided in accordance with the quality.

TABLE 33   GRAIN PRICES (In marks, per 1,000 kg.)

YEAR	WHEAT	RYE	OATS
1905	174.8	151.9	137.2
1906	179.6	160.6	154.6
1907	206.3	193.2	166.8
1908	211.2	186.5	148.9
1909	233.9	176.5	167.3
1910	211.5	152.3	143.4
1911	204.0	168.3	159.3

SOURCE: *Statistisches Jahrbuch für das deutsche Reich*, 1915, p. 302. Also see Walther Hoffmann, *Das Wachstum der deutschen Wirtschaft seit der Mitte des 19. Jahrhunderts* (Berlin, 1965), pp. 552–55.

Grain prices not only rose, but they exceeded the amount anticipated by all forecasters. Coincidental with the imposition of the duty, world grain prices began to edge upward for two reasons. By 1906 the United States population was multiplying so rapidly from immigration and a falling death rate that grain surpluses available for export had declined. In addition, the Russian harvests from 1905 to 1908 were mediocre, leaving little for export. Therefore, the prices of wheat and rye had increased measurably in Odessa, Vienna, and Paris. In 1906 rye fetched 101 marks in Odessa, 120 in Vienna, and 132 in Paris; three years later the prices were 132, 178, and 137 respectively.[1] The average difference in wheat prices in the three cities was fifty marks between 1906 and 1909. German prices rose in excess of the Bülow rates because of the shortage in world grain supplies. Theodor von der Goltz, who certainly bore no hostility to the legitimate interests of agriculture, drew up a sliding scale of rye rates in 1902, which he believed would provide a fair price for farmers without unnecessarily burdening the consumer.[2] It is of some interest to compare his projected rates to the price levels after 1905. If his sliding scale had been followed, the

1. Karl Diehl, *Zur Frage der Getreidezölle*, (Jena, 1911), p. 137.
2. Goltz, *Agrarwesen und Agrarpolitik* (Jena, 1904), p. 278.

rye duty would have been 30.0, 25.0, 10.0, 12.50, 10.75, 30.0, and 10.25 marks respectively for the years from 1905 to 1911, instead of a flat 50 marks. The fears expressed earlier by the Social Democrat Molkenbuhr came to fruition: prices exceeded the levels necessary for an adequate return for the farmers, and the duties remained in effect although they now imposed a great burden on the consumers.

An important objection of Brentano to higher duties had been his belief that agricultural prosperity would not be restored, but rather, that many Junkers would use the accompanying rise in land prices to sell their heavily indebted estates. That is, the Junkers were seeking a "bullish" event to escalate the price of their estates artificially. The 1902 yearly report of the East Prussian Agricultural Chamber states: "A significant number of large and small estates, many of which have been in the hands of the seller's family for many years, have been sold in the period covered by this report. The inclination to sell is very strong. . . . The prices paid were very high when compared with those paid in previous years."[3]

In order to determine the correctness of Brentano's forecast, the price of land in various Prussian provinces will be examined along with the frequency of selling in comparison with previous years. Table 34, derived from official tax tables, presents the increase of

TABLE 34 INCREASE OF LAND PRICES
BASED ON AVERAGE LAND TAX

	1895–97	1901–03	1907–09
Königsberg	100	116	147
Gumbinnen	100	122	135
Danzig	100	116	143
Stettin	100	111	119
Posen	100	130	154
Breslau	100	102	118
Prussia	100	117	133

SOURCE: W. Rothkegel, "Die Bewegung der Kaufpreise für ländliche Besitzungen und die Entwicklung der Getreidepreise, 1895–1909," *Schmollers Jahrbuch* 34 (1910): 102. According to Hoffmann, land prices rose by about 8 percent from 1890 to 1904 and by about 42 percent from 1904 to 1914. Hoffmann, *Das Wachstum*, pp. 569–70.

3. *Jahresbericht der Landwirtschaftskammer Ostpreussen* 1901/02 (Berlin, 1902), p. 112.

land prices between 1895 and 1909. The average percent rise according to the size of estates in East Elbian Prussia from 1896 to 1917 was: zero, 13, 26, 74, and 92. In West Elbian lands it was: 1, 8, 24, and 20.[4] Even more interesting is the fact that the prices rose only moderately, if at all, from 1896 to 1901. Only when it was certain that grain duties would be significantly higher did land prices soar. Before Bülow's proposals were announced, land prices reflected the relatively declining state of agriculture. Afterward, the prices bore no relation at all to the health of agriculture because they were based on the hopes of continued and augmented government support rather than real value.

Not surprisingly, there was a rash of selling by estate owners as soon as the new duties took effect. Between 1897 and 1900 the percentage of estates of: between 125 and 250 acres, between 250 and 500 acres, and 500 acres and over, changing hands by sale, was 4.35, 5.8, and 5.8 respectively. In the year 1906 it was 4.7, 8.0, and 7.3 respectively.[5] More specifically, 23,000 more farms in Prussia were sold in 1906 than in 1903. The percentage sold in East and West Prussia was twice that of the farms in the west. All in all, it would seem that the tariffs set off a new wave of speculation and enhanced the opportunities for indebted Junkers to sell their estates.

Whether the duties restored agriculture to a healthy state can be judged from table 35, which presents the indebtedness in selected provinces after 1906. It must be remembered that agrarians

TABLE 35   INDEBTEDNESS (In thousands of marks)

YEAR	EAST PRUSSIA	WEST PRUSSIA	POSEN	SILESIA	RHINE-LAND
1887–1912	29,006	19,002	17,284	45,414	66,848
1908	52,398	26,116	32,989	47,265	99,000
1909	54,232	42,916	40,251	63,444	78,000
1910	57,446	51,450	54,055	97,927	76,000
1911	65,297	53,202	63,138	77,135	79,000
1912	91,815	50,145	55,656	82,882	69,000

SOURCE: *Statistisches Jahrbuch für Preussen*, 1914.

4. W. Rothkegel, *Schätzungslehre*, 2 vols. (Berlin, 1930), appendix.
5. *Statistisches Jahrbuch für Preussen 1908–14.*

claimed the duties would enable estate owners to reduce their debts. Indebtedness not only did not decline in East Elbian Prussia but appears to have increased at a faster pace than in previous years. On 7 February 1907, the minister of agriculture in Prussia, von Arnim Kriewen, told the House of Deputies, "I cannot conceal my impression that the favorable nature of the tariff legislation for agriculture has been exaggerated. I cannot conceal my conviction that the high land prices we presently have are not a sufficient pillar for agriculture . . . and indebtedness is in my view one of the main cancers from which agriculture suffers."[6] Apparently the primary problem of agriculture under Bismarck and Caprivi remained under Bülow. If anything, the duties aggravated the problem.

Bülow's introduction of new *Fideikommiss* regulations was described in the previous chapter. Alarmed by the spread of this institution, which worked against the colonization of the eastern areas by peasants, Bülow had stipulated a minimum income for the beneficiaries of *Fideikommiss*. Weber argued that the new rules would foster the anachronistic institution, and that this was another in the long line of the chancellor's concessions to agriculture. Table 36 contains the relevant statistics about the progress of *Fideikommiss*. Even Max Sering admitted that the growth of *Fideikommiss* hindered the increased productivity of agriculture. Its defenders always used social and historical justifications but rarely economic ones.

TABLE 36   ENTAILED ESTATES

YEAR	NUMBER	ACRES	PERCENT OF LAND SURFACE
1890	981	4,800,000	5.6
1895	1045	5,250,000	6.1
1900	1100	5,350,000	6.3
1905	1170	5,650,000	6.5
1910	1251	6,017,000	6.9
1914	1311	6,167,000	7.0
1918	1314	6,266,000	7.2

SOURCE: *Handwörterbuch der Staatswissenschaften,* 4th ed., 3:998.

6. *Schulthess' europäischer Geschichtskalender,* 48 (1907).

Beginning in 1870, the number of farm animals in the empire grew rapidly, even more so after Caprivi's duties. The expansion was a result of both increasing prosperity and the declining profitability of grain. As meat prices were high, farmers found it more profitable to fodder their grain rather than take it to market. This development was desirable because it gave evidence of the adaptability of German farmers to changing world conditions and it ultimately provided more nutritious food for the consumer. Bülow's tariff policy, however, brought this trend of events to a halt. The decline in livestock after 1907 is immediately apparent. On those estates broken up into peasant holdings the number of cattle multiplied immediately, which disproved the Junkers' contention that weather and soil forbade cattle raising in the east. Sering acknowledged in 1909 that cattle and pigs seemed to thrive only on peasant farms.

TABLE 37   NUMBER OF COWS AND PIGS

YEAR	COWS	PIGS	COWS PER 100 PERSONS	PIGS PER 100 PERSONS
1892	17,556,000	12,174,000	34.8	24.1
1900	18,940,000	16,807,000	33.6	29.8
1904	19,332,000	18,921,000	32.3	31.6
1907	20,631,000	22,147,000	33.0	35.4
1912	20,182,000	21,924,000	30.3	32.9

SOURCE: F. Wilken, *Volkswirtschaftliche Theorie der landwirtschaftlichen Preissteigerung* (Berlin, 1925), appendix. The situation of the nineties repeated itself during the first World War. Grain prices remained low while meat prices rose sharply. Again farmers used their grain for fodder instead of marketing it. In contrast to the nineties, however, real income declined during the war with disastrous consequences on the working-class diet.

An argument adduced on numerous occasions to justify higher duties was the blockade theory. According to this view, Germany had to become self-sufficient in grain because of the possibility of blockade in wartime. Tariffs were suggested as the best method to achieve this result. The ineffectiveness of tariffs in realizing autarky is attested to by the following statistics. During the 1880s Germany spent an average of 45 million British pounds on food imports; in the 1890s the amount rose to 75 million and in 1912 it reached 160 million.[7] While Germany ceased to import rye and oats (the two grains grown on Junker estates), the demand for wheat and barley increased precipitously. By 1911 wheat imports were 8 percent higher and barley imports 15 percent higher than they had been in 1901.[8] Since these developments were coincidental with the fall in meat production, it is doubtful whether the duties prepared Germany for war. Also, the imports of rye and wheat might have been even greater if penurious consumers had not switched to potatoes as the staple of their diets.

After World War I, many economists looked back upon the turnip winter and thanked Oldenberg and other autarkists for having sought to increase food production before the war. Few perceived that his methods brought about the reverse effect. Several points seem to indicate that the food shortage during 1915 and 1916 were not the result of insufficient production in any case. First, both Kehr and Zickursch recognized that had the war broken out in September, after the summer grains were exported in order to gain identity passes, Germany would not have been able to survive the winter.[9] If the autarkists had been correct, one would expect a sharp increase in food production in the last decade before the war. This is not the case. To be sure it increased, but no faster than in the preceding decade.[10]

Most important in this connection is the point made by Adolf von Batocki, the head of the *Kriegsnährungsamt* during the war. It was his opinion that Germany produced enough grain in the first two years of the war to feed the population, but poor administration of even poorer regulations hindered the distribution of foodstuffs.[11]

7. J. H. Clapham, *Economic Development of France and Germany* (Cambridge, 1921), p. 361; Hoffmann, *Das Wachstum der deutschen Wirtschaft seit der Mitte des 19. Jahrhunderts* (Berlin, 1965), p. 524.

8. *Deutsche Landwirtschaft* (Berlin, 1913), p. 261.

9. Johannes Ziekursch, *Politische Geschichte des neuen deutschen Kaiserreiches* (Frankfurt/M, 1930), 3:62; Eckart Kehr, *Schlachtflottenbau und Parteipolitik, 1894–1901* (Berlin, 1930), p. 342.

10. R. Wagenfuhr, "Das Geheimnis der Gegenseitigkeit im Wirtschaftsleben," *Vierteljahrsheft für Konjunkturforschung* 2, pt. A (1936), pp. 149, 159; Hoffmann, *Das Wachstum*, p. 294.

11. Adolf von Batocki, *Schluss mit Kriegszwangwirtschaft* (Berlin, 1921).

At the outset of the war, price controls were placed on grain, potatoes, sugarbeets, and other items in short supply. Not being able to take advantage of the demand for grain, the wily German farmers ignored the regulations against foddering in order to exact high prices for meat. Thus, quality grain was being fed to cows and pigs while German citizens were eating potatoes or turnips. Finally, in 1917, price controls were placed upon meat and severe punishments introduced for the foddering of grain. Those who could afford meat did not have to reduce their consumption in the early years of the war. August Skalweit concurred with Batocki's conclusions.[12] In 1932 Sering confirmed Batocki's views—he attributed the near-starvation of many Germans to the omission of meat from the goods under control.[13]

In summation it can be said that the tariffs in no way restored agriculture to a healthy state. The decline of grain agriculture that had begun in the 1870s continued unabated until the war. The seeds of the postwar crises in German agriculture were already laid in 1902. When grain prices slumped to all-time lows in the 1920s, the German farmers were less able to survive because they had ignored the warnings of the prewar years. If Bülow had fostered the adaptation to livestock farming, as Caprivi had done, the slumps of the 1920s might have been considerably mitigated. Those farmers surviving through the Weimar Republic did so by introducing pigs and dairy farming, hitherto considered impossible on the East Elbian lands. Indebtedness, entail, and high land prices —the three hindrances to a sound German agriculture—were all aggravated by the tariffs which were designed to initiate prosperity among the German farming community.

INDUSTRY

The industrial expansion during the years just before World War I was the brightest spot in the economic picture at the time. Despite

12. August Skalweit, *Die deutsche Kriegsernährungswirtschaft* (Stuttgart, 1927).

13. Max Sering, "Wehrwirtschaftliche Studien zur deutschen Volksernährung vor, in, und nach dem Weltkriege," (unpublished manuscript), pp. 34, 46.

the equivocating predictions of exporters, German industrialists showed their flexibility in adjusting to the disadvantageous terms of the new treaties. These years were prosperous ones in all of Europe, and 1913, in particular, was the biggest boom year in exports to that time. The amount of foreign trade per capita remained stationary at 245 marks until 1910, when a new upswing caused the figure to reach 318 marks by 1913.[14] The increase in trade with treaty nations is shown in Table 38. The statistics hardly need am-

TABLE 38   TRADE WITH TREATY NATIONS
(In thousands of tons)

	1905		1912		1913	
	IM-PORTS	EX-PORTS	IM-PORTS	EX-PORTS	IM-PORTS	EX-PORTS
Russia	1090.8	368.4	1527.9	679.8	1424.6	880.2
Romania	94.1	44.1	138.2	131.7	79.7	140.0
Austria	773.2	494.9	830.0	1035.3	825.5	1104.8
Switzerland	190.3	369.8	205.7	495.3	213.3	551.0

SOURCE: *Statistisches Jahrbuch für das deutsche Reich,* 1894, 1900, 1906, 1914.

plification. Exports increased at a much faster pace than imports. The deficits with Russia and Austria-Hungary had been reduced, and in the case of the latter a favorable balance had set in. In 1905 Germany had imported 32.7 percent of its goods from treaty nations and exported 29 percent of total exports to them. By 1913 the imports had dropped to 24.5 percent and the exports risen to 31.8 percent. Writing in 1924, Sartorius von Walthershausen scoffed at those who had expected the tariffs to result in the decline of German industry. Instead, industry enjoyed an unprecedented period of prosperity.

Yet, oddly enough, these sentiments were not shared by the very industrialists who were presumably experiencing the profitable years. It must be remembered that the dissidents among industrialists had always been the leaders of light industries dependent upon exports. That the iron and steel manufacturers saw their exports soar was not surprising since they had been the recipients of ex-

14. Ernst Wagemann, *Konjunkturlehre,* (Berlin, 1928), p. 277.

traordinarily high duties in 1902. Having a monopoly of the domestic market assured, they were able to undercut competition in foreign markets because their profits were virtually guaranteed. Light industry, however, depended on the tariff schedules of their market nations, tariffs which had been increased in response to Germany's duties of 1902. Speaking to a group of industrialists in 1913, the head of the Bund der Industriellen said, "We members of the Bund der Industriellen cannot conceal that we see severe damage to industry in the activities of the Farmers' League over the last two decades. . . . It has struggled against industry and its further development."[15]

The evidence of industrial dissatisfaction was even more pointed. Both linen and paper industry executives wrote of the bleak future that they anticipated under the treaties.[16] In 1910 the *Deutsche Handelstag* expressed its concern about the state of German industry. It found that exports and imports had not increased as much as the statistics had indicated.[17] Bülow had changed the terms used from *Ausfuhr* to *Bestimmungsland* and *Einfuhr* to *Herstellungsland*—a change, the Deutsche Handelstag claimed, that caused the amount of foreign trade to be exaggerated. The *Handelstag* also noted that many exporters had borne the increase in rates; thus trade increased but profits did not. On 2 September 1906, the Ministry of the Interior requested the Ministry of Trade to investigate rumors that numerous German enterprises were opening branches in Austria to avoid the handicap imposed by the treaties.[18] The Ministry of the Interior had been stirred to this action by a series of articles in the *Berliner Tageblatt* on industries fleeing the country in response to the new rates. The reply of the Ministry of Trade was not heartening. Ten major concerns had moved in part or in toto to Austria, with an accompanying loss of jobs to Germans. Among the firms listed were the Upper Silesian Iron Industry, the United Dye

15. Hansabund no. 7 (1913).
16. Heinz Potthoff, "Die Leinenindustrie und die Handelsverträge," *Deutsche Wirtschaftszeitung* 1, no. 22 (8 November 1905); Eugen Hagen, "Die papierverarbeitende Industrie und die Handelsverträge," ibid.
17. *Der deutsche Handelstag* 2:552.
18. DZA, *Abschrift vom Innernministerium*, 2 September 1906, Rep. 120 CXIII Nr. 79 vol. 1.

Works, and the Elberfeld Dye Works.[19] On 10 September 1906, the Ministry received a letter from the professional organization of the dye industry pleading for aid before all the manufacturers moved to Austria.[20]

Two years later, the Ministry reported to the chancellor of the declining profits in the industries manufacturing "chemicals, textiles, wood products, paper, toys, glass, clocks, and musical instruments."[21] When Bülow issued a pamphlet in 1909 claiming great success for his treaties, he received nine- and fourteen-page reports from the Wiesbaden Chamber of Commerce and an association of paper manufacturers with contrary views. According to the Chamber, Great Britain was replacing Germany in Russia and elsewhere as a main source of industrial supplies.[22] The declining prices of exports also received mention. The Association for Commercial Treaties got into the act with a booklet severely critical of the business situation, in which the city of Mannheim was cited as having lost twenty firms because of the tariffs. That many firms were not producing at full capacity was given as further evidence of the tariff's malevolent effects. Lastly, the German consul in Prague wrote to the chancellor in 1911 of the growing number of German factories in the city—a development he attributed to the "tariff relations between Germany and Austria-Hungary."[23] He then proceeded to list forty-two plants, employing 3,700 workers, that had settled in the Bohemian capital in the preceding five years.

Perhaps the most convincing evidence of industrial dissatisfaction with the economic developments during Bülow's years as chancellor was the establishment of the *Hansabund* on 12 June 1909. On that day in Berlin, representatives of 100 chambers of commerce, 400 professional organizations, bankers, and merchants met to plan a campaign against the favoritism shown agriculture by the government. Delegates from the Krupp firm, the chairman

19. DZA, *Abschrift vom Handelsministerium*, 10 September 1906, Rep. 120 CXIII Nr. 79 vol. 1.
20. DZA, *Brief an das Innernministerium von dem Verein betr. Farberstoff und Gerbstoff*, 10 September 1906.
21. DZA, *Abschrift an den Reichskanzler*, p. 198.
22. DZA, *Handelskammer zu Wiesbaden*, p. 79.
23. DZA, *Abschrift von Handelsvertragsverein*, p. 27.

of the Centralverband deutscher Industrieller, and the head of the Deutsche Bank attended. Geheimrat Riesser, the first chairman of the Hansabund, opened by criticizing the long-standing apathy of industry toward the contemporary economic situation, in which "agriculture has not only political and economic advantages but also has been able to extend its political power, when primacy in trade and industry has been yielded. Political power is used ruthlessly, and more often than ever before, to create privileges, subventions, and gifts of love, which the other classes must pay for."[24] The Hansabund was bent on preventing the use of political power for economic advantage and on countering the anti-industrial policy of agriculture. Bülow's tariff was roundly criticized. "The crass egotism and irreconcilability" of the Junkers was to be fought on every occasion.[25]

If the Hansabund had been founded in 1900, its chances of succeeding would have been greatly enhanced. After the tariff issue had been more or less settled in 1902 in favor of agriculture, the industrialists had lost the right moment and the moral suasion necessary for victory in the struggle with agriculture. In any event, the promising beginning of the Hansabund was not lived up to, for in 1911 the Centralverband withdrew over differences on social and tariff policy. When a member said that "the Social Democrats were a lesser evil than the agrarians," the heavy industry members demurred.[26] They gradually became alienated as the Hansabund policy gave evidence of seeking to moderate the hostility of the Socialists to the empire by concessions in social welfare. After the members agreed that high tariffs had to be rejected at the next opportunity, the Centralverband walked out.[27] It was more profitable

24. *Schulthess'* 50 (1909): 198, 302. An immediate reason for the Hansabund's foundation was the failure of Bülow's tax program to get Reichstag approval. The proposal would have increased the burden on agriculture moderately.

25. *Jahrbuch des Hansabundes*, 1912, p. 56. On the organization, see Jakob Riesser, *Der Hansabund* (Jena, 1912).

26. *Jahrbuch des Hansabundes* 1912, p. 62. According to Kaelble, Emil Kirdorf and other representatives of the Centralverband joined the Hansabund as a tactical maneuver and expected it to be a stillborn child. Kaelble, p. 76.

27. *Schulthess'* 50 (1909): 302.

to be an adjunct of those in power than a leader among the opposition. Thereafter, the Hansabund became more closely identified with merchants, those engaged in light industry, and bankers. It struggled against the election of agrarian candidates on the local level, but never quite reached the size of the Farmers' League.

The seven years during which the tariffs were in effect were favorable to those industries organized into cartels and having a secure home market. For the others it depended very much on the reaction of their foreign markets to Germany's imposition of high agricultural duties. In general, industry was extremely fortunate that the years after 1906 were prosperous ones for Europe; this, in some part, moderated the effect that the tariffs otherwise would have had. A final judgment on the state of industry would have to be favorable, although certain dangerous precedents were being set in the cartelization of heavy industry, and the prosperity was partially due to a Europe-wide boom.

CONSUMERS

"The economic results of the new trade treaties were good," wrote Karl Bachem in the late 1920s. "Agriculture entered a period of stability and steady growth. The higher duties struggled for so desperately by the Farmers' League proved not to be necessary. The protection in combination with self-help measures initiated a new period of prosperity . . . which enabled Germany to approach the aim of feeding herself. . . . From the industrial upswing the industrial worker slowly but steadily improved his economic position. . . . A considerable worsening of his situation through exaggerated prices of necessities did not occur."[28] Thus Bachem closed a section on the trade treaties in his history of the Center party. Like most of his colleagues in the party, Bachem ignored the *Schattenseiten* resulting from the action of the Center. From his vantage, the prewar years appeared to be the best of all possible worlds. Only a cynic could hint that the conditions of postwar Germany were a logical development from prewar events.

Did the laborer in fact profit as much as Bachem implies? (It

28. Bachem, *Vorgeschichte, Geschichte, und Politik der deutschen Zentrumspartei, 1815–1914,* (Cologne, 1927–32), 4:250.

may be noted first that even Bachem admitted the Trimborn plan was an unmitigated failure, and in 1911 a comprehensive insurance scheme including widows and orphans had to be introduced.) The duties were expected to hit the consumer hardest in the prices paid for bread. Most Junkers and some economists denied the existence of a correlation between the prices of grain and bread. From table 39, bread prices appear to have risen more quickly in Germany

TABLE 39   BREAD PRICES

	1894–98	1899–1903	1904–9	1909–13
Berlin (pennies)	21.8	24	28	30.2
Cologne (pennies)	20	22	27	30
Baden (pennies)	24	25	27.5	28.7
France (index)	100	100	100	99
London (index)	104	100	100	105

SOURCE: *Statistisches Jahrbuch der Stadt Berlin*, 1913; *Statistisches Jahrbuch für Baden*, (1911); von Tyszka, "Löhne und Lebenskosten," *Schriften des Vereins für Sozialpolitik* 145 (1914): 20, 21, 113; Hoffmann, *Das Wachstum*, pp. 571–75; Kuczynski, *Die Geschichte der Arbeiter unter dem Kapitalismus* (Berlin, 1962), 4:331.

than in France or England. The major rise in Germany actually occurred in 1906 and 1907—the same years that the Bülow duties were introduced. But the rise in bread prices was only one effect of the duties. By causing meat and dairy production to slump, the duties influenced the price of most necessities used by the laboring classes. Table 40 shows that the price of meat and eggs rose even

TABLE 40   PRICE INDEX, BAVARIA

YEAR	RYE BREAD	BEEF	PORK	POTA-TOES	MILK	EGGS
1881	100	100	100	100	100	100
1890	106	131	106	99	93	105
1905	93	151	119	110	106	118
1910	106	172	141	111	112	126

SOURCE: *Statistisches Jahrbuch für Bayern* (Munich, 1911), p. 211. According to Hoffmann and Kuczynski, meat consumption scarcely changed from 1906 to 1914. Hoffmann, *Das Wachstum*, pp. 626–29; Kuczynski, *Die Geschichte*, 4:332.

more precipitously than bread. Inducements to export grain or sell it had become so great in 1909 and 1910 that shortages of fodder for livestock were not rare. Horsemeat once again became a common sight in Munich butcher shops. For a comprehensive account of food costs we can turn to Bry's compilation (table 41), in which six different studies are included. These statistics showing an approximately 32 percent rise in twelve years correspond closely to the price charts for sundry foods in the statistical yearbooks for Prussia. According to the yearbook for 1914, the prices of beef, veal, and mutton rose from 143, 161 and 147 pennies a pound in 1905 to 181, 201, and 191, respectively, in 1913.[29]

From an examination of the kinds of foods consumed by the population under the treaties as compared with the last decade of the nineteenth century, it would appear that consumption of wheat re-

TABLE 41   COST OF LIVING INDEX

YEAR	KUC-ZYNSKI	JUNGST	KRUPP	BRUTZE	ZAHN	RICHTER
1900	100	100	100	100	100	100
1901	101	101	102	102	103	103
1902	102	102	105	103	103	103
1903	102	101	103	102	103	104
1904	103	101	98	101	104	106
1905	107	106	105	105	111	114
1906	113	112	113	111	115	117
1907	114	113	107	115	114	116
1908	114	113	108	117	116	116
1909	117	116	113	117	121	121
1910	120	119	—	—	126	121
1911	124	123	—	—	—	125
1912	130	131	—	—	—	134

SOURCE: G. Bry, *Wages in Germany* (Princeton, 1960), pp. 354–55.

mained stable while that of beef and rye declined and that of potatoes rose. Thus, the least nutritious food, the one associated with poverty, experienced the largest increase in consumption in prewar years. Having risen by four kilograms during the tenure of Caprivi's rates, meat consumption fell back to just above what it had

29. *Statistisches Jahrbuch für Preussen*, 1914, p. 263.

been in 1892. Lastly, the increased exportation of rye is now easily explained by the switch to potatoes because of the expense incurred in buying grain. Using 1913 as an index of 100 for Germany, Great Britain, and America, one finds the cost of living to have been 82, 90, and 91 respectively in 1905.[30] Germany thus endured by far the largest increase in the cost of living of the three major powers. In Hoffmann's view, the percentage by which average caloric intake surpassed the necessary minimum fell between 1904 and 1913.

TABLE 42   CONSUMPTION PER CAPITA (In kilograms)

YEAR	RYE	WHEAT	POTATOES	BEEF
1893–99	150	88	566	15.9
1906–7	143	90	592	16.4
1907–8	142	83	625	15.5
1908–9	152	93	631	16.3
1909–10	139	87	624	17.6
1913	—	—	—	14.1

Source: F. Wilken, *Volkswirtschaftliche Theorie der landwirtschaftlichen Preissteigerung* (Berlin, 1925), appendix.

Before the changes in real income can be assessed, the wages of the German worker should be analyzed. Those like Bachem who believed that protection aided the worker assumed that wages would rise much faster than costs as a result of industrial growth. This did not occur. Wages in all the major industries edged upward at about 1.5 percent yearly during the 1890s, and with few exceptions the pace continued until the war.[31] There are no natural break points in wages, as the year 1906 is in the cost-of-living index. Wages in the Ruhr coal mines, for instance, fluctuated considerably although the pattern was generally higher. In 1910 and 1911, however, wages were lower than in 1907 and 1908.[32] Bry's graph of wages showed a small steady increase yearly from 1895 to 1913.

The studies of German real income between 1900 and 1913 have

30. Gerald Bry, *Wages in Germany* (Princeton, 1960), pp. 464–65.
31. Ibid., pp. 472–73; Kuczynski, *Die Geschichte der Lage der Arbeiter unter dem Kapitalismus* (Berlin, 1962), 4:326–27.
32. Wagemann, p. 277.

all come to different conclusions, but that the rise experienced in the 1890s almost leveled off completely is universally agreed upon. Carl von Tyszka's work of 1913 pictured the real income falling by 18 percent in thirteen years.[33] His predisposition for free trade, no doubt, caused him to exaggerate his findings. The investigation conducted by the Prussian Statistical Bureau in 1932 was prejudiced in the opposite direction. According to its findings, the increase was about 6 percent in the 1890s and 4 percent from 1900 until the war—hardly a testimonial for the tariffs.[34] Bry's study, which appears more comprehensive as well as more objective, indicated the change to be somewhere between the two extremes. Using 1913 as an index of 100, he found 1890 to be 87, and 1900 to be 98. He concluded, "After a steep rise during the 1890s and part of the subsequent decade, the growth [of real income] lost momentum and weekly real earnings began to level out."[35] To be more exact, weekly real earnings were higher in 1900 and 1904 than in 1912. The upward trend of the real income graph declined after 1905 and leveled out to around the average of 1903 and 1904. Hardest hit were the unskilled workers with large families, whose food requirements were great.

These developments were simultaneous with one of the longest periods of expansion in German industrial history. Heavy industry recorded record profits at a time when the laborer struggled to live as well as he had a decade earlier. The number of Prussians in high tax categories increased prodigiously during these years.[36] The economic cleavages in German society were perhaps never greater than in 1913, and this was not a result of greedy capitalistic policy but of the Junkers' protectionism. Distressed by the extreme division of wealth in society, which was alienating the workers from

33. Carl von Tyszka, "Löhne und Lebenskosten in Westeuropa im 19ten Jahrhundert," *Schriften des Vereins für Sozialpolitik* 145 (1914): 289.

34. *Das deutsche Volkseinkommen vor und nach dem Kriege:* Einzelschriften zur Statistik des deutschen Reiches, Nr. 24 (Berlin, 1932), p. 68.

35. Bry, *Wages in Germany*, pp. 71–73. According to Kuczynski, "Since the 1860s, real income stagnated for the first time—in fact, it would have fallen had the 1902–14 economic cycle continued normally." Kuczynski, *Geschichte*, 4:331.

36. *Statistisches Jahrbuch für Preussen*, 1913.

the empire, Wagner had determined to reduce the gap. His methods merely increased the inequalities.

By 1913 Germany was clearly the continent's foremost industrial country; large-scale urbanization had taken place, the tax structure relied heavily on income from commercial and industrial sources, and the nation boasted the best-organized working-class party in the world. Yet Germany resembled a two-headed hydra because Bülow's tariffs had clearly enabled the large estates to persist in an otherwise paradigmatic industrial nation. In a sense the conflict between agriculture and industry had not been resolved; both continued to receive state subventions in an uneasy alliance based primarily upon their mutual hostility to the workers. Since the natural trend of events favored industry, Wagner and other agrarians rightly interpreted this pattern as a victory for agriculture. In the decade before the war the Junkers could choose to sell their estates at a handsome price or cultivate them with the assurance of government subsidies. Junker incentive to improve and modernize the estates declined as their reliance on the state to bail them out of any difficulties now appeared justified. The enormous subsidies provided by the Republic during the crisis-ridden twenties was merely a logical and almost inevitable step, once Bülow's policy had triumphed.

8 Conclusion

A country-keeping lord who minds his own
    business
It is we country lords who know the country
And we who know what the country needs.
It is our country. We care for the country.
We are the backbone of the nation.

T.S. Eliot
"Murder in the Cathedral"

In the preceding pages, I have sought to show that the tariff debates, the economic growth, and the intellectual life of Germany from 1890 to 1902 were intertwined and must be treated together if the period is to be properly understood.

Until the 1890s, parliamentary debates over tariffs had often been prolonged and sometimes acrimonious, but never had they been as bitter as during Caprivi's and Bülow's chancellorships. The debates were reflecting the response of various segments of society to the severe agricultural crisis of the early nineties. Artisans and peasants moved to the right by voting for anti-Semitic candidates or for the Farmers' League. Professors who had been critical of

271

capitalism edged towards irrational agrarian romanticism and sought a wider audience for their views. And the Junkers came to challenge the emperor and the chancellor in order to preserve their privileged position.

At the same time, industrialists were momentarily more concerned with expanding trade than with forming alliances with agrarians. The depression of 1873 and the succeeding years of recession, capped by a decline of trade in the 1890s, caused them to seek new trade agreements. Economic motives impelled heavy industry to break with agriculture in the nineties, whereas it had brought them together in the late seventies. The professors' virulent hostility to industrial capitalism now found a welcome audience in the Junkers, who felt abandoned in their hour of need. Interpretations of these years that rely on the purely economic issue of free trade versus protection or of struggles between vested interest groups are too narrow in scope. They fail to take into account the sudden blossoming of antimodernism and its increasing effect on the political process.

A period of instability began after 1890 as the old power equilibrium of big agriculture and big industry broke down. Concentrating on what he believed the long-run interests of Germany to be, Caprivi found himself creating a new equilibrium in economic policy—one consisting of the left, the Center, and the National Liberals. The voting strength of these parties derived overwhelmingly from classes brought into being by industrialization. The tenuous coalition was immediately subjected to a sustained attack. Junkers and agrarian professors used all their power and persuasiveness to prevent the new alliance from cementing.

To the Junker-dominated Conservative party, all its opponents seemed united against grain tariffs through one principle—industrialism. Labor, industry, merchants, and free trade economists, all were seeking to foster a thriving industrial economy. The survival of the eastern estates as well as the social and political position of the gentry would not be allowed to stand in the way of this aim. With the founding of the Farmers' League in 1892, the agrarian campaign took on a decidedly anti-industrial character. The virtues of the land and rural way of life increasingly preoccupied Conservative speeches on the tariff question, and conversely the shadowy sides of industrialism were expounded at great length. When von Plötz of the Farmers' League said that the speculators of the stock exchange would collapse in the face of a cavalry charge, he was expressing the common Conservative belief that the new industrial magnates were incapable of replacing the Junkers as a ruling class. The hostility to industrialism was manifested openly in the Prussian lower house and by the strict regulation of the stock exchange in 1896. That Caprivi was not a landowner and therefore had no vested interest in a prosperous agriculture, was severely criticized by agrarians, who proposed that all future chancellors be landowners.

In their campaign to preserve a profitable agriculture and their power, the Junkers found staunch allies among political economists. Theorists of Wagner's ilk deemed industrial capitalism a threat to the nation's security. Political unity was considered too fragile to withstand the divisions created by rapid economic change. No less than Marx, they foresaw a decline in religious observance and the triumph of naked self-interest with the rise of industrialism. In their writings and speeches, therefore, the economists and many others gave contemporary agricultural society a romantic halo. The hardihood of the peasants was emphasized along with their morality. Their devotion to the empire was compared with the revolutionary nature of the workers. The very real differences separating the interests of peasant and Junker were obscured in a synthesis on a higher level. Having adopted an analysis similar to Marx's, these economists found in a return to a rural society the only means, after 1890, of preventing Marx's ominous predictions from being realized.

The impassioned conservative critique of industrial capitalism, building up through the nineteenth century, has all too often been obscured by the rise of socialism. Actually, the conservative theorists were a greater threat to the new order. While the condition of the workers gradually improved, the preindustrial groups—Junker, peasant, artisan—facing severe dislocation, provided a growing audience for the irrationalism of the conservative theorists. A deep reservoir of antimodernism in German public opinion helped feed the controversy.

The professors' reservations, on both ethical and national

grounds, about industrial capitalism meshed neatly with the pragmatic fears of the Junkers. Despite their differing approaches, both could agree on the virtues of bimetallism, the Kanitz plan, and higher tariffs. While the former contributed scholarly respectability and a theoretical base for the equilibrium that emerged after 1902, the latter provided the ruthlessness and the power necessary for success.

By their victory in the tariff debates of 1902 the Junkers and their academic supporters performed no mean task, for they managed to insure the continued predominance of a landed squirearchy in a nation whose wealth and population had shifted to the cities. The power given to the Junkers in 1867, when industrialism was in its infancy, was to be maintained despite vast economic and social transformations. In the new *Sammlung*, heavy industry received considerable privileges in the domestic market.[1] Those engaged in

1. Recently both J. C. G. Röhl (in *Germany without Bismarck* [Berkeley, 1967]) and Hartmut Kaelble (in *Industrielle Interessenpolitik in der wilhelminischen Gesellschaft* [Berlin, 1967]) have offered theories about the reconstitution of the *Sammlung*. In his excellent book, Röhl suggests 1897 as the year in which Miquel brought big agriculture and big industry together again after a seven-year hiatus. While this is true, I would argue that Miquel's *Sammlung* was a temporary phenomenon, and that 1902 is a much more crucial year. Agrarians, particularly in the Farmers' League, remained very hostile to industry after 1897, as evidenced by their rejection of the Canal Bill in 1899 and 1901. It is worth remembering that Miquel died after failing to change the agrarians' position on the canal. The period after 1897 was also marked by the strident anti-industrial and anticapitalist rhetoric of agrarian organizations, which only abated when Bülow's duties received Reichstag approval. After Bülow's success the agrarians also allowed a modified Canal Bill to pass through the Landtag. As Hans-Jürgen Puhle has pointed out, the Farmers' League was content with Bülow's tariffs, despite its decision for rejection in the Reichstag. Only after 1902 could the agrarians be assured of adequate state support, with the aid of heavy industry, to survive the rigors of the international grain competition.

Kaelble believes that the *Sammlung* restored by Miquel fell apart around the turn of the century and was not reestablished until the outbreak of war in 1914. He argues that sharp conflicts separated agriculture from industry, and that those industrialists in the Centralverband favoring alliance with the Junkers declined in power after 1900. For a number of reasons I find Kaelble's case unconvincing. First, he himself is contradictory and frequently makes points contrary to his general thesis. For instance, on page 170 he writes of the close cooperation between agriculture and industry through 1905. Subsequently, he admits that the Centralverband lost interest in the Hansabund

light industry and commerce were unhappy with the settlement but found the effects mitigated by a rapidly developing economy. The workers were expected to remain content with additions to Bismarck's social legislation. Once the Junkers were safely protected, Posadowsky began to show a patriarchal interest in the proletariat. As with Wagner, the degree of his social concern was directly proportional to the profitability of agriculture. Thus, a new equilibrium was created in which industry was allowed to expand as long as the gentry's right to enjoy economic, social, and political prerogatives was clearly recognized.

That the new distribution of power still reflected society in 1867 did not disturb the industrialists. Only when their economic interests were diametrically opposed to the Junkers as in 1893 and 1894 were they willing to give battle. Otherwise, economic concessions satiated their appetite. In 1902 they demonstrated their lack of combativeness when a favorable opportunity presented itself.

(1909) because its majority of light industry men and merchants adopted an uncompromising attitude toward big agriculture. The sharp conflicts over a stock exchange bill in 1904 and a new *Gewerbeordnung* in 1907 referred to by Kaelble strike me as petty squabbles. Heavy industry may not have found its relations with agriculture running smoothly after 1902, but the alternative of a *Sammlung* with light industry and commerce promised even greater discord, for the latter supported low tariffs, opposed cartels, and did not view Social Democracy as an uncompromising enemy. The issues dividing big agriculture from big industry pale in importance before those outlined above. Neither in 1902 during the tariff controversy nor in 1907 with the founding of the Hansabund did the Zentralverband make meaningful attempts to ally with light industry or commerce.

Kaelble ignores the importance of the cooperation between agrarians and industrialists over the Bülow tariff because he associates the agrarians almost solely with the Farmers' League. Actually, nearly all of the agrarian magnates in the Conservative and Free Conservative parties supported the compromise worked out by Kardorff, and the small contingent from the Farmers' League rejected the final rates to save face and because they were bound to pass anyway. As pointed out above, league members were not disgusted with the final settlement. I believe Kaelble's error lies in his narrow interpretation of the word *Sammlung*. Although there was no formal alliance between agriculture and industry after 1902, they both united around a system of state protection at the expense of the consumer to mitigate the effects of foreign competition. While disputes may have occurred in the decade before the war, neither partner challenged the framework established in 1902. See Röhl's criticism of Kaelble in *Central European History,* June 1968, pp. 182–86.

By withdrawing from the *Hansabund* in 1911 they again retreated from a coalition with light industry and commerce. Alliance with the authoritarian monarchy offered security against the traditionally exaggerated socialist menace. Although they did not actively seek political primacy, men such as Krupp, Ballin, and Dernberg could use their personal contacts with the emperor and the bureaucracy to see that their interests were not neglected. Social status was easily attainable by the purchase of an estate, by being received at court, or by getting a reserve commission in the army. However imperfect the empire was, the industrialists identified with it because it met their needs better than any available alternative.

Nor was the intelligentsia uniformly alienated from the post-Bismarckian empire. True, the socialist leaders despised Junker domination, and liberals sought to abolish the three-class suffrage. Nevertheless, a sizeable number of intellectuals including the majority of professors believed the imperial government superior to the British, French, or Russian forms of government. The almost unanimous hostility to the old regime by Russian intellectuals in the early twentieth century had no counterpart in Wilhelmian Germany. This is in part explained by the military contributions of the Junkers to German unity—a goal that had long been dreamed of by most of the intelligentsia. Generations of despair came to an end in 1871 when academics could for the first time hold their heads up with the pride of residing in a powerful empire, one in which professors had great social prestige, and academic freedom was scrupulously respected. No longer did professors have to repeat the experiences of Wagner, who taught in five sovereign states within a decade. It was highly unlikely that professors would deem economic and political patterns inadequate so soon after they had been established in Germany (having been transferred from Prussia). To be critical of such patterns would undermine the empire's strength, in the opinion of nationally minded academics.

The truth of the matter is that the equilibrium established in 1902 was not unpopular, except among the Social Democrats. And as Carl Schorske has shown, their revolutionary rhetoric was waning and the imperial parliament increasingly looked to for redress of grievances. If there had not been an ideological framework for the 1902 settlement, it is doubtful whether widespread acceptance would have been achieved so quickly. In speech after speech, the economists reiterated that the Junkers were struggling in behalf of the commonweal and not for their own interests. These academic efforts were not without their effect on the popular mind.

Nevertheless, because an equilibrium is workable and supported by a consensus of opinion does not necessarily mean that it is sound. For numerous reasons I believe Bülow's solution to have been hazardous for Germany's future. One of the ironies of the anti-industrial campaign was that its success led to its proponents' greatest fear—a weakening of German security. The exclusion of the workers from a meaningful place in society (so lamented by the agrarian economists) was increased. Higher tariffs jeopardized the chances of moderating socialist militancy. Only the facade of patriarchal concern remained among the *Sammlung* partners. Working-class hostility to a power structure that scorned its most moderate aspirations prevented the evolution of a well-integrated society. Bülow's victory not only increased the divisions in society but made agrarians and industrialists even greedier by whetting their appetites.

In the sphere of foreign policy the effects were more ominous. As Kehr has pointed out, agrarian antipathy to industrialism led to a hatred of Great Britain, where the despised values set the tone of society. Although no essential conflicts of interest existed, cordial relations with Britain were hindered by the commitment of those in power to the myth of the virtuous *Landvolk*. Public opinion, after a decade of anti-industrial propaganda, readily responded to an anti-British foreign policy. The belief of many Germans during World War I that Britain and Germany represented unalterably opposed cultures had roots in the industrialization controversy.[2]

On the other hand, good relations with Russia were precluded because of competition with Junker grain farmers. The hostility of Count Witte and other Russian leaders to Germany's protective tariff policies was recounted in chapter 6. An explanation for the

2. See Werner Sombart, *Händler und Helden* (Munich, 1915); and Max Scheler, *Der Genius des Krieges und der deutsche Krieg* (Leipzig, 1915).

aggressiveness of middle-class opinion in foreign affairs may, perhaps, be found in the sublimation and rerouting of power drives away from the domestic scene, where they had long been frustrated.

It can also be questioned whether the nation was strengthened for war. The long-vaunted grain surpluses of the estates were produced in spite of gross inefficiency and would have been larger had the land been more equitably distributed. The nutritional value of agricultural products would have increased with adaptation to foreign competition. The influx of Slavs, fostered by artificially high grain prices, certainly did not bolster the empire's strength. Much as German wealth increased by 1914, the increase could have been even larger if Caprivi's policy had been maintained.

Perhaps the greatest irony lies in the failure of Wagner and his fellow academic conservatives to retard the spread of an acquisitive capitalist spirit. Despite their partial victory in preserving the Junkers' privileged position, industrial capitalism expanded its sway after 1902. In fact, it grew more quickly and in a distorted fashion because of the protection accorded heavy industry. The eastern estates themselves were commercial ventures. The Junker habit of speculating in land belied the faith placed in them as bulwarks against capitalism. Acquisitiveness and crass egotism were more marked after the controversy than before, and particularly among those groups who were the supposed purveyors of the patriarchal spirit. Karl Helfferich showed better foresight than his contemporaries in 1901 when he stated, "I see the greatest danger not in an industrial state per se, but in that we pursue an agrarian policy in an industrial state." This was indeed the legacy of the controversy over German industrialization.

Bibliography

ARCHIVAL SOURCES

Bundesarchiv Koblenz: BA — Brentano Papers, Bülow Papers

Deutsche Staatsbibliothek: Berlin-Ost: DSB — Althoff Papers, Harnack Papers

Deutsche Staatsbibliothek: Marburg/L: DSB II — Darmstaedter Sammlung, Tippel Papers

Deutsches Zentralarchiv, Abteilung Merseburg: DZA — Schmoller Papers (Schmoller Nachlass), Sombart Papers, Akta betr. Handelsverträge: Reichkanzlei, Akta betr. Massregeln zur Hebung der Landwirtschaft, Akta betr. österreichische Verträge, Minutes of Prussian Ministry of State, 1890–94.

CONSERVATIVE ECONOMISTS

Oldenberg, Karl. "Arbeitseinstellungen." *Handwörterbuch der Staatswissenschaften.* 2d ed. Vol. 1.

——————. "Arbeitslosenstatistik, Versicherung und Arbeitsvermittlung." *Schmollers Jahrbuch* 28 (1895).

——————. "Aushungerungskrieg; Englische Sorgen seit 100 Jahren." *Schmollers Jahrbuch* 43, no. 2 (1919).

——————. *Deutschland als Industriestaat.* Göttingen, 1897.

Oldenberg, Karl. "Deutschland als Industriestaat." *Soziale Praxis* 8, no. 28 (13 April 1899).

_____. "Englische Agrarpolitik." *Die Zeit* 2 (1903).

_____. "Die Gewerkvereine in Deutschland." *Handwörterbuch der Staatswissenschaften,* vol. 1 (1895).

_____. "Die heutige Lage der Commis nach neuerer Literatur." *Schmollers Jahrbuch* 14 (1892).

_____. "Kann ein Industriestaat im Kriegsfalle ausgehungert werden?," *Zeitschrift für Agrarpolitik* 1, no. 7 (20 July 1903).

_____. "Die Konditorei Arbeiter." *Soziale Praxis* 2 (1893).

_____. "Konsumption." *Grundriss der Socialökonomik* 2, no. 1 (1923).

_____. "Landarbeitermangel und Abhilfe." *Zeitschrift für Agrarpolitik* 5, no. 2 (Feb. 1907).

_____. *Der Maximalarbeitstag im Bäcker- und Konditoreigewerbe.* Leipzig, 1894.

_____. "Neue Wege der Bevölkerungspolitik." *Schmollers Jahrbuch* 41 (1917).

_____. "Die rheinisch-westfälische Bergarbeiterbewegung." *Schmollers Jahrbuch* 14 (1890): 603-73, 913–66.

_____. "Der Rückgang der Geburten." *Archiv des deutschen Landwirtschaftsrat,* 1912.

_____. "Die slawische Gefahr." *Das neue Deutschland* 4, no. 17 (19 Feb. 1916).

_____. "Über den Rückgang der Geburten- und Sterbeziffer." *Archiv für Sozialwissenschaft und Sozialpolitik* 33 (1911).

_____. "Über Volksernährung im Industriestaat." *Die Zeit,* 9 July 1903.

_____. "Die volkswirtschaftliche Lage der deutschen Fleischversorgung." *Archiv der deutschen Landwirtschaftsrat* 31 (1907).

Oldenberg, Karl. "Über den Weizenpreis der bevorstehenden Handelsvertragsperiode." *Zeitschrift für Agrarpolitik* 1 (30 May 1903).

————. "Die Ziele der deutschen Sozialdemokratie." *Evangelische Soziale Zeitfragen,* ser. 1 nos 8/9 (1891).

————. "Zum Verständnis der Geburten Rückgangsziffer." *Zeitschrift für Säuglingsfürsorge* 9 (1916).

————. "Zur Theorie Volkswirtschaftlicher Krisen," *Schmollers Jahrbuch* 27 (1903).

Sering, Max. "Agrar und Industriestaat." *Wörterbuch der Volkswirtschaft.* 2d ed. vol. 1.

————. *Agrarkriser und Agrarzölle.* Berlin, 1925.

————. "Arbeiterfrage und Kolonization in den östlichen Provinzen Preussens," *Deutsche Landwirtschaftliche Presse* 9 (13 Feb. 1892).

————. "Die Bauern." *Deutsche Monatschrift* 2 (Nov. 1901).

————. "Die Bedeutung der landwirtschaftlichen Bevölkerung für die Wehrmacht des deutschen Reiches." *Archiv des deutschen Landwirtschaftsrat* 24 (1902).

————. "Bemerkungen zum vorläufigen Entwurf eines preussischen Gesetzes über Familienfideikommiss." *Schmollers Jahrbuch* 28 (1904).

————. "Die Bodenbesitzverteilung und die Sicherung des Kleingrundbesitzes." *Verhandlungen des Vereins für Sozialpolitik* 58 (1893).

————. "Fideikommiss." *Wörterbuch der Volkswirtschaft.* 3d ed. 1911.

————. "Die Handelspolitik der Grossstaaten und die Kriegsflotte." *Handels- und Machtpolitik.* Stuttgart, 1900.

————. *Die innere Kolonization im östlichen Deutschland.* Leipzig, 1893.

Sering, Max.   "Jährliche Anspräche." *Landwirtschaftliches Jahrbuch* 23–38 (1894–1909).

―――――. *Die landwirtschaftliche Konkurrenz Nordamerikas in der Gegenwart und Zukunft.* Leipzig, 1887.

―――――. "Die preussische Agrarkonferenz." *Schmollers Jahrbuch* 18 (1894).

―――――. "Rede." *Archiv der Landwirtschaft.* 1902.

―――――. "Rede." *Deutsche Landwirtschaftsrat.* 1902.

―――――. "Rede." *Königliches Landwirtschaftliches Kollegium.* 1911.

―――――. "Rede." *Landes-Ökonomie-Kollegium.* 1912.

―――――. "Rede." *Landwirtschaftliches Jahrbuch* 23 (1894), supp. vol. 2.

―――――. "Reden." *Verhandlungen des königlichen Landes-Ökonomie-Kollegium.* 1909–14.

―――――. "Rede," *Verhandlungen des Vereins für Sozial Politik.* 1901.

―――――. *Sinken der Getreidepreise und Konkurrenz des Auslands.* Berlin, 1894..

―――――. *Die Ursachen und weltgeschichtliche Bedeutung des Krieges,* Berlin, 1914.

―――――. *Die Verteilung des Grundbesitzes und die Abwanderung vom Lande.* Berlin, 1910.

―――――. "Wehrwirtschaftliche Studien zur deutschen Volksernährung vor, in, und nach dem Weltkriege." Unpublished manuscript, 1937.

―――――. Untitled article. *Deutsche Kolonialblatt* 18 (1907).

―――――. Untitled article. *Die Flotte* 15 (1912).

Wagner, Adolf. *Die Abschaffung des privaten Grundeigentums.* Leipzig, 1870.

―――――. "Agrar- und Industriestaat." *Die Zukunft* 5 (8 Sept. 1894).

―――――. *Agrar- und Industriestaat; Eine Auseinandersetzung mit den Nationalsozialen und mit Professor Lujo Brentano über die*

Wagner, Adolf.
Kehrseiten des Industriestaats und zur Rechtfertigung agrarischen Zollschatzes. Jena, 1901; 2d ed. 1902.

—————. *Die akademischer Nationalökonomie und der Sozialismus.* Berlin, 1895.

—————. *Allgemeine oder theoretische Volkswirtschaftslehre.* Leipzig, 1876.

—————. "Die Auswanderung." *Allgemeine Zeitung,* supp., 8 June 1880.

—————. "Anwortbrief an Arthur Dix." *Die Zukunft* 26 Nov. 1899.

—————. "Bankbrüche und Bankkontrolle." *Deutsche Monatschrift* 1 (1901).

—————. *Beiträge zur Lehre von den Banken.* Leipzig, 1857.

—————. "Bimetallismus und Handelsverträge." *Bericht über die Verhandlungen der 19ten Generalversammlung der Vereinigung der Steuer und Wirtschaftsreformer.* 1894.

—————. Comments from the floor. *Verhandlungen des Evangelisch-sozialen Kongresses,* 1896, 1897. 1901, 1904.

—————. *Elsass und Lothringen und ihre Wiedergewinnung für Deutschland,* Leipzig, 1870.

—————. "Die Erhöhung der Getreidezölle." *Die Woche,* 2 March 1901.

—————. *Die finanzielle Mitbeteilung der Gemeinden an kulturellen Staatseinrichtungen.* Jena, 1904.

—————. *Finanzwissenschaft.* Leipzig, 1890.

—————. "Finanzwissenschaft und Staatssocialismus." *Tübingen Zeitschrift für Staatswissenschaft,* 1887.

—————. "Flottenverstarkung und unsere Finanzen." *Handels- und Machtpolitik.* Stuttgart, 1900.

—————. "Die Freude am neuen Deutschen Reich." *Die Woche* 2, no. 30 (1900).

Wagner, Adolf.   *Für bimetallistische Münzpolitik Deutschlands.* Berlin, 1881.

————. *Gegen England.* Berlin, 1912.

————. *Die Geld- und Credittheorie der Peel' schen Bankacta.* Vienna, 1862.

————. "Grundbesitz." *Handwörterbuch der Staatswissenschaften.* 2d ed. Vol. 4 (1894).

————. *Grundlegung der politischen Ökonomie.* 3d ed. 2 vols. Leipzig, 1892–94.

————. *Die Kartellierung der Grossindustrie und ihr Einfluss auf die Arbeiter,* Essen, 1906.

————. *Landwirtschaftliches Jahrbuch* 23 (1894), supp. vols. 1 and 2.

————. "Lassalle und Rodbertus." *Allgemeine Zeitung,* 9 October 1878.

————. *Mein Konflikt mit dem Freiherrn von Stumm.* Berlin, 1895.

————. "Meine Duellangelegenheit mit dem Freiherrn von Stumm," *Die Zukunft* 10 (1895).

————. *Die neueste Silberkrisis und unser Münzewesen.* Berlin, 1894.

————. *Das neue sozialdemokratische Programm.* Berlin, 1892.

————. *Offener Brief an Herrn H. B. Oppenheim* Berlin, 1872.

————. *Rede über die sociale Frage.* Berlin, 1872.

————. "Rede." *Verhandlungen des Vereins für Sozialpolitik* 22 (1893).

————. "Die Reichsfinanznot, und die Pflichten des deutschen Volks sowie seiner politischen Parteien." *Die Woche,* 29 Aug. and 12 Sept. 1908.

————. *Die sozialen- und wirtschaftlichen Gesichtspünkte.* Berlin, 1901.

————. *Sozialismus, Sozialdemokratie, Kathedersozialismus und Staatssozialismus,* Rede in Barmen, Berlin, 1895.

Wagner, Adolf. "Staat." *Hwb. d. Staatswissenschaften,* supp. vol. 1.

——————. "Staatsbürgerliche Bildung." *Soziale Streitfragen* 59 (1916).

——————. *Die Strömungen in der Sozialpolitik und der Katheder- und Staatssozialismus.* Berlin, 1912.

——————. *Theoretische Sozialökonomie.* Berlin, 1894.

——————. *Unternehmergewinn und Arbeitslohn.* Speech in Bochum, Göttingen, 1897.

——————. *Die Veränderungen der Karte von Europa.* Berlin, 1871.

——————. *Der Verein für Sozialpolitik und seine Verbindung mit dem Volkswirtschaftlichen Kongress.* Leipzig and Heidelberg, 1878.

——————. "Volksmehrung und Auswanderung." *Münchener Allgemeiner Zeitung,* 8, 10, 11 June 1880.

——————. *Vom Territorialstaat zur Weltmacht.* Kaisergeburtstagsrede. Berlin, 1900.

——————. "Wohnungsnot und städtische Bodenfrage." *Soziale Streitfragen,* 1901.

——————. "Zur Frage von Industriestaat und wirtschaftlicher Entwicklung." *Der Lotse* 17 and 24 Nov. 1900.

LIBERAL ECONOMISTS

Brentano, Lujo. *Agrarpolitik.* Stuttgart, 1925.

——————. *Die Arbeiterwohnungsfrage in den Städten.* Munich, 1909.

——————. *Die deutschen Getreidezölle.* Stuttgart, 1910.

——————. *Das Freihandelsargument.* Berlin, 1901.

——————. *Die Getreidezölle als Mittel gegen die Not der Landwirte.* Berlin, 1903.

——————. "Handel und Krieg." *Österreichische Rundschau,* 15 February 1915.

Brentano, Lujo. *The Industrial Organization of Germany under the Influence of Protection.* London, 1908.

——. *Ist das System Brentano zusammengebrochen?* Berlin, 1918.

——. "Justus Möser der Vater der neuesten preussischen Agrarreform." *Beilage zur Münchener Allgemeinen Zeitung,* 12 and 13 Feb. 1897.

——. "Die Krisis der deutschen Wirtschaftswissenschaft." *Die Nation* 14 (1896-97).

——. *Mein Leben im Kampfe um die soziale Entwicklung Deutschlands.* Jena, 1931.

——. *Die Schrecken des überwiegenden Industriestaats.* Volkswirtschaftliche Zeitfragen, nos. 7–8. Berlin, 1901.

——. "Der Streit über die Grundlage der deutschen Wehrkraft." *Patria,* 1906.

——. "Über Ausfuhrprämien." *Jahrbuch der Hilfe,* 1904.

——. *Über den Wahnsinn der Handelsfeindseligkeit.* Munich, 1916.

——. *Über die Ursachen der heutigen Sozialnoth,* Leipzig, 1889.

——. "Über eine zukünftige Handelspolitik des deutschen Reichs." *Schmollers Jahrbuch* 9 (1885).

——. "Wagner und die Getreidezölle." *Die Hilfe,* 7 (1901).

——. "Wollen oder Erkennen." *Die Nation* 14 (1896–97).

——. and Kuczynski. *Die heutige Grundlage der deutschen Wehrkraft.* Stuttgart, 1900.

Conrad, Johannes. "Die Agrarzölle in der Zolltarifvorlage." *Jahrbuch für Nationalökonomie und Statistik.* Feb. 1902.

——. *Grundriss zum Studium der politischen Ökonomie.* Jena, 1902, 1908.

Conrad, Johannes. "Die Stellung der landwirtschaftlichen Zölle." *Schriften des Vereins für Sozialpolitik* 90 (1900).

Dietzel, Heinrich. Comment from the floor. *Verhandlungen des Vereins für Sozialpolitik* 98 (1901).

_____, "The German Tariff Controversy." *Quarterly Journal of Economics*, May 1903.

_____. *Kornzoll und Sozialreform*. Berlin, 1901.

_____. "Die Theorie von den drei Weltreichen." *Die Nation* 17, nos. 30–34 (1900).

Drill, Robert. *Soll Deutschland seinen ganzen Getreidebedarf selbst produzieren?* Stuttgart, 1895.

Gerlach, Helmut von. "Die agrarische Bewegung." *Die Hilfe* 35 (1 Sept. 1901).

_____. *Von Rechts nach Links*. Zurich, 1937.

Goltz, Theodor von der. *Agrarwesen und Agrarpolitik*. Jena, 1904.

_____. *Geschichte der deutschen Landwirtschaft*. 2 vols. Stuttgart, 1902.

Helfferich, Karl. *Deutschlands Volkswohlstand 1888–1913*. Berlin, 1917.

_____. *Handelspolitik*. Leipzig, 1901.

_____. Comment from the floor. *Schriften des Vereins für Sozialpolitik* 98 (1901).

Huber, Fritz D. *Deutschland als Industriestaat*. Stuttgart, 1901.

Lotz, Walther. "Die agrarische Stimmung unter den Gebildeten Deutschlands." *Der Lotse* 2 (25 Jan. 1902).

_____. "Die Erziehung des deutschen Bürgertum durch die Agrarier." *Der Lotse* 1 (16 Feb. 1901).

_____. "Die Handelspolitik des deutschen Reiches unter Caprivi und Hohenlohe. "*Schriften des Vereins für Sozialpolitik* 92 (1901).

_____. *Der Schutz der deutsche Landwirtschaft und die Aufgaben der künftigen deutschen Handelspolitik*. Berlin, 1900.

Lotz, Walther.	"Wirkungen der gegenwärtigen und Ziele der künftigen Handelspolitik." *Schriften des Vereins für Sozialpolitik* 92 (Berlin, 1901)
Mombert, Paul.	*Die Belastung Arbeitereinkommens durch die Kornzölle.* Jena, 1901.
Naumann, Freidrich.	*Demokratie und Kaisertum.* Berlin, 1900.
—————.	*Neue deutsche Wirtschaftspolitik.* Berlin-Schönberg, 1906
—————.	*National-sozialer Katechismus.* Berlin, 1897.
—————.	*Nationale Sozialpolitik.* Göttingen, 1898.
Schacht, Hjalmar.	"Inhalt und Kritik des Zolltarifentwurfs." *Schmollers Jahrbuch* 26 (1902): 330–53.
—————.	*76 Jahre meines Lebens.* Bad Wörishofen, 1953.
Schäffle, Albert.	*Aus meinem Leben.* 2 vols. Berlin, 1905.
—————.	*Die Gefahren des Agrarismus für Deutschland.* Tübingen, 1901.
—————.	*Ein Votum gegen den neuesten Zolltarif.* Tübingen, 1901.
—————.	"Zur wissenschaftlichen Orientierung über die neueste Handelspolitik." *Zeitschrift für Staatswissenschaften* 49 (1893).
Schulz, Arthur.	*Kornzoll, Kornpreis, und Arbeitslohn.* Königsberg, 1902.
Weber, Adolf.	Comment from the floor. *Schriften des Vereins für Sozialpolitik* 48 (1901).
—————.	"Review of Deutschland am Scheidewege." *Schmollers Jahrbuch* 26 (1902).
—————.	*Volkswirtschaftslehre* 4 Bde., Berlin, 1928.
Weber, Max.	"Agrarstaat und Sozialpolitik." *Gesammelte Aufsätze zur Social- und Wirtschaftsgeschichte.* Tübingen, 1924.
—————.	Comment from the floor. *Verhandlungen des 7. Evangelisch-sozialen Kongresses* (1896).
—————.	"Critique of Oldenberg." *Verhandlungen des 8. Evangelisch-sozialen Kongresses* (1897).

Weber, Max.   "Der Nationalstaat und die
                           Volkswirtschaftspolitik" (1895).
                           Gesammelte politische Schriften.
                           Tübingen, 1958. Pp. 7–30.

OTHER SOURCES CONSULTED

Abel, Wilhelm.   *Agrarpalitik.* Stuttgart, 1957.

Aereboe, Friedrich.   *Agrarpolitik.* Berlin, 1928.

————————.   *Die Beurteilung von Landgütern und
                           Grundstücken.* Berlin, 1921.
                           Allgemeine Zeitung.

Anderson, Pauline   *The Background of Anti-English Feeling
                           in Germany.* Washington, D.C., 1939.

Andreas, Willy, ed.   *Bismarcks Gesammelte Werke,*
                           vol. 9. Berlin, 1926.

Angermann, Erich.   *Robert von Mohl, 1799–1875.* Neuwied, 1962.

Ashley, Percy.   *Modern Tariff History.* London, 1910.

Ashley, W. J.   *The Progress of the German Working Class.*
                           London, 1904.

Bachem, Karl.   *Vorgeschichte, Geschichte, und Politik der
                           deutschen Zentrumspartei, 1815 1914.*
                           9 vols. Cologne, 1927–32.

Batocki, Adolf von.   *Schluss mit Kriegszwangwirtschaft.*
                           Berlin, 1921.

Bechtel, Heinrich.   *Wirtschaftsgeschichte Deutschlands.*
                           3 vols. Munich, 1951–56.

Berlepsch,   *Sozialpolitische Erfahrungen und
  Hans Freiherr von.   Erinnerungen,* Mönchen-Gladbach, 1925.

Boese, Franz.   *Geschichte des Vereins für Sozialpolitik.*
                           Berlin, 1939.

Böhme, Helmut.   *Deutschlands Weg zur Grossmacht.*
                           Cologne and Berlin, 1966.

Born, Karl E.   *Staat und Sozialpolitik seit Bismarcks Sturz.*
                           Wiesbaden, 1957.

————————.   "Der soziale und wirtschaftliche
                           Strukturwandel Deutschlands am Ende des
                           19. Jahrhunderts," *Vierteljahrsschrift für
                           Sozial- und Wirtschaftsgeschichte* 50 (1963).

Bowen, Ralph. *German Theories of the Corporative State,* New York, 1947.

Brünstad, Friedrich. *Adolf Stöcker, Wille und Schicksal,* Berlin, 1935.

Bry, Gerald. *Wages in Germany.* Princeton, 1960.

Buchenberger, Adolf. "Agrarwesen und Agrarpolitik." In Adolf Wagner's *Lehr- und Handbuch der politischen Ökonomie,* vol. 3. Leipzig, 1892.

Buchheim, Karl. *Geschichte der christlichen Parteien in Deutschland.* Munich, 1953.

Bueck, H. A. *Der Centralverband deutscher Industrieller 1876–1901.* 3 vols., Berlin, 1902–05.

——————. *Der Centralverband deutscher Industrieller und seine 30-Jährige Arbeit.* Berlin, 1913.

Bülow, Fürst Bernhard von. *Denkwürdigkeiten,* 4 vols., Berlin, 1930–31.

——————. *Imperial Germany.* New York, 1914.

Bürger, Kurt. *Die Agrardemagogie in Deutschland.* Berlin. 1911.

Bussmann, Walter. *Staatssekretär Herbert von Bismarck.* Göttingen, 1964.

Caprivi, Leo von. *Die Reden des Grafen von Caprivi.* Ed. R. Arendt. 1894.

Clapham, J. H. *Economic Development of France and Germany.* Cambridge, 1921.

Clark, Evelyn. "Adolf Wagner: From National Economist to Nazi," *Political Science Quarterly* 55 (1940).

Conrad, J., and Hesse A. *Grundriss zum Studium der politischen Ökonomie.* 39th ed. Jena, 1924.

Cowing, Cedric. *Populists, Plungers, and Progressives.* Princeton, 1965.

Croner, Johannes. *Die Geschichte der agrarischen Bewegung in Deutschland.* Berlin, 1909.

Dahrendorf, Ralf. *Society and Democracy in Germany.* Garden City, N. Y., 1967.

Dawson, W. H. *The Evolution of Modern Germany.* London, 1908.

Dawson, W. H.   *Protection in Germany.* London, 1904.
Der deutsche Handelstag. 2 vols. Berlin, 1913.
Deutsche Landwirtschaft. Ed. Kaiserliche
Statistische Amt. Berlin, 1913.
Deutsche Landwirtschaftliche Presse.
*Das deutsche Volkseinkommen vor und nach
dem Kriege.* Einzelschriften zur Statistik des
deutschen Reiches, no. 24. Berlin, 1932.
Die Grosse Politik.

Diehl, Karl.   *Zur Frage der Getreidezölle.* Jena, 1911.

Dietze, Constantin von. "Fideikommiss." In *Wörterbuch der
Volkswirtschaft,* 3d ed. 1931.

————————————."Max Sering." In *Gedanken und Bekenntnisse
eines Agrarpolitikers.* Göttingen, 1962.

Dietzel, Heinrich.   *Karl Rodbertus.* Jena, 1888.

Dorpalen, Andreas.   *Heinrich von Treitschke.* New Haven, 1957.

Eckardt, Julius von.   *Lebenserinnerungen.* Leipzig, 1910.

Eger, Hans.   *Der evangelisch-soziale Kongress: ein Beitrag
zu seiner Geschichte und Problemstellung.*
Heidelberg, 1930.

Eulenberg, Franz.   "Aussenhandel und Aussenpolitik," *Grundriss
der Sozialökonomik,* vol. 8. Tübingen, 1929.

Eyck, Erich.   *Das persönliche Regiment Wilhelms II.*
Erlenbach-Zurich, 1948.

Farnsworth, Helen.   "Decline and Recovery of Wheat Prices in the
'Nineties." *Wheat Studies of the Food
Research Institute* 10 (June and July, 1934).

Feitelberg, Dr.   "Bekleidung." In *Interesse an der neuen.
Handelsverträge.* Berlin, 1901.

Feldman, Gerald.   *Army, Industry and Labor in Germany,
1914–18.* Princeton, 1966.

Finckenstein,
  H. W. Graf von.   *Die Entwicklung der Landwirtschaft in
Preussen und Deutschland.* 3 vols. Basle, 1959.

Frank, Walther.   *Hofprediger Adolf Stöcker und die
christlichsoziale Bewegung.* Berlin, 1928.

Frauendorfer,
  Sigmund von.   *Ideengeschichte der Agrarwirtschaft und
Agrarpolitik.* 2 vols. Munich, 1957.

Gehrig, Hans.   *Die Begründung des Prinzips der Sozialreform.* Jena, 1914.

Geiger, Walter.   *Miquel und die preussische Steuerreform, 1890–93.* Göppingen, 1934.

Geis, Robert.   *Der Sturz des Reichkanzlers Caprivi.* Berlin, 1930.

Gerloff, Wilhelm.   *Die Finanz- und Zollpolitik des deutschen Reiches nebst ihren Beziehungen zu Landes und Gemeindefinanzen.* Jena, 1913.

Gerschenkron, Alexander.   *Bread and Democracy in Germany.* Berkeley, 1943.

Gilg, Peter.   *Die Erneuerung des demokratischen Denkens im wilhelminischen Deutschland.* Wiesbaden, 1965.

Haberler, Gottfried von.   *The Theory of International Trade.* London, 1956.

Hagen, Eugen.   "Die papierverarbeitende Industrie und die Handelsverträge." *Deutsche Wirtschaftszeitung* 1, no. 22 (8 Nov. 1905).

Haller J.   *Aus dem Leben des Fürsten Philipp zu Eulenburg-Hertefeld.* Berlin, 1924.

Hamburger Nachrichten.

Handwörterbuch der Staatswissenschaften. 6 vols. 1st ed. 1890–94.

Hartung, Fritz.   *Verfassungsgeschichte.* Leipzig, 1914.

Haushofer, Heinz.   *Die deutsche Landwirtschaft im technischen Zeitalter.* Stuttgart, 1963.

Hellwig, Fritz.   *Carl Freiherr von Stumm-Halberg, 1836–1901.* Heidelberg and Saarbrücken, 1936.

Hennig, Hermann.   "Die Entwicklung der Preise in der Stadt Chemnitz." *Schriften des Vereins für Sozialpolitik* 145 (1914).

Herold, Carl.   *Die wichtigsten Agrarfragen.* Munich, 1900.

Herzfeld, Hans.   *Johannes von Miquel.* 2 vols. Detmold, 1938.

Heuss, Theodor.   *Friedrich Naumann: der Mann, das Werk, die Zeit.* Stuttgart, 1937.

Hintze, Otto. *Soziologie und Geschichte*. ed. G. Oesterreich. Göttingen, 1964.

Hoffmann, Walther. *Das Wachstum der deutschen Wirtschaft seit der Mitte des 19. Jahrhunderts*. Berlin, 1965.

Hofmann, Hermann. *Fürst Bismarck 1890–1898*. 3 vols. Stuttgart, 1914.

Hohenlohe, C. zu. *Denkwürdigkeiten der Reichskanzlerzeit*. Ed. K. A. von Müller. Stuttgart, 1931.

Horn, Hanelore. "Die Rolle des Bundes der Landwirte im Kampf um den Bau des Mittellandkanals." *Jahrbuch für die Geschichte Mittel- und Ostdeutschlands* 7 (1958).

Hubatsch, Walter. *Die Ära Tirpitz*. Göttingen, 1955.

——————, ed. *Schicksalswege deutscher Vergangenheit*. Düsseldorf, 1950.

Huber, Ernst. *Verfassungsgeschichte*. 3 vols. Stuttgart, 1963.

Hunter, Dorothy. *Professor Brentano on the German Corn Duties*. London, 1911.

Jahrbuch des Hansabundes. Berlin, 1909–14.

Jahresbericht der Landwirtschaftskammer Ost/Preussen.

Jenson, Jens. "Karl Oldenberg." *Schmollers Jahrbuch* 61 (1936).

Jordan, Henry. "Der Einfluss der Schutzzollpolitik auf die Beziehungen zum Ausland." Unpublished manuscript, 1927.

Kaelble, Hartmut. *Industrielle Interessenpolitik in der wilhelminischen Gesellschaft: Centralverband deutscher Industrieller, 1895–1914*. Berlin, 1967.

Kanitz, Graf von. *Die Festsetzung von Mindestpreisen*. Preussisch- Holland, 1894.

Kantorowicz, Hermann. *Der Geist der englischen Politik und das Gespenst der Einkreisung Deutschlands*. Berlin, 1929.

Kardorff, Siegfried von. *Wilhelm von Kardorff*. Berlin, 1936.

Kardorff, Wilhelm von. *Gegen den Strom*. Berlin, 1875.

Kehr, Eckart. *Der Primat der Innenpolitik*. Ed. Hans-Ulrich Wehler. Berlin, 1965.

——————. *Schlachtflottenbau und Parteipolitik, 1894–1901*. Berlin, 1930.

Keup, Erich, and Mührer, Richard. *Die volkswirtschaftliche Bedeutung von Gross- und Kleinbetrieb in der Landwirtschaft*. Berlin, 1913.

Kiesenwetter, Otto von. *Fünfundzwanzig Jahre wirtschaftspolitischen Kampfes*. Berlin, 1918.

Korrespondenz des Bundes der Landwirte.

Korte, S., ed. *Deutschland unter Wilhelm II*. 3 vols. Berlin, 1914.

Krausse, R. "Die Handelsverträge und die Lederindustrie." *Deutsche Wirtschaftszeitung* 1 Dec. 1905.

Kreuzzeitung.

Kroger, Karl. *Die Konservativen und die Politik Caprivis*. Rostock, 1937.

Krzymonski, R. *Geschichte der deutschen Landwirtschaft*. Berlin, 1961.

Kuczynski, Jürgen. *Die Geschichte der Lage der Arbeiter unter dem Kapitalismus*, vols. 3, 4. Berlin, 1962.

——————. *A short History of Labour Conditions under Industrial Capitalism*, vol. 3 part 1. London, 1945.

Lambie, Ivo. *Free Trade and Protection in Germany*. Wiesbaden, 1963.

Landwirtschaftliche Jahrbücher 23 (1894), supp. vol. 2.

Lenz, Friedrich. *Agrarlehre und Agrarpolitik der deutschen Romantik*. Berlin, 1912.

Lindenlaub, Dieter. *Richtungskämpfe im Verein für Sozialpolitik*. 2 vols., in *Vierteljahrsschrift für Sozial- und Wirtschaftsgeschichte*, Supps. 52, 53. Wiesbaden, 1967.

List, Friedrich. *Das nationale System der politischen Okonomie* (1841). Basel, 1959.

Lorenz, Robert. *The Essential Features of Germany's Agricultural Policy from 1876–1937.* New York, 1941.

Lubovics, Herman. "Agrarians vs. Industrializers." *International Review of Social History* 12 (1967).

Lütge, Friedrich. *Deutsche Sozial- und Wirtschaftsgeschichte.* Berlin, 1960.

Mannheim, Karl. "Conservative Thought." In *Essays on Sociology and Social Psychology,* ed. Paul Kecskemeti. New York and London, 1953.

Marienfeld, Wolfgang. *Wissenschaft und Schlachtflottenbau in Deutschland, 1897–1906.* Supp. 2, Marine Rundschau. April, 1957.

Martin, Rudolf. *Deutsche Machthaber.* Berlin, 1910.

Massing, Paul. *Rehearsal for Destruction.* New York, 1949.

Mitzman, Arthur. "Sociology and Disenchantment in Imperial Germany." Unpublished dissertation, Brandeis University, 1963.

Mommsen, Wolfgang. *Max Weber und die Deutsche Politik 1890–1920.* Tübingen, 1959.

Müller, Adam. *Elemente der Staatskunst.* 2 vols. ed. J. Baxa. Jena, 1922.

————. *Friedrich II.* Berlin, 1810.

Müller, Ernst. "Zolltarif-Reichsverfassung und Geschäftsordnung des deutschen Reichstages." *Annalen des deutschen Reiches für Gesetzgebung, Verwaltung, und Volkswirtschaft,* 1902.

Nichols, J. Alden. *Germany after Bismarck.* Cambridge, 1958.

Nipperdey, Thomas. "Interessenverbände und Parteien in Deutschland vor dem ersten Weltkrieg." *Politische Vierteljahresschrift* 2 (1961).

Nitzsche, M. *Die handelspolitische Reaktion in Deutschland.* Stuttgart and Berlin, 1905.

Oberschall, Anthony. *Empirical Social Research in Germany, 1848–1914.* The Hague, 1965.

Oldenburg-Januschau. *Erinnerungen.* Leipzig, 1936.
 Elard von.

Philipovich, "Auswanderung and Auswanderungspolitik in
 Eugen von, ed. Deutschland. *Schriften des Vereins für
 Sozialpolitik* 52 (1892).

Pohle, Ludwig. *Deutschland am Scheidewege.* Leipzig, 1902.

——————. "Wirkungen der gegenwärtigen und Ziele der
 künftigen Handelspolitik." *Verhandlungen
 des Vereins für Sozialpolitik* 98 (1901).

Poschinger, H. von. *Aktenstücke zur Wirtschaftspolitik des Fürsten
 Bismarck.* 3 vols. Berlin, 1980.

——————————. *Fürst Bismarck als Volkswirt.* Berlin, 1890.

Potthoff, Heinz. "Die Leinenindustrie und die Handelsverträge."
 Deutsche *Wirtschaftszeitung* 1, no. 22
 (8 Nov. 1905).

Puhle, Hans-Jürgen. *Agrarische Interessenpolitik und preussischer
 Konservatismus im wilhelminischen Reich,
 1893–1914.* Hanover, 1966.

Radacanu, Jon. "Vom Leben und Werk Adolf Wagner."
 Schmollers Jahrbuch 63 (1939).

Richter, Dr. "Die Chemische Industrie und die Zölle."
 Schriften der Zentralstelle 92 (1900).

Riesser, Jacob. *Der Hansabund.* Jena, 1912.

Ringer, Fritz. *The Decline of the Mandarins.*
 Cambridge, Mass., 1969.

Ritter, Emil. *Die katholisch-soziale Bewegung Deutschlands
 im 19. Jahrhunderts und der Volksverein.*
 Cologne, 1954.

Rodbertus, Johann K. *Zur Erklärung und Abhülfe der heutigen
 Kreditnot des Grundbesitzes.* Jena, 1876.

Rodbertus, Karl. *Das Kapital.* Berlin, 1884.

Röhl, J.C.G. *Germany without Bismarck.* Berkeley, 1967.

——————. "Higher civil servants in Germany,
 1890–1900." *Journal of Contemporary History*
 2, no. 3 (July 1967).

Rohr, Donald. *The Origins of Social Liberalism in Germany.*
 Chicago, 1963.

Rosenberg, Arthur. *Die Entstehung der deutschen Republik.* Berlin, 1928.

Rosenberg, Hans. *Grosse Depression und Bismarckzeit.* Berlin, 1967.

_____. "Political and Social Consequences of the Great Depression of 1873–1896 in Central Europe." *Economic History Review* 12 (1943).

_____. "The Rise of the Junkers in Bradenburg Prussia, 1410–1653," *American Historical Review* 49, nos. 1, 2 (Oct. 1943 and Jan. 1944).

Rothfels, Hans. *Theodor Lohman und die Kampfjahre der staatlichen Sozialpolitik.* Berlin, 1927.

Rothkegel, W. "Die Bewegung der Kaufpreise für ländliche Besitzungen und die Entwicklung der Getreidepreise, 1895–1909." *Schmollers Jahrbuch* 34 (1910).

_____. *Schätzungslehre.* 2 vols. Berlin, 1930.

Sachse, Arnold. *Friedrich Althoff und Sein Werk.* Berlin, 1928.

Sartorius von Waltershausen, A. *Deutsche Wirtschaftsgeschichte 1815–1914.* 2d ed. Jena, 1925.

Schelling, Thomas. *International Economics.* Boston, 1958.

Schmitz, O. *Die Bewegung der Warenpreise.* Berlin, 1903.

Schmoller, Gustav. "Analekten und Randglossen zur Debatte über Erhöhung der Getreidezölle." *Schmollers Jahrbuch* 9 (1885).

_____. "Einige Worte zum Antrag Kanitz," *Schmollers Jahrbuch* 19 (1895).

_____. "Die wirtschaftliche Zukunft Deutschlands und die Flottenvorlage." *Handels- und Machtpolitik.* Stuttgart, 1900.

_____. *Zwangiz Jahre deutscher Politik, 1897–1917.* Munich, 1920.

_____, and Sering, Max. "Reden zu Adolf Wagners 70 Geburtstag." *Schmollers Jahrbuch* 29 (1905).

Schneider, Walter. *Adolf Wagners Beziehungen zum Sozialismus.* Neubrandenburg, 1921.

Schneidewin, Max.   "Briefe des Reichkanzler Caprivi." *Deutsche Revue* 1 (1922).

Schulthess' europäischer Geschichtskalender. 79 vols. Munich, 1860–1938.

Schulz, Gerhard.   "Über Entstehung und Formen von Interessengruppen in Deutschland seit Beginn der Industrialisierung." *Politische Vierteljahresschrift* 2 (1961): 124–54.

Schumacher, H.   "Adolf Wagner." *Schmollers Jahrbuch* 42 (1918).

Schüssler, Wilhelm.   *Weltmachtstreber und Flottenbau.* Witten-Ruhr, 1956.

Shanahan, William O.   "Friedrich Naumann: A Mirror of Wilhelminian Germany." *Review of Politics* 13 (1951).

——————————.   *German Protestants Face the Social Question.* Notre Dame, 1954.

Sheehan, James.   *The Career of Lujo Brentano.* Chicago, 1966.

Siemens, G. von.   *Rede über die Handelsverträge.* Berlin, 1901.

Simon, W. H.   *Failure of the Prussian Reform Movement.* Cambridge, 1955.

Skalweit, August.   *Die deutsche Kriegsernährungswirtschaft.* Stuttgart, 1927.

Skarzynski, W. von.   *Agrarkrisis.* Berlin, 1894.

Sombart, Werner.   *Die deutsche Volkswirtschaft im 19. und im Anfang des 20. Jahrhunderts.* Berlin, 1927.

——————————.   "Die neuen Handelsverträge." *Schmollers Jahrbuch* 16 (1892).

Sonnemann, R.   *Die Auswirkungen des Schutzzolles auf die Monopolisierung der deutschen Eisen- und Stahlindustrie, 1879–92.* Berlin, 1960.

Stadelmann, Rudolf.   "Der neue Kurs in Deutschland." *Geschichte in Wissenschaft und Unterricht* 9 (September, 1953).

Statistisches Jahrbuch der Stadt Berlin. 1913.

Statistisches Jahrbuch für Baden. 1905–13.

Statistisches Jahrbuch für Bayern.

Stadelmann, Rudolf.   *Statistisches Jahrbuch für das deutsche Reich.* Berlin, 1890–1914.

Statistisches Jahrbuch für Preussen. Berlin, 1890–1914.

Steinbrück, Karl.   *Die deutsche Landwirtschaft.* Berlin, 1902.

Stenographische Berichte der Verhandlungen des Preussischen Abgeordnetenhauses.

Stenographische Berichte der Verhandlungen des Reichstages.

Stopler, Gustav.   *German Economy 1870–1940.* New York, 1940.

Struve, Emil.   "Die neuen Handelsverträge und die deutsche Brauindustrie." *Deutsche Wirtschaftszeitung* 1 (1 Nov. 1905).

Teichmann, Ulrich.   *Die Politik der Agrarpreisstützung.* Cologne, 1955.

Thier, Erich.   *Rodbertus, Lassalle, und Wagner.* Jena, 1930.

Tippelskirch, G. Dieter von.   *Agrarhistorische Ausschnitte aus der Zeit von 1893 bis 1924 im Lichte des Wirkens von Dr. Gustav Roesicke.* Stollhamm, 1956.

Tirrell, Sarah.   *German Agrarian Politics after Bismarck's Fall.* New York, 1951.

Tönnies, Friedrich,   "Adolf Wagner." *Deutsche Rundschau* 174 (1918).

Towle, Lawrence.   *International Trade and Commercial Policy.* New York, 1947.

Treue, Wilhelm.   *Die deutsche Landwirtschaft zur Zeit Caprivis und ihr Kampf gegen die Handelsverträge.* Berlin, 1933.

Tyszka, Carl von.   "Löhne und Lebenskosten in Westeuropa im 19ten Jahrhundert." *Schriften des Vereins für Sozialpolitik* 145 (1914).

Veblen, Thorstein.   *Imperial Germany and the Industrial Revolution.* New York, 1915.

Die Verhandlungen der kirchlichen Oktober-Versammlung in Berlin von 10. bis 12. Oktober, 1871. Berlin, 1872.

Verhandlungen des Evangelisch-sozialen Kongresses. 1896–1904.

Verhandlungen des Vereins für Sozialpolitik. 1893.

Vierteljahrsheft zur Statistik des deutschen Reiches. Berlin, 1902.

Vosberg-Rekow, Dr. *Die Zolltarifvorlage und ihre Begründung.* Berlin, 1902.

Wagemann, Ernst. *Konjunkturlehre.* Berlin, 1928.

Wagenfuhr, R. "Das Geheimnis der Gegenseitigkeit im Wirtschaftsleben," *Vierteljahrsheft zur Konjunkturforschung* 2, part A (1936).

Wahl, Adelbert. *Deutsche Geschichte.* 3 vols. Stuttgart, 1932.

Waldersee, Graf von *Denkwürdigkeiten II 1888–1890.* Stuttgart, 1922.

Walker, Mack. *Germany and the Emigration, 1816–1886.* Cambridge, Mass., 1964.

Weber, Adolf. *Agrarpolitik.* Berlin, 1928.

Wilken, F. *Volkswirtschaftliche Theorie der landwirtschaftlichen Preissteigerung.* Berlin, 1925.

Wippermann, Karl, ed. *Deutscher Geschichtskalender.* Leipzig, 1885–1934.

Witte, Sergei. *Memoirs of Count Witte.* Trans. Abraham Yarmolinsky. London, 1921.

Woodward, C. Vann. *The Burden of Southern History.* Baton Rouge, 1960.

Wunderlich, Frieda. *Farm Labor in Germany, 1810–1945.* Princeton, 1961.

Zechlin, Egmont. *Staatsstreichpläne Bismarcks und Wilhelms II 1890–1894.* Stuttgart and Berlin, 1929.

Ziekursch, Johannes. *Politische Geschichte des neuen deutschen Kaiserreiches.* 3 vols. Frankfurt/M, 1930.

Index